Kant's Impact on Moral Philosophy

THE LEGACY OF KANT

Series editor
Paul Guyer

Immanuel Kant transformed every area of philosophy, from epistemology, philosophy of science, and philosophy of mathematics to moral philosophy, political philosophy, philosophy of religion, philosophy of history, and more. Almost every major philosopher since Kant has responded to him, whether by developing some aspect of his views or by seeking an alternative. To tell the story of Kant's influence on modern philosophy would be beyond the powers of any single person. For that reason *The Legacy of Kant* will be a series of single-authored volumes by leading scholars in particular areas of Kant's work and impact. Topics will include Kant's impact on general metaphysics and epistemology, philosophy of science, moral philosophy, political philosophy, and aesthetics and teleology; others may be added.

Kant's Impact on Moral Philosophy

PAUL GUYER

OXFORD
UNIVERSITY PRESS

Great Clarendon Street, Oxford, OX2 6DP,
United Kingdom

Oxford University Press is a department of the University of Oxford.
It furthers the University's objective of excellence in research, scholarship,
and education by publishing worldwide. Oxford is a registered trade mark of
Oxford University Press in the UK and in certain other countries

Published in the United States of America by Oxford University Press
198 Madison Avenue, New York, NY 10016, United States of America

British Library Cataloguing in Publication Data
Data available

Library of Congress Control Number: 2023944410

ISBN 978–0–19–959245–6

DOI: 10.1093/oso/9780199592456.001.0001

Printed and bound by
CPI Group (UK) Ltd, Croydon, CR0 4YY

Contents

PART III. GERMAN IDEALISM
AND ITS OPPONENTS

PART IV. THE ANGLOPHONE RECEPTION:
IDEALISM PRO AND CON

PART V. THE ANGLOPHONE RECEPTION:
CONSEQUENTIALISM AND CONSTRUCTIVISM

Acknowledgments

I have talked about this project with too many people and at too many places over too many years to thank them all. Many of the teachers who have influenced my thought are no longer alive. In addition to Stanley Cavell, John Rawls, and Morton White, I should certainly also remember Dieter Henrich. I might regard conversations with Derek Parfit when we were both visiting at Harvard in 2002 as part of the origination of the project. Conversations with Jerry Schneewind a decade later were also seminal—and Jerry, along with our dear friend the late John Cooper, always deserves my thanks for getting my career started with my initial appointment at the University of Pittsburgh. Indeed, I would be very happy if this book were seen as carrying on from where Schneewind left off in his great book *The Invention of Autonomy*, which told the history of modern moral philosophy up to and through Kant.[1] I have talked about pieces of it over the years with my former colleagues and longtime friends Alexander Nehamas (who provided detailed comments on Chapter 11), Samuel Freeman, and Jay Wallace; with Onora O'Neill, Barbara Herman, Adrian Piper, Jens Timmermann, and Marcus Willaschek; and with former students including Fred Rauscher, Jennifer Uleman, Julian Wuerth, Kate Moran, and Mike Nance. Michael Walschots has generously provided me with valuable comments on Part II. And two people deserve special thanks for their remarkable patience with this project: my editor Peter Momtchiloff at Oxford University Press, and my wife Pamela Foa, who has had to put up with a perverse form of Kantianism: the time taken up by this work, and the space taken up by all the books and papers involved, cluttering three successive homes.

I would also like to thank the Office of the Dean of Faculty of Brown University and the Dean during the time on which I was working on this book, Kevin McLaughlin, for research leave in 2014, 2016, and 2021.

The chapters on Schiller, Fichte, and Hegel and the section on Adrian Piper draw on previously published papers.[2]

---

[1] Schneewind 1998a.   [2] Guyer 2014d, Guyer 2015a, Guyer 2018d, and Guyer 2023.

Abbreviations

Editions used are cited in the Bibliography. For works by Kant, if the title of the work abbreviated differs from the title of the Cambridge Edition volumes in which it is contained, then the title of the latter is included in parentheses, with the full entry in the Bibliography.

Locke

EHU	*An Essay Concerning Human Understanding*
TG2	*Second Treatise of Government*

Hume

THN	*A Treatise of Human Nature*
EPM	*Enquiry Concerning the Principles of Morals*

Kames

EC	*Elements of Criticism*

Kant

APV	*Anthropology from a Pragmatic Point of View (Anthropology, History, and Pedagogy)*
Collins	*Moral Philosophy Collins (Lectures on Ethics)*
Corr	*Correspondence*
CPuR	*Critique of Pure Reason*
CPracR	*Critique of Practical Reason (Practical Philosophy)*
CPJ	*Critique of the Power of Judgment*
G	*Groundwork for the Metaphysics of Morals (Practical Philosophy)*
ID	Inaugural dissertation, *On the Form and Principles of the Sensible and Intellectual World (Theoretical Philosophy 1755–1770)*
JL	*Jäsche Logic (Lectures on Logic)*
MM	*Metaphysics of Morals (Practical Philosophy)*
DR	Doctrine of Right
DV	Doctrine of Virtue
Mrongovius I	*Moral Philosophy Mrongovius (Lectures on Ethics)*
R	*Reflection, from Handschriftliche Nachlaß (Notes and Fragments)*
RBMR	*Religion within the Boundaries of Mere Reason (Religion and Rational Theology)*

TP   "On the Common Saying: That May be Correct in Theory, but it is of no
                Use in Practice" (*Practical Philosophy*)
Vigilantius   *Metaphysics of Morals Vigilantius* (*Lectures on Ethics*)

Ulrich

E   *Eleuthereiologie*

Schmid

VMP   *Vorlesungen zur Moralphilosophie*

Reinhold

BKP2   *Briefe über die kantischen Philosophie*. Volume 2

Schiller

GD   *On Grace and Dignity*

Fichte

CR   *Critique of All Revelation*
FNR   *Foundations of Natural Right*
SE   *System of Ethics*
WNM   *Wissenschaftslehre Nova Methodo*

Schelling

EHF   *The Essence of Human Freedom*
STI   *The System of Transcendental Idealism*

Hegel

NL   *Natural Law*
P   *Phenomenlogy*
PR   *Philosophy of Right*

Schopenhauer

BM   *Basis of Morality*
FW   *On the Freedom of the Will*
WWR   *The World as Will and Representation*

Nietzsche

BG	*Beyond Good and Evil*
GM	*The Genealogy of Morals*
HATH	*Human All Too Human*

Bradley

ES	*Ethical Studies*

Green

LK	*Lectures on Kant*
PE	*Prolegomena to Ethics*

Caird

CP	*The Critical Philosophy of Immanuel Kant*

Royce

PC	*The Problem of Christianity*
PL	*The Philosophy of Loyalty*

Paton

GW	*The Good Will*

Sidgwick

LPK	*Lectures on the Philosophy of Kant*
ME	*Methods of Ethics*
OHP	*Outlines of the History of Moral Philosophy*

Moore

PE	*Principia Ethica*

Williams

ELP	*Ethics and the Limits of Philosophy*
ML	*Moral Luck*

Hare

LM	*Language of Morals*
FR	*Freedom and Reason*

Baier

MPV	*The Moral Point of View*

Singer

GE	*Generalization in Ethics*

Parfit

OWM	*On What Matters*

Rawls

KC	"Kantian Constructivism"
LHMP	*Lectures on the History of Moral Philosophy*
PL	*Political Liberalism*
TJ	*A Theory of Justice*

Nagel

PA	*The Possibility of Altruism*

Korsgaard

CKE	*Creating the Kingdom of Ends*
KFH	"Kant's Formula of Humanity"
SN	*The Sources of Normativity*
SC	*Self-Constitution*

Piper

RSS	*Rationality and the Structure of the Self*

Introduction

The project of this work is a description and assessment of Kant's impact on the subsequent history of moral philosophy. It is not intended as a history of scholarship on Kant's moral philosophy, which by this point would be a Sisyphean task, and of interest only to specialists. The aim is rather to examine the impact of Kant's moral philosophy on notable philosophers since Kant who were influenced by him in one way or another, either constituting their own approaches to moral philosophy by adapting elements of his moral philosophy or founding their approaches on what they took to be important criticisms of his work. Some of these philosophers and their work will be very well known, such as Johann Gottlieb Fichte, Georg Wilhelm Friedrich Hegel, Arthur Schopenhauer, Friederich Nietzsche, and of course John Rawls and a number of his students such as Thomas Nagel, Onora O'Neill, and Christine Korsgaard. Others will be less well-known, although they may have once been better known, such as Friedrich Schelling (at least as moral philosopher), the idealists Francis Herbert Bradley, Thomas Hill Green, Edward Caird, Josiah Royce, and Herbert James Paton, or some of those who preceded Derek Parfit in attempting to reconcile Kantianism with consequentialism. Some omissions will no doubt also be obvious: I do not discuss John Stuart Mill at any length, because I think that his engagement with Kant was minimal, while others such as Jeremy Bentham (of course), Auguste Comte, Wilhelm von Humboldt, and Samuel Taylor Coleridge (the turn-of-the-nineteenth-century poet and literary theorist, that is, not the turn-of-the-twentieth-century composer) had much more influence on him; and I omit any discussion of Jürgen Habermas and such prominent subsequent Frankfurt philosophers as Axel Honneth and Rainer Forst, mostly because of lack of time and my own expertise but partly because my account of the twentieth-century reception of Kant's moral philosophy has a certain coherence as the history of the Anglophone reception of Kant. For some of the authors I discuss, for example Kant, Hegel, and Rawls, there is an extensive secondary literature; for some, such as Fichte and Sidgwick, there is a smaller but growing literature; for some, for example Schelling, Royce, and various of the more recent authors, almost none at all. Where literature does exist, I try to provide some suggestions about further reading and to signpost some of my agreements and disagreements with it, but for good Kantian reasons of space, time, and fairness, I have limited my commentary upon the commentaries—doing so would swell an already big book beyond reason. This caveat applies particularly to Part I, my review of Kant's own moral

Kant's Impact on Moral Philosophy. Paul Guyer, Oxford University Press. © Paul Guyer 2024.
DOI: 10.1093/oso/9780199592456.003.0001

philosophy as background to the rest of the book, where thorough annotation of my agreements and disagreements with other commentators would be virtually endless. My focus is on primary sources and my aim is to chart my own path through the rich field of philosophically interesting responses to Kant's moral philosophy, and to provide readers with enough orientation to pursue their own investigations of this field further.

However, I should mention two monumental histories of moral philosophy that do cover many of the authors I will discuss, namely volume 3 of Terence Irwin's three-volume *The Development of Ethics: A Historical and Critical Study*, subtitled *From Kant to Rawls* (Oxford University Press, 2009), and John Skorupski's *Being and Freedom: On Late Modern Ethics in Europe* (Oxford University Press, 2021). Each of these books has its own agenda. Irwin's aim is to show the enduring importance of what he calls naturalist yet normative eudaimonism, inspired by Aristotle and further developed by Thomas Aquinas, Francesco Suarez, and Joseph Butler, and to argue that subsequent philosophers such as Kant were at their best when they came closest to this tradition. Skorupski aims to show the centrality to modern moral philosophy of a conception of freedom or autonomy that was absent from the ancient tradition but moved to center stage by Kant, but then developed in different ways by philosophers such as Hegel, Mill, Sidgwick, and Rawls. While I am more focused on tracing the influence of and response to Kant than either of these works, there are certainly affinities between my approach and theirs: like Skorupski, I think that the preservation and promotion of freedom is the essence of morality for Kant, and that those subsequent philosophers who understood him best understood that; and since I have long been underwhelmed by Kant's arguments for his peculiar position of transcendental idealism, like Irwin I am most comfortable with those parts of Kant's moral philosophy that can be understood in more naturalistic terms. I will not note every point where I agree with these authors, though I will point out some differences between my interpretations and theirs.

As I worked my way through this project over the last dozen or more years, first with my students at the University of Pennsylvania and then at Brown University, it became apparent to me that many of the issues that have stimulated or troubled responses to Kant's moral philosophy had been quickly raised in the immediate response to his work, that is, in the short decade from the publication of his *Groundwork for the Metaphysics of Morals* in 1785 to that of Friedrich Schiller's essay "On Grace and Dignity" in 1793 and Kant's response to it in his *Religion within the Boundaries of Mere Reason* in the same year. Following Part I of this book, an orientation in Kant's moral philosophy and my approach to it with an eye to what follows, Part II therefore concerns that initial reception in more detail than either Irwin or Skorupski offer. The issues raised in that period that I discuss include: (1) The objection that Kant's categorical imperative is an "empty formalism," famously associated with Hegel's treatment of Kant in his essay on *Natural Law* from 1802 and the *Outlines of the Philosophy of Right* from 1821, but already raised in the first substantive review of the *Groundwork* published in 1786 by Hermann Andreas Pistorius, who also raised objections to Kant's conception of the highest good in his later review of the *Critique of Practical Reason* and to Kant's doctrine of the postulates of pure practical reason. (2) The question whether Kant has any convincing deduction of, that is, argument for, the categorical imperative. (3) The issue of the proper place of happiness within Kant's moral philosophy, an issue implicitly raised by Pistorius's early reviews and explicitly raised by Christian Garve's objection that Kant's characterization of the highest good as a combination of virtue plus happiness mars the purity of Kant's philosophy, to which Kant responded in his 1793 essay "On the Common Saying: That may be Correct in Theory, But it is of No Use in Practice." Issues about the justification of the categorical imperative, whether it is indeed an empty formalism, and the proper place of happiness in Kantian morality have been addressed ever since. (4) In 1788, the Jena philosopher Johann August Heinrich Ulrich raised the objection that on Kant's account of freedom of the will as achieved by its conformity to the moral law, there could be no explanation of the possibility of imputable, that is, freely chosen immorality, a charge that Kant's disciples Carl Christian Erhard Schmid, Karl Leonhard Reinhold, and then Kant himself, again in *Religion within the Boundaries of Mere Reason*, sought to refute. The problem of free will and the question of the success of Kant's attempt to address it by means of his general doctrine of transcendental idealism have also been central to the reception of Kant ever since, although perhaps more so in the nineteenth century than in the twentieth, which in this regard might be thought to have begun with an incisive critique of Kant's approach in one of the earliest publications of the Cambridge philosopher and one of the founding fathers of "analytic" philosophy, G. E. Moore. (5) Finally, the question of the proper role of feeling in Kant's or a Kantian model of moral motivation has been an issue for many from Friedrich Schiller to Adrian Piper, and will also be one of our themes.

But beneath these issues, there is another, perhaps deeper question that has driven my own work on Kant's moral philosophy since my first publication in the field in 1993, after my early work on Kant's aesthetics (1979) and on his epistemology and metaphysics (1987), namely the question of whether Kant's approach to moral philosophy is ultimately grounded on the value of the adherence to *law*, to rationality defined as the pursuit of universal and necessary validity *for its own sake*, or on the value of *freedom*, specifically the freedom of human beings to set their own ends, with the adherence to universally valid moral law functioning as the *means* to the realization of this end, or the condition under which each may indeed set his or her own ends compatibly with the freedom of all to do the same, thus within the limits of compossibility among the freely set ends of all.[1] My own position has been, as my former student Kate Moran has elegantly put it, that it is

---

[1] See Guyer 1993b.

a "mistake . . . to think that Kantian agents ought to act for the sake of duty just for the sake of acting from duty as if they were compelled to follow rules just for the sake of following rules,"[2] and that the real driver of Kant's approach to moral philosophy is rather the idea that it is only by all following rules that the end of freedom can be most fully realized for all. So in the course of this work I will suggest that those who understood this, such as the nineteenth-century idealists T. H. Green and Josiah Royce and in the most recent period above all John Rawls, have been the most interesting readers of and builders upon Kant, rather than those who have focused too much on the first formulation of the categorical imperative simply as the demand that agents act only on universalizable maxims, without much concern for the end—universal freedom—to which that might merely be the means. Especially those who have entirely rejected Kant from a consequentialist standpoint, such as John Stuart Mill, as well as those who have attempted to reconcile Kant and consequentialism, most recently Derek Parfit, might be thought to fall into this category, as well as those who have accused Kant of promulgating a thinly disguised ethics of divine command, such as Arthur Schopenhauer and Elizabeth Anscombe. The organization of the book is basically chronological rather than thematic, so its remaining parts (III, IV, and V) are not directly organized around either the set of issues that emerged in the first decade of the reception of Kant's moral philosophy or this issue of whether Kant thought that adherence to law is the intrinsic value at the bottom of moral philosophy or only the means to realize the value of the maximal freedom of all. But I will touch upon these themes throughout.

I begin with a survey of the central points of Kant's moral philosophy as I have come to understand it, beginning in my first year of college with several lectures on Kant's *Religion within the Boundaries of Mere Reason* by Stanley Cavell in his famous course "Hum 5" and in graduate school with lectures on Kant's moral philosophy by John Rawls in his course on the history of moral philosophy.[3] This survey builds upon my previous work on Kant's moral philosophy, but has been written with an eye to the issues to be discussed in this volume, and should also be of use to those who may come to this book from an interest in one or some of the later figures I discuss without a prior grounding in Kant, or who look into this book from a general interest in moral philosophy without much prior acquaintance with its history at all.[4] Of course the account of Kant's moral philosophy offered here cannot be complete, since a thorough presentation of it would at least double the size of what has already become a large book.

---

[2] Moran 2022, p. 53.

[3] Barbara Herman edited a late iteration of this course as Rawls 2000. I took Rawls's course in the fall of 1970, which was still fairly early in his tenure at Harvard, and the year before the publication of *A Theory of Justice*. I do not recall that he spent as many lectures on Kant as in the course Herman edited; he certainly did not discuss Leibniz's "perfectionism" as he did in the later course; and as I remember he spent more time on the contrast with utilitarianism, which was much on his mind as he was finishing *A Theory of Justice*.

[4] My prior work on Kant's moral philosophy includes papers collected in Guyer 1993a, Guyer 2000, Guyer 2005a, Guyer 2016a, and the monographs Guyer 2007c, 2014a, and 2019.

PART I
KANT'S MORAL PHILOSOPHY

1
The Development of Kant's Moral Philosophy from 1764–5 to 1781

In the Introduction to the *Metaphysics of Morals*, his final work in moral philosophy, the detailed account of moral duties for human beings that he had been working toward throughout the evolution of this philosophy, Kant states that "a practical philosophy...has not nature but freedom of choice for its object."[1] This comes at the end of a paragraph that begins with the statement that "the teachings of morality command for everyone, without taking account of his inclination, merely because and insofar as he is free and has practical reason" (*MM*, Introduction, 6: 216). The claim that the teachings of morality command everyone insofar as they are free was a commonplace in Kant's time and holds for any moral theory: morality concerns norms for agents capable of making choices (however a philosopher may have conceived of freedom of choice,, whether in libertarian or compatibilist form),[2] not inanimate objects, nor animate objects driven solely by reflexes and instincts, and perhaps not even a God who can do only what is good.[3] The claim that the teachings of morality command for everyone is also hardly unique to Kant's moral philosophy. The claim that

---

[1] Chief works on the development of Kant's moral philosophy prior to the publication of the *Critique of Pure Reason*, thus on his "pre-critical" moral philosophy, include Schilpp 1960 (originally 1938); Henrich 1957–8, Henrich 1960 (translated in Henrich 1994), and Henrich 1963; Schmücker 1961; Ward 1972; and Allison 2020, chapters 1–5. For the historical background to Kant's moral philosophy, see Beck 1969, Schneewind 1998a, and Irwin 2008. Older works that place Kant in the history of moral philosophy include Stäudlin 1822, written by a follower in the generation after Kant's death, and Jodl 1929. Hunter 2001 places Kant in a "university" and "metaphysical," Wolffian tradition in moral philosophy contrasted to a "civil," more exoteric tradition associated with Leibniz and Christian Thomasius; that Kant was, as so often, attempting to find a middle way between two rival approaches, in this case "rival enlightenments," would be closer to the truth.

[2] "Compatibilists" are committed to thoroughgoing determinism, and define freedom of choice as just a specific variety of causal determination; "libertarians" hold that freedom of choice is the ability to choose either way between alternatives, no matter what the chooser's prior history might seem to determine. Most early modern philosophers were compatibilists, including Hobbes, Locke, Leibniz, Hume, and Jonathan Edwards; the chief representative of libertarianism in Kant's time was Christian August Crusius. Kant is unique in the history of philosophy in attempting to reconcile determinism and libertarianism by means of his doctrine of transcendental idealism, on which more later. See also Wood 1984.

[3] Whether it makes any sense to attribute freedom to God, who can never "choose" anything but the best, was an issue for theology before and during Kant's time; see Insole 2013.

Kant's Impact on Moral Philosophy. Paul Guyer, Oxford University Press. © Paul Guyer 2024.
DOI: 10.1093/oso/9780199592456.003.0002

morality commands independently of anyone's particular desires or inclinations[4] is characteristically Kantian, and distinguishes Kant's approach to moral philosophy from that of some of his immediate predecessors and contemporaries, notably the philosophers of the "moral sense" school such as Francis Hutcheson, David Hume, and Adam Smith (see *Collins*, 27: 253 and *CPracR*, 5: 40–1).[5] The suggestion that the source of the independence of morality from all inclination is practical reason, specified further as pure practical reason, is also characteristic of Kant's approach. But the suggestion that morality commands everyone *because* of their freedom, that freedom is the *object* of morality, that freedom is not only the necessary condition of being subject to the commands of morality but that its fullest possible realization is the *goal* of morality, is the deepest claim of Kant's moral philosophy: the moral law, or its specification in the form of the various duties of human beings, is aimed at the maximization of human freedom for each compatible with the greatest possible equal freedom for all. This principle is not liable to the objections that might be brought against a principle of the maximization of either aggregate or average happiness or utility, namely that it might be achieved at the cost of great inequality, or against some principle of equality as such, that it might be satisfied by a low level of happiness itself or of resources, e.g., income, as means to happiness, for everyone;[6] the principle requires the greatest possible freedom for *each* compatible with equal freedom for *all*, and concerns happiness only indirectly, as what people will naturally use their freedom to strive for, *within* that constraint.

1.1. Kant's Earliest Thoughts

That this is the central idea of Kant's moral philosophy is *not* immediately evident from the way he presents the chief elements of this philosophy in the two works that are ordinarily taken to be its foundational documents, namely the *Groundwork for the Metaphysics of Morals* of 1785 and the *Critique of Practical Reason* of 1788. But it is clear in some of the very earliest documentation of Kant's

---

[4] Kant's formal definition of "inclination" (*Neigung*) is "habitual desire," or impulse or desire that has become entrenched (*RBMR*, 6: 28–9, see also *MM*, Introduction, 6: 212, and *APV*, §73, 7: 251, where Kant defines it as "habitual sensible desire"). But Kant himself frequently uses "inclination" to mean simply impulsive desires without any implication of duration, as in the crucial argument for the formal character of the categorical imperative at *G*, 4:399–402. Commentators generally follow Kant in this looser usage, and I will too.

[5] Kant interprets the attempt of these "moral sense" philosophers to ground moral principles on "sentiments" or feelings (e.g., Hume, *THN*, book III, part 1, sections 1–2), as an attempt to ground it on contingent features of *human* nature and therefore ill-suited for deriving universal and necessary moral laws. Terence Irwin's argument is that this is an unduly narrow conception of what a "naturalist" approach would be, and that if naturalism is understood more broadly, Kant's own approach can also be understood as naturalist. See Irwin 2009, e.g., §897, vol. 3, p. 5.

[6] For the criticism of utilitarianism, see, e.g., Rawls 1999, §5, p. 23, and §§27–8, pp. 139–52.

moral thought, namely notes that he wrote in his personal copy of his 1764 book *Observations on the Feeling of the Beautiful and Sublime*, and in both the political philosophy and the ethics, that is, as he used the terms and as I will use them in this work, namely the coercibly enforceable and the non-coercibly enforceable duties of human beings (see *MM*, Introduction, 6: 218-19), that he presented in his last work in moral philosophy, the *Metaphysics of Morals* of 1797. (I return to this distinction in Chapter 3.) Since the *Groundwork for the Metaphysics of Morals* was intended to be the groundwork for the metaphysics of morals or doctrine of human duties as Kant finally presented it a dozen years later, it makes as much sense to interpret the intentions of the *Groundwork* retrospectively from the *Metaphysics of Morals* as it does to interpret the *Metaphysics of Morals* on the basis of the *Groundwork*. Since the *Groundwork*, and the *Critique of Practical Reason*, are thus both preceded and succeeded by clear statements that the fundamental object or goal of morality is the greatest yet equal freedom possible for all human beings, I take it that this was the core idea of Kant's moral philosophy all along. Note that I say "greatest yet equal freedom possible for all human beings": Kant always insists that the fundamental principle of morality must be valid for all *rational* beings; but since the only rational beings upon whom we can act and with whom we can interact are ourselves and each other, the duties that follow from the fundamental principle of morality for us human beings can be only the duties comprised under the requirement to preserve and promote the greatest possible yet equal freedom for all human beings.

Kant's 1764 *Observations on the Feeling of the Beautiful and the Sublime* was not primarily a work in moral philosophy, or even in aesthetics, as its title might suggest, but was an essay in what Kant called anthropology, the study of human nature in its cognitive, affective, and conative dimensions and its varying manifestations in what Kant took to be the different sexes, nations, and races of humankind.[7] But at some time, presumably shortly after the publication of that work, Kant used his interleaved copy of the book to write notes, some directly connected to topics of the book but some not directly connected, including some general observations on morality. These notes reveal how Kant was thinking about morality as he entered into his philosophical maturity (we think of the *Observations* as an early work, but Kant was already 40 when he published it). Among the most revealing of these notes is this:

[W]hat is harder and more unnatural than [the] yoke of necessity [from nature] is the subjection of one human being under the will of another. No misfortune

---

[7] There is an extensive literature on this subject. For the main texts of Kant's anthropology, see Kant 2007 and Kant 2012. For a few key commentaries on Kant's anthropology, including its applications on the issues of race and sex, see Brandt 1999, Louden 2000, Kleingeld 2012, Varden 2020, and Klemme 2023.

can be more terrifying to one who is accustomed to freedom...than to see himself delivered to a creature of his own kind who can compel him to do what he will (to give himself over to his will)....There is in subjection not only something externally dangerous but also a certain ugliness and a contradiction that at the same time indicates its injustice...that a human being should as it were need no soul himself and have no will of his own, and that another soul should move my limbs, is absurd and perverse   (*NF*, pp. 11–12)

There are two different ideas here. One, suggested by such terms as "harder," "ugliness," and "perverse," is overtly axiological, with a psychological, even aesthetic foundation: people, especially people who have already been accustomed to freedom, just do not *like* being deprived of their freedom, of their own will, of the right to make their own decisions about how to act, beginning with how to move their own bodies. This might be an entirely plausible thought, but it is not clear that it would satisfy the criterion of being a principle of pure practical reason, as Kant will subsequently insist the fundamental principle of morality must be, rather than an empirical fact about human inclination. But the other thought, suggested by such terms of logical criticism as "contradiction" and "absurd," would satisfy this criterion. This is the idea that there is some sort of contradiction in treating a being that does have its own will as if it did not, and a contradiction is a violation of the most fundamental law of reason in general and hence of pure reason, namely the law of non-contradiction, the rule that contradictions must be avoided. It might take some work that Kant does not do in this brief note to work this idea out, but his thought might be, first, that to treat people as if they do not have wills of their own is tantamount to asserting that they do not, and second, that we all know and cannot deny that all human beings have wills of their own, so that, third, to treat people who do have wills of their own as if they did not is tantamount to both asserting and denying that they do have their own wills, and thus a flagrant violation of the most fundamental rule of reason.[8] Of course, although Kant does not say so in this passage, this would apply in one's own case as well: to treat *oneself* as if one did not have a will of one's own, by letting mere inclination or desire dictate one's behavior, would be tantamount to both asserting and yet denying that one has a genuine will oneself, and likewise a violation of the law of non-contradiction.

Kant never spells this argument out completely, but he supplies all of the premises for it, and it might be considered the most fundamental level of his moral thought, even when he is using different terminology, as he does in the *Groundwork*. This argument applies the basic law of logic to what Kant takes to be the most fundamental *fact* about us, that we each have our own will, our own

---

[8] See Guyer 2019, pp. 12–34, for development of this approach.

ability to determine how our bodily and other capabilities are to be used and to what ends. But the psychological argument that is also suggested by Kant's note treats freedom as our most fundamental *value*, and other, less overtly psychological passages in Kant will do that as well, as we will next see. Perhaps Kant never clearly distinguished between these two approaches to the fundamental principle of morality, hence never clearly chose one over the other or recognized any need to do so. He often seems to have been more interested in working out the implications of his approach to morality, as in the theories of justice and ethics that comprise the *Metaphysics of Morals*, than in working out the foundation of his approach as clearly and completely as contemporary philosophers, or even some of his more immediate successors, might demand.[9] Nevertheless, it might be that the more logic-based argument suggested by our passage from Kant's notes in the *Observations* is the part of his thought that comes closest to fulfilling his claim to ground moral philosophy in pure reason.

1.2. The Lectures on Ethics

This approach is evident in our next significant source for the evolution of Kant's moral philosophy, the lectures on ethics in the form in which he gave them during the 1770s; and here the application of this approach to one's own case, thus to duties to oneself, is foremost. Kant foregrounds freedom as a fundamental value in these lectures, while in the *Groundwork*, although with different terminology, he will foreground the argument from the fact that every human being (indeed, every rational being) possesses his or her own will. To get from 1764–5 to the mid-1770s, the period of the lectures on which the first group of surviving extensive transcriptions of Kant's lectures on ethics are based, we need to skip over a number of Kant's publications, including *On the Form and Principles of the Sensible and Intelligible Worlds*, the inaugural dissertation that he gave upon the occasion of his installation of Professor of Logic and Metaphysics at Königsberg in 1770.[10] This work is important in the story of Kant's overall philosophical development, for it is here that he first introduces his arguments for space and time as mere forms of our representation rather than of reality itself, what he would come to call in the *Critique of Pure Reason* "transcendental idealism," and which would provide the basis for his approach to the problem of free will by means of the doctrine that events must appear to be fully deterministic at the "phenomenal" level of reality itself but our choice between good and evil *could* be "spontaneous" and not determined by antecedent events at the "noumenal" level

---

[9] This is a point that Dieter Henrich suggested to me many years ago.
[10] For accounts of Kant's development providing coverage of these works, see Schönfeld 2000 and Kuehn 2001.

of reality itself, that is, at the level of our real wills.[11] But although Kant regarded this solution to that problem as a necessary condition of morality itself, and almost twenty years later would devote the *Critique of Practical Reason* in good part to that problem, this doctrine does not yet appear in the inaugural dissertation. All that it has to say on the subject of morality is that it must be a product of pure reason; Kant says that "moral philosophy... is not cognized except by pure intellect, and itself belongs to pure philosophy" (*ID*, §9, 2: 396), but he offers no account of what moral principle pure intellect cognizes. In the lectures on ethics that he was giving to his students around the time of the inaugural dissertation, Kant emphasizes the normative content rather than metaethical foundations of his position.[12]

Although a partial transcription of Kant's lectures on ethics from the 1760s by Johann Gottfried Herder, who was Kant's student at the time, survives, our primary source for Kant's lectures in the 1770s is a transcription that bears the name Georg Ludwig Collins and date "Winter Semester 1784–85." But it is virtually identical to a transcription from 1777, the so-called "Kaehler" transcription. Both of these seem to be copies of an original transcription from around 1775.[13] The Collins transcription thus well represents Kant's lectures as he gave them during the 1770s. Later transcriptions, such as those from the 1780s by another student, Carl Celestin Mrongovius, and from 1794–4 by Kant's attorney, Friedrich Vigilantius, differ in some regards, and use more of the language of Kant's published works on moral philosophy. But in all cases Kant based his lectures on ethics on two textbooks by Alexander Gottlieb Baumgarten, whose textbook on metaphysics Kant also used for his courses on metaphysics and anthropology.[14] Following in the tradition of Christian Wolff, Baumgarten had divided his material on ethics into two parts, an *Initia* or *Elements of First Practical Philosophy* followed by a normative *Ethics*.[15] Kant criticized Wolff and by implication Baumgarten because their "universal practical philosophy" was not based on *pure* practical reason and was not based on a conception of "a will of any special kind, such as one that would be completely determined from *a priori*

---

[11] For my interpretation of Kant's inaugural dissertation, see Guyer 1987; see also Beiser 1992, pp. 46–52; Laywine 1995; and Stang 2021.

[12] Up until his appointment as Professor of Logic and Metaphysics in 1770, Kant was a *Privatdozent*, living on the fees that he could charge auditors of his lectures, including his popular lectures on ethics. After his appointment as professor, his lectures on logic and metaphysics were part of his salaried duties, but he could and did continue giving his lectures on ethics for student fees, as well as the popular lectures on "physical geography" that he had been giving and the lectures on "anthropology" that he began giving in 1772–3. These fees, later earnings from his books, and good investments made Kant a prosperous man by the time of his death in 1804.

[13] See Kant 2004, and *LE*, pp. xv–xvii.   [14] Baumgarten 2013.

[15] Baumgarten 2019 and 2020. Baumgarten's *Ethica* has not yet been translated into German or English; the Latin text is printed in volume 19 of the *Akademie* edition of Kant. Kant's division between the *Groundwork for the Metaphysics of Morals* and the later *Metaphysics of Morals* follows Baumgarten's division between the *Initia* and the *Ethica*, a fact that is reflected in the division of Kant's lectures on ethics as well.

principles"; in his view "the metaphysics of morals has to examine the idea and the principles of a possible *pure* will and not the actions and conditions of human volition generally, which for the most part are drawn from psychology" (*G*, preface, 4: 390–1). Kant repeated this meta-ethical claim, definitive for his mature moral philosophy, in the section "Of the Principle of Morality" in the first part of his lectures, which is titled, following Baumgarten's textbook, "Universal Practical Philosophy." Here he criticizes, as he would later do in the *Critique of Practical Reason*, "empirical" approaches to morality, whether they attempt to ground morality in "vanity and self-interest," as in Epicurus, Helvétius, and Mandeville, or in "moral feeling," as in Shaftesbury and Hutcheson (*LE*, 27: 253). He holds instead that the proper approach to morality is "the intellectual one," in which the philosopher judges that "the principle of morality has a ground in the understanding, and can be apprehended completely *a priori*": in virtue of that fact, "the moral law expresses categorical necessity, and not a necessity fashioned from experience. All necessary rules must hold good *a priori*, and hence the principles are intellectual." And he immediately states the content of the principle that "resides in the understanding" and provides an "injunction" that is "absolute": "If I consider my free choice, it is a conformity of free choice with itself and others. It is thus a necessary law of free choice" (*LE*, 27: 254). Or, in a further text from a contemporaneous transcription, "*Morality* is the conformity of the action to a universally valid rule of free choice, all morality is the relation of action to the universal rule" (*Mrongovius I, LE*, 27: 1426)—*but the universal rule is that freedom itself must be universal*. The object of morality, what morality requires to be preserved and promoted, is free choice, but the free choice of each as far as is compatible with the free choice of all.[16] Kant does not present any new argument for this claim, but takes the next step of suggesting that the goal of equal freedom for all is achieved *through* adherence to universalizable maxims, that is, principles of action that could freely be accepted by all, not just by one agent considering a course of action while others are *not* allowed to adopt that maxim—a "universal rule which holds good at all times and for everyone" (*LE*, 27:1427), a maxim that one could act upon even if everyone else also chose to act upon it.[17] This is what Kant will subsequently introduce as the first formulation of the categorical imperative, and he then illustrates it with two examples that he will

---

[16] See also Schneewind 1998a, pp. 486–7.

[17] "Maxim" is a term that will become central to Kant's moral philosophy. It means a general principle that in certain sorts of circumstances a certain type of action could be performed, perhaps adding for the sake of a certain goal or end. The structure of a maxim is often represented as "In circumstances *C* to perform (or refrain from) actions of type *A* in order to achieve end *E*." Among the large literature on maxims, see esp. O'Neill 1985, O'Neill 2013, and McCarty 2009. A maxim is "subjective" in the sense that it is the principle on which a person (a "subject") actually acts, but it *should* be "objective" or "universalizable" in the sense of being able to be adopted by any agent in the relevant circumstances without contradiction of either the specific intention or the generally rational will of the original agent; see *G*, 4: 420n.

also use to illustrate the categorical imperative in the *Groundwork*. "For example, to keep one's promise as a means of procuring happiness is not moral," that is, to choose whether to keep one's promise only if doing so at the time at which it might be kept seems to promise happiness is not moral, because "if everyone wishes to keep his promise as he might choose," that is, *only* as he might choose, "then in the end it would be of no use at all." That is, in the end making promises would not be possible, because no one would accept promises knowing that they will be kept only if and when the promisor feels like it when the time comes to keep it; so the agent's original goal of using promises he might not keep as a means of securing his own happiness would not be possible after all. Similarly, if one were to attempt to universalize a maxim of being indifferent to the needs of others rather than being benevolent, helping others when one can, that would be willing that others "should be equally indifferent to me," but this could "not accord with my choice," which as a matter of prudential rationality would be to get help from others when I need it; so the universalization of my maxim—or "intention," as Kant calls it further down the page—would undermine the possibility of achieving my own goals, and would thus be immoral, irrational rather than rational. In the one case, the universalization of my maxim must be compatible with the freedom of others, in the other case the universalization of my maxim must be compatible with my own continued exercise of my freedom, which includes being able to freely choose my ends because I have done everything I can to ensure that I have means to realize them.

A crucial point in this train of thought—one that we will see in the sequel has been widely misunderstood—is that the reasoning that Kant describes as *following* the universalization of an intended maxim may be prudential or consequentialist, but the universalization itself is *not* undertaken for prudential reasons.[18] One is not asking whether it is likely that if one adopts some maxim everyone else will too and then whether one would like the outcome; one is asking whether one's maxim *could be* universalized consistent with one's own intention *because morality requires that universalization* and then reason in general requires that consistency. "In all moral judgments we frame the thought: What becomes of the [intended] action if it is taken universally? If, when it is made into a universal rule, the intention is in agreement with itself, the action is morally possible; but if not, then it is morally impossible" (*Collins*, 27: 1428). And even more deeply, one *must* ask that question because acting only on maxims that everyone, including one's own continuing, future self, *could freely accept* is the way to ensure that one's maxim is compatible with the freedom of all.

After discussing some of the general concepts of ethics that Baumgarten also discusses, such as obligation, necessitation, and imputation (ascription of

---

[18] See also Walschots 2021.

responsibility), Kant then presents the specific contents of ethics in two parts, duties to self and duties to others. This division will remain a constant through Kant's final *Metaphysics of Morals* in 1797. Baumgarten and others before him such as Wolff and Samuel Pufendorf had recognized *three* classes of duties, duties to God, self, and others; but from an early date Kant held that, since God as a perfect being could *need* nothing from us, our only possible duty to God could be the fulfillment of our duties *to ourselves and others*, and that in turn not from fear of divine punishment or hope of divine reward, which would possess only external correctness and no moral worth, but simply because it is the right thing to do— "*rectitudo actionum ex principio internum*," or correctness of action from an internal principle (*Collins*, 27: 300). This position will lead to Kant's insistence in *Religion within the Boundaries of Mere Reason* almost twenty years later that our only duty to God is to fulfill our moral duties to ourselves and others (*RBMR*, part three, e.g., 6: 103–4), a position that Kant shares with many other enlightened thinkers.[19] Here Kant is also introducing one of his most characteristic positions, namely that doing the right thing for any reason is always blameless, but only doing the right thing for the *right* reason—respect for the moral law itself, nothing less and nothing more—entitles one to "moral worth" or "esteem," that is, is praiseworthy or positively meritorious (see *MM*, DV, Introduction, section VII, 6: 390–1). So Kant is left with two classes of duty, duties to oneself and duties to others, plus the requirement that in order to deserve esteem or earn merit for fulfilling one's duty one must be motivated by respect for the moral law, not fear of God, concern for one's reputation, or any other motivation that in his opinion would really be a matter of mere inclination. In conjunction with this idea, Kant also introduces a conception of virtue that will remain characteristic in his later work as well, that virtue "means strength in mastering and overcoming oneself, in regard to the moral disposition.... a certain self-coercion and self-command" (*Collins*, 27: 300). Moral worth consists in being motivated by respect for the moral law, and does not directly refer to self-constraint; virtue consists in the strength to make that one's motivation in the face of other inclinations, inclinations to do something (or anything) other than what morality requires, so it is a form of self-constraint. Kant believes that human beings typically do have inclinations to do other than what morality requires, so for us moral worth typically does require virtue, but that is synthetic, a fact about us, not a fact about all possible rational beings—for example, strange as it might sound, God, an angel, or a Stoic sage might have moral worth, but not virtue. In Kant's later work, he will treat virtue as a property of the phenomenal self, the self as it appears in space and time, not necessarily of the noumenal self, because space and time are the natural home of inclination and therefore of the strength to overcome it; but he does not yet

---

[19] E.g., Shaftesbury, *The Moralists* (1709), part II, section iii, in Shaftesbury 1999, vol. 2, pp. 45–6; Mendelssohn, *Jerusalem* (1783), in Mendelssohn 1983, p. 58.

employ the distinction between phenomenal and noumenal in the lectures on ethics of the 1770s.

One should also note here Kant's description of virtue as self-*coercion*, or in his later terminology as a form of self-*constraint* (*MM*, DV, Introduction, section IX, 6: 394). This is because Kant will later distinguish the duties of right or justice from the duties of virtue by the criterion of permissible coercion: duties of right are the subset of moral duties that can and should be coercively enforced by the juridical and penal mechanism of the state, while duties of virtue (actually, as will later become clear, a broader class of ethical duties) cannot be. But this does not mean that duties of virtue allow or require *no* coercion; they just allow or require *internal, self-coercion* rather than *external coercion* through the public offices of a state (*MM*, Introduction, 6: 218–19; *MM*, DV, Introduction, section IX, 6: 394). In sum, moral worth does not by definition require overcoming obstacles presented by inclinations, while virtue, as the strength to overcome such obstacles, can be thought of as the ability and readiness to do so, but it can only be verified and measured when it actually does so. (This topic will be pursued further in Chapter 3 below.)

Let us now return to Kant's division of duties in the lectures. The division between duty to self and duty to others reflects that morality requires consistency *within* each agent's use of freedom of choice, that is, the use of freedom of choice only in ways consistent with the possibility of further use of free choice on other occasions, and consistency *between* one person's use of free choice and that of all others. Kant develops his conception of consistency in the use of freedom most fully in his account of duties to oneself, which he in fact regards as the foundation of morality.[20] Kant says that "He who violates duties toward himself, throws away his humanity, and is no longer in a position to perform duties to others.... the man who has violated the duties to himself has no inner worth. Thus the infringement of self-regarding duties takes all his worth from a man" (*Collins*, 27: 341). Kant does not fully explain this claim. At one level, what he might mean is obvious: as he will ultimately explain in the *Metaphysics of Morals*, duty to self or self-regarding duty includes the perfection of one's physical and mental capabilities, and these are obviously necessary means to any possible ends, including fulfilling possible duties to others, such as rendering assistance to another in some particular circumstance; so one may not be in a position to fulfill duties to others unless one has fulfilled these duties to oneself. But at another level, what Kant has in mind is that, unless one has preserved one's own humanity—one's own freedom—and, in the terms of the *Metaphysics of Morals*, strived to perfect

---

[20]   My use of "consistency" follows *LE*, 27: 344–6, but also suggests O'Neill's usage in O'Neill 1985. In that paper she fleshes out the conditions for consistency between one's formation of an intention under a maxim on one occasion and the universalization of a maxim, but discusses it primarily with respect to the interpersonal case, not the intrapersonal case.

one's innate *moral* potential, that is, moral worth plus virtue—one might act towards others in outward conformity with demands of duty, but might do so merely from some form of self-interest—love of a good reputation, fear of ostracism or punishment, and so on—and not be acting in a genuinely moral, that is, morally worthy way. Thus, unless one fulfills one's self-regarding duty to perfect one's natural capacities, one may not even be capable of outward compliance with the demands of duties owed to others, but if one does not fulfill one's self-regarding duty to perfect one's moral capacity, then whatever one does for others will not be morally worthy and will not fully satisfy the demands of duty.[21]

But let us return to the foundation of the content of the duties both to self and to others, namely, intra- and interpersonal consistency in the exercise of freedom. In the section "Of Duties to Oneself" that begins the section "On Morality," a title that pointedly begins only after the section "On Religion," Kant provides both a general account of the foundation of such duty and examples of duties to oneself explicated on the basis of this foundation. His general thesis is that "the inner worth of the world, the *summum bonum*, is freedom according to a choice that is not necessitated," something that, among the creatures known to us, is available only to human beings. "Freedom is thus the inner worth of the world," but this must be freedom "restricted by objective rules," for otherwise "the result is much savage disorder" (*Collins*, 27: 344). Kant goes on to explain that the "prime rule whereby I am to restrict freedom," which must come from our own understanding, "is the conformity of free behavior to the essential ends of mankind" (27: 345). This statement seems to leave open what the "essential ends" of mankind are, and could be included in any moral theory that treats human choices as actions as free in any sense; it does not say that the preservation or maximization of freedom is itself the object of morality. But Kant says exactly that a page later when he says that "The conditions under which alone the greatest use of freedom is possible, and under which it can be self-consistent, are the essential ends of mankind." Freedom "has to be restricted, not, though, by other properties and faculties, but by itself"; only thus can "any use of powers" be "compatible with the greatest use of them" and "freedom be consistent with itself" (27: 346). The fundamental requirement of morality is that freedom not be limited by our choices but preserved and extended as far as possible. Of course, there are limits to human freedom that are beyond our control. Individual human lives and, we have every reason to believe, the life of the entire human species as well are finite, not infinite,

---

[21] In the *Metaphysics of Morals* Kant will describe the duty to perfect one's natural and moral capacities as the duty to adopt the *end* of self-perfection. Walschots 2022 correctly argues that one can never be forced to adopt an end, only to perform external actions, so it is necessarily true that one can be motivated to adopt this end only from one's own respect for the moral law. He also argues that Kant does not consider it a distinct duty to act from (respect for) duty, which would lead to an infinite regress; however, Kant will argue that it *is* a duty to *cultivate* and *strengthen* our natural and inborn disposition to act from respect for duty. See Guyer 2010a and 2010b.

so the greatest possible freedom cannot be infinite in duration. There are natural forces other than finitude or mortality itself that limit our freedom—we cannot eat a rock, for example, so cannot rationally choose to do so; if someone tried to do so, that would be evidence of irrationality rather than freedom. Kant is not worrying about limits on our freedom like those, however. He is worrying about limits on freedom that we might unnecessarily impose upon ourselves and each other, and arguing that no limits on freedom are permissible except those that are necessary to preserve freedom itself, that is, intra- and interpersonal freedom, and that morality positively commands that we extend our freedom in any ways we can, again though consistent with the preservation of freedom. In these lectures Kant thus suggests that the necessity of rendering the use of freedom self-consistent and as great as possible is the foundation for all the negative and positive duties of morality, or our duties of omission and commission as they were often designated in eighteenth-century Germany.[22]

Kant provides straightforward examples of what he means in the case of duties to self. First, he explains that suicide is prohibited because in it "a man uses his freedom to destroy himself, when he ought to use it solely to live as a man; he is able to dispose over everything pertaining to his person, but not over that person itself, nor can he use his freedom against himself" (*Collins*, 27: 343). What Kant means by this, at least as if it is understood in terms of his general statement that the greatest self-consistent use of freedom is the essential end of mankind and the inner worth of the world, is that an act of suicide, considered by itself, might be a freely chosen act, as free as any other, but it is one that would undermine all possible further exercise of freedom by the suicide, that is, all further exercise of freedom that would be permitted to him by the ordinary course of nature (of course he would die eventually no matter what); it is morally prohibited for that reason. Introducing language that will become prominent a decade later in the *Groundwork for the Metaphysics of Morals*, Kant also states that "A man can indeed dispose over his condition, but not over his person, for he himself is an end and not a means. It is utterly absurd that a rational being, who is an end whereto every means exists, should use himself as a means" (27: 343). This passage is important, because in saying that it is absurd that something that is an end should be used as a means, Kant is suggesting that this is actually self-contradictory, thus reminding us of the argument from a decade earlier in his notes in his copy of the *Observations on the Feeling of the Beautiful and Sublime*. But since Kant has not explained what he means by the claim that a human being is an end and that it should not be used as a means, we need to understand this claim on the basis of his

---

[22] Christian Wolff, e.g., entitled his ethics *Vernünfftige Gedancken von der Menschen Thun und Lassen*, that is, *Rational Thoughts on Human Action and Omission*—although he added, in a way characteristic of everyone before Kant, *zur Beförderung ihrer Glückseligkeit*, that is, *for the Promotion of their Happiness*; Wolff 1733.

thesis that the self-consistent, maximal use of freedom is the essential end of mankind, rather than vice versa: to treat something, including oneself, as an end is to treat it as something whose freedom must be preserved or restricted by nothing other than freedom itself—that is, in the case of the prohibition of suicide, its own further freedom, while to treat it (merely, as Kant will later add) as a means is to treat it as something whose freedom may be restricted by or used for some purpose other than freedom itself.

Kant's second example is the prohibition of drunkenness. Here Kant admits that the choice to give in to inclination, including the inclination to get drunk, is, considered by itself, as much of a free choice as any other, indeed that "Everything harmful is the product of [human] invention and...freedom," indeed that by means of their freedom humans "can remodel the whole of nature to satisfy [their] inclinations." But although it is the result of a free choice, "if I have drunk too much today, I am incapable of making use of my freedom and my powers," just as "if I do away with myself, I likewise deprive myself of the ability to use them. So this conflicts with the greatest use of freedom...it abolishes itself." That is, although considered by itself the decision to get drunk is a free choice, considered in its whole context it is one that may or certainly will destroy some if not all of my potential further freedom: it will undermine my powers of choice and action for some time, and could even lead to my own injury or death and/or to the injury or death of another, for example if I drive while drunk, and therefore to the limitation or destruction of what would otherwise be my further freedom and/or the limitation or destruction of the freedom of another. In order to preserve and maximize rather than limit or altogether destroy the otherwise possible further freedom of myself and/or others, I must therefore adopt the "supreme rule: In all self-regarding actions, so to behave that any use of powers is compatible with the greatest use of them." For "Only under certain conditions can freedom be consistent with itself; otherwise it comes into collision with itself" (*Collins*, 27: 345–6). Freedom can conflict with itself not when we consider a single exercise of it, but when we consider the possibility of multiple exercises of freedom within a single human life and among multiple human lives, and since it is all of that possible freedom that constitutes the "inner worth" of the world, such self-destruction of freedom must be avoided.[23]

These examples of self-regarding duties, the duties to refrain from suicide and drunkenness because they destroy or compromise one's freedom, are examples of negative duties or duties of omission. Kant does not here discuss positive duties to oneself, such as the duties to develop or (of course never completely) perfect one's

---

[23] Christine Korsgaard has argued that Kant's principle of morality is what it takes for a person to be unified rather than a mere heap of impulses; see Korsgaard 2009, esp. chapter 7. My interpretation of Kant emphasizes that it is the consistency or unifiability of one's *free choices* with one's own continuing freedom and that of others that is the gist of morality. We will return to Korsgaard in Chapter 16.

physical, mental, and moral abilities. However, those duties can be understood as duties to maximize rather than merely not minimize one's freedom. A rational agent can freely and rationally set ends only for which she (believes she) has adequate means, and by developing one's abilities or potential talents one provides oneself with more or greater means to possible ends and thereby expands the range of ends one could rationally choose to adopt, and in that way expands one's freedom itself. Such positive duties to self will figure more prominently in Kant's subsequent discussions of duties to self in the *Groundwork* and the *Metaphysics of Morals*, however, so we can save further discussion of them until we come to those works.

The boundary between duties to self and duties to others may not always be as sharp as Kant suggests. In his own presentation of the duty to avoid drunkenness, Kant mentions only its effects on the agent's own further freedom; the reference to its possible effects on others is my addition. But one person's choice to get drunk might damage the freedom of others as well as his own, as the case of drunk driving makes all too clear. For that matter, a suicide can affect others than the person who commits it, not just emotionally, as the loss of a loved one, but in ways that limit their freedom as well: if someone who was financially dependent on the person who committed suicide now has to get a job instead of continuing in college, for example, that is case of the free choice of one person reducing the free choice of another in a way that would not otherwise have happened. We can distinguish between duties to self and to others, but few of our actions take place in a purely self-affecting bubble.

Indeed, it is helpful to see from these examples that duties to others can be understood within the framework of not necessarily restricting their freedom and where possible expanding it, affording them a greater range of choices by maximizing rather than minimizing means available to them, because Kant does not bring this out in his account of duties to others in the lectures of the 1770s. He divides duties to others into "Duties of good-will, or benevolence," and "Duties of indebtedness, or rectitude" (*Collins*, 27: 413), foreshadowing his subsequent division between duties of virtue and duties of right, but he provides a conventional basis for these two classes of duty, founding them on human needs on the one hand and rights on the other. His account of the foundation of the duty of benevolence, to do good to others, is reminiscent of the type of argument that we could find a century earlier, for example in John Locke. We might be benevolent toward others out of mere inclination, "well-wishing from inclination," but of course inclination is never a universally valid basis for moral obligation—some have it, some do not, it comes and goes, so it cannot provide a basis for universal and necessary rules. A duty of benevolence must rest on a principle.

What, then, is the source of the obligation to do good to others on principle? Here we must survey the worldly stage upon which nature has set us as guests, and on which we find everything needed for our temporal welfare. Everyone has a right to enjoy the good things of this world. But now since each has an equal interest therein, though God has not parceled out his share to anyone, but has left it to men to divide these goods among themselves, everyone must so enjoy these good things of life that he is mindful also of the happiness of others, who have an equal interest in them, and must not preempt anything from his fellows. For since the provision made for us is universal, one must not be indifferent to the happiness of others.   (*Collins*, 27: 413–14)

This passage basically takes Locke's account of the limits on appropriation of natural resources, that it is right to take from nature what one needs but subject to the proviso that because God has given mankind the earth in common, one must leave as well and as good for others,[24] and adds to it an argument for benevolence—perhaps the idea is that, because God has given us the good things of nature for our collective happiness, we must each have a concern not just for our individual happiness but for the happiness of others, and do what we can to promote that consistent with promoting our own happiness. Perhaps the idea is even the ancient idea of the *imitatio Dei*: because God has a concern for the happiness of all, we must each imitate God in that regard. Here there is no mention of the maximization of free choice as the foundation of the duty of benevolence, nor of the requirement not to minimize the free choice of others as the foundation of duties of rectitude or justice. Later Kant will explicate the duties of justice explicitly in those terms. It may take more work to find him grounding the affirmative duty of benevolence in those terms. That work can wait until we discuss the *Groundwork* and Kant's final *Metaphysics of Morals*. However, we might now just note this tantalizing passage from the transcription of Kant's lectures on the metaphysics of morals from 1793–4 by his lawyer Vigilantius: "The love for others can be considered in its generality, and to that it extent it rests on this, that our ends coincide with those of others in such a way that they are able to co-exist together according to the universal rule of duty" (*Vigilantius*, 27: 673). This formulation is close to the "Universal Principle of Right" that Kant will later enunciate, not a principle of benevolence, but differs in its use of the term "ends," that is, in its demand that we make the ends of others our own, which justice does not require. The point then would be that ends are freely set, or are themselves the products of free choice, and Kant would thus be explaining the requirement of love or benevolence as a duty to promote the free choice of others as well as of ourselves. This is at least a hint how to ground the duty of benevolence in freedom as the "inner worth of the world."

---

[24] Locke, *TG2*, chapter 5, "Of Property," §§26–7, pp. 304–6.

1.3. The *Critique of Pure Reason*

Before we turn directly to Kant's published works in moral philosophy, however, we must pause over the contributions to Kant's emerging moral philosophy made by the *Critique of Pure Reason*.[25] It might seem surprising that we need to discuss a work that we now think of as concerning issues of epistemology and metaphysics in an account of Kant's moral philosophy. However, Kant originally conceived of the first *Critique* as a sufficient foundation for *all* of his philosophy, and originally intended to proceed directly from it to his substantive metaphysics of nature and metaphysics of morality. Thus on February 21, 1772, Kant had written to his former student Marcus Herz, then studying medicine in Berlin, that he was working on a project titled *The Limits of Sensibility and Reason*, which would "consist of two parts, a theoretical and a practical," in which

> The first part would have two sections (1) a general phenomenology and (2) metaphysics, but this only with regard to its nature and method. The second part likewise would have two sections, (1) the universal principles of feeling, taste, and sensuous desire and (2) the first principles of morality.
>
> (10: 129; *Corr*, p. 132).

After he finally published the *Critique of Pure Reason* almost a decade later, in 1781, Kant decided that more foundational work needed to be done than he had accomplished there before he could proceed to the metaphysics of morals as the account of the actual duties of human beings, and thus he wrote the *Groundwork* and then the *Critique of Practical Reason* before he finally produced the *Metaphysics of Morals*. But the *Critique of Pure Reason*, incomplete as it turned out to be as a foundation for Kant's moral philosophy, nevertheless introduced several key presuppositions of that philosophy as well as one of its key concepts, that of the highest good for human beings, although not in its final form.

The *Critique of Pure Reason* makes two fundamental contributions to the development of Kant's moral philosophy. First, it develops Kant's conception of pure reason and thereby provides the framework for his elaboration of a moral philosophy grounded in pure reason; second, it exploits the doctrine of transcendental idealism for which the first *Critique* argues to make room for the *possibility* of free will at the level of our real, "noumenal" selves, even though at the "phenomenal" level all appearances, including those of ourselves, our choices, and our actions are fully determined by causal laws and antecedent events—although Kant will argue in the second *Critique* that only morality itself can

---

[25] Of course there are a vast number of commentaries on the *Critique of Pure Reason*. In addition to Guyer 1987 and Guyer 2014a, a very small list of comprehensive commentaries in English would include Caird 1889, Kemp Smith 1923, Paton 1936, Weldon 1958, Strawson 1966, Bennett 1966 and 1974, Allison 2004, and Bird 2006.

confirm the *reality* of free will, which Kant always believes to be a necessary condition of moral responsibility or in his term imputability. There are three crucial steps in Kant's elaboration of his conception of pure reason. First, Kant introduces the conception of *ideas of reason*, ideas that reason generates from the categories of the understanding such as substance, ground, and community (*CPuR*, A76–83/B102–9) by applying to them its own idea of the "unconditioned," that is, by imagining them as complete and perfect in a way that the application of the categories to the intuitions or data of sensibility to provide our ordinary knowledge of objects never can be because sensibility itself is always conditioned, not unconditioned (*CPuR*, A307–8/B364–5, A322–3/B379). Any space that we can represent can always be represented as contained in a larger space, any time that we can represent can always be represented as contained in a larger time, so, since empirical objects are always represented in space and/or time, our representation of any empirical objects whatsoever, whether in ordinary life or in advanced natural science, is always conditioned by that fact. That means that our *cognition* of the world, the subject of theoretical philosophy, is always incomplete and indefinitely extendable—conditioned rather than unconditioned. But in the practical sphere, which concerns what *ought* to be done rather than what does exist and *is* done, we are free to imagine perfection, even if it "can never be fully expressed in experience" (*CPuR*, A318–19/B375). Or, "objective **laws of freedom**...say **what ought to happen**, even though perhaps it never does happen," while "**laws of nature**...deal only with that **which does happen**" (*CPuR*, A802/B830). The difference between the role of the ideas of reason in the theoretical and practical cases is perhaps subtle, for in the practical sphere we know well that people are not always fully moral, indeed are often far from it, and perhaps that they *might* never be, but in the theoretical sphere we know that the world of objects in space and time which is the object of our inquiry and knowledge *cannot* ever be complete. So ideas of reason in the theoretical context, like the idea of a world complete in space and time and completely knowable or a complete causal explanation of the world, can only ever be what Kant calls regulative ideals (*CPuR*, A672–3/B700–1, A680/B708), to which we can at best approach asymptotically; but in the practical sphere ideas of reason, such as the idea of a complete community of rational beings, can be norms that we can and must strive to realize fully—even if we never do fully realize these norms, at least under ordinary conditions (more about that in a moment), there is nothing to say that we *could not* do so. In the theoretical case, there is no chance that the "**totality of conditions to a given conditioned thing**" can ever actually be given to us (*CPuR*, A322/B379), but in the practical sphere our task is precisely to try to realize the unconditioned, to bring about perfection or complete compliance with the moral law.[26]

---

[26] A restriction of this claim will be that what Kant calls imperfect duties, under the general headings of developing one's own talents and promoting the happiness of others, can always be fulfilled only to a degree, never completely, or perfectly.

Second, in addition to advancing in this way over the inaugural dissertation's passing remark that the moral law is known by pure intellect, not yet divided into two separate faculties of understanding and reason, Kant also suggests something more about the actual content of the moral law, which he had not done in the dissertation. The moral law is derived by reason from the third category of relation, community, or interaction (*CPuR*, A80/B106), and is really the idea of perfect community among *agents*, beings with wills and ends of their own, in their actions and interactions, transformed into a norm of what ought to be rather than a knowledge-claim about what is. With a nod to Plato, who had first "made use of the expression **idea** in such a way that we can readily see that he understood by it something that not only could never be borrowed from the senses, but that even goes far beyond the concepts of the understanding (with which Aristotle occupied himself)" (*CPuR*, A313/B370), and who in his *Republic* explored the idea of justice at great length (A316/B372), Kant illustrates his initial discussion of the ideas of reason with his own interpretation of the ideal of perfect justice: "A constitution providing for the **greatest human freedom** according to laws that permit **the freedom of each to exist together with that of others** (not one providing for the greatest happiness, since that would follow of itself) is at least a necessary idea, which one must make the ground not merely of the primary plan of a state's constitution but of all the laws too" (A316/B373). Although Kant makes no attempt here to derive this norm from anything more fundamental, it is pregnant with Kant's entire moral philosophy, and in a more straightforward form than we will find it in the *Groundwork* and *Critique of Practical Reason*. Kant's statement is virtually identical to the definition of the condition of right or justice that he will offer almost two decades later in the Doctrine of Right of the *Metaphysics of Morals*, although there he makes clear that justice proper, the domain of laws properly coercively enforced by the mechanisms of the state, is restricted to the external use of choice, that is, the use of one's freedom to choose actions that can affect the freedom of others to choose their actions. Justice concerns "the external and indeed practical relation of one person to another, insofar as their actions, as deeds, can have (direct or indirect) influence on each other" (*MM*, DR, Introduction, section B, 6: 230). But as we have already seen from Kant's lectures on ethics, the entire content of the moral law, including the duties that cannot be enforced by juridical and penal institutions as well as the part that can be, can be expressed in terms of the "greatest human freedom": maximal consistency in any agent's intrapersonal use of her freedom of choice, and maximal consistency in the interpersonal use of freedom of choice. This conception of what morality requires, the "essential ends of humankind," is still clearly present in the *Critique of Pure Reason* in 1781. Although Kant's way of presenting the fundamental requirement of morality will look different in the *Groundwork* and the *Critique of Practical Reason*, it would be remarkable if Kant had radically changed his fundamental idea in the four years between that and the publication of the *Groundwork* in 1785.

Kant's third application of the concept of ideas of reason in the *Critique of Pure Reason* is his introduction of the "ideal of the highest good" as the "complete good for our reason" (*CPuR*, A813/B841), or as he will subsequently call it, the "necessary object of a will determinable by the moral law" (*CPracR*, 5: 122) or the "final end assigned by pure reason and comprehending the whole of all ends under one principle" (*TP*, 8: 279n.)—under each name, an idea of unconditioned moral completeness conceivable only by pure practical reason, that is, pure reason in its application to actions, or practice. Kant introduces the ideal of the highest good in a chapter of the second main part of the *Critique of Pure Reason*, its "Doctrine of Method," which in the tradition of early modern logic textbooks[27] concerns the application of the first part of the *Critique*, its (much longer) "Doctrine of Elements," comprised by the "Transcendental Aesthetic" in which he argued for his transcendental idealist interpretation of space and time as merely the forms of human sensibility, the "Transcendental Analytic" in which he presented the categories and principles of the understanding and argued that they yield knowledge only in application to the deliverances of our senses, and the "Transcendental Dialectic," in which he argued that the ideas of pure reason can have only a regulative function in theoretical cognition but, as we have just seen, provide the foundations for the practical use of reason in morality. This chapter is titled the "Canon of Pure Reason." By a canon, Kant means a body of laws (as in canon law), "the sum total of the *a priori* principles of the correct use of certain cognitive faculties in general" (*CPuR*, A796/B824), and he uses this title for a presentation of some elements of his moral philosophy because of his claim that it is only in the practical context that reason can provide outright laws—the moral law and the duties that derive from it—rather than mere regulative ideals. The ideal of the highest good, which we are commanded by reason to realize, is the idea of "happiness in exact proportion with the morality of rational beings, through which they are worthy of it ... a world into which we must without exception transpose ourselves in accordance with the precepts of pure but practical reason" (A814/B843). Kant claims that our conception of a perfect world in which perfect morality is combined with perfect happiness—a world in which both morality and happiness are completely unconditioned, that is, unlimited—is a necessary idea of reason:

> Now in an intelligible world, i.e., in the moral world, in the concept of which we have abstracted from all hindrances to morality (of the inclinations), such a system of happiness proportionately combined with morality can also be thought as necessary, since freedom, partly moved and partly restricted by moral laws, would itself be the cause of the general happiness, and rational beings, under the

---

[27] See Tonelli 1994.

guidance of such principles, would themselves be the authors of their own enduring welfare and at the same time that of others. (*CPuR*, A809/B837)

Kant calls this concept the idea of a "system of self-rewarding morality." He does not explain this statement, but if we interpret it in light of both what he has already said about the use of freedom and what he will say in his subsequent works we can see what he has in mind: morality does not directly command the pursuit of happiness, rather it requires the greatest possible consistent intra- and interpersonal use of freedom of choice; but if happiness consists simply in people getting what they choose, or realizing the ends that they freely choose, as Kant will indeed define it, then the greatest possible consistent use of choice will, under ideal circumstances, result in the greatest possible happiness.[28] Such happiness would not be the *object* or direct aim of morality, but it would, under ideal circumstances, be its *consequence*.

However, we do not live under ideal circumstances; nature outside of human beings can frustrate us, but more importantly, as we know perfectly well, human beings do not always behave morally and thus frustrate each other and for that matter themselves as well. That is why this "system of self-rewarding morality" is the *idea* of an "intelligible" world, not a "sensible world" that could be the object of theoretical cognition (*CPuR*, A814/B 842). And here is where Kant then appeals to ideas of pure reason, now in the specific form of ideas of God and of personal immortality, in the form of what he will subsequently call "postulates of pure practical reason," although he does not yet use that phrase in the *Critique of Pure Reason*. Nor is Kant's account of the postulates the same as he will subsequently, at least sometimes, suggest. His argument in the first *Critique* is that in order for one to maintain the "resolve" to be moral in the face of knowledge that not everyone else will be and that the immoral actions of others might frustrate one's own expectation of happiness in the natural world, the agent who is moral has to be able to believe in "God and a future life," in "a world that is now not visible to us but is hoped for," in which the "whole end that is [both] natural for every rational being and determined *a priori* and necessarily through...pure reason" (*CPuR*, A811–13/B 839–41) is realized. That is, even though an individual who is herself entirely moral cannot expect to be fully happy in the natural world, she must still be able to believe that if she is fully moral she will be fully happy—not as a *motivation* to be moral but as a condition, given human psychology, of

---

[28] Francis Hutcheson, an author well known to Kant, defined happiness as "the highest and most durable Gratifications of, either all our *Desires*, or, if all cannot be gratify'd at once, of those which tend to the greatest and most durable *Pleasures*, with exemption either from all *Pains* and Objects of *Aversion*, or at least from those which are most grievous"; Hutcheson 2002, treatise I, section IV, subsection V, pp. 80–1. Substitute "realization of freely chosen ends" for Hutcheson's gratifications of desire and exemption from pains and you have Kant's conception of happiness.

maintaining her resolve to be moral[29]—so she must be believe in the existence of God, as the "highest original good" who can provide happiness to the morally worthy, and in a future life, that is, her own immortality, as the time when this will happen. One *can* believe these things, Kant argues, because as he has previously shown, although one cannot *prove* the existence of God or personal immortality, neither can one *disprove* it—these ideas are simply beyond the reach of theoretical confirmation or disconfirmation; and one *must* believe these things, because otherwise one's resolve to be moral may be weakened. This is what Kant calls in the final section of the Canon of Pure Reason rational *belief* or *faith* (*Glaube*) rather than theoretical knowledge or cognition (*CPuR*, A820–31/B848–59).[30]

Kant's doctrine of the postulates of pure practical reason drew criticism immediately and has done so ever since. Kant himself soon modified or at least amplified this theory, whether or not in response to external criticism, and at least sometimes shifted from the individualistic conception of the highest good of the first *Critique*—that moral individuals must be able to believe in the eventuality of *their own* happiness, not as the incentive to be moral but as the condition of possibility of maintaining the resolve to be moral—to a collective conception of the highest good, namely that the human species as a whole must be able to believe that its collective efforts to be moral could eventually result in happiness for the human species, indeed at some point in human history, not in an afterlife, and still facilitated by God, although not as a divine rewarder but as the author of nature itself. We will see this transformation of his doctrine of the highest good in Kant's works from the 1790s. But first we must examine the final contribution of the *Critique of Pure Reason* to Kant's mature moral philosophy: its attempt to resolve the problem of freedom of the will.[31]

This occurs back in the Transcendental Dialectic of the Doctrine of Elements, specifically in the chapter titled "The Antinomy of Pure Reason" (A405–567/ B432–595). This is the longest single chapter in the *Critique*, thus perhaps dearest to Kant's heart. Indeed it is the heart of Kant's "critique" in the negative sense, his critique of all previous metaphysics. Here he argues that the attempted application of the ideas of pure reason to what is given by human sensibility gives rise to four "antinomies," apparently intractable conflicts between apparently cogent arguments for both sides on the four fundamental issues of philosophical cosmology.

---

[29] See also Kant's discussion of a "righteous man (like Spinoza) who takes himself to be firmly convinced that there is no God": he may well know what morality requires and be motivated to do it, but without belief in God he will not be able to "remain attached to the appeal of his inner moral vocation" and the "respect, by which the moral law immediately influences him to obedience," will inevitably be weakened; *CPJ*, §87, 5: 452.

[30] On Kant's conception of rational belief or faith, see Wood 1970 and Chignell 2007, 2021a, and 2021b.

[31] For my survey of the evolution of Kant's treatment of freedom of the will, see Guyer 2014a, pp. 245–65; see also Timmermann 2003, Schönecker 2005, and, for the most detailed treatment of freedom of the will throughout Kant's career, Allison 2020.

These issues are the extent of the cosmos in space and time, the divisibility of the cosmos in space and time, the possibility of spontaneity or creation of the cosmos *ex nihilo*, and whether there is any necessary ground of all the contingencies of the cosmos. In each case, Kant opposes a "thesis" to an "antithesis," all of which could be associated with historical positions in philosophy although Kant does not do that, because he holds that these are natural, inevitable conflicts of human reason unless resolved by his own philosophy of transcendental philosophy.[32] Kant calls the first two antinomies the "mathematical" antinomies because they concern issues of size and duration, the latter two the "dynamical" antinomies because they concern relations between ground and consequence.[33] The first antinomy is a conflict over what completeness (the unconditioned) in extent in space and time would mean, thus whether an unconditioned cosmos must be completely finite in spatial and temporal extent, or completely infinite. The second antinomy concerns completeness in the division of spatio-temporal extent, thus whether completeness in division must terminate in indivisible simples or atoms, or whether reality must be infinitely divisible. The third antinomy, the first of the dynamical antinomies, debates whether the complete or unconditioned application of causation, or of the principle of sufficient reason, must terminate in something itself uncaused or spontaneous, or instead only in an actually infinite chain of causes and effects in which nothing is ever a first cause or spontaneous. And the fourth antinomy is the conflict between the position that the complete series of objects and events in the cosmos must have a necessary ground outside of themselves, and the position that all that exists is the series of objects and events causally necessary relative to each other within the series of events which is however contingent as a whole, with no necessary ground.

Kant's resolution of these antinomies on the basis of his doctrine of transcendental idealism, that space and time are merely the forms in which reality appears to us, not the forms of reality itself, which, as in his view the only possible resolution of these conflicts, is also intended to be a confirmation of this doctrine (*CPuR*, Bxix–xxi), is this. In the mathematical antinomies, both sides explicitly concern space and time, and both are wrong because they assume that space and time are independent realities that must be either finite or infinite. Space and time are rather indefinitely extendable forms of intuition, so the world of objects and events in space and time is neither finite nor infinite in extent or divisibility, only ever indefinitely extendable or divisible. In the case of the dynamical antinomies, however, both sides *could be true*, because the antitheses concern the world in space and time but the theses concern the possible *grounds* of this world *outside* of

---

[32] Although for an attempt at an historical interpretation of the antinomies as Kant's representation of a conflict between Leibnizians and Newtonians, see Al-Azm 1972. See also Falkenburg 2020. For a detailed examination of Kant's antinomies, see Proops 2021, pp. 209–333.

[33] For Kant's previous distinction between mathematical and dynamical principles of judgment, that is, a priori principles of empirical judgment rather than metaphysics, see *CPur*, A160–1/B199–200.

it. Thus, the world of appearances may be a series of causes and effects that is completely deterministic internally, with relations of only hypothetical necessity among its constituent events, but there *could be* a spontaneous and absolutely necessary *ground* (although not spatio-temporal *cause*) of this world outside of and not a part of it.

> The dynamic regress has in itself this peculiar feature, distinguishing it from the mathematical one: that since the latter really has to do only with the combination of parts into a whole, or with the dissolution of a whole into its parts, the conditions of this series always have to be seen as parts of it, hence as being of the same kind,... whereas in the former regress, which has to do not with the possibility of an unconditioned whole... but with the derivation of a state from its cause or of the contingent existence of a substance itself from the necessary existence of one, the condition need not necessarily constitute one empirical series along with the conditioned.   (*CPuR*, A560/B588)

Thus there is conceptual room for the *possibility* of a spontaneous and necessary ground of the world of appearances outside of the world, although precisely because this would be outside of the world we can never *know* that it exists. Still, we can *believe* that it exists, at least if that turns out to be necessary on some practical ground (*CPuR*, Bxxvi–xxxi).

And then Kant makes the move that is the key to his resolution of the problem of free will: if we can at least conceive of and believe in *one* spontaneous ground of appearance, there is no reason why we cannot conceive of and believe in *more than one*—namely, conceive and believe that, at the level of reality, *our own wills* are the spontaneous grounds of what seem to be merely deterministic series of events at the level of appearance, in which our choices are always *in media res* and thus determined by long chains of events before them. This possibility would not *follow* from the possibility of one spontaneous ground of appearance, namely God, but the possibility of spontaneity in the case of God at least leaves room for the possibility of our own spontaneity, in the form of the freedom of the will (although just as there is a theological difficulty in conceiving of God as free, so there would be a theological difficulty in reconciling divine freedom with human freedom).[34] The distinction between spatio-temporal, causally determined appearance, on the one hand, and reality, on the other, not subject to these conditions, makes room for spontaneity in general, not just in one case: "By freedom in the cosmological sense... I understand the faculty of beginning a state **from itself**, the causality of which does not in turn stand under another cause determining it in time in accordance with the law of nature. Freedom in this signification is a pure

---

[34] See again Insole 2013.

transcendental idea, which...contains nothing borrowed from experience" (*CPuR*, A533/B561). This is the conceptual space for freedom of the human will.

Kant himself states that in the *Critique of Pure Reason* "we have not been trying to establish the **reality** of our freedom," indeed he goes so far as to say that "we have not even tried to prove the **possibility** of freedom...because from mere concepts *a priori* we cannot cognize anything about the possibility of any real ground or any causality....that nature at least **does not conflict** with causality— that was the one single thing we could accomplish" (*CPuR*, A588/B586). This statement might seem self-contradictory, but it assumes Kant's distinction between *logical* possibility, the mere freedom of a concept from self-contradiction, and *real* possibility, which has to include a reason for thinking that its object can be given to us in some way. Most interpreters have ignored this subtlety, and adopted the position that the *Critique of Pure Reason* is meant to establish the possibility of human freedom, but only the subsequent works on the foundations of morality, the *Groundwork* and the second *Critique*, are intended to establish its reality, although then only on practical rather than theoretical grounds. Rather Kant seems to mean that he has established only the logical possibility of freedom of the will, not even its real possibility, which will require a *ratio essendi*. In spite of his own statement, however, and in spite of the subsequent tradition of interpretation, in the *Critique of Pure Reason* Kant *does* anticipate the arguments by which he will later attempt to establish the reality of human freedom of the will. In fact, Kant anticipates *both* of the arguments he will later develop, one in the *Groundwork* and the other in the second *Critique*, the latter of which conforms to the restriction that the positive argument for freedom of the will can be based only on practical grounds, but the first of which seems to be a straightforwardly theoretical argument for the reality of freedom of the will. These two arguments come in two successive paragraphs.

First, Kant writes:

> In the case of lifeless nature and nature having merely animal life, we find no ground for thinking of any faculty which is other than sensibly conditioned. Yet the human being, who is otherwise acquainted with the whole of nature solely through sense, *knows himself also through pure apperception*, and indeed in actions and inner determinations which cannot be accounted at all among impressions of sense; he obviously is in one part phenomenon, but in another part, namely, in regard to certain faculties, he is a merely intelligible object, because the actions of this object cannot at all be ascribed to the receptivity of sensibility. We call these faculties understanding and reason
>
> (*CPuR*, A546–7/B574–5, emphasis added),

including practical reason, the source of the idea of the moral community of free agents and of the moral law. This passage anticipates the argument that Kant will make for the reality of human freedom and the bindingness of the moral law in section III of the *Groundwork*, although here as well as there it seems to violate Kant's stricture on any positive knowledge of things as they are in themselves— Kant seems to be saying that apperception, or self-consciousness (Kant borrows the term from Leibniz), is genuine knowledge of ourselves as we are in ourselves, and includes knowledge of our "cosmological" freedom.[35]

Kant is usually thought to have replaced this forbidden metaphysical, theoretical argument with a permissible argument from purely practical grounds in the *Critique of Practical Reason*. But he already states the latter argument too in the *Critique of Pure Reason*, immediately following that just quoted.

> Now that this reason [practical reason] has causality, or that we can at least represent something of the sort in it, is clear from the **imperatives** that we propose as rules to our powers of execution in everything practical. The **ought** expresses a species of necessity and connection with grounds which does not occur anywhere else in the whole of nature. In nature the understanding can cognize only **what exists**, or has been, or will be. It is impossible that something in it **ought to be** other than what, in all these time-relations, it in fact is; indeed, the **ought**, if one has merely the course of nature before one's eyes, has no significance whatsoever.   (*CPuR*, A547/B575)

But in the practical sphere, "the law of reason ... regards reason as a cause that, regardless of all the empirical conditions just named, could have and ought to have determined the conduct of the person to be other than it is" (A555/B583), and in the practical sphere we hold that *ought implies can*, thus that persons are, at their core, free to act as morality requires, even if they all too obviously do not always or even ever do so. We cannot explain *how* persons are free to be moral, that is, what noumenal causality in accordance with the moral law is actually like, because our explanations are always confined to the phenomenal level of spatio-temporal reality, but we can and must believe that we are free to act in accordance with the moral law, no matter what. This is the position Kant will adopt in the *Critique of Practical Reason* under the name of the "fact of reason."

If Kant's argument in section III of the *Groundwork* is indeed a violation of the proscription of theoretical metaphysics by the *Critique of Pure Reason*, it cannot be considered merely a momentary lapse from which he recovered in the *Critique of Practical Reason*; whether they are compatible or not, the arguments of both works are already present in the first *Critique*. And as we will see throughout this book, Kant's solution to the problem of free will, which seems controversial in his own hands, would remain controversial. But let us leave that issue for now, and finally turn to the overall form of Kant's mature moral philosophy as presented in the two foundational books of 1785 and 1788.

---

[35] On the argument of *Groundwork* III, see Guyer 2007a, Schönecker 1999, and Schönecker 2015.

2

The Foundations of Kant's Mature Moral Philosophy in the *Groundwork* and *Critique of Practical Reason*

2.1. Kant's Two Foundational Works in Moral Philosophy

As noted, Kant originally intended the *Critique of Pure Reason* to be the complete foundation for his substantive metaphysics of both nature and morals. Thus when he wrote it he had no plan yet to write a separate *Groundwork for the Metaphysics of Morals*, and when he published the latter, he apparently had no plan yet for a subsequent *Critique of Practical Reason*. He seems to have hatched the plan for a *Critique of the Power of Judgment*, which brings the topics of aesthetics and teleology—judgments of beauty and sublimity and judgments about purposes in nature—into the framework of his critical philosophy only as he was completing the *Critique of Practical Reason*.[1] Some have argued that the composition of the *Groundwork* was prompted by the popularity of Christian Garve's 1783 translation of and commentary on Cicero's *De officiis*:[2] Kant would have wanted to counter the eclectic and pluralistic ethics of Cicero with his own rationalistic foundations for moral philosophy.[3] And although the third section of the *Groundwork* is titled "Final Step from Metaphysics of Morals to the Critique of Pure Practical Reason" (*G*, 4: 392), by this Kant does not seem to have meant that this section, or the *Groundwork* as a whole, was the transition to an already planned *Critique of Pure Practical Reason*; rather, he seems to have meant that the third section of the *Groundwork* itself contained the necessary critique of pure practical reason. The need for a full second *Critique* appears to have become clear to him only during his work on the revisions of the *Critique of Pure Reason* for its

---

[1] On or about September 11, 1787, Kant wrote to Ludwig Heinrich Jacob that, with the *Critique of Practical Reason* now at the printer, he was ready to "turn at once" to a book to be titled the *Critique of Taste*, which he thought would appear by the following Easter (10: 493–4; *Corr*, pp. 262–3). But it was only in a letter to Karl Leonhard Reinhold, written on December 28 to 31, 1787, that he suggested that the work would also address teleology, that is, purposiveness in nature; he still predicted that the work would be completed by the following Easter, i.e., 1788, but the third *Critique* was not finished and published until the Easter book fair of 1790 (10: 513–16; *Corr*, pp. 271–3).

[2] Cicero 1783 and Garve 1783.

[3] Most famously, Klaus Reich in Reich 1935. See also Kuehn 2001, pp. 278–83, and Wood 2006, at pp. 361–5.

Kant's Impact on Moral Philosophy. Paul Guyer, Oxford University Press. © Paul Guyer 2024.
DOI: 10.1093/oso/9780199592456.003.0003

second edition, which appeared in 1787; the *Critique of Practical Reason* was then written in 1787 and published in 1788. For the new edition of the first *Critique*, its first half by volume, that is, the Transcendental Aesthetic, the Transcendental Analytic, and the first part of the Transcendental Dialectic, the Paralogism of Pure Reason, in which Kant limits metaphysical insight into the nature of ourselves, were extensively revised, but the rest of the Transcendental Dialectic and the Doctrine of Method were left untouched. Although we have virtually no record of Kant's thoughts about the revision of the first *Critique*,[4] it seems reasonable to speculate that as he thought about the two central topics in this remaining half of the book, namely his treatment of freedom of the will in the third Antinomy and of the highest good in the Canon of Pure Reason, he realized that those needed far more discussion than he could give them within the framework of a revised first *Critique* and thus called for a critique of their own. In any case, those are the two main topics of the second *Critique* and much of what it adds to the *Groundwork*. The new *Critique of the Power of Judgment* then appeared just two years later in 1790. Kant obviously wrote at white heat throughout the "critical decade" of the 1780s, which in addition to all three critiques and the *Groundwork* also saw the publication of his metaphysics of nature, the *Metaphysical Foundations of Natural Science* in 1786. The complementary *Metaphysics of Morals*, the application of the fundamental principle of morality established in the *Groundwork* and the second *Critique* to yield a substantive doctrine of human juridical and ethical duties, would, however, wait until 1797, with the main work in the intervening period being Kant's philosophy of religion, *Religion within the Boundaries of Mere Reason*, as well as the pamphlet *Toward Perpetual Peace*. *Religion within the Boundaries of Mere Reason* continued Kant's attempt to clarify his position on freedom of the will, while *Perpetual Peace* began Kant's effort to apply his general principle of morality to the political sphere.

To orient ourselves amidst this group of works we must realize that Kant actually means two different things by the phrase "metaphysics of morals." In the *Groundwork*, Kant states that "the metaphysics of morals has to examine the idea and the principles of a possible *pure* will and not the actions and conditions of human volition generally, which for the most part are drawn from psychology" (*G*, 4: 390–1), or what Kant also calls anthropology. The purpose of a metaphysics of morals in this sense is "nothing more than"—but also nothing less than—"the search for and establishment [*Aufsuchung und Festsetzung*] of the **supreme principle of morality**" (*G*, 4: 392). The task of a metaphysics of morals in this sense is the formulation and justification of the fundamental principle of morality, or at least the defense of this principle, once properly formulated, from any

---

[4] The notes that Kant made in his own copy of the first edition of the first *Critique*, which are reproduced in the Guyer-Wood translation, cover only the parts of the book that he did in the end revise, not the parts that were not revised.

reasonable objection.[5] But why then is the *Groundwork* called a "groundwork" for the metaphysics of morals rather than the metaphysics of morals itself, given that it does not merely prepare but completes, at least to Kant's satisfaction in 1785, the tasks of formulating and defending the supreme principle of morality? This is because in a second sense a metaphysics for Kant is body of principles or doctrines that results from the *application* of a pure, a priori principle to certain fundamental, *empirical* but indisputable facts. Thus, Kant's metaphysical foundations of natural science apply the synthetic a priori principles of nature deduced in the *Critique of Pure Reason* to the fundamental empirical fact that we perceive substance as matter in motion; and the parallel metaphysics of morals applies the pure, a priori fundamental principle of morality, valid as Kant always stresses for all rational beings, to "the particular *nature* of human beings, which is cognized only by experience, in order to *show* in it what can be inferred from universal moral principles. . . . This is to say, in effect, that a metaphysics of morals cannot be based upon anthropology but can still be applied to it" (*MM*, Introduction, 6: 217). This application yields the juridical and ethical duties of human beings. In the sense of metaphysics of morals first defined in its Preface, the *Groundwork* is the complete formulation and defense of the fundamental principle of morality (although Kant would revisit some of its arguments in the *Critique of Practical Reason*); in the sense of metaphysics of morals defined in the Introduction to the work titled *Metaphysics of Morals*, the *Groundwork* supplied only the a priori principle for the derivation of our actual juridical and ethical duties. The empirical facts required for this derivation are above all that we humans are embodied beings, that we need the use of various physical objects in order to survive, and that we unavoidably interact with each within the finite space of the surface of our globe. Kant's twofold usage of the phrase "metaphysics of morals" must be kept in mind when we consider subsequent criticisms of his approach as excessively aprioristic and formalistic.

A few words about the organization of the *Groundwork* and the *Critique of Practical Reason* are necessary before we can plunge into their doctrines.[6] Two facts about the *Groundwork* must be noted. First, it is divided into three sections, which Kant calls the "Transition from common rational to philosophical moral cognition," the "Transition from popular moral philosophy to metaphysics of morals," and, as already mentioned, the "Final step from metaphysics of morals to

---

[5] For an interpretation of the *Groundwork* as intended to provide a defense rather than a deduction of the moral law, see also Rosen 2022, p. 75.

[6] There are far too many commentaries on the *Groundwork* for me to engage with them in detail (except for Ross 1954 and Rawls 2000, which are considered in Chapters 13 and 15 below as part of the more general discussion of those philosophers). Useful commentaries include Paton 1947; Williams 1968; Wolff 1973; Aune 1979; Sullivan 1989; Höffe 1989; Wood 1999, part I, and Schönecker and Wood 2015; Guyer 2007c; Timmermann 2007; Sedgwick 2008; Uleman 2010; Allison 2011; Kim 2015; Cholbi 2016; Klemme 2017; Ludwig 2020. Commentaries on the *Critique of Practical Reason* include Beck 1960 and Sala 2004.

the critique of pure practical reason" (*G*, 4: 392). But the relation among these sections is not a linear succession, in which each begins from the conclusion of the previous one. Rather, in order to understand their more complex relation, we have to take account of the second feature, expressed in Kant's statement that "I have adopted in this work the method that is, I believe, most suitable if one wants to proceed analytically from common cognition to the determination of its supreme principle, and in turn from the examination of this principle and its sources back to the common cognition in which we find it used" (*G*, 4: 392). This suggests that the argument of the book is not strictly linear but both progressive and regressive. Actually, the method of the work is even more complicated than this, because it involves two different movements from analysis to synthesis. One characterizes the overall structure of Kant's argument. In the first section, Kant analyzes what he takes to be a common conception of good will and duty that every normal human being accepts, even if he or she does not formulate it in the technical language of philosophy, to yield a first formulation of the fundamental principle of morality. In its general form, this principle would be valid for any rational being, because "the ground of obligation here must not be sought in the nature of the human being or in the circumstances of the world in which he is placed, but *a priori* simply in concepts of pure reason" (*G*, 4: 389), but in the case of humans, who have inclinations to do otherwise than what morality requires and thus can find its demands constraining, Kant calls this principle the "categorical imperative" (*G*, 4: 413). The results of the analysis of the concepts of good will and duty, however, are strictly hypothetical, as are all results of purely or merely conceptual analysis: *if* those concepts apply to us, then we are bound or obligated by the categorical imperative. The transition of the second section is not directly from this result to the synthetic proposition that we are in fact bound by the categorical imperative, however; rather, it continues the analytical phase of the argument. For the "popular moral philosophy" with which Kant begins the second section is not the "common rational cognition of morality" of the first section, but rather a natural but misguided moral philosophy, which is essentially utilitarianism, the idea that morality simply requires the maximization of happiness. Kant then *replaces* this with a line of argument that is independent of the first section of the book but comes to the same conclusion, namely a formulation of the categorical imperative, although now more complex, as Wood calls it a "system of formulas,"[7] which however still need to be proven to apply to and obligate us human beings. The synthetic phase of the overall argument, namely proving the synthetic proposition that the categorical imperative actually *does* obligate us, then seems to be the task left for the final part of the *Groundwork*, and Kant says as much at the end of the second section (*G*, 4: 445). However, Kant also employs

---

[7] Wood 2001 and Wood 2017.

what can be considered another synthetic method *within* the second section that also fits his description of a synthetic move from the pure principle of morality to "the common cognition in which we find it used" (G, 4: 392), namely, the demonstration twice over in the course of his formulations of the categorical imperative in this section that his principle really does yield the "usual division" of human duties "into duties to ourselves and to other human beings and into perfect and imperfect duties" (G, 4: 421). The distinction between perfect and imperfect duties goes back to Hugo Grotius and Samuel Pufendorf, so Kant could well take it as a commonplace, even though he will change the criterion of perfect duty from enforceability to specificity, which is a necessary but not sufficient condition for enforceability.[8] Demonstrating that his version of the fundamental principle of morality does yield what were commonly taken to be the actual duties of human beings, regardless of their varying philosophical theories of these duties, would offer confirmation that Kant's analysis of the fundamental principle of morality is correct, although precisely because the classification of duties is compatible with other moral theories this would not constitute proof. The proof of the synthetic proposition that the fundamental principle of morality, in the form of the categorical imperative, really does apply to us, is then what awaits the third section of the *Groundwork*, and then the unforeseen *Critique of Practical Reason*. The more detailed description and derivation of our particular duties as human beings will await the final *Metaphysics of Morals*.

The *Critique of Practical Reason* also has a complicated structure, based on the structure of the *Critique of Pure Reason* although with subtle but important variations. Like the first, the second *Critique* is divided into a Doctrine of Elements and a Doctrine of Method; in the latter Kant argues that moral education should proceed by giving examples of people who have done the right thing even in the face of terrible costs, which will convince the young that they are also always free to do what morality requires, even if in their ordinary lives it will never require as much. This approach makes sense for him, because since the moral law is a priori, Kant assumes that it becomes known to everyone early in life, and what we all really need to learn, and can learn by example, is that it is always possible for us to act in accordance with it.[9] The philosophical basis for that assurance, in turn, is the primary subject of the Transcendental Analytic of the *Critique of Practical Reason*, as in the first *Critique* the first half of its Doctrine of Elements, followed by a Transcendental Dialectic. The latter presents Kant's next version of the doctrine of the highest good and of the postulates of the existence of God and personal immortality, somewhat revised from the Canon of Pure Reason in the first *Critique*. The Analytic of Pure Practical Reason, like the Analytic of the first *Critique*, is divided into three chapters, "On the Principles of Pure Practical

---

[8] See Schneewind 1998a, pp. 79, 131–4.   [9] See Guyer 2011b.

Reason," "On the Concept of an Object of Pure Practical Reason," and "On the Incentives of Pure Practical Reason." Kant explains that this is the reverse of the order of exposition from "that in the critique of pure speculative reason," which proceeded from intuitions to concepts to principles, for:

> in the present *Critique* we shall begin with *principles* and proceed to *concepts*, and only then, where possible, from them to the senses, whereas in the case of speculative reason we had to begin with the senses and end with principles. The ground for doing so lies ... in this: that now we have to do with a will and have to consider reason not in its relation to objects but in relation to this will and its causality; thus the principles of empirically unconditioned causality must come first, and only afterward can the attempt be made to establish our concepts of the determining ground of such a will, of their application to objects and finally to the subject and its sensibility.   (*CPracR*, 5: 16)

This passage expresses two distinct but related points. The first is that morality concerns not how the world is, but how it ought to be, so the task in morality is not to conform our will to the world as it is presented to our senses but to make that world conform to the causality of the moral will. So while speculative reason has to begin with the world as it is given to sensibility, although on Kant's view sensibility has its own a priori forms of intuition inherent in us rather than the world, in morality we begin with the principles that we are to impose on the world, in the first instance of course by imposing them upon ourselves as beings in the world. Kant's second reason for beginning the Analytic of the *Critique of Practical Reason* with principles and only then progressing to the objects of morality and then to the senses of the moral subject is to emphasize that the principles of morality are given to us by pure reason, not by inclination or feeling of any kind nor by mere objects of inclination. Pure reason gives us a purely formal principle of morality, which we then apply to our circumstances to define the object of morality, and which also produces its own characteristic effect on our feelings, namely the feeling of respect, which plays a necessary part in acting upon the principle of morality but no part in establishing the content and validity of that principle. This last point is Kant's concession to but critique of the "moral sense" school of Francis Hutcheson, David Hume, and Adam Smith: moral feeling, in Kant's account the feeling of respect, does play a role in executing but not defining the demands of morality.[10] Only reason establishes the latter.

---

[10] In Francis Hutcheson's terminology, the moral feeling of respect can and must play the role of an "exciting reason," but can never serve as the "justifying reason" that determines which of our exciting reasons it is permissible to act upon; see Hutcheson 2002, p. 138. For Kant, feeling may provide the proximate cause of moral action, but only the faculty of pure reason can provide its justifying reason.

Kant's claim in the second *Critique* that we must begin with the principles of morality and only then move on to its objects and its incentives in sensibility is another version of his argument in section I of the *Groundwork* that duty is not defined by inclination or its objects but by a formal principle of reason. We can see this as we now turn from the organization to the contents of Kant's two books. The following issues will all be of importance throughout the subsequent reception, appropriation, and/or criticism of Kant's moral philosophy. First, we will look at Kant's attempts to formulate and establish the categorical imperatives in both the *Groundwork* and the *Critique of Practical Reason*. Next we will consider his efforts to move from analysis to synthesis by proving that the moral law does apply to us, as well his intimately connected arguments that we are always free to do as it commands whether we like that or not, whether we do so or not, and whether or not our doing so could be predicted from our prior history. Then we can turn to Kant's account of moral feeling as part of his model of how in fact we do what morality demands. Finally we can consider the evolution of his conception of the highest good and his account of the postulates of pure practical reason. These will be recurring issues throughout the subsequent reception of Kant's work.

2.2. The Categorical Imperative and its Formulations

Both the *Groundwork* and the *Critique of Practical Reason* begin by deriving and formulating the fundamental principle of morality, in its human form as the categorical imperative. There are superficial differences in the approaches of the two works, but the underlying train of thought is the same, namely that a universally and necessarily valid principle of morality must be a formal principle given by pure reason alone.[11] Neither work explicitly associates the fundamental principle of morality with the idea of the greatest possible use of freedom that animated Kant's earlier presentation of his moral philosophy, especially in his

---

Kant's version of Hutcheson's distinction in his lectures is his distinction between the "*principium der dijudication*" and "*principium der Execution*," or the "principle of appraisal of obligation" and the "principle of its performance or execution" (*Collins*, 27: 274); his mature view will be that the former, i.e., the moral law, or the determination of our will by the moral law, produces the feeling of respect, or moral feelings more generally, as the proximate cause or causes of actual action, i.e., performance or execution.

[11] Here is where I see one difference between my approach and Skorupski's. He presents Kant as beginning from the concept of *autonomy*, as setting one's own ends, and then trying, with less than complete success, to derive the fundamental principle from that; Skorupski 2021, e.g., I.2.4, p. 91; I see Kant as beginning in both section II of the *Groundwork* and the *Critique of Practical Reason* with the idea of a moral law as universal and necessary, then deriving from this premise that such a law must be purely formal, that is, concern only the universalizable form of our maxims, and only then introducing the concept of autonomy to characterize (i) the character of a purely formal principle of morality, expressing the pure form of the will without reference to any arbitrary object of the will, and (ii) the character of a rational agent who governs her actual choices by the pure form of the will.

lectures on ethics. But we will see that this idea still underlies Kant's approach in his two critical works, and that it becomes explicit again in the final *Metaphysics of Morals*.

In the first section of the *Groundwork*, Kant derives the first formulation of the categorical imperative from what he takes to be common conceptions of a good will and duty. This section includes some of Kant's most famous statements in moral philosophy, but has also caused endless criticism. It was only intended as a prelude to the more formal derivation of the categorical imperative in the second section of the book, however, an appeal to common cognition of morals rather than to any special philosophy, and Kant does not use its approach in the second *Critique* at all. So if there are problems with Kant's approach in the first section they should not be taken to undermine Kant's entire project.

Kant famously begins with the assertion that "It is impossible to think of anything at all in the world, or indeed even beyond it, that could be considered good without limitation except a **good will**" (G, 4: 393). This statement needs no argument, perhaps only illustration, because it is supposed to be part of "common rational moral cognition," and in any case because, as just said, section I of the *Groundwork* is only a prelude to the more philosophical argument of section II. The statement means several different things. First, it means that other goods, goods of nature such as strength and intelligence and goods of fortune such as wealth and position, are good only if accompanied by a good will. Otherwise they can be put to evil use. Any moral theory can accept this.[12] Second, it means that moral appraisal should focus on what an agent was sincerely trying to accomplish, not necessarily on the actual outcome of her efforts, because this may have gone awry for reasons beyond her control. "Even if, by a special disfavor of fortune or by the niggardly provision of a stepmotherly nature, . . .—if with its greatest efforts it should yet achieve nothing and only the good will were left . . . then, like a jewel, it would still shine by itself, as something that has its full worth in itself" (G, 4: 394). Again, any moral theory can accept that moral evaluation should be based on the intended rather than the actual outcome of an agent's action (unless the failure to attain the intended outcome is itself due to the agent, as in the case of failure to take reasonable precautions). Neither of these points establishes the distinctive content of Kant's moral philosophy. What does point toward Kant's distinctive position is his further claim that "Usefulness or fruitlessness can

[12] Hutcheson's *Inquiry concerning Moral Good and Evil*, the second treatise of his 1725 volume *An Inquiry into the Original of our Ideas of Beauty and Virtue*, likewise begins with what he takes to be the universally accepted distinction between "moral Goodness" and "natural Goodness," the latter including gifts of nature and fortune such as beautiful fields and commodious habitations, but also such traditional virtues as temperance and courage; Hutcheson 2008, section I.I, pp. 89–90, and section II.I, pp. 101–2. Hutcheson's argument could have been a model for Kant's method in the first, but only in the first section of the *Groundwork*. A rare exception to the distinction between moral virtues and gifts of nature is Hume, who treats all qualities of character that we love from a general point of view as virtues, whether voluntarily acquired or not; e.g., *THN*, 3.3.4.

neither add anything to this worth nor take anything away from it. There is ... something so strange in this idea of the absolute worth of a mere will, in the estimation of which no allowance is made for any usefulness" (*G*, 4: 394). That is, according to Kant it is not even the utility, the contribution to happiness, of the *intended outcome* of an action that makes it morally worthy or obligatory, as other theories would have it;[13] it is something about the will itself, precisely its independence from any concern with utility, that makes it morally special. Kant says that "the true vocation of reason must be to produce a will that is good, not perhaps **as a means to other purposes**, but good in itself" (*G*, 4: 396). (We should also note that Kant's apparent throw-away remark that there is nothing *in* nature *or outside it* that is good without limitation is a dig at divine-command or voluntaristic morality; Kant's position is that nothing is good simply because God wills it, but, assuming that there is a God, what it wills is good because it too conforms to pure reason.[14])

To explain what he means, Kant turns to what he takes to be the common conception of "**duty**, which contains that of a good will though under certain subjective limitations and hindrances, which, however, far from concealing it and making it unrecognizable, rather bring it out by contrast and make it shine forth all the more brightly" (*G*, 4: 397). The subjective limitations and hindrances that Kant has in mind are human inclinations[15] that can urge the performance of actions in particular circumstances that are other than what morality requires; in that case, doing what morality requires, thus having and realizing a good will, presents itself to us in the form of duty. Kant's idea is the same as in section II when he argues that the fundamental principle of morality presents itself to us as a categorical imperative, a constraint that allows no exceptions, because we, unlike perfectly rational beings, have inclinations that can offer resistance to the demands of morality (*G*, 4: 412). Kant then analyzes the common conception of duty by means of three propositions, the first of which is not explicitly stated but is implied by Kant's examples. These examples, which have caused endless difficulty because readers have taken them to be Kant's complete model of moral motivation rather than mere thought-experiments designed for the single purpose of elucidating the character of the fundamental principle of morality, are the examples of a person who restrains from suicide just because he happens to enjoy life and of one who is philanthropic just because helping other people makes him feel good

---

[13] See Hutcheson, *Inquiry concerning Moral Good and Evil*, in Hutcheson 2008, section III.XI, pp. 128–30.

[14] For a particularly clear statement of Kant's position on this issue, see *Collins*, 27: 263–4; in *Lectures on Ethics*, pp. 56–7. Schneewind 1998a, pp. 510–13, explains Kant's rejection of voluntarism, as does Rosen 2022, e.g., pp. 61–3, although Rosen thinks that the alternative to voluntarism is Platonic realism, akin to contemporary moral realism. He does not see Kant's form of rationalism, that it is reason itself, which is at least in part our own, that is the source of the moral law, as a way between these traditional alternatives.

[15] See Chapter 1 n. 10 above.

(G, 4: 397–8).[16] Refraining from suicide and being philanthropic are in fact human duties, among the examples Kant will use in section II and explicate more fully in the *Metaphysics of Morals*, so there is nothing *immoral* in the outward behavior of these stick-figures, indeed their behavior "deserves praise and encouragement" because we want people to behave in these ways, no matter how they come to do it. But only if they do such actions "**from duty**" rather than from mere inclination, as they clearly would if they were to lose these inclinations but still force themselves to refrain from suicide or be charitable anyway, would their actions merit "esteem" or have "moral content" or moral worth. As we will see, Kant does not mean that the only morally worthy action is that done in the absence of *all* feeling, let alone only action done in the face of contrary inclination; but he does mean that morally worthy action must be done on the basis of a fundamental principle that does not derive the value of actions from our mere inclinations. This is what the first two steps of his analysis mean. The first proposition is that actions derive their moral worth by being done from duty, not from inclination. This entails the second proposition, namely that if actions do not derive their moral worth from inclination, they cannot derive their moral worth from the *objects* of inclination, from goodness supposed to be inherent in the objects to which we are inclined (food, sex, wealth, whatever): "an action from duty has its moral worth **not in the purpose** to be attained from it but in the maxim in accordance with which it is decided upon, and therefore does not depend upon the realization of the object of the action but merely upon the **principle of volition** in accordance with which the action is done without regard for any object of the faculty of desire" (G, 4: 399–400). By a "maxim" Kant means the particular principle upon which an intended action is performed: it might be something like "Enrich myself in any way I can," or more formally "In circumstances that allow it, perform any action that should have the result of adding to my riches"—obviously not a moral maxim—or "Help other people whenever I can," more formally "In circumstances that call for it, perform any action in my power to assist other persons"— obviously a morally commendable maxim.[17] Maxims in this sense should be distinguished from intentions, that is, intentions to perform particular actions in

---

[16] For a clear statement of the strictly heuristic import of Kant's examples, see Moran 2022, pp. 34–5, 55. Timmermann 2007, pp. 26–36, and Sedgwick 2008, pp. 59–68, discuss the examples of dutiful actors in detail, although without stressing the strictly heuristic role of the examples; Sedgwick suggests that the examples are epistemologically rather than methodologically motivated, i.e., the absence of inclination to the morally requisite act would be evidence of moral motivation in real life, which is not Kant's real point. Schönecker and Wood 2015, p. 75, make it clear that these examples are not intended to present Kant's full picture of moral motivation, which comes only in the *Metaphysics of Morals*.

[17] Maxims can be expressed in the form "In circumstances of type C (I should) do an action of type A in order to achieve end E," although the last term is often left implicit. Maxims of this sort have a certain level of generality, such as "Whenever I can get away with it, I should do that action that most enriches me" or "Whenever I have the opportunity and the means, consistent with my other duties, I should help someone in need," and while their precise level of generality is a controversial issue, they should be distinguished from what Kant will later characterize as the two most fundamental maxims,

light of one's maxims, and also from what Kant will later treat as an agent's *fundamental* or "supreme" maxim, that is, whether to subordinate self-love to the demands of morality, or to subordinate morality to the demands of self-love (*RBMR*, 6: 36), in the light of which the agent will choose more particular maxims, such as to be benevolent even when it costs one something, or only if it does not cost one anything or even adds to one's own riches. Maxims are intermediate between our most fundamental maxim and the specific intentions we formulate in particular circumstances.

From the first two propositions in the analysis of the concept of duty Kant then infers the third proposition: "**duty is the necessity of an action from respect for law**.... Now an action from duty is to put aside entirely the influence of inclination and with it every object of the will"—that is what the first two propositions require—"hence there is left for the will nothing that could determine it except objectively the **law** and subjectively **pure respect** for this practical law, and so the maxim of complying with such a law even if infringes upon all my inclinations" (*G*, 4: 400–1); this is what Kant will call in the *Religion* the supreme maxim of morality, or the fundamental maxim to which we ought to subordinate the gratification of self-love and that ought to govern our selection of all more particular maxims. Now, in this statement, the moral law is the content that determines the morally worthy will, and the attitude of respect for that law is the determination of the will to make the law its supreme maxim. These characterizations are abstract, and do not entail any specific phenomenology, thus that respect is a *feeling*.[18] In a footnote attached to this passage, however, Kant does introduce the idea of a specific *feeling* of respect, which has an "analogy" both with fear and inclination—it is unpleasant, because it is associated with self-constraint, but it is also pleasant, because it is the positive "representation of a worth that infringes upon self-love." This feeling is special, because it is "**self-wrought** by means of a rational concept," but Kant suggests that it is entirely the *effect* of the determination of the will by respect for the moral law, not that it plays any *causal* role in the performance of morally worthy action. In subsequent works Kant will assign a causal role to the feeling of respect not in the formulation and adoption of the fundamental principle of morality but in the transition from that to action, and will also differentiate it into a complex of moral feelings.[19]

---

expressions of anyone's basic moral character, namely the maxims to always put self-love ahead of morality or morality ahead of self-love (*RBMR*, 6: 35–6). Kant characterizes maxims as "subjective" principles of volition, i.e., the principles that agents actually attempt to act upon (*G*, 4: 401n.); but since the first formulation of the categorical imperative is that we should act only on maxims that could also be universally accepted, obviously our maxims can and should also be "objective." On maxims, see Paton 1947, pp. 58–62, O'Neill 2013 (1975), Albrecht 1994, and Wood 1999, pp. 40–2; for the distinction between fundamental maxims and more particular maxims, see McCarty 2009. For view that treats as maxims only an agent's most fundamental maxims, see Höffe 1994, p. 149, and Kuehn 2001, pp. 144–8.

[18] See Timmermann 2007, pp. 41–4, and Sedgwick 2008, pp. 75–6.

[19] See *MM*, DV, Introduction, section XII, 6: 399–403, to which we will return in Chapter 3.

But the crucial point now is the conclusion that Kant draws from this tripartite analysis of the concept of duty.

> But what kind of law can that be, the representation of which must determine the will, even without regard for the effect expected form it, in order for the will to be called good absolutely and without limitation? Since I have deprived the will of every impulse that could arise for it from obeying some law, nothing is left but the conformity of actions as such with universal law, which alone is to serve the will as its principle, that is, **I ought never to act except in such a way that I could also will that my maxims should become a universal law.**   (G, 4: 402)

This is Kant's first formulation of what he will name in the next section the categorical imperative. His argument is simply that if moral worth has nothing to do with action from inclination or the objects of inclination, and consists only in acting on or out of respect for the moral law, the moral law itself can have nothing to do with inclination and its objects—and all that this leaves is the requirement of lawfulness or universal validity itself. The moral law requires nothing more but nothing less than that one's maxim, that is, one's particular maxim, could be a law, valid for all.[20] Kant then both illustrates what this means and confirms the correctness of his analysis with another example. "Common human reason also agrees completely with this in its practical judgments and always has this principle before its eyes." The ordinary person might not formulate the fundamental principle of morality in exactly these terms or know that a philosopher calls it the categorical imperative. But faced with an opportunity to get something he wants by making a lying promise, that is, a promise he has no intention of keeping,[21] he asks himself whether he could perform the action he is contemplating if everyone else also adopted the maxim of making lying promises when they think they can get away with it—and then realizes that "in accordance with such a law there would properly be no promises at all," that is, no rational agent would accept any purported promises so no promises at all could be made, and so his "maxim, as soon as it were made a universal law, would have to destroy itself" (G, 4: 403). The universalization of the maxim to make lying promises would undermine—or contradict—the maxim itself; an agent with this maxim could not do what he wants if everyone were to do it.

Kant's argument has frequently been understood as consequentialist in spite of his ambition for a non-consequentialist moral philosophy, that is, that he is arguing that the problem with immoral action is that it has bad consequences

---

[20] For this formulation, see Korsgaard, SN, p. 98. There is a good brief account of this argument at Timmermann 2007, pp. 44–5.

[21] A lying promise is one that the agent never intends to keep, and is not the same as a sincerely made promise that as it turns out the agent cannot later keep. The maxim "Do not make a false promise" is not equivalent to "Keep every promise that you make."

for oneself, or is imprudent.[22] This is a misunderstanding: prudence requires you to consider the foreseeably *actual* consequences of your action, thus to ask whether acting on a supposedly immoral maxim would *actually* cause others to do the same and thereby undermine itself. But Kant just requires you to ask whether you could go ahead with your maxim *if* everyone else Chose to act upon it as well, because pure reason itself requires you to ask whether your maxim *could be* a universally valid law. And on the approach to Kant that I advocate, morality requires you to ask this question, which is not about prudence at all, not because it values lawfulness as such, but because it requires you to ask whether your proposed action is consistent with the greatest possible freedom, thus whether you could freely choose to act upon your proposed maxim even if everyone else freely chose to do so as well. If your action remains possible under that condition, fine, but if not, it does not preserve the greatest possible freedom and is immoral. Kant's argument thus does concern the possible consequences of proposed maxims of action for the greatest possible freedom, but that is not what anyone usually means by consequentialism. We will come back to the objection that Kant's reasoning is just disguised consequentialism in later chapters. At this point, however, let's see how Kant makes the same argument he has offered in his analysis of the concept of duty in different language in the opening of the *Critique of Practical Reason.*

Kant starts this work in *more geometrico,* with a more formal argument than in the *Groundwork.* He begins with the assumption that a practical *law* must hold "for the will of every rational being" (*CPracR,* chapter 1, I, definition, 5: 19). He then states as his "Theorem I" that "All practical principles that presuppose an **object** (matter) of the faculty of desire as the determining ground of the will are, without exception, empirical and can furnish no practical laws" (5: 21). This is a restatement of the second proposition in the *Groundwork*'s analysis of the concept of duty, although it makes clear what the problem with basing the fundamental principle of morality upon inclination and its objects would be: inclinations vary over time and among different persons, so there would be no way to base a universally and necessarily valid principle on them—but a genuine law, moral law included, must be universally and necessarily valid. Kant also adds what he calls "Theorem II," although it would be better named "Definition II": "All material practical principles as such are, without exception, of one and the same kind and come under the general principle of self-love or one's own happiness" (5: 22); as a matter of definition, happiness just is a matter of gratifying as many of

---

[22] Notoriously by Arthur Schopenhauer, in *WWR,* I.555–6, and by John Stuart Mill, who wrote that when Kant "begins to deduce from" the categorical imperative "any of the actual duties of morality, he fails, almost grotesquely, to show that there would be any contradiction...in the adoption by all rational beings of the most outrageously immoral rules of conduct. All he shows is that the *consequences* of their universal adoption would be such as no one would choose to incur"; *Utilitarianism,* section I, in Mill 1969, p. 207. We will return to Schopenhauer's criticism in Chapter 10 below.

one's own inclinations as one can, or some maximal set of one's inclinations—even if, as might contingently be the case, one has an inclination toward the happiness of others, that is, takes pleasure in their pleasure and acts for the sake of that, that is, one's own pleasure. Thus, at least in Kant's view, to act out of inclination is always to act for the sake of one's own happiness, or out of self-love—and that is obviously not moral.[23] Then Kant infers, his "Theorem III," that "If a rational being is to think of his maxims as practical universal laws, he can think of them only as principles that contain the determining ground of the will not by their matter"—not because of any object of inclination—

> but only by their form.... all that remains of a law if one separates from it everything material, that is, every object of the will (as its determining ground), is the mere **form** of giving universal law. Therefore, either a rational being cannot think of **his** subjectively practical principles, that is, his maxims, as being at the same time universal laws or he must assume that their mere form, by which **they are fit for a giving of universal law**, of itself and alone makes them practical laws.
> (CPracR, 5: 27)

Kant has added to the argument of the *Groundwork* the contrast between matter and form as well as the definition that satisfaction of the sum total of one's inclinations would be self-loving happiness, but the argument is otherwise the same: if the fundamental principle of morality cannot be founded on inclination and its objects, all that is left is that it requires simply the universal validity—or universalizability, as it is commonly called—of one's proposed more particular maxims of action.

Kant's argument is an argument by elimination: inclination or matter and universal form are the only two alternatives for determining grounds for the will, so if the moral law cannot concern the former it must concern the latter. However, in the *Critique of Pure Reason* Kant had argued that "transcendental proofs," the kind of proofs getting down to the principles of possibility of understanding or rationality that philosophy demands, can never be "apagogic" but must always be "ostensive," that is, they cannot be mere arguments by elimination—because you can never be sure that your list of alternatives is in fact completely exhaustive—but must be positive arguments producing "insight into the sources" of that which is to be proven, that is, insight into its *ground*

---

[23] Here Kant is just ignoring the argument of Joseph Butler, in the Preface to his *Fifteen Sermons Preached in Rolls Chapel* (1726; in Butler 2017, pp. 11–14), that to act for the sake of another's happiness is *not* the same as acting for the sake of one's own happiness even if it does also produce pleasure in oneself. Butler's argument would be taken up by Francis Hutcheson in his *Illustrations Upon the Moral Sense* (1728) and then in turn by David Hume and Adam Smith, thus becoming crucial to the position of the moral sense school, contrary to Hobbes, that utilitarianism does not entail egoism. If Kant was aware of and understood this position, he was not impressed by it.

(*CPuR*, A789/B817). To return to the *Groundwork*, Kant does not explicitly state this requirement, but we can read its second section as not merely putting the results of its first section more formally or philosophically, in its first formulation of the categorical imperative, but, in its second main formulation, as also attempting to replace its merely apagogic proof with an ostensive proof, an explanation of the ground for accepting his interpretation of the moral law as strictly formal. Kant does not repeat the ostensive proof of the moral law from the *Groundwork* in the *Critique of Practical Reason* because that work merely summarizes the result of the search for the moral law from the earlier work and then focuses on the question of whether we really are free to act in accordance with that law and the issue of the highest good. But the ostensive proof of the categorical imperative in the *Groundwork* is the foundation of Kant's mature normative philosophy.

So we now turn to Kant's derivation and formulation of the categorical imperative in section II of the *Groundwork*.[24] This section is designated "Transition from Popular Moral Philosophy to Metaphysics of Morals" (*G*, 4: 406). As already mentioned, by "popular moral philosophy" Kant does not mean the same as the "common rational moral cognition" of section I, and the transition he has in mind is not a further inference from the result of that section. Rather, by popular moral philosophy he means an empirical approach to morality that would infer its fundamental principle from actual examples of human experience, and the transition he has in mind is the replacement of this by a proper metaphysics of morals (in his first sense), the derivation of an a priori principle of morality from pure concepts of reason. The problem with attempting to derive morality from examples of actual human conduct is twofold. First, there may be no actual examples of completely moral conduct, for it is unclear "whether any true virtue is to be found in the world." Indeed, we cannot be sure even that our own conduct is purely moral when we think that it is, for self-love is very good at hiding itself, and "we can never, even by the most strenuous self-examination, get entirely behind our covert incentives"—even when we have performed morally correct actions, we cannot be sure they have resulted from the morally correct "inner principles of action that one does not see" (*G*, 4: 407). But second, there is also a conceptual rather than an epistemological problem in attempting to derive morality from example: we cannot tell that something *is* an example of proper moral conduct unless the example can "first be judged in accordance with principles of morality." We have to know the principle in order to recognize an example of it. This premise also underlies Kant's critique of any attempt to ground the fundamental principle of morality in religious belief: "Even the Holy One of the Gospel must

---

[24] Detailed discussion in English of the several formulations of the categorical imperative and their relations in *Groundwork* II goes back to Paton 1947, book III, chapters XIII–XVIII. See also Wood 1999, chapters 3–5, and Wood 2017; Timmermann 2007, pp. 73–114; Irwin 2009, pp. 2–49; and Allison 2011, pp. 176–236. For my own previous approach, see Guyer 1995.

first be compared with our ideal of moral perfection before he is cognized as such" (*G*, 4: 408; see also *Collins*, 27: 263–4). Kant's morality has implications for religious belief: as we saw in the discussion of the Canon of Pure Reason of the first *Critique*, and will see in our further review of the *Critique of Practical Reason*, Kant thinks that we have to believe in the existence of God and in immortality as the conditions of the possibility of realizing the *object* of morality, beliefs necessary to make it rational to attempt to carry out what it commands. But Kant is always clear that we must already acknowledge the fundamental principle of morality to ground this *rational* faith; the principle itself cannot be grounded in *religious* faith.

Kant's argument against deriving the principle of morality from examples might appear to contradict his argument in section I of the *Groundwork*, which featured examples such as the would-be suicide and the philanthropist. But there is no contradiction, for, again, those examples are only thought-experiments designed to clarify a principle that is already tacitly acknowledged, not examples of actual human conduct from which the principle is to be derived by some empirical procedure of observation or induction. Reasoning with thought-experiments is a priori, not empirical.

Kant's claims that even when the actions of others or ourselves are in outward compliance with morality we can never be sure about the agent's ulterior motive, thus the morality of the motivation of others or even ourselves might also seem problematic: isn't morality precisely the business of making such judgments? Not according to Kant. While he will later emphasize the importance of developing self-knowledge so that we can be on the lookout for our own temptations and weaknesses (*MM* DV, §§14–15, 6: 441–2), Kant always insists that the primary perspective of morality is *prospective*, determining what we *should do* and on what ground. The *retrospective* business of moral judgment, the assessment of what *has been done* and why, is best left to God—or best represented *as if* left to God, "him who scrutinizes the heart (through his pure intellectual intuition)" (*RBMR*, 6: 68), since for Kant God is an idea of reason and of rational belief but not of theoretical knowledge.[25] Passing moral judgment upon each other is not an essential part of Kantian morality, and even passing moral judgment upon ourselves is not its primary concern; we need to cultivate our disposition to do this only to improve our moral judgment and performance in the future.[26]

Kant does assert that "descending to popular concepts is certainly very com-mendable, provided the ascent to the principle of pure reason has first taken place

---

[25] Rosen 2022, chapter 2, bases his defense of Kant's philosophical theology on the supposed necessity of a divine judgment of human moral worth, but does not ask whether Kant's commitment to the necessity of such judgment is grounded in anything more fundamental in Kant's philosophy, nor how belief in God as judge is to be reconciled with Kant's epistemological strictures on claims to knowledge about God.

[26] On this point, see also Moran 2022, p. 35.

and has been carried through to complete satisfaction" (*G*, 4: 409). But this just means, as he has already suggested in the preface to the *Groundwork*, that once he has clearly determined the content and foundation of the fundamental principle of morality, the correctness of his own analysis can and must be confirmed by showing that the fundamental principle as he has formulated it does give rise to the duties that ordinary people in their good sense commonly recognize—whether or not they commonly fulfill them, which is a different matter. This is why examples of duties, or more precisely of what Kant takes to be the commonly and properly recognized four main *classes* of duty, figure prominently in section II of the *Groundwork*. But Kant is not deriving the fundamental principle from these examples; he is showing how these examples of duty can be derived from the fundamental principle.

Kant's methodological alternative to attempting to derive the principle of morality empirically from examples is to derive it "from the universal concept of a rational being as such," a concept valid for any possible rational being and not just for actual human beings (*G*, 4: 412).[27] Of course an analytic connection between the concept of rationality and the moral law will have no existential implications, that is, it does not entail that there *are* any rational beings other than human beings or even that we ourselves actually *are* rational or even capable of being rational—the latter is the synthetic step that Kant will save for section III of the *Groundwork*, and as for the former, only the postulate of the existence of God by pure practical reason as the condition of the possibility of the highest good will imply, in the epistemic modality of practical belief rather than theoretical knowledge, the existence of any rational being other than human beings—nothing in Kant's repertoire could imply in any epistemic modality the existence of any rational beings other than humans and God, though neither could that be excluded. Kant's argument then proceeds through the premise that although "Everything in nature works in accordance with laws," "Only a rational being has the capacity to act **in accordance with the representation** of laws, that is, in accordance with principles, or has a **will**" (*G*, 4: 412). Kant next states that (if we humans are rational at all) we are not completely rational; we can have inclinations contrary to *any* principle of reason even if we accept it; so principles of reason present themselves *to us* in the form of imperatives, constraints on our will "to which this will is not necessarily obedient" (*G*, 4: 413). Kant's search for the proper formulation of the moral law then proceeds by looking for an imperative that is universally and necessarily valid for all rational beings, that is, categorical. Since he assumes from the outset that the fundamental principle of morality must

---

[27]   This point is well brought out by Irwin, beginning on the first page of his treatment of Kant (Irwin 2009, p. 1). His larger argument with Kant, rather than his interpretation of Kant, is that this concept should be understood as part of the concept of a human being available to a naturalist rather than any sort of non-natural concept. I do not fundamentally disagree with him.

be universally and necessarily valid, if he can find one and only one imperative that is categorical, that will be the moral law.

Kant proceeds by canvassing three possible kinds of imperative to see if one and only one is the categorical imperative. His argument thus at least initially has the form of an argument by elimination, although since he has stated that arguments in transcendental philosophy must be ostensive and not merely apagogic, this may only be the first stage of his overall argument. He says that "all imperatives command either **hypothetically** or **categorically**."

> The former represents the practical necessity of a possible action as a means to achieving something else that one wills (or that is at least possible for one to will). The categorical imperative would be that which represented an action as objectively necessary of itself, without reference to another end.   (G, 4: 414)

This statement distinguishes two kinds of imperatives, not three, but Kant draws a distinction within the first class of hypothetical imperatives. On the one hand are what Kant calls imperatives of skill or technical imperatives, that tell you that *if* you want to achieve a certain end you should or must use a certain means; for example, if you are a physician who wants to cure a patient, you should use this drug, but *if* you are a murderer who wants to poison someone, you should use that one (G, 4: 415). This example makes it clear that the end to which a particular hypothetical imperative states the means—which is a matter of causal law, so really a matter for theoretical cognition that can be adapted for purposes of practical reason[28]—is not only optional, but can even be immoral. So hypothetical imperatives obviously cannot be the foundation of morality, although their underlying principle is, in Kant's view, entirely analytic and correct as far as it goes: "in the volition of an object as my effect, my causality as acting cause, that is, the use of means, is already thought" (G, 4: 417)—that is, *if* you really will some end, you must will some sufficient means to it, and, conversely, if you cannot will the means, then you cannot rationally *will* the end, much as you might *wish* for it. But this principle, although *necessary* for moral rationality too, is not *sufficient* for it.[29] The second kind of hypothetical imperative that Kant considers is imperatives of prudence rather than skill, or general prescriptions for happiness rather than prescriptions of particular means to particular ends. Kant calls these supposed imperatives "assertoric" rather than problematic, because they are not,

---

[28] Thus Kant refers to hypothetical imperatives by the hybrid description "technically practical" at *CPJ*, Introduction, section I, 5: 172.

[29] Skorupski introduces what he calls the "General Hypothetical Form," "If you ought to *make it the case that E* then you ought to *do what brings it about that E*" (Skorupski 2021, p. 96). For Kant, this must be a hybrid of a moral and non-moral imperative, for only a moral principle—the categorical imperative that he is about to introduce—could ground the "ought" in the antecedent of this conditional.

so to speak, technical solutions to particular problems that only some people have, but rather statements of means to one end that everyone is supposed to have, namely (their own) happiness, "a maximum of well-being in my present condition and in every future condition" (G, 4: 418), or the greatest possible satisfaction of desires. Here is where Kant makes his basic criticism of utilitarianism: even leaving aside the question of how one could really know what the happiness of any other persons would require, let alone the question of why one should care, no one ever really knows with any certainty what their *own* long-term happiness requires. Experience can offer "counsels of prudence," general policies or rules of thumb like "You should set aside enough money while you are still working for a comfortable old age"—but can you be sure that you will live to an old age, or that if you do you will care about money? If not, might you not be better off spending the money on something fun now? Who can be sure which rule of thumb actually makes most sense for one? Mere counsels of prudence are no basis for a universal and necessary principle of morality.

So neither imperatives of skill nor counsels of prudence are candidates for the basis of morality. What then can the categorical imperative be? Here Kant restates the key argument of section I of the *Groundwork*, in more technical terms, and of the *Critique of Practical Reason*, in slightly different technical terms, by saying that the very form of the concept of a categorical imperative entails its content. The categorical imperative must be universally and necessarily valid, so it cannot depend on anything contingent including inclinations and their objects, thus it can concern only the form of maxims, and is nothing other than the requirement that the particular maxims on which we can or must act themselves be universally and necessarily valid:

> For, since the categorical imperative contains, beyond the law, only the necessity that the maxim be in conformity with this law, while the law contains no condition to which it would be limited, nothing is left with which the maxim of action is to conform but the universality of a law as such; and this conformity alone is what the imperative properly represents as necessary.

> There is, therefore, only a single categorical imperative and it is this: **act only in accordance with that maxim through which you can at the same time will that it be a universal law.**   (G, 4: 420–1)

The moral law does not have some independent content that then has to be shown to be universally and necessarily valid and binding on each of us for that reason; the moral law is simply the requirement that our proposed principles of action be universally and necessarily valid.

This time, however, Kant's analysis does not stop here. The first addition that he makes to the argument of section I of the *Groundwork* is a reformulation that helps in the application of the categorical imperative: "**act as if the maxim of your** action were to become by your will a universal law of nature " (*G*, 4: 421). The first formulation is often called the Formula of Universal Law, this second one the Formula of the Law of Nature, but the second formulation only makes explicit how the first is to be applied, and does not introduce any new idea.[30] Kant makes this clear in the *Critique of Practical Reason* when he introduces the second formulation under the title of the "typic of pure practical judgment" and compares this role in practical philosophy to that of a "schema" for a category of pure understanding in theoretical philosophy, defined as "a universal procedure of the imagination (by which it presents *a priori* to the senses the pure concept of the understanding which the law determines)." A schema in theoretical philosophy outlines how a concept of the understanding is to be applied to the objects of our senses (*CPuR*, A137–47/B176–87); the typic of pure practical judgment shows how we are to apply the requirement of universalizability to the maxims of action that our sensible nature—our natural embodiment, complete with needs, desires, and so on—suggests to us. Kant then formulates this "typic" in precisely the same terms as the Formula of the Law of Nature:

> The rule of judgment under laws of pure practical reason is this: ask yourself whether, if the action you propose were to take place by a law of the nature of which you yourself were a part, you could indeed regard it as possible through your will.... If the maxim of action is not so constituted that it can stand the test as the form of a law of nature in general, then it is morally impossible.

In a remarkable commentary, Kant adds:

> This, then, as the typic of judgment, guards against **empiricism** of practical reason, which places the practical concepts of good and evil merely in experiential consequences (so-called happiness)...The same typic also guards against **mysticism** of practical reason, which make what served as a **symbol** into a **schema**, that is, puts under the application of moral concepts real but not sensible intuitions (of an invisible kingdom of God) and strays into the transcendent. Only **rationalism** of judgment is suitable for the use of moral concepts, since it takes from sensible nature nothing more than what pure reason can also think for itself, that is, conformity with law, and transfers into the supersensible nothing but what can, conversely, be really exhibited by actions in the sensible world in accordance with the formal rule of a law of nature in general.
>
> (*CPracR*, 5: 69–71)

---

[30] These names for Kant's several formulations, including the ones yet to be introduced, go back to Paton 1947. On the Stoic origins of Kant's Formula of the Law of Nature, see Reich 1935 and Timmermann 2007, pp. 77–9.

These comments can help us understand how Kant means the categorical imperative's requirement of universalizability to be applied and, to use Kant's term, to guard against the objection already mentioned that Kant's position is just consequentialism in disguise. By a nature Kant means a domain subject to exceptionless laws, as for example (Kant supposed), physical nature is subject to Newton's laws of motion without exceptions. The test required to apply the categorical imperative is then to ask whether one could act on a proposed maxim, which will be suggested to one by one's needs and desires in the actual world, *if* everyone else were also to act on the same maxim.[31] In the terms suggested by John Rawls and Onora O'Neill, as we will see in Chapters 15 and 16, we are to ask whether acting on our proposed maxim would be compatible with its "universalized typified counterpart" or with the "adjusted social world" in which everyone else also acts on our maxim. This question is not what Kant calls the empiricist question, whether the actual consequences of our action would make us happy (any us, oneself or everyone), but neither is it some mystical question about some altogether transcendent world that has no connection to the actual world. It is the hypothetical question whether, holding everything else about the actual world constant, we could still act upon our proposed maxim *if* everyone else were to do so as well. Once again, it must be understood that the question we are to ask is not whether everyone else *will* act on our proposed maxim if we do and whether we would like the consequences when they do, which is a question of prudence; morality simply requires us to ask whether our maxims would be universalizable, that is, whether we could act on our proposed maxims if everyone else were to do so as well.[32]

Kant tries to show how this test, in the form of the Formula of Universal Law, is to work by means of four examples (again, thought-experiments, not empirical examples of actual human conduct). To show that the moral law as he has interpreted it is consistent with common rational moral cognition, Kant takes

[31] John Skorupski's main criticism of Kant is that he does not recognize that acting to realize non-moral ends suggested by feeling rather than by pure reason itself is "reasonable," or that feelings rather than pure reason can give rise to "reasonable interests." Thus he thinks that Kant's official formulation of the universalizability test (FUL), "Act only on that maxim through which you can at the same time will that it should become a universal law," has to be replaced with "FUL*," namely "Act only on a maxim through which you can at the same time will—*after taking into account everyone's reasonable interests in an impartial way*—that it should become a universal law" (Skorupski 2021, pp. 98, 102). But this seems to neglect Kant's view that the universalizability test is a test of the *permissibility* of maxims that are of course *suggested* by natural conditions such as desires and needs, and which in turn can lead to the rational adoption of *hypothetical* imperatives, but that the only test of whether everyone's interests are "reasonable" in "an impartial way" is the universalizability test (or the other formulations of the categorical imperative to follow), so that the inclusion of his italicized clause in FUL* is question-begging or redundant. Both Moran 2022, pp. 12–13, and previously Wood 1999, chapter 3, have made it clear that Kant's FUL is a test of the *permissibility* of maxims that are not themselves suggested by pure reason (although Wood thinks this makes FUL inadequate as a principle for imperfect duties, pp. 97–107).

[32] See Rawls 2000 pp. 167–70, O'Neill 2013, chapter 5, pp. 136–93, and Korsgaard 1985, esp. pp. 92–101.

his examples from the commonly recognized division of duties into perfect and imperfect duties, that is, proscriptions of particular action-types and prescriptions of general ends or policies, and regarding either oneself or others.[33] Kant provides one example from each of the four classes of duty in that classification: his example of a perfect duty to oneself is the duty to refrain from suicide; the duty not to make false promises is a perfect duty to others; the duty to cultivate one's own potential talents is an imperfect duty to self; and the duty to assist others in need when one can is an imperfect duty to others. The perfect duties are typically duties of omission, obligations to refrain from certain actions, which can be perfectly fulfilled simply by so refraining;[34] the imperfect duties are duties of commission, duties to do something rather than refraining from doing something, and they are imperfect because they are open-ended and can never be perfectly, in the sense of completely, fulfilled: no one could completely perfect any potential talent, let alone perfect all of her potential talents, and no one could possibly help everyone else in the world in all the ways they might need help. But one can do more, or less, or nothing at all, to fulfill these duties. Kant also says that the violation of the perfect duties "cannot even be **thought**, without contradiction," or would be what is commonly called a contradiction "in conception," whereas the violation of the imperfect duties would not be such a conceptual contradiction, but "it is still impossible to **will** that their maxim be raised to the universality of a law of nature because such a will would contradict itself," or be what is commonly called a "contradiction in willing" (*G*, 4: 424). What Kant means is that it in the first case it would not be logically possible for one to act on one's proposed maxim in a world in which everyone did, or more precisely that in a world in which everyone proposed to act on the maxim in question no one could, while in the second case acting on one's proposed maxim would be logically possible even if everyone acted upon it but in spite of this no one could rationally will to do so because of some general canon of rationality. This of course presupposes some underlying conception of rational willing and not just the logical law that contradictions must always be avoided. But applying the law of non-contradiction always requires some substantive consideration: after all, the rule to avoid asserting "*p* and not-*p*" does not itself tell you which it is, *p* or not-*p*, that must be rejected. Something additional must tell you that.

---

[33] As already noted, this division was well-entrenched in both German and British moral philosophy in the eighteenth century as the distinction between those duties that are coercibly enforceable and those that are not, e.g., Hutcheson, *Inquiry concerning Moral Good and Evil*, VII.VI, in Hutcheson 2008, pp. 183–4. Kant will ultimately revise this standard distinction, defining *juridical* duties as only the coercibly enforceable subset of our perfect duties regarding others, those the violation of which would interfere with their freedom of action, while perfect duties in general are those that prescribe or more typically proscribe particular actions types rather than prescribing general ends. See *MM*, Introduction, section IV, 6: 218–19.

[34] Perhaps a duty like that of repaying one's debts is a perfect but positive duty or duty of commission rather than omission; of course, this distinction may be flexible, as in this case where the duty could be restated as "do not fail to repay your debts."

Kant's examples are meant to illustrate what all this means, although some do so better than others; he also repeats these examples after his next main formulation of the categorical imperative, and in some cases the second illustration works better than the first. Kant's first example, the prohibition of suicide, is problematic: he argues that the maxim "from self-love I make it my principle to shorten my life when its longer duration threatens more troubles than it promises agreeableness." His objection to this maxim is that "a nature whose law it would be to destroy life itself by means of the same feeling whose destination is to impel toward the furtherance of life would contradict itself" (*G*, 4: 422). But here Kant does not even reach the question whether one could conceive of committing suicide if everyone else were also to do so; he is arguing rather that a principle that a feeling could have one effect in some circumstances but the opposite effect in others is self-contradictory and thus not even a candidate for a law of nature. However, such a law would not be self-contradictory, just complex, as many laws of nature really are.[35]

Kant's other examples are better. The duty not to make false promises can be understood as Kant proposes: if everyone were to make false promises, and were known to do so, then, holding the rest of human nature constant—here is where Kant's approach is "rationalism" but not "mysticism"—no one in their right mind would accept any promise, thus promises could not be made, so one could not act on one's own maxim of making false promises after all. The universalization of one's maxim would contradict, that is, undercut, the possibility of one's acting on that maxim oneself. Again, Kant is not making a factual claim that if one were to make a false promise oneself in the actual world then everyone else would do so as well, nor is he saying either that a world without promising cannot exist nor that we would not like a world without promising, as Mill would have it. He is saying that *if* everyone were known to be trying to make false promises then no one could make any kind of promises; but it is morality, not prudence, that requires one to consider the universalization of one's maxim and thus to ask whether one could act on one's maxim if everyone did so as well. Switching from contradiction in conception to contradiction in willing, the same sort of reasoning is at work in Kant's examples of imperfect duty to self and others, although his illustration of the latter brings the point out more clearly than his illustration of the former. In the case of the duty to develop one's own talents, he argues that one "necessarily wills that all the capacities in him be developed, since they serve him and are given to him for all sorts of possible purposes" (*G*, 4: 423). This statement needs to be cleaned up. First, perhaps no one could develop *all* their possible talents, because the development of some might be incompatible with the development of others— perhaps someone could have the potential to become either a fine defensive tackle

---

[35] Paton 1947, pp. 149–55, tried to defend Kant's treatment of the suicide case as a "teleological" argument. For criticism, see Korsgaard 1985, at pp. 89–92.

or a fine violinist, but couldn't become both because the thickening of the hands and frequent broken fingers that would result from the former would be incompatible with the latter. Second, the suggestion, again teleological, that nature alone might set norms for us that is contained in the phrase that our capacities are *given* to us for all sorts of possible ends is irrelevant. Third, one might be able to achieve one's own ends well enough as a free rider, that is, if one let one's own talents rust while others did not but wittingly or unwittingly shared the results of their labors. But the argument would be correct that if one's maxim of laziness, i.e., not cultivating one's potential talents, were universalized, thus if *no one* cultivated their talents, then *everyone*, including oneself, might lack otherwise possible means to their ends—and, Kant assumes, no one could rationally will *that*. This presupposes something like a complement to the principle of hypothetical imperatives, namely a canon of rationality that one should will the availability of means to ends that one might adopt;[36] but that does seem like it should be part of any reasonable conception of rational willing or practical reason. And that principle seems to be clearly at work in Kant's final example, the imperfect duty to contribute to the welfare of others by providing assistance to them when they need it and when one can. One might find oneself in circumstances where one does not need anything from others, but that fact would be contingent and it would be short-sighted and ignorant about how the real world works to think that such a situation must always be true; so if one were to try to universalize the maxim of *not* helping others when they need it, then "a will that decided this would conflict with itself, since many cases could occur in which one would need the love and sympathy of others and in which, by such a law of nature arisen from his own will"—that is, the universal law that people do *not* help others in need—"he would rob himself of all hope of the assistance he wishes for himself" (*G*, 4: 423). Again, Kant is not assuming that in the ordinary course of nature if one does not help others they will never help one, nor is he assuming just that one would not like it if others did not help one when one needed help. Rather, he is supposing that morality requires that you adopt a maxim only if everyone could do so *and* you could still satisfy the general canon of rational willing that you must will the availability of means to your ends in order to be able to rationally will the ends. If you willed that no one ever help anyone else, then, in the real world, you could not satisfy that canon of practical reason. Again, this is neither empiricism nor mysticism, but rationalism.

Kant will present a much more detailed system of the actual duties of human beings based on the a priori principle of morality on the one hand and some basic facts about human existence in the real world on the other in the *Metaphysics of Morals*, which we turn to in Chapter 3. But his introduction of a preliminary

---

[36] For the idea of canons of rationality, see O'Neill 1985.

version of this system of duties in section II of the *Groundwork* and of the Formula of the Law of Nature (or the "typic" in the *Critique of Practical Reason*) is not section II's only advance over the argument of section I. What comes next is Kant's advance from a merely apagogic argument to an ostensive one: although he does not say this is what he is doing, his next step in section II is to provide a positive ground for the categorical imperative's requirement of universalizability. This is what he does with the Formula of Humanity as an End in Itself.[37] Kant signals that he is taking his argument to a new level with this formulation by beginning his discussion with the question "is it a necessary law **for all rational beings** always to judge their actions in accordance with such maxims as they themselves could will to serve as universal laws?" (*G*, 4: 426). Thus he is not assuming that the correct formulation of the categorical imperative as the require-ment of universalizability of maxims through the argument by elimination that he has deployed thus far is sufficient to establish the validity of that imperative. Instead, he now says, "in order to discover this connection we must, however reluctantly, step forth, namely into metaphysics, although into a domain of it that is distinct from speculative philosophy, namely into metaphysics of morals" (*G*, 4: 426–7). Only this will provide "the ground of a possible categorical imperative, that is, of a practical law" (*G*, 4: 428). We might think of this step as itself comprising two stages. First, Kant needs to find a positive ground for the catego-rical imperative, thus far attained only through an argument by elimination, in the concept of a rational being. Second, in order truly to establish the categorical imperative, as he said he would do in the Preface to the *Groundwork*, he needs to prove that this concept really applies to *us*. The first of these stages is Kant's next concern; the second is what he will try to do in section III of the *Groundwork*. (Kant's "step into a metaphysics of morals" also suggests yet another sense for this phrase: now the metaphysics of morals is not so much the *formulation* of the fundamental principle of morality but the *establishment* of it by adducing a *ground* for it.)

The first stage of this larger argument proceeds as follows. Kant adds to his analysis that rational beings act in accordance with their representations of laws that they also always act for the sake of some *end*, some state of affairs of value to be realized, in some way, through their adherence to a law. But if this law is to be "objective," that is, universally and necessarily valid, then the end to be achieved through adherence to it must also be universally valid: it must be "something **the**

---

[37] My chief objection to Irwin's interpretation of Kant is that he speaks of Kant's "Formula of Humanity" as intended to "explain the Formula of Universal Law" or "to explicate the previous formulae" (Irwin 2009, p. 38). "Explain" and "explicate" might not mean exactly the same, "explain" could just mean to clarify, while "explicate" could mean to show in some detail how the formula applies to the examples Kant offers. But either way, this language fails to capture the way in which the conception of humanity is supposed to *ground*, that is, presumably *justify* ("deduce") the first formulation of the categorical imperative as the Formula of Universal Law.

existence of which in itself has an absolute worth, something which as **an end in itself** could be a ground of determinate laws." Only such an end could be the ground of a possible categorical imperative. Kant then asserts that "the human being and in general every rational being **exists** as an end in itself, **not merely as a means** to be used by this or that will at its discretion" (*G*, 4: 428). This leads to the imperative, "**so act that you use humanity, whether in your own person or in the person of any other, always at the same time as an end, never merely as a means**" (*G*, 4: 429). These statements immediately raise several questions: What does Kant mean by humanity here? What does it mean to treat humanity always as an end and never as a means? What is the argument for this claim? And how would the status of humanity as an end in itself ground what has to this point in the argument been treated as *the* categorical imperative, that is, the Formula of Universal Law or its "typic," the Formula of the Law of Nature?

Kant does not mean by "humanity" either humankind collectively or anything biological that might be thought to distinguish members of the human species from members of other species, such as a common genome.[38] Nor does he mean what he identifies as humanity in the *Religion* (6: 27), namely self-love and a tendency to compare ourselves to others, leading to either pride or envy (perhaps this could be better translated as "humanness," which could connote the weaknesses as well as strengths typical of actual human beings); these are certainly common human dispositions, but precisely what at least sometimes we need to overcome for the sake of morality. Indeed, Kant cannot mean by "humanity" any property necessarily restricted to biological human beings, since he has claimed from the outset that the moral law which is to be grounded and which can be expressed as the imperative always to treat humanity as an end in itself and never merely as a means to some other end must be valid for any and all possible rational beings, not just biological human beings. However, "humanity" can be the name for a property common to all rational beings insofar as it is instantiated in human beings. What then is this property? Kant gives us a clue in the *Groundwork* when he says that "Rational nature is distinguished from the rest of nature by this, that it sets itself an end" (*G*, 4: 427), and offers a similar definition as a definition of humanity in the Introduction to the Doctrine of Virtue of the *Metaphysics of Morals*: "A human being has the duty to raise himself from the crude state of his nature, from his animality…, more and more toward humanity, by which he alone is capable of setting himself ends" (*MM* DV, Introduction, section V.A, 6: 387), and "The capacity to set oneself an end—any end whatsoever—is what characterizes humanity (as distinguished from animality)" (section VIII, 6: 392). I suggest that the ability to set our own ends is the essence of human freedom—if

---

[38] More precisely, resemblances among the genomes of human individuals that suffice to distinguish the genomes of that population from those of others, e.g., other primates.

every rational choice begins with the choice of an end, only then proceeding to a choice of means, then free choice is at bottom the free choice of ends. To be sure, what Kant will refer to as the external use of choice in the formulation of the foundational principle of justice (*MM*, DR Introduction, 6: 230–1), that is, the ability to execute actions designed to realize one's ends, is part of what we commonly think of as freedom, namely what philosophers in the British tradition such as Hobbes, Locke, and Hume call "liberty," the ability to carry out what one wills independent from interference with others, but for Kant freedom begins with the ability to choose one's own ends—not part of the conception of liberty or freedom in, for example, Hume. Thus, what Kant calls humanity in the *Groundwork* is precisely what he meant by freedom in the lectures on ethics, and his position in the *Groundwork* that humanity must always be treated as an end and never as a means is the same as his position in the lectures that freedom of choice is the "inner worth of the world," the "essential end" of human beings, and that the greatest consistent use of which must be attained in moral conduct. Kant's language has changed, but his underlying view has not.

Some authors have interpreted "humanity" as Kant uses it in the formulations of the categorical imperative to mean an agent's either *actually* being moral or having the *capacity* to be moral.[39] But this would mean that what morality requires is simply that being moral or having the capacity to be moral be treated always as an end and never merely as a means, which may well be true—surely we should not exploit someone else's disposition to be moral as a means to our own non-moral ends—but is not very informative: it presupposes that we know what being moral requires of us rather than telling us what it does. And Kant himself tells us that our punishments for criminals must still respect their humanity (see *MM*, DR, Appendix, section 5, 6: 362–3); so actually being moral certainly cannot be a condition of being treated morally. Neither being moral nor being capable of being moral seems like either a sufficient condition for determining the content of morality nor a necessary condition for being treated morally. But treating the capacity of human beings to set their own ends as an end and never merely as a means can define the content of what morality demands non-vacuously and non-circularly. That is what Kant did in his early notes, in terms of will, and in the lectures on ethics, in terms of freedom, and he does the same thing in the *Groundwork* in terms of humanity. Moreover, defining humanity as the capacity to set our own ends, at least if that is assumed to implicate the capacity to do so freely and rationally, *includes* the capacity to be moral, that is, to set our own ends in a way that respects the freedom of both ourselves and others.On Kant's own principle that nothing should be included in a definition that is already implied by what is essentially included ("*conceptus rei adaequatus in minimis terminis*,"

---

[39] For the former, see Dean 2006, part I; for the latter, Allison 2011, pp. 215–29.

JL, §99, 9: 140), the capacity to be moral is implied by the freedom to set our own ends and therefore does not need to be included in the definition of humanity.

To be sure, it could not satisfy morality to treat my *own* capacity to choose my ends freely as an end and never merely as a means but not treat humanity in *others* the same way. Kant makes that plain enough when he formulates the requirement to treat humanity as an end, *whether in my own person or that of any other*, always as an end and never merely as a means. Whatever else may be true of morality, it certainly seems to require that everyone be treated in the same way, or more precisely, that like cases be treated alike, that everyone in similar circumstances be treated the same way, at least as far as that is in our power.[40] Kant makes this clear when he writes in the *Groundwork* that:

> If, then, there is to be a supreme practical principle and, with respect to the human will, a categorical imperative, it must be one such that, from the representations of what is necessarily an end for everyone because it is an **end in itself**, it constitutes an **objective** principle of the will and thus can serve as a universal practical law. The ground of this principle is: **rational nature exists as an end in itself.** The human being necessarily represents his own existence in this way; so far it is thus a **subjective** principle of human actions. But every other rational being also represents his existence in this way consequent on just the same rational ground that also holds for me; thus it is at the same time an **objective** principle from which, as a supreme practical ground, it must be possible to derive all laws of the will.   (*G*, 4: 429)

Kant then states the Formula of Humanity as an End in Itself in imperatival form, previously quoted. Now, if Kant means to state an inference that because I treat *my own* rational nature or humanity as an end in itself I must treat *everyone's* in the same way, or that if everyone treats *his or her own* humanity as an end in itself they must treat *everyone's* humanity in the same way, that would obviously be fallacious. It hardly follows from the fact that I love my own spouse that I should love everyone's spouse or partner. But Kant is not committing such a fallacy; on the contrary, he is saying that everyone can treat *their own* humanity as a *subjectively* valid end, indeed everyone actually does this, as a matter of inclination; but if they treat their own humanity as an *objectively* valid end, that everyone else must also treat as an end, then they must be doing so on the basis of some

---

[40] That like cases be treated alike is the essence of morality has long been held in modern moral philosophy. "Those things which are equal, must needs all have one measure," wrote Richard Hooker in *Of the Laws of Ecclesiastical Polity* (1593), book I, chapter 8, in Hooker 2013, vol. 1, p. 65, cited by Locke, *TG2*, chapter II, §5, p. 288; and "Whoever therefore judges *truly*, must judge the *same* things, which he thinks truly are lawful to *himself*, to be lawful to *others* in a *like Case*" wrote Richard Cumberland in *A Treatise of the Laws of Nature* (1672), in Cumberland 2005, chapter II, p. 381.

objective ground that is valid for everyone. In this passage Kant is elucidating what he means by saying that humanity is an end in itself, not arguing for this thesis. The question of how or even whether he means to argue for this thesis remains open.

But before we turn to that question, there is the question what it means to treat humanity as an end and never merely as a means, whether in one's own case or that of others. What does it mean to treat our capacity to set our own ends as an end in itself and never merely as a means? Kant gives no sign that he means that everyone must make it their end to produce more human beings; although he treats continuing the species as a *natural* end of human beings, he never suggests that it is a moral end obligatory on anyone who can do so to participate in procreation. (If he had meant that, then, as a lifelong and as far as anyone knows celibate bachelor Kant would have been derelict in duty on his own account.) Indeed, Kant seems to deny that the duty always to treat humanity as an end is a duty to bring about any antecedently non-extant state of affairs at all; following the statement that "Rational nature . . . sets itself an end" Kant continues:

> This end would be the matter of every good will. But since, in the idea of a will absolutely good without any limiting condition (attainment of this or that end) abstraction must be made altogether from every end to be *effected* [*zu bewirkenden*, to be brought about] (this would make the will only relatively good), the end must here be thought not as an end to be effected but as an **independently existing** [*selbstsändiger*] end, and hence thought only negatively, that is, as that which must never be acted against . . .   (G, 4: 437)

The idea that our capacity to set our own ends must never be acted against fits Kant's first two examples of perfect duties to self and others: the duty to refrain from suicide is a duty not to destroy an existing instance of humanity, and the duty not to make false promises is a duty not to limit others' use of their capacity to set their own ends by exploiting that as a means to one's own ends without regard to theirs. But Kant's other examples of duty belie understanding humanity merely as something not to be acted against in the sense of being destroyed or restricted. On the contrary, in revisiting his examples of imperfect duties to self and to others after his statement of the Formula of Humanity as an End in Itself, he says of the duty to cultivate talents that,

> with respect to contingent (meritorious) duty to oneself, it is not enough that the action does not conflict with humanity in our person as an end in itself; it must also **harmonize** with it. Now there are in humanity predispositions to greater perfection . . . ; to neglect these might admittedly be consistent with the **preservation** of humanity as an end in itself but not with the **advancement** [*Beförderung*, promotion] of this end;

and he says of the duty to provide assistance with others when one can,

> there is still only a negative and not a positive agreement with **humanity as an end in itself** unless everyone also tries, as far as he can, to further [*befördern*] the ends of others. For, the ends of a subject who is an end in itself must as far as possible be also **my** ends, if that representation is to have its **full** effect in me.
>
> (*G*, 4: 430)

Humanity as an end in itself is not merely an end not to be acted against; it does require positive promotion of some new states of affairs. How can this be understood if humanity is defined as the capacity to set our own ends freely? Well, if an agent can only set an end rationally if he knows that he has some adequate means to bring it about, and cultivating our natural predispositions or potential talents can expand the range of means available to us, whether in the form of physical or mental capacity, external goods that we might earn through our talents, such as wealth, and so on, then expanding the means available to us also expands the range of ends we could rationally set for ourselves, and thereby promotes or expands rather than merely preserving our freedom to set our own ends. Likewise, assisting others by providing them with means to their ends, when we can, expands the range of ends that they can rationally set for themselves, and thus expands or promotes their freedom.[41] Thus, what it is to treat humanity always as an end and never merely as a means in both ourselves and others is not to destroy or unnecessarily restrict the ability of all to choose their own ends freely but also to enhance or expand the freedom of both ourselves and others to set ends freely—of course, the latter is an open-ended task, so the duty to preserve humanity as an end itself is a perfect duty but the duty to promote or advance humanity is an imperfect duty. And this whole, complex duty with regard to humanity in both ourselves and others can serve as a limiting condition on each individual's merely natural inclinations, summed up as their pursuit of happiness, without being reduced to a merely negative duty. This just means that the satisfaction of any of one's mere inclinations must always be subordinated to treating humanity as an end and never merely as a means, which itself comprises both negative and positive duties—do not destroy or restrict but as far as possible expand and promote the capacity of all to set their own ends.

Kant confirms this interpretation of what it means to treat humanity as an end and not merely a means by his treatment of ethical rather than juridical duties in the *Metaphysics of Morals*. We will come back to his treatment of the virtues in Chapter 3. Our next question here is what sort of proof that humanity is an end in itself Kant intended to provide in the *Groundwork*. The *Critique of Practical*

---

[41] For this analysis, see O'Neill 1985; Johnson 2011, pp. 89, 94; Guyer 2016a, pp. 87–104; and Guyer 2019, pp. 27–8.

Reason adduces only the Formula of Universal Law and its "typic," and as we have seen employs only a version of the argument by elimination that Kant used in section I of the *Groundwork* in the introduction of the Formula of Universal Law and Formula of the Law of Nature in section II, at *G*, 4: 420–1. No further proof of the categorical imperative or explanation of its ground is attempted there. If there is a proof of the Formula of Humanity as an End in Itself to be found anywhere, it seems that it must be found in the *Groundwork*.

But what Kant actually says in support of the assertion that humanity is an end in itself and must be treated as such does not look like an argument at all. As we saw, Kant just asserts—"Now I say"—"that the human being and in general every rational being **exists** as an end in itself, **not merely as a means** to be used by this or that will at its discretion." He adds that "rational beings are called **persons** because their nature already marks them out as an end in itself, that is, as something that may not be used merely as a means, and hence to that extent limits all choice (and is an object of respect)" (*G*, 4: 428). This looks like a straightforward assertion of fact, reminding us of Kant's early supposition that it is just a fact that human beings have wills of their own. If supplemented by the further claim that it would be a violation of the law of non-contradiction to both assert and deny that rational beings are ends in themselves, it might be the basis of an argument, but Kant does not make such an argument explicit. It does not look like Kant is starting from an underivable assertion of value, as when in the lectures on ethics he asserted that freedom is the inner value of the world. At the conclusion of the paragraph that begins with the assertion that the human being and in general every rational being is an end in itself, however, Kant adds what some have interpreted as an argument for the absolute value of humanity or rational being: persons

> are not merely subjective ends, the existence of which as an effect of our action has a worth **for us**, i.e., beings the existence of which is in itself an end, and indeed one such that no other end, to which they would serve **merely** as means, can be put in its place, since without it nothing of **absolute worth** would be found anywhere; but if all worth were conditional and therefore contingent, then no supreme practical principle for reason could be found anywhere.   (*G*, 4: 428)

On the basis of this remark Christine Korsgaard has attributed to Kant, as already noted, the argument that for anything to have conditional value there has to be something of unconditional value, in particular for us to *confer* conditional value on the ordinary objects of our desire we have to *confer* unconditional value upon ourselves as valuers.[42]

---

[42] Both Korsgaard and Allen Wood have endorsed an interpretation of Kant's argument according to which in order to place value on particular, conditional ends—ends associated with a "practical identity," as a parent, firefighter, whatever, on Korsgaard's version—we have to place an intrinsic and

There are problems with attributing such an argument to Kant. In the case of theoretical metaphysics, Kant insists that it is impermissible to assume that because a series of conditions is given, an unconditioned ground for it must also be given, or to assume that a series of conditions necessarily terminates in something unconditioned; so why should this not likewise be a mistake in practical philosophy? In more ordinary terms, why should we not assume that there just are things that happen to be valued, but that there is no one thing that is necessarily valued or valuable from which they derive their value? Such an assumption was precisely David Hume's position, after all: we might value exercise for the sake of health, he argued, but must there be an explanation of why we value health? We just do.[43] What entitles Kant to reject this position? Yet another way to put the objection is that, if Kant's own statement is intended as a proof, it is question-begging: maybe there does need to be something of absolute worth to ground a supreme practical principle, but isn't the present question precisely whether there *is* something of absolute worth that could ground a supreme practical principle? That there is such a thing has to be proven in order to prove the validity of the moral law; it cannot be inferred from the validity of the moral law if that is not yet proven. In other words, it seems that we have to some independent reason to place unconditional value on something in order to stop a potentially infinite regress of merely conditional values of the form "A is valuable as the means to B, C is valuable as the means to A, . . ." But in Kant's view we are never entitled from a theoretical point of view to simply assume that the uncon-ditioned for everything conditioned actually exists, so the argument for the existence of something actually unconditioned would have to be a practical rather than theoretical argument. But for Kant our obligation under the moral law is always the premise of a practical argument for something else, such as the existence of God or immortality, so the idea of a practical argument for the unconditional value that grounds all other moral arguments is problematic. The actual structure of Kant's argument at *G*, 4: 428–9 seems rather to be just that a necessary—if you like, intrinsically and unconditionally valuable—end is the only possible ground for any necessary law, and humanity is self-evidently such a necessary end. Or that it is a necessary end is just a "fact of reason," *not derived* from any prior premise, as Kant will claim in the *Critique of Practical Reason* that the moral law itself is (*CPracR*, 5: 31). And finally, Kant adds in a footnote that "Here I put forward this proposition"—that rational being does have uncondi-tional, objective worth—"as a postulate. The grounds for it will be found in the last Section" of the *Groundwork* (*G*, 4: 429n.). In other words, Kant himself does *not*

---

unconditional value on ourselves as the setter of such ends; see Korsgaard 1986; Korsgaard, *SN*, pp. 120–3; and Wood 1999, pp. 124–32. For criticism of this argument, see Wuerth 2014, pp. 274–318, and Rosen 2022, pp. 136–7. We will return to Korsgaard's argument in Chapter 16.

[43] Hume, *EPM*, appendix I, p. 88.

think that he has here, in section II, *proven* that rational being is an end in itself that can therefore ground a possible categorical imperative. For the moment, it is only a supposition. For the moment we must therefore defer the question of whether he actually proves his assertion until we can discuss section III of the *Groundwork*.

Before we can do that, there are not only remaining formulations of the categorical imperative to consider, but also the last question about the Formula of Humanity: how would it serve as a ground for the Formulas of Universal Law and the Law of Nature? Why would acting only on universalizable maxims be the way in which to treat humanity whether in oneself or others always as an end and never merely as a means, or to preserve and promote the freedom of everyone possibly affected by action on one's proposed maxim? One clarification must be made up front: in all sorts of morally permissible actions we *do* treat others as means to our own ends; for example, when I enter into a lawful contract with another to produce some good or perform some service for me, I *am* using the other as a means to realize my own end of acquiring that good or service. The moral requirement is that I not use the other *merely* as a means, for example that I can use a contract with another as a means to some end of my own only if she can freely consent to the contract. If the other can agree—freely, without coercion or duress—to "my way of behaving toward" her, that would be because the proposed contract in some way serves some end of her own and therefore she herself can also "contain the end of this action" (G, 4: 430), or an end for this action. The case in which the other person can and does give actual consent is, of course, the simplest case in which she is being treated as an end and not merely as a means. There are all sorts of cases in which another cannot give actual consent— infants and children prior to what is commonly called the age of consent, people who are temporarily or permanently incapacitated and need medical consent, and so on. In such cases, perhaps the fact that the person is *not* being treated as a means to anyone else's end but is being treated on someone else's reasonable conception of their interest will have to suffice. This can of course be a contro-versial criterion in practice; what it takes to treat someone as an end and not merely as a means may sometimes require judgment and social consensus, not a mechanical rule or algorithm.

This point noted, we can see how the first formulation of the categorical imperative can be the means toward the satisfaction of the second. If I could perform my intended action on my intended maxim only if others could *not* adopt my maxim for themselves, that means I could freely adopt *my* maxim only by restricting *their* freedom to adopt it—so I would not be treating their humanity, that is, their freedom, as an end to be preserved. But if I were to freely choose a maxim that they *could* also freely choose to adopt, then I would (in that regard) be preserving the freedom of everyone involved, i.e., treating the humanity in everyone involved as an end and not merely as a means. I would not be willing that they *do* adopt my maxim, which would itself be a restriction of their freedom, but I am leaving them free to adopt it if they choose. In the self-regarding case, I might freely choose to perform a destructive action on a maxim that would destroy or limit *my own* future freedom, and that would not be to treat the humanity in myself—in all my actions, not just the present one—as an end in itself; but if I freely choose some possible alternative maxim or course of action now that does leave my future freedom intact as can be, then I am treating the humanity in myself—now and later—as an end in itself. Thus, although Kant's Formulas of Universal Law and the Law of Nature might obscure the self-regarding part of this by their focus on the requirement of interpersonal universalizability, we can see in the case of the Formula of Humanity how the freedom of all involved can be preserved by acting only on maxims that could be freely adopted by all involved, whether that means oneself and all others or one's present and future selves.

It might look as if positive duties to promote the humanity of oneself or others will need a different treatment. Sometimes this is accomplished by supposing that the duty to treat humanity as an end in itself is the bipartite duty to allow all to set their own ends and to facilitate their pursuit of ends. I have already suggested that the apparently distinct abilities to choose ends and to pursue them are not entirely independent, because a restriction of one's ability to pursue ends effectively limits the range of ends one can rationally set for oneself in the first place, and vice versa an expansion of one's ability to pursue ends effectively also expands the range of ends from which one can freely choose. Thus both negative and positive duties can be explained by the single idea of treating humanity—the freedom to set one's own ends—always as an end and never merely as a means.

Let us now turn to Kant's remaining formulations of the categorical imperative in section II of the *Groundwork*. An immediate problem is that Kant refers to a "third practical principle of the will" (*G*, 4: 431), clearly regarding the Formula of Universal Law and the Formula of the Law of Nature as two versions of the same principle, or one principle and its "typic," that is, as the first principle, and the Formula of Humanity as the second; but he offers two apparently very different candidates as the third practical principle or formulation of the categorical imperative. First he states as the third formulation, although not in the form of an imperative, "the idea **of the will of every rational being as a will giving universal laws**" (*G*, 4: 431). This formulation stresses that we must not regard the moral law simply as *applying* to us, but as being *given* to us *by ourselves*, an expression not of some alien will but of our own pure practical reason, and that we must regard all to whom the moral law applies not merely as *subjects* of the moral law but as themselves *authors* of the moral law, who must therefore legislate the moral law and apply it to their own maxims just as we do. Because this formulation brings out that the moral law is given to human beings by themselves, and given to all human beings by all human beings, not by any external source, Kant calls "this basic principle the principle of the **autonomy** of the will in contrast with every other, which I accordingly count as **heteronomy**" (*G*, 4: 433); autonomy was originally a political concept applying to a colony capable of legislating its own laws rather than depending on a mother-city. This is Kant's first introduction into the text of the *Groundwork* and into his moral discourse generally of the term "autonomy," which figures largely in the following pages and in many subsequent versions of Kantian moral philosophy.[44] But while this term clearly makes a meta-ethical point, about the source of the moral law, it does not obviously add any additional normative content to the moral law as already analyzed in the first two main formulations of the categorical imperative. However, a second statement of the Formula of Autonomy, as it has come to be called, might. Here Kant says that "the **principle** of every human will **giving universal law through all its maxims**...would be very **well suited** to be the categorical imperative" (*G*, 4: 432). This is a principle of autonomy in Kant's new sense of independence from anything other than pure reason itself because it obviously cannot be based on any particular inclination of anyone ("**it is based on no interest**"), but it also brings out that the test of universalizability is not really to be applied to single maxims of single persons considered in isolation; rather, all the maxims of each person and everyone must be consistently universalizable—maxims must comprise an intra- and interpersonally coherent system. This is a genuine clarification of if not an addition to the Formula of Universal Law. And it recaptures Kant's original idea of the "greatest possible" intra- and interpersonal use of freedom: any morally permissible maxim must be consistent with the rest of an agent's maxims but also with the maxims of all agents.

This version of the Formula of Autonomy also explains Kant's statement that it "leads to a very fruitful concept dependent upon it, namely that of an **empire of ends**" (*G*, 4: 433).[45] Kant introduces this key concept and basis for the final formulation of the categorical imperative thus:

> By an **empire** I understand a systematic union of various rational beings through common laws. Now since laws determine ends in terms of their universal validity, if we abstract from the personal differences of rational beings as well as from all the content of their private ends we shall be able to think of a whole of

---

[44] Kuehn 2001, p. 278, attributes Kant's use of the term "autonomy" in the *Groundwork* to his engagement with Garve's Cicero. It is striking that the term does not figure in Kant's earlier hints towards a moral philosophy nor in his works after the *Groundwork*.

[45] Kant's phrase is *Reich der Zwecke*. This is usually translated as "kingdom of ends," but the more accurate translation of *Reich* would be "empire," as in "Holy Roman Empire" (or, less fortunately, in "Third *Reich*." The term "kingdom" implies a single authority ruling over mere subjects, while "empire" suggests a union of sovereign authorities under some overall head. The latter image would better capture Kant's idea that the *Reich der Zwecke* is composed of multiple, equal agents each of whom gives herself the moral law, all under the authority only of the moral law itself, or of God as merely the personification of the moral law. For further argument and references on this point, see Guyer 2022.

all ends in systematic connection (a whole both of rational beings as ends in themselves and of the ends of his own that each may set himself), that is, an empire of ends, which is possible in accordance with the above principles.

(*G*, 4:433)

Kant then refers to the imperative based on *this* conception, namely "all maxims from one's own lawgiving ought to harmonize with a possible realm of ends as an empire of nature" (*G*, 4: 436), as the third formulation of the categorical imperative; he says that

> The above three ways of representing the principle of morality are at bottom only so many formulae of the very same law, and any one of them unites the other two in it.... All maxims have, namely,
>
> 1) a **form**, which consists in universality, and in this respect the formula of the moral imperative is expressed thus: that maxims must be chosen as if they were to hold as universal laws of nature;
>
> 2) a **matter**, namely an end, and in this respect the formula says that a rational being, as an end by its nature and hence as an end in itself, must in every maxim serve as the limiting condition of all merely relative and arbitrary ends;
>
> 3) **a complete determination** of all maxims by means of that formula, namely that all maxims from one's own lawgiving ought to harmonize with a possible empire of ends as an empire of nature. A progression takes place here, as through the categories of the **unity** of the form of the will (its universality), the **plurality** of the matter (of objects, i.e., of ends), and the **allness** or totality of the system of these. (*G*, 4:437)

Not only does the concept of the empire of ends constitute the "complete determination" of maxims and culminate the series of formulations of the categorical imperative; Kant goes so far as to say simply that "Morality consists, then, in the reference of all action to the lawgiving by which alone an empire of ends is possible" (*G*, 4: 434). Ultimately, the empire of ends is what is to be realized—the idea of the moral world that is to be transformed into an actual natural world (see *CPuR*, A808/B836)—by the compliance of everyone with the moral law. To treat all persons as ends in themselves requires acting only on universalizable maxims, indeed only on an intra- and interpersonally consistently universalizable system of maxims, and what would result from that is the empire of ends. That is, at least thus far, the ultimate object of morality.

Two connected points about the Formula of the Empire of Ends have to be treated carefully. First, Kant does not say just that the empire of ends is an empire of all persons treated as ends in themselves, in virtue of the defining legislation of the realm and their own status as mutual legislators; the empire of ends is also a systematic connection of the particular, of course permissible ends of these persons. This follows from a proper understanding of what it is to treat persons as ends and not merely as means: as we saw, this means not only refraining from destroying or restricting their capacity to set their own ends, but also positively promoting their ends—everyone's ends, thus even one's own—to the extent that one can, and to the extent that so doing is compatible with the first requirement. So if the empire of ends is the state of affairs that would be brought about by everyone treating everyone as ends in themselves, then it will include the promotion of everyone's permissible ends. But then—this is the second point—how do we reconcile this conclusion with Kant's statement that in order to think of a possible empire of ends we have first to "abstract from the personal difference of rational beings as well as the content of their private ends"? Is Kant contradicting himself? No; rather, what he means is that adopting the empire of ends as one's moral goal is not a matter of prudence or personal preference, depending on any particular end one happens to have, but a moral necessity, commanded by pure reason in the form of the moral law—but then what this law commands is that everyone promote the particular, of course morally permissible, ends of all, insofar as this is possible. There is no contradiction here.

One last point to mention here is that after Kant says that the formulae of the Law of Nature, of Humanity as an End in Itself, and of the Empire of Ends are "only so many formulae of the same law," he adds that there is a difference among them which is only subjective rather than objective, "intended namely to bring an idea of reason closer to intuition (by means of a certain analogy)" (G, 4: 436), but that "in moral **judging** it is better always to proceed by the strict method, and to make the foundation the universal [law] formula of the categorical imperative: **act according to the maxim that can make itself at the same time a universal law**," even though the other formulations and their sequence are "very useful" to "obtain **access** for the moral law" (G, 4: 436–7). This suggests that although the second and third formulae may be very persuasive, perhaps therefore useful in moral education, one should always use the first formulation of the categorical imperative—the Formula of Universal Law and its "typic," the Formula of the Law of Nature—as the actual decision-procedure in moral judgment; one should test proposed maxims, that is, chiefly, one's own proposed maxims for prospective actions, by that formulation. Is Kant right about this? We will see that over two centuries many objections have been raised to Kant's first formula, objections that any maxim may be universalized, that some immoral maxims pass the test but some obviously morally permissible maxims flunk, and so on. We will also see that at least some of these objections may be answered. But we can also suggest now that if the empire of ends is the ultimate goal of morality, perhaps, contrary to what Kant thought, that idea might be most useful as the test for proposed maxims—the question is whether acting on a proposed maxim would contribute to the realization of the empire of ends, or not. Such judgments may not always be easy to make. Kant himself might have been tempted by the idea that the first formulation of the categorical imperative provides a decision-procedure that offers a determinate result in every case, but perhaps using the idea of an empire of ends as an ideal for moral judgment, even if it is less determinate, would be a sounder paradigm. There may be no way to get away from the need to exercise good judgment under less than complete conditions of knowledge.[46]

In summing up his argument in section II of the *Groundwork*, Kant also stresses the importance of the third formulation of the categorical imperative by fore-grounding the concept of autonomy, which as we saw figures in his first version of the third formulation of the imperative. Kant did not *start* his overall argument from a concept of autonomy or from the premise that the fundamental goal of morality is autonomy, rather he sums his position up with this term: only after having analyzed the concept of a categorical imperative (or a practical law, as he calls it in the second *Critique*) does he state, as a matter of definition, that "Autonomy of the will is the property of the will by which it is a law to itself (independently of any property of the objects of volition). The principle of auton-omy is, therefore: to choose only in such a way that the maxims of your choice are also included as universal law in the same volition" (*G*, 4: 440; note that this is connected to what he called the principle of autonomy by its reference to maxims in the plural). Adopting a principle on the basis of mere inclination would be what Kant calls heteronomy; adopting a principle independently of mere inclination, which is what is necessary in order to adopt a universal and necessary principle, and adopting it instead solely on the basis of the mere form of rational willing, is what Kant now calls autonomy. In other words, his argument has not been an argument *from* the moral necessity of autonomy, but *to* the moral necessity of autonomy; that our moral principle must be autonomous is not the premise of Kant's argument but its conclusion. And it must also be noted here that Kant's concept of autonomy applies in the first instance to the principle of morality itself, and to the legislation—the adoption—of that principle; his concept is not identical to the contemporary conception of autonomy, which is something more like self-expression, or more crudely always getting to do what you want to do. Kant's conception of autonomy *makes room* for self-expression through the individual adoption of morally *permissible* ends a key *consequence* of morality, but the morality of autonomy in that sense is based on the morality of autonomy in Kant's own sense, the foundation of the principle of morality in reason rather than mere inclination.[47]

---

[46] In recent years Wood has argued for conceiving of the categorical imperative as an ideal for human action rather than a decision-procedure (e.g., Wood 2008, p. 57), as has Rosen (Rosen 2022, pp. 108, 124–5). In the end this may be right, but it should above all be the empire of ends formula that spells out the ideal.

[47] Onora O'Neill has stressed the difference between contemporary conceptions of autonomy and Kant's, e.g., O'Neill 2000, chapter 2. It is crucial to stress that Kant's conception of autonomy can both ground and limit contemporary conceptions.

In the paragraph in which Kant introduces his concept of autonomy, he goes on to say:

> That this practical rule is an imperative, that is, that the will of every rational being is necessarily bound to it as a condition, cannot be proved by mere analysis of the concepts to be found in it, because it is a synthetic proposition; one would have to go beyond a cognition of objects to a critique of the subject, that is, of pure practical reason … This business, however, does not belong in the present section. (G, 4: 440)

Up to this point Kant has shown us what is required by the categorical imperative, but not that we human beings are actually bound by it. That is the next, synthetic stage of the argument. Let us now turn to that, and to Kant's associated attempt to prove that we really are free always to act in accordance with the moral law.

2.3. The Freedom to be Moral

Kant's footnote to the Formula of Humanity as an End in Itself in section II of the *Groundwork* (4: 429n.) is naturally read as promising a proof that humanity is indeed an end in itself in section III, or a proof that freedom is indeed of fundamental and absolute value, as he had stated his premise in the lectures on ethics. However, proving that something is a fundamental value is problematic: if its value could be demonstrated from any other premise, then it would not be fundamental after all. Kant does not in fact attempt to prove that humanity is an end in itself in section III. Instead, at the conclusion of section II he states: "That morality is no phantom—and this follows if the categorical imperative, and with it the autonomy of the will, is true and absolutely necessary as an *a priori* principle—requires a possible **synthetic use of pure practical reason**, which use, however, we cannot venture upon without prefacing it by a **critique** of this rational faculty itself, the main features of which we have to present, sufficiently for our purpose, in the last section" (G, 4: 445). And what Kant attempts to demonstrate in section III is that we really are capable of autonomy of the will, that is, willing, or at least choosing the fundamental maxim of our will, independently of any object or matter of inclination, indeed that our real will or "proper self" (G, 4: 457) *is* autonomous in this sense. Since the moral law is the law of an autonomous will, this means that we are capable of being governed by the moral law, indeed that our real will *must* adopt the moral law. Rather than trying to prove that humanity is an end and the only end in itself, Kant's direction of proof, that we are autonomous and therefore are governed by the moral law, seems intended to obviate the need to prove that freedom itself is our fundamental value and humanity an end in itself, although our action in accordance with the moral law means that we always will treat humanity as an end and never merely as a means. Here is where Kant comes closest to contemporary "constructivism," that is, attempting to derive the moral law from the sheer fact of our rationality (see Chapter 16)—but he also does so on the problematic premise of his transcendental idealism.

A problem with this approach was immediately noticed by Kant's first critics: if our will really is autonomous and therefore determined by the moral law, then how can we ever will anything *other* than that, that is, how can we freely will to be evil? How is freedom of the will, that is, not merely the freedom to set our own ends independently of the inclinations of ourselves and others, which is what we have been discussing so far, but freedom to choose between alternatives no matter what, independently of one's past history, even possible on Kant's account? This objection was raised in 1788 by Johann August Heinrich Ulrich, in a book called *Eleutheriologie* or "Theory of Freedom," which we will examine in Part II, Chapter 5. Kant could not have seen this work when he was writing the *Critique of Practical Reason* because the two books came out at the same time, although he and some of his supporters would certainly respond to it after 1788. But Kant must already have realized that there was a problem with his view, for in the second *Critique*, written in 1787 and finished by Christmas of that year, he takes a different approach to the relation between freedom of the will and the moral law: instead of trying to prove first that we have freedom of the will and therefore must be bound by the moral law, Kant simply asserts, as the fundamental "fact of reason," that we are aware of our obligation under the moral law, and therefore that we must be free to act in accordance with it. Kant's argument may turn on the premise that "ought implies can," but "ought" does not imply "does," so on this approach Ulrich's problem need not arise. Actually, the argumentative situation is a little more complicated than this suggests. In the *Critique of Practical Reason* Kant uses the premise "ought implies can" only in his illustration of the fact of reason, and his formal statement of his position, which seems to equate our will with pure reason, may still be liable to Ulrich's objection. But *Religion within the Boundaries of Mere Reason* relies frequently and heavily on "ought implies can" yet centrally insists that freedom is always the freedom to choose between good and evil. So at least the *Religion* contains a definitive resolution of the Ulrich problem. We will come back to this issue briefly in the Chapter 3 of this Part and then more fully in Part II, Chapter 5.

But first, Kant's argument in *Groundwork* III: Kant starts with a distinction between two *conceptions* of freedom, or aspects of the conception of freedom. This is not a distinction between two different *kinds* of freedom—Kant's argument would collapse immediately if there were two different kinds of freedom such that an agent could have one without the other. Freedom of the will may be conceived **negatively**, as independence "from alien causes **determining** it," that is, mere inclinations. But as a type of causality, freedom of the will must have some sort of law that positively determines it, or that can be included in a positive conception of freedom of the will: "it is not for that reason lawless but must instead be a causality in accordance with immutable laws but of a special kind" (G, 4: 446). Given Kant's arguments in sections I and II, if the causality of the free will can have nothing to do with inclination and its objects (alien causes), then it can only be determined by the purely formal law to give our maxims the form of reason and thus law itself: "what, then, can freedom of the will be other than autonomy, that is, the will's property of being a law to itself" (G, 4: 447). This is the source of Ulrich's problem: if the moral law is the causal law of the free will, then how can a free will freely will to be immoral? Kant does not raise that problem, but he is aware that he cannot move past the analytic conclusions of the previous sections, that is, their analyses of our obligations if we are indeed bound by the moral law, merely by a full or fuller *definition* of freedom of the will. To reach a synthetic a priori conclusion, he needs some *fact*, although one that we somehow know a priori.

Some commentators[48] think that Kant discharges his obligation to prove that we are free a page later when he says that "every being that cannot act otherwise than **under the idea of freedom** is just because of that really free in a practical respect, that is, all laws that are inseparably bound up with freedom hold for him just as if his will had been validly pronounced free also in itself and in theoretical philosophy" (G, 4: 448). But whatever Kant might have meant by saying this—one thing he clearly did mean, and reiterates in the second *Critique*, is that we cannot give a theoretical *explanation* of our freedom and therefore have no obligation to do so—he clearly did not mean it to be the end of the present argument, only the beginning. Because of the analytical connection between the moral law and freedom of the will that has been brought out by the concept of autonomy and the connection between the negative and positive aspects of the concept of freedom, it is clear that if agents are free then they are also bound (at least obligated) by the moral law; but Kant signals that he has *not* yet made the actual argument that we are free and therefore bound by the moral law two pages after this comment:

> It must be freely admitted that a kind of circle comes to light here from which, as it seems, there is no way to escape. We take ourselves as free in the order of efficient causes in order to think ourselves under moral laws in the order of ends; and we afterwards think ourselves as subject to these laws because we have ascribed to ourselves freedom of the will: for, freedom and the will's own law-giving are both autonomy of the will and hence reciprocal concepts, and for this very reason one cannot be used to explain the other or furnish a ground for it but

---

[48] E.g., Hill 1985 and Hill and Zweig 2002, pp. 97–9.

can at most be used only for the logical purpose of reducing apparently different representations of the same object to one single concept... (G, 4: 450)

This is what Henry Allison has called Kant's "reciprocity thesis,"[49] and what Kant himself expresses in the *Critique of Practical Reason* with the statement that "freedom and unconditional practical law reciprocally imply each other" (*CPracR*, 5: 29). But for Kant a "reciprocal" and "logical" connection of this sort is purely analytic, and it would indeed be circular, or begging the question, to try to prove one side of the equation *from* the other: rather, Kant needs *first* to prove that one of the terms applies to us, and *then* the other will follow. He has to get outside the tight little circle of the reciprocal connection between freedom of the will or autonomy (which for now he still identifies) and the moral law by proving either that we really are free *or* that we really are subject to the moral law, in which case the other will follow.

This is what Kant now attempts to do in *Groundwork* III. He says next that "One resource, however, still remains to us, namely to inquire whether we do not take a different standpoint when by means of freedom we think ourselves as causes efficient *a priori* than when we represent ourselves in terms of our actions as effects that we see before our eyes" (G, 4: 450). From the standpoint of purely theoretical philosophy, we think of ourselves as just nodes in the great causal chain of nature, governed by deterministic laws by which our past entirely determines our future, just like everything else; but from another standpoint we can apparently think of ourselves as initiating action not in accordance with such causal laws but in accordance with the moral law. But again, while some commentators have written as if we can just help ourselves to both standpoints, and simply ignore the natural standpoint of causal determinism from the practical standpoint,[50] Kant is *not* just helping himself to the practical standpoint. Rather, he now tries to prove that we are fully *entitled* to and *must* adopt this standpoint.

Here is his argument. From a theoretical point of view, even the "commonest understanding" distinguishes between appearances and "something else that is not appearances," that is, "**things in themselves**"—Kant makes this remarkable statement even though he had needed the entire *Critique of Pure Reason* to explain and demonstrate this distinction! He then says that we all also apply this distinction to the representation of ourselves when we distinguish between "the constitution of [our] own subject, made up of nothing but appearances," such as our sensations of our inner states, and "something else lying at their basis, namely [our] I as it may be constituted in itself... belonging to the **intellectual world**" (G, 4: 451). So far, so good, although Kant would argue in the second edition of the *Critique of Pure Reason* that we are entitled to conceive of things in themselves only as noumena

---

[49] Allison 1990.   [50] E.g., Beck 1975.

"in the negative sense," as *not* the same as appearance although the ground of appearance, and not as noumena "in the positive sense," with their actual characteristics known by pure reason (which would be the proper sense of the term "noumenon," namely an object of *nous* or pure reason) (*CPuR*, B307–9). However, here in the *Groundwork*, before the second edition of the *Critique of Pure Reason*, Kant apparently goes on to assert precisely that we *do* have positive knowledge of the nature of our selves as they are in themselves, namely that we find in ourselves reason as "pure self-activity" (*G*, 4: 452). From there, the rest of Kant's argument follows: if we really do have, or are in our essence, pure self-activity, and pure self-activity is obviously not determination by alien causes, then there is no alternative but that we are determined by our own pure will, that is, by the pure form of the will, that is, by the moral law. Kant now takes himself to be entitled to the premise that we really are rational beings, and that "As a rational being, and thus as a being belonging to the intelligible world, the human being can never think of the causality of his own will otherwise than under the idea of freedom"—what was merely assumed a few pages earlier but has now become a fact—"for independence from the determining causes of the world of sense (which reason must always ascribe to itself) is freedom. With the idea of freedom the concept of **autonomy** is now inseparably combined, and with the concept of autonomy the universal principle of morality" (*G*, 4: 452). Now Kant thinks that he has established as a fact that we are self-active and free, and then that the moral law really does apply to us can safely be inferred, for autonomy, the will giving itself its law, can yield nothing other than the moral law. By this means "the suspicion that a hidden circle was contained in our inference from freedom to autonomy and from the latter to the moral law" has now been "removed" (*G*, 4: 453).

It is difficult to read this argument as other than the kind of speculative metaphysics that Kant seemed to outlaw in the *Critique of Pure Reason*. It is also clear that Kant does not quite know what to do with it, for a few pages later, when he should present our rational self as the ground of all our actions at the phenomenal level (even though that would raise Ulrich's problem), he instead presents our reason and our sensible nature, thus our inclinations, as if they were in *competition* for our actual volition. Instead of presenting the rational noumenal self as the *ground* of the self of appearance, Kant suddenly presents pure reason as *part* of our one and only self, potentially at war with its other part, mere sensible inclination. If I were only "a member of the intelligible world...all my actions **would** always be in conformity with the authority of the will; but since at the same time I intuit myself as a member of the world of sense, they **ought** to be in conformity with it" (*G*, 4: 454). This is certainly a traditional picture of human nature, going all the way back to Plato's image of the soul being pulled in two different directions by its rational and appetitive parts (*Republic* 4.439d–440e), and would avoid Ulrich's objection, but only at the cost of undermining Kant's previous claim that the moral law is the *causal* law of our real self and the self-activity of reason the real nature of that self.

Kant does not say that he is revising the *Groundwork*'s approach to freedom of the will in the *Critique of Practical Reason*. Yet this statement seems to be a tacit admission that he regarded his previous approach as a failure and is taking a different tack; referring back to what seems to be the strategy of *Groundwork* III to provide a deduction of the moral law, Kant writes:

> But something different and quite paradoxical takes the place of this vainly sought deduction of the moral principle, namely that the moral principle conversely itself serves as the principle of the deduction of an inscrutable faculty which no experience could prove but which speculative reason had to assume as at least possible (in order to find among its cosmological ideas what is unconditioned in its causality, so as not to contradict itself), namely the faculty of freedom, of which the moral law, which itself has no need of justifying grounds, proves not only the possibility but the reality in beings who cognize this law as binding upon them.   (*CPracR*, 5: 47)

Here Kant seems to argue that, while the possibility of freedom of the will at the noumenal level was necessary in order to resolve the (third) antinomy in the first *Critique* (although that antinomy *required* only divine spontaneity, but *allowed* for the possibility of human spontaneity by analogy), morality requires its actuality, and that this can be deduced from our awareness of our binding obligation under the moral law.[51] Kant is suggesting that the circle that he worried about in the *Groundwork* is to be broken in the opposite direction: freedom and the moral law still reciprocally imply each other, thus are conceptually connected, but instead of first asserting the self-activity of reason and then inferring the validity of the moral law from that, here Kant seems to assert the self-evidence of our obligation under the moral law and infer the freedom of our will from that. This inference is called Kant's argument from the "fact of reason," from his statement that "This Analytic shows that pure reason can be practical—that is, can of itself, independently of anything empirical," and thus of the causal laws of the empirical world, "determine the will—and it does so by a fact in which pure reason proves itself actually practical, namely autonomy in the principle of morality by which reason determines the will to deeds" (*CPracR*, 5: 42).[52] Indeed, Kant explains that he calls the book a critique of practical reason, not a critique of *pure* practical reason, because while the task of the critique of theoretical reason was to criticize

---

[51] For an argument that the *Critique of Practical Reason* reverses the direction of Kant's argument from *Groundwork* III, see Ameriks 2000, chapter VI. For an argument for the continuity of the two texts, see Henrich 1975.

[52] For detailed discussions of the "fact of reason" argument, see Beck 1960, chapter X, pp. 166–70, and Rawls 2000, pp. 253–72.

its pretensions to knowledge from pure reason alone, the present task is to criticize the assumption that practical reason can only be empirical, i.e,, prudential and instrumental, and to prove instead that there *is* such a thing as pure practical reason, as the source of both the moral law and action in accordance with it (*CPracR*, 5: 15–16). The actual inference from the fact of reason, our awareness of our binding obligation under the moral law, to our freedom of will then looks as if turns on the premise that "ought" implies "can," that if we truly ought to do something, then we must be able to do it.

Actually, it is Kant's illustration of his first statement of the connection between the moral law and freedom of the will in the second *Critique* that involves "ought implies can." Kant offers the example of someone who is threatened with being hanged if he does not control his lust, who certainly knows that he could do that; he then asks whether someone could similarly refrain from bearing false witness even if threatened with certain death if he does not. Kant then says of his imagined character: "He would perhaps not venture to assert whether he would do it or not, but he must admit without hesitation that it would be possible for him. He judges, therefore, that he can do something because he is aware that he ought to do it and cognizes freedom within him, which, without the moral law, would have remained unknown to him" (*CPracR*, 5: 30). Kant apparently just assumes that "ought implies can," because he makes no attempt to argue for this premise.

In fact, the premise "ought implies can" is problematic, because it can support *modus tollens* ((p implies q and not-q) implies not-p) as well as *modus ponens* ((p implies q and p) implies q): that is, while from "ought implies can" and "I ought to do ϕ" I might be able to infer "I can do ϕ," from "ought implies can" and "I cannot do ϕ" I could infer "It is not the case that I ought to do ϕ." The premise "ought implies can" cannot prove our obligation to act in accordance with the moral law unless somehow that obligation is unshakeable, which at least in the *Groundwork* was the question that needed to be answered in order to break the circle or reciprocity between freedom and the moral law.

But it is not clear that the argument from "ought implies can" is Kant's most fundamental argument in the *Critique of Practical Reason* rather than just a statement of its conclusion that Kant could then use in subsequent work such as the *Religion*. For what Kant says before he offers the example, which is just supposed to "confirm" the fact of our freedom, is this:

> It is therefore the **moral law**, of which we become immediately conscious (as soon as we draw up maxims of the will for ourselves), that **first** offers itself to us and, inasmuch as reason presents it as a determining ground not to be outweighed by any sensible conditions and indeed quite independent of them, leads directly to the concept of freedom. But how is consciousness of that moral law possible? We can become aware of pure practical laws just as we are conscious of pure theoretical principles, by attending to the necessity with which reason prescribes them to us and to the setting aside of all empirical conditions to

which reason directs us. The concept of a pure will arises from the first, as consciousness of a pure understanding arises from the latter.... morality first discloses to us the concept of freedom ...   (*CPracR*, 5: 29–30)

Kant's claim here seems to be that, just as in proposing ordinary theoretical judgments, for example the causal judgments of everyday life and natural science, we can become aware that we possess certain a priori categories and principles (e.g., the category of causation) and can make our ordinary judgments only because we do, so in the proposing maxims of conduct to ourselves we realize that we inevitably evaluate them by the a priori principle of morality, which is thus as unimpeachable as the categories themselves. This is the fact of reason: the criterion for morally correct maxims that we discover in considering them. Kant then makes a further claim, but without any invocation of the principle that "ought implies can": instead he asserts that from our practice of evaluating maxims by the moral law we become aware not only that we have pure *reason* but also that we have a pure *will*—and what could that be but a will that is determined not by "alien causes," that is, mere inclinations, but by the rational form of maxims themselves, thus by pure and spontaneous reason. This argument avoids invoking "ought implies can" with its potential liability to *modus tollens* instead of *modus ponens*. But it also ends up foregoing the potential benefit of "ought implies can," namely that "ought" does *not* imply "does." Instead, it appears to work by *identifying* pure reason with "a pure will," throwing Kant back to the position of (the first part of) *Groundwork* III and thus in the end still leaving open Ulrich's objection that if Kant simply identifies free will with pure reason then he cannot explain the possibility of freely willed and thus imputable evil.

We will see that in the *Religion* Kant thought that he could avoid this problem by splitting the will into two parts, one, pure will (*Wille*), which prescribes the moral law but does not choose whether or not to accept it, and the other, the faculty of choice (*Willkühr*), which decides whether or not to accept the moral law, or as Kant puts it in the *Religion*, whether to make it one's fundamental maxim to subordinate self-love to the moral law or the moral law to self-love (*RBMR*, 6: 36). But this solution presupposes that we have a free *Willkühr* as well as a rational *Wille*, and Kant does not add any further argument for this presupposition in the *Religion*. We will see that philosophers from Kant's contemporaries (Part II, Chapter 5) to such later figures as Henry Sidgwick and G. E. Moore (Part IV, Chapter 13) have found Kant's treatment of freedom unsatisfactory, and few have attempted to defend it since Moore wrote at the turn of the twentieth century.[53] However, we can also suggest that Kant's difficulties with the metaphysics of the freedom of the *will* do not necessarily undermine the value of his

---

[53] Henry Allison has attempted to defend the idea that we can *conceive* of ourselves as free to follow the moral law no matter what, or to adopt the practical point of view, because we can *conceive* of ourselves as things in themselves, without subjection to space, time, and ordinary spatio-temporal

normative theory of the fundamental value of freedom of *choice and action*. The latter might be a good account of the content of what morality valorizes and demands even if, as a matter of empirical fact, we are *not* always, each or all of us some of the time and perhaps even some of us all of the time, able to do what morality requires. Perhaps it is an empirical question to what degree and when particular people are fully aware of and able to respond to the demands of morality, thus liable to the imputation of responsibility. That would not plunge morality "into an abyss of skepticism" (*CPracR*, 5: 3), as Kant fears; it would just mean that we need to be humane rather than unforgiving in our judgments about moral shortcomings or failure, and perhaps rethink our practices of blame and punishment.[54]

So much for now on the issue of freedom. Before we can turn to the final main issue in Kant's foundational works in moral philosophy to be discussed here, namely the continuing development of his conception of the highest good and his doctrine of the postulates of pure practical reason, which is the central issue in the Dialectic of the *Critique of Practical Reason*, we need to pause over the further development of Kant's conception of the role of the feeling of respect in moral motivation in the second *Critique*. Kant discusses this topic in the third chapter of the Analytic of Pure Practical Reason under the title "On the Incentives of Pure Practical Reason" (*CPracR*, 5: 71). In spite of the plural title, however, Kant allows only a single incentive for pure practical reason, namely the feeling of respect for the moral law.

2.4. The Feeling of Respect in the *Critique of Practical Reason*

Kant had introduced the feeling of respect in a footnote in section I of the *Groundwork*. There he had treated this feeling as the "self-wrought" *effect* of the determination of the will by the moral law, or the "**subordination** of my will to a law without the mediation of other influences on my sense." He described the feeling of respect as the "consciousness" of such determination of the will (*G*, 4: 401n.), suggesting that its role was purely epiphenomenal: the feeling of respect is how what Kant will later describe as the noumenal determination of the will by the

---

causality, rather than as appearances; see Allison 1990, pp. 247–9, and Allison 2011, pp. 326–7. This is difficult to square with Allison's general interpretation of transcendental idealism, in which he claims that appearances and things in themselves are the very same things (the "one-world" interpretation) although conceived in two different ways, one of which includes the spatio-temporality of things and the subjection to causality that follows from that and the other of which omits this aspect of things (see Allison 1983, revised 2004). The problem is that simply omitting their spatio-temporality from one way of *conceiving* of things does not change any facts about them as they actually are; so merely omitting our subjection to causality from one *conception* of ourselves does not make us free from ordinary causality.

[54] See Guyer 2008b.

moral law makes itself known empirically or phenomenally, but it seems to play no causal role in our performance of moral action. In the *Critique of Practical Reason*, however, Kant suggests that the feeling of respect does play a causal role in the transition from the determination of the will by the moral law to the performance of particular actions, or the selection of particular maxims for the performance of particular actions. Following a suggestion already made in the *Groundwork*, he presents the feeling of respect as complex: it is in part a painful feeling engendered by the restriction or "humiliation" of "self-conceit," self-love made into a principle, by the determination to be moral; but it is also "a positive feeling that is not of empirical original and is cognized *a priori*," that is, a feeling of pleasure at the facts that the moral law that restricts self-conceit is produced by our own reason and that we know ourselves to be capable of acting in accordance with the moral law (*CPracR*, 5: 73). But what Kant adds in the second *Critique* is that through this feeling, which although it is initially painful must be on balance pleasurable and positive, "the hindrance to pure practical reason is lessened and the representation of the superiority of its objective law to the impulses of sensibility is produced, and hence, by removal of the counterweight, the relative weightiness of the law (with regard to a will affected by impulses) in the judgment of reason" is rendered effective (*CPracR*, 5: 75–6). That is, while at some level—for Kant, at the noumenal level—the moral law must determine the will, at the level of empirical psychology, the disposition to self-love—which is always present in mere human beings, even the best of us—is accompanied by impulses to action, even the entrenched ones that Kant calls inclination, that must be outweighed if the determination of the will by the moral law is to be what determines our actions. That is the role of the feeling of respect—it is not the basic incentive to be moral, for Kant at the noumenal level, but it plays a causal role in rendering the determination of the will causally effective, at the level where we can understand the causality involved, for Kant the phenomenal level.

Kant makes his revised conception of the role of the feeling of respect even more precise a few pages later when he states that "respect for the moral law must be regarded as also a positive though indirect effect of the moral law on feeling insofar as the law weakens the hindering influence of the inclinations by humiliating self-conceit, and must therefore be regarded as a subjective ground of activity—that is, as the incentive to compliance with the law—*and as the ground for maxims of a course of life in conformity with it*" (*CPracR*, 5: 79, emphasis added). That is, the specific point in the empirical etiology of action at which the feeling of respect plays its indispensable causal role is in the transition from the general determination of the will by the moral law to the adoption of particular maxims, for example, the maxim to help others in need whether one expects a benefit in return or not rather than the maxim to help others only when one expects a benefit in return. The selection of such maxims, whether on the basis of one's respect for morality or out of self-love, must be supposed to occur in the phenomenal world of ordinary experience, because the content of such maxims—whether to pay back deposits, help others in need, and so on—concerns the world of ordinary experience. Commitment to such maxims, rendered possible by the feeling of respect, is then expected to translate into particular actions in particular circumstances. Thus the feeling of respect, as the phenomenal effect of the noumenal determination of the will by the moral law, can enter into the etiology of action in the phenomenal world.

We will see that Kant refines this model of motivation even further in the *Metaphysics of Morals*, where the single feeling of respect is transformed into a complex of morally relevant feelings through the cultivation of which the will's commitment to its maxims is rendered causally efficacious. But before we can come to that, we must complete our survey of the key topics in the *Critique of Practical Reason* with a discussion of its development of Kant's conception of the highest good.

2.5. The Highest Good and the Postulates of Pure Practical Reason in the *Critique of Practical Reason*

Kant returns to the topic of the highest good under the rubric of a "Dialectic of Pure Practical Reason" in the second *Critique* because the concept of the highest good is that of "the unconditioned totality of the object of pure practical reason," and ideas of unconditioned totalities always generate dialectical inferences (*CPracR*, 5: 107–8). In this case, the dialectical inference is supposed to take the form of an antinomy (5: 113). Kant's argument would be clearer if he had said that the antinomy was in practical reason in general, not pure practical reason. For he presents the idea of the highest good as the complete object of morality as arising from the combination of the supreme condition of *morality*, of course complete compliance with the moral law given by pure practical reason, with the ultimate object of each agent's own empirical and *natural* or merely prudential practical reason, namely her own happiness as the satisfaction of a maximally compossible set of her own desires. Without explanation, Kant says that both virtue and happiness, for an agent, is required "not merely in the partial eyes of a person who makes himself an end but even in the judgment of an impartial reason, which regards a person in the world generally as an end in itself. For to need happiness, to be also worthy of it, and yet not to participate in it cannot be consistent with the perfect volition of a rational being" (*CPracR*, 5: 111). Kant does not explain why being virtuous would make one worthy of happiness, or for that matter why being vicious would make one worthy of unhappiness—although that the vicious should be punished with unhappiness to make their (lack of) virtue proportionate to their (un)happiness will play *no* role in Kant's argument. In spite of occasional turns of phrase, Kant's conception of the highest good is not that happiness should be proportionate to virtue, whatever the level of virtue is, but that the *greatest* happiness should accompany the *greatest* virtue.[55]

What Kant does do is to reject two ancient views which as he sees it would make the connection between (individual) virtue and (individual) happiness analytic, that is, conceptually necessary. The Epicurean view is that virtue is nothing but the pursuit of happiness (which the true Epicurean places only in the simplest possible satisfaction of natural needs, easily obtained, not in the refined pleasures of table or wine cellar of the modern "Epicurean"), the Stoic view is that happiness is nothing but the achievement of virtue (*CPracR*, 5: 111). Either way, satisfying one of the terms of the equation automatically satisfies the other. In Kant's view, however, virtue and happiness are two different things, one a matter of pure practical reason in the form of "the moral disposition of the will," the other a matter of "the laws of nature and the physical ability to use them for one's purposes." Thus "no necessary connection of happiness with virtue in the world, adequate to the highest good, can be expected from the most meticulous observance of moral laws," but neither can virtue result from the most prudent use of the laws of nature for one's own happiness. Yet still the two things should be connected, and indeed necessarily so; this is what Kant calls the antinomy of pure practical reason.

As with the antinomies of pure theoretical reason in the first *Critique*, Kant's resolution of this antinomy ultimately depends upon transcendental idealism. He does not say this explicitly, but both parts of his solution require that we be able to coherently conceive of and believe in things that are not given in appearance but could be true at the level of noumenal reality. Kant's solution has two parts, each a "postulate of pure practical reason, which is a theoretical proposition affirmed on practical grounds" (*CPracR*, 5: 122), as a necessary condition of the possibility of morality, or a presupposition "having a necessarily practical reference" that does not "extend speculative cognition" but is nevertheless is justifiably affirmed by us (5: 132). The two postulates that resolve the antinomy are the postulate of personal immortality on the one hand and of the existence of God as the author of nature on the other. Personal immortality, which of course we never observe in the spatio-temporal world of experience and can only be conceived as a property of the self as it is in itself, would allow for "**endless progress** toward that complete conformity" with the moral law that we also never observe in the natural world but which is required by the conception of the highest good; on the basis of this

---

[55] See also Rawls 2000, p. 313. I do not deny that Kant may well have believed that the vicious should be made unhappy and based an argument for the existence of God as judge on this belief, as is central to the interpretation of Rosen 2022, e.g., pp. 57–9, but I do not see that this (inherited?) religious belief has any foundation in Kant's basic arguments for the highest good, either as the combination of the moral goal of virtue with the natural goal of happiness or as the product of the (ideal) perfection of virtue itself. Kant's "antinomy" assumes the first of these conceptions, but says nothing about punishing the vicious.

postulate we can at least believe that what morality says *must* be realized *can* be accomplished. (Although thinking of immortality as "endless progress" shows that we cannot in fact escape thinking about ourselves in temporal terms, even though our real selves are not supposed to be literally temporal.) The "existence of God as a postulate of pure practical reason" allows us to believe that "the highest good in the world is possible . . . insofar as a supreme cause of nature having a causality in keeping with the moral disposition is assumed" (*CPracR*, 5: 124–5). That is, although our initial impression of the natural world may be that it gives us no reason at all to think that our efforts to be virtuous will be succeeded by happiness, once we conceive of the laws of nature as written by a God who is also of course completely aware of and committed to the moral law, we realize that it must be possible that our efforts to be moral will be accompanied with happiness (so perhaps our failure to find such a connection in nature thus far is due merely to inadequate efforts to be moral). The synthetic connection between virtue and happiness that initially appeared to be missing can be established through belief in the existence of God as the author of both nature and the moral law. Finally, once he has resolved the antinomy of practical reason through these two postulates, Kant retrospectively characterizes his argument for the reality of freedom of the will as the condition of the compliance with the demands of the moral law as a postulate of pure practical reason as well, a postulate flowing from "the necessary presupposition of independence from the sensible world and of the capacity to determine one's will by the law of an intelligible world, that is, the law of freedom" (*CPracR*, 5: 132). The postulate of freedom is in a different position than the postulates of immortality and of the existence of God, however: the first is required simply by the supposition that we must always be able to do what morality demands, or *is* that supposition; the other two are required only by the additional assumption that morality specifically requires the highest good, the juxtaposition of complete happiness with perfect morality.

As already suggested, Kant's argument for complete freedom of the will has not met with a friendly reception; the same is true in the case of Kant's affirmation of the other two postulates. One problem that has largely gone unnoticed is that the argument for those two postulates as Kant presents it in the second *Critique* is not even internally coherent. Kant's version of the postulates in the first *Critique* was at least internally coherent, in that the realization of both virtue and happiness were deferred to a non-natural, non-experienced "world that is future for us" (*CPuR*, A811/B839), where there is no danger that the realization of happiness would *precede* the achievement of virtue which is however supposed to be its necessary condition. In the version of the postulates in the second *Critique*, however, while the achievement of complete virtue is deferred to the non-natural time (or perhaps better "time," not literal time) of personal immortality, God is conceived of as the author of *nature* precisely in order to make the realization of complete happiness possible in the real time of that nature. This opens the possibility that happiness might be achieved before virtue is, or quasi-before, since the noumenal realm in which immortality might be possible is not supposed to be really temporal. This would violate Kant's insistence that the achievement of virtue and thus of worthiness to be happy must be the condition of the realization of happiness in the eyes of "impartial reason."

3

Kant's Moral Philosophy in the 1790s

Perhaps Kant quickly noticed this problem; in any case, he soon suggested an alternative conception of the highest good and the conditions of its possibility on which this problem does not arise. This was one three main refinements of his moral philosophy that he accomplished in the 1790s, his final decade of philosophical publication. The other two were the further refinement of his theory of free will (even though, as already suggested, this still might not have been successful) and fleshing out the system of human moral duties that he had sketched in the *Groundwork* only as far as was necessary to confirm the correctness of his analysis of the categorical imperative. These three refinements are found, respectively, in the *Critique of the Power of Judgment* (1790) as well as in the 1793 essay "On the Common Saying: That May Be Correct in Theory, but It is of No Use in Practice" (1793), in *Religion within the Boundaries of Mere Reason* (also 1793), and in the *Metaphysics of Morals* of 1797. Kant discusses the ethical duties of human beings, distinguished by the fact that they be enforced only by our own respect for the moral law, in the Doctrine of Virtue of the latter work; its Doctrine of Right, along with the pamphlet *Toward Perpetual Peace* (1795), present Kant's theory of our juridical duties, those of our moral duties that can and should be enforced with the coercive means of the state. This theory will not be discussed here, however, since Kant's legal and political philosophy and its influence will be the topic of a separate volume in this series by Howard Williams.[1]

3.1. The Highest Good in the *Critique of the Power of Judgment* and "Theory and Practice"

Kant seems to have decided upon a third *Critique* as soon as he had completed the second.[2] Initially, he had in mind a "critique of taste," that is, a theory of aesthetic experience and judgment, which had been a topic in his lectures on anthropology and metaphysics since the early 1770s. (Alexander Gottlieb Baumgarten, the

---

[1] There are few commentaries on the *Metaphysics of Morals* as a whole, but see Gregor 1963 and the edited volumes Timmons 2002, and Denis 2010. On the Doctrine of Virtue, see Trampota et al. 2013, and esp. Herman 2021. On the distinction yet relation between juridical and ethical duties, see Guyer 2002, Guyer 2005b, and Guyer 2014a, chapters 7 and 8.

[2] See Kant's letters to Ludwig Heinrich Jacob, September 11, 1787, *Corr*, 10: 493–5, and to Carl Leonhard Reinhold, December 28 and 31, 1787, *Corr*, 10: 513–16.

Kant's Impact on Moral Philosophy. Paul Guyer, Oxford University Press. © Paul Guyer 2024.
DOI: 10.1093/oso/9780199592456.003.0004

founder of the discipline of aesthetics in Germany, had included some of his views in the chapter on "Empirical Psychology" in his *Metaphysica* of 1739, which was the textbook for Kant's course on metaphysics, with that chapter in particular being the text for Kant's course on anthropology.) But, as noted previously, by the end of 1787, Kant had broadened his conception of the new work to include a critical approach to the teleological judgment of nature—the judgment of purposiveness in nature—which however had also been a topic for him as early as his 1755 *Universal Natural History and Theory of the Heavens* and his 1763 book *The Only Possible Basis for a Demonstration of the Existence of God.* In the new critique aesthetics and teleology were somehow to be combined to "bridge" the "incalculable gulf" or "great chasm" that separates the two separate "legislations" of nature and morality, the laws of nature and the moral law (*CPJ*, Introduction, section II, 5: 175–6, and section IX, 5: 195). It is not clear what this "gulf" or "chasm" was supposed to be, since Kant had already reconciled the noumenal freedom of the will with the causal determinism of the phenomenal world in the first and second *Critiques* and had also bridged the threatened gulf between virtue and happiness in the second with the postulate of the existence of God as the condition of the possibility of the highest good in his capacity as author of the laws of both nature and morality. Yet since Kant does not revisit the problem of freedom of the will in the third *Critique* (although he would a few years later in the *Religion*), but does revisit the topic of the highest good, indeed in the culminating section of the book, the Doctrine of Method of its second half, the Critique of the Power of Teleological Judgment, it seems plausible that offering a better account of the highest good and the conditions of its possibility were at least part of what Kant had in mind as bridging the gulf between nature and freedom.[3]

Be that as it may, Kant does suggest a new account of the highest good in the third *Critique*, one that averts the objection raised in the previous section and that was perhaps intended to do so. As in the second *Critique*, Kant's new conception of the highest good follows the presentation of an antinomy, this time the "Antinomy of Teleological Judgment."[4] This is the antinomy between the thesis that everything in nature must be judged in accordance with strictly mechanical laws that make no reference to purpose, and the antithesis that some things in nature—"organized beings," or organisms—can be understood only in terms of purposes, since their organs seem to have various purposes necessary to the maintenance and reproduction of the whole but yet depend upon the whole (*CPJ*, §§64–5). In the latter regard, the parts depend on the whole; but since we cannot comprehend backward causation, we can understand this relation only in analogy to human intentional production, where the antecedent conception and design of the whole can play a causal role in the production of the parts. Thus,

---

[3] I suggest some other aspects to Kant's bridging of the gulf in Guyer 1990.
[4] For discussion, see McLaughlin 1990.

Kant supposes, we can understand the latter only by conceiving of organisms as if they were designed. But we have no direct experience of a designer in nature. However, Kant then exploits his transcendental idealism by arguing that we can at least *conceive* of organisms *as if* they were designed by a designer outside of nature even though we experience no such thing (§73). Further, Kant argues, once we conceive of purposiveness *within* nature, in the form of particular organisms, it is natural for us to conceive of nature as a whole as if it were purposive, that is, the product of a design for some end (§67), for surely an author of nature would not confine his efforts at design to part of nature, but would design the whole of nature coherently. We must also conceive of such a designer as having some purpose or end in mind for the whole of nature; a design without a purpose would be irrational. We must conceive of both the designer of nature and of its end or purpose as "supersensible," that is, standing outside of nature itself, which transcendental idealism makes it possible for us to do. But then, Kant further supposes, we can conceive of the possible end of nature as a whole only as something unconditioned, that is, of unconditional value, and the only possible candidate for such an end is the complete realization of human freedom—that is, the end of morality (§84).[5]

Kant then adds that, while human freedom is supersensible—that is, freedom of the will stands outside of nature, in the noumenal realm—we must also suppose, in conjunction with this "final end" of nature, an "ultimate end" *within* nature, and this can be nothing other than the highest good possible *within nature*, or the realization of human virtue and human happiness *within* nature:

> Now we have in the world only a single sort of beings whose causality is teleological, i.e., aimed at ends and yet at the same time so constituted that the law in accordance with which they have to determine ends is represented by themselves as unconditioned and independent of natural conditions but yet as necessary in itself. The being of this sort is the human being, though considered as noumenon: the only natural being in which we can cognize, on the basis of its own constitution, a supersensible faculty (**freedom**) and even the law of the causality together with the object that it can set for itself as the highest end (the highest good in the world.   (*CPJ*, §84, 5: 435)

Several sections later, in his presentation of the "moral proof of the existence of God," Kant further clarifies the relation between freedom and the highest good:

> The moral law, as the formal rational condition of the use of our freedom, obligates us by itself alone, without depending on any sort of end as a material

---

[5] For more detail, see Guyer 2001.

condition; yet it also determines for us, and indeed does so *a priori*, a final end, to strive after which it makes obligatory for us, and this is the **highest good in the world** possible through freedom.   (*CPJ*, §87, 5: 450)

These two passages sum up and clarify much in Kant's moral philosophy. The second passage can be compared to Kant's introduction of the idea of the empire of ends in the *Groundwork* (4: 433): it makes clear that, while the moral law does not derive its validity from any merely personal inclinations in its favor, it does, in some way, require efforts toward the realization of particular ends, summed up in the happiness that is included in the highest good. And the two passages together make it clear that, while freedom is something that must ultimately be conceived of as "supersensible," or as having a noumenal ground, not directly experienced, the highest good that freedom commands us to realize is to be realized "in the world," that is, in the natural world. Kant makes no allusion here to a world that is "future for us." Kant appeals to our supersensible freedom, to be sure, but seems to avoid any suggestion that the highest good is something to be realized outside of nature. Further, personal immortality plays no role in Kant's present argument, although he does invoke it a few sections later (§90). His view seems to have become that, although human *freedom*, in the sense of the freedom of the will, can only be something supersensible, that is, noumenal rather than phenomenal and experienced, both human *virtue* and human *happiness* must be achievable *within* nature, made possible by a supersensible author of nature outside of nature. Thus any problematic suggestion that human happiness might be achieved within nature before human virtue is completed in personal immortality is averted.[6] Further, since it is clear that the actual achievement of virtue in particular human lives has not always been accompanied by happiness, it is also clear that what Kant is now supposing is that we must imagine the achievement of both virtue and happiness to be possible sometime in the future but natural existence of the human *species*. The idea of the highest good as the reward of personal happiness for personal virtue that was suggested in the first *Critique* and was still at work in the second seems to have disappeared entirely, to be replaced by a conception of the highest good as the ultimate realization of both virtue and happiness by and for the human species, something that is clearly not yet real but which we can at least believe to be possible if we can believe a divine author of nature to be actual—all of which we have to be able to believe if our efforts to be moral are to be rational, since it would not be rational to try to do something that we know to be impossible.[7]

---

[6] See Guyer 2020a, chapter 4.

[7] This does raise the problem of the failure of morally worthy souls who live before this happy day in the history of the human species to realize the happiness of which they are nevertheless worthy. Kant offers no solution to this problem in the third *Critique*, but neither does he premise the possibility of the highest good in this work on the assumption that virtue is the worthiness to be happy.

Kant confirms this impression by his further discussion of the highest good in the essay on "Theory and Practice." In three parts this essay offers crucial commentary on Kant's moral philosophy, his nascent political philosophy, and his philosophy of history, in the form of responses to Christian Garve, Thomas Hobbes, and Moses Mendelssohn. In each case, Kant argues that what ought to be the case—what is correct in theory—must be possible—is of use in practice. Part I takes up the objection of Garve that Kant's introduction of the highest good undermines the purity of his moral philosophy by making the promise of personal happiness the motive for morality after all (*TP*, 8: 280), thereby denying that pure moral motivation—the good will—is possible. Kant objects to this objection; even in the first *Critique* he had held only that the promise of one's own happiness in a future life as a reward for virtue in this life is necessary to maintain one's resolve to be virtuous, not to motivate it in the first place. But in "Theory and Practice" he goes further. First, he makes it clear that the highest good is the *object* of morality but not the *incentive* for it. But second, and perhaps even more important, he formulates his description of the highest good in a way that makes clear that it is not an individual goal but the collective moral goal of humankind. The concept of the highest good

> **introduces** another end for the human being's will, namely to work to the best of one's ability toward the highest good possible in the world (universal happiness combined with and in conformity with the purest morality throughout the world), which, since it is within our control from one quarter but not from both taken together, exacts from reason belief, **for practical purposes**, in a moral ruler of the world and in a future life.   (*TP*, 8: 279–80)[8]

Kant insists that the *principle* of morality remains "the **limitation** of the will to the condition of a giving of universal law possible through a maxim adopted, whatever the object of the will or the end may be (thus happiness as well), from which, as well as from every end one may have, we here abstract altogether" (*TP*, 8: 280). This makes clear that the incentive to be moral can never be the promise of one's own happiness. But he also makes tolerably clear that in the final analysis every action has some end, that happiness is the result of action that successfully realizes its end, and that morality prescribes the realization of the freely chosen ends of all and thus of a collective form of happiness even though the prospect of their own happiness is not the incentive of morally good agents. He explains all this in a long footnote to the previous extract:

---

[8] Here Kant obviously does continue to refer to the postulate of personal immortality.

The need to assume, as the final end of all things, a good that is the **highest good** in the world and is also possible through our cooperation is a need not from a deficiency in moral incentives but from a deficiency in the external relations within which alone an object as end in itself (as moral **final end**) can be produced in conformity with [moral] incentives. For without some end there can be no **will**, although, if it is a question only of lawful necessitation of actions, one must abstract from any end and the law alone constitutes its determining ground. But not every end is moral (e.g., that of one's own happiness is not), but this must rather be an unselfish one; and the need for a final end assigned by pure reason and comprehending the whole of all ends under one principle (a world as the highest good and possible through our cooperation) is a need of an unselfish will **extending** itself beyond observance of the formal law to a production of an object (the highest good). This is a special kind of determination of the will, namely through the idea of a whole of all ends...   (*TP*, 8: 279–8n.)

The promise of one's own happiness is never a morally worthy incentive, and the formal law that one must adopt has nothing to do with one's own happiness. But an action must always have some end, and willing an action without willing some end would be "deficient." If this end cannot be the selfish end of one's own happiness, it can only be the unselfish end of the realization of the collective, morally permissible ends of all, the "whole of all ends," which would in turn constitute the greatest possible happiness of all consistent with the greatest morality throughout the world.

Here Kant proceeds once again by an argument through elimination: even moral action needs an end, the end cannot possibly be any or all of one's own personal ends, thus one's own happiness, so it can only be the (compossible set of the) ends of all, so the happiness of all. The argument might have been more persuasive if Kant had explicitly appealed back to the empire of ends formulation of the categorical imperative, thereby emphasizing that to treat everyone as ends in themselves is to treat their (compossible) particular ends as ends for all, and thus collective happiness as the end for all. But the direction of Kant's thought is clear enough. The role of belief in a "moral ruler of the world" is also clear enough: being moral is entirely in our own power, that is, it is in the power of each of us to be moral, although it is not in the power of any of us to make everyone moral; but that even our best intentions should always have their intended outcomes does not seem to be in the power of any or all of us, so for that we need cooperation from another quarter—or nature needs to be more cooperative than it initially appears to be, because, at least so we can believe, its laws are ultimately written by a moral author. Whether the postulate of a future life is to play any role in this argument, however, is unclear; Kant's continuing reference to that may be a sincere expression of his personal belief, but has no obvious basis in his present argument. In "Theory and Practice" Kant has not argued that the attainment of virtue has to be deferred to a future life, and the only postulate that seems to be necessary on that front is that complete morality be possible in the natural life of the human species, from which the collective happiness of the species, or at least the greatest collective happiness for the species *possible in this world*, as Kant now formulates the happiness component of the highest good, would follow.

3.2. Kant's Theory of Freedom in *Religion within the Boundaries of Mere Reason*

That the postulate of personal immortality plays no serious role in Kant's final formulation of his conception of the highest good is, surprisingly, confirmed by Kant's further treatment of freedom of the will in *Religion within the Boundaries of Mere Reason*.[9] This work, published at the same time as the essay on "Theory and Practice," reinterprets central dogmas of Christianity in terms of Kant's rationalistic morality. Since resurrection and therefore personal immortality is a central dogma of Christianity, indeed one that Kant himself treats as a central dogma of any genuine religion (*RBMR*, 6: 126), it would seem that the postulate of personal immortality should play a large role in this book. But it does not; on the contrary, the chief point of the book is that a complete conversion in our fundamental maxim from evil to good is possible for each of us *at any time*, and the idea of immortality is only a symbol or metaphor for the continuing commitment to such a conversion that each of us must make. So let us turn now to Kant's return to the topic of freedom of the will in the *Religion*.

The first essay of Kant's *Religion*, on "Radical Evil in Human Nature," was published in the *Berlinische Monatsschrift*, the leading organ of the late German Enlightenment, in 1792. It had been approved by the official philosophy censor of the Prussian regime, but its doctrine was radical—that human evil is not due to the original sin of Adam and Eve, but to the free choice of each and every human being, yet precisely because the choice of evil is free, each and every human being is also free to choose to be morally good, and divine grace can never be more than a supplement to the human "change of heart"—and earned Kant the disfavor of the conservative government of Friedrich Wilhelm II, the nephew who had succeeded the free-thinking patron of Voltaire, Friedrich II, in 1786, and who

---

[9] Kant's *Religion* has drawn increasing commentary in recent years, much of it focused on Kant's opening assertion of the "radical evil" of human nature. A selection includes Muchnik 2009, DiCenso 2011, DiCenso 2012, Pasternack 2014, Miller 2015, Palmquist 2016, and Wood 2020, as well as the anthologies Anderson-Gold and Muchnik 2010, and Michalson 2014. Insole 2013 is not a commentary on the *Religion* but deals with Kant's views on human as well as divine freedom. See also the articles Morgan 2005 and Sussman 2005. A movement that attempts to bring Kant closer to orthodox Christianity is represented by Firestone and Jacobs 2008 and Firestone and Palmquist 2006.

was far less well-disposed to the Enlightenment than his uncle had been. Kant had three more essays in mind, but was blocked from publishing them in the journal. Eventually he published the four essays as a book with the approval of the philosophy rather than theology faculty in Königsberg, which was permissible, although Kant's publisher nevertheless had the book printed in Jena, outside of Prussian territory, in the hope of avoiding trouble. This hardly appeased the Prussian government, and in October 1794 Kant was enjoined from any further publication on matters of religion. He acceded to this injunction, although he interpreted his concession as a personal promise to Friedrich Wilhelm II, and when that king died in 1797 Kant immediately published *The Conflict of the Faculties*, in which he argued that, although the university faculties of law, medicine, and theology are supported by the state in order to train officials or licensed professionals and therefore have to teach material approved by the state, the official role of the state-supported philosophical faculty (what we would now call the faculty of arts and sciences) is simply to search after and teach the truth on any subject, to the best of its ability, without interference by any other faculty or organ of the state. It is thus a proper part of the task of the philosophical faculty to criticize the dogmas of the other three faculties. In spite of this provocation, the new regime took no action against Kant, who had in any case now retired, and if anything his position became the creed of the nineteenth-century German university, led by the new Prussian royal university founded in Berlin in 1810 under the leadership of Wilhelm von Humboldt.[10]

The overall project of the *Religion* is to interpret central concepts and dogmas of Christianity—original sin, grace, the savior, and the idea of personal immortality—as symbols or "aesthetic" presentations of the truths of morality founded in pure reason, while arguing against any priesthood or ecclesiastical establishment that would have anything other than the moral improvement of mankind as its aim. (Having been brought up Protestant, Kant would have no truck with an intercessionary role for the priesthood, but his criticism of "priest-craft" goes beyond that; see *RBMR*, part IV.) As for the freedom of the human will, Kant offers no new argument for its reality, taking this to be a settled fact; but he does repeatedly and explicitly invoke the principle that ought implies can to represent this established fact: even though human beings have often, perhaps always, proven themselves evil, "the command that we **ought** to become better human beings still resounds unabated in our souls; consequently, we must also be capable of it" (*RBMR*, 6: 45; see also 6: 41, 47, 49n,, 50, 62, and 66). Kant's innovations on the subject of freedom are rather these two. First, as we will see in more detail in Chapter 5, he responds to the objection raised by Ulrich that on his view only a will acting in accordance with the moral law is free, so that

---

[10] This whole story has often been told; for a reliable summary, see the Translator's Introduction (by George di Giovanni) to the *Religion* in Kant 1996b, pp. 41–54.

conversely a will violating the moral law cannot have chosen to do so freely, by clearly distinguishing between legislating and recognizing the moral law on the one hand and choosing to act in accordance with it on the other—the former is attributed to what Kant now consistently calls *Wille* but the latter to the "faculty of choice," *Willkühr* (also sometimes translated as "elective will," in reference to the root *Wahl*, the modern German term for "election"). Or, what we generally refer to as will is now clearly divided into *Wille* proper, which is identical with pure practical reason, and *Willkühr*, the ability to choose between adhering to the command of pure practical reason or not.[11] Insofar as it is identical with pure practical reason, *Wille* is not capable of corruption, "as if reason could extirpate within itself the dignity of the law itself, for this is absolutely impossible"; but the human power of choice, *Willkühr*, is capable of corruption, for it is nothing less than the power to choose whether to make the moral law into one's "supreme maxim as sufficient determination," or not. Kant also now makes it clear that the choice between good and evil, whether to be moral or not, takes the form of deciding which of two principles, both of which are inherent in human nature, the moral law and self-love, to "**make the condition of the other**," or which to subordinate to the other (*RBMR*, 6: 36). That is, concern for one's own interest—one's own happiness—is entirely natural to human beings, it neither can nor should be extirpated, and often it is perfectly permissible to act in one's own interest, namely when this does not conflict with any moral obligation. But coincidence between the demands of self-love and the demands of morality is always contingent; thus they can come into conflict with each other, and then the decision has to be made: will one satisfy the demands of morality only if that is consistent with one's own self-love, or will one satisfy the demands of self-love only when that is consistent with morality? Kant supposes that every human being gives herself and is aware of the moral law through her pure practical reason or *Wille*, but also that every human being has the freedom to choose between fully respecting that law or giving priority to self-love, the choice that faces *Willkühr*.

The second innovation in the *Religion*'s treatment of freedom is to emphasize that freedom is always the choice between two alternatives, but also that we *always* have this freedom: so if a person is evil—as experience, although not any a priori ground, seems to suggest that we are (*RBMR*, 6: 32–3)[12]—that evil has been freely chosen, yet the person *remains* free to choose to become good. There are two parts to this doctrine. The first is that we are not evil because of purely natural

---

[11] There is a concise description of the distinction at Rosen 2022, pp. 90–1, and extended discussions in Silber 1960, at pp. xcv–cvi, and Beck 1962.

[12] Contrary to Morgan 2005 and Sussman 2005, I do not take Kant to intend to provide any a priori proof that humans are in fact always evil; on the contrary, since on his theory the noumenal location of free choice makes it "inscrutable," or inexplicable by any causal law why any human being chooses one way or the other, he *could* not provide an a priori proof of radical evil. (This point is clearly made at Dalferth 2014, p. 68.) All that could be proven a priori, following from the very concept of freedom, is the *possibility* of radical evil.

dispositions or inclinations, such as the instincts to seek food or sex; in fact, Kant is convinced, contrary to those who think that humans are inherently sinful, that our natural predispositions are "predispositions to good," to the preservation and promotion of the individual human being and the species, and their potential for perfection, although these can be perverted by the choice to subordinate morality to self-interest (*RBMR*, 6: 26–7). We cannot blame our choice to be evil on mere nature.[13] Second, and this is Kant's main point in the book, if we have freely chosen evil, we can still freely choose to become good. If we, rather than mere nature, are to be responsible for our choice of evil, that must be a free choice; but if it is a free choice, then it must also be possible for us to choose the alternative, namely to be or become good:

> The human being must make or have made **himself** into whatever he is or should become in a moral sense, good or evil. These two must be an effect of his free power of choice [*Willkühr*], for otherwise they could not be imputed to him and, consequently, he could be neither **morally** good nor evil. If it is said, The human being is created good, this can mean nothing more than: He has been created for the **good** and the original **predisposition** in him is good; the human being is not thereby good as such, but he brings it about that he becomes either good or evil...
>
> (*RBMR*, 6: 44)

But since this choice is free, it must be reversible:

> Now if a propensity to this [inversion of the proper subordination of self-love to morality] does lie in human nature, then there is in the human being a natural propensity to evil; and this propensity itself is morally evil, since it must ultimately be sought in a free power of choice [*Willkühr*], and hence is imputable. This evil is **radical**, since it corrupts the ground of all maxims; as natural propensity, it is also not be **extirpated** through human forces... Yet it must be equally possible to **overcome** this evil, for it is found in the human being as acting freely.   (*RBMR*, 6: 37)

Genuinely free choice is the choice between two alternatives, so if we are free to choose one, we are also free to choose the other. Precisely because our evil is freely

---

[13] Allen Wood's "anthropological" approach to radical evil, as originally presented in Wood 1999, pp. 283–91, blames this evil on the "unsocial sociability" of human beings, our mix of dependence upon and antagonism toward each other. This is at odds with Kant's insistence that our choice whether to subordinate morality to self-love or vice versa is "inscrutable," i.e., causally inexplicable. More recently Wood has qualified his position, claiming that his account is "not a causal explanation of the propensity to evil," and that the "social context of evil provides evil with the only kind of (very limited) intelligibility Kant thinks evil can have" (Wood 2014, pp. 49–50). This comes closer to a plausible interpretation of Kant, which is that unsocial sociability might provide a temptation to evil at the phenomenal level, but that the choice to give in to evil for Kant remains noumenal, free, and reversible.

chosen, in the form of choosing to subordinate morality to self-love, we are free to choose good, in the form of choosing to subordinate self-love to morality.

I am assuming that for Kant, once free, always free, that is, that our choice between good and evil is not a choice one time for all time, but always remains open, thus a change of heart is always possible even for the most reprobate. This has not always been understood; sometimes it is assumed—we will see this when we come to Arthur Schopenhauer's response to Kant in Chapter 10—that because for Kant free choice takes place at the noumenal, timeless level of reality rather than at the phenomenal, temporal level of experience governed by causal law, it must also be unique—that is, that the timelessness of noumenal choice implies that each agent has only one opportunity for choice. But that is a mistake: thinking of ourselves as having only a single opportunity for choice would be just as much a temporal way of thinking as is thinking of ourselves as having sequentially multiple opportunities for choice (one is just as much a number as any other). Rather, Kant's view has two premises: first, that reality is really non-temporal, although we have no other way of representing it except temporally; second, that we can attribute to our noumenal selves nothing more but nothing less than is required to understand morality. Then, since we must attribute freedom to ourselves, we must attribute to ourselves the freedom to choose good over evil, and even if we have already chosen evil; we have no way to represent that freedom except by representing ourselves as *still* free to choose good even if we have *already* chosen evil; and we certainly have no knowledge of our noumenal reality that could *block* that inference.[14]

That we necessarily represent our freedom in temporal terms even though it obtains at the noumenal level is implied by Kant's brief discussion of immortality in the second essay of the *Religion*. At this point Kant is responding to the concern that if the change of heart from evil to good ("which must be possible because it is a duty") really takes place at the noumenal level, "which transcends the senses," then we, "who are unavoidably restricted to temporal conditions in our conception of the relationship of cause to effect," can never actually know whether we have successfully effected a change of heart. We can at best know that we seem to be making progress toward "conformity to the law," and even then that might be only outward compliance with morality, not a real change of heart. We should not worry about that, he says, because our moral task is not to *know* whether we are good or evil but simply to try to *be* good, while judgment about our change of heart can be left up to "him who scrutinizes the heart (through his pure intellectual intuition)" and can know whether our change of heart is a "perfected whole"

---

[14] Only in the "General Remark" to the first essay of the *Religion* does Kant suggest that we make "a single and inalterable decision" (*RBMR*, 6: 48), but that is the decision to become good after having already chosen evil—so it is already a second decision. And Kant offers no reason why the decision to become good is inalterable, that is, to exclude the possibility of moral backsliding.

even if we cannot, in other words, God. But "notwithstanding his permanent" epistemic "deficiency, a human being" who has in fact undertaken the change of heart "can still expect be **generally** well-pleasing to God, *at whatever point in time his existence be cut short*" (*RBMR*, 6: 67, emphasis added). This implies that, on the one hand, we do *not* have to be immortal to undertake the change of heart—and this is what obviates Kant's postulate in the *Critique of Practical Reason* that we need immortality to perfect our virtue—but, on the other hand, the only way that *we* have *of representing* the actual occurrence of our change of heart is by representing—or imagining—ourselves as making endless progress toward the good. And that is not a bad thing, either, because it reminds us that, even having chosen good over evil, we are still, until our life is actually cut short, as it certainly will be at some point or other, free to revert to evil. The change of heart, even though noumenal, is not a one-time thing; if we are really to be good, we must repeatedly or perhaps better constantly choose to be good—which we can do, because we ought to do it. The way to make sense of all this is simply to suppose that change is always possible at the level of our real, free, noumenal will, even though we cannot represent the possibility of this change in our ordinary temporal terms—and at the same time have no other way of representing it.

Kant's position on the possibility of divine grace in the *Religion* is less clear than his position on our freedom to undertake a change of heart from evil to good. But one thing is clear: if there is such a thing as God and as grace, and whatever grace might add to human effort, there can be no grace without the human agent first undertaking his or her own moral reform. Thus Kant continues the already quoted statement that "The human being must make or have made himself into whatever he is or should become in a moral sense, good or evil," with the further statement that "Granted that some supernatural cooperation is also needed to his becoming good or better, whether this cooperation only consist in the diminution of obstacles or be also a positive assistance, the human being must nonetheless make himself antecedently worthy of receiving it . . . in this way alone is possible that the good be imputed to him" (*RBMR*, 6: 44). This is the same stance that Kant has taken with regard to happiness: in the eyes of impartial reason, human beings must make themselves worthy of whatever happiness they receive; when it comes to grace, if there is such a thing and however it might contribute to the facilitation or completion of human efforts to be moral, human beings must show themselves worthy of grace by undertaking their own moral reform first. Here Kant is taking a distinct position relative to standard Protestant doctrines of salvation. He is certainly rejecting the Calvinist idea that people are pre-elected for salvation or damnation regardless of their own efforts. Yet he is also rejecting, although more subtly, any idea that people earn their salvation through their good works, or at least through good works alone, because it has been throughout part of his view that our external actions, thus our works, can be in conformity with morality for all sorts of reasons other than respect for morality itself, but that only good actions performed out of the proper disposition—respect for the moral law—are worthy of esteem. Translated into theological terms, this becomes the doctrine that grace can only be a response to our own change of heart. Perhaps this view is reminiscent of the Pietism with which Kant grew up, although of course in his mature view the existence of neither God nor grace can be a matter either of theoretical knowledge or of an ungrounded leap of faith, but only an idea of pure reason affirmed on practical rather than theoretical grounds.[15]

3.3. The *Metaphysics of Morals* and the Doctrine of Virtue

Kant's second chief work in moral philosophy in the 1790s was the long-promised *Metaphysics of Morals*, a work that had been part of Kant's plan since his conception of the critical philosophy in the 1770s and which had been preceded by the parallel *Metaphysical Foundations of Natural Science* in 1786.[16] As the *Metaphysical Foundations of Natural Science* had applied the principles of judgment deduced in the first *Critique* to our experience of motion, so the *Metaphysics of Morals* is to derive the specific duties of human beings by applying the fundamental principle of morality valid a priori for all rational beings to the most basic although empirically known circumstances of human existence. In Kant's words, "a metaphysics of morals cannot dispense with principles of application, and we shall often have to take as our object the particular **nature** of human beings, which is cognized only by experience, in order to **show** in it what can be inferred from universal moral principles" *(MM*, Introduction, 6: 217). Kant's account of the fundamental principle of morality is not a naturalistic moral theory, but his theory of duties is a theory of human duties given our own nature in its entirety and the rest of nature as we find it.

The work was published in two parts, the *Metaphysical Foundations of the Doctrine of Right* or Doctrine of Right *(Recht)* in January 1797 and the *Metaphysical Foundations of the Doctrine of Virtue* or Doctrine of Virtue *(Tugend)* in August, with a consolidated edition with appendices to the Doctrine of Right following in 1798. Both sections of the work take much of their outward form and content from the works of previous authors, the Doctrine of Right from the "natural right" tradition in political philosophy culminating in the *Law of Nature* of Gottfried Achenwall which Kant used as the textbook for his course on natural right, and the Doctrine of Virtue from the *Ethics* of Alexander Gottlieb Baumgarten, which Kant used as one of the textbooks for his lectures on moral

---

[15] The term "leap of faith" is of course associated with the theology of Søren Kierkegaard, who wrote fifty years after Kant, although clearly in response to Kant; but the idea was present in the work of Friedrich Heinrich Jacobi, a major interlocutor of Kant as well as Moses Mendelssohn in the 1780s. See Jacobi 1994 and Beiser 1987, chapter 2.

[16] E.g., letter to Christian Gottfried Schütz, September 13, 1785, *Corr*, 10: 406–7.

philosophy.[17] Because the form and much of the content of these works would therefore have been familiar to his readers, Kant could afford to be brief, even telegraphic. The two parts of Kant's book nevertheless represent a radical departure from the traditions on which they built, because the foundation of Kant's concepts of both legal obligations and ethical duties is always the preservation or promotion of human freedom and never either happiness or perfection for its own sake (or the former through the latter, as in Wolff).

Since Kant included his doctrines of both right or justice and virtue or ethics (as he also calls it) under the single title and within the single covers of a *Metaphysics of Morals*, it is clear that he intended his theory of justice as well as his ethics to be parts of morality, contrary to the thesis of the "independence" of right from morality that a number of recent commentators have asserted.[18] Kant's formulation of what he calls the "Universal Principle of Right," "Any action is **right** if it can coexist with everyone's freedom in accordance with a universal law, or if on its maxim the freedom of choice can coexist with everyone's freedom in accordance with universal law" (*MM*, DR, Introduction, section C, 6: 230), is, in spite of its formulation as a definition rather than an imperative, so clearly an application of the first formulation of the categorical imperative to those of our actions, or maxims of action, that can interfere with the freedom of others, rather than our own, that it is difficult to understand why anyone would think that it could have any other foundation, or, if it did how, in Kant's view, that could be anything other than mere prudence, in other words the Hobbesianism that Kant so clearly rejects (see *TP*, section II, subtitled "Against Hobbes," 8: 289–307). Assuming that for Kant the doctrine of right is part of morality in general, however, the question is what distinguishes right from the doctrine of virtue or ethics proper? (In translating and discussing Kant, the word "ethics" should thus not be used as a synonym for "morality," although many commentators do use it this way, and Kant does not always avoid this himself, and sometimes, of course, as in the title of the *Groundwork*, Kant's word *Sitten* can only be translated as "morality.")

3.3.1. Kant's Division of Duties

The problem is that Kant suggests two different criteria for this distinction that are not co-extensive, although in the end the principle of his division of duties is clear enough. In the Introduction to the work as a whole he writes:

[17] See Achenwall 2019 and Baumgarten 2020. Baumgarten's *Ethica* has not yet been translated into German or English, but the Latin text is available in Kant 1900–, vol. 19.

[18] The "independence" thesis that Kant's doctrine of right is not part of his moral philosophy has been defended by a number of authors beginning with Julius Ebbinghaus, and continuing more recently with Thomas Pogge, Marcus Willaschek, and Allen Wood. For my arguments against this thesis, as well as references to their arguments, see Guyer 2002 and Guyer 2016d.

> All lawgiving can…be distinguished with respect to the incentive (even if it
> agrees with another kind with respect to the action that it makes a duty, e.g., these
> actions might in all cases be external). That lawgiving which makes an action a
> duty and also makes this duty the incentive is **ethical**. But that lawgiving which
> does not include the incentive of duty in the law and so admits an incentive other
> than the idea of duty itself is **juridical**. It is clear that in this latter case this
> incentive which is something other than the idea of duty must be drawn from
> **pathological** determining grounds of choice, inclinations and aversions, and
> among these, from aversions; for it is a lawgiving which constrains, not an
> allurement, which invites.   (*MM*, Introduction, 6: 218–19)

By "pathological" Kant means based in pleasure or pain, or in the prospect of
pleasure or pain, not anything sick or abnormal; and what he is saying is then that
although the fulfillment of ethical duties can be motivated only by respect for the
idea of duty—or the moral law—itself, compliance with juridical duties can be
enforced by the prospect of pain or if necessary the infliction of pain, that is, by
actual exercise of coercion or the threat of it. Kant argues that it is morally
acceptable to enforce duties of right by coercion, indeed morally necessary to do
so because of the weakness of human nature, precisely because violations of duties
of right are hindrances to the freedom of others, and coercion, or the threat of
coercion, is therefore a hindrance to the hindrance of freedom, or in Kant's view
necessary for the preservation of freedom and indeed analytically connected to the
concept of right (*MM*, DR, Introduction, section D, 6: 231). Although Kant does
not give this example, assault or homicide certainly damage or destroy the
freedom of others; the examples that he is concerned with, the prohibitions of
violations of property, contracts, or lawful personal relationships such as marriage
and parenthood, likewise concern damage to the free exercise of permissible
rights. Since the coercive enforcement of such duties cancels out potential hindrances, in Kant's view such enforcement preserves freedom. To be sure, Kant
adds, it is *possible* to fulfill duties of right from respect for the moral law, so
juridical lawgiving is that the incentive for compliance with which "can *also* be
external" (emphasis added), whereas in the case of ethical duties the motivation
for compliance can *only* be, so Kant thinks, internal, namely respect for the moral
law (*MM*, Introduction, 6: 220). This would make no sense if juridical duties did
not depend on the moral law in general, just as ethical duties do.

   This is all clear enough; the problem is that Kant also suggests a criterion for
ethical rather than juridical duties that seems to let some moral duties that he does
not include among the juridical duties fall between the cracks. In the Introduction
to the Doctrine of Virtue he says that:

> The doctrine of right dealt only with the **formal** condition of outer freedom (the
> consistency of outer freedom with itself it is maxims were made universal laws),

that is, with **right**. But ethics goes beyond this and provides a **matter** (an object of free choice), an **end** of pure reason which it represents as an end that is also objectively necessary, that is, an end that, as far as human beings are concerned, it is a duty to have.—For since the sensible inclinations of human beings tempt them to ends (the matter of choice) that can be contrary to reason, lawgiving reason can in turn check their influence only by a moral reason set up against the against the ends of inclinations, an end that must therefore be given *a priori*, independently of inclinations.... this would be the concept of an **end that is in itself a duty**. But the doctrine of this end would not belong to the doctrine of right but rather to ethics, since **self-constraint** in accordance with (moral laws) belongs to the concept of ethics alone.

For this reason ethics can also be defined as the system of the **ends** of pure practical reason.   (*MM*, DV, Introduction, section I, 6: 380–1)

The law, that is, the juridical law of obligations and rights, the law that can be penally enforced, does not care about anyone's underlying motivations and therefore their ultimate ends as long as their particular actions are in outward compliance with the law: you will not earn any moral esteem from anyone if you pay your debts or refrain from assault solely from fear of the unpleasant consequences of not doing so, but you will avoid penal consequences by not doing so for that or any other reason. Ethics, however, concerns what ends you have—what you are trying to accomplish in life, for yourself or for others—as well as requiring "self-constraint," that is, control of your morally wayward inclinations solely by respect for the moral law. Although Kant never fully spells this out, self-constraint is required and is the only form of constraint allowed in ethics because failure to fulfill ethical obligations is not an immediate hindrance to the freedom of others, although it may be failure to promote it, and coercive enforcement of such duties would therefore not be a hindrance to a hindrance to freedom justifiable on that account.[19]

The problem, however, is that some of the duties that Kant includes as ethical duties in the Doctrine of Virtue are not positive duties to *promote* any *specific* ends, although they are duties not to *destroy or damage* beings that are *ends in themselves*, namely human beings—but this is true of the duties of right as well. Among duties to oneself, Kant includes his favorite example, the duty to refrain from suicide, but also duties not to damage one's own capabilities through gluttony or drunkenness and duties not to sell vital body parts such as one's

---

[19] Walschots (forthcoming) also points out that, since the adoption of ends is an internal matter, as contrasted to the performances of actions, only an internal conditions can motivate the adoption of ends This is correct if stated carefully enough to exclude fear of coercion, which is an internal condition, although one directly linked to and dependent upon an external condition (the threat of coercion).

teeth for pecuniary advantage (*MM*, DV, §§6–8; the story might be different when it comes to selling one's hair, for that can grow back); these are all duties not to destroy or damage a being, namely oneself, that is an end in itself, but they are not duties to promote any particular ends. Among duties regarding others, Kant includes what he calls duties of love, which are duties to promote the freely chosen ends of others by various forms of assistance (*MM*, DV, §§29–36), but also what he calls duties of respect, namely the prohibition of arrogance, defamation, and ridicule (§§37–44), which are duties not to violate the dignity of others and their status as free beings in their own right, but not duties to promote any particular ends of theirs in any particular way. These duties do not seem to involve ends that are also duties, yet Kant does not include these prohibitions regarding oneself or others among the duties of right.

These duties thus do not satisfy the stated criterion for duties of virtue, yet Kant does not include them among the duties of right. He does not explain why, but obviously he does not think that the violations of these duties is an outright hindrance to the freedom of others and therefore that their coercive enforcement could not be justified by the argument that a hindrance to a hindrance to freedom is justified as the way to preserve freedom. This seems obvious in the case of self-destruction or damage, although in some cases an act like suicide can damage the interests and even the freedom of others, such as dependents or creditors (but then the offense might be the violation of contractual or parental obligations, not the suicide itself); and it also seems reasonable to suppose that such violations of the duties of respect as arrogance, defamation, and ridicule do not directly destroy or limit the freedom of their victims, although common and statutory law have found defamation by libel or slander to be punishable. But if Kant's reason for excluding these sorts of duties from the duties of right is basically acceptable, his classification still needs to be neatened up—not all the duties that cannot be coercively enforced are duties to promote any specific ends.

Kant does suggest a way to resolve this issue, namely a contrast between ethical duties in general and duties of virtue in particular. He says that:

> to every ethical **obligation** there corresponds the concept of virtue, but not all ethical duties are thereby duties of virtue. Those duties that have to do not so much with a certain end (matter, object of choice) as merely with **what is formal** in the moral determination of the will (e.g., that an action in conformity with duty must also be done **from duty**) are not duties of virtue. Only **an end that is also a duty** can be called a **duty of virtue**.

He continues that "For this reason there are several duties of virtue ... whereas for the first kind of duty only one (virtuous disposition) is thought, which holds for all actions" (*MM*, DV, Introduction, section II, 6: 383). Here Kant is treating the requirement to act out of respect for the moral law itself as a duty, and supposing that this is ethical rather than juridical—which it obviously is, since penal coercion can enforce only outward compliance with any sort of demand, not any motivation other than that of fear of the sanction. But this duty is not the duty to promote any specific end, for it is the motive for all other ethical duties, and as we saw it *can* be the motive even for compliance with juridical duties. One might balk at calling this requirement a duty at all, since doing the right thing for the right reason seems like something more than just doing the right thing, and to entitle one to special esteem precisely because it is above and beyond the call of duty proper.[20] But since Kant believes that if self-constraint is needed to fulfill more specific duties of virtue, it can only be the self-constraint of respect for the moral law itself, we can see why he might be prepared to call respect for the moral law—doing duty *from duty*—itself a duty.

That being said, it seems that Kant should have allowed more than one duty into the class of ethical duty, that is, duty that is to be complied with out of respect for the moral law but is unsuited for juridical coercion. Then there would be a place for the duties like refraining from suicide or arrogance to others: they would be duties to treat oneself or others as ends in themselves, but not duties to promote any particular ends, yet also not coercively enforceable, for the reason already mentioned: they do not fall under the concept of hindrances to the freedom of others that can and should be hindered by penal means. If this result is accepted, then Kant's system of duties can be divided thus: the basic distinction between juridical duties and ethical duties is the distinction between those duties that are enforceable by penal means, the threat of coercion, or actual coercion, and those duties that it would not be morally permissible to so enforce, which can thus be enforced only by the self-constraint of respect for the moral law itself. Then the latter class would itself be divided into two classes, namely ethical duties that are not duties of virtue, and ethical duties that are duties of virtue. The latter would be the duties to promote the ends that are also duties, while the former would be those ethical duties that do not fit that description. These not only would include the general duty to have or develop a virtuous disposition, as Kant points out, but also would include specific duties such as the duties to refrain from suicide or disrespect of other persons that do not satisfy the condition for coercive enforcement and so can be enforced only by moral self-constraint.

Kant further divides the class of duties of virtue proper, that is, those ethical duties that require moral self-constraint but are also duties to promote specific ends, into two main groups, regarding ourselves and regarding others. But before we examine that division, let us say a little more about Kant's concept of virtue and of virtuous dispositions.

---

[20] See again Walschots (forthcoming).

3.3.2. Virtue and Moral Feelings

Kant's phrase "duties of virtue" refers to specific non-coercively enforceable duties to oneself and others. The noun "virtue" by itself means "the moral capacity to constrain oneself" (*MM*, DV, Introduction, section IX, 6: 394), "the will's conformity with every duty, based on a firm disposition" (6: 395), or "the moral strength of a **human being's** will in fulfilling his duty, a moral **constraint** through his own lawgiving reason, insofar as this constitutes itself an authority **executing** the law" (section XIII, 6: 405). In the doctrine of the postulates of pure practical reason in the first two *Critiques*, virtue is something that a person could, indeed could only, perfect in a future life (*CPuR*, A811/B839, *CPracR*, 5: 122), so it must be a quality of the noumenal will that is not experienced in phenomenal, that is, ordinary spatio-temporal reality. In the *Metaphysics of Morals*, however, while Kant must still be presupposing his transcendental idealist theory as the basis for his confidence that we do have freedom of the will, he does not explicitly invoke the distinction between our noumenal and phenomenal selves, and his emphasis on the phrase "human being" in the last quotation suggests that he is here regarding virtue as strength of will as something that is manifest in ordinary experience. Kant also expresses this point by calling his treatment of virtue part of an "aesthetic of morals...a subjective presentation in which the feelings that accompany the constraining power of the moral law (e.g., disgust, horror, etc., which make moral aversions sensible) make its efficacy felt, in order to get the better of **merely** sensible inducements" (*MM*, DV, Introduction, section XIII, 6: 406). Both sensible inducements to be moral and the feelings that help overcome them obtain only in the natural, phenomenal world, as does any state that Kant calls "aesthetic." Kant also describes the "true strength of virtue [as] a **tranquil mind** with a considered and firm resolution to put the law of virtue into practice" (*MM*, DV, Introduction, section XVI, 6: 409). Here the phrase "law of virtue" means the moral law itself, but "strength of virtue" refers to the strength of will to put that law into effect in one's actions in the phenomenal world. In a Remark on this passage, Kant adds that

> Virtue is always **in progress** and yet always starts **from the beginning.**—It is always in progress because, considered **objectively**, it is an ideal and unattainable, while yet constant approximation to it is a duty. That it always starts from the beginning has a **subjective** basis in human nature, which is affected by inclinations because of which virtue can never settle down in peace and quiet with its maxims adopted for once and for all but, if it is not rising, it is unavoidably sinking.   (*MM*, DV, Introduction, section XVI, 6: 409)

The remark in Kant's *Religion* that God could know that a human agent had fully undertaken a change of heart, even if the person himself could represent only continued progress toward the good, assumed that the change of heart took place at the noumenal level where only God could know that it had (*RBMR*, 6: 67). It left implicit that, even in the noumenal world, once free, always free, thus that the human agent who has undertaken a change of heart from evil to good is still free to revert to evil, that is, once again subordinate morality to self-love. In the present passage, Kant is assuming that virtue is something that obtains in the natural world of space and time, where it is only ever in progress and where the possibility of relapse in ordinary time is always present. Finally, although real-world virtue is the *capacity* to overcome obstacles to being moral, it does not require that a virtuous agent actually have obstacles to overcome, although, Kant suggests, anyone's *degree* of virtue can be assessed, judged, or measured "only by the magnitude of the obstacles that the human being himself furnishes through his inclinations," that is, his inclinations toward actions contrary to morality (*MM*, DV, Introduction, section XIII, 4: 405). This again assumes that virtue is a property of persons in the natural world: strength of will comes in degrees in the natural world, and empirical evidence of overcoming obstacles for the sake of measuring the degree of virtue is only to be had in the natural world.[21]

That virtue is a property of human beings in the natural world is also evident in Kant's treatment of moral feeling in the Doctrine of Virtue.[22] In general, feelings exist only in the natural world. Specifically, Kant refines his earlier references to undifferentiated respect or moral feeling (*CPracR*, 5: 76) into a theory of four "Aesthetic preconditions of the mind's receptivity to concepts of duty as such" (*Ästhetische Vorbegriffe der Empfänglichkeit des Gemüts...*), where the phrase "aesthetic preconditions" connotes something in the natural world of feelings and where Kant's term *Gemüt* is his word for mind as an empirical phenomenon, the subject of the empirical disciplines of psychology and anthropology. Kant makes it clear that he is offering a theory of motivation and action at the empirical level by stating that "Every determination of choice proceeds **from the representation of a possible action to** the deed through the feeling of pleasure or displeasure, taking an interest in the action or its effect" (*MM*, DV, Introduction, section XII.a, 6: 399). This does not deny that the underlying determination of the will to subordinate self-love to the moral law (or vice versa) must take place at the noumenal level, but since both feelings and deeds are events in the phenomenal world, it says that the transition from the choice of fundamental maxim, perhaps also the choice

---

[21] Richard Henson distinguished between "fitness report" and "battle citation" interpretations of Kant's conception of the good will, the former being the ability to do what the moral law requires even if it is never tested and the latter requiring actually overcoming obstacles from inclination. See Henson 1979, and Barbara Herman's response in Herman 1981. The present passage makes it clear that Kant's theory of virtue actually lies in between: as strength of will, virtue is simply the capacity to overcome obstacles, but *measuring* someone's actual degree of virtue requires (empirical evidence of) their having actually overcome obstacles. For an overview of Kant's conception of virtue, see Louden 2011, pp. 16–24.

[22] See Guyer 2010b and Falduto 2014, chapter 5.

of more particular maxims, to deeds in the natural world takes place through feelings of pleasure or displeasure in the natural world. The four "aesthetic preconditions" are then "moral feeling" in general, by which Kant now means specifically the feeling, as we have previously seen a combined feeling of pleasure and displeasure, directed at the moral law itself, that is, what he previously called respect; "conscience," which is not itself a feeling at all but rather "practical reason's holding the human beings duty before him for his acquittal or condemnation in every case that comes under a law" (section XII.b, 6: 400), that is, the disposition to hold particular prospective actions before the court of the moral law (see also *MM DV*, §13, 6: 438), which however no doubt results in a feeling of pleasure or displeasure at the prospect of performing the action;[23] "love of human beings," which is a feeling that follows (although given his initial statement Kant should say prompts) acts of beneficence (section XII.c, 6: 401–2; in §§34–5 Kant will replace the feeling of love of human beings with feelings of sympathy, and make clear that these *do* prompt rather than follow beneficent actions); and finally a feeling of "respect," by which Kant now means not general moral feeling directed at the moral law but a feeling of "**self-esteem**," "**respect** for [one's] own being," which prompts compliance with duties regarding oneself (section XII.d, 6: 402–3). The strength together of these aesthetic preconditions, which all obtain in the phenomenal world, is what constitutes virtue in that world. Kant makes it clear that these are "natural predispositions of the mind," "antecedent predispositions" of an "aesthetic character," and that it cannot be a duty simply to *have* them, because without them one cannot be susceptible to concepts of duty at all (section XII, 6: 399), but that they need to be "cultivated" and "strengthened" (section XII. a, 6: 400), because that is something that can be done in the natural world. Our duty with regard to these aesthetic preconditions is to cultivate and strengthen them; and that must be an ethical duty but not a specific duty of virtue, because it is a precondition of fulfillment of the specific duties of virtue. Anything that can be cultivated and strengthened, of course, can exist in some degree, as qualities, powers, or capabilities in the natural world do (see the "Anticipations of Perception" in the *Critique of Pure Reason*, A165–76/B207–18). Kant's mature theory of virtue is thus a psychological theory about the phenomenal self, not a metaphysical theory about the noumenal self.

3.3.3. The Ends that are Also Duties

Let us now return to Kant's account of the duties of virtue proper, the duties that can be enforced only by moral self-constraint but that involve ends that are also

---

[23] On Kant's conception of conscience, see Kahn 2021.

duties. Kant had not made this distinction in his fourfold division of duties for the examples of the first two formulations of the categorical imperative in the *Groundwork*. There he had simply divided duties into perfect duties to self and others, the examples of which were the prohibitions of suicide and false promises, and imperfect duties to self and others, the examples of which were the development of one's own talents and beneficence to others. The former were perfect duties in that anyone can comply with them completely simply by avoiding the prohibited behavior, while the latter are imperfect duties in that they are open-ended: in principle there is no limit to what might be done toward these goals, but in practice there are always both alternatives and limits to what anyone can do— so the application of these duties always requires judgment. Under the designation as ends that are also duties, what were formerly just supposed to be examples of imperfect duties now become the two comprehensive duties to perfect oneself and promote the happiness of others. These two generic duties subsume several more specific duties, as we will see in a moment. But as already noted, Kant also includes in the Doctrine of Virtue perfect duties that are not, however, suitable for coercive enforcement, namely the perfect duties not to destroy or damage oneself and the perfect duties of respect to others.

Kant's arguments that the imperfect duties of virtue to self and others are the duties to perfect oneself and promote the happiness of others are too brief and harbor some problems. Regarding the duty of self-perfection, he first says that anyone's potential talents or "predispositions" are "mere **gifts** for which he must be indebted to nature," which are thus not the products of his own deeds, therefore not proper subjects of duty; the duty pertaining to them, which is a deed for which one can properly be praised, is that of "**cultivating**" or perfecting them (*MM*, DV, Introduction, section V.A, 6: 386–7). This argument has the same structure as Kant's argument for the necessity of cultivating the mind's natural "aesthetic preconditions of susceptibility to concepts of duty," and is acceptable as far as it goes. But it really states only a necessary condition for self-perfection being a duty, not a sufficient condition. Kant points towards a positive argument for this duty when he continues that "A human being has the duty to raise himself from the crude state of his nature, from his animality, more and more toward humanity, by which he alone is capable of setting himself ends; he has a duty to diminish his ignorance by instruction and to correct his errors" (6: 387). This links the cultivation of talents to humanity as our ability to set ends; assuming that this is equivalent to freedom, and freedom is the underlying value to be promoted in imperfect duties to self, as he had argued in the lectures on ethics, Kant still needs an additional premise to make his argument complete. This is the lemma that failing to develop one's potential talents limits the means one has available for realizing ends one might otherwise freely set for oneself, thus limits one's freedom to rationally set those ends, since one cannot rationally will an end for which one has (or believes oneself to have) no adequate means. Conversely, developing our talents as much as we can expands the range of means available to us and thus expands the range of ends that we can freely yet rationally set for ourselves. Thus cultivating our predispositions to talents is the means to promoting our freedom to set our own ends.

This argument is straightforward. Kant complicates matters somewhat when he divides the duty of self-perfection into two parts, namely the duty to cultivate one's *natural* predispositions to talents, which he further divides into powers of body, spirit, and soul, meaning by the latter two powers of theoretical reason on the one hand and other cognitive powers such as imagination and memory on the other (*MM*, DV, §19, 4: 444–5), and one's *moral* powers of conscience and self-knowledge, specifically knowledge of one's own tendencies to morality and its opposite (§§13–15, 6: 437–42). Kant is hardly wrong to conceive of such a duty; the problem is just that the duty to cultivate one's moral powers is not a specific end that is also a duty, but is more like the general condition for successfully fulfilling any and all of one's duties, whether perfect or imperfect and whether to self or others. It is really just a more detailed account of what it is to become virtuous in general. That this duty is in fact quite general should be clear from the fact that it includes the duty to perfect one's conscience, yet the duty to cultivate and strengthen one's conscience had already been included as part of the duty to cultivate the mind's susceptibility to concepts of duty in general. It need not be included as part of the specific duty of self-perfection because it underlies successful performance of all duties.

The other problem in Kant's treatment of the duty of self-perfection is his quick dismissal of a possible duty regarding the perfection of others. Kant asserts that "it is a contradiction for me to make another's **perfection** my end and consider myself under obligation to promote this. For the **perfection** of another human being, as a person, consists just in this: that he **himself** is able to set his end in accordance with his own concepts of duty" (*MM*, DV, Introduction, section IV, 6: 386). It is certainly true that no one can set another's ends if those ends are to be freely set by the other, which is what morality requires that we allow; more generally, no one can exercise will for another if that will is to be free. This was the insight with which Kant had begun his moral philosophy thirty years earlier. But of course one person can *assist* others in all sorts of ways in the development of their *natural* talents, that is, naturally endowed potentials—this is what education is all about—and can also assist others in the development of their "minds' susceptibility to concepts of duty," such as understanding what the moral law requires in specific sorts of circumstances, which is part of conscience.[24] We just cannot make others' free decisions for them. Kant's remarks about moral education in both the *Critique of Practical Reason* (5: 151–61) and the *Metaphysics of*

---

[24] See Kitcher 2022, e.g., pp. 101–3.

Morals (§§49–52, 6: 477–84) make it clear that he was perfectly well aware of this fact, and of our duty to assist in the moral education of others, and in his lectures on pedagogy he insists on the necessity of both theoretical and moral education.[25] Kant's wholesale restriction of the duty of perfecting the natural and moral predispositions of human beings to oneself is excessive in view of his own theory of education.

Kant's argument regarding the duty to promote the happiness of others also starts off with an unnecessary restriction. He begins with the negative argument that our duty regarding happiness can be *only* a duty to promote the happiness of *others* because we all naturally desire our *own* happiness, and "an end that every human being has (by virtue of the impulses of his nature)...can never without self-contradiction be regarded as a duty" (*MM*, DV, Introduction, section IV, 6: 385–6). The word "impulses" gives away the problem here: it is true that people can have all sorts of short-term impulses, immediate desires for gratification, but if their happiness is anything like the long-range satisfaction of a consistent set of desires over their whole lives or long periods of their lives, then this can certainly conflict with their immediate impulses. Kant himself gives a perfectly good example of this possibility when he imagines a man "suffering from gout" who nevertheless chooses "to enjoy what he likes and put up with what he can since, according to his calculations, on this occasion at least he has not sacrificed the enjoyment of the present moment to the perhaps groundless expectation of a happiness that is supposed to lie in health" (*G*, 4: 399). And Kant defines happiness precisely in terms of a lifelong satisfaction of a sum of desires rather than in satisfaction of merely momentary impulses considered in isolation: happiness is "a maximum of well-being in my present condition and in every future condition" (*G*, 4: 418). The conditions for realizing happiness in this sense can conflict with my immediate impulses just as much as the conditions for the happiness of others can conflict with the gratification of my immediate impulses. So if the happiness of others is a necessary object of my reason rather than a merely natural object of my desire, my own long-term happiness could also be an object of reason rather than a merely natural object of desire.

Perhaps this objection is partially although not entirely answered when we think through the implications of Kant's argument that promotion of the happiness of others is a genuine duty of each. Kant does not really give any positive argument for this duty in the Introduction to the Doctrine of Virtue, only the negative argument that the duty to promote happiness cannot be a duty to promote one's own happiness. When he does come to offer a positive argument in the body of the Doctrine of Virtue, he does not develop the argument he suggested in the fourth example of the Formula of Humanity as an End, namely

---

[25] See Louden 2011, pp. 136–49.

that making the humanity of others a positive end rather than merely not treating it as a means to one's own ends requires making their ends one's own, because their humanity is their ability to set their own ends and thus promoting their humanity means promoting their ends. Rather, he renews the kind of argument that he had suggested in the fourth example of the initial Formulas of Universal Law and Laws of Nature, namely that no one could rationally will that others not help *him* if he were to need help, but if he is to universalize a maxim of getting help or active "love and sympathy" from others, he must be prepared to give it to others as well (*G*, 4: 423). He develops the same sort of argument for the general duty of love to others in the Doctrine of Virtue: "I want everyone else to be benevolent toward me; hence I ought also to benevolent toward everyone else." It is a simple matter of universalizing the maxim I have of wanting benevolence from others (this is a good example of Kant's conception of maxims as general policies for action rather than more specific intentions formed in specific circumstances). However, Kant here continues, "But since all **others** with the exception of myself would not be **all**, so that the maxim would not have within it the universality of a law, which is still necessary for imposing obligation, the law making benevolence a duty will include myself, as an object of benevolence, in the command of practical reason" (*MM*, DV, §27, 6: 451). Kant does not go on, however, to say that each person has a duty to promote her own happiness. But neither does he need to, for here is where the logic of generalization kicks in: if *everyone* adopts the maxim of promoting the happiness of others and acts on it as appropriate, then of course *others* will have the duty of benevolence toward *me* in appropriate circumstances, and I do not need to have a special duty to promote my own happiness. To be sure, there will be many circumstances in which it is perfectly *permissible* for me to seek my own happiness, that is, seek to realize my own ends, indeed many circumstances in which I can most effectively contribute to the happiness of all by tending to my own;[26] there will be some circumstances in which I might have to forego the promotion of some end of my own in order to be benevolent towards some other or others; but there will equally be some circumstances in which others will have a duty to promote my happiness. Thus all human beings collectively have the duty to promote the collective happiness of all human beings, although of course there will still be certain things necessary for their long-term happiness that people can do only for and by themselves—no one except himself can, or rather has the right, to stop the sufferer with gout from having another pint of ale.

In addition to pointing toward this implication of the duty to promote the happiness of others, Kant adds to his previous treatment of this duty in two ways. First, he makes it explicit that since the duty of benevolence is grounded in the duty to promote the freely chosen ends of others, it is always a duty to promote

---

[26] As Hutcheson had already noted; see *Inquiry concerning Moral Good and Evil*, section III, subsection VI, in Hutcheson 2008, p. 123.

their conception of their happiness, not *my* conception of it: "It is for them to decide what they count as belonging to their happiness." At the same time, since the duty to promote the happiness of others is an imperfect duty of wide obligation, that is, I cannot possibly fully promote the happiness of everyone in the world in all the ways they might need help, I have to pick and choose who, when, and how much I can help, in light of my other duties and my actual means. Thus "it is open to me to refuse" some others "many things that **they** think will make them happy but that I do not, as long as they have no right to demand from them from me as what is theirs" (*MM*, DV, Introduction, section V.B, 6: 388), that is, have no enforceable claims of right against me, such as a debt that I owe them. Indeed, I have no choice but to choose whom to help and how to help them even if they are right about what they think will make them happy; since I cannot possibly help everyone in every possible way in which they could use help, I must help how and when and where I think best, not every way everywhere everyone else thinks best.

This is a sound and important restriction on the duty to make the ends of others my own ends: I cannot make all of everyone's ends my own ends, so I must use my judgment how best to satisfy this general imperative. The other refinement that Kant adds to his earlier treatment of the general duty of love of others is to differentiate it into the three specific duties of beneficence, gratitude, and sympathy (*MM*, DV, §§29–35, 6: 452–8). These may be understood as the general duty or "maxim of making others' happiness one's end" (§29, 6: 452), the specific duty of "**honoring**" and when necessary helping "a person because of a benefit he has rendered us" (§32, 6: 455), and then the general duty of cultivating a type of feeling—sympathy—that will help us satisfy these first two duties. Two points are worth special notice here. First, Kant makes it clear that gratitude is a duty, "not merely a **prudential** maxim of encouraging the other to show me further beneficence by acknowledging my obligation to him for a favor he has done" (6: 455). That is, showing gratitude is not merely a good strategy to get more help from a benefactor in the future if in fact that person might give more help in the future, but otherwise a waste of time; it is a universal and unremitting obligation (although perhaps Kant does not fully explain why). Second, it is not Kant's view that it would be best for people to assist others directly motivated by pure reason alone, but that sympathetic feelings that would prompt one to action should be cultivated as some sort of back-up in case pure reason by itself is not strong enough. Far from it: Kant's view is that "Nature has already implanted in human beings receptivity" to sympathetic feelings "as so many means to sympathy based on moral principles" (*MM*, DV, §§34–5, 6: 456–7). Remember Kant's statement that the transition from the determination of the will to the deed is *always* through the "feeling of pleasure or displeasure" (*MM*, DV, Introduction, section XII.a, 6: 399), or, we might add, through specific sorts of pleasure or displeasure, for example pleasure at the thought of helping someone else or displeasure at the thought of their continued suffering: even if the ultimate cause of our moral action is to be pure reason itself, at the phenomenal level of action—"nature"—the proximate cause of action is *always* some feeling, and thus our duty to perform certain types of actions *includes* the duty to develop the kinds of feelings that can prompt us to such actions in appropriate circumstances. This is not a duty *in addition* to the duty to be benevolent, nor a back-stop, but it is part and parcel of that duty, how we prepare ourselves to fulfill the duty of beneficence in the real world—just as cultivating the feeling of self-esteem must be part and parcel of fulfilling our duties to ourselves.

That being said, Kant also notes that the duty to cultivate sympathetic feeling is a "conditional" duty (*MM*, DV, §35, 6: 456). That means not merely that this duty is derivative from the duty to perform beneficent actions, because the feelings are the means to the necessary action. It also means that the feelings might sometimes, in particular circumstances, prompt one to perform a morally inappropriate action—as when, for example, one's well-cultivated readiness to help others in need might prompt one to help the driver of what is actually a getaway car change a flat tire, when what one should do is call the police. Sometimes even the best feelings have to be checked by reflection on what morality really requires in those particular circumstances. That is precisely the role of conscience. So our conclusion should be that Kant's four "aesthetic preconditions of the mind's susceptibility to concepts of duty"—moral feeling or respect for the moral law in general; conscience; love of human beings, now broken down into beneficence, gratitude, and sympathy; and the feeling of self-esteem, now understood as the prompt to both natural and moral self-perfection—must be cultivated and applied together, not one to the exclusion of any other.

This completes our survey of essential elements of Kant's moral philosophy. Now we are ready to see how other philosophers have responded to these elements in the nearly two and a half centuries since Kant first expounded them, accepting some, rejecting some, and transforming them as seems to have been required by the merits of Kant's views, problems in his views, the philosophical sensibilities and commitments of particular subsequent philosophers, and general developments in philosophy and/or changes in philosophical style. We begin with the responses to Kant's moral philosophy in the first decade of its reception, while the late works that have been discussed in this chapter were still being written and published, because so many of the issues that have been discussed ever since were raised in that period.

PART II
THE EARLY RECEPTION OF KANT'S MORAL PHILOSOPHY

4

The Categorical Imperative, Empty Formalism, and Happiness

The Early Criticisms

4.1. Introduction

Although Kant had complained about the slow reception of the *Critique of Pure Reason*, by 1785 it had garnered enough attention to ensure a rapid response to his first main publication in moral philosophy, the *Groundwork for the Metaphysics of Morals*. At least six reviews appeared that same year and six more in 1786, including the detailed and challenging review by Hermann Andreas Pistorius (1730–98) in the influential *Allgemeine deutsche Bibliothek* in May and an anonymous but loyal defense of Kant's work against the first book-length critique of Kant's ethics, *Über Herrn Kant's Moral Reform* by Gottlob August Tittel (1739–1816), in the generally pro-Kantian *Allgemeine Literatur-Zeitung* for October. The appearance of the *Critique of Practical Reason* in 1788 would be greeted with an equal level of attention, and a decade later the appearance of the two parts of Kant's *Metaphysics of Morals* would also be noticed, especially by Kant's early publicist Carl Leonhard Reinhold, although by then the post-Kantian idealists Fichte and Schelling had already taken center stage in the German philosophical theater. The interest of this early reception of Kant's moral philosophy is that within the first ten or fifteen years of the publication of the *Groundwork*, sometimes indeed in that first year or two, many of the issues with Kant's position that have occupied philosophers ever since were already identified.[1]

This Part will discuss five issues or groups of issues that have been at the center of the reception of Kant's moral philosophy ever since its appearance. Some subsequent philosophers still taking a generally Kantian approach have attempted

---

[1] Two detailed studies of the period to be covered in this chapter are Beiser 1987 and di Giovanni 2005. Both of these texts cover more issues and more figures, especially F. H. Jacobi, than I will cover here. My focus is more narrowly on the five issues about Kant's moral philosophy now to be enumerated. This is not the focus of Beiser's book at all, while di Giovanni focuses on the debate about freedom begun by Kant but not on the other issues I will discuss. Translations of some of the material on the debate over freedom of the will that I have translated myself in this volume are now available in Noller and Walsh 2022. Other material is translated in Walschots 2023.

Kant's Impact on Moral Philosophy. Paul Guyer, Oxford University Press. © Paul Guyer 2024.
DOI: 10.1093/oso/9780199592456.003.0005

to fix or to sidestep these problems, while for other philosophers these problems have led to the rejection of Kant's approach to moral philosophy in favor of an alternative. Indeed, all of these issues were already incipient in the reviews of the *Groundwork*, although some of them were more fully elaborated only subsequently, in reviews of Kant's further works or in other forms of response within this early period.

First, one review of the *Groundwork* raised the question of whether Kant had actually offered a "proof" (*Beweis*) or in Kant's own language a "deduction" of his formulation(s) of the fundamental principle of morality and of our freedom to act in accordance with it; this was not a central issue in the earliest responses, but this issue or the underlying issue of the proper method for moral philosophy would surely become a central issue not only for critics of Kant but also for philosophers inspired by the substance of Kant's moral philosophy, especially its normative substance, from Johann Gottlieb Fichte to John Rawls.

Second, the charge that Kant's categorical imperative, especially in its first formulation as the requirement that maxims be universalizable, is an "empty formalism," a charge associated with Hegel, who raised it in his 1802 essay on natural law as well as in his 1821 *Outlines of the Philosophy of Right*, was clearly raised by Pistorius in his 1786 review of the *Groundwork*; indeed, it had already been suggested a few months earlier in a harsh review in the *Kritische Beyträge zur neuesten Geschichte der Gelehrsamkeit*. In the hands of Pistorius, this issue led directly to the question of whether Kant's moral law could be established without an antecedent conception of a fundamental good, or, in terms that would become popular in the twentieth century, whether deontology could be independent of teleology. That would become a major issue for twentieth-century moral philosophers in general and in the final decades of the century for Kantians as well, some of whom would break with the prevailing interpretation that for Kant deontology (the "right") must precede teleology (the "good").[2]

Third, and of course not unconnected with the previous issue, some of the earliest reviewers of the *Groundwork* objected to Kant's claim that morality has nothing to do with happiness, and argued against Kant that a universally valid morality, or at least one valid for all *human* beings, which is all we need to care about, could be grounded on a sufficiently refined and enlightened conception of happiness. Kant's increasing emphasis on his idea of the highest good in works from the *Critique of Practical Reason* through the *Critique of the Power of*

---

[2] Jeremy Bentham introduced the term "deontology" in a posthumously published text of that name of 1834, but the contrast between "deontological" and "teleological" moral theories is usually ascribed to Broad 1930; Herman 1993, p. 208 n. 1, ascribes it to Muirhead 1932. Anscombe 1958 introduced the now more customary "consequentialism" for Broad's "teleology," rightly so since the latter term has such a different meaning in the philosophy of nature, for example in Kant's *Critique of the Power of Judgment*. For an argument that "deontology" is too loosely defined to be of much philosophical use, see Timmermann 2015. See my Chapter 13.

Judgment to his essay on "Theory and Practice" and the book form of *Religion within the Boundaries of Mere Reason*, both published in 1793, is a response to this objection meant to show that properly understood happiness does have a place in his moral theory. But Kant's theory of the highest good would in turn raise questions about the persuasiveness of the postulates of pure practical reason that are meant to support or legitimize our belief in its possibility. The doctrine of the postulates of pure practical reason was what inspired Carl Leonhard Reinhold to publish his first series of *Letters on the Kantian Philosophy* in 1786 and 1787, but would also provide fodder for the criticisms of subsequent philosophers, such as Arthur Schopenhauer, and many twentieth-century Kantians would attempt to separate the core of Kant's moral philosophy from this controversial doctrine. More generally, discomfort with Kant's apparent exclusion of happiness from the fundamental principle of morality would lead to numerous attempts to reconcile Kant's deontological ethics with some form of consequentialism, culminating in Derek Parfit's *magnum opus*, *On What Matters* (Parfit 2011).[3]

Fourth, Kant's theory of freedom of the will would quickly prove contentious. One of the earliest reviews of the *Groundwork* raised the question of whether Kant had proven the reality of the freedom of the will, while several others argued that section III of the *Groundwork* was only meant to *defend* the possibility of the freedom of the will from criticism, not to provide a positive proof of its reality. But this issue would pick up steam after the publication of the *Critique of Practical Reason*, and in particular the question of whether the free will could be both governed by the moral law and yet responsible for immoral actions, which was formulated in a famous article by Henry Sidgwick in 1888,was in fact already raised by 1790. Kant and Reinhold in particular would perform a complicated dance on this question, Reinhold proposing a defense of Kant in a second series of *Letters on the Kantian Philosophy* in 1792 that seems similar to Kant's own apparent solution to the problem in part one of the *Religion*, first published as an article in the *Berlinische Monatsschrift* in April of that year (Kant 1792), but Kant then rejecting Reinhold's position in the *Metaphysics of Morals* without any suggestion that he might be modifying his own position of 1792—and Reinhold in turn criticizing that! Many subsequent philosophers would grapple with Kant's position on the freedom of the will, whether by focusing on the problem of responsibility for evil, as Schelling did in his 1809 *Essay on the Essence of Human Freedom*, or more generally, as for example Schopenhauer and Nietzsche. One of G. E. Moore's earliest papers offered a scathing criticism of Kant's theory of free will, and perhaps caused this problem to fade from the forefront in the reception of Kant in the twentieth century.[4]

---

[3] See my Chapter 14.
[4] On Moore 1898, see my Chapter 12. Although there are still those who defend Kant's solution in the twenty-first century, e.g., Baiasu 2020.

Finally, in a famous distich in their joint *Xenien* Friedrich Schiller and Johann Wolfgang von Goethe raised a question about the place for sympathetic feelings in morally praiseworthy motivation, and Schiller is ordinarily understood to have pressed Kant further on this issue in his famous essay "On Grace and Dignity" in 1793. In the second edition of the *Religion* and in his contemporaneous lectures on the metaphysics of morals, Kant himself certainly understood Schiller to have been pressing him on this issue, although as we shall see it is unclear just how much difference there really was between them. But in any case, the issue had already been raised by the reviewer defending Kant from Tittel, and it would continue to be an issue for many later philosophers, and one that has continued to attract much interest among recent interpreters of Kant.

In the case of a number of these issues, we will see that what is really at the bottom of debate is whether Kant's moral philosophy should be understood as one that demands that we act only on universalizable maxims because that is what it is to be *rational* or because that is what it takes to be *free*, or to *preserve and promote* freedom both in one's own person and that of every other. This issue has been central to much of the history of Kant's impact on subsequent moral philosophy, and in particular some of those who have been most hostile to Kantian moral philosophy have understood his approach in the former way while at least some of those who have been most receptive to Kant's philosophy and who have developed it in the most interesting and promising ways have understood it in the latter way, although until recently without reference to the texts in which Kant himself suggested that interpretation most explicitly. For the moment, this remark will remain a promissory note, while the remainder of this chapter explores the earliest reception of Kant's moral philosophy with an eye to the five issues just enumerated. In subsequent chapters we will see how one or the other of these issues has animated the reception or rejection of Kant's moral philosophy up to the recent work of John Rawls, Derek Parfit, and others such as Onora O'Neill and Christine Korsgaard, although some, like Rawls, have addressed many of them.

4.2. The Demand for Proof

The question of whether Kant could actually prove any of his claims in the *Groundwork* was not widely debated in the immediate response to the work, but was pressed in at least one review. The first review to appear, in the *Allgemeine Literatur-Zeitung*, as early as April 7, 1785, consisted largely of quotations from the Preface to Kant's book, but said, in the few of the reviewer's own words, that "Mr. Kant's chief concern in this most remarkable text is to *discover* the supreme principle of all morality," while featuring Kant's own statement that a presentation of the moral law in all its "purity and genuineness" is necessary in order to preserve morality from "all sorts of corruption" stemming from a mixture of empirical principles with the pure one.[5] Others emphasized that at least when it comes to the freedom of the will, Kant's project was to defend our assumption that we have such freedom from objections rather than to prove it *ab novo*. For example, a review in the *Gothaische gelehrte Zeitungen* in August 1785 emphasized that Kant's appeal to the distinction between the two standpoints of phenomena and noumena in the central argument of *Groundwork* III meant that "Although freedom cannot be explained, those who simply hold freedom to be impossible have nevertheless not won their point; one can *defend* themselves against them, fend off their objections, by showing them that their putative objection lies in still considering the human being as appearance when they should be conceiving him, as an intelligence, as a thing in itself."[6] This and similar reviews did not demand that Kant *prove* either the validity of the moral law or the reality of freedom of the will. But at least one reviewer did press a demand for proof upon Kant. This was the anonymous review published in Tübingen in February, 1786—Tübingen, where the theology professors who would teach the young Schelling, Hegel, and Hölderlin in the next decade would try to appropriate Kant's philosophy of religion for their own dogmatic purposes. This hostile review opened with the statement that although the *Groundwork*, like all the other words of the philosopher from Königsberg, "quite unmistakably bears the stamp of an original, deep-thinking mind," it, like Kant's previous works, "in place of a *proof* often places a *dialectical illusion*, or (to use [Kant's] own expression), places a cloud in the place of Juno."[7] Specifically, the author demands that Kant demonstrate (*erwiesen*), "*in accordance with the principles of his critique*," that there are rational beings other than humans and that "the principles of *human* morality ... be valid for *all rational beings in general*," as well as that there is a "specific difference" between the principles of "well-being" and "good conduct" (*Wohlbefinden* and *Wohlverhalten*), or between happiness and virtue, a distinction which he takes to have been undermined by "the best of the empirical moral philosophers (e.g., [Johann August] Eberhard)."[8] The reviewer himself admits that the question of whether apart from God there actually are rational beings other than human beings, an existential assertion that Kant never made, can be left to one side, but presses the other two questions, which are essentially the questions of whether there really must be a principle of morality valid even for all human beings and, even if so, whether it still might not be grounded on a suitably refined conception of happiness. He clearly takes Kant's assumption of the former to be inadequately grounded and Kant's arguments in sections I and II of the *Groundwork* that a universally valid moral principle cannot be grounded on any

---

[5] Anonymous 1785a, at pp. 139 (emphasis added) and 138.
[6] Anonymous 1785b, p. 196 (emphasis in original).
[7] Anonymous 1786a, p. 277 (emphasis in original).
[8] Anonymous 1786a, p. 278. The reference is to Eberhard 1781, republished 1786.

conception of happiness to be too hasty; he specifically rejects Kant's argument in section I that since reason is not always good at producing happiness that cannot be the goal of reason at all but only of instinct to be based on a failure to distinguish between the "*specific kind* of happiness that "*presupposes no reason*" and "*another kind*" that does.[9] He further states that he "absolutely fails to see" how Kant could "derive [*herleiten*] the foremost kinds of duties from his principles *without any recourse to experience*—entirely *a priori*, without regard to the consequences, which we know only through experience"[10]—in other words, he charges that Kant has failed to prove that the four specific duties that he discusses in section II of the *Groundwork*, the duties to refrain from suicide and false promises and to develop one's talents and provide assistance to others in the pursuit of their own ends, follow from his fundamental principle of morality (although here one might object that Kant merely means to show in the *Groundwork* that his formulations of the categorical imperative *can accommodate* these commonly recognized duties, actual *derivations* or *proofs* of them being reserved for the *Metaphysics of Morals* that was not to appear for another dozen years).[11] Finally, the reviewer states that Kant's "idea of freedom also seems problematic," although he begs off from discussion of freedom for reasons of space.[12]

The Tübingen reviewer does not use Kant's term "deduction," but after the publication of the *Critique of Practical Reason*, where Kant specifically abjures the possibility of a deduction of the moral law itself but insists upon the legitimacy of a deduction of the reality of our freedom *from* our immediate and undeniable consciousness of our obligation under the moral law (*CPracR*, 5: 47), the famous "fact of reason" argument, the question of whether Kant had successfully deduced either the moral law or the freedom of the will would be repeatedly pressed. We will see that the question of whether Kant provided a deduction of his central claims, and whether, if not, such a deduction could nevertheless be provided, would become central in Fichte's *Theory of Ethics*, published a decade after Kant's foundational works and at the same time as Kant's own *Metaphysics of Morals*, and that the more general question of the proper method for practical philosophy and the epistemic status of its claims would remain central down to the times of the most prominent recent Kantian moral philosopher, John Rawls, and his most important followers, who have debated this issue under the name of "constructivism."[13] For now let us turn to the next issue raised by Kant's early reviewers, namely the charge of "empty formalism."

---

[9] Anonymous 1786a, p. 281.   [10] Anonymous 1786a, p. 282 (emphasis in original).

[11] Some recent commentators deny that Kant intended specific duties to be straightforwardly derived from the categorical imperative at all; see the discussion of Barbara Herman in Chapter 16.

[12] Anonymous 1786a, p. 283.   [13] See Chapters 15 and 16.

4.3. The Charge of "Empty Formalism"

The objection that Kant's categorical imperative, particularly in its first formulation as the Formula of Universal Law, the requirement that agents act always only on maxims that they could at the same time will be to be universal law, is an "empty formalism," in fact compatible with any maxim an agent might actually will, is most famously associated with Hegel, who pressed it first in his 1802 essay on natural law and then raised it again in his 1821 handbook on *The Philosophy of Right*.[14] But it may be regarded as having been raised immediately, first in a very hostile review of Kant's *Groundwork* in the Leipzig *Kritische Beyträge zur neuesten Geschichte der Gelehrsamkeit* in its first number for 1786 and then in May of that year in a more respectful but still critical review in the *Allgemeine deutsche Bibliothek* published anonymously but known to have been written by Hermann Andreas Pistorius (1730–98), a well-educated pastor on the Baltic island of Rügen who wrote numerous reviews for the journal, including a subsequent review of the *Critique of Practical Reason* that was not published until 1794 because it had been mislaid![15] The Leipzig review is hostile from the outset: its second sentence says that because "It so overheated my head, I could have read [Kant's book] through only with difficulty had it been more than a little work of 128 pages and one sheet of preface"![16] The review omits an exposition of Kant's work, instead proceeding directly to criticism. Its first objection is that Kant is hardly original in distinguishing morality from self-love, for that has been the position of all serious moralists since even the "ancient Epicurean party," who, although Cicero "ascribed *sensual pleasure* [*Wollust*] to them as their *finem bonorum*," nevertheless, the author insists, like every other "honorable sect," distinguished the *honestum* or right thing to do from "the advantage for his own person" that anyone might derive from doing the right thing.[17] The review's next objection actually intimates a point that would soon become another major bone of contention, and to which we will return later in this chapter, namely that Kant's claim that "only a rational being has the capacity to act *in accordance with the representation* of a law, i.e., in accordance with principles, or a *will*," leads either to "*fatalism*" or to a mere "*play* with the word 'law'."[18] He does not explain this remark, but presumably means that Kant is unclear whether his version of the moral law is supposed to be a *norm* for human agents, to which they *may or may not* conform, or a descriptive *generalization* or *uniformity* to which their conduct always *does*

---

[14] Hegel 1802–3, translated as Hegel 1975; Hegel 1821, translated as Hegel 1991.

[15] Pistorius coyly does not say whether it was mislaid by himself or by the journal. For an account of Pistorius and the texts of his five most important reviews of Kant and Kantians, see Gesang 2007. In what follows, I will cite Pistorius from this more readily accessible source rather than from Landau 1991, which in any case does not contain the 1794 review of the *Critique of Practical Reason*. Pistorius also translated David Hartley's associationist *Observations on Man* (1749) into German (1791).

[16] Anonymous 1786b, p. 318.   [17] Anonymous 1786b, p. 319.

[18] Anonymous 1786b, p. 320.

conform, or in accordance to which they are as it were fated to act, which would then make it impossible to explain how humans ever act *immorally*. The Leipzig reviewer does not draw this inference, but others quickly would, so we will defer further discussion of that point until the next section of this chapter. Rather, the reviewer immediately turns to Kant's conception of an imperative and its three subvarieties, namely the two forms of hypothetical imperative, the imperatives of skill and of prudence, and then the "imperative of morality" or the categorical imperative. He first objects that these are merely new names for old ideas, but then, more importantly, objects that the Kant's categorical imperative, "*act only in accordance with those maxims through which one can at the same time will to become a universal law*," has "not the least *determinate content*." All he says to explain this charge is that "nobody would hold" Kant's ensuing examples of duties "to be entirely more suitable [*passend*] than any others."[19] This suggests that *any* maxim or proposed course of conduct could be universalized by an agent willing to accept the consequences of so doing. But again, the reviewer does not pause to elaborate his criticism. Rather, he hurries on to cast aspersions on Kant's idea that humanity whether in one's own person or that of any other is an end in itself of absolute value, and instead asserts that only God could be a ground of absolute value and complains that Kant's moral philosophy leaves "God off to one side."[20] The reviewer makes no reference to Kant's first statement of his doctrine of the postulates of pure practical reason in the "Canon of Pure Reason" in the first *Critique*, and of course he could not yet have been acquainted with Kant's explicit elaboration of this doctrine in the second *Critique*. But we may safely assume that he would not have been satisfied with Kant's position that we can and indeed must postulate the existence of God on practical grounds but cannot claim to know it on theoretical grounds, and that even in the practical case our rational insight into what is right and wrong must precede and underlie our postulation of the existence of God and is not derived from divine command.

The review by Pistorius that appeared in May, 1786, thus about a full year after the original publication of the *Groundwork*, is a more serious and careful piece of work. Pistorius begins with Kant's own opening claim that there is nothing that can be held to be good without restriction except a good will, and immediately expresses his wish that Kant had begun with a "general concept of what is *good*."[21] But his objection applies not just to the case of a good will, but to anything called good adjectively when no substantive good to which it conduces has been adduced. Thus he questions what could be meant by "a good principle, a good law, following which makes a will good," if the question "what is good? is to recur." On his view, "we must finally come to some object or some final end [*Endzweck*] of the law, and must seek help in the matter [*das Materielle*] because

---

[19] Anonymous 1786b, p. 320.   [20] Anonymous 1786b, p. 321.   [21] Pistorius 1786, p. 27.

with the formal [*dem Formalen*] neither the will nor the law will suffice."²² He makes it clear that exploring the consequences of this point will be his concern throughout his review: "What follows from this for the entire moral system we will subsequently see." But we can already see that his general position is that having the form of universal law does not by itself *explain* why following that law is valuable. As he continues, it becomes clear that Pistorius's objection is that we cannot explain why following a law (or having a pure will to follow only that law) should be good unless so doing leads to a good result, to be sure not just for the individual but for all. This is not to make the objection that would become famous with Hegel, that any maxim can be universalized if the agent is willing to accept the consequences, but it may go straight to the larger point that Hegel too ultimately wants to make.

As he proceeds to Kant's first formulation of the categorical imperative as the requirement to act only on universalizable maxims, Pistorius correctly characterizes Kant's argument that attempting to act on a maxim that cannot be universalized will lead to a contradiction in the very conception of the intended action: my action, e.g., making a promise I do not intend to keep, would be in vain if my maxim were universalized, or "if everyone were to repay me in the same coin," for if everyone were known to be trying to make false promises then no one would accept a promise and no promises of any kind could be made, thus my own attempt to make a false promise would be in vain, "and thus my maxim, as soon as it was made into a universal law, would destroy itself."²³ Pistorius thinks that we need an explanation of what is wrong with attempting to act on a maxim that would have this result, however, a perfectly reasonable question since it is not obvious that my trying to make a false promise would *in fact* lead to everyone trying to make false promises and thus bring down the whole practice of promising. He proposes that the only possible explanation of the impermissibility of false promises is (what we would now call) consequentialist, namely, "that is right the universal performance of which would be *generally beneficial* [*gemeinnützig*], or in accordance with the interest of rational beings, and that that is wrong the universal performance of which would be *generally harmful* [*gemeinschädlich*], or opposed to the interest of rational beings." In other words, the explanation of why following the fundamental principle of morality is in fact right, or why it is the fundamental principle of morality, cannot be, as Kant thinks, that it is merely "formal, and excludes everything material," but rather that following the law is in fact beneficial to all and contravening it is harmful to all.²⁴ As he puts it a page later, we need an explanation of the "necessary connection between the law and the will of a rational being," and such an explanation can be either "the truth or the utility of the law, its harmony with the power of thought or its concordance with

²² Pistorius 1786, p. 27.   ²³ Pistorius 1786, p. 30.   ²⁴ Pistorius 1786, p. 31.

the power of desire"; only through one of these middle terms, and in the case of a practical rather than a theoretical law only through the latter alternative, the concordance of the law with the—enlightened, universal rather than merely self-serving—faculty of desire, can "the law interest a rational being."[25] And then, Pistorius further argues, anticipating an objection that would be made in the mid-twentieth century in a famous article by Philippa Foot,[26] Kant's conception of a categorical imperative, or of a strict distinction between the categorical and hypothetical imperatives, collapses.

> Now precisely that on which the validity of [the moral law] is grounded, or by means of which it can be known, constitutes the *condition* of its validity, hence there is no other moral law than a hypothetical one, and no merely formal law can be thought to be valid, as little as I can know a will to be absolutely good merely because it is in conformity to law, or because the law alone is the maxim of its will, but it also comes down to whether its law is also good. This leads us back to what I remonstrated at the beginning, that moral inquiry must begin with the concept of the *good*, and the question must first be investigated, whether in relation to the conduct of human beings anything can be declared good other than what is actually good for the human being as a sensitive [*empfindendes*] and thinking being.[27]

The objection that would later often be brought against Kant's examples of duties as following from the categorical imperative, for example Hegel's objection that there would be nothing wrong with refusing to return deposits unless the practice of making deposits were thought to be useful to the agent concerned or the objection of many that providing assistance for others will seem rational only if one expects to need their reciprocal assistance on some other occasion, is here made by Pistorius in a much more general form: the moral necessity of willing to act only in accordance with universal law can be explained only if such a practice is beneficial to mankind.[28] Pistorius's objection is that Kant's deontological principle of morality makes sense only if presupposes an enlightened consequentialism, an interest of all in the well-being of all. He is not objecting that Kant's formulation of the moral law is invalid because a widespread interest in the welfare of all cannot be presupposed, but is rather making the methodological objection to Kant that his principle does depend upon the perfectly sound presupposition of such an interest. This is also to say that Pistorius's objection that Kant's fundamental principle of morality is ultimately a hypothetical rather than a categorical imperative is not that it is *optional* in the sense that hypothetical

---

[25] Pistorius 1786, p. 32.   [26] See Chapter 13.   [27] Pistorius 1786, p. 33.
[28] For Hegel's version of the empty formalism charge, see Hegel 1975, pp. 76–8, and Hegel 1991, §135, pp. 162–3. For discussion, see Wood 1990, Freyenhagen 2012, and my Chapter 9.

imperatives likes rules of etiquette ("If you want to be invited again, be sure to send a thank-you note") or rules of skill ("If you want to win, open with queen's pawn") are, but rather that it is not *self-standing* or *independent* of a more fundamental conception of the good. Again, his objection is not to the universal validity of Kant's formula, nor is it the objection that it does not yield determinate results. His objection is just that the validity of Kant's formula depends upon an antecedent conception of the good. We will see in Chapter 14 that Pistorius's objection that Kant's deontology presupposes a teleology has continued to animate attempts to reconcile Kantianism with consequentialism from R. M. Hare to Derek Parfit.

As Pistorius continues, it becomes clear that his objection to Kant is made from the standpoint of Stoicism, that is, that he thinks that an interest in the welfare of all is *natural* for human beings and that Kant's principle ultimately depends upon the virtue of living in conformity with (human) nature. As he puts it in his discussion of Kant's third main formulation of the categorical imperative, the so-called Formula of Autonomy, if the will, as Kant maintains, is not to be determined by the character of a particular object:

> Nevertheless something must determine it, something must bind it to the law; now if this is not to be the particular character of the object (and all the consequences of the choice of this object), then absolutely nothing remains that can and should determine it other than [the agent's] own nature and the universal interest of every rational being that is grounded in it. To make a deceitful lie is opposed to this interest, and solely this circumstance (not the possible good or bad consequences that his lying promise might have for the agent himself) should determine him not to make such a promise. I cannot attribute any other sense than that founded in the doubled interest in truth and utility grounded in the common nature of rational beings... to [Kant's concept of] autonomy; I also cannot conceive of or wish for any more free legislation than that which as it were my own nature exercises, and which the Stoics expressed through these formulas, *naturam, optimam ducem, tanquam Deum sequi, naturae convenienter vivere*, etc. [let nature lead you to the best as if it were God; live in accordance with nature].[29]

Pistorius's objection is not that Kant's formal principle of morality is indeterminate, as the Leipzig reviewer would hold, or compatible with any maxim, as Hegel would argue, but that it must be grounded in a common human interest in the common weal. This does not render Kant's principle invalid, as some might hold, because in Pistorius's confident view there is such a common interest, but it renders Kant's methodology unsound or at the very least incomplete.

---

[29] Pistorius 1786, pp. 35–6.

In his review of the *Critique of Practical Reason*, however (although as previously mentioned that did not actually appear until 1794), Pistorius did formulate something closer to what would subsequently become Hegel's "empty formalism" objection.[30] Here his thesis is that "the validity of a maxim or of its opposite for universal legislation cannot be judged from its reasonableness [or] unreasonableness [*Vernunftmäßigkeit und Unvernunftmäßigkeit*] alone," because one might act on one maxim or the other "consistently" (*consequenter*), that is, presumably, act on it while being prepared to accept the consequences of others doing so as well. This may not be the case when universalizing a maxim would be self-defeating in the sense of making one's proposed action impossible, as in Kant's example of the maxim of making false promises, the universalization of which would make it impossible to make any promise at all, *a fortiori* a false one, but it will apply in other cases, ones that we might think of as more general moral policies. Pistorius's argument is worth quoting at length:

> Suppose that one has to decide between the two opposed maxims, each of which is suited for universal legislation, that we might observe with respect to our conduct toward our enemies, those, namely, which Christianity prescribes and which the Hurons follow, the latter of which might be expressed thus: Never spare your enemy, but persecute him until he is incapable of ever injuring you or if that is not otherwise possible then until you have destroyed him. Here it is, it seems to me, evident that the merely rational or consistent that is supposed to lie in the one case and the self-contradictory that is supposed to lie in the other cannot be used as the ground of cognition, because I neither act consistently if I follow the one nor contradict myself if I practice the other. This case is not like the case presented by Kant, whether or not I may get myself out of an embarrassment through a false promise, or the case of whether I may steal or not, for in both those cases I would contradict myself: I would will something and at the same time not will it—namely, will that promises should be valid and also that they should not be valid; will that there be property and also that there not be. But whether I act toward my enemy in the Christian way or the Huron way, I do not act more consistently in the one case nor more self-contradictorily in the other.... I must always remain undecided between my two maxims or, if it is important for me to choose between them, then search for a higher consideration, from which I can decide the legitimate value or disvalue [*Werth oder Unwerth*] of my maxims; and that this consideration or ground of cognition is not to be further sought in pure reason, this, it seems to me, is obvious... it

---

[30] A rare discussion of Pistorius's review of the *Critique of Practical Reason* is Walschots 2021 (published after I originally drafted this material). Walschots argues that Kant's response to Pistorius is primarily methdological, his insistence on the "priority of the right over the good." In the following section, I will emphasize that the second *Critique* also contains a substantive response to Pistorius in its argument that happiness does have a proper although subordinate place in the idea of the highest good.

is undeniable that ... in asking this question one would know more than what is consistent or not, but what is in accordance with nature and with the universal interest of rational beings grounded therein.[31]

Pistorius goes on to make explicit that his rejection of Kant's formalism is grounded in his own "Stoic moral principle" that there are actions or maxims of action that are consistent with our common nature as human beings and others that are not, even if from a purely formal view conduct on both those that are and those that are not consistent with our nature are nevertheless equally self-consistent. The Huron who is willing that his enemy try just as hard to destroy him as he tries to destroy the enemy is not inconsistent, but his maxim is nevertheless contrary to human nature and its interest in the well-being of all. Pistorius thus concedes that there are some easy cases in which the universalization of maxims would lead to self-contradiction and where those maxims can be rejected for that reason, but in other cases, perhaps the morally more significant cases, the formal requirement of consistency is not enough, and material considerations—as he put it in his review of the *Groundwork*, a conception of the good—must also be invoked to settle the moral question. Thus Pistorius does not anticipate Hegel's subsequent objection in its full force, but his version may be all the more plausible precisely because he does not deny that *some* maxims are obviously self-defeating.

As I argued in the Part I, Kant's fundamental principle of morality is not so purely formal as either Pistorius or Hegel suppose, but through the Formula of Humanity includes and is in fact grounded on a conception of the good, although a conception very different from the kind of conception of the good that Pistorius at least has in mind, namely a conception of the intrinsic value of freedom itself. Kant's underlying position is that the universalization of some maxims is incompatible with the greatest possible use of freedom by oneself and others but the universalization of other maxims not, and that acting only on the latter sort of maxims is what morality requires because freedom is the essential end—or good—of mankind. His position is not formally or methodologically so different from that of Pistorius, but differs substantively in taking freedom rather than some other conception of happiness to be the good served by morality. But Pistorius could hardly be faulted for having failed to recognize this, for as I have suggested Kant made this theory clear in his lectures on ethics but not in either the *Groundwork* or the second *Critique*, where it can be readily found only with the hermeneutical assistance of the lectures and other unpublished materials.

Pistorius's objection that Kant's theory omits any material good also takes the form of an objection to Kant's attempt to separate morality from a concern with

---

[31] Pistorius 1794, pp. 87–8.

happiness, and he further objects to what he regards as Kant's "problematic conception of freedom."[32] These are our next two topics, so rather than continuing directly with the exposition of Pistorius's reviews, we can now turn to these two topics more generally.

4.4. Morality and Happiness

As we have already seen, many among the earliest reviewers of Kant's *Groundwork* objected to his apparent severance of any connection between morality and happiness. Kant's lengthy argument in the Dialectic of the *Critique of Practical Reason* that there is a proper connection between morality and happiness, in what he calls the highest good, as long as the priority of morality over happiness is properly understood, must surely be understood as a response to this objection; this would explain why Kant felt the need to expand at such length on the brief treatment of the highest good already included in the first *Critique*, in the "Canon of Pure Reason" buried deep in its Doctrine of Method, and to return yet again to this topic in the *Critique of the Power of Judgment*. In particular, Kant's objection to the Stoics' way of connecting virtue and happiness in their own conception of the highest good might be considered to be intended as a reply to the unnamed Pistorius's invocation of Stoicism in behalf of his own argument that, even if Kant's formulation of the categorical imperative is in one sense valid (although not, as we saw Pistorius argue, sound in its claim to be categorical in the sense of independent of any presupposition), it nevertheless depends on the presupposition of a natural human interest in the well-being—which is to say happiness—of all. For this reason, I will first consider the objection that Kant's theory of morality disregards the connection between morality and happiness.

We have already seen that the Tübingen review published in February 1786 questioned Kant's radical separation between virtue and happiness. More specifically, the reviewer argued that there is a contradiction between Kant's general claim that in the case of a hypothetical imperative if we do not like the means to our end then we can always give up the end and his claim about happiness, the end in the case of the hypothetical imperative of prudence, that *"It is an end that one can presuppose as real in all rational beings (insofar as imperatives apply to them, as dependent beings), and thus an aim [Absicht] that they not merely can have but that one can safely assume that they all have in accordance with a **natural necessity**, and that is the aim of **happiness**."*[33] The reviewer's claim is that, while Kant's account of morality requires the agent to be able to simply give up any claim to happiness that conflicts with duty, on Kant's own theory this is "an

---

[32] Pistorius 1786, p. 37.   [33] Anonymous 1786a, pp. 278–81.

impossible condition": it may be contingent that rational beings with an interest in happiness exist in nature, but once they do it is hardly contingent that they aim for happiness and they cannot be expected to give this interest up. The reviewer archly suggests that perhaps Kant's apparent contradiction is another of the "*antinomies* of *Kantian* reason," and even goes so far as to say that, if Kant's text were a couple of hundred years older, "the temptation to doubt the authenticity of one of the passages adduced could hardly be resisted"![34] The reviewer's objection is not well-formed. To be sure, any action of an agent must always have some end or other, so an agent can never act without some end in view. But happiness is not some particular end at the same level as other particular ends, whether those be getting oneself an ice cream cone or saving the world from starvation. It is rather simply the condition that ensues upon the satisfaction of first-order ends, whatever they might be, and thus perhaps a second-order end, but one at which one cannot directly aim—agents can aim at happiness only by aiming at particular ends. Conversely, it is not merely naturally but rather conceptually impossible for rational agents to give up the end of happiness as long as they have any particular ends, but that fact is not incompatible with agents acting only for the sake of morally permitted or mandated particular ends; they can, in Kant's view freely, place their happiness in the realization of such ends only. Morality may proscribe always acting to realize narrow, self-centered ends, such as getting some ice cream for oneself now (no matter what), and can prescribe acting to realize broad, altruistic ends, such as saving the world from starvation (and of course there are various possible extensions for the abstract concept of happiness in between these two extremes, such as one's own happiness throughout one's life, the happiness of the narrow circle of one's family, the happiness of the somewhat wider circle of one's family and friends, the happiness of the yet wider circle of one's classmates or compatriots, and so on). Kant will ultimately make it clear, above all in the 1793 essay on "Theory and Practice," that what morality requires is not the abnegation of any interest in happiness at all, which is indeed impossible for rational agents as long as they are agents, that is, initiators of end-directed action, at all, just because all action aims at realizing some end and happiness just is the realization of ends; nor does morality require that one have no interest at all in one's own happiness. But morality does require that when they conflict then one act on behalf of the greatest happiness possible throughout the world rather than just for one's own, selfish happiness. Kant's real task is to explain *how* universal rather than personal happiness can and must become the interest of the morally good agent. Unlike a utilitarian, he never simply presupposes that the greatest happiness of the greatest number is simply a self-evident good or the sole self-evident good. Rather, the unselfish goal of the

---

[34] Anonymous 1786a, p. 281.

greatest happiness possible in the world must somehow become a moral goal *through* the moral law.

In fact, in none of his treatments of the highest good in each of the three critiques does Kant make sufficiently clear how morality itself generates the interest in unselfish happiness. But I suggested in Part I that there is a route to this conclusion for Kant, through the argument from the premise that morality requires the preservation and promotion of the *freedom* of all and the interpretation of that freedom as the *freedom of each to set their own ends* but compatibly with the like freedom of all others, to the conclusion that the condition that would result from the success of all in pursuing their own ends subject to this condition of equality, namely the greatest happiness possible throughout the world consistent with morality as the universal satisfaction of this condition. But it took Kant the whole period from the first *Critique* to the essay on "Theory and Practice" to even come close to stating this argument clearly, and the first reviewers of the *Groundwork*, in which Kant is concerned only to "search out and establish" (*aufsuchen und festsetzen*) (4: 392) the fundamental principle of morality, could hardly have been expected to divine the argument that Kant might still only intimate almost a decade later.

As already suggested, Pistorius too was concerned about the wedge that Kant had apparently driven between morality and happiness. In his review of the *Groundwork*, this is manifest in his objection that Kant's argument that not happiness but the good will must be the goal of reason because while reason must be well-suited for some goal it is not well-suited for the realization of happiness (*G*, 4: 395–6) is too hasty. First, Kant's argument does not bear on "true inner happiness" as obviously as it might on some cruder conception of happiness, equated with merely sensuous gratification, nor does it recognize the possibility of a "progressive happiness, namely one that is not complete all at once, in one determinate moment of our existence," but that rather might emerge gradually in tandem with a "gradually developing reason."[35] We can take Kant to be responding to part of this objection in the Dialectic of the *Critique of Practical Reason* when he argues that the happiness that must be part of the highest good is indeed *natural* happiness, what results from the satisfaction of natural desires, and *not* the mere "contentment" or satisfaction (*Zufriedenheit*) with one's "person," that is, one's moral disposition or character, that results from knowing that one has done or attempted to the right thing, whatever the cost to one's natural happiness (*CPracR*, 5: 119). This argument is part of Kant's rejection of precisely the version of Stoicism that Pistorius defended on the ground that when it comes to happiness Stoicism actually settles too cheaply for the kind of satisfaction that follows automatically ("analytically") from virtue rather than

---

[35]   Pistorius 1794; Gesang 2007, p. 28.

natural happiness, the real thing, that should accompany virtue in the highest good, although for reasons that Kant does not yet spell out very clearly in the second *Critique*. However, Kant might also be seen as ultimately accepting part of Pistorius's critique in his argument, in works other than the foundational treatises in practical philosophy, that in fact the perfection of both the virtue and the happiness of mankind can be expected to be realized only gradually, over the life span of the species, and not in the lifetime of any one individual. Since Kant had already suggested this point in the 1784 essay "On the Idea of a Universal History" (Third Proposition, 8: 20), thus prior to the publication of the *Groundwork* and of course Pistorius's review of it, we cannot take this idea itself to have been formulated in response to Pistorius's objection, but perhaps Kant's subsequent connection of this point with his conception of the highest good in works such as the third *Critique* might be seen as a response to the objection.

Be that as it may, Pistorius continued to press his defense of Stoicism against Kant's treatment of the highest good in the *Critique of Practical Reason*, where Kant had himself presented his theory as an alternative to both Epicureanism and Stoicism.[36] Kant had argued that both Epicureans and Stoics made the connection between virtue and happiness "analytic," the Epicureans equating virtue with being happy, although Kant always recognized that their conception of happiness was far from one of mere animal, sensory gratification, and the Stoics equating being happy with being virtuous. Kant took it to be obvious that virtue, or being moral, and happiness are two different things, even if being moral is what makes one *worthy* of happiness, and that their connection could be at most causal or synthetic, not analytic. He also took it to be obvious that at least individual happiness does *not* appear to be directly caused by being virtuous, at least in the phenomenal world of experience, or at least by our own efforts, and postulated the existence of God ("the highest original good") to ground the possibility of a causal connection between virtue and happiness after all ("the highest derived good") (*CPracR*, 5: 125). It is far from clear precisely what Kant's final position even in the *Critique of Practical Reason* which Pistorius had before him is supposed to be, since there God is the postulated as the author *of a nature* in which it turns out that worthiness to be happy and actually being happy can reasonably be expected to be connected after all, and since he makes no suggestion that our happiness in nature will be brought about by processes independent of our own efforts, as by manna falling from the sky (or, in the terms of Kant's *Religion within the Boundaries of Mere Reason*, by grace), he must mean that once we postulate *our own* origin from God we may realize that *our own efforts* to link happiness to virtue can be more effective than they initially seemed.

---

[36] Although Kant's position that the highest good comprises virtue as the supreme good but also natural happiness as the completion of the good may be closer to Stoicism as we now understand it than to Stoicism as both Pistorius and he may have understood it; see Guyer forthcoming (b).

But Kant's obscurity on this point is not Pistorius's worry. His worry is rather that Kant does not explain why natural happiness, the happiness that arises from the satisfaction of natural desires, should be part of his conception of the highest good in the first place. Pistorius maintains that the Stoics "did not need to provide any special proof that happiness belongs to the highest good" since in what he calls their "coalition system" they expressly place the highest form of "happiness in the exercise of virtue." But Kant, he correctly says, "does not seem to have this happiness in mind, but rather one that is called happiness in the popular sense, which presupposes sensory needs, drives, and inclinations, and which at least in part consists in the satisfaction of these."[37] In this case, "one can always ask, what justifies him in connecting happiness with virtue in the concept of the highest good, or in demanding that to the highest good there must also accede a degree of happiness proportionate to the degree of virtue, and indeed a happiness demanded not only by the rational but also by the sensible nature of the human being?"[38] This is a question that every reader of the *Critique of Practical Reason* must ask, and to which the *Critique* offers no very clear answer. By 1794, when Pistorius's review was finally published, Kant had already attempted to answer this question in the *Critique of the Power of Judgment*, in the essay on "Theory and Practice," and in the Preface to *Religion within the Boundaries of Mere Reason*, but if we are to credit Pistorius's note that he had written the review much earlier and that it had then been mislaid, he could not have read any of those answers when he wrote the review. Whether they would have satisfied him even if he had is another question.

Pistorius continues by saying that "in a word" Kant "has not fit his theory of happiness and his theory of virtue together but has set them in a striking misrelation," namely, "that in the doctrine of virtue he seems to be stricter than *Zeno*" (the original Stoic) "and in his doctrine of happiness laxer than *Epicurus*." He then appeals to the "quite correct remark of Herr *Garve* in his notes on the moral philosophy of *Ferguson*, that it is nonsensical to make it our *duty* to despise and sacrifice happiness for the sake of virtue...when such goods and gratifications [are treated] as the real reward for virtue in a future state of life."[39] Since Kant explicitly replies to the objection by Christian Garve (1742–98) to his original presentation of the doctrine of the highest good in the 1793 essay on "Theory and Practice," let us now turn specifically to Garve's objection before evaluating Kant's response to the objection. But since the object of Kant's concern in 1793 was the version of his objection that Garve had published shortly before, in his 1792 *Essays on various Objects from Morals, Literature, and Social Life*, rather than Pistorius's as yet unpublished review of the second *Critique*, we must first look at Garve's text.

---

[37] Pistorius 1794; Gesang 2007, p. 92.   [38] Pistorius 1794; Gesang 2007, p. 93.
[39] Pistorius 1794; Gesang 2007, p. 93.

Garve's objection to Kant's separation between virtue and happiness comes in a long note appended to the first essay in this volume, "On Patience." Garve makes his own teleological approach to moral philosophy plain on the very first page of the essay, which he opens with the claim that we "would do well to measure the value of the virtues more by their general utility than by their difficulty," that is, how much "force and effort" it takes to fulfill them"; he will then argue that "patience is not only a difficult but also a generally useful virtue."[40] He makes clear both what he means by "utility" and what he takes to be the foundation of the normative force that makes the pursuit of the general utility clear some pages later, when he equates utility with happiness and says that the happiness of sensitive creatures is the aim of God, which, it hardly needs to be stated, we humans are also obliged to pursue. "He who says that there is a God says at the same time that the world has a purpose [Zweck], and this purpose is the happiness of sensitive [empfindenden] beings."[41] He also quickly makes it clear that he does not infer from this premise that the pinnacle of virtue is to aim strictly at one's *own* happiness, but rather that it is both virtuous *and natural* for each of us to aim at the happiness of all: "It is not self-love [Eigenliebe] but reason and truth that we find [in happiness] in ourselves and in other beings similar to us...the final purpose [Endzweck] of creation."[42] On the next page he says further that "The representation that all of nature works for our weal [Wohl] cannot be separated from the concept of God." To be sure, events like earthquakes and storms seem to be exceptions to this rule, but they are "local, contingent, changeable, and restricted in time and place," and we can rest assured that even "displeasure and pain must be compatible with joy and happiness in some way, even if it is hidden from us."[43] On this point, perhaps itself a reply to Kant's argument in the *Critique of the Power of Judgment* that our happiness could not possibly be the final end of nature, only our supersensible freedom could be (*CPJ*, §83), Garve did not depart from Leibniz's *Theodicy*, published eighty years before his debate with Kant, or the prevailing view of many writers in both Germany and Britain (hence the justice of Garve's designation as a "popular philosopher").

It is to the first of these claims, that to assert the existence of God is to assert that the world has a final purpose that is nothing other than our own (collective) happiness, that Garve attaches the long endnote to the essay "On Patience" that includes his direct confrontation with Kant on the relation between happiness and virtue.[44] Here he defines the debate as whether "moral perfection or happiness is the ultimate end [letzte Zweck] of creation."[45] He does not explictly name his target as the "Kantian philosophy" until the second page of the note, but it is clear that he has a single target throughout, so he is characterizing Kant's moral philosophy as a version of perfectionism. This might seem erroneous, since Kant

---

[40] Garve 1792, pp. 3–4.   [41] Garve 1792, p. 81.   [42] Garve 1792, p. 81.
[43] Garve 1792, p. 82.   [44] Garve 1792, pp. 111–16.   [45] Garve 1792, p. 111.

explicitly abjures perfectionism in the *Critique of Practical Reason* (CPracR, 5: 41),
but as I have argued Kant's position *can* be seen as a form of perfectionism,
namely one on which it is the will itself, as the capacity (in all) to set ends, that is to
be perfected in the name of morality, and indeed in his lectures on ethics, which of
course Garve could not have known unless by hearsay, Kant did put his own
position in the place of perfectionism in his classification of approaches to moral
theory.[46] But Garve immediately says that "those who assert the former," that is,
that it is moral perfection rather than happiness that is the ultimate purpose of
nature and of ourselves, "do not trust themselves to separate happiness from
virtue for ever." They want "the observation of the moral law without regard to
happiness to be the sole final end [*Endzweck*] for human beings," but nevertheless
also insist that virtue lends the virtuous agent "the *worthiness* to be happy," and
further—Kant's doctrine of the postulates of pure practical reason—that belief in
the existence of God and in immortality are necessary "to give the moral system
support and stability [*Halt und Festigkeit*]."[47] On Kant's principles, "The virtuous
agent strives... unceasingly to be worthy of being happy but never—insofar
as he is truly virtuous—strives to be happy."[48] Garve finds the distinction
between striving for worthiness to be happy and actually striving for happiness
unconvincing—he can understand it "in his head" but not "find it in his heart"—
and does not see how anyone could strive to be worthy of happiness without also
striving to be happy.[49] His position is rather that to strive for happiness is the
natural condition of human beings, that the drive to seek happiness is "earlier and
more original than the concept of *moral* purposes," and that it must "be allowed to
speak of happiness as the only conceivable purpose of things,"[50] but that it is also
natural for human beings to come to care about and strive for the happiness of all,
all human beings and indeed other sentient even if not self-aware creatures. Thus
we are "obligated to include the promotion of this good," that is, the happiness of
all, "and the avoidance or diminution of this evil," that is, the hindrance of the
happiness of all, "in our own final end," because it is the happiness of all and not
just of one or another of us that is God's final purpose in the creation of nature.[51]
Garve's objection is thus that Kant's separation between virtue as the worthiness
to be happy and happiness itself is artificial, and that there is rather a natural
connection between virtue and happiness, namely that striving for the happiness
of all is both our own natural end and the end of God in the creation of nature, at
once both natural and normative for us precisely because it is God's end in the
creation of nature. Garve's objection to Kant is thus rooted in natural law tradition
and in the moral sense school of the eighteenth century, with which Garve, as an
active translator of British authors such as Lord Kames, Edmund Burke, Adam

---

[46] See Kant, e.g., *Moral Philosophy Collins*, 27: 254, and Guyer 2011a.   [47] Garve 1792, p. 111.
[48] Garve 1792, pp. 111–12.   [49] Garve 1792, p. 112.   [50] Garve 1792, p. 114.
[51] Garve 1792, p. 116.

Smith, and Adam Ferguson, was well-acquainted: the idea that we each have a natural interest in the happiness of all, grounded in our creation by God, is the underlying premise of the ethics of Francis Hutcheson, for example.[52]

Kant addresses Garve's objection in the 1793 essay "On the Common Saying: That may be Correct in Theory, But it is of No Use in Practice." The essay is divided into three parts, the first on general issues in moral theory in response to Garve, the second being Kant's first published text on political philosophy, cast in the form of a response to Hobbes, and the third an essay on the philosophy of history cast in response to a position of Moses Mendelssohn. The brief introduction to the essay as a whole makes the general point that "it would not be a duty to aim at a certain effect of our will if this effect were not also possible in experience (whether it be thought as completed or as always approaching completion)" (*TP*, 8: 277). The introduction does not spell out in detail what the three parts of this essay add to what Kant had already said in the *Critique of Practical Reason*, namely, that "ought implies can." But we might take Kant's general point to be that "ought implies can" does not entail (or better require) just the noumenal possibility of free choice, but also the phenomenal possibility of effective choice. We could then see the three parts of the essay as addressing the general theme in the following way. The second part is intended to show that it is possible for rulers to rule in accord with the ideal of a just state, and for subjects to encourage although not to compel their rulers to do so; the third part is aimed to show that human history at least can become the progressive realization of global ("cosmopolitan") justice, not just an endless oscillation between progress and regress; and the first part can be considered to acknowledge that it will not in fact be possible for human beings as they actually are, sensible as well as rational, to be moral if they have no prospect for happiness, but it is crucial to be clear about what the proper relationship between individual happiness, morality, and the collective happiness of mankind is. That at least is the issue for the first part of the essay.

Garve had presented his arguments against Kant quite respectfully, concluding his note with the remark that Kant's philosophy is "rightfully universally esteemed,"[53] and Kant opens his response, in the first section of the "Theory and Practice" titled "On the relation of theory to practice in morals generally," on an equally respectful note: "I call this worthy man's contesting of my propositions *objections* to matters in which (as I hope) he wishes to reach agreement with me, not attacks, which, as disparaging assertions, should provoke a defense; this is not the place to defend them nor am I inclined to do so here" (*TP*, 8: 278n.). But it is clear that there are fundamental differences between Kant's approach to moral philosophy and Garve's more traditional teleological-theological approach. There are two main points to Kant's response. First, although he hardly wants to suggest

[52] Hutcheson 2008.   [53] Garve 1792, p. 116.

that human beings can simply set aside their natural interest in their own happiness (which, although Kant does not say so, might *contingently* include an interest in the happiness of selected others, for example one's children, or maybe only some of them), this interest must be *subordinated* to the demands of morality if there is a conflict between them. Second, morality itself generates an interest in the happiness of all, so the concept of the highest good as the complete object of morality must indeed include the happiness of all, not just one's own, but this is because of the character of pure practical reason, not mere human nature. Thus Kant draws a firmer contrast between the happiness of the individual and of the species: the former is a purely natural interest, the latter a rational interest. Kant could have made this response to the anonymous Tübingen reviewer as well. As a subsidiary to this point, Kant also insists that the postulates of the existence of God and immortality are not meant to give morality "support and stability"— Kant quotes Garve's terms for his own position, although Garve could have had in mind Kant's own, only slightly different words in the *Critique of Pure Reason* (A813/B841)—by promising the individual the just reward for his own worthiness to be happy, but are rather necessary to make the effort to realize the object of morality itself rational by making belief in the conditions of its possibility and of the realization of its prescribed object rational. The existence of God and of immortality do not guarantee the realization of the highest good, for which the virtue of (all) individuals will always be a necessary condition, but they at least make it *possible* for virtue to be both perfected and effective.

Kant begins his response by reiterating his general view that "morals" is "a science that teaches, not how we are to become happy, but how we are to become worthy of happiness" (*TP*, 8: 278). He immediately defends himself from Garve's objection that he can "conceive" Kant's separation between happiness and virtue as the worthiness to be happy "in his *head*" but cannot find it "in his *heart*" (*TP*, 8: 284) by saying that he nevertheless "did not fail to remark that the human being is not thereby required to *renounce* his natural end, happiness, when it is a matter of complying with his duty; for that he cannot do, just as no finite rational being whatever can; instead, he must *abstract* altogether from this consideration when the command of duty arises; he must on no account make it the *condition* of his compliance with the law prescribed to him by reason" (*TP*, 8: 278–9). Kant's view is thus that the human interest in happiness is indeed natural, but what is natural is an interest in one's own happiness—Kant's reference to happiness here is singular—and this interest must not be renounced but must be subordinated to the moral law and its command of duty. Garve could have justly complained that Kant still has not explained his constant equation of virtue with the worthiness to be happy, and no doubt Kant's response would have been more complete if he had explicitly argued here that a commitment to being *worthy* of happiness is the form that the natural interest in happiness must take in a being who is both naturally interested in happiness and rationally interested in morality, just as the feeling of respect is the form that awareness of the moral law must take in a being who is cognizant of that law but also has inclinations to act contrary to it (for the sake of his own happiness, of course). But instead of providing what could have been a useful explanation of this fundamental point, Kant quickly moves to his second point, which he puts by saying that his

> concept of duty does not have to be grounded on any particular end but rather *introduces* another end for the human being's will, namely to work to the best of one's ability toward the *highest good* possible in the world (universal happiness combined with and in conformity with the purest morality throughout the world), which, since it is within our control from one quarter but not from both taken together, exacts from reason belief, *for practical purposes*, in a moral ruler of the world and in a future life.

And he adds to this his subsidiary point:

> It is not as if the universal concept of duty first gets "support and stability" only on the presupposition of both, that is, gets a sure basis and the requisite strength of an *incentive* [*Triebfeder*], but rather that only in that ideal of pure reason does it also get an *object*.   (*TP*, 8: 279)

By his reference to an "incentive" Kant makes it clear that his theory is not that the promise of a personal reward of happiness in exchange for the individual's worthiness to be happy is any kind of incentive for being moral, or that it is necessary to strengthen one's purely moral motivation to comply with duty, as the *Critique of Pure Reason* might have suggested (see again A813/B841). His claim is rather that the effort to be moral would be incoherent or irrational if the realization of its object, the state of affairs it is supposed to bring about, could not be thought to be possible, in the phenomenal world where the effects of our choices are intended to be realized. This has implications for motivation, to be sure: no matter how independent of any promise of reward the motivation of a rational agent to pursue any end might be, if such an agent also has no ground to believe the realization of that end is possible, or at least if she has ground to believe it to be impossible, then just insofar as she is rational she will not in fact act on that motivation. But the purity of the motivation is not undermined by this consideration, as it would be if the agent needed the promise of reward to be fully motivated to act for the realization of a possible end in the first place.

Although Kant's response certainly makes clear the difference between the natural interest in one's own happiness and a moral interest in "universal happiness" or happiness "throughout the world," the big question about it is whether Kant succeeds in making clear *why* such universal happiness should be the "object" of a morality that was initially claimed to have nothing to do with happiness. Even if we accept Kant's claim that morality is not concerned with nor does it build upon one's interest in one's own happiness, on what basis are we supposed to accept his equally strong claim that it is ultimately concerned with universal happiness? Here it has to be acknowledged that his response to Garve (and thus also his possible answer to Pistorius's not yet published review of the *Critique of Practical Reason*) does not say everything that needs to be said. His key claim comes in a note to the last quoted statement that the postulates of pure practical reason are not necessary for our incentive to be moral but for the object of our morality. Here Kant says:

> The need to assume, as the final end of all things, a good that is the *highest good* in the world and also possible through our cooperation is a need not from a deficiency in moral incentives, but from a deficiency in the external relations within which alone an object as end in itself (as moral *final end*) can be produced in conformity with these incentives. For without some end there can be no *will*, although, if it is a question only of lawful necessitation of actions, one must abstract from any end and the law alone constitutes its determining ground. But not every end is moral (e.g., that of one's own happiness is not), but this must rather be an unselfish one; and the need for a final end assigned by pure reason and comprehending the whole of all ends under one principle (a world as the highest good and possible through our cooperation) is a need of an unselfish will *extending* itself beyond observance of the formal law to production of an object (the highest good).   (*TP*, 8: 279–80n.)

This takes us part of where we need to go but not all the way there. It is an argument by elimination, thus subject to the limitations of any such argument. It tells us that the rational will always needs an object (to act without an end in view is not rational but irrational), that one's own happiness (or any particular object in the realization of which one might set one's own happiness, or in the sum of particular objects in which one might set one's own happiness) is a morally ineligible object for the moral will, and then immediately infers that instead the happiness of all—the whole of all the (particular and compossible) ends people might have—is the only alternative. Perhaps it is supposed to be obvious that there are none but particular ends, so the only alternative to the morally ineligible object of one's own happiness is some larger set of ends, perhaps only the set of the (compossible) ends of all. But an argument by elimination is not persuasive if it is not obvious that what it offers as the only possible alternative is in fact the only possible alternative. A positive argument is always more persuasive. And on the basis of the interpretation of Kant's moral philosophy proposed in Part I he could have offered one: he could have argued that the unconditional good and in that sense the primary object of morality is humanity itself, in all persons, not just one's own, and that since humanity includes the freedom of agents to set their own ends, then universal happiness as the realization of the (compossible) ends freely set by all moral subjects is the inevitable ultimate object of morality, that to which the primary object of morality inevitably leads. I would suggest that Kant needed to spell this point out to make his response to Garve completely satisfying.

This brings us to a different problem about freedom, however. We have just been considering the possibility of deriving Kant's conception of the highest good as the object of morality from his conception of the freedom of all to set their own ends, Kant's fundamental normative notion. We will now turn from the normative to the metaphysical conception of freedom, that is, to Kant's theory of the freedom of the will and the objections that it immediately triggered.

5

Freedom and Immorality

Ulrich, Schmid, Reinhold, and Kant

5.1. Freedom of the Will and the Problem of Evil

So far we have considered only responses to Kant published within the first few years of his own publication of seminal works in moral philosophy. Now let us jump ahead for a moment. Exactly a century after the publication of the *Critique of Practical Reason*, the Cambridge moral philosopher Henry Sidgwick published an article on "The Kantian Conception of Free Will" in *Mind* (1888), which was subsequently included as an appendix in the sixth and the final, seventh editions of his *magnum opus The Methods of Ethics* (*ME*, pp. 511–16). Sidgwick is widely thought to have made the objection in this article that Kant equated the free will with a fully rational will, a fully rational will with one that fully adheres to the moral law, and thereby to have precluded the possibility of free yet immoral action: Kant does not exclude the possibility that the human being "often acts contrary" to moral law, Sidgwick grants, but does imply that "its choice in such actions is determined not 'freely' but 'mechanically,' by 'physical' and 'empirical' springs of action" (*ME*, p. 515), for which, however, the individual is not responsible. Such an interpretation of Sidgwick is not correct. What Sidgwick actually argues is that Kant had two different conceptions of freedom, namely "Rational" or "Good Freedom," which can be realized only by action in accordance with the moral law, or on which "a man is a free agent in proportion as he acts rationally," but also "Neutral" or "Moral Freedom," on which "'man has a freedom of *choice* between good and evil,' which is realised or manifested when he deliberately chooses evil just as much as when he deliberately chooses good." Sidgwick says that "if we say that a man is a free agent in proportion as he acts rationally, we cannot also say, in the same sense of the term, that it is by his free choice that he acts irrationally when he does so act" (*ME*, p. 511), or that an agent acts both immorally yet freely, but his point is not that Kant is committed to this conclusion, which would undermine any ordinary conception of responsibility for immoral actions. His point is only that Kant uses the term "freedom" ambiguously, thereby opening himself up to the charge by the unwary that by "freedom" he always means Rational Freedom and thus makes the imputation of

Kant's Impact on Moral Philosophy. Paul Guyer, Oxford University Press. © Paul Guyer 2024.
DOI: 10.1093/oso/9780199592456.003.0006

responsibility for immoral actions impossible. Sidgwick's point is that, had Kant disambiguated his own usage, he could have readily avoided this charge.[1]

But Sidgwick's charge of ambiguity is based solely on passages from Kant's *Groundwork* and the *Critique of Practical Reason*, and ignores the subsequent *Religion within the Boundaries of Mere Reason*, which makes a distinction between *Wille* as the source of the moral law and identical with pure practical reason and *Willkühr*[2] as the power or faculty of choice, the ability to choose between subordinating self-love to the moral law or vice versa, and which thus seems to make exactly the terminological distinction between two different senses of freedom that Sidgwick is looking for. Kant seems to have made this distinction in the *Religion* precisely because he needed it to avoid an objection very much like the one that Sidgwick is ordinarily thought to have made, an objection that was made within two years of the publication of the *Critique of Practical Reason* and did not have to wait a hundred years to be made. But in reviewing the history of this early objection to Kant's theory of freedom of the will we may find a comedy of errors. For in the eighth letter of his second series of *Letters on the Kantian Philosophy*, which appeared in 1792 around the same time as Kant published part one of the *Religion* in the *Berlinische Monatsschrift* and therefore independently of it, Carl Leonhard Reinhold, who had spread favorable word about Kant's philosophy in the first series of *Letters* in the 1780s, attributed to Kant pretty much the same distinction that Kant himself made in the *Religion* and to the same end, namely to avert the charge that Kant's theory of free will undermines responsibility for immoral or evil action. But instead of welcoming Reinhold's support, Kant subsequently repudiated the distinction, and did so as if it had been entirely Reinhold's invention and not his own. In this chapter, we will retrace the fate of the objection and what seems to be the natural response to it and then consider Kant's reason for rejecting this natural response.[3]

---

[1] Sidgwick's own terminology might also be considered confusing. By "Rational" or "Good Freedom" he means freedom from "non-rational impulses," which can be achieved only by acting in accordance with the moral law; by "Neutral" or "Moral Freedom" he means the freedom to do good or evil, to override non-rational impulses when necessary or to give in to them when they should be overridden. By calling the latter "Moral Freedom" he means to connote that this kind of freedom is the necessary *condition* for imputation or moral responsibility, but the term might just as naturally connote a *morally successful* use of freedom of choice, which is to say "Rational" or "Good Freedom." So Sidgwick's own argument might have been clearer if he had called freedom of choice "Neutral Freedom," which is not misleading, but not "Moral Freedom," which is.

[2] Because the authors to be discussed in this chapter, namely Ulrich, Schmid, Reinhold, and Kant, all used this older spelling of what is now spelled *Willkür*, I will use the older spelling throughout the chapter.

[3] Di Giovanni 2005, chapter 4, covers some of the same ground as this chapter, although di Giovanni does not discuss Kant's response to Reinhold in the Introduction to the *Metaphysics of Morals* and does include a discussion of Jacobi's appropriation of a Spinozistic approach to freedom, which I will not. Di Giovanni's chapter also includes a valuable discussion of the Hannoverian and therefore empiricist-influenced August Wilhelm Rehberg, known primarily as a political writer but who also published a review of the *Critique of Practical Reason* in 1788 that influenced Reinhold. See di Giovanni 2005, pp. 126–36. A translation of Rehberg's review is now available in Walschots 2023.

5.2. Ulrich

Kant's theory of freedom drew immediate attention. As early as 1788, the Jena professor Johann August Heinrich Ulrich (1746–1813), who would years later serve on the committee for Hegel's habilitation, published a work with the remarkable title of *Eleutheriology*—"Theory of Freedom"—*or on Freedom and Necessity*, in which he argued that there could be no "middle way" between determinism and indeterminism, thus no room for Kant's approach. He further argued that there could be neither a priori argument nor empirical evidence for indeterminism, and finally argued that determinism is compatible with and indeed necessary for all our sound practices of moral assessment, evaluation, praise and blame, and punishment and reward.[4] The last phase of his argument was very much along the lines of British compatibilists such as Hobbes, Locke, and Hume, whose work Ulrich clearly knew, as well as of the American compatibilist Jonathan Edwards, whose 1757 treatise *On the Freedom of the Will* was not known in Germany or elsewhere in Europe. Since Ulrich's book appeared in the same publishing season as Kant's *Critique of Practical Reason* and was thus written before Ulrich could have read Kant's new book, his argument with Kant was based on Kant's treatment of the freedom of the will in the Third Antinomy of the *Critique of Pure Reason* and in the *Groundwork*. But it seems unlikely that reading Kant's next work would have changed his view of Kant's position.

Ulrich begins with the argument against Kant that "there is absolutely no middle way between necessity and contingency, determinism and indeterminism" (*E*, chapter 1, §5, p. 16).[5] He complains that Kant's attempt to "unite the freedom of actions with their thoroughgoing necessity" is as hard to understand as Spinoza, (*E*, chapter 1, §10, p. 22), but in fact he lays out Kant's position quite clearly and raises objections against it that have been repeated ever since. Kant's "middle way" is his attempt to combine thoroughgoing determinism at the phenomenal level with transcendental freedom or spontaneity at the noumenal level, or, as Ulrich also puts it, following Kant's terminology from the first *Critique*, determinism at the level of empirical character with transcendental freedom at the level of intelligible character. "As *appearance*, and in accordance with its *empirical character*," the agent's "actions . . . are connected in accordance with constant laws of nature, and can be derived from them as their conditions, thus constitute in

---

[4] Apart from a brief discussion in di Giovanni 2005, pp. 108–18, there is little scholarship on Ulrich. For translation of an extract from *Eleutheriology*, see Noller and Walsh 2022, pp. 9–23. This volume consists entirely of translations except for an "Historical and Systematic Introduction," pp. xvi–xlvii. It also includes translations of selections (pp. 63–82) from Carl Christian Erhard Schmid, whom we will discuss in the next section. Most of the same selections can be found in their original German in Imhof and Noller 2021.

[5] Di Giovanni also characterizes Ulrich as a thoroughgoing determinist and compatibilist, although he does not use the latter term and does not link Ulrich's position to the standard historical British position on free will. See di Giovanni 2005, pp. 112–14.

connection with the latter a single series of natural order," while "*in accordance with its intelligible character* the acting subject and its capacity to act do not stand under any *temporal determination* and *temporal condition. For time is the condition of appearance, but not of the thing in itself,*" and "In it no action *begins* or *ceases.*" From this it follows that intelligible character "is not subject to the law of all temporal determination, of everything *alterable,* namely, that everything that *happens in appearances* ... has its cause" (*E*, chapter 1, §10, pp. 24–5). Thus, although "this *intelligible character* can never, to be sure, be immediately cognized," we can, on Kant's account, allow it "*Transcendent freedom, absolute spontaneity* ... to begin a series of successive things or states of affairs *of itself*" (*E*, chapter 1, §10, p. 23) and in accordance with the moral law given by pure reason in spite of the thoroughgoing determinism of empirical character at the phenomenal level. So, although at the phenomenal level of choice (*Willkühr*) there is "*not a single human action that we cannot foresee with certainty and cognize as necessary from its antecedent conditions,*" the intelligible character of an agent of whom that is true "must be pronounced *free* from all influence from sensibility and determination by appearances, and since in it, insofar as it is *noumenon.* nothing *happens,* no *alteration,* which requires temporal determination, hence there is no connection with appearances as causes, this active being in its actions is independent and *free* from all *natural necessity,* which is encountered only in the sensible world" (*E*, chapter 1, §10, p. 26).

Ulrich makes several objections to this model of free will. For one, he claims that Kant has not proven that "time is a *merely subjective form of appearances,*" thus that there *is* a noumenal level of agency not subject to time, to change, and therefore to causal determinism (*E*, chapter 1, §12, p. 33). Kant's argument for the transcendental ideality of time is certainly questionable, and indeed had been questioned since it first appeared in Kant's inaugural dissertation of 1770;[6] but Ulrich provides no detail here. And since Kant did not allege to have proven that there *is* transcendentally free and spontaneous will in the *Critique of Pure Reason,* only that it is *possible* that there is, this might be set aside as an objection to the first *Critique.* Kant would claim to prove the actuality of transcendental freedom in the second *Critique,* but Ulrich was not yet responding to that book. Second, and more interestingly, Ulrich raises the question of whether there might not be "grounds of the determination of the intelligible capacity" for choice "which are not temporally antecedent grounds but are nevertheless grounds, in which case there would be *natural necessity in another sense*" (*E*, chapter 1, §12, p. 32). In other words, he asks whether excluding intelligible character from our ordinary (spatio-temporal) conception of causation is really enough to liberate it from necessity of some other kind, and this is a reasonable question. Most importantly,

---

[6] See Kemp Smith 1923, pp. 138–40, and Guyer 2020a, pp. 14–15.

Ulrich asks how the transcendentally free will can actually have a choice between the "application" of the faculty of reason or the "omission of the application of this faculty." If reason is considered a ground or (non-spatio-temporal) cause of the determination of the will, then how can it be possible that there is a free choice either to apply reason to one's action or not to? This question is only exacerbated by the assumption that, since it is not in time, an agent's intelligible character is "original and inalterable" (*E*, chapter 1, §12, pp. 33–4): even if we could make sense of the idea that the noumenal will could *be* rational or not, what sense could we make of the idea that a non-temporal and inalterable will could *choose* to be rational or not, or to apply the demands of reason to its desires (or the desires of its empirical character) or not? In other words, Ulrich asks what sense we can make of the idea that the noumenal will makes a choice at all, but even if we can make sense of that, what sense could we make of the idea that the noumenal will can *choose* to be irrational and immoral? How can immorality be imputed to the noumenal will?

Ulrich is really asking two separable questions, although both are based on the premise that for Kant our noumenal or "intelligible" character is pure reason itself. One question is, how could such a character ever choose anything *immoral* if its own law is nothing other than reason itself, pure reason, and reason's law is the moral law? Another question, however, is how could the intelligible character ever *change* if it is not in time—"In the human being's *intelligible character*, which is not appearance, nothing can arise and case, *nothing alters*" (*E*, chapter 1, §12, p. 33)—but isn't a *choice* always a *change*, either from a determined state to a different determined state, or from an undetermined state to a determined state? These questions need to be separated. On the one hand, it might be true that insofar as pure reason is the source of the moral law, and the law as never changes, then pure reason never changes—as Ulrich continues, "In *reason, as an intelligible faculty*, nothing begins and nothing ceases." But then, as Kant will finally make clear in the Introduction to the *Metaphysics of Morals* (*MM*, Introduction, 6: 226), pure reason cannot count as a faculty of *choice* at all, and insofar as moral responsibility requires choice, reason cannot be considered the locus of moral responsibility. *This has nothing to do with whether pure reason is considered a faculty of the noumenal self or will.* On the other hand, insofar as *choice* is to be attributed to the *noumenal* will, it is fallacious to think that such a will can make only a *single* choice, and thus is subject to fatalism rather than freedom. For although this point has bedeviled many, and occasionally even seem to confuse Kant himself,[7] all that follows from transcendental idealism is that we cannot

---

[7] At *RBMR*, part I, 6: 25, Kant says that "The disposition, i.e., the first subjective ground of the adoption of the maxims, can only be a single one, and it applies to the entire use of freedom universally." If this is meant as an expression of Kant's rigorism, that *at any one time* an agent is either committed to the subordination of self-love to the moral law, or not, then it is correct; but if it were to mean that an agent can never *change* her fundamental maxim, or rank-ordering of the two

represent the possibility of noumenal change in our usual phenomenal, that is to say, temporal form—but if moral conversion is possible, and moral conversion can only take place at the noumenal level, then noumenal change must be possible, even if we cannot represent it as ordinary temporal change. That is certainly one reason for Kant to call the change of heart, as he so often does, inscrutable: "the moral law thus determines that which speculative philosophy had to leave undetermined" (*CPracR*, 5: 47).

5.3. Schmid

Ulrich would go on to defend determinism and its compatibility with all of our normal practices of imputation, of praise and blame, of punishment and reward, but the details of that argument, readily foreseen by anyone familiar with the British tradition of compatibilism, are not our concern here. Instead, we may now turn to the 1790 *Essay toward a Moral Philosophy* of Carl Christian Erhard Schmid (1761–1812), a student of Ulrich's at Jena.[8] Schmid is typically thought to have pressed the same objection against Kant's conception of free will that his own teacher Ulrich had raised two years earlier, namely "intelligible fatalism" or the impossibility of change at the noumenal level that is supposed to be the ultimate locus of moral responsibility. He indeed may have been thought by Reinhold and by Kant himself to have raised that objection. To this reader, however, Schmid seems to have tried to defend Kant from Ulrich's objection, and the positions that Reinhold and Kant simultaneously took in 1792 can be read as restating Schmid's proffered defense in more orthodox Kantian language rather than rejecting it.[9] To compound complexity, however, in his *Metaphysics of Morals* five years later Kant himself appears to reject Reinhold's 1792 position, and in so doing also to reject not only Schmid's 1790 defense but his own resolution of the problem in the *Religion*. This suggests that the problem of reconciling Kant's conception of the will as rational with responsibility for immoral action remained a problem for Kant's moral philosophy after the first decade of debate.

Schmid studied theology as well as philosophy at Jena. During an interlude in his education, he served as the tutor for the young Friedrich von Hardenberg, later

---

possible fundamental maxims, however we are to understand the possibility of noumenal change, which we cannot represent as literally temporal, then the entire argument of the *Religion* would be undermined.

[8] There is little scholarship on Schmid. Some relevant extracts from his writings have been translated in Noller and Walsh 2022, pp. 63–82.

[9] Di Giovanni adopts the position that Reinhold is criticizing Schmid rather than joining Schmid in criticizing Ulrich; see di Giovanni 2005, pp. 118–25. I will suggest in the next section that the relation between Reinhold and Schmid is more complicated than that, with Reinhold nominally disagreeing with Schmid but in fact agreeing with him on crucial points of substance.

to become renowned as the Romantic poet Novalis. He also became a friend of Friedrich Schiller, and indeed officiated at Schiller's wedding. He was briefly an adjunct at Jena and then a pastor, during which period he published a primer on Kant's *Critique of Pure Reason* (Schmid 1788) and then the *Essay toward a Moral Philosophy* (Schmid 1790). These works earned him first a professorship at Gießen and then, in 1793, a permanent professorship at Jena, where he remained the rest of his career. He published an *Outline of Natural Right* (Schmid 1795) before Kant published his own "Doctrine of Right" as the first part of the *Metaphysics of Morals*, but in the remainder of his career otherwise concentrated on theoretical philosophy and psychology, indeed editing a *Psychological Magazine* in 1796–8 and an *Anthropological Magazine* in 1803 and 1804. In his later works he argued that Kant's transcendental philosophy needs empirical confirmation, and that Kant's claims for the synthetic a priori status of the forms of intuition, conceptualization, and judgment have to be relativized to the human condition. He was thus far from an orthodox Kantian.[10]

Nevertheless, Schmid modestly presents his *Essay toward a Moral Philosophy* as a handbook for lectures following the lead of the *Meisterhand* of Kant, and indeed his work is an orthodox and clear—or orthodox but clear—exposition of Kant's moral philosophy as far as it had been published by 1790, with a venture into the realm of the metaphysics of morals, or theory of specifically human duties, and an "applied morals," areas that Kant himself would not reach until 1797. Those two parts of the work are preceded by what Schmid calls a "Critique of Practical Reason," so his intention to expound Kant's own moral philosophy could not be clearer. Schmid's discussion of the problem of freedom and responsibility occupies the final sections of this part of the work (*VMP*, §§220[11]–61). But before we turn to that, some comments on the preceding argument are in order.

On Schmid's account, the "Critique of Practical Reason" deals with "Practical principles, which are elevated above [*erhaben*] all contingent conditions as cognizable as absolutely necessary, and which should be pure, thus which, as in the case of every absolutely universal and necessary truth, can lie nowhere but in the essence of reason itself" (*VMP*, §11, p. 10). The critique of practical reason thus concerns the general principles of morality, valid for all rational beings, rather than duties specific to human beings, although in including an account of moral feeling and of the nature of human as contrasted to divine freedom, the critique of practical reason does address some issues specific to human beings. But as far as principles are concerned, Schmid presents Kant's formulations of the categorical imperative as derived straightforwardly from the nature of reason itself, and thus his interpretation of Kant might be seen as a forerunner of contemporary "constructivist" approaches to Kant (see Chapter 16). Schmid begins with what he

---

[10] See van Zantwijk 2010.
[11] In the first edition, a typographical error mislabels §220 as "§120."

calls a search for four "absolutes": "a *universally valid*, absolutely necessary practical *rule*"; a "*universally valid*, absolutely necessary *goal*—a highest absolute good for reason"; a "*universally valid*, absolutely necessary *incentive* [*Triebfeder*]"; and a "*universally valid*, absolutely necessary *condition*, through which the will to follow the moral law, to strive for the highest good, and to be determined by the rational incentive can assert itself *against all hindrances* from conditionally necessary opposed impulses, [and] united with all otherwise natural efforts of the faculty of desire" (*VMP*, §20, pp. 17–18). Schmid's premise seems to be that any rational action has a principle, a goal, an incentive, and conditions of its possibility, and that pure reason imposes the requirement that all of these be absolutely valid and necessary—as he later argues, that is just what it is to be rational, and to ask for any further reason for being rational would itself be irrational. In his words, "I can also ask, why I should act *morally*, and beyond the answer 'because it is rational' there is no higher answer for a rational being, which therefore cannot ask further nor will without denying its own reason." (*VMP*, §123, p. 123). This is what I mean by saying that Schmid's approach anticipates contemporary constructivism: the principles of morality are supposed to follow immediately, we might say analytically, from the concept of rational action.

Although under the headings of the four "absolutes" Schmid will expound orthodox Kantian ideas, there is some divergence between his terminology and Kant's that might cause confusion. Specifically, under the heading of the "highest absolute good" as the goal of rational action Schmid does not mean Kant's conception of the *complete* good for a natural yet rational being, the conjunction of virtue and happiness, but only the *supreme* good, which is nothing other than rational being itself, the object of Kant's second main formulation of the categorical imperative. Perhaps Schmid avoids using Kant's term "humanity" here to avoid a misleading restriction of the concept of rational being to human beings, although later in his career Schmid will argue that all of Kant's a priori concepts must be so restricted. Kant's notion of the highest good, more precisely the highest derived good, as the complete object of the will of a rational yet animal being, instead comes into Schmid's account as one of the conditions of the possibility of rational action for such a being, namely that what morality demands be compatible with what nature demands, that is, happiness. This implies the specific interpretation of Kant's conception of the highest good, most obviously suggested by the *Critique of Practical Reason*, as the combination of individual morality with individual happiness, rather than by Kant's later versions in the third *Critique* and in the essay on "Theory and Practice," which treat the happiness of *all* as the object of the morality of *each*, and which Schmid could not have seen when he published the first edition of his *Essay*. More importantly for our present purposes, the possibility of the complete good is only one of the conditions for the possibility of rational action. The other is nothing less than the freedom of the moral agent to choose to adhere the principles of morality, to aim for its supreme goal and his own complete goal, and to act on the incentive of moral feeling—but also the freedom not to do so. This is the main topic to be reached in this section.

But first, to continue with our brief exposition of Schmid's version of the critique of practical reason: having stated the four absolutes of reason, the first part of his critique focuses on the issue of universally valid and absolutely necessary moral principles. He follows Kant in explaining why no empirical principles of skill or prudence, no empirically grounded conception of human perfection, and no divine commands can be the source of such moral law: they are all either contingent or else, as in the case of divine commands, presuppose an antecedent recognition of moral law by pure reason. Schmid then derives Kant's three main formulations of the categorical imperative from the idea of a purely rational principle for action as such. Or as he puts it, "by means of [the] relation of the pure knowledge of reason [*Vernunftwissens*] to a sensible [yet] rational faculty of desire the following imperative[s] (command[s]) of reason are produced" (*VMP*, §118, p. 115). The derivations are preceded by a fuller exposition of the concept of rational action (*vernünftige Handlungsweise*) on which they will be based. Schmid lists six features of rational action. Such action (1) is "in accordance with principles, i.e., supremely universal, all-encompassing rules." (2) It takes place "in accordance with *a priori* representations, i.e., concepts of objects that are not known from experience . . . in relation to ends, that it does not *receive* from a sensible faculty of desire." (3) It is "therefore self-active and free in the strictest sense, not coerced and not bound with respect to the way it acts by anything outside it." (4) It is "systematic, i.e., thoroughly in harmony [*übereinstimmend*] with itself. " (5) It is "*absolutely necessary*, i.e., such that it cannot act otherwise, that its mode of acting cannot alter," and "*absolutely universal*, for itself and for every other rational being," or, as Schmid strikingly puts it, "Reason considered as reason is always the same." Finally, reason is free in another way than that mentioned in (4), namely (6) "It acts without restriction, free from all restricting conditions." (*VMP*, §107, pp. 103–4). By definition, then, reason acts only according to universal, necessary, therefore a priori, systematic or self-consistent, and inalterable principles, and is free in the double sense of being free from anything outside it either setting ends for it or otherwise hindering it. In either case, the freedom that Schmid has in mind seems to be negative freedom, or more precisely freedom negatively conceived, freedom from internal or external interference. On this account, freedom is just a property of reason, or a necessary condition of it. Schmid makes no suggestion that freedom is a value to be realized through adherence to reason, rather it is a product of reason. So Schmid does not attempt to interpret or reconstruct Kant's moral philosophy on a conception of freedom as our fundamental value or the fundamental value of rational beings. Rather, again like a contemporary constructivist, he attempts to derive morality from the concept of rationality or the conditions of rational agency alone.

Thus, first, subtending both what are sometimes distinguished as the "Formula of Universal Law" and the "Formula of the Law of Nature" under the single heading of "First Formula," Schmid argues that the very concept of "applying laws of reason to a restricted (sensible [yet] rational) nature" implies the formula "*So act that you could will that your maxim* (the subjective rule that grounds your action) *should become a universal law for yourself as well as for every other rational being*" or (as he explicitly says) "Act according to such maxims which could fit into a universal legislation" or further "direct yourself in your actions according to such maxims which, if they were to become through your conduct universal laws of nature, would produce an arrangement of nature [*Natureinrichtung*] that could be self-consistent" (*VMP*, §118, pp. 115–16). In these versions of the first formulation of the categorical imperative, Schmid simply takes it to be obvious that to be rational is to act only in accordance with "supremely universal" rules, as he stated in the first clause of his analysis of the concept of rational action.

Kant's second main formulation of the categorical imperative, the "Formula of Humanity," has often been considered the most attractive of his formulations, especially recently, but its derivation is also less obvious than that of the Formula of Universal Law: Kant famously introduces it with the bald assertion "Now I say…" (*G*, 4: 428). Schmid is clearly trying to explain what Kant has left obscure. On his account, "The universality of practical rules, as laws"—the basic requirement of reason for universality—"requires the most complete unity, thus the subordination and coordination of ends [*Zwecke*]—absolute, universal, and necessary purposiveness [*Zweckmäßigkeit*] of rules" (*VMP*, §119, p. 116). Here he seems to be assuming that every action has some distinct end, so a plurality of actions has a plurality of ends, but reason as such demands coherence among them. This might seem unproblematic, but Schmid then takes the step of assuming that such coherence among ends can only be provided by the subordination of all ends to a single, highest, or absolute end: "A free, rational being must relate all actions, all particular and relative ends and the means to their attainment to an end that is not only universal but also absolute, final, and self-sufficient [*selbständigen*]." He then further infers that "Everything that is an end is finally related to a being that sets forth [*vorsetzt*] ends, and to that power or that faculty by means of which it is capable of setting ends. This being is a *rational being*; this faculty is *reason*," and thus we get the imperative "*So act that you consider rational being* (e.g., humanity) in general, in your own person as well as in the person of every other, *always at the same time as an end, never merely as a means*" (*VMP*, §119, pp. 116–18). There seems to be no obvious justification for Schmid's transition from the necessary *coordination* of particular ends to their necessary *subordination* to a single highest end, and the equation of that in turn with rational being itself.But perhaps we can read him generously to be arguing that if it is a demand of reason that we *coordinate* our ends, then the power to set ends *rationally*, in a coordinated way, must be a necessary condition or constraint on all our setting of ends, and treating that power as a limiting condition on all other setting of ends is equivalent to treating it an end in its own right, indeed one that is superior to and limits all other ends. Setting ends, any ends whatsoever, would simply be what agents do, but setting them in a coordinated way and thus privileging above all else the power that can coordinate them would be what *rational* agents by definition do. This might indeed be a constructivist derivation of the Formula of Humanity.[12] Note also that Schmid clarifies something that is less than clear in Kant's own presentation, namely that "humanity" (*Menschheit*) is an *example* of rational being, as a matter of fact, the only one with which we are acquainted, but not necessarily *co-extensive* with it. However, Schmid fails to make it explicit at the outset of his argument that rationality in any one agent demands coordination of the ends of *all* agents, and that if the derivation of the second formula is not to be circular, that is, not just to presuppose that all rational beings are ends in themselves, then this must be regarded as an "absolute" demand of reason.

Finally, Schmid derives a "third formula" that neatly combines Kant's own two variant forms of what he himself calls the third formula, namely the "Formula of Autonomy" and the "Formula of the Empire of Ends." Schmid's version is "Each of your maxims includes in itself the will that it become a universal law for a system of rational beings and ends; [thus] *act in accordance with such maxims that you can give as yourself a law-giver for a realm of rational beings*" (*VMP*, §120, p. 119). If my insertion of "thus" into Schmid's sentence may be allowed, the sentence shows his inference of the imperative to legislate as if for a realm of ends to follow directly from the requirement of reason to act only in ways consistent not only with the universal validity of any particular maxims but also with the systematic coherence of all of one's maxims, all of everyone's maxims, and all of everyone's ends. To demand systematicity is also just what it is to be a rational agent, as Schmid has stated, and his argument, already quoted, that no further reason can be given for why we should be rational, follows immediately.

Schmid has thus dealt with his first two moral absolutes, the absolute law and the absolute goal of morality, in the course of expounding the three formulae of the categorical imperative. That leaves two other moral absolutes, the absolute incentive and the absolute conditions of the possibility of morality. He attempts to resolve the problem of responsibility for immoral action in what he clearly takes to be a Kantian way under the last rubric, but also provides his account of what Kant calls the highest good, i.e., the complete good for a natural yet rational will, under this rubric; and under the idea of an absolute incentive he provides his theory of

---

[12] But it is not identical to the "regress" argument of Christine Korsgaard, which we will consider in Chapter 16: it does not infer the unconditional value of humanity from the conditional value of any particular end (or "practical identity"), but infers that rationality itself is the supreme end from the assumption that all particular ends must be coordinated.

moral feeling. So a brief comment on each is in order before we turn to his treatment of the problem of responsibility. In both cases, he clearly presents Kant's ideas as deriving from his insight into the dual sensible and rational nature of human beings, thus perhaps compromising the generality of his critique of practical reason but not its interest. His treatment of moral feeling (*VMP*, §§146–66) begins with a definition of an incentive (*Triebfeder*) as the subjective ground of action, which may or may not coincide with a motivating ground (*Bewegungsgrund*) as an objectively valid ground for action: an individual's actual cause for acting may also be a valid reason for action, or it may not be (*VMP*, §146, p. 132). He then states that "a feeling, which is produced by the representation of [an] action itself insofar as it is moral (in its form) and depends on the law of reason, can yield a necessary and purely moral incentive" (*VMP*, §153, p. 140). His view is thus that moral feeling is produced by a cognitive state, the recognition that the moral law requires a prospective action or omission, and that this feeling, an effect of reason on sensibility, is in turn the proximate cause of action in the empirical world, or at least of the effect of the recognition of the moral law "on the sensible powers." As Schmid writes,

> The real [*eigentliche*] moral incentive is thus the moral law or reason itself, whose own proper activity, not aroused through any feeling nor dependent on any antecedent sentiment [*Empfindung*] as its determining ground, produces the sensible sentiment that has been described, and thereby sets the sensible drives themselves into an efficacity [*Würksamkeit*] that corresponds to the moral law itself. The feeling is the *consequence* of the free activity of the faculty of reason; [and] cause of the corresponding efficacity of the sensible powers.
>
> (*VMP*, §162, p. 145)

As he says at the start of the next main section, which begins with his discussion of the complete good for beings both natural and rational and thus links his discussion of moral feeling to the discussion of the highest good, moral feeling is the bridge between the rational and sensible natures of human beings: "By generating a feeling, the moral law obtains a necessary influence on a rational will that is sensibly affected" (*VMP*, §167, p. 148). This is precisely the position that Kant ultimately reaches in the Introduction to the Doctrine of Virtue of the *Metaphysics of Morals*,[13] but it is certainly not implausible to argue that Schmid presented this position more clearly in 1790 than Kant himself had done to that point in time, and that some of the arguments or misunderstandings over the place of feelings in Kant's conception of moral motivation that we will consider in the next section might have been averted had Kant himself been equally clear by

---

[13] See Guyer 2010b.

that date. Schmid's final remark about moral feeling is also entirely consistent with Kant's own conception of the relation between the phenomenal and the noumenal: in what is his first employment of Kant's distinction between appearances and things in themselves, as opposed to the common-sense distinction between sensibility and reason that he has thus far employed, he concludes that "The determination of the sensible by the non-sensible, of a feeling by a pure idea of reason, is however not a *cognizable* causal relation, where a temporally antecedent cause produces an effect that follows in time, but an effect out of freedom.... The feeling itself is cognizable; its ground is only thinkable; its origination is thus just as incomprehensible as is every free activity in general" (*VMP*, §166, p. 148). That is, things in themselves may be conceived but not known by means of spatio-temporal representations; thus we can conceive of moral feeling as in some abstract sense grounded in a pure reason that is noumenal, but we cannot understand this on our ordinary, temporal model of causation. Of course that is what Kant thought as well.

Schmid's claim that freedom is "incomprehensible" will be important in his reconciliation of responsibility with immorality, and is part of why I will argue that he did not mean to be criticizing but only to be explicating Kant. But before we get to that, finally, the promised word about the complete good. What is interesting here is that he adopts Kant's simplest and least interesting model of this concept, namely that it is just the sum of the individual agent's rational interest in morality combined with his natural interest in his *own* happiness, which must be brought together simply because of the agent's rational interest in self-consistency. The premise of Schmid's argument, quite close to Kant's own commencement of his argument in the Dialectic of the second *Critique* (*CPracR*, 5: 110–11), is:

> *Morality* is the *supreme* [*oberste*] *good*, which comprises the condition under which reason can recognize anything else as good; at the same time it is *complete* only for pure reason, and cannot take the place of other goods for the rational being in general, and for one that is capable of sensible pleasure and displeasure, thus for finite rational beings it is *incomplete* and inadequate for fulfilling all their rational (sensibly modified) wishes. *Well-being* must therefore be added, though not for itself, but subordinated to the *highest* [*höchsten*] good, and combined with it into a *complete good*, which corresponds to all the possible strivings of a rational being. (*VPM*, §171, pp. 150–1; see also §199, pp. 165–6)

On this account, a finite rational being's interest in happiness is a purely natural interest, and thus presumably an interest chiefly in his own happiness and only contingently in the happiness of others insofar as that happens to be part of his own. It is an interest that must be combined with although subordinated to our purely rational interest in morality, but it is not an interest that is generated by morality. Perhaps morality dictates an interest in the happiness of others under certain circumstances, but such an interest in happiness would not be what is referred to in the concept of the highest good. Under this concept, the rational finite individual is interested in the unification of his own happiness with his own complete morality, whatever the latter requires of him, and the "absolute" conditions of possibility in which he is interested are thus the conditions of the possibility of that combination. It is those conditions of possibility that Schmid describes as the postulates of practical reason: "A proposition that reason must assume to be true in order to conceive of the demands of the (unconditionally necessary) moral law as unifiable with the (conditionally necessary) rules of the same reason in its empirical employment is practically necessary, and on account of this relation can be designated as a *postulate of practical reason*" (*VMP*, §185, p. 156). Schmid then goes on to adduce the existence of a deity that can be the source of the laws of both nature and reason and thus of their unifiability (*VMP*, §203, p. 168) and of our own infinitely enduring existence to allow for the completion of progress toward the unification of our two moral and natural goals (*VMP*, §199, p. 166) as the conditions of the possibility of the unification of our moral and natural interests that have to be postulated.

It is certainly not unreasonable to read Kant's first two critiques as offering this approach to the highest good, and thus to see Schmid as simply expounding what he reasonably takes to be Kant's own doctrine. However, this is also the way of thinking about the highest good to which Garve objected in 1792, and perhaps his concern with the issue at that date, four years after the publication of Kant's *Critique of Practical Reason* but only two years after that of Schmid's, was triggered as much by Schmid's clear exposition of this version of the doctrine as by Kant's less clear account. Perhaps in trying so hard to argue against Garve in "Theory and Practice" that the happiness component of the highest good is the object of morality itself and not a merely natural desire that is extraneous to morality although it has to be constrained by it, Kant was trying to distance himself from the interpretation placed on his own words by his erstwhile defender Schmid, although without naming him.

In any case, the precise meaning of Kant's concept of the highest good as well as the propriety of its place in his pure moral philosophy would continue to be contested, for example by a nineteenth-century philosopher like Schopenhauer and a twentieth-century scholar such as Lewis White Beck.[14] But let us leave that issue for now and turn finally to the Schmid's other "absolute condition" of the

---

[14] See Beck 1960, ch. 13, esp. pp. 242–5. Beck had a well-known debate with John Silber over whether Kant's doctrine of the highest good added anything to his account of duties derivable from the categorical imperative, Silber arguing "pro" and Beck "con." See also Silber 1963 and other papers collected in Silber 2012. Beck was correct that the concept of the highest good does not add anything to the list of duties for human beings compiled in the *Metaphysics of Morals*, but that does not mean that it does not play an ineliminable role in Kant's argument for the postulates of pure practical reason.

possibility of morality, for it is here that he broaches the problem of reconciling freedom with immorality.

Schmid presents the problem of freedom as part of the problem of reconciling the natural and sensible aspects of humankind with the rational and moral aspects (*VMP*, §222, p. 184), for determinism is part of our theoretical conception of human beings as part of nature but freedom, at least in some sense, as we saw in Schmid's initial analysis, is equally part of our practical conception of rational agency. Determinism, he quickly argues, is the "only true and rational philosophy" of nature (*VMP*, §224, p. 187), so there can be no question that at least in some way we human beings are subject to determinism. There can also be no question that we are different from other animals, thus that our actions are not determined solely by "*the immediate impressions of the representation of an object on the sensible faculty of desire* (instinct)," but that "*rational considerations and motives [Bewegursachen] also have influence on human actions*" (*VMP*, §226, p. 188). The difficult question is only "*whether our will is determined solely and only by grounds of empirical reason*, i.e., of reason insofar as it proceeds by inference from sensible experiences and yields means and designs for sensibly determined ends, *or whether pure ideas of reason also produce a volition [Wollen]*, or *can* modify the same?" (*VMP*, §227, p. 189). In other words, is practical reason strictly Humean, able to determine means to ends that are given entirely empirically, thus are only contingent, or is it able to give the human being other ends and other than merely instrumental rules? But even if the latter is the case, Schmid immediately argues, it would not by itself breach the iron rule of determinism: if even pure practical reason is still part of nature, then our actions and omissions even when under the guidance of its ideas would still be as fully determined and predictable as when they are determined by anything else (*VMP*, §228, p. 191). This is what Schmid means by "intelligible fatalism," a term he uses only once and defines more precisely as "intelligible *natural fatalism*," i.e., a doctrine that even practical reason or intelligence is still part of nature, its operations thus determined inexorably by natural law. However, contrary to what may have been assumed either by Schmid's contemporaries or by more recent commentators,[15] this is not Schmid's own position. Rather, Schmid argues that this outcome may be *avoided* precisely by Kant's distinction between the phenomenal and the noumenal person or will. As soon as Schmid has described the "obvious conflict" between the determinism demanded by theoretical or "speculative" reason and the absolute freedom demanded by practical reason, he proceeds to their "possible unification" (*VMP*, §237, p. 196) by introducing Kant's distinction between "I, as an object of experience" and "I, as a thing in itself" (*VMP*, §§239–40, p. 193). He then argues, in orthodox fashion, that while my "sensible perceptible character" is subject to

---

[15] E.g., van Zantwijk 2010, p. 1035; Ameriks 2012, p. 73; and Bondeli 2012, p. 135.

time and therefore to determinism and in-principle predictability, my self as a thing in itself is not in time and can be the origin of a series of events in the phenomenal, temporal "without itself being determined to produce one member of this series (which I ground in its entirety) by an antecedent member" of it (*VMP*, §240, p. 199). On the contrary, "It is morally necessary, i.e., necessary because I regard the moral law as a law of my will, to represent myself as an absolutely free being," and there is no objection to doing so. The distinction between appearance and thing in itself means that absolute freedom "regarded merely theoretically is not impossible, although it is in no way demonstrable" (*VMP*, §244, p. 202). That is the entirely Kantian point that Schmid then develops at some length: absolute freedom is "rationally *conceivable*," "*not applicable to objects of experience*" but "*applicable to merely conceivable objects*," not theoretically cognized, explained, or comprehended, but necessarily assumed from a practical point of view (*VMP*, §258, pp. 212–15). Determinism may be demonstrated to be true *of appearances*, but to apply determinism to "the finite rational being, the human being," would be "indemonstrable," provable neither by an "analogy with experience" nor from the "*logical principle of the ground*," and above all "practically damaging," a subordination of reason "entirely to sensible nature," and an obstacle to my "virtuous striving" to become better than I may currently be (*VMP*, §260, pp. 220–3). In all of this, Schmid clearly means to be saying nothing other than what Kant himself had said, not to be criticizing Kant.

However, Schmid may nevertheless have laid himself open to the criticism that he is usually thought to have brought against Kant. For he says both that "I consider the moral law to be an essential law of my supersensible self" (*VMP*, §245, p. 203), which would seem to imply that at the noumenal level I have no choice but to act in accordance with the moral law and that insofar as my noumenal choice grounds my phenomenal self, my phenomenal self does not either, but also that my actions may not be influenced solely or at all by reason. Thus he says that neither moral nor immoral actions "can be ascribed to any coercion by temporal conditions," as would be the case if they were phenomenally determined, but that they represent rather "an expression or an omitted expression of the self-active faculty of reason" (*VMP*, §251, p. 206). Explicitly explaining the possibility of imputation, he continues that "Reason is the law-giving faculty of the human being and of every rational being," thus not itself capable of *legislating* immoral action, rather that "immoral action arises not from the efficacy of reason but from the activity of other (non-rational) powers" (*VMP*, §252, p. 207). Thus reason is never itself the source of immoral action, but neither can it be after all the causal law of the noumenal self—it may be the ideal or normative law *for* the noumenal self, but not the law *of* that self or of its phenomenal expression. Thus, Schmid thinks he has "saved" the "universal validity of the moral law for all actions of rational beings at any time ... by having come to recognize reason as a faculty for acting independently of all appearances in time," but that, precisely because this has been shown by employing the distinction between knowable appearances and thinkable but unknowable things in themselves, the answers to two questions remain "incomprehensibilities," namely "(1) how is reason and its self-activity possible? how does it produce appearances and natural laws?" and "(2) Why isn't the same self-activity, the same morality revealed in all perceivable actions? why is it sometimes the determining faculty of the will that is revealed, sometimes the determinable faculty of the will?" (*VMP*, §254, p. 203). That is, why does reason sometimes determine the will but sometimes the will is determined by something other than reason? Because of the distinction between appearances and things in themselves, we have no theoretical reason to deny these possibilities and every practical reason to affirm them, but again because of that distinction we have no way to explain them. Schmid thus does not mean by his phrase "intelligible fatalism" that the noumenal will is fated to act only in accordance with the moral law, but why it should ever not so act remains a mystery.

5.4. Reinhold

In 1792 both Reinhold and Kant took it upon themselves to respond to Schmid by introducing a distinction between the will as the faculty, equivalent to pure practical reason, that legislates the moral law, and the will as the power of choice that decides whether or not to act in accordance with the moral law, in Kant's terminology the distinction between *Wille* and *Willkühr*, although this may only verbally make room for the gap between the determination of the will by pure practical reason and its determination by something else that Schmid had exposed rather than genuinely explaining why the will should ever choose against the dictates of morality. Kant's own interpretation of his distinction between phenomenal causality and noumenal spontaneity is that this choice, like anything at the noumenal level, *must* remain inexplicable by any causal laws accessible to us.

Let us begin with Carl Leonhard Reinhold (1757–1823) before coming back to Kant himself.[16] While Reinhold's first series of *Letters on the Kantian Philosophy*,

---

[16] In eighteenth-century German orthography, Reinhold's first name was spelled with a "C," in contemporary German orthography with a "K." In spite of the fact that the "K" is now standardly used, e.g. in the current critical editions of Reinhold's works and correspondence, Reinhold 2007—and Reinhold 1983—I will avoid anachronism by using the original spelling. Reinhold has recently become the focus of intensive scholarly study, primarily in German but to some extent in English as well. For monographs, see Lazzari 2004 and Marx 2011; for collections of essays, Valenza 2006; di Giovanni 2010; and Stolz et al. 2012. For chapters in histories of German philosophy, see Beiser 1987, pp. 226–65; Pinkard 2002, pp. 96–104; di Giovanni 2005, pp. 91–107 and 118–25; and Jaeschke and Arndt 2012, pp. 38–58. Except for di Giovanni's, however, these works focus on Reinhold's attempt to refound Kant's theoretical philosophy on a single concept of representation as containing a reference to both

published in journal form in the *Teutsche Merkur* in 1786–7,[17] thus largely on the basis of the first edition of the *Critique of Pure Reason* and before the appearance of the *Critique of Practical Reason*, and then in revised book form in 1790 (after several pirated editions in 1789),[18] had focused on the large issue of the relation between reason and faith, the second series, published in the journal in 1790 and 1791 and in book form in 1792 (Reinhold 1792), concentrates on more details of Kant's moral philosophy, by then known from both the *Groundwork* and the *Critique of Practical Reason*. Much of the material in the second series of letters concerns the relation between morality in general and *Recht* or coercively enforceable law in particular, but the eighth letter is devoted to an "Elucidation of the concept of the freedom of the will" (*BKP2*, p. 262). That is our concern here.

Reinhold begins by observing that "determinists" (*BKP2*, p. 264) are not restricted to holding that all human actions are fully determined by selfish [*eigennützig*] drives for their own pleasure and avoidance of their own pain, but can also allow actions to be determined by "the absolute independence of reason in its practical laws from pleasure and pain" without breaching the general rule of causal law (p. 267). But in his view certain initially unnamed "friends of the Kantian philosophy" make a mistake if they take "this single characteristic of freedom," that it is rational, for the whole story, for if they treat determination by reason as just another form of causal determination, different from determination by pleasure and pain in its particular motive but just as deterministic, then there could be no possibility of an agent for whom reason is its causal law ever doing anything contrary to that law, anything irrational or immoral. As he boldly puts it,

> From the confusion between the to be sure self-active but nothing less than free action of practical reason—which gives nothing but the law—with the action of the will, which acts as the *pure* [will] only insofar as it freely grasps this law—nothing less than the impossibility of freedom for all *immoral* actions must result. As soon as it is assumed that the freedom of *pure volition* consists merely in the self-activity of practical reason, then one must also concede that *impure volition*, which is not effected through practical reason, is by no means free. Some of the foremost writers from the Kantian school have actually attempted to prove against Kant himself that in the case of immoral actions not merely the occasioning but even the *determining* ground of volition are to be sought outside the person, and that the will is free only in moral actions.   (*BKP2*, pp. 268–9)

object and subject; this is true also of Henrich 2003, pp. 113–39, and, in the context of Reinhold's reception in Tübingen, Henrich 2004, vol. 1, pp. 227–440. On Reinhold's position in the post-Kantian debate about freedom of the will, see Noller 2016, pp. 206–35, and Walsh 2020.

[17] The *Teutsche Merkur* was a major organ of the German Enlightenment, edited in Jena by Reinhold's father-in-law, Christoph Martin Wieland.

[18] Reinhold 2005. For details on the publication history of the letters, see p. x. Ameriks and Hebbeler present the letters first in their original journal form, and then provide the almost equally long additions in the 1790 book edition (101 pages to 120 pages) as an appendix.

If the free will is identified with pure practical reason, the normative law of pure practical reason becomes the causal law of the free will, and the free will can will nothing immoral. Reinhold clearly thinks that this view and its consequence, which he is about to reject, are not Kant's own view, so that in raising the problem of the possibility of free but immoral actions he does not mean to criticize Kant, but rather to defend him from other, misguided supporters.

Having initially attributed the problematic result to unnamed friends of the Kantian philosophy, Reinhold then names names, explicitly criticizing Schmid (*BKP2*, p. 269) as one who takes the freedom of the will to be the "dependence of the will on reason immediately determining it, [by] the pure moral law," and who thus equates freedom of the will with the "autonomy of the will." By means of this identification, however, "freedom is assigned only to the *pure* will and is consequently denied of the *impure*" or immoral will (p. 271). Reinhold appeals to Schmid's definitions of freedom in his *Dictionary for the Easier Use of the Kantian Writings* for his attribution of this view to him, although as we saw this is not where Schmid had ended up in his *Essay towards a Moral Philosophy*, where "intelligible fatalism" was not his final position but rather a threat to be avoided by insisting upon inexplicable but incontrovertible transcendent freedom. Perhaps Reinhold divined in 1792 that this was not a position that Schmid would sustain; at least in the fourth edition of his dictionary, in 1798, Schmid adds to his definitions that "*The freedom of the faculty of choice* [*Willkühr*] cannot (with *Reinhold*) be defined through the capacity of choice to act either for or against the law (*libertas indifferentiae*)."[19] As we will see later, Schmid could have been influenced by Kant's own attack upon Reinhold in the Introduction to the *Metaphysics of Morals* of the previous year to retract his earlier insistence upon what is after all a form of *libertas indifferentiae*, under the name of transcendent or absolute freedom. But whether or not the dreaded consequence was correctly attributed to Schmid in 1792, Reinhold proposes to avoid the problem by clearly distinguishing between pure practical reason as the source of the moral law and the ability to choose or decide *whether or not* to act in accordance with that law. In the first instance he does that by making it clear that what practical reason offers is a "restriction" or a norm for the will, but not a causal law for it:

> The dependence of the will on practical reason is so little freedom from anything whatsoever for a will that it is rather a *restriction* of it; but a restriction by which freedom is not canceled [*aufgehoben*], for it posits only the freedom to follow or overstep the law of practical reason. Practical reason only prescribes the law, its

---

[19] Schmid 1798, p. 251. In the 2nd edition of the *Dictionary*, Schmid had defined "practical freedom" in the "negatively determined sense" as "dependence of the will on reason, which determines it immediately, on the pure moral law; autonomy of the will" (Noller and Walsh 2022, p. 64). This is the kind of passage that Reinhold seems to have in mind.

execution is up to freedom. Only the latter, not the former, acts *morally*, and the autonomy of the will does not consist merely in the giving of the law by reason, in which the person is to be sure self-active but acts involuntarily [*unwillkührlich*], but in the self-determination of the will for this law, to which it binds itself.

(*BKP2*, p. 271)

Without using our contemporary terminology, Reinhold here clearly treats the moral law legislated by pure reason as a norm to which the will ought to conform but which it must decide to do, in which case it is moral, but can also decide to reject, in which case it is obviously not moral. Autonomy, he also makes clear, is not a condition automatically established by pure reason, but rather a state that must be achieved by the will, in which it succeeds in making the norm held before it by pure reason the actual law of its conduct—although it could do otherwise. It may also be noted about this passage that although Reinhold uses the ordinary adverb *unwillkührlich*, he does not here make his point by distinguishing a faculty of *Willkühr* from either pure reason or the will; he just distinguishes between the will and reason rather than identifying them, ascribing decision (*Entschluß*) to the will rather than to reason. Schmid had also distinguished between them in his *Essay towards a Moral Philosophy*. Both therefore distinguish themselves from Ulrich, who portrayed Kant as having ascribed choice or decision to pure reason itself, which he thought incoherent.[20]

In the next paragraph, Reinhold makes the same point by distinguishing between pure reason and the *person* as the subject of actual choice. Here he defines freedom of the will as "The capacity [*Vermögen*] of the person to determine himself to the satisfaction or non-satisfaction of a desire either in accordance with the practical law or contrary to it," and explains that it thus consists "neither in the mere independence of the will from coercion by instinct . . . nor in the mere independence of practical reason from everything that is not itself . . . but also *in the independence of the person from necessitation by practical reason itself.*" And then here, as Kant would do, he introduces the term *Willkühr* as a name for the faculty that can choose whether to act in accordance with the moral law or against it: "In the *negative* sense [freedom] comprises these *three* forms of independence; and in the *positive* sense it is the faculty of self-determination through choice [*Willkühr*] for or against the practical law" (*BKP2*, pp. 271–2). Here Reinhold appropriates but, it might be argued, also subtly revises Kant's distinction between negative and positive conceptions of freedom at the outset of section III of the

[20] I agree with Martin Bondeli that Reinhold's distinction between reason and will as the faculty of decision (*Entschluß*) differs only terminologically from Kant's distinction in the *Religion* and the *Metaphysics of Morals* between *Wille* as equivalent to pure practical reason and *Willkühr* as the power of choice. See Bondeli 2012, pp. 134–6.

Groundwork precisely in order to avoid the problem about the possibility of free yet immoral action that seems to arise there more obviously than in any of Kant's other moral writings to date. There Kant had said that freedom negatively defined is the property of the will to be determined "independently of alien causes" and that freedom positively defined is the property of the will to be determined by a law of its own, but had also defined the will's own law as "a causality in accordance with immutable laws but of a special kind" (*G*, 4: 446), namely, of course, the moral kind. Reinhold borrows the terminology, but calls the will's independence from determination by mere instinct a negative property and its ability to choose for *or against* the moral law its positive property.

Reinhold also borrows the terminology of his (supposed) opponent Schmid in calling the freedom of the will as he has defined it "absolute" freedom: "*Absolute freedom*," he says, "belongs to the will neither insofar as it acts as a *pure* nor insofar as it acts as an *impure* will, but rather insofar as it can act in both ways [*Eigenschaften*]" (*BKP2*, p. 273). It might seem as if he means to be hoisting Schmid by his own petard by appropriating Schmid's favored term to mean the opposite of what he thinks Schmid meant by it, but in fact he seems to mean by "absolute freedom" precisely the same thing that Schmid had meant: the indemonstrable but entirely conceivable property of the will to act either in accordance with pure reason or contrary to it (*VPM*, §258, pp. 211–12, 214–15). It may be noted, however, that while Schmid had said that absolute freedom could be attributed to but not demonstrated of the *supersensible* will, Reinhold has not mentioned that part of Kantian orthodoxy, nor does he throughout the remainder of the eighth letter. The most significant difference between Reinhold and Kant will be that Kant appeals to his transcendental idealism to secure the possibility of the freedom of the power of choice or *Willkühr*, while Reinhold does not: he just asserts it as a "fact of consciousness."[21]

As already suggested, Reinhold clearly meant his position to be a defense of Kant, even from his own self-appointed "friends," not a critique of Kant. Thus he says that "Kant has too often and too expressly asserted that he acknowledged even immoral actions to be freely willed [*freywillig*] for anyone to be able to hold that he has restricted freedom merely to the *pure will*... and wanted the will to be regarded as nothing but the *causality of reason* in the case of desire" (*BKP2*, p. 285). Reinhold does not cite of any of Kant's supposedly frequent assertions of that point, and there is certainly language at least in Kant's *Groundwork* that seems to assert precisely the opposite (above all *G*, 4: 446).[22] He does try to prevent the appearance of any conflict with Kant in another passage that is worth quoting in full:

---

[21] See also Bondeli 2012, pp. 137–8, and Marx 2011, pp. 273–4.
[22] Fugate 2012 emphasizes this sort of language in Kant.

The will ceases to be free if one considers it one-sidedly, and lets its nature subsist either solely in its relation to unselfish drives or solely in relation to selfish drives, if one conceives of it as *subjected* either the practical law or to the natural law of desire. Through either of these two laws it would be independent of the other, but through the faculty of self-determination it is dependent on itself alone. Without the practical law it would depend on the mere natural law of desire, and would not only not be free, but would not even be a *will*, but would be an involuntary [*unwillkührlich*] desire, and without the natural law of desire it would depend on the mere practical law, mere practical reason itself, and consequently would be self-active, but not free and would not be a *will*, a faculty for determining itself to the satisfaction or non-satisfaction of a desire. In this respect the assertion of the *Critique of Practical Reason* "that the concept of freedom first receives its reality through the consciousness of the moral law" is indisputably true. The person can only be conscious of the faculty to determine himself insofar as he is conscious of the faculty to determine himself in accordance with two different laws, and consequently insofar as he is conscious of these different laws themselves. But precisely for that reason freedom can by no means consist in the faculty of following only one of those laws, and that Kantian assertion can by no means have the sense "that the reality of freedom depends on the consciousness of the moral law *alone*." (*BKP2*, pp. 274–5)

Reinhold recognizes that Kant is making an argument about the *ratio cognoscendi* rather than *ratio essendi* of freedom in the *Critique of Practical Reason*, that he has argued that our consciousness of the moral law is the basis for our belief in the possibility of our freedom to act in accordance with it, which can never be attested to by mere experience. But since Reinhold understands freedom to be nothing less than the freedom to choose to act in accordance with the moral law or contrary to it, a choice that he describes as that between unselfish and selfish "drives" (Reinhold would hand the term "drive" on to Fichte), he assumes that we can know that we have such freedom only from our consciousness of both the moral law and merely natural laws of desire: if we were conscious of only one or the other, we would not infer that we have genuine freedom, but could only infer that we are entirely dependent on the one law or the other, that it completely determines our action. Disingenuously or not, he takes Kant to mean the same thing, thus to mean that it is our consciousness of the moral law *as an alternative* to the natural law of desire that is the *ratio essendi* of our freedom. As we will see, five years later Kant would deny that this is what he meant. But first, we must look at Kant's argument in part one of *Religion within the Boundaries of Mere Reason*, published about the same time as Reinhold's second series of letters, where it looks as if Kant is taking exactly the same position that Reinhold has taken.

5.5. Kant's Response to Reinhold

The first essay of *Religion*, "Concerning the indwelling of the evil principle alongside the good, or of the radical evil in human nature," submitted to the *Berlinische Monatsschrift* in February, 1792 and published in the April edition, argues for the possibility of human conversion from evil to good, and presupposes the existence of an ability to choose between evil and good throughout. Kant does not discuss his own previous views on freedom of the will or any criticisms of them, and makes no suggestion that he is in any way departing from what he has previously held rather than simply applying it. Kant rarely admitted that he had changed his mind, although he was sometimes willing to concede that he had clarified a previous argument (e.g., *CPuR*, Bxxxvii–xxxviii). But with the exception of one passage, Kant's position throughout the essay is that we have the—to be sure inscrutable and inexplicable—ability to choose between good and evil and that we always have this ability no matter what our prior choices may have been. Thus while the moral law is the norm for our power of choice, the law to which we ought to choose to subordinate all self-interest, it cannot be the causal law for our power of choice, the only law that we can freely choose to observe. So there does seem to be a fundamental difference between Kant's position in the *Religion* in 1792 and the position that he took at least at the outset of section III of the *Groundwork* in 1785.[23] Kant's position in *Religion* is often described as depending upon a contrast between *Wille*, a legislative faculty that is identical to practical reason and thus can indeed only legislate the moral law, and *Willkühr*, the faculty of power or choice, an executive power that can choose *either* to prioritize the moral law offered to it by *Wille* or to subordinate that law to the principle of self-love, acting in accordance with the moral law when that is consistent with self-love but not acting from the moral law or making the moral law its fundamental maxim. In fact, Kant does not make an explicit contrast between *Wille* and *Willkühr* in part one of *Religion*, but instead simply asserts the absolute spontaneity of *Willkühr* or our unrestricted freedom to make a choice (*Wahl*) between making the moral law or self-love our supreme principle, that is, between subordinating self-love to morality (for morality hardly requires that we always thwart self-love) or subordinating morality to self-love. But if *Wille* is identified with pure practical reason, as Kant had done in the *Groundwork* and *Critique of Practical Reason*, then a distinction between *Wille* and *Willkühr* is implicit even if not explicit.

---

[23] Fugate 2012 argues that Kant's position on freedom in the *Metaphysics of Morals* is not a radical departure from his position in the *Groundwork*, and thus cannot be the same as Reinhold's position in 1792. This interpretation seems to me to be incompatible with Kant's argument in the *Religion*, however that is to be reconciled with his remarks in the *Metaphysics of Morals* (6: 226–7), to which I will return below.

Kant's argument, such as it is, is simply that an ability to choose freely between good and evil, between the superiority of morality and the superiority of self-love, is presupposed by the imputability of evil, the fact that we are rightly held responsible for our evil deeds as well as for our good ones. This is clear from the outset of the essay. Kant first maintains that "We call a human being evil... not because he performs actions that are evil (contrary to law), but because these are so constituted that they allow the inference of evil maxims in him" (*RBMR*, 6: 20). Just as actions that are in outward conformity with the moral law might be performed out of self-love in circumstances in which self-love contingently calls for the same actions that would be required by the moral law, so actions that outwardly violate the moral law might do so only accidentally, having actually been intended to comply with the moral law. The real locus of moral good and evil is thus not the actions themselves but the maxims on the basis of which they were performed, indeed, as Kant subsequently makes clear, the agent's *fundamental* maxim, the overall intention either *always* to prioritize morality over self-love or conversely the overall intention to subordinate morality to self-love *whenever* that seems desirable. (*RBMR*, 6: 36). Kant's claim is then that the choice of fundamental maxim or "subjective ground" underlying "the exercise of the human being's freedom in general" in any particular choice of maxim and action "must in turn always be a deed [*Actus*] of freedom (for otherwise the use or abuse of the human being's power of choice [*Willkühr*] with respect to the moral law could not be imputed to him, nor could the good or evil in him be called moral)" (*RBMR*, 6: 21). It is now simply the premise of Kant's argument that responsibility for either good or evil presupposes the freedom to choose between good and evil, whether or not this is inconsistent with what he had previously held. Kant reiterates the point with equal clarity at the start of the General Remark that concludes part one of the *Religion*: "The human being must make or have made *himself* into whatever he is or should become in a moral sense, good or evil. Either must be an effect of his free power of choice [*Willkühr*], for otherwise it could not be imputed to him and, consequently, he could be neither *morally* good nor evil" (*RBMR*, 6: 44).[24]

The point is likewise repeated several times between the beginning and the end of part one, in ways that raise additional issues. Several passages make the basic point that imputability implies freedom while adding that the evil that results from the choice to subordinate morality to self-love is both "radical" and "innate." First, Kant introduces the idea of a "propensity" (*Hang*) to evil. This is somewhat

---

[24] Both early in his career and late, from Wood 1970 to Wood 2020, Allen W. Wood has contributed more to our understanding of Kant's *Religion* than any other commentator. However, I cannot accept his "anthropological" interpretation of Kant's account of evil, that "evil has its *source* in social comparisons and antagonisms" and that "Kant explicitly attributes the corruption of human nature to the *social* condition of human beings," in Wood 1999, p. 288. Such "anthropological" facts may be prominent in Kant's empirical, deterministic etiology of evil, but that story has to be compatible with the completely free choice to subordinate morality to self-love at the noumenal level for the account to be Kant's.

confusing, for Kant initially defines a propensity as "the subjective ground of the *possibility* of an inclination (habitual desire, *concupiscentia*), insofar as this possibility is contingent for humanity in general" (*RBMR*, 6: 29, emphasis added), which suggests that it is merely the *possibility* of evil that might then turn out to be innate and radical in human beings. This makes perfectly good sense if the *possibility* of choosing immorality is simply the complement of the possibility of choosing morality, in other words, if freedom itself is simply the possibility of choosing between good and evil rather than the necessity of choosing good. However, Kant then complicates matters when he suggests that the propensity to evil is not in fact the mere possibility of choosing the evil fundamental maxim of the superiority of self-love to morality, but rather the actual choice of this maxim. This comes in the course of his argument that, although human beings are free to choose either good or evil, as a matter of fact, "in view of the multitude of woeful examples that the experience of human *deeds* parades before us," it seems that all actually do choose evil, but nevertheless all remain free to choose good:

> We may presuppose evil as subjectively necessary in every human being, even the best. Now, since this propensity [*Hang*] itself can be considered morally evil, hence not a natural predisposition [*Naturanlage*] but something a human being can be held accountable for, consequently must consist in maxims of the power of choice [*Willkühr*] contrary to the [moral] law [*gesetzwidrig*] and yet, because of freedom, such maxims must be viewed as accidental, a circumstance that would not square with the universality of evil at issue unless their supreme subjective ground were not in all cases somehow entwined with humanity itself and, as it were, rooted in it; so we can call this ground a natural propensity [*natürlichen Hang*] to evil, and since it must nevertheless always come about through one's own fault [*da er doch immer selbstverschuldet sein muß*], we can further even call it a *radical* innate *evil* in human nature (not any the less brought upon us by ourselves).   (*RBMR*, 6: 32)

Now it is the actual rather than possible disposition toward evil, that is, choice of the evil subordination of maxims, that Kant calls a propensity, but the key point remains that this choice must still be considered a free choice, something for which we are ourselves responsible (*selbstverschuldet*) and have brought upon ourselves—although Kant's ultimate point will be that precisely because we have brought this evil upon ourselves by ourselves, we can also undo it by ourselves. This evil is "innate" in the dual sense that it is essential to our freedom itself that it is a freedom to choose between good and evil and that it is not essential to our freedom or to our species that we choose evil but nevertheless is an empirical fact that we pretty much all do choose evil. In a further key passage, Kant again insists that our freedom to choose between good and evil is a necessary condition of the imputability of evil and then explicates what he means by the otherwise unexplained term "radical" in the previous passage:

> Now if a propensity to [the subordination of morality to self-love] does lie in human nature, then there is in the human being a natural propensity to evil; and this propensity itself is morally evil, since it must ultimately be sought in a free power of choice, and hence is imputable. This evil is *radical*, since it corrupts the ground of all maxims; as natural propensity, it is also not to be *extirpated* through human forces, for this could only happen through good maxims—something that cannot take place if the subjective supreme ground of all maxims is presupposed to be corrupted. Yet it must equally be possible to *overcome* this evil, for it is found in the human being as a freely acting being.
>
> (*RBMR*, 6: 37, translation of final clause modified)

This passage represents the core of Kant's argument in part one of the *Religion*: evil is radical in the sense that it consists in the choice of a fundamental maxim—the subordination of morality to self-love—that underlies all of an agent's other maxims, and it is radical in another sense in that its possibility is inherent in the very nature of freedom of choice itself. For that reason the possibility of evil cannot be extirpated, but for the very same reason the actuality of evil can also always be overturned. If the very nature of freedom means that there is always a possibility of choosing evil, then it also means that there is also always a possibility of choosing good. The nature of our power of choice—*Willkühr*—is precisely that it is always a power to choose between good and evil, between the moral law given to us by pure practical reason and the self-love given to us by nature, or one aspect of our nature. Historically speaking, Kant's position that human beings are always free to choose between good and evil on their own is also radical in constituting a radical departure from the doctrines of pre-election and grace that are essential to every form of official Protestantism, whether Lutheran, Calvinist, or otherwise,[25] and would get Kant into serious hot water with the Prussian establishment.[26]

Now the conclusion that we always have the power to choose between good and evil, including the power to choose good even though we have already, apparently always already chosen evil, seems to conflict with a suggestion on Kant's part that the choice of evil is innate and radical in a further sense, namely that everyone gets just *one* chance to choose between good and evil. In a passage that I previously quoted in part, Kant says:

---

[25] See Hall 2019, pp. 23–8.
[26] For a brief account of the trouble with the Prussian crown that the *Religion* caused for Kant, see Kant 1996b, editors' Introduction, pp. xix–xxii, and translator's (di Giovanni's) Introduction to *RBMR*, pp. 41–8.

To have one or the other disposition by nature as an innate characteristic does not mean here that the disposition has not been earned by the human being who harbors it, i.e., that he is not its author, but rather that it has been earned in time (that he has been the one way or the other *always, from his youth on*). The disposition, i.e., the first subjective ground of the adoption of his maxims, can only be a single one, and it applies to the entire use of freedom universally. This disposition too, however, must be adopted through the free power of choice [*Willkühr*], for otherwise it could not be imputed.

He then continues to explain that by calling the disposition (to evil) "a charac-teristic of the power of choice that pertains to it by nature" he only means that because we cannot derive the choice of fundamental maxim from any other, more fundamental maxim, and indeed cannot explain the choice at all, we treat it as if it were a matter of nature "even though the disposition is in fact grounded in freedom" and must be in order to be imputable (*RBMR*, 6: 25). The passage thus begins and ends with Kant's statement of his position throughout part one of *Religion*, that since it is imputable the human choice of evil can only be a product of the absolute freedom of the human power of choice. But in between, Kant makes it sound as if the maxim of subordinating morality to self-love must not only be fundamental or radical in the sense of underlying all of one's choices of more particular maxims at so to speak any one moment or stage of life, but that is further single or unique in that one gets to make the fundamental choice of maxim only once, indeed in youth, and has no chance to reverse this choice. The suggestion seems to be that since one's disposition "has not been earned in time," it must have been chosen in youth, and cannot be reversed.

But this would fly in the face of Kant's message throughout *Religion*, and moreover is not entailed by his transcendental idealist explanation of the possi-bility of freedom of choice. This is that, since the self as it is in itself is not subject to the temporality that pervades the appearance of the self to itself, so the ordinary, temporal conception of causation and the determinism that it grounds need not, indeed cannot be applied to the self as it is in itself, and there is at least room for the conception of it as absolutely spontaneous, not causally determined in its choice by antecedent events, a possibility the actuality of which is then attested by our awareness of our obligation under the moral law and the recognition that we must at least be able to fulfill that obligation. But the non-temporality of noumenal choice does not imply that each agent gets to make only *one* such choice; as I previously suggested, it implies only that *everything* about noumenal choice, including its frequency, is completely *non-representable* and therefore *indetermi-nate* from a theoretical point of view, and that whatever we can say about noumenal choice, including what we can say about its frequency, can be said only on *practical* grounds. And what practical grounds tell us is that, since we are *always* aware of our obligation under the moral law, we must *always* be free to choose that law over self-love, even if we have previously chosen self-love over the moral law—*even if we cannot represent what that continued possibility of choice by our noumenal selves would be like by means of any temporal model, since time is only the form of our empirical intuition of our selves.* The possibility of multiple noumenal choices is just as "inscrutable" as why any particular noumenal choice is made one way or the other, but is nevertheless implied, or perhaps better said demanded, by our inexorably continuing obligation under the moral law.

Kant makes this clear in a subsequent passage in which he argues against applying any of our normal temporal representations to our choice of maxims, thus against thinking of that choice as taking place at any determinate moments or moment of time, and instead explains that what he now calls the "originality" of our choice of fundamental maxims means precisely that we are *always* free to make this choice anew, *as if* for the first time, no matter what has gone before in our phenomenal lives—and that *this* is what pure practical reason tells us.[27] He begins this crucial passage by telling us that "first origin" can mean "either *origin according to reason*, or *origin according to time*," and then argues:

> If an effect is referred to a cause which is however bound to it according to the laws of freedom, as is the case with moral evil, then the determination of the power of choice to the production of this effect is thought of as bound to its determining ground not in time but merely in the representation of reason; it cannot be derived from some *preceding* state or other, as must always occur, on the other hand, whenever the evil action is referred to its natural cause as *event* in the world. To look for the temporal origin of free actions as free (as though they were natural effects) is therefore a contradiction;[28] and hence [it is] also [a contradiction to look for] the temporal origin of the moral constitution of the human being, for constitution here means the *exercise* of freedom which (just like the determining ground of the free power of choice) must be sought in the representation of reason alone....
>
> Every evil action must be so considered, whenever we seek its rational origin, as if the human being had fallen into it directly from the state of innocence. For whatever his previous behavior may have been, whatever the natural causes influencing him, whether they are inside or outside him, his action is yet free and not determined through any of these causes; hence the action can and must always be judged as an *original* exercise of his power of choice.

---

[27] My interpretation thus differs from Wood's, which is that the "non-temporality" of the choice of fundamental maxim means that it is lifelong commitment of the phenomenal self, not anything noumenal (e.g., Wood 2020, p. 289). It is not clear to me how this can model the possibility of a radical change of heart to which Kant is committed, even if we cannot represent this change in our ordinary temporal terms.

[28] This is why Wood's anthropological account of radical evil cannot be Kant's own account.

This in turn means that "However evil a human being has been right up to the moment of an impending free action (evil even habitually, as second nature), his duty to better himself was not just in the past: it is still his duty *now*; he must therefore be capable of it." Kant concludes that "we cannot inquire into the origin in time of this deed but must inquire only into its origin in reason" (*RBMR*, 6: 39–41). We cannot appeal to our ordinary assumptions about temporality to tell us *anything* about our freedom, thus we cannot appeal to it to tell us that we are incapable of choosing morality even if we have already chosen self-love. We can appeal only to reason, and reason tells us without regard to temporality at all that as long as we are obligated by the moral law we are also free to choose to observe the moral law, no matter what has gone before in our temporal lives, indeed no matter how often we have chosen evil before in those lives.

Throughout part one of *Religion*, therefore, Kant insists, like Reinhold in his simultaneous eighth letter, that freedom is freedom to choose between right and wrong, although Kant does not put this in terms of a contrast between *Wille* and *Willkühr* but rather simply in terms of the absolute freedom of *Willkühr* to choose between the law of pure practical reason and the law of self-love. Notice that I say *pure* practical reason: one key passage in part one of *Religion* makes it clear that Kant does not think that our possession of reason in *any* form, for example, merely instrumental reason, entails our obligation under the moral law, but only our possession of *pure* practical reason does so. This passage is Kant's footnote to his distinction between the original predispositions of mankind to "humanness"[29] and to "personality." In this passage Kant treats humanness as something like the possession of merely instrumental reason,[30] while personality is defined as "the susceptibility to respect for the moral law *as of itself a sufficient incentive to the power of choice*" (*RBMR*, 6: 27), and he then observes that "We cannot consider this predisposition as already included in the concept of the preceding one," the disposition to humanness, "but must necessarily treat it as a special predisposition. For from the fact that a being has reason it does not follow that...this reason contains a faculty for determining the power of choice unconditionally...The most rational being in the world...might apply the most rational reflection to... objects—about what concerns their greatest sum as well as the means for attaining the goal determined through them—without thereby even suspecting the possibility of such a thing as the absolutely moral law" (*RBMR*, 6: 26n.). In other words, a being could have instrumental reason without having pure, moral reason; our obligation

---

[29] Kant's term here is *Menschheit*, not *Menschlichkeit*. Jens Timmermann has suggested translating this as "humaneness" rather than "humanity." But since to be humane is always something good, whereas Kant is talking about a disposition that can be used for good but can also be perverted, it would seem better to use "humanness" here: it is precisely human to be capable of evil as well as good.

[30] Although in this passage Kant seems to have Rousseau rather than Hume in mind, and his conception of humanity here is perhaps closer to Rousseau's conception of self-love or *amour-propre*, or prideful comparison of oneself to others—something Kant thinks is never morally warranted.

FREEDOM AND IMMORALITY 167

under the moral law is not a general condition of rationality as such, but a self-standing obligation, given to us by pure practical reason and not by practical reason in general. This is indeed why Kant had always rejected Wolff's project of a "universal practical philosophy in favor of his own "metaphysics of morals" and "critique of pure practical reason" (see *G*, 4: 390).

The footnote from which I have just quoted concludes with the statement that the moral law "is the only law that makes us conscious of the independence of our power of choice from determination by all other incentives (of our freedom) and thereby also of the imputability [*Zurechnungsfähigkeit*] of all our actions" (*RBMR*, 6: 26n.). Although Kant's insistence throughout the *Religion* that the freedom of our power of choice is essentially a freedom to choose between good and evil may be an unacknowledged departure from his earlier work, certainly from the opening of section III of the *Groundwork*, this claim does not seem to differ from his assertion in the *Critique of Practical Reason* that our awareness of the moral law is the way we become aware of our freedom, what Kant considers our *ratio cognoscendi* of our freedom. This statement can certainly be interpreted to mean that, unless we were aware of our obligation under the moral law *as well as* being aware of various inclinations toward our own gratification, we would not be able to become aware that we are free to choose between subordinating the gratification of our inclinations to the moral law and the reverse. To know that we ought to be moral may be sufficient to entail that we know that we can *choose* to be moral and thus are absolutely free (although as we saw Ulrich denied this), but it does not entail that we *will* be moral and thus that we cannot also freely choose to be evil—"ought" implies "can" but not "does." The doctrine that the moral law is the *ratio cognoscendi* of our freedom thus seems to be entirely consistent with the position of part one of *Religion* as thus far described. Indeed, it could be argued that Kant's characterization of the form in which the moral law presents itself to us as a *categorical imperative* always entailed the possibility of our choosing to act contrary to the moral law and our awareness of that possibility (see *G*, 4: 412, 414).

One sentence, however, might seem to threaten this conclusion. Just before he describes our fundamental moral choice as whether to subordinate self-love to the moral law or vice versa, Kant says that "To think of oneself as a freely acting being, yet as exempted from the one law commensurate to such a being (the moral law), would amount to the thought of a cause operating without any law at all (for the determination according to a natural law is abolished on account of freedom); and this is a contradiction" (*RBMR*, 6: 35). This suggests that if our freedom is not to be governed by mere laws of nature as causal laws, the only alternative is that it be governed by the moral law as its causal law. This in turn sounds just like what Kant said at the outset of *Groundwork* III (4: 446). Yet it cannot be what he means here. For what he next says is:

even though the existence of this propensity to evil in human nature can be established through experiential demonstrations of the actual resistance in time of the human power of choice against the law, these demonstrations still do not teach us the real nature of that propensity or the ground of this resistance; that nature, rather, since it has to do with a relation of the free power of choice (the concept of which is not empirical) to the moral law (of which the concept is equally purely intellectual), must be cognized *a priori* according to the laws of freedom (of obligation and imputability).　(*RBMR*, 6: 35)

Even if our awareness of our *obligation* under the moral law is the *ratio cognoscendi* of our freedom, the condition for the possibility of *imputability* gives us a priori knowledge that our freedom is the freedom to choose between good and evil. The two claims should be entirely compatible: only if we know that we should live up to the moral law can we know that we are free to do so, but that we know that we are responsible for our evil as well as for our good teaches us that our freedom is nothing less than the freedom to choose between good and evil.

Thus it seems as if Kant ends up in *Religion* in exactly the same place that Reinhold ended up in his eighth letter of the same time, and indeed, whether or not either of them realized it, in pretty much the same place as Schmid had ended up two years earlier—all of them were in fact rejecting the conclusion of Ulrich that, while the moral law is certainly an ideal for us, we have no reason to think we can all always live up to this ideal. In an ensuing comedy of errors, however, Kant seems to have been led by a desire to distance himself from Reinhold to distance himself from the view of freedom that he had just so clearly expounded in *Religion*.

Reinhold published a lengthy review of *Religion within the Boundaries of Mere Reason* in the *Allgemeine Literatur-Zeitung* in March 1794, in which he took Kant to be asserting the same position that he had himself maintained in his eighth letter, namely that of the "*unconditional freedom* of the will [*des Willens*]."[31] On his account, Kant "presupposes a freedom in the person, which must be conceived as just as different from the self-activity of practical reason as it is from being determined by pleasure or displeasure," and which consists in the faculty "to determine oneself *either* through the law *or* contrary to it, through pleasure or displeasure, to the satisfaction or non-satisfaction of a desire" (Reinhold 1794, column 684). He thus had nothing critical to say about Kant's treatment of freedom of the will in *Religion*, or anything else—the review is entirely positive. Nor did Kant see any need to reply to the review, if in fact he read it; he did write to Reinhold only two weeks after it appeared, but only to congratulate Reinhold on his acceptance of a professorship in Kiel and to apologize for not having read his book on natural law from the previous year—he makes no mention of the

---

[31] Reinhold 1794. For the attribution of the unsigned review to Reinhold, see di Giovanni 2005, p. 353.

review at all.[32] (Although since the *Allgemeine Literatur-Zeitung* was a strongly pro-Kantian journal, Kant probably did read it.) The next and last surviving letter from Reinhold is from a year later, and merely recommends a student to Kant,[33] nor does Kant's final surviving letter to Reinhold a couple of months later make any mention of the review.[34] So there is no evidence that Kant saw any daylight between Reinhold's position on the freedom of the will and his own.

However, in the Introduction to the *Metaphysics of Morals* published with its first part, *The Metaphysical Foundations of Right*, in 1797, Kant criticizes "some" who "have tried to define" freedom of choice (*Willkühr*) as "the ability to make a choice [*Wahl*] for or against the law (*libertas indifferentiae*)" (*MM*, Introduction, 6: 226). This has been taken to be intended as a rejection of Reinhold's position in the eighth letter of five years earlier,[35] on which Kant had not previously commented, and indeed the language Kant uses is very much Reinhold's[36]—although if Kant now rejects Reinhold's position from 1792, then he also seems to reject his own position of that year! So it is necessary to examine Kant's grounds for rejecting Reinhold's position to see whether he has good grounds for rejecting his own previous position.

Kant's criticism comes in a section of the Introduction devoted to the "Preliminary Concepts of the Metaphysics of Morals," which he subtitles, now in an homage to Wolff although in the *Groundwork* Kant had rejected precisely this terminology (*G*, 4: 390), as *Philosophicia practica universalis* (*MM*, Introduction, 6: 221).[37] Kant begins this section by defining the concept of freedom as a "pure rational concept" that is entirely "transcendent" for theoretical philosophy, since it is not empirically attested but neither is it an a priori theoretical concept. In other words, theoretical philosophy has nothing to say about freedom, and everything that we can and must say about freedom depends upon practical philosophy. Kant then goes on to define the concepts of moral law, obligation, and duty and to give a brief recapitulation of his derivation of the categorical imperative, or more precisely of its first formulation, the Formula of Universal Law (*MM*, Introduction, 6: 224–5). He then states that while "Laws proceed from the will [*dem Willen*], maxims from the faculty of choice [*Willkühr*]," and further that since the will is "not directed to actions but immediately to giving laws for the maxims of actions" it is in fact identical to "practical reason itself" and "cannot be called either free or unfree," therefore "Only the *faculty of choice* can be called *free*." It is natural to assume that what Kant means is that while the will, identical as it is to (pure) practical reason, always gives only one

<hr />

[32] Kant, letter to Reinhold, March 28, 1794, 11: 494–6.
[33] Reinhold, letter to Kant, March 29, 1795, 12: 9–10.
[34] Kant, letter to Reinhold, July 1, 1795, 12: 27.   [35] E.g., di Giovanni 2005, p. 205.
[36] See *BKP2*, pp. 276, 281, 293, 297, and 306–7.
[37] The section containing this passage was numbered "IV" in the original edition and in the Academy edition of the text, but renumbered "III" in Bernd Ludwig's 1989 edition of the *Rechtslehre* and in Mary Gregor's edition in *Practical Philosophy*.

and the same law, namely the moral law, which *ought* to be adopted as our fundamental maxim and to which our more particular maxims *ought* to confirm, it is the faculty of choice which actually decides whether or not to conform our fundamental maxim and our particular maxims to the moral law—it is the faculty of choice, after all, that *chooses*. Thus far, Kant seems to be saying the same thing he said in *Religion*, although by means of an explicit contrast between *Wille* and *Willkühr* that was only implicit there.

But now Kant introduces his criticism of Reinhold and argues for it. The passage needs to be quoted in full:

> But freedom of choice [*Willkühr*] cannot be defined—as some have tried to do— as the ability to make a choice [*das Vermögen der Wahl*] for or against the law (*libertas indifferentiae*), even though choice [*die Willkühr*] as a *phenomenon* provides frequent examples of this in experience. For we know freedom (as it first becomes manifest to us through the moral law) only as a *negative* property in us, namely that of not being *necessitated* to act through any sensible determining grounds. But we cannot present [*darstellen*] freedom as a *noumenon theoretically*, i.e., considered in accordance with the ability of the human being merely as an intelligence, as it is *necessitating* in regard to the sensible faculty of choice [*Willkühr*], hence in its positive constitution. But we can indeed well see that although experience shows that the human being as a *sensible being* is able to choose [*wählen*] not only in accord with but also contrary to the law, his freedom as an *intelligible being* cannot be defined through this, since appearances cannot make any supersensible object (of the sort that the free faculty of choice is) comprehensible, and that freedom can never be located in the fact that the rational subject can also make a choice in conflict with his (legislative) reason, even though experience often enough shows that this happens (the possibility of which we still cannot comprehend).—For it is one thing to accept a proposition (of experience), something else to make it into a *principle of definition*[38] and universally distinguishing mark (of the concept of freedom)...because the former [accepting a proposition from experience] does not assert that the mark *necessarily* belongs to the concept, which is however requisite in the case of the latter [making it into a definition].—Only freedom in relation to inner legislation is properly an ability [*Vermögen*]; the possibility of deviating from [this legisla- tion] is an inability [*Unvermögen*]. How can the former be defined by the latter?   (*MM*, Introduction, 6: 226–7, translation modified)

---

[38] *Erklärungsprincip*; this could also mean a principle of explanation, since Kant himself famously stated that the German word *Erklärung* could equally well be translated by the Latinate words "exposition," "explication," "declaration," and "definition" (*CPuR*, A730/B758). But since he has announced at the outset of the paragraph is how freedom is to be "defined" (*definirt*), it seems better to translate *Erklärung* now as "definition." Gregor translated the compound term *expository principle*, which seems evasive.

Kant's reasoning is hardly easy to follow. He begins with what seems to be a straightforward statement of the *ratio cognoscendi* argument he had been making since the *Critique of Practical Reason*: we do not know our freedom from experience, but we know that we are not necessitated to act only in accordance with sensible incentives, thus that we are free to act in accordance with the moral law, from our non-empirical—therefore a priori—knowledge of the moral law and our obligation to act in accordance with it. So far, so good: that we know that we are free not to act only on sensible incentives from our awareness that we must also be able to act in accordance with the moral law does not imply that we actually will. Kant's next claim is that we cannot *theoretically* present or perhaps better exhibit (*darstellen*) freedom as a noumenon, or the freedom of our noumenal selves, nor can we have theoretical insight into *how* the noumenal self can constrain the sensible incentives of the phenomenal self—at this point, one would see no reason not to add "if the noumenal self so chooses"—and this is entirely consistent with Kant's position, indeed since the first *Critique*, that we can have no theoretical knowledge of or insight into the noumenal, *a fortiori* into noumenal freedom, only practical faith therein. Again, so far, so good.

But then Kant's argument takes a strange turn: he next argues that we cannot define the freedom of a human being as an intelligible being, or the freedom of choice at the noumenal level, as the freedom to choose either in accordance with or contrary to the moral law *because* "appearances cannot make any supersensible object comprehensible." The ability of human beings to choose maxims either in accordance with or contrary to the moral law cannot be made the "defining principle" of noumenal freedom because a definition must be *necessarily* true, or a mark ascribed to an object by a definition must "belong to the concept *necessarily*." But both of these points seem confused. First, although perhaps Reinhold had attempted to infer the absolute freedom of the faculty of choice *from experience*, that is, from the empirical knowledge that people do both right and wrong, the earlier Kant certainly had not, yet had nevertheless *characterized* freedom as the ability to choose either good or evil. In *Religion*, for example, Kant had clearly argued that although experience attests to the fact that people typically choose evil and that fact needs *no* other proof, the freedom of humans to choose either good or evil was *not* inferred from any such empirical observation, but from the conditions of imputability and from the very concept of freedom itself: that people freely choose evil was inferred from their responsibility for evil, and the possibility of their moral conversion was inferred from the very nature of the freedom thus attributed to them. Indeed, while the "fact of reason" argument of the *Critique of Practical Reason* infers our freedom from our awareness of the moral law, the argument of *Religion* actually infers our freedom from the imputability of evil—but in neither case is the argument an empirical theoretical argument. Finally, Kant claims that freedom cannot be defined as the ability to choose to act *either* in accord with the moral law or contrary to it, but can be defined *only* as the ability to act in accordance with the moral law, because while the possibility of acting in accordance with the law is an ability, the possibility of acting contrary to it is not an ability but an inability. This seems just a verbal point, and not a very plausible one: if an ability is so to speak just the nominalization or reification of a "can," and if people can, as indeed experience attests, act contrary to the moral law, then they have the ability to do so, whatever one wants to call it.[39]

In short, Kant seems to have offered no good reason not to accept the conception of freedom as the possibility of choosing either to accept or to reject the moral law (to subordinate self-love to it, or it to self-love), and thus no good reason for retracting his account of *Willkühr* from five years previous. Moreover, if he were to insist now that the noumenal will can be defined only by its adherence to the moral law and therefore, presumably, can only choose in accordance with the moral law, then he would indeed be left with the position of "intelligible fatalism" (which Schmid had not himself adopted), that the noumenal will is not free at all but necessarily acts in accordance with the moral law, or that it is nominally but not really free only when it so acts, and further left with the conclusion that when a phenomenal person acts contrary to the moral law he is acting out of merely sensible grounds *instead of being determined by his noumenal self*. This would fly in the face of Kant's position in both the first and the second *Critiques* that our empirical character is in fact always grounded in our intelligible character or noumenal self, even when it seems to be determined by the whole history of the phenomenal world (*CPracR*, 5: 97–8).

There is a way to avoid these untoward consequences, however, namely to take Kant to be talking about what he calls "real definition," not just "nominal definition." I suggest that what is moving Kant in this passage is his conception of *real* definition as "one that suffice[s] for cognition of the object according to its inner determinations, since [it] present[s] the possibility of the object from inner marks" (*JL*, §106, 9: 143): what Kant is arguing is that the possibility of choosing contrary to the moral law should not be included in the real definition of freedom of the *Willkühr* because it is only the possibility of choosing in accordance with the law that reveals the fact of this freedom to us. In other words, Kant is here relying upon and reminding us of the doctrine of the second *Critique* that "morality first discloses to us the concept of freedom" (*CPracR*, 5: 30), thus that our awareness of (our obligation under) the moral law is the *ratio cognoscendi* of freedom even if freedom is the *ratio essendi* of the moral law. On Kant's theory of real definition, the *ratio cognoscendi* of the *definiendum* must be included in the definition, and here he is assuming that only the *ratio cognoscendi* can be included. This would

---

[39] Fugate 2012, however, defends Kant's claim that freedom cannot be defined as including the ability to choose evil because that is merely an incapacity, and ends up defending the interpretation that for Kant choosing evil is merely a misapplication of the moral law. This is hard to square with Kant's insistence in the *Religion* that the choice of evil is fully imputable and thus as fully a choice as the choice to be moral.

explain Kant's own explanation of his restriction on the definition of freedom of the *Willkühr* by means of the premise that "we know freedom (as it first becomes manifest to us through the moral law)," which is the turning-point in his argument. But this exclusion of the possibility of choosing contrary to the law from the *definition* of freedom does not exclude the possibility of choosing contrary to the law from freedom itself, as indeed seems to be conceded in Kant's continuation that we know freedom "only as a *negative* property in us, namely that of not being *necessitated* to act through any sensible determining grounds." What our awareness of (our obligation under) the moral law discloses to us is precisely that we are not necessitated to act from merely sensible incentives, and are instead capable of acting out of respect for the moral law itself, by choosing to act on maxims in accordance with it. But neither does our awareness of our obligation under the moral law disclose to us that we *are* necessitated to act under the moral law. That is why the subject confronted with an unjust demand by his tyrannical ruler, described in Kant's example in the second *Critique*, does not know whether he *will* act in accordance with the moral law at the risk of his own death, even though he knows that he *could*. What the moral law discloses to us is just that we always *can* choose to act in accordance with the moral law—that we have the capacity to choose for it, even though we also have the capacity to choose against it. If we take Kant to be claiming only that the *ratio cognoscendi* of our freedom of choice must be included in its real definition, there is nothing in the present argument to put in doubt his otherwise usual position that the *Willkühr* is not automatically determined by the *Wille* and thus that immoral but free action is possible.[40]

But Reinhold apparently did not appreciate this technical point, and instead reacted to Kant's apparent rejection of his solution to the problem of immorality with what can only be described as astonishment. This is the tone of the "Remarks on the Concepts of the Freedom of the Will presented in the Introduction to the Metaphysical Foundations of the Doctrine of Right by I. Kant" in the same year in which Kant's work appeared. Right at the start, Reinhold says that in light of the

---

[40] I have borrowed this paragraph from Guyer 2018c. Several other writers connect Kant's denial that the freedom of the *Willkühr* can be defined as the freedom to choose between good and evil to his theory of definition, but on grounds different from mine. Manfred Baum argues that Kant cannot include the ability to choose evil rather than good in the definition because a definition must include only necessary attributes of its *definiendum*, and it is obviously not necessary that the free will choose evil; the whole *Religion* would be in vain if that were true. See Baum 2012, p. 160. But this argument depends on a misplaced modal modifier: Baum proceeds as if Kant would need to define freedom as "Necessarily (the free agent chooses evil)," or the free agent necessarily chooses evil, when all that the definition of freedom would require is "Necessarily (the free agent can choose between good and evil)," which certainly would not imply that the free agent chooses evil, let alone does so necessarily. Jörg Noller argues that Kant cannot define freedom of the will as the capacity to choose evil rather than good because why anyone does this is inscrutable, since it takes place at the noumenal level; Noller 2016, pp. 275–81. It is certainly true that for Kant moral freedom obtains at the noumenal level and it is therefore inscrutable *why* anyone chooses one way rather than the other, but a *definition* is not an *explanation*, and Kant is happy to define other things that must be supposed to exist at the noumenal level—God and immortality, obviously—in terms of properties that cannot actually be experienced.

position that Kant had taken in *Religion within the Boundaries of Mere Reason*, he finds the account of "*the faculty of desire, will* [*Willen*], *the faculty of choice* [*Willkühr*] *and freedom*" that Kant offers in the Introduction to the *Metaphysics of Morals* "either *incomprehensible* or *untenable*" (Reinhold 1797). At his usual length, Reinhold makes several points, one of which has already been suggested. First, Reinhold argues against Kant's separation of *Wille* and *Willkühr* with its concomitant identification of *Wille* with pure practical reason; he argues that *Willkühr* is rather an aspect of the human will, its ability to choose in light of either pure reason or merely sensible gratification, with the human *Wille* thereby differing both from purely animal *Willkühr*, which cannot choose in light of reason, and divine *Wille*, which cannot choose in light of merely sensible incentives. So he wants to distinguish pure reason from both human *Wille* and *Willkühr* instead of just distinguishing *Wille* from *Willkühr*. As he puts it, "the *human Willkühr* is the capacity *to choose* characteristic of the [human] *Wille*" (Reinhold 1797, p. 369), while the human *Wille*, now including the *Willkühr*, "can be identified neither with a *faculty of desire* nor with *practical reason*" (p. 371); in his view, will is precisely the ability to choose between mere desire and reason. Reason is "always *one* and the *same*," but the will is not a will at all unless it can be "either a good or an evil will" (p. 373). Reinhold may be right that his usage is closer to common usage (p. 367), which does not distinguish between *Wille* and *Willkühr*, but the point is nevertheless merely verbal: he still insists that the human will, *Wille* including *Willkühr*, is the ability to choose in accordance with the moral law or contrary to it, and, although in different terminology, that seems to be what Kant had accepted in 1792 by distinguishing between reason and *Willkühr* but suddenly, although as I have suggested only apparently, rejected in 1797. This point is just terminological. However, Reinhold also continues to make several more substantive points.

First, he insists that neither he nor in fact the author of *Religion within the Boundaries of Mere Reason* derived the conception of a will—call it *Wille* or *Willkühr*, it makes no difference—that is free to choose between good and evil from any merely empirical evidence. On the contrary, he insists, both he and Kant derived the freedom of the will from purely moral concepts. He claims that "My concept of freedom as a capacity to act for and against the law, not *any sort of law* of reason but the *moral law*—consequently to act not merely *legally* and *illegally*, but *morally good* and *morally evilly*, is not drawn from *experience* at all, not derived from *appearances*." Rather, "like the concept of the *morally evil* action, which *Religion within the Boundaries of mere Reason* (as it calls itself) presents in accordance with the *mere law of freedom*, it is drawn strictly from the consciousness of the moral law itself, from the *categorical imperative*" (Reinhold 1797, pp. 392–3). For several pages preceding this, Reinhold had also argued that *conscience* (*Gewissen*) teaches us both that we are capable of acting in accordance with the moral law but also capable of overstepping it. He asked rhetorically

"Whether through the *moral law* as we know it through an immediate *consciousness*, as a *fact of conscience*, freedom is announced as a *mere capacity of reason*?" or "Whether through the moral law *morally good* actions in accord with it but also *morally evil* actions contrary to it are conceivable and must be conceivable?" (p. 384)—and the answer is clearly supposed to be the latter. Or again, "Does conscience deceive us when it seeks the worth and lack of worth of our actions of the will not in reason but in the use and misuse of reason, which reason does not make for itself and of itself, but which *we ourselves* make of reason?" "Does consciousness deceive us" in teaching us *both* "the *absolute necessity of the moral law*" but also "the *possibility of overstepping it?*" (pp. 385–6)—and again the answer is clearly intended to be "no." Reinhold does not offer a moral epistemology of his own that would clearly explain how conscience is non-empirical, but he clearly thinks that it is, or that it is more like a pure moral concept than an empirical observation. Whether Reinhold's appeal to a "fact of consciousness" is really non-empirical might be disputable, but then again Kant's claim that the "fact of reason," our consciousness of the moral law, is entirely non-empirical could also be debated (*CPracR*, 5: 30–1). But Reinhold clearly does not think he has drawn his definition of freedom of the will from mere observation that humans commonly violate as well as observe the moral law, nor did he think that Kant had done so in *Religion*. Kant's clear distinction in that work between empirical evidence for the *existence* of evil and an a priori or "formal" argument that the very nature of freedom entails both the *possibility* of evil but also the possibility of conversion from evil to good is on Reinhold's side.

Second, and here Reinhold makes a fundamental contrast between Kant's position and his own, he argues that he could never have attempted to make an inference about a noumenal or intelligible being from merely empirical evidence because he does not distinguish between a noumenal and phenomenal will and thus is not attempting to make any claim about a noumenal will at all. As he puts it,

> It never occurred to me to want to define the freedom of the human being as an *intelligible* being. I am concerned only with the freedom of the *human will*; for me the human being is neither an *intelligible being* nor a *sensible being*, but *both at the same time*; and I hold the human being to be free *because* and *insofar as* he is both at once, while Kant seems to hold him to be free only insofar as he is an intelligible being. The *subject* of the transcendental faculty [of freedom] is at the same time to be the subject of the empirical [faculty], if that faculty is not *transcendent* but *transcendental*—i.e., to relate *a priori* to the empirical.
>
> (Reinhold 1797, p. 393)

Reinhold has in mind Kant's usage of "transcendental" in the eponymous Aesthetic and Analytic of the first *Critique*, where it is properly used to refer to the a priori conditions of the possibility of cognition of the empirical world (even mathematical cognition, although it is itself synthetic a priori, is actually *knowledge* insofar as cognition of the form of the empirical world; see *CPuR*, B147), and thus holds that the concept of the freedom of the will, non-empirically entailed by morality and conscience, applies to the empirical subject, the human being in the natural world.[41] This means that Reinhold does not offer an account of how the human being in the natural world can be liberated from the grip of determinism in order to be free to be moral or not, but is simply confident that conscience suffices to tell us that we are free in this way. His position may thus seem incomplete. However, since few have ever been willing to follow Kant in using transcendental idealism to secure the freedom of the will, Reinhold's response to Kant marks one of the two ways forward possible in this debate: either accept determinism and offer some redefinition of freedom compatible with it ("compatibilism"), or insist that freedom is incompatible with determinism but nevertheless find space for it in a single, empirical world that includes human beings and their wills ("incompatibilism").

Finally, Reinhold observes that, if Kant does not stand by the position he had reached in *Religion*, then he will indeed be saddled with "intelligible fatalism" (Reinhold 1797, p. 387), the view that the will is free if and only if it is acting in accordance with pure practical reason, thus that an immoral act cannot even be imputed to a free will. As he puts it, on Kant's supposed new position (although as we have seen Kant may well not have actually modified his position about the fact of freedom, but had only made a point about proper definition), "The power of choice [*Willkühr*], which" on his own account "by no means *gives* the law but *ought to follow* it, and *can* follow it only insofar as it is *free*, would be free only *insofar* as it is not a *power of choice* [*Willkühr*] but rather also—like the will [*Wille*]—*practical reason itself*" (Reinhold 1797, p. 375). In other words, in Reinhold's view Kant by his distinction between reason and *Willkühr* in the *Religion* had properly avoided the problem of intelligible fatalism originally raised by Ulrich, but by insisting in the Introduction to the *Metaphysics of Morals* that the positive freedom of the noumenal will can only be its ability to act only in accordance with the moral law and never against it, he has stepped right back into this morass. As our description of Kant's remarks in the Introduction to the *Metaphysics of Morals* suggested, this may not have been what Kant intended, but one cannot but feel some sympathy for Reinhold in his dismay, as Kant's intent in that passage is certainly obscure.

Be that as it may, the argument over the necessity of a radical theory of free will would continue. We will see that at least one writer in the wake of Kant, namely Friedrich Schelling in his 1809 essay on *The Essence of Human Freedom*, tried to

---

[41] See again Bondeli 2012, pp. 137–8, and Baum 2012, p. 156.

regain the ground occupied by Kant's *Religion*, while others, such as Arthur Schopenhauer, rejected any attempt to escape from determinism at all, and a few, such as Hegel, tried to make room for both rationality and contingency in their conception of human freedom without invoking transcendental idealism. As mentioned at the outset of this Part, G. E. Moore's early article on Kant's theory of freedom may well have pushed that theory off the table for most twentieth-century moral philosophers. The debate between Reinhold and Kant just recounted was only the opening shot in an ongoing war over freedom of the will.

We will return to the issue of free will at various points during the subsequent narrative. But before we start our examination of how subsequent philosophers have grappled with the issues raised thus far, there is one last issue identified in the initial response to Kant that must be discussed. This is the issue of the proper role of feeling in morally acceptable or praiseworthy motivation, identified above all with Friedrich Schiller.

6

Moral Feelings in Kantian Ethics

At least among philosophers, the most frequently quoted of the *Xenien*, a compilation of satirical distiches that Friedrich Schiller (1759–1805) and Johann Wolfgang von Goethe (1749–1832) published in 1796, is the following:

Scruples of Conscience
I like to serve my friends, but unfortunately I do it by inclination
And so often I am bothered by the thought that I am not virtuous.

Decision
There is no other way but this! You must seek to despise them
And do with repugnance what duty bids you.[1]

This is often taken as meant to be a biting criticism of Kant. Some have rather held that it is meant to be a parody of poor readers among Kant's critics,[2] and given that the *Xenien* jabbed at many in the contemporary literary world but were in part at least meant to defend the younger Jena philosophers—Fichte and the emerging Schelling—from shallow Berlin critics such as Friedrich Nicolai,[3] there may be something to be said for this interpretation.[4] In any case, whether Schiller and Goethe were lampooning them or joining them, there were certainly critics who thought that Kant was committed to precisely such a ridiculous conclusion. Thus, in his ill-tempered screed *On Mister Kant's Moral Reform*, which has previously been mentioned in connection with the problem of happiness, Gottlob August Tittel first crudely paraphrased Kant's position in the following terms, obviously transforming one of Kant's thought-experiments in *Groundwork* I, meant to lead to a clear formulation of the moral principle from cases of agents who *could* act on it without inclination, into a requirement that a morally worthy

---

[1] Translation quoted from Wood 1999, p. 28. As a piece of poetry, I prefer the translation by A. B. Bullock, quoted by Hastings Rashdall in *The Theory of Good and Evil* and in turn quoted from him by H. J. Paton (1947, p. 48): "Gladly I serve my friends, but alas I do it with pleasure. / Hence I am plagued with doubt that I am not a virtuous person. // Sure, your only resource is to try to despise them entirely, / And then with aversion to do what your duty enjoins." But here I have used Wood's translation because his use of "inclination" rather than "pleasure" brings out better the issue we are about to discuss.

[2] Beck 1960, p. 231 n. 63.   [3] Boyle 2000, pp. 400–1.

[4] But note that Schiller and Goethe were also capable of poking fun at Kant's followers as well. *Kant and His Interpreters*: 'But how can a single rich man provide nourishment for so many beggars! / When kings build, the charnel houses have plenty to do." (My translation from Schiller 1966, vol. 3, p. 145.) The *Xenien* spared no one.

Kant's Impact on Moral Philosophy. Paul Guyer, Oxford University Press. © Paul Guyer 2024.
DOI: 10.1093/oso/9780199592456.003.0007

agent *have no* inclination in favor of what morality demands: "In the case of a good will, the human being always acts from duty. Thus—not on account of any use. Also not—merely in accord with duty, but from inclination; but also contrary to his inclination, only because it is his duty to so act, as for example an unhappy person preserves his life without loving it." Tittel then responds that "The moral worth of a human being consists in the fact that in him duty has become his dominant inclination. The strength of this inclination elevates his worth. The more reservations or stimuli lie in the way, which this inclination conquers, all the stronger must it be" (Tittel 1786, p. 12). Tittel might seem to contradict himself, first rejecting Kant's alleged view that the good will has to overpower inclination and then arguing that moral worth is to be measured precisely by the strength of resistance to inclination, but what he means is that moral worth consists in having an *inclination* in favor of duty that is stronger than all other *inclinations* and capable of overpowering them, and this he takes to be a criticism of Kant.

This seems an unfair criticism of Kant, who in *Groundwork* I was certainly not attempting to give a psychologically complete picture of the actual motivation of a morally worthy person. Rather he was offering narrowly defined thought-experiments, examples of cases in which persons could be imagined to be acting with moral worth but without any inclination in behalf of their actions, from which it would follow that the fundamental *principle* of morality, the criterion for distinguishing between right and wrong, cannot depend on inclination, and must instead directly concern only the form of our maxims rather than the matter of our happiness. As we saw previously, Tittel's larger argument is directed precisely against that position, so it cannot be argued that in general he simply misunderstood Kant. But in taking Kant to be intending to provide a complete phenomenology of morally worthy motivation in *Groundwork* I, he was being unfair to Kant.

6.1. Kames, Schiller, and Kant on Grace and the Ideal of Beauty

But whether in the notorious distich Goethe and Schiller meant to be parodying a critic like Tittel or to be taking his side, in his famous essay *Anmut und Würde* ("On Grace and Dignity") of 1793, thus seven years after Tittel's little book but three years before the poem, Schiller offered what seems to be a more subtle criticism of Kant's position on the role of feelings in moral motivation. The argument of this essay is complex, however, and by no means directed solely against Kant's ethical theory, so it will take a moment to reach the point of dispute between Schiller and Kant, if there really is one. Schiller begins with a debate in aesthetics rather than ethics, and initially his target seems to be Henry Home, Lord Kames (1696–1782), rather than Kant. Indeed, Kames's 1762 *Elements of*

Criticism, widely popular in Germany,[5] includes a chapter (11) titled "Dignity and Grace," so although Schiller reverses the order of Kames's title, it is also clear that Kames is more than just an ancillary target for Schiller. In that chapter, Kames first states that "These terms must belong to sensitive beings, probably to man only" (*EC*, 1.245). Schiller agrees with this, although from his point of view, on this issue entirely Kantian, both dignity and grace will belong to humans as the only sensitive *and rational* beings. Kames further argues that "we never attribute dignity to any action but what is virtuous," and that the term "dignity" is further "appropriated" to express the human being's "SENSE of the worth and excellence of his nature: he deems it more perfect than that of the other beings around him; and he perceives that the perfection of his nature consists in virtue, particularly in virtues of the highest rank." He states further that "to behave with dignity, and to refrain from all mean actions, is felt to be, not a virtue only, but a duty" (*EC*, 1.246). Acting with dignity is thus acting in a way that expresses the agent's own sense of his moral worth, and it is a duty for human beings to so act. Of course, for Kames, as a moral sense theorist, the dignified person does not merely act with a sense of his own worth, but duty and virtue are defined by our moral sense, not by any form of pure reason. Schiller will take the part of Kant rather than Kames on this score.

Having devoted the bulk of his chapter, which is in any case not one of the longer ones in the *Elements of Criticism*, to dignity, Kames then devotes two pages to grace. He says first that it is displayed externally, and in particular to sight; this is in line with his initial definition of beauty in general as in the first instance a quality for sight and only secondarily for the other senses (*EC*, 1.141-2). He then argues that, unlike beauty, which can be found in static objects, grace "is undoubtedly connected with motion; for when the most graceful persons is at rest, neither moving nor speaking, we lose sight of that quality as much as of colour in the dark" (*EC*, 1.251). In particular, grace "is too deep for any cause purely corporeal," and instead lies in motions "which indicate mental qualities, such as sweetness, benevolence, elevation, [and] dignity." "Collecting these circumstances together, grace may be defined [as] that agreeable appearance which arises from elegance of motion and from a countenance expressive of dignity" (*EC*, 1.252). Thus, for Kames grace and dignity are hardly mutually exclusive, but grace is a feature of the appearance of motions stemming from moral qualities of mind and above all from dignity. For him, grace is the appearance of dignity in the motions of a human agent. Thus dignity is a purely moral notion, while grace is more of an aesthetic

---

[5] According to Jane Curran, Schiller "consulted the third German edition of 1790–93, with commentary by Georg Gottlob Schatz" (Schiller 2005, p. 134 n. 5.) I have not been able to identify this edition. There is Home 1790–1, But there were earlier German translations of Kames as well, beginning in 1766. There can be no doubt that Schiller had ready access to Kames's work.

concept, although like other eighteenth-century Britons Kames did not use the term "aesthetic" that Alexander Gottlieb Baumgarten had introduced into German.

In a general way, Schiller is in complete agreement with Kames that grace is an expression of the moral quality of an agent, but it is not an expression of dignity as he defines it. At the same time, his ultimate ideal of human perfection is that grace and dignity should coincide. Schiller deals with grace first, and in the course of his analysis his target shifts from Kames to Kant. He contrasts grace first with beauty, then with "static" beauty, then with "architectonic" beauty. But the key idea remains the same: beauty under its several names is an enduring feature of an object, while grace is a "movable beauty, a beauty that can appear in a subject by chance and disappear in the same way," or "beauty of movement" (*GD*, p. 125). As Kames had held that grace is "elegance in motion," thus far there is no difference between him and Schiller. Next, he argues that "if grace is a prerogative of human development, then none of those movements that humans have in common with merely natural beings can lay claim to it," for example the rippling of curls in a beautiful head of hair (*GD*, p. 126). Again, there is still no difference with Kames, nor is there when Schiller adds that this is because grace is an expression of the moral quality of the graceful agent, or in his Kantian language, an "expression of purpose" (*GD*, p. 128). His analysis diverges from Kames's, however, when he argues, now drawing on the central notion of Kant's aesthetics that beauty lies in a free play that appeals to and unifies our sensible and intellectual capacities, that grace "is always only beauty of the physique that *freedom sets in motion*" (*GD*, p. 134), that it must be connected to both the intentional expression of moral purpose and yet to motions that are entirely natural to human beings, and therefore locates it in "*sympathetic* movements" (p. 135), or movements that "accompany moral sentiment or moral attitude" (p. 136), that is, in the unintended accompaniments of intentional actions. As Schiller explains, "Whatever is left undetermined by either will or purpose can be sympathetically determined by the emotional state of the person and serve as the expression of that state." Thus grace is the natural accompaniment of actions dictated by reason, but expresses the harmony between reason and nature, that is, between reason and the person as natural being. In particular, a person's "sympathetic" movements are the best expression of his real intentions and moral character because while intentional movements can easily be faked, their unintended accompaniments cannot be. For example, "one can deduce from a person's words how he would *like to be viewed*, but what he *really* is must be guessed from the mimic gestures accompanying the speech, in other words, from the *uncontained* movements" (p. 137). This is a subtlety that is not present in Kames's account, and is part of what Schiller means when he says later that he "takes up characteristics of dignity into grace... His observations are usually correct, and the rules he *initially* forms from them, true; but one should not follow him further than this" (p. 164n.). Dignity is strictly an expression of the morality and rationality of an agent, but the motions that Kames had correctly identified as constituting grace must be natural, and therefore must be the unintended accompaniments of intended action rather than the intended movements of the action themselves.

Schiller also criticizes Kames for assuming "too *narrow* a meaning for the idea of grace" when he argues that it disappears entirely when a person is at rest (*GD*, p. 134n.). Schiller's objection is that a person's movements, intentional or sympathetic and graceful or not, leave enduring traces on her physiognomy: "The rigid features were originally nothing other than movements that through frequent repetition became habitual and left lasting traces" (p. 134). Schiller's original training as a physician always gave him a stronger sense of the intimate connection between mind and body than many of his philosophical contemporaries had.

This would seem like a minor point, but it is part of Schiller's inexplicit criticism of Kant's conception of the "ideal of beauty." In the Analytic of the Beautiful in the *Critique of the Power of Judgment*, Kant had argued that an ideal of beauty would be a uniquely maximal sort of beauty, that such an ideal would have to be in some way fixed by a concept or idea even though beauty is never *determined* by a concept, and that the only candidate for such a role is the idea of human morality itself, the capacity of the human beings "to determine his ends himself through reason" (*CPJ*, §17, 5: 233), thus that the ideal of beauty can be found "only in the *human figure*" as "the expression of the *moral*," as the "visible expression of moral ideas, which inwardly govern human beings" (5: 235). In fact, Kant's account is doubly problematic: he treats the ideal of beauty as a species-wide ideal for human beings, but of course some human beings are moral and some are not—though all have the capacity to be moral, some choose not to be, as we have just discussed—and therefore presumably only some human beings will express morality in their outward appearance. Further, but for the exception noted in Schiller's criticism of Kames, the expression of morality, when it is present, will not lie in the fixed form of a human figure or face, which is a product of nature alone, but in an individual's graceful movements, the unintended accompaniments of intended actions that are the product of reason and nature together. The "human form is expressive" of individual morality "only in those appearances that accompany and serve to express its moral attitude" (*GD*, p. 140), not in the natural beauty of an individual and certainly not in that of the species, should there be such a thing. And "We are thus not satisfied when a human form presents to our eyes the universal concept of humanity or perhaps the degree to which *nature* has fulfilled it in the individual... In the former case one can easily see that nature *planned* for a human being, but only in the second case does it emerge whether it *actually* became one" (*GD*, p. 141). This cannot be a criticism of Kames, because he had said no such thing; it is a criticism of Kant, who tried to find the expression of human morality in the architectonic beauty of the species when it can lie only in the graceful movements of the individual.

Thus far, Schiller seems to be arguing only with Kant's aesthetics, not with his moral theory. And when he proceeds beyond a mere analysis of the concept of grace to explain what he takes to be the expectation or even demand for grace, he makes it clear that this issues not from our expectation of morality alone but from our demand for beauty:

> Human beings, as appearance, are also an object of the senses. Where the *moral* feeling finds satisfaction, the *aesthetic* feeling does not wish to be reduced, and the correspondence with an idea may not sacrifice any of the appearance. Thus, however rigorously reason demands an ethical expression, the eye demands beauty just as persistently.

To be sure, these two demands have to be conjointly satisfied, because they are to be satisfied in one and the same object:

> Since both these demands are made of the same object, although they come from different courts of judgment, satisfaction for both must be found in the same source. The frame of mind in which a human being is most able to fulfill his moral purpose must permit the type of expression that is also most advantageous for him as simple appearance. In other words: moral capacity must reveal itself through grace.   (*GD*, pp. 144–5)

This double requirement, Schiller goes on to argue, can be satisfied only when the person who is to satisfy the demands of both morality and aesthetics (the person as object, who presumably might be the same as the subject who is making both a moral and an aesthetic judgment on the object, but who will typically be numerically distinct) satisfies something like the Kantian condition of free play between intellect and sensibility, the condition by which Kant defines the aesthetic but which Schiller has now extended to the relation between aesthetics and morality: "When neither *reason dominating the sensuous*, nor *sensuousness dominating reason* is compatible with beauty of expression, then...the state of mind *in which reason and sensuousness*—duty and inclination—*coincide* will be the condition under which the beauty of play appears" (p. 148). Now it may seem that by his lengthy argument Schiller has reached the same point that Tittel quickly asserted against Kant, namely that duty and inclination must coincide, but it might also seem that he has cast this demand not as a purely moral demand, but as a demand of our dual sensuous and rational nature, our aesthetic and moral character, and thus that while superficially agreeing with Tittel, he has in fact offered Kant a defense—for Kant should have no objection to an *aesthetic* demand for grace, or for the idea that while *morality* alone may have no interest in inclination coinciding with duty, our dual moral-aesthetic nature might well have such an interest. Schiller continues to emphasize that the demand for grace is a demand that originates in our whole, complex nature, not in our capacity for morality alone: it is nature, not morality, that "gave the human being notice of his obligation not to separate what it had bound together and, even in the purest expressions of his divine part, not to neglect the sensuous, and not to base the triumph of the one on the subjugation of the other" (p. 150). Schiller also puts the point in terms of his famous concept of the "beautiful soul": "One refers to a beautiful soul when the ethical sense has at last so taken control of all of a person's feelings that it can leave affect to guide the will without hesitation and is never in danger of standing in contradiction of its decisions"; but he makes it clear that the demand for a "beautiful soul" is an aesthetic demand, or a jointly aesthetic and moral demand, but not a demand of morality alone. In a "beautiful soul that sensuous and reason, duty and inclination, are in harmony, and grace is their expression as appearance" (pp. 152–3). The demand for grace is not a demand of duty alone.[6]

6.2. Schiller and Kant on Grace and Dignity

Schiller concedes that Kant has laid himself open to the criticism of insisting on a necessary opposition between duty and inclination, that "the idea of *duty* ... repels all grace," which might "tempt a weak intellect to seek moral perfection by taking the path of a somber and monkish asceticism," but argues that Kant was "incensed" by the "moral state of his time, as he found it in theory and practice," to exaggerate this contrast. Only thus, Schiller suggests, could Kant counter the hedonistic utilitarianism which is always a temptation for people and which was being encouraged by the "inappropriately accommodating" and "lax" philosophers around him (*GD*, p. 150). But his position remains that the demand for grace in our performance of duty, thus for harmony between duty and inclination, is a demand of our dual nature, not of our moral nature alone. Moreover, when he turns from grace to dignity, his position seems to become, just like Kant's position, that in case there is a conflict between the demands of duty and of inclination—which, given the frailty of human nature, there inevitably will be—then inclination must give way to duty, and the person must act with dignity, the "expression in appearance" of "control of impulses through moral strength" rather than the appearance of harmony between impulse and duty (p. 158). Schiller's concept of

---

[6] Frederick Beiser puts it thus: "*Anmut und Würde* is a treatise more on the aesthetic aspects of moral conduct than on aesthetics itself"; Beiser 2005b, p. 80. I would put the point slightly differently, by saying that it is a treatise more on the aesthetic aspects of moral conduct than on morality itself. I do agree with Beiser's further suggestion that Schiller's essay "is less an attempt to correct Kant's moral theory than to complete it" (p. 81), although Kant did not recognize this. For further discussion of Beiser's interpretation, see Baxley 2008. Ehrenspeck 1998, pp. 146–8, interprets Schiller's essay as criticizing Kant for a morally rather than aesthetically defective picture of the role of inclination on moral motivation.

dignity is not the same as Kant's: for Kant, dignity is a strictly moral concept, the expression of or response to the absolute value of humanity or the *capacity* for rational free being in human beings (*G*, 4: 434–5),[7] while for Schiller it is a phenomenological, perceptual, or aesthetic concept, the concept of the *appearance* of the actual triumph of morality over contrary impulse in a particular individual. (Kant does refer at least once to a "certain sublimity and *dignity* in the person who fulfills all his duty," which is part of Schiller's conception of dignity, but he does not refer to the sensible appearance of such a person's fulfillment of duty, which is the other part of Schiller's concept; *G*, 4: 440.) But Schiller does not seem to disagree with Kant's position that human beings do not always do their duty gladly, and that when they do not, then we must settle for dignity rather than grace:

> Human beings do have the task of establishing an intimate agreement between their two natures, of always being a harmonious whole, and of acting with their full human capacity. But this beauty of character, the ripest fruit of humanity, is only an idea that they can vigilantly strive to live up to, yet, despite all efforts, can never fully attain.
>
> The reason they cannot reach it is the unchanging outlines of their nature; the physical conditions of their existence hinder them.   (*GD*, p. 154)

In this case, it seems, humans must at least achieve dignity, a claim that Schiller illustrates with his own take on a common topic in German cultural life of his time, the famous Roman statue of the Trojan priest Laocoön and his sons being destroyed by Neptune's serpents. Unlike Johann Joachim Winckelmann, he does not think that the composure of the priest's face in contrast to the struggle of his body represents a merit of Greek culture as a whole, and unlike Gotthold Ephraim Lessing he does not think it represents a concession to the laws of beauty in a visual medium like sculpture as contrasted to a verbal medium like epic poetry (where Virgil's Laocoön, *vox clamantes ad sidera*, can scream all he wants); in his view, Laocoön's composed face represents his individual *"peace in suffering*, in which dignity actually consists*,"* the visible expression of the moral freedom of an individual who knows he is doing the right thing (*GD*, p. 160).[8] Schiller uses the iconic statue to illustrate his conception of dignity as the appearance of the best moral condition that human beings as conceived by Kant can sometimes although not always achieve. As he puts this last point, now using Kant's term "humanity" to designate the combined rational and sensuous character of human beings

---

[7] For a careful analysis of Kant's concept of dignity as a term expressing the unconditional value of humanity rather than as the property that itself has unconditional value, see Sensen 2011.

[8] For their respective views see Winckelmann 2006 and Lessing 1984. For my discussion of their debate, see Guyer 2014c, vol. 1, pp. 363–76. On the discovery of the statue, see Barkan 1999, and on Winckelmann's aesthetic more generally, Potts 1994.

rather than their free and rational character alone, "In general, the law is valid here that humans should do everything with grace that can be carried out within humanity, and everything with dignity that requires going beyond humanity" (GD, p. 162).

This would seem to be the final step in Schiller's argument, and nothing to which Kant would object. But he does not quit while he is ahead, and makes two further claims. First, he makes the epistemological claim that only grace, not dignity, offers conclusive evidence of a person's commitment to morality:

> Dignity alone displays a certain restriction of desires and inclinations whenever we encounter it. Only the grace associated with it can establish beyond doubt whether what we take to be control is not actually a dullness (hardening) of sensibility and whether it is really one's own moral activity and not rather the preponderance of another emotion, deliberate exertion, that holds the outbreak of the present one in check. Grace gives evidence of a peaceful, harmonious disposition and a sensitive heart.   (GD, p. 163)

Second, essentially returning to his previous conception of the beautiful soul, Schiller argues that only the union of grace with dignity satisfies our complex conception of human perfection rather than our strictly moral conception of human virtue:

> If grace, supported by architectonic beauty, and dignity, supported by strength, are *united* in the same person, then the expression of humanity is complete in that person, and he stands there, justified in the world of spirit and affirmed in appearance. The two legislations are in such close contact here that their boundaries flow together.   (p. 163)

But his position still seems compatible with Kant's, namely, that although our overall conception of human perfection, grounded in our distinct interests in moral achievement on the one hand and aesthetic pleasure on the others, demands the union of dignity and grace, morality alone demands that if there is a conflict between duty and inclination then duty must trump inclination, and dignity without grace must manifest itself in appearance. Of course it is nice when duty and inclination coincide, but if they do not, then duty must be done. Schiller's claim about the complete expression of humanity does not conflict with this, and his epistemological claim that only grace gives adequate evidence of a complete commitment to morality does not contradict the normative claim that in case of conflict duty must trump inclination, thus dignity must appear without grace.

In the Vigilantius transcription of Kant's lectures on the metaphysics of morals, from a course that began on October 14, 1793, Kant is reported within a few days of the start of the course as digging his heels in, taking just the position a critic like Tittel imputed to him, and seeing no common ground between himself and Schiller: he insists that there is always a felt conflict between duty and inclination:

> It is also certain that every obligation is forthwith associated with a moral constraint, and that it is contrary to the nature of duty to *enjoy* having duties incumbent upon one; it is necessary, rather that man's impulses should make him disinclined to fulfill the moral the laws.

It is not just contingent whether our inclinations would move us to actions contrary to the moral law, and thus contingent whether there is a conflict between duty and inclination; Kant insists here that it is inevitable. This leads to a rejection of what Kant takes to be Schiller's position in *Grace and Dignity*:

> Assuming that man's fulfillment of the moral laws can be accomplished only under a necessitation, it cannot therefore be claimed, as Schiller does in his *Thalia*,[9] where he takes issue with the Kantian critique of reason, that such fulfillment has a certain *grace*[10] about it, though otherwise, by man's nature, the necessitation requires obedience to the moral laws; if we wish, with Schiller, to assume a worth arising therefrom, it is nothing more than man's respect for the moral law, and that provides no ground for supposing a grace that attracts us to fulfilling it. That is contradicted by the authority of the laws, which enjoins absolute obedience, and awakens resistance and struggle, which we perceive in fulfilling them.

Kant continues that a person may take reflexive or second-order pleasure in the fact *that* it has become easy for him to fulfill duty by the strength of his own will, but he denies that a person can simply enjoy doing his duty without any such further reflection:

> It is true that we can find pleasure in virtue and the contemplation of it, but only by the time, and for the reason, that we have already become equipped to fulfill duties, and it is thus easy for us to follow the prescriptions of reason; we thereby take satisfaction in our actions, and in the strengthening of our will to comply with the prescriptions of reason... Finally, even psychological experience tells against Schiller's view: *We would do many things, if only they did not have to be done from duty* ... It would be good if men were so perfect that they fulfilled their

---

[9] Schiller's journal, in which he first published *Anmuth und Würde*.
[10] In his translation of the lectures, Peter Heath translates *Anmuth* as "charm" rather than "grace." For the sake of consistency with the rest of my discussion, I am translating it as "grace." See Kant 1997, p. 259.

duties from a free impulse, without coercion and law; but this is beyond the horizon of human nature.   (*Metaphysics of Morals Vigilantius*, 27: 490–1)

Kant evinces no recognition either that Schiller was criticizing his conception of the ideal of beauty *in aesthetics* or that he was attempting to defend Kant in moral philosophy, and that in his discussion of dignity, at least in its initial phase, Schiller was actually agreeing with him that to assume that human beings could always fulfill their duties with grace is unrealistic. Later in the lectures, he says that "Schiller is right to this extent, that [moral] worth lies in the intellectual nature of the determination to duty," but he still insists that there will always be a felt conflict between duty and inclination: "But the moral law also engenders worth through the very compulsion that fetters us in obedience" (27: 623). In other words, it is not enough for moral worth to be motivated by the moral law; that motivation has to be in conflict with one's inclination for one to deserve the accolade of moral worth. Kant does not appear to be making an epistemological argument, that it is only in the case of a conflict with inclination that we can *know* that someone is being motivated by the moral law; his claim seems to be the normative point that it is only when an agent has to overcome contrary inclination that he deserves esteem—but no need to worry, for the human agent always will have inclinations contrary to morality to overcome. Towards the very end of the lecture notes, finally, Kant reverts to Schiller one more time, and here acknowledges Schiller's claim that "we must couple virtue with grace," but still supposes that there will inevitably be conflict between grace and virtue (here indicated by the Latin words *decorum* and *honestum*), and that in such a case "strict duty" must always be preferred to grace or *decorum* (27: 707).

Kant's response to Schiller in a note added to part one in the second edition of *Religion within the Boundaries of Mere Reason*, which came out in 1794, is more complex. Kant appends this note to a discussion of rigorism, to which it is not actually relevant. Kant defines rigorism as the position that there is no intermediate between good and evil, but then argues that although there may be *actions* that are morally indifferent, neither good nor evil, agents' *fundamental maxims* can be only either good or evil, as he will subsequently put it, the maxim to subordinate self-love to morality in any case of conflict or the maxim to subordinate morality to self-love in any case of conflict. What he means by rigorism is thus that either one is committed to the subordination of self-love to morality or one is not, even though in the latter case many or even most of one's actions may be in conformity with what morality requires in their circumstances; if one is not fully committed to morality, then it is only contingent that one's actions, motivated by self-love, happen to be in outward conformity with what morality requires.[11] The footnote

---

[11] The discussion of rigorism is at *RBMR*, 6: 23–4; the subsequent characterization of the two possible fundamental maxims at 6: 36.

on Schiller concerns rather whether or not there must be a conflict between duty and inclination in moral motivation. Kant does not immediately reject Schiller's position wholesale; rather, he begins by saying that "Since we are however at one upon the most important principles, I cannot admit disagreement on this one, if only we can make ourselves clear to one another." But then he seems to take the same negative stance toward what he supposes Schiller's position to be that he took in the Vigilantius lectures, saying that "the concept of duty includes unconditional necessitation, to which grace[12] stands in direct contradiction," although he is willing to concede that "the glorious picture of humanity, as portrayed in the figure of virtue, does allow the attendance of the *graces* [*Grazien*], who, however, maintain a respectful distance when duty alone is at issue." Presumably the graces are the personification of grace, and thus, although Kant is attempting to be more conciliatory to Schiller in this public forum than he was in the relative privacy of his classroom, he is still insisting that grace cannot be too closely connected to duty, thus that there can never be an immediate inclination to fulfill duty and a feeling of complete freedom from conflict in so doing. "These same attendants of Venus Urania become wanton sisters in the train of Venus Dione as soon as they meddle in the business of determining duties and try to provide incentives for them," Kant adds, although Schiller certainly did not say that grace, sympathetic movements, or inclination could determine what our duties are and indeed did not even suggest that inclination could become an incentive for the fulfillment of duties the content of which is determined by reason. His position was really only that the involuntary grace of an agent's voluntary movements would prove that his moral motivation was genuine and not faked.

However, Kant now takes a break (marked by a one-em dash), and suddenly seems to agree with Schiller after all that something like grace can and must serve as *evidence* of genuine virtue:

> [I]f we ask, "What is the *aesthetic* constitution, the *temperament* so to speak of *virtue*: is it courageous and hence *joyous*, or weighed down by fear and dejected?" an answer is hardly necessary. The latter slavish frame of mind can never be found without a hidden *hatred* of the law, whereas a heart joyous in the *compliance* with duty (not just complacency in the recognition of it) is the sign of genuineness in virtuous disposition.

Kant continues that a "firm resolve to improve in the future…encouraged by good progress, must needs effect a joyous frame of mind, without which one is never certain of having gained also a *love* for the good" (*RBMR*, 6: 23–4n.). Kant's position by the end of the note thus seems to be that human agents *can* have a firm

---

[12] In this case, George di Giovanni translates *Anmuth* as "gracefulness"; again I am using "grace" for the sake of consistency. See Kant 1996b, p. 72n.

resolve to make continuous progress in being good and that their grace—grace in Schiller's sense, not in the sense of a divine gift, which Kant questions in the *Religion* (*RBMR*, 6: 43–53)—can be conclusive evidence of this. In this regard, Kant seems in the end to go further than Schiller, who seemed to suppose that, even though our ideal of perfection demands grace as well as dignity, we can never realistically suppose that human beings can always accompany dignity with grace, and sometimes will have to settle for dignity—the manifestation of the struggle to be good in the face of contrary inclinations—alone.

It might seem strange for Kant to go further than Schiller on this point, it might seem indeed that he has been carried away, but this conclusion is in fact entirely consistent with the central argument of the *Religion*, namely that since evil is imputable it must be the product of freedom, but if it is the product of freedom that means that human beings are also free to choose good rather than evil, and thus can effect a moral conversion from evil to good: radical evil implies the possibility of radical goodness (*RBMR*, 6: 237). Indeed the argument of the *Religion* may out-Schiller Schiller. At the same time, there does seem to be one tension between Kant's position in the footnote and his position in the remainder of the *Religion*. In the note, he seems to be adopting Schiller's position that grace (and only grace) can be adequate evidence of the firmness of resolve to make continuous moral progress. In the body of the work, however, Kant seems to argue both that our moral conversion can be *complete*, not a mere firm resolve to make moral progress, but also that because our exercise of our absolute freedom to be good rather than evil is noumenal, not something for which we can have evidence in experience, in fact we have neither the possibility nor the need of having adequate evidence for the true condition of our will, that is, technically, *Willkühr*. In fact, Kant argues, only God can have adequate evidence of a human's real moral disposition, not the human being himself. More precisely, Kant argues that because of the inescapably temporal character of human self-representation, human beings can represent their moral conversion to themselves *only* in the form of continuous moral progress, continuous progress in submitting their inclinations to the fundamental maxim of morality, even though their moral conversion is in fact complete and can and indeed must be known to be so by God. As Kant puts it,

> According to our mode of estimation, [to us] who are unavoidably restricted to temporal conditions in our conceptions of the relationship of cause to effect, the deed, as a continuous advance *in infinitum* from a defective good to something better, always remains defective, so that we are bound to consider the good as it appears to us, i.e., according to the *deed*, as *at each instance* inadequate to a holy law. But because of the *disposition* from which it derives and which transcends the senses, we can think of the infinite progression of the good toward conformity to the law as being judged by him who scrutinizes the heart (through his pure

intellectual condition) to be a perfected whole even with respect to the deed (the life conduct). And so notwithstanding his permanent deficiency, a human being can still expect to be *generally* well-pleasing to God, at whatever point in time his existence be cut short.   (*RBMR*, 6: 67)

So, contrary to Schiller, Kant believes that a complete moral conversion *is* possible, not mere progress in morality, and thus one would think that grace, or the complete joyousness of heart that he describes in the footnote to part one, should be available to human beings along with dignity, which Schiller actually denied.[13] At the same time, Kant thinks that because of the distinction between the phenomenal and noumenal character of human beings, even complete moral conversion can *appear* to human beings only in the form of continuous *progress* toward morality, which is closer to what Schiller seems to have held possible, and that only God can know that a human being has in fact undergone moral conversion, a conclusion that the thoroughly secular Schiller did not suggest at all. This in turn undercuts Kant's adoption of Schiller's suggestion that the aesthetic quality of grace in a person's conduct might be both possible and necessary evidence of his completion of moral conversion. For Kant, no such evidence should be either possible or necessary for human beings.

So Kant's position on the harmony of inclination and duty in his controversy with Schiller in 1794 seems unresolved or at least unclear. But this is not Kant's last word on the possible role of feeling in moral motivation. In the *Metaphysics of Morals*, not the classroom lectures of 1794–5 but the book of that name finally published in two parts in 1797, Kant returns to the subject of moral feeling as he calls it there as an "aesthetic precondition of the mind's susceptibility to the concept of duty." Here Kant seems to present an unconflicted position on the possibility and indeed necessity of moral feeling, or several kinds of moral feelings, in the empirical manifestation or phenomenology of moral motivation. Yet since this very late work of Kant did not have the degree of influence in its time as his earlier works, because the next generation of philosophers led by Fichte and Schelling had begun to stake out their own positions on many issues before this book even appeared, Kant's late incorporation of moral feeling into his account of moral motivation has not always been appreciated. So this chapter will conclude with a brief comment on Kant's final position on moral feeling before we begin to

---

[13] It should be obvious that grace in Schiller's sense is not identical to the religious concept that Kant discusses in the General Remark to part one of the *Religion*, namely a divine gift to a finite being to make up for the shortcomings of its will (*RBMR*. 6: 43–53). Kant is adamant that if there is such a thing as grace in that sense, "the human being must nonetheless make himself antecedently worthy of receiving it" by his own moral effort (6: 43)—the Calvinist doctrine of pre-ordained election is completely off of Kant's table.

see what subsequent philosophers have done with this issue and the others that have been raised in this chapter.[14]

In the previous chapter we discussed Kant's response to Reinhold on freedom of the will in the Introduction to the *Metaphysics of Morals* as a whole. Kant does not return to the abstract question of free will in the Doctrine of Virtue, the second part of the work, which enumerates those of our duties that as a matter of morality itself cannot be coercively enforced, and therefore can be enforced only by the individual's own commitment to the moral law. This is of course on Kant's view a commitment made by the choice of the free will (*Willkühr*), but that is now taken as settled, and Kant instead focuses on virtue in a double sense, the specific non-coercively enforceable duties or virtues such as self-perfection and beneficence to others, and the general virtue that is itself the strength of motivation to fulfill these particular duties. Kant describes virtue in this general sense as "the strength of a human being's maxims in fulfilling his duties." But he immediately continues that "Strength of any kind can be recognized only by the obstacles that it can overcome, and in the case of virtue these obstacles are natural inclinations." Virtue "is a self-constraint in accordance with a principle of inner freedom" (*MM*, DV, Introduction, section IX, 6: 394), namely the moral law, but since it has to overcome natural inclinations, it cannot simply be the determination of the noumenal will to act only in accordance with the moral law, but must be a force in the natural, phenomenal world where those inclinations lie, or a force that bridges the gulf between the noumenal and the phenomenal world—the medium through which the determination of the noumenal will is effective in the phenomenal world. The same can then be said about the "aesthetic preconditions of the receptivity of the mind to concepts of duty in general" that Kant describes several sections later (*MM*, DV, Introduction, section XII, 6: 399):[15] there may be a transcendental, noumenal act that can be described simply as the determination of the will by the moral law, or the determination of the will to make the moral law its fundamental maxim—nothing Kant says suggests he is taking back this cornerstone of his philosophy—but these "aesthetic preconditions" are conditions in the phenomenal world through which the duties of virtue are fulfilled in that world.[16] Kant

---

[14]   I have discussed what follows in more detail in Guyer 2010b.

[15]   Mary Gregor translated Kant's German section title "Ästhetische Vorbegriffe der Empfänglichkeit des Gemüths für Pflichtbegriffe überhaupt" as "Concepts of What is Presupposed on the Part of Feeling by the Mind's Receptivity to Concepts of Duty as Such" (Kant 1996a, p. 528). I have preferred the literal translation "aesthetic" to "on the part of feeling" because among what Kant is about to discuss, one item, conscience, cannot be properly called a feeling, although it is empirical, something we somehow sense, and therefore properly called aesthetic; and I have translated *Vorbegriffe* as "preconditions" not only because Kant refers to them in Latin as *praedispositio[nes]*, for which that seems a good translation, but also because he is not about to engage in conceptual analysis, but in psychological explanation. Finally, it should be noted that Kant's use of the term *Gemüth* here suggests that he is talking about the mind as a phenomenon in the natural world, not in any other sense.

[16]   More precisely, these aesthetic preconditions are the only conditions through which fulfillment of the duties of virtue can be enforced in the empirical world; duties of justice can be enforced through

further says that "Every determination of choice [*Willkühr*] proceeds *from the representation of a possible action to* the deed *through the feeling of pleasure or displeasure*," which is a "state of feeling" (*MM*, DV, Introduction, section XII, 6: 399, second emphasis added). This makes it clear that for Kant, at least at this late stage of his thought, however pure the determination of the noumenal will may be, *the empirical etiology of every action involves feeling*, thus even action that is at some level motivated by respect for the moral law itself *must also, in the phenomenal world, involve feeling*. Kant is now not talking about a contingent coincidence of inclination and duty, or postulating a special feeling or expression of grace as a *sign* of moral motivation, but rather maintaining that feeling is a normal part of moral motivation at the empirical level.

Specifically, Kant identifies four aesthetic preconditions, namely "moral feel-ing," "conscience," "love of human beings," and "respect," and of each of these says that our duty is not to create it out of whole cloth, since if we did not at least have a predisposition to it we would not be able to be "put under obligation at all"—we would not be susceptible to concepts of duty *aesthetically* or in the empirical world, and would be as good as "morally dead"—but instead "to *cultivate* it and strengthen it" (*MM*, DV, Introduction, section XII, 6:400). The identity of and relations between these four aesthetic preconditions are not obvious. In the *Critique of Practical Reason*, Kant had identified only a single "moral feeling," namely the feeling of respect at the moral law, a complex feeling involving both an unpleasant feeling at the striking down of self-conceit and an exhilarating feeling of pleasure at the recognition that it is one's own pure practical reason that is striking down one's self-conceit (*CPracR*, 5: 72–3, 76), but here moral feeling and respect are being distinguished from each other, so must refer to different things. And although love of human beings certainly sounds like a feeling, at least if it is what Kant calls "pathological" love, conscience is not exactly a feeling at all, but rather "practical reason holding the human being's duty before him for his acquittal or condemnation in every case that comes under a law" (*MM*, DV, Introduction, section XII, 6: 400). I suggest the following interpretation of the four aesthetic preconditions. "Moral feeling" is identical with what Kant previ-ously called respect: it is our general awareness at the empirical, felt level of "the constraint present in the thought of duty," it is a precondition—as Kant calls it—of the fulfillment of particular duties in the phenomenal world and of everything that might involve, and it is to be cultivated and strengthened, although Kant does not say much about how this is to be done except that it is to be done "through wonder at its inscrutable source"—focusing our attention on the source of the moral law in pure reason will somehow strengthen our motivation to act in

external, politically instituted juridical and penal sanctions, but *can* also be enforced through the inner—although not noumenal—"aesthetic preconditions." See Kant, *MM*, Introduction, 6: 219–20, and Kant, *MM*, DV, Introduction, section II, 6: 383.

accordance with this law.[17] That means in turn that strengthened moral feeling in this general sense is an indispensable factor in the phenomenal motivation to cultivate the *other* aesthetic preconditions, which are further, more proximate causes of the fulfillment of duty at the phenomenal level. Conscience, as I have already suggested, does not seem like a feeling, but more like the disposition to bring particular proposed actions or their maxims before the bench of the moral law for judgment, particular possibilities of action that suggest themselves in and only in the natural world and that must be judged in the natural world. We have a disposition to conscience, but it too must be strengthened through our general moral feeling, presumably through the motivation to do whatever is necessary to be moral that this feeling strengthens and the recognition that the development of conscience is so necessary. Love of other would then be feelings that specifically motivate beneficence or other proper treatment of others, or what Kant later in the text calls "sympathetic feelings" (*MM*, DV, §§34–5, 6: 456–7), and such feelings too would be both cultivated with the encouragement of moral feeling in the first sense but also subjected to the constraints of conscience, checking whether acting on feelings of love or sympathy would in fact be appropriate in specific circumstances—Kant says that we have a "conditional" duty to cultivate sympathetic feelings as a "means to promoting active and rational benevolence" (*MM*, DV, §34, 6: 456), presumably because although we need to cultivate our sympathetic feelings as the proximate cause of beneficence, helping others is not in fact morally appropriate or permissible in every circumstance (helping a thief), so these feelings, even when properly cultivated, or precisely when properly cultivated, sometimes also have to be checked. Finally, by the aesthetic precondition of respect Kant now means not the general feeling of respect for the moral law but rather "*self-esteem*," respect for "one's own being," which is "the basis of certain duties, that is, of certain actions that are consistent with [one's] duty to himself" (*MM*, DV, Introduction, section XII, 6: 402–3). Thus, just as the feeling of love for others is the proximate cause for fulfillment of (non-juridical) duties to others, so the feeling of self-esteem is the proximate cause for fulfillment of specific duties to oneself (all of which are non-juridical, because their violation does not directly hinder the freedom of others and thus does not give others, in the collective person of the state and its juridical system, the right to enforce them coercively). The fulfillment of duties to oneself is also a distal if not proximate cause of the fulfillment of duties to others, since one needs to cultivate some talents, for example, not only for one's own sake, but also in order to be able to benefit others when that is necessary or appropriate. And the feeling of self-esteem can be

[17] Grenberg 2013 argues that phenomenological "awareness" is the source of our knowledge of the content of the moral law. I do not find that a plausible interpretation of Kant, but I do think her notion of focused awareness could be used in the interpretation of the cultivation of the motivation to obey the law, the content of which is given (for Kant) by pure reason rather than by anything merely empirical.

cultivated with the impetus of the general moral feeling as well as constrained when necessary by conscience.

Kant has thus concluded his moral philosophy not with Schiller's account of grace but with a complex account of the role of a variety of moral feelings or "aesthetic preconditions" in the phenomenal etiology of moral motivation. Unfortunately, the battle lines over the role of feelings in Kant's moral philosophy had been drawn as soon as the *Groundwork* had been published, long before this account was published, and it was neglected by Kant's immediate successors and for many generations to come.

We can now turn to his successors, beginning with Johann Gottlieb Fichte, to see how the various issues identified in the first decade of response to Kant's moral philosophy inspired them either to do better within the spirit of Kant or to reject Kant because they thought that only a radically different approach to moral philosophy could resolve one or the other of these issues.

PART III

GERMAN IDEALISM AND ITS OPPONENTS

7

Fichte

7.1. The Challenges for a Transcendental Moral Philosophy

Johann Gottlieb Fichte (1762–1814) began his public career in 1792 with an anonymous book, *Attempt at a Critique of All Revelation*,[1] that was published by Kant's publisher and initially taken by many as Kant's expected work on the philosophy of religion. And not unreasonably so, since on many points it was close to Kant, although very different from Kant's own book on religion, the *Religion within the Boundaries of Mere Reason*, which appeared the following year. As Fichte's philosophy developed, it continued to be inspired by Kant, above all by Kant's conception of the primacy of practical reason and by the thought that freedom is the central concept of morality, the core value to be promoted by moral law. In some ways, Fichte attempted to go further than Kant, arguing that recognition of the moral law is a necessary condition of the possibility of self-consciousness itself, thus deriving moral philosophy from the basic premise of theoretical philosophy in a way that might be taken as the forerunner of recent constructivist interpretations of Kantian ethics, perhaps especially that of Adrian Piper, which will be discussed in the final chapter of this book. Owen Ware implies this when he says that "Fichte's aim in the *System of Ethics* is to derive the concept of morality from the principle of I-hood as a means of establishing ethics as a science," although he does not make the connection to recent constructivism explicit.[2] In other ways, Fichte did not go as far as Kant, arguing for the independence of the demands of justice or right from the demand of morality and at least leaving open the possibility that the decision to accept the burdens of justice might be prudential in a way that, on at least one interpretation, Kant did not. Moreover, not being privy to Kant's lectures on ethics with their explicit use of the self-consistency of freedom rather than the vaguer concept of humanity as the foundation of morality, Fichte might not have entirely realized how Kantian his approach to ethics was. In this chapter, I will examine Fichte's attempt to develop a Kantian approach to moral philosophy that would be immune to the chief objections that had already been raised against Kant's own version of Kantian ethics, and consider whether Fichte succeeded in resolving these difficulties. This

---

[1] Fichte 2010.
[2] Ware, 2020, p. 11. See also Wood 2016, pp. 184–6, and Jaeschke and Arndt 2012, p. 127.

Kant's Impact on Moral Philosophy. Paul Guyer, Oxford University Press. © Paul Guyer 2024.
DOI: 10.1093/oso/9780199592456.003.0008

will require some comments on Fichte's philosophy as a whole, although a complete interpretation of Fichte's philosophy can hardly be attempted here.[3]

Fichte's philosophy took many forms during his years as a professor in Jena (1794–9), and independent lecturer in Berlin, and then finally as a professor at the new royal university in Berlin from its founding in 1810 until his sudden death in 1814. My main focus will be Fichte's *System of Ethics* (*Das System der Sittenlehre nach den Principien der Wissenschaftslehre*), published in 1798,[4] which, considered with regard to Kant, can be counted as two or three books for the price of one. In its first two parts, it deals with the foundational issues for practical philosophy that Kant had dealt with in the *Groundwork for the Metaphysics of Morals* of 1785 and the *Critique of Practical Reason* of 1788, while in its third part it deals with the duties of virtue that Kant had dealt with in the second half of his *Metaphysics of Morals*, the "Doctrine of Virtue," first published separately in August 1797 and then unified with the first half of the work, the "Doctrine of Right," in 1798, thus the same year as Fichte's work. (Fichte dealt with the subject-matter of the "Doctrine of Right," namely legal and political obligations, in his *Foundations of Natural Right* of 1796, thus before he could have seen Kant's "Doctrine of Right," and it is quite likely that his *System of Ethics*, although published in March 1798, was also conceived and largely drafted before he could have seen Kant's "Doctrine of Virtue."[5] Fichte argued for the independence of the theory of right from morality in the *Foundations of Natural Right*, and therefore does not return to the subject in the *System of Ethics*.) But Fichte's *System of Ethics* does not merely cover the same territory as Kant's foundational works in practical philosophy on the one hand and more specific or applied theory of ethical duties on the other: his work is also clearly an attempt to improve upon Kant's foundations for practical philosophy, to use the method of transcendental philosophy as he conceives it to solve outstanding problems in Kant's own attempt to ground moral philosophy within the framework of the transcendental philosophy. Examining the success of Fichte's attempt at a transcendental moral philosophy is thus a way at least to begin considering the prospects for such an enterprise beyond Kant's own attempt at it.[6]

Here are four outstanding problems in Kant's foundations for practical philosophy, as we have seen all already raised in initial reception of that philosophy, that

---

[3] For works on Fichte's philosophy as a whole that emphasize the centrality of his approach to ethics within it, see Neuhouser 1990 and Zöller 1998. Wood 2016 and Ware 2020 put Fichte's moral philosophy in the context of his *Wissenschaftslehre* and also provide detailed studies of the connections and differences between Fichte's moral philosophy and Kant's. Kosch 2018 is another important recent study of Fichte's approach to moral philosophy. La Vopa 2001 is a detailed study of Fichte's life and works through 1799, while Kuehn 2012 covers Fichte's entire life and career. Gottlieb 2016, contains valuable papers on Fichte by Neuhouser, Wood, and others.

[4] Fichte 2005, cited here as "*SE*."   [5] See Wood 2016, p. xi, and Kosch 2018, p. 5.

[6] For my diagnosis of the flaws in Kant's own attempt at a transcendental practical philosophy, see Guyer 2007a.

Fichte can be thought of as attempting to resolve by the use of the transcendental method of philosophy as he understands it in the *System of Ethics*. First, as we saw, critics objected that Kant had failed to provide a transcendental deduction of the validity of the fundamental principle of morality for human beings of the kind that his own philosophical method should have required, that is, a deduction of the categorical imperative (the former presents itself to us as the latter, of course, for even if the fundamental principle of morality is valid for human beings it does not exhaust our possible motivations, but rather presents itself to us as a constraint on at least some of our desires, thus as a categorical imperative, "the relation of an objective law of reason to a will that by its subjective constitution is not necessarily determined by it (a necessitation)") (*G*, 4: 413). In section III of the *Groundwork*, Kant attempted to demonstrate that the moral law is the law for our authentic or proper (*eigentlich*) selves by arguing that the moral law is necessary for any rational being and that the uniqueness of our faculty of reason shows that at the noumenal level *we are* rational beings (*G*, 4: 451–3), an argument that obviously depends upon a transcendent claim about our noumenal selves rather than any merely transcendental analysis of or argument about the conditions of the possibility of our phenomenal consciousness. Then in the *Critique of Practical Reason* Kant insisted that all human beings are immediately aware of the obligatory status of the moral law as soon as they attempt to reason their way through any moral issue (*CPracR*, 5: 30), a "fact of reason" that cannot be reasoned "out from antecedent data of reason" but that "forces itself upon us of itself as a synthetic *a priori* proposition that is not based on any intuition" (5: 31) and which can, even though its own deduction would be "vainly sought," serve "as the principle of a deduction of an inscrutable faculty which no experience could prove . . . namely the faculty of freedom" (5: 47). This looks like a concession that the categorical imperative cannot be demonstrated by the methods of transcendental philosophy at all, even if once it is granted the reality of freedom might be derived from it by an argument that employs the method of transcendental philosophy. This is a result on which Fichte attempts to improve.

Second, both the need for a concept of the highest good, its consistency with Kant's conception of the purity of moral motivation, and the plausibility of Kant's doctrine of the postulates of pure practical reason as the conditions of the possibility of the highest good had all quickly come under fire. Fichte can be read as attempting to improve upon Kant's treatment of the highest good, although he may only have succeeded in getting himself into difficulties at least as great as any Kant may have had with this topic.

Third, Kant supposes not just that we human beings are immediately aware of the binding force of the moral law in the form of the categorical imperative, but that we are aware of it by means of or at least in conjunction with a distinctive *feeling*, the feeling of "respect" or "reverence" (*Achtung*). He claims that "though respect is a feeling, it is not one *received* by means of influence; it is, instead, a feeling *self-wrought* by means of a rational concept and therefore specifically different from all feelings of the first kind, which can be reduced to inclination or fear" (*G*, 4: 402n.), and even that "this feeling is the only one that we can cognize completely *a priori* and the necessity of which we can have insight into" (*CPracR*, 5: 73). But even if we were to overlook Kant's first problem and suppose that he does have a theory of our a priori knowledge of the content and the binding force of the moral law itself, it is not at all clear on what grounds he thinks that we can know a priori that this moral law must make its presence and force known *through a feeling*, that is, it is not clear how we know not just that this feeling "has an intellectual cause, which is known *a priori*" (*CPracR*, 5: 79), but how we also know a priori that this intellectual cause must produce a specific feeling. Fichte attempts to improve upon this aspect of Kant's foundations of morality also.

Finally, at least up through the *Religion* Kant had a problem about the compatibility of his proof of the reality of freedom with the undeniable fact that human beings do not always act as morality demands. At least he has such a problem in the *Groundwork*, where his proof that the moral law is the law of our noumenal selves because the noumenal self is essentially rational amounts to a proof that the moral law is the *causal* law of the noumenal self, a "causality in accordance with immutable laws but of a special kind" (*G*, 4: 446), which, if the noumenal self is the complete ground of the phenomenal self, as Kant at least initially supposes when he states that "the world of understanding contains the ground of the world of sense and so too of its laws" (*G*, 4: 453), would in turn mean that the phenomenal self also cannot but act in accordance with the moral law, that is, cannot act immorally—although obviously people do so all the time. As soon as he has introduced his transcendent proof that the moral law is the law of our noumenal will in *Groundwork* III (4: 451-2), Kant attempts to avert this implication by writing as if the moral law of our noumenal selves is only an *ideal* for our phenomenal selves, and as if our actions in the phenomenal world are the outcome of a struggle *between* our noumenal selves governed by the moral law and our phenomenal selves that "conform wholly to the natural law of desires and inclinations" (*G*, 4: 453), or *between* our "proper" or authentic and our inauthentic and lesser selves (*G*, 4: 457). But the treatment of our inclinations as a separate source of agency not grounded in our noumenal selves and competing with the rationality that is characteristic of our noumenal selves is inconsistent with the supposition that our noumenal selves are the complete ground of our phenomenal selves, thus Kant's theory of freedom in the *Groundwork* looked incoherent. As we saw, this problem was quickly pointed out by Ulrich, and Kant, following Schmid and accompanied by Reinhold, attempted to resolve it by the time he wrote the essays put together as *Religion within the Bounds of Mere Reason* by retaining the supposition that the noumenal self is the complete ground of the phenomenal self but jettisoning the supposition that the moral law is the *causal* law of the noumenal self, supposing instead that the noumenal self can freely choose (through its *Willkühr* or faculty of choice) whether to subordinate the moral law (which is given to it by pure practical reason or *Wille*) to the principle of self-love or rather to prioritize self-love over the moral law, thereby retaining the premise that the phenomenal self will faithfully reflect this noumenal choice while leaving room for immoral choice. This renders the possibility of freely choosing to do evil at least *conceivable* or *consistent* with Kant's theory of the noumenal basis of the phenomenal self, but at the cost of rendering the nature of noumenal choice, to use Kant's own term, *inscrutable*, and it certainly puts the last nail in the coffin of any attempt to derive the validity of the moral law from the essential character of our noumenal selves. Fichte will attempt to do better than Kant on this issue as well.

Determining whether Fichte *does* do any better than Kant in applying the transcendental method to any foundational issue in moral philosophy naturally depends on how we understand this method in the first place. What Kant meant by transcendental method has of course been long discussed and debated; what Fichte means by such a method has been more recently discussed.[7] For purposes of the present discussion of Fichte's attempt to improve upon Kant's transcendental moral philosophy, focusing on the *System of Ethics*, it seems most natural to derive one's conception of his transcendental method in general not only from this work itself but also from the version of the *Wissenschaftslehre* that Fichte promulgated during the period of the composition of this work, namely that preserved in the lectures that he gave during the period 1796–9 that has now become known as the *Wissenschaftslehre Nova Methodo*.[8] Two points that are essential to the method of transcendental philosophy as Fichte conceives of it in the period represented by this work may be emphasized here. First, transcendental philosophy aims to describe the structures of thought that make self-consciousness possible, structures that will include awareness of the self's activity on representations thought of as originating from something without the self but where the latter thought is recognized to be part of the self's own thought: transcendental philosophy is thus supposed to be immanent rather than transcendent, that is, to confine itself to describing the structures of thought that are the conditions of the possibility of experience rather than anything outside of experience, even though experience itself includes the thought of something outside of itself.[9] As Fichte puts it in the *Wissenschaftslehre Nova Methodo*,

---

[7] See work by Daniel Breazeale, such as Breazeale 2006 and 2007. See also Wood 2016, pp. 30–48, and Ware 2020, chapter 3, pp. 54–5 and esp. his argument with me at pp. 70–1; basically, Ware considers Fichte's transcendental method as explicative, unfolding the basic facts about consciousness, whereas I see the transcendental method as regressive, attempting to show that the conclusions follow deductively from premises which must be given a priori.

[8] Fichte 1992, cited below as *WNM*.

[9] An approach that would later be taken up in Edmund Husserl's conception of the phenomenological *epochē* or "bracketing" of "ontological" questions in favor of description of the structure of consciousness itself (see Wood 2016, p. 33), although whether either Fichte or Husserl could successfully maintain this stance is another question.

We are not talking about anything more than the occurrence of this representation [of the self]!... Here we are dealing with nothing but an immediate positing of the I, and this is a representation. The idealist's principle is present within consciousness, and thus his philosophy can be called 'immanent'.... Dogmatism is transcendent; it soars beyond consciousness. Idealism is *transcendental*; for though it remains within consciousness, it shows how it is possible to go beyond consciousness. That is to say, it shows how we come to assume that there are things outside of ourselves which correspond to our representations.

(*WNM*, pp. 94–5)

In other words, transcendental philosophy concerns itself with the self's *representation* of its relation to objects other than itself, but does not concern itself directly with those things apart from the fact of their being represented by the self. Or as Fichte puts it in *The System of Ethics* itself, "Anyone familiar with the spirit of transcendental philosophy will share our presupposition that this thinking of something subsisting must itself be based on our laws of thinking and that, accordingly, what we are seeking is only the essence of the I for the I, and by no means the latter's essence in itself, as a *thing* in itself" (*SE*, p. 33). In Fichte's language, "the essence of the I for the I" refers to the conditions for the possibility of self-consciousness, and in this statement Fichte is essentially endorsing Kant's own bipartite conception of transcendental philosophy as consisting in the analysis of the conditions of the possibility of self-consciousness on the one hand (the core of the Transcendental Analytic of the *Critique of Pure Reason*) and the critique and rejection of the transcendent metaphysics of the substantial self on the other (the topic of the Paralogisms of Pure Reason).

Second—and here is where Fichte departs from and aims to improve upon Kant's conception of transcendental philosophy—what transcendental philosophy reveals is that the essence of the self's thought of both itself and the things beyond itself that it represents is its *activity*, that representing and thinking are forms of activity, and that this cannot be understood except by thinking of the self as an agent in the world, or from the practical standpoint.[10] "The I is nothing but its own activity," Fichte states, "The representing subject is identical with its own self-activity, which constitutes its very essence, and thus, in every specific situation, its essence consists in a certain, specific self-activity" (*WNM*, p. 97). But particularly in the *Wissenschaftslehre Nova Methodo*, Fichte stresses that concrete human individuals can only come to understand the active nature of thought by understanding what is distinctive in action in the quotidian sense, goal-directed

---

[10] See the interpretation of Fichte, due largely to my co-author, in Guyer and Horstmann, 2023, pp. 75–84. The novelty of Fichte's interpretation of self-consciousness as an activity rather than mere reflection on a given object was pioneered by Dieter Henrich in Henrich 1966, expanded in Henrich 1967 and translated in Henrich 1982.

bodily intervention in the course of the world, so that "Considered from an a priori perspective and within the context of its place within a genetic account, the [philosophical] viewpoint is found to arise in the course of acting, and thus it can also be called 'the practical point of view'" (*WNM*, p. 106). The key to understanding the nature of self-consciousness in general thus becomes understanding human action, and the key to understanding this is understanding freedom. The key to understanding freedom, in turn, is to understand that activity must have its own law distinct from the laws that govern that which is represented merely as object, and the key to Fichte's transcendental derivation of the moral law is then the insight that the moral law is the only candidate for such a law of the distinctive activity of the self. The key to Fichte's system of ethics but also to his entire philosophy in the period 1796 to 1798 or 1799 is thus the argument that understanding the self requires understanding its activity but understanding its activity requires understanding its subjection to the moral law. It is because it makes such a direct transition from the necessary condition of self-consciousness as such to recognition of the validity of the moral law that Fichte's view may be considered as the precursor of the most radical form of contemporary constructivism.

Because of his direct transition from self-consciousness to the moral law, Fichte emphasizes in this period that he no longer recognizes the traditional distinction between theoretical and practical philosophy. The first presentation of his philosophy in 1794, Fichte now writes,

> was made somewhat awkward by the fact that the discussion of the conditions for the possibility of the principles [of transcendental philosophy] did not present these conditions in their natural order, but was instead divided into a "theoretical" and a "practical" part. As a result of this division, many directly related issues were separated too widely from one another. This will no longer occur in the present version, [which will follow] {a method of presentation that is just the opposite of that followed by the author in his compendium of 1794, where he proceeded from the theoretical portion of philosophy (i.e., from what had to be explained) to the practical part (i.e., to what was meant to serve *as the basis* for explaining the former). In the present lectures, however, the hitherto familiar division between theoretical and practical philosophy is not to be found. Instead, these lectures present philosophy *as a whole*, in the exposition of which theoretical and practical philosophy are united. This presentation follows a much more natural path, beginning with the practical sphere ... in order to explain the [theoretical] in terms of the former ...}   (*WNM*, pp. 85–6)[11]

---

[11] Material enclosed between squiggly brackets {} is from a secondary manuscript of *Wissenschaftslehre Nova Methodo*, the "Hallesche" manuscript, while the primary manuscript for Breaezeale's edition and translation is the "Krause" manuscript. See *WNM*, p. 61.

If *The System of Ethics* is truly composed in the spirit of this methodological remark from the *Wissenschaftslehre Nova Methodo*, then it should not be considered as an addendum to Fichte's transcendental philosophy but as its foundation, and his attempt to provide a satisfactory transcendental derivation of the central concepts of practical philosophy should not be regarded just as an attempt to improve upon Kant's use of the transcendental method in practical philosophy but as an attempt to improve upon Kant's use of the transcendental method *überhaupt*.

To be sure, some aspects of what Fichte intends by his practical foundations for transcendental philosophy as a whole are obscure. From the time of the first *Wissenschaftslehre* of 1794, the *Foundations of the Entire Science of Knowledge*,[12] through the works of the end of the decade, it remains unclear whether Fichte means by what he calls in that work the I positing the non-I merely that any subject must, whether on purely theoretical or on practical grounds, *recognize* that there must exist something other than the individual self, or rather that the self, each ordinary human self or perhaps ultimately some sort of super-self, *constitutes* an external reality, which in some ontological sense is therefore not ultimately independent of the individual self. In the *Wissenschaftslehre Nova Methodo* and perhaps in the earlier *Wissenschaftslehre* Fichte seems to mean primarily the former, although he was at pains to avoid the appearance of leaving an unknowable Kantian thing in itself, while in work beginning with the 1800 *Vocation of Mankind*[13] Fichte began to speak of an "absolute" that had elements of both subject and object but was in any case independent of and prior to individual selves like you, me, and Fichte himself. Fichte may have been pushed in this direction by his desire to improve upon Kant's theory of the postulates of pure practical reason, although in moving toward this view he may have put his immanent interpretation of the transcendental method at risk. But for much of our purposes we will not need to enter into the depths of Fichtean ontology, but can confine ourselves to the question of what Fichte supposes to follow from the individual's consciousness of him- or herself as a free agent. Many of both the strengths and weaknesses of Fichte's attempt to improve upon Kant's moral philosophy on the issues previously mentioned will be apparent at this level of discourse.

7.2. The Transcendental Deduction of the Categorical Imperative

Here I will comment briefly on Fichte's general argument in the *Wissenschaftslehre Nova Methodo* that awareness of activity is the condition of the possibility of the

---

[12] Fichte 1982.   [13] Fichte 1956.

awareness of selfhood, before discussing in more detail his argument in *The System of Ethics* that recognition of the moral law is the condition of the possibility of the awareness of activity. The overall argument is stated compactly in a series of "dictata" with which Fichte summarized his lectures during the course of giving them and which the transcriber of the lectures, Karl Christian Friedrich Krause, placed at the beginning of his transcription of them (*WNM*, pp. 35, 65).

Here Fichte states that the philosophical task at hand is to "Construct the *concept of the I* and observe how you accomplish this." Fichte then claims that if one does this "one will discover that one is *active* and will discover in addition that one's activity is directed upon *one's own active self*. Accordingly, the concept of the I comes into being only by means of a *self-reverting activity*" in which "*one posits oneself as self-positing*" (*WNM*, p. 65). By this, Fichte means that representing an object is a form of activity and representing oneself as representing an object is also a form of activity: thus understanding oneself as a self representing a world of objects requires understanding the activity of representing objects and the activity of representing oneself as representing objects. Fichte stresses that the mental activity that is involved twice over here cannot be reduced to a passive event of copying or merely receiving an impression; rather, "The activity involved in this transition is called *real activity* and is opposed to that *ideal* activity which merely copies the former" (*WNM*, p. 67). Fichte does not pause at this stage in his summaries to spell out in exactly what way or ways the self must be active in order to represent objects or to represent itself representing objects, although he subsequently illustrates at least part of why representing is active, tacitly drawing on Kant's "Transcendental Aesthetic," by arguing that the first condition for the possibility of representing objects is representing them as occupying different places in space and that this in turn requires the activities of *constructing* ("drawing") space itself and representing or *placing* objects at different locations in the space thus constructed. He does not, however, directly allude to the argument of Kant's "Transcendental Analytic" that *judging* that different representations are representations of a single object also requires the *activity* of combining or synthesizing representations, so that since knowledge requires judgment there is no knowledge without activity. Rather, what he does do is to stress that any form of activity at all, of which self-consciousness has been asserted to involve at least two instances, requires a conception of oneself as *free*, as *self-determining*, as oneself determining how one's mental capacities are to be exercised rather than as merely being acted upon by external agencies. His claim is that "*Freedom* is therefore the ultimate ground and the first condition of all being and of all consciousness" (*WNM*, p. 68). The starting-point of Fichte's transcendental philosophy in the period of the *Wissenschaftslehre Nova Methodo* and *The System of Ethics* thus consists of the claims that understanding oneself as a self involves understanding oneself as not merely having representations but as acting upon representations, and that this in turn requires understanding oneself as free or self-determining.[14]

One might have thought that this sense of freedom and Kant's sense of freedom as the ability to choose our own maxims and set our own ends are two different things. But Fichte's next and for our purposes crucial claim is that understanding oneself as self-determining requires the concepts of practical philosophy and ultimately the recognition of oneself as governed by the moral law rather than by mere laws of nature. The first of these steps is asserted in the *Wissenschaftslehre Nova Methodo* and the latter is spelled out in *The System of Ethics*. In the former work, Fichte states that "*Free self-determination* is intuitable only as a determination to become 'something,' of which the self-determining or practical {power} must possess a {freely constructed} concept," where in turn "A concept of this sort is called 'the *concept of a goal*.' Consequently, for the intuiting subject, the same subject who possesses *practical power* at the same time possesses the power to form concepts, just as, conversely, the *comprehending subject*, or {the power of} *the intellect*, must necessarily be practical" (*WNM*, p. 68). Fichte's claim here is that the activity of representing can only be understood as the act of determining one's general capacity or potential—determinability—to represent in some specific or determinate way, to represent some specific object, and that this must in turn be conceived of as realizing a goal or engaging in a goal-directed activity. "A *free action* is possibly only if it is guided by a freely constructed concept of this action," or a freely chosen goal. The next task is then to understand what it takes to represent oneself as a being that can choose a goal and choose to act in a way intended to realize such a goal.

Fichte develops the second stage of this argument, that one can represent oneself as freely choosing a goal only by representing oneself as subject to the moral law, the argument by which he intends to resolve the first challenge in improving upon Kant's use of the transcendental method in practical philosophy, in the Introduction to *The System of Ethics*. The argument of the *System* proceeds in three stages, the first in which the need, role, or *concept* of the moral law is deduced; the second in which the condition of the *applicability* of the moral law in the form of conscience and conscientiousness is deduced; and the third in which the *application* of the moral law in the form of particular duties is derived.[15] (Since Kant's *Metaphysics of Morals* had not yet appeared when Fichte devised this structure, he does not point out its obvious affinity to Kant's formulation of the moral law in the *Groundwork* and first chapter of the *Critique of Practical Reason*,

---

[14] This emphasis on the activity in representing would be Fichte's advance, if it is that, over his Jena predecessor Reinhold's *Satz des Bewußtseins* or "proposition of consciousness" that in representing the self is aware of both subject and object, which does not stress the element of activity. See Reinhold, *Versuch einer neuen Theorie des menschlichen Vorstellungsvermögens* (1789), "Essay on a New Theory of the Human Capacity for Representation"; modern editions Reinhold 2010 and 2011.

[15] See Wood 2016, pp. 137–8, and Jaeschke and Arndt 2012, pp. 122, 124–5.

his derivation of the "incentive" of the feeling of respect in the third chapter of the second work, and the derivation of the particular duties of human beings in the *Metaphysics of Morals*.) The premise of the whole argument is provided in the Introduction, which begins with a statement of the "direction of fit" contrast that Elizabeth Anscombe was to make well-known among Anglo-American philosophers a century and a half later: "*The entire mechanism of consciousness rests on the various aspects of* [the] *separation of what is subjective from what is objective, and, in turn, on the unification of the two*," he begins.[16] There are two ways in which the subjective and the objective may be unified, he then continues, namely in cognition, where the subjective is supposed to agree with the objective, and "when *I act efficaciously* [*wirke*]," where "the two are viewed as harmonizing in such a way that what is objective is supposed to follow from what is subjective," where "a being is supposed to result from my concept (the concept of an end)" (*SE*, pp. 7–8). But in fact the activity of the self must be recognized in order for the distinction between subjective and objective even to be made in the first place, for self can be distinguished from object only by recognition of one's activity in the world: "I find myself to be acting efficaciously in the world of sense. All consciousness arises from this discovery. Without this consciousness of my own efficacy, there is no self-consciousness; without self-consciousness, there is no consciousness of something else that is not supposed to be I myself" (*SE*, pp. 9–10). Presumably Fichte's thought is that if I were entirely passive, just a mirror for changes going on in an entirely objective world, I would have no way of distinguishing myself from that world: a mirror, after all, which passively receives images, is just another piece of furniture in the world. It is only because I can initiate changes in the world, myself determine what happens there in accordance with my own concepts of my goals, that I can have a sense of myself as distinct from the rest of the objects of the world in the first place, and then in turn conceive of objects as distinct from that self. In order to have a sense of myself as distinct from the world, I have to have not only "a representation of the *stuff*" of the world but also a representation of the "*properties* of this stuff... that are changed by my efficacy" and "a representation of this *progressive process of change*, which continues until the shape that I intend is there" (*SE*, p. 9). Thus, Fichte begins with the claim that the most fundamental feature of self-consciousness, the very distinction between subjective and objective, presupposes a conception of the purposive activity of the self, because it is only by conceiving of itself as acting on the world that the self can distinguish itself from the world. "Accordingly, insofar as I know anything at all I know that I am active." In the terminology of Fichte's 1794 *Foundations of the Entire Wissenschaftslehre*, the I can posit the not-I, which is essential to its consciousness of itself as an I, only by conceiving of itself as actively

---

[16] On direction of fit, see also Wood 2016, e.g., pp. 111, 126–8.

intervening in the world of the not-I; positing turns out to be a practical and not merely theoretical activity.

But the key move in Fichte's deduction of the moral law is the argument that being conscious of oneself as active requires being conscious of oneself as acting not merely in accordance with a concept of an end or purpose, but with a concept of an end or purpose that is independent of and self-sufficient from any merely objective laws of nature, because if one did not so conceive of one's activity, one's conception of it would collapse back into a representation of oneself as a merely passive object of nature, which would not be sufficient for a conception of one's own consciousness after all. Fichte claims that "the principle of all practical philosophy" is derived from the explanation of "how I come to assume that something objective follows from something subjective, a being from a concept." "This assumption arises," he states, "because I have to posit myself absolutely as active, and, since I have distinguished something subjective and something objective within myself, I cannot describe this activity otherwise than as the causality of a concept.... Absolute activity in this shape is also called *freedom*. Freedom is the sensible representation of self-activity, and it arises through opposition to the constrained state both of the object and of ourselves as intelligence, insofar as we relate an object to ourselves" (*SE*, p. 14). If I were to try to conceive of myself as acting in according with concepts of ends but were to suppose that those concepts of ends were simply given to me from elsewhere, I could not conceive of myself as anything but another part of the objective world, and thus could not conceive of myself as active and as a self after all; I can only conceive of myself as a self acting on the world insofar as "I presuppose a concept designed [or 'projected': *entworfen*] by myself." Fichte continues, "the concept of an end, as it is called, is not itself determined in turn by something objective but is determined absolutely by itself. Were this not the case, then I would not be absolutely active and would not be immediately posited in this way; instead, my activity would depend on some being and be mediated by that being—which contradicts our presupposition," that is, the presupposition that I am active, which is in turn the presupposition of my recognition of myself as a self at all. Fichte concludes:

> The most important result of all this is the following: *there is an absolute independence and self-sufficiency of the mere concept* (that which is "categorical" in the so-called categorical imperative), due to a causality of what is subjective exercised upon what is objective—just as there is supposed to be an absolutely self-posited *being* (of the material stuff), due to a causality of what is objective exercised on what is subjective. With this we have joined together the two extremes of the entire world of reason.   (*SE*, p. 15)

Fichte's argument is that we cannot conceive of freedom of thought without also conceiving of freedom to set ends of action. And in order to conceive of ourselves as freely acting, we have to conceive of a world of stuff on which to act, things with properties that we have to modify, and no doubt we have to conceive of that stuff as having its own laws with which we have to cope; but we cannot conceive of ourselves as also governed entirely by those laws, because then we will not be able to conceive of ourselves as different from and acting on that stuff after all. We must conceive of our action as governed by the principle of acting in accordance with or for the sake of ends that are determined independently of the mere laws of stuff, thus for the sake of ends that are "independent" from and "self-sufficient" with regard to the mere laws of stuff. Put in other words, a deterministic interpretation of human action is incompatible with the very possibility of self-consciousness.[17]

This is the gist of Fichte's deduction of the moral law, but he amplifies his presentation of it in part I of the *System of Ethics*, the explicit "Deduction of the Principle of Morality." Here Fichte presents his premise that I must think of myself as acting in order to think of myself as a self at all as the "Theorem" that "I FIND MYSELF AS MYSELF ONLY AS WILLING" (*SE*, p. 24), and his deduction then proceeds by means of a description of the conditions of the possibility of willing. His argument is thus analogous to Kant's derivation of the categorical imperative from the concept of a rational will in section II of the *Groundwork*, with the key difference that whereas Kant presents his analysis as yielding merely analytical truths about any possible rational wills that can be shown to apply to us, thus to be synthetic a priori, only if he can give a further proof that we actually are rational beings with wills, Fichte has already paved the way for our acceptance of the results of this analysis by means of his previous argument that the recognition of our activity is the condition of the possibility of self-consciousness itself. In this way, Fichte thinks that he can do better than either Kant's argument in section III of the *Groundwork* or Kant's subsequent insistence, or resignation, that the validity of the moral law must be accepted as an indemonstrable "fact of reason," a doctrine to which Fichte alludes several times (*SE*, pp. 19, 56). Fichte does not deny that moral philosophy must begin from the acknowledgement of a fact, or even from what he calls "faith," but he insists that the only fact from which moral philosophy can and must begin is the fact of self-consciousness itself, "I-hood" (*SE*, pp. 20, 23, 31), because self-consciousness presupposes the consciousness of willing.

Fichte's analysis of willing proceeds thus. On the one hand, "WILLING ITSELF...IS THINKABLE ONLY UNDER THE PRESUPPOSITION OF SOMETHING DIFFERENT FROM THE I," namely, something to be acted

---

[17] The gist of Michelle Kosch's interpretation of Fichte's conception of "independence" and "self-sufficiency" as the goal of morality is that this goal is the control of nature; see Kosch 2018, pp. 165, 178. Wood 2016 criticizes this interpretation (in earlier work by Kosch) as excessively "maximizing consequentialist" (pp. 148–53).

upon but also some particular way in which that external thing is to be acted upon, because "All willing that is actually *perceivable*...is necessarily a determinate willing, in which *something* is willed." Thus, "what I will is never anything but a modification of an object that is actually supposed to exist outside of me" (*SE*, p. 29). On the other hand, "IN ORDER TO FIND MY TRUE ESSENCE I MUST... THINK AWAY ALL THAT IS FOREIGN IN WILLING. WHAT THEN REMAINS IS MY PURE BEING" (*SE*, p. 30); in other words, I cannot think of the determinate change that I will in an external object as dictated by that object, because then I will not be thinking of myself as willing after all. Thus, "Insofar as willing is something absolute and primary,...it simply cannot be explained on the basis of any influence of some thing outside the I, but only on the basis of the I itself; and *this absoluteness* of the I is what would remain following abstraction from everything foreign" (*SE*, p. 30). So "THE ESSENTIAL CHARACTER OF THE I, THROUGH WHICH IT DISTINGUISHES ITSELF FROM EVERYTHING OUTSIDE OF IT, CONSISTS IN A TENDENCY TO SELF-ACTIVITY FOR SELF-ACTIVITY'S SAKE" (*SE*, p. 34); in other words, in order to think of the self as willing, it must have an end, but in order to think of it as genuinely active, this end cannot be imposed upon it by external objects and their laws, so the only alternative is to think of the self itself as an end—in other words, to think of the self as an end in itself, and of that conception as the ground of the law in accordance with which the self acts.

This argument is clearly supposed to parallel Kant's argument that rational being as an end in itself is the ground of a possible categorical imperative, but to derive that rational being is an end in itself from the conditions of the possibility of self-consciousness rather than merely to assert it, as Kant did in his exposition of the formula of humanity as an end in itself (*G*, 4: 428) or in the fact of reason doctrine (*CPracR*, 5: 30–1). But the argument might seem open to the objection that it is only *my own* self-activity that it makes into the non-externally imposed end of my willing, and thus that it does not give rise to a genuine moral law, equivalent to Kant's second formulation of the categorical imperative as "*So act that you use humanity, whether in your own person or in the person of any other, always at the same time as an end, never merely a means*" (*G*, 4: 429), after all. I take it that Fichte's assumption is that in arguing that self-consciousness must distinguish the end of its willing and action from any particular end merely imposed upon it by particular external, empirical circumstances, he has already shown that a genuine will must will a general rather than merely personal end, thus that self-activity in general, whether in one's own empirical person or that of any other, must be the ultimate end of willing, although of course an end that can lead to determinate action only insofar as it implies some determinate object of willing in one circumstance or another. I think that this thought is implicit in Fichte's characterization of the results of his argument as applying to "a rational being," that is, to *any* rational being. Thus he writes, "Strictly speaking, our deduction is now concluded. Its proper and final goal was, as we know, to derive from the system of reason as such the necessity of thinking that we ought to act in a certain manner and to demonstrate that if any rational being whatsoever is assumed, such a being must think such a thought," and he continues:

> A rational being is *itself* supposed to produce everything that it is ever actually to be. You therefore have to ascribe to such a being some sort of existence prior to all actual (objective) being and subsistence... This manner of existing can be none other than existing as an intellect in and with concepts. In your present concept [of yourself] you therefore must have thought of a rational being as an intellect...   (*SE*, pp. 52–3)

There is nothing personal in the thought of oneself as a rational being, although that thought is a condition of the possibility of self-consciousness; therefore there is presumably nothing personal in the thought of self-activity as the ultimate end of willing, one's end as a rational rather than merely natural being, either. Fichte makes the same point even more explicitly when he argues that the principle that is necessary in order to conceive of oneself as willing, thus as active, thus as self-conscious, and that is imposed upon oneself to this end, cannot be conceived of as a self-referential rule suggested by particular circumstances, because then it would not be a rule of genuine activity after all, but can only be a general rule furnished by the pure intellect. Thus, beginning his somewhat protracted conclusion of part I of *The System* (like a Bruckner symphony, the section seems to reach repeated climaxes before it finally ends), he states that "the thought just deduced has been called a '*law*' or a '*categorical imperative*'," and proceeds to explain why this is appropriate:

> We are able to think of freedom as standing under absolutely no law, but as containing the ground of its determinacy purely and entirely within itself—the determinacy of a thinking that is subsequently thought of as the ground of a being; and this is how we must think freedom if we want to think it correctly, for its essence lies in its concept, and the latter is absolutely indeterminable through anything outside itself. Since what we are thinking of is freedom, and freedom is determinable in all possible ways, we can also think it as subject to a hard and fast rule. The concept of such a rule, however, is something that only a free intellect could design for itself, and only a free intellect could freely determine itself in accordance with such a rule. The intellect could thus make for itself a great variety of different rules or maxims—for example, rules pertaining to self-interest, laziness, the oppression of others, and other similar rules—and could obey these rules steadfastly and without exception, and always freely. Let us now assume, however, that the concept of such a rule imposes itself on the intellect, i.e., that the intellect is, under a certain condition, required to think a certain rule,

and only this rule, to be the rule governing its own determinations. We may rightly assume something of this sort, since the intellect, thought absolutely free with regard to the sheer occurrence of an act of thinking, still stands under determinate laws with regard to its way and manner of thinking.

In this way, the intellect would be able to think of a certain way of acting as conformable to the rule and another way of acting as contradicting it.

(*SE*, pp. 56–7)

Here Fichte seems to be arguing as follows. It might seem possible to think of such self-referential maxims as to serve self-interest whenever one can, always to indulge in laziness, or to oppress others whenever one wants—examples that seem quite carefully chosen to echo the maxims that are to be excluded by Kant's own illustrations of the categorical imperative, specifically his second through fourth illustrations (see *G*, 4: 422–4 and 429–31)—as freely chosen rules. But in fact they could not furnish genuine rules that could be genuinely observed or violated, because since they are merely self-referential and arbitrary, they can be changed at any time. Instead, what is to serve as a genuine rule for the free intellect and will must be something that such an intellect and will chooses to follow independently of the mere desires that would ground such self-referential maxims, and such a rule could only be genuine, valid for any free intellect and will and comprehending all free intellects and wills in its scope. This is nothing other than "independence and self-sufficiency" as such. "The concept of such a rule is something purely and simply primary, something unconditioned, which possesses no ground outside itself, but is grounded completely in itself. Hence the action in question is not one that ought to occur for this or that reason, or because something else has been willed . . . instead, this is an action that ought to occur purely and simply because it ought to occur" (*SE*, pp. 57–8). Genuine freedom can be obtained only through generality, thus if freedom is a condition of the possibility of self-consciousness then so is generality.[18] But it is a question whether such a conception of "independence and self-sufficiency" as independence from all natural desires, not allowing them even to suggest possible ends for adoption by the free self, does not completely hollow out the conception of action, turning Fichte's conception of action into an "empty formalism" just as Kant's categorical imperative was alleged to be.[19]

---

[18] A difference between my approach and Ware's is thus that I see Fichte as attempting to derive the generality of the moral law abstractly in the first stage of his argument, whereas on Ware's account the general applicability of the moral law is not derived until the third stage of the argument, where Fichte adduces embodiment, intelligence, and relation to others as (supposedly) transcendental though material conditions of selfhood; see Ware 2020, chapter 7, esp. pp. 148–51 and 155–8.

[19] It seems to me that Wood's interpretation of Fichte's conception of "independence and self-sufficiency" is open to this objection. Kosch's approach, even if her inference from "self-sufficiency" to control of nature is open to the criticism that it is too empirical and too restrictive, seems to me on a better trajectory when she equates "self-sufficiency" with *perfecting the exercise of rational agency, by promoting the necessary external conditions of good deliberation in ourselves and others, and*

In addition to explaining how his own deduction of the moral principle satisfies Kant's demand for a categorical imperative, Fichte also tries to show how his argument yields a principle of autonomy (*SE*, p. 58), thus further confirming his own ambition to be giving a transcendental argument for the moral law as Kant conceives it.[20] I will not comment on this further step, however, but will instead conclude this section with a general comment on Fichte's strategy for a transcendental method in practical philosophy and then a comment on a tension in Fichte's practical philosophy as a whole that threatens the defense of his deduction that has just been given. The first point is this. Kant, as we earlier noted, seemed to recognize only two options with regard to a proof of the moral law: either it needs to be grounded not by a transcendental proof but by a step into transcendent metaphysics, that is, the argument of *Groundwork* III that the moral law is equivalent to the law of reason and is the law of our noumenal selves because the noumenal self is essentially rational, or else the moral law cannot be grounded at all, but can only be accepted on faith, as a "fact of reason," although once accepted it can ground an argument for the reality of freedom. Fichte, however, has attempted to argue that the recognition of self-activity as the end of willing for its own sake is necessary in order properly to conceive of oneself as willing, and that to conceive of oneself as willing is a condition of the possibility of self-consciousness itself; if the argument must start from faith, it starts from self-consciousness itself as an act of faith. Then if an argument to the condition or conditions of the possibility of self-consciousness itself is the paradigmatic form of a transcendental argument, as could well be argued if Kant's own transcendental deduction of the pure concepts of the understanding is supposed to be the paradigm of a transcendental argument, then Fichte's deduction of the moral law does have the form of a transcendental argument for the moral law, which eluded Kant. This is not, of course, to say that Fichte's transcendental argument for the moral law is compelling, although I have tried to show how Fichte can be seen as having attempted to avert one obvious objection to it, namely the objection that it merely makes the recognition of *one's own* self-activity as an end in itself the condition of the possibility of one's own self-consciousness. Fichte can be thought to have argued, I have suggested, that it is only by conceiving of oneself as willing an entirely general end that one can conceive of oneself as genuinely willing at all, and not merely as being acted upon by contingent and idiosyncratic desires. The key to the success of this defense is his underlying assumption that one needs to conceive of oneself as genuinely acting in order to conceive of oneself as a self at

---

broadening the scope of possible rational plans of action" (Kosch 2018, p. 45). This interpretation aligns Fichte's concept of "self-sufficiency" with Kant's account of what it is to treat our capacity to set ends as itself our end in itself, as I understand it.

[20] See also Kosch 2018, pp. 167–71.

all, and that to conceive of oneself as being moved by merely accidental desires would not be to conceive of oneself as genuinely acting at all.

There is a substantive problem with Fichte's defense, but before I turn to that I want to raise one issue concerning his general strategy for a transcendental deduction of the moral law. The problem is that, if recognition of the moral law is necessary for the achievement of self-consciousness, it might seem as if there is no further necessity to acknowledge or abide by the moral law *once self-consciousness has been achieved*. That is, if the achievement of self-consciousness is construed as an historical event in the life of any (or every) individual person, might not the acknowledgement of the moral law itself be construed as a one-time event, to which the agent need pay no further attention once he has become self-conscious? Perhaps Fichte has a different model of the necessary conditions of self-consciousness or the consciousness of the activity of the self in mind, but that alternative model would have to be spelled out to avoid this objection. More generally, Fichte owes us an explanation of how a necessary condition for the possibility of self-consciousness becomes *normative*, or an *ideal* to which we *ought* to conform our behavior.[21] One half of "deducing" Kant's categorical imperative would be deducing the inevitable presence of the *resistance* to our obligation—what Kant calls "inclination"—which makes the fundamental principle of morality into an *imperative* for us, but the other half would be deducing the normativity of this principle itself, its status as something to which we *should* conform our conduct whether or not doing so seems like a burden to us or in any way unpleasant. Fichte may indeed be attempting to sidestep such an issue with an approach that separates the abstract and general conditions of self-consciousness from anything like a narrative of the achievement of self-consciousness as a psychological fact in the life of particular human beings.[22] But that will solve one problem only to raise another, namely how general conditions for self-consciousness become a norm or ideal for the actual individual. We will return to that problem.

---

[21] Wood's treatment of this, e.g., Wood 2016, p. 123, seems very quick.

[22] Zöller's approach to Fichte emphasizes the difference between these, thus distinguishing between the "absolute I" and "our human, finite I," and then describing the former as an "ideal" to which the latter "always strives" (Zöller 1998, p. 102). This seems correct for Fichte, certainly beginning with *The Vocation of Mankind*, but leads to problems. Frederick Beiser has argued that by separating an absolute I from individual selves, the German idealists end up with precisely the same sort of epistemological problem with the traditional model of knowledge as a relation between subject and ontologically independent object that they were trying to avoid by bringing the object into the subject in the first place: the individual self still ends up having to know something other than itself; see Beiser 2002, p. 594. He is talking about Schelling there, but I suggest the same problem would arise for Fichte once he introduces the distinction between the individual and the absolute I. The problem I am raising here is an analogous problem for practical rather than theoretical problems, not how the individual self may know the absolute I but rather why what might be true of an absolute I becomes normative for the individual self.

7.3. Relation to Others in Fichte's Doctrine of Right

On the strategy for defending the deduction of the moral law from the necessary condition of self-consciousness that has just been discussed, this condition and the law that follows from it are both entirely general and thus make no reference to any particular self, thus not to any particular self whose individual self-consciousness must be founded on these general conditions. Fichte does discuss relations among actual individuals in his philosophy of right (*Naturrecht*), or the foundations of political philosophy. Fichte insists upon the independence of right from ethics, in part because on his view ethics concerns entirely *self-sufficiency* and *internal* motivation or conscience, whereas right does not concern either self-sufficiency or motivation.[23] Thus what he has to say in the area of right may not have been intended as part of his response to Kant's moral philosophy. But it can be taken as another attempt to deduce the moral law, and indeed has been so in contemporary moral philosophy.[24]

Fichte wrote the *Foundations of Natural Right* in 1795–6 and published it in 1796–7,[25] thus just before his *System of Ethics* and also just before Kant published his own *Metaphysical Foundations of the Doctrine of Right* in January 1797, and its combination with the *Metaphysical Foundations of the Doctrine of Virtue* of August 1797 into the *Metaphysics of Morals* of 1798. In the *Foundations of Natural Right* Fichte argues that "The finite rational being cannot assume the existence of other finite rational beings outside it without positing itself as standing with those beings in a particular relation, called a relation of right" (*FNR*, p. 39), yet he also argues, against what he takes to be position of "Kantians" if not clearly of Kant himself, that entering into the relation of right with others is voluntary (*willkürlich*) rather than mandated by morality and conscience. This seems to risk undermining his transcendental argument for the principle of right as a condition of the possibility of self-consciousness itself, but I am going to ignore that and just consider Fichte's own transcendental argument for the principle of right as if it were a further attempt to deduce the moral law. If the argument were successful, it could supply both a deduction of the very fact of the existence of other people as moral subjects, a fact that Kant seems simply to

---

[23] On Fichte's account of the independence of right from ethics, see among others, Neuhouser 2016, Clarke 2016, and Wood 2016, pp. 255–9. In Kant, right and ethics are two parts of morality as a whole, right differentiated from ethics as the coercively enforceable part of morality while ethics is that part of our moral duties compliance with which can be motivated only by respect for the moral law. Clarke distinguishes right from ethics in Fichte as *permissive* law distinguished from *prescriptive* duty; if that is correct, then Fichte's distinction is not so far from Kant's, but if Fichte's distinction is taken to mean that right is founded on prudence rather than morality, then his position is Hobbesian rather than Kantian.

[24] See Stephen Darwall, *The Second-Person Standpoint: Morality, Respect, and Accountability* (Cambridge, MA: Harvard University Press, 2006).

[25] See Fichte 2000, p. vii.

take for granted, as well as a deduction of the necessity of relating to them in a way that respects their freedom as well as one's own.

As is his wont, Fichte first states his argument briefly in the Introduction to the *Foundations of Natural Right* (pp. 8–12) and then states it at greater length in the form of a "deduction of the concept of right" (pp. 18–52). The brief argument consists of two main steps. First, Fichte asserts that "the rational being cannot posit itself as a rational being with self-consciousness without positing itself as an *individual*, as one among several rational beings that it assumes to exist outside itself, just as it takes itself to exist" (p. 9). This passage is important, because it suggests how Fichte's sometimes ambiguous talk of the I positing the non-I is to be taken, at least in the present context: although passages such as this later comment in the same work, that "The transcendental philosopher must assume that everything that exists, exists only *for* an I, and that what is supposed to exist for an I, can exist only *through* the I" (p. 24), might suggest that in positing the non-I the self *constitutes*, that is, literally *creates* the non-I, Fichte's opening assertion in the initial exposition of the deduction of the concept of right suggests rather that by the I positing the non-I what he means is just that the I must *assume the existence* of the non-I, or, at least in the case of other rational beings, *assume the existence* of other rational beings like itself. Of course, in some sense one I always directly experiences only its own representations of the non-I, whether the non-I is ordinary external objects or other selves, but its *positing* the non-I consists precisely in interpreting its representations *as* representations of something other than itself, whether ordinary objects or other rational beings. Fichte does not make the basis for this assertion very clear.

In the fuller exposition of the deduction of the concept of right, he explains that in positing itself as a rational being such a being "must ascribe to itself an activity whose ultimate ground lies purely and simply within itself," but that insofar as it is to posit or conceive of itself as a *finite* rational being, it must also conceive of its activity as *limited* in some way (*FNR*, p. 18), and that in turn to do this it must conceive of its own activity as limited by that *of other finite rational beings*, who must also be active in order to be rational but limited in order to be finite. His basis for this step is still less than clear. Perhaps he means it to follow from the further thought that "a rational being perceives itself immediately only in willing, and would not perceive itself and thus would also not perceive the world (and therefore would not even be an intelligence), if it were not a practical being" (*FNR*, p. 21), combined with the assumption that a will becomes aware of its own limits not in the resistance of inanimate or irrational objects to its wishes but only in the opposition of *another will* to its intentions. This might be intended by his subsequent statement that "there is no limitation without something that does the limiting. Thus the subject, insofar as it has posited this influence upon itself, must have simultaneously posited something *outside itself* as the determining ground of this influence" (*FNR*, p. 34), at least if there is supposed to be an emphasis on the idea that what is posited outside the finite rational self is *doing* the limiting, that is, if it must be considered another source of *activity*, another will. This would be consistent with Fichte's suggestion that in understanding ourselves as finite rational beings we do not merely posit an "external check" (*Anstoß*) (*FNR*, p. 32) on our own activity but a "summons" (*Aufforderung*), a "being-determined to be self-determining" (*FNR*, p. 31), something that cannot emanate from a mere rock, plant, or animal that we might choose to throw or eat, but only from another active, rational being. But Fichte does not make this argument, important and perhaps as plausible as it might ultimately be, very clear.[26]

What he does do, however, is to argue that conceiving of others around me as free in order to conceive of myself as free, I *limit* my freedom by theirs:

> I posit myself as rational, i.e., as free. In doing so, the representation of freedom is in me. In the same undivided action, I simultaneously posit other free beings. Thus, through my imagination I describe a sphere for freedom that several beings share. I do not ascribe to myself all the freedom I have posited, because I posit other free beings as well, and must ascribe to them a part of this freedom. In appropriating freedom for myself, I limit myself by leaving some freedom for others as well. Thus the concept of right is the concept of the necessary relation of free beings to one another. (*FNR*, p. 9)

This is the core of Fichte's deduction of the concept or principle of right: to think of myself as a finite rational being is to think of myself as freely willing, to think of myself as freely willing is also to conceive of my free willing as limited by the free willing of other finite rational beings, and to conceive of my free willing as limited by the free willing of other finite rational beings is to leave room for them to exercise their freedom—to grant them some rights as well as to claim some for myself.

In the second main step of his deduction, Fichte adds that to think of ourselves as freely willing is not just to think of ourselves as forming intentions, but also as acting upon such intentions in the external world: "what is required, therefore, is that something in the world outside the rational individual follow from the thought of his activity," or that his activity have "possible efficacy" (*Wirksamkeit*) (*FNR*, p. 9). He does not make the ground for this addition explicit either, though one might well see it as heir to Kant's distinction between mere wish and actual

---

[26] The role of the "summons" of the other as the basis of morality has been emphasized by interpreters of Fichte such as Allen Wood (Wood 2016, pp. 91–100) as well as by moral theorists taking inspiration from Fichte, such as Stephen Darwall in *The Second-Person Standpoint*. As I said, this is supposed to be the key to Fichte's doctrine of *right*, which is supposed to be rigidly separated from his *ethics*, and thus for him cannot be the basis of a general moral theory including ethics. This is of course just an historical point, and does not mean that Fichte's approach to right might not be used for a general moral theory other than Fichte's own.

will (e.g., *MM*, Introduction, 6: 213). What he does do is to make it clear that if this principle applies to one rational will, then it must also be seen by that rational will as applying to the other rational wills whom it must recognize as the condition of its own self-consciousness, thus a rational will that must be able to see the external world as an arena for the efficacy of its own intentions must also see it as an arena for the efficacy of the intentions of others as well. So "freedom in this sense would be possible for persons who stand with one another in this state of mutual influence only on the condition that all their efficacy be contained within certain limits, and the world, as the sphere of their freedom, be, as it were, divided among them." From this we would in turn derive the "complete object of the concept of right," namely "a community among free beings as such" (*FNR*, p. 10), but more precisely a community of *property*, that is, a world of external objects in which each has a sphere of efficacy. Thus a system of property rights, spheres of freedom of action in the external world, becomes a condition of the possibility of self-consciousness, at least insofar as that is understood as our self-conception as finite rational beings with wills.

Needless to say, Fichte's concept of rights is highly abstract, hardly specifying what sorts of things in the external world can become property and precisely what rights to property people must have in order to make their self-consciousness possible.[27] That is of course only what we should expect in the initial deduction of the bare concept of right. More worrisome is that the deduction does not specify *how many* others any one I must conceive as free and efficacious agents in order to be able to conceive of itself in this way, or *how much* freedom I must concede to them in order to conceive of my own. Must I conceive of *all* other human beings as *equally* free as myself, or would it suffice for the purpose of constituting my own self-consciousness that I just conceive of *one* other or *some* others as entitled to *some* of the freedom I claim for myself? Perhaps we would hope that the general deduction of the concept of right would address this issue, as Kant's Universal Principle of Right does. While leaving this issue open, Fichte has nevertheless offered a model for an argument that we must limit our own exercise of freedom by the freedom of others that could serve for a deduction of the moral law in general. However, Fichte himself blocks the generalization of this argument to a deduction of the moral law by his assumption that, while right necessarily concerns the freedom of multiple persons, morality is ultimately concerned only with the self-consistency of the individual—it is not merely concerned with the purity of an individual's motivation, but with the internal consistency of an agent's

---

[27] That is, Fichte does not conceive of the right to property, as the legal theorist Wesley Newcomb Hohfeld did, as an abstract concept that can be instantiated by varying bundles of rights—the permission to use something and the claim to enforce that permission against another are distinguishable and separable, for one thing, but so are the right to exclusive use, the right to transfer or alienate, the right to destroy, etc. See Hohfeld 1919.

actions. This is revealed in his description of the moral law as "the law of absolute agreement with oneself" (*FNR*, p. 11). Had Fichte been familiar with Kant's treatment of duties to oneself in the lectures on ethics in the form that Kant gave them from the mid-1770s to the mid-1780s, the period marked by the Kaehler transcription at one end and the Collins transcription at the other, he could have felt justified in asserting that Kant does treat those duties as a matter of self-consistency in the use of one's own freedom or power of choice, that is, making particular choices in ways that do not undermine but rather preserve and enhance one's capacity for choice on others.[28] However, in the seminal formulation of the categorical imperative in the *Groundwork*, the one that is to provide the "ground of a possible categorical imperative" and thus the foundation for the other formulations, Kant states that one must always act so "that you use humanity, whether in your own person *or in the person of any other*, always at the same time as an end, never merely as a means" (*G*, 4: 429, emphasis added), and given that he subsequently defines humanity as "the capacity to set oneself an end—any end whatsoever" (*MM*, Doctrine of Virtue, Introduction, section VIII, 6: 392), this means that the most fundamental requirement of morality is always to treat the capacity to set ends—freedom—consistently, in a way that preserves and enhances rather than undermining it, in oneself *and others*. Fichte thus misses the chance to himself explicitly improve upon Kant's deduction of the moral law.

7.4. The Realization of Morality

We have seen how the assumption that our intention must be potentially efficacious in order to count as willing figures in Fichte's derivation of the principle of right. In his "popular" work of 1800, *The Vocation of Mankind* (*Die Bestimmung des Menschen*), which can be seen as either the culmination of the first period of his philosophizing or the start of his second, Fichte makes a more general argument that we must assume, as he puts it in this work as a matter of faith, that our action can be efficacious, in order to conceive of ourselves as acting at all, and that we can do this because we must assume that our entire world, the world of theory as well as practice, is our own creation. We do not need an independent postulate of God or our own immortality to support our belief in the possible efficacy of our morality, although it may well be argued that this avoidance of separate postulates of pure practical reason is achieved only at the cost of transforming the positing self into something that is itself more immortal and God-like than in Fichte's earlier works. For this reason *The Vocation of Mankind*

---

[28] See Kant 1997, "Moral Philosophy Collins," 27: 343–6.

can be seen as marking the transition to a more "absolute" form of idealism than Fichte had earlier advanced.[29]

Fichte's attempt in *The Vocation of Mankind* to resolve the problem of the efficacy of morality without infinitely deferring the realization of its goals is a departure from his original, orthodox Kantian position in the *Critique of All Revelation*. There he had been content to say:

> This concept of infinite Happiness with infinite right and worthiness—*blessedness*— is an indeterminate idea, which is nevertheless established for us by the moral law as the ultimate goal, and which we continually approach, since the inclinations in us come ever closer to agreement with the moral law and our rights should thus extend themselves further and further. But we can never reach this goal without destroying the limits of finitude. And then the concept of the entire highest good, or *blessedness*, would be deducible from the legislation of practical reason.
>
> (CR, p. 27)

It may be noted that at this early stage in his career Fichte had not yet separated right and morality, as he would later. But that is not my concern here. Rather, I am pointing out only that at this early stage Fichte was content to regard the highest good as a goal that is legislated by morality but must always remain only an ideal for finite beings, which is to say for us, always. In *The Vocation of Mankind*, however, Fichte seems to want to undermine the dualism of ideal and actuality that his earlier argument presupposes and that Kant had attempted to get around with the expedient of postulated immortality. We will see, however, that he can do this only by introducing a distinction between individual selves and an absolute I that just reproduces the problem in another form. His initial instinct, that the gap between actual, imperfect virtue and happiness on the one hand and ideal, perfect virtue and happiness on the other, is an inescapable aspect of human finitude, was right.[30]

There are actually two interesting aspects to Fichte's argument in *The Vocation*. First, addressing an issue that sometimes bothers readers of Kant, who assume that morality in general prescribes ways of acting toward other persons as free agents even though we can have no theoretical proof of their freedom or of their existence as more than mere bodies at all, Fichte analyzes the command of conscience, which is the condition of the applicability of morality in Fichte's

---

[29] Allen Wood interprets Fichte's apparent turn to more traditional theology in 1800 and afterwards as only a symbolic expression of his earlier, non-transcendent views (Wood 2016, pp. 248–50). This is controversial, although in line with Wood's immanentist approach to Kant's moral theology as well.

[30] Regarding Fichte's earlier view, Wood's distinction between a "maximizing" conception of an infinite ideal that always remains unattainable for finite beings like us and a "recursive" conception of the "final end" on which we can fully attain our moral goal on a particular occasion but new moral situations and demands will inevitably arise is illuminating; see Wood 2016, pp. 179–84.

three-staged exposition, to *include* the commitment to the existence of others as free agents even though we have no theoretical proof of such existence. Here is the key passage:

> There appear before me in space certain phenomena to which I transfer the idea of myself; I conceive of them as beings like myself. Speculation, when carried out to its last results, has indeed taught me, or would teach me, that these supposed rational beings external to me are but the product of my own presentative power; that, according to certain laws of my thought, I am compelled to represent out of myself my conception of myself; and that, according to the same laws, I can transfer this conception only to certain definite objects. But the voice of my conscience thus speaks: "Whatever these beings may be and for themselves, you shall act toward them as self-existent, free, substantive beings, wholly independent of yourself. Assume it, as already known, that they can give a purpose to their own being, wholly by themselves and quite independently of you; never interrupt the accomplishment of this purpose, but rather further it to the utmost of your power. Honor their freedom, take up their purposes with love as if they were your own." Thus I ought to act; by this course of action all my thought *ought* to be guided; and it will necessarily be so guided if I have resolved to obey the voice of my conscience.   (Fichte 1956, pp. 94–5)

One striking feature of this passage is that it now clearly includes recognition of and respect for the freedom of others as part of the demand of conscience, thus apparently undermining the rigid separation between right and morality for which Fichte had argued just a few years previously. What is more important here is his claim that, even though from a theoretical point of view we have to recognize that we are only ever acquainted with *our own representations* of other persons, from a practical point of view, for Fichte always the most fundamental, we must regard other persons as genuinely independent centers of freedom. We might think of this commitment to the reality of other free agents as following from an "ought implies can" argument, as Fichte's last sentence hints: since we *ought* to treat others as independent centers of freedom, we must *be able* to treat them as such, and in order to be able to treat them as such we must regard them as *being* such. Thinking of them in any other way would undermine the command of conscience.

But such an argument might be in tension with Fichte's next argument, which is that we can be assured of the possible efficacy of our own agency just because we must think of the world as our own creation. Fichte introduces this argument, which may reflect his post-1800 transcendent metaphysics more than his pre-1800 immanentism, with the statement:

> My world is the object and sphere of my duties, and absolutely nothing more; there is no other world for me, and no other qualities of my world; my whole

united capacity, all finite capacity, is insufficient to comprehend any other. Whatever possesses an existence for me can bring its existence and reality into contact with me only through this relation, and only through this relation do I comprehend it; for any other existence than this I have no other organ whatever.   (Fichte 1956, pp. 96–7)

This might initially seem like a pompous way of saying that fulfillment of our moral duties is more important than anything else in our lives. But Fichte means it more literally: from the view that the external world is posited by our mental activity he is inferring that our mental activity is in turn intelligible only through our practical activity, that is, not merely on the model of our practical activity but on the ground of that activity, and thus that we have no way of representing an external world but as one that is a suitable arena for our practical activity, one in which our ends can be achieved. In *The Vocation of Mankind* he states this in the language of faith, thereby revealing the affinity of his view with Kant's postulates of pure practical reason but also showing that on his view the realization of our moral goals need not be deferred to an afterlife.

Our consciousness of a reality external to ourselves is thus not rooted in the operation of supposed external objects, which indeed exist for us, and we for them, only in so far as we already know of them; nor is it any empty vision evoked by our own imagination and thought, the products of which must, like itself, be mere empty pictures; it is rather the necessary faith in our own freedom and power, in our own real activity, and in the definite laws of human action, which lies at the root of all our consciousness of a reality external to ourselves—a consciousness which is itself but faith, since it is founded on another faith of which however it is a necessary consequence. We are compelled to believe that we act, and that we ought to act in a certain manner. We are compelled to assume a certain sphere for this action: this sphere is the real, actually present world, such as we find it—and the world is absolutely nothing more than this sphere, and cannot in any way extend beyond it. From this necessity of action proceeds the consciousness of the actual world and not the reverse way; the consciousness of the actual world is derived from the necessity of action.   (*VM*, p. 98)

Although in his deduction of the moral law in the *Doctrine of Ethics* Fichte had rejected Kant's position in the second *Critique* that the moral law is simply given as a fact of reason, here he is willing to use the term "faith" to characterize the epistemic status of our recognition of the law. But he then doubles the act of faith involved to include our affirmation of the character of the world that is posited as the arena of our action as well as the law according to which we are to act. The key thought is that we posit the laws of the world, and we posit them once, not twice: we do not posit separately theoretical laws of nature and practical laws of conduct and then worry how they are to cohere. Nor, even worse, do we defer the satisfaction of our moral objectives to another world because we have posited a natural world in which these objectives cannot be satisfied. Rather, we posit a single world in which the laws of nature cohere with the moral law.

But this attempt to avoid postulating a non-natural arena for the realization of our moral goals may be difficult to sustain. It might seem as if Fichte tries to make this radical conception of positing the world plausible by a kind of pantheism— what may well have been the basis of the charge of "atheism" that cost Fichte his post in Jena the year before[31]—namely by not resting with our ordinary conception of the human will as limited in its efficacy by all sorts of natural forces but by instead seeing it as a manifestation of a "sublime" or divine and omnipotent will.[32] On this account, the powers of the human will would simply be infinitely greater than they appear to be to common sense, so nothing could get in the way of its efficacy. In the end, that position may have seemed implausible to Fichte himself, as well it should have, and driven him to take refuge in the position that the only thing that the moral will really aims at is its own purity of motivation, which can be achieved in an inner or "spiritual" realm quite apart from the laws of nature. Thus he writes:

> Such a view of my will as I have taken, however, is not attained merely through the conviction that the will is the highest active principle for this world—which it certainly might be, without having freedom in itself, by the mere energy of the system of the universe, such as we must conceive of the formative power in Nature. The will rejects absolutely all earthly purposes, all purposes lying outside itself, and recognizes itself, for its own sake, as its own ultimate end. By such a view of my will I am at once directed to a supersensual order of things in which the will, by itself alone and without any instrument lying outside of itself, becomes an efficient cause in a sphere which, like itself, is purely spiritual, and is thoroughly accessible to it. That moral volition is demanded of us absolutely for its own sake alone... (VM, p. 126)

Fichte seems to offer us two ways around whatever problem might lie in Kant's postulates of pure practical reason as the necessary conditions for the rationality of acting morally. On the one hand, we can disambiguate his initial conception of the I positing the non-I, which seemed ambiguous between the idea that the self necessarily creates its *representation* of what is not itself and the idea that the self literally creates the non-self, in favor of the latter. This would leave us free to create

---

[31] See La Vopa 2001, chapters 12–13, pp. 368–424, and Kühn 2012, chapter 7, pp. 376–401.
[32] Wayne Martin opts for a non-transcendent interpretation of the conditions for "a form of harmony between 'things' and 'the pure form of the I'" (Martin 2019, p. 302), but makes this plausible by confining his attention to Fichte's pre-1800 works.

an external world that is fully hospitable to our moral objectives. On the other hand, we can stop worrying that the goals of morality have to be achieved in an external world at all and think of them entirely internally, as being nothing but the achievement of purity of intention, which we are always free to realize no matter what may transpire beyond our own minds. This option, it might be noted, would be consistent with Fichte's premise in his argument for the independence of right from morality that the latter concerns only what is within our minds, namely, our intentions and their self-consistency. But it seems to revert to a caricature of Kantian morality rather than to improve upon it.

Fichte's attempt to improve upon Kant's postulates of pure practical reason thus seems caught between the Scylla of an implausible metaphysics and the Charybdis of an implausible morality. Thus far, it looks as if it might have been better had he limited his efforts to the deduction of the moral law, and as if we might be better off confining our attention to the *Doctrine of Ethics* rather than venturing beyond. So let us now return to that work, but to look at a different attempt to improve upon Kant, namely Fichte's attempt at a deduction of moral *feeling*.

7.5. The Transcendental Argument for Moral Feeling

Kant claimed that the feeling of respect is "self-wrought" by reason (*G*, 4: 401n.) and the only feeling that we can in some way know a priori (*CPracR*, 5: 73), but he certainly did not explain the latter claim. A distinctive feature of Fichte's attempt to apply the transcendental method to practical philosophy in the *Doctrine of Ethics* is that he does attempt to give an argument that the moral determination of the will must be accompanied with a distinctive feeling, indeed that the moral determination of the will must make itself effective *through* a distinctive kind of feeling and the relation of that feeling to other feelings.[33] And while Kant, for example in the *Critique of Practical Reason*, treated the feeling of respect as a pendant to the moral law, an "incentive" that could be described after the presentation of the "fact of reason" or consciousness of the moral law and the deduction of freedom from it had been completed, Fichte includes the premise for his account of moral feeling in his original deduction of moral law and his fuller account of it under the rubric of a "Deduction of the Reality and Applicability of the Principle of Morality" (*SE*, p. 65), the second stage of his exposition. His thesis is that human freedom and its direction by the concept of the end of activity for its own sake can only be empirically manifest to the human being in the form of a distinctive feeling, a feeling that stands in a distinctive relation to other feelings, so

---

[33] This is a central theme in Ware's interpretation of Fichte's moral philosophy; Ware 2020, pp. 105–10.

that the existence of a distinctive form of moral feeling is not an unexplained accident but a condition of the possibility of consciousness of the self as a moral being and agent at all. In this sense Fichte attempts to give a transcendental deduction of moral feeling. Although he is attempting to go one better than Kant by actually providing such a deduction rather than merely asserting that we know a priori that the moral law must produce a feeling of respect, he can also be taken to be defending the centrality of moral feeling to a Kantian approach against those who thought that Kant's moral philosophy had no room for feeling at all.[34]

There are two underlying premises of Fichte's argument. The first is that the moments of self-consciousness, including both what can be thought of as its content and as the activity it performs on that content, must be manifest to consciousness in some empirical form, that is to say, in some spatio-temporal form. The second is that self-consciousness requires the unification of the objective and the subjective, but a unification that is really a reunification, that is, a unification of something objective and something subjective that are really already within the self. Putting these together, he reaches the conclusion that both the objective and the subjective moments of consciousness must be represented to us in some temporal form. In the context in which it has been customary for us to start thinking about self-consciousness in the philosophical tradition, namely the context of the perception of external objects, we think of the objective as presented by sensations and of the subjective as manifested in the activity of organizing and conceptualizing these sensations. Against this background it would seem that Fichte's general desideratum could be satisfied by supposing that we have some form of empirical awareness of our activity of conceptual organization as well as of sensation—the former being precisely what he called, beginning with the *Wissenschaftslehre Nova Methodo*, and so misleadingly from a Kantian point of view, "intellectual intuition," by which he means not an intuition of objects by pure reason alone, which is what Kant denied to human beings, but an intuition of the activity of reasoning itself (which Kant also denied, but without making this denial central to his critical project).[35] In the context that Fichte himself thinks is primary for the explication of self-consciousness, namely, the conscious of our own activity, there must also be two forms of empirical consciousness, namely some empirical consciousness of freedom itself, but also some consciousness of that on which freedom is exercised—that which is objective for freedom as subjective, and which is analogous to the sensation that is organized by conceptual activity in the cognitive case. Fichte first introduces the empirical manifestation of

---

[34] Wood devotes a chapter to conscience (Wood 2016, chapter 5, pp. 137–71), but does not discuss moral feeling.

[35] See Kant, "Answer to the Question: Is it an Experience that we Think?," Reflection 5661, 18: 318–19; translation in Kant 2005, pp. 289–90.

freedom itself as the subjective moment in practical activity. He maintains that "THE I BECOMES CONSCIOUS OF ITS OWN TENDENCY TOWARD SELF-ACTIVITY ... IN RELATION TO THE ENTIRE I AS A DRIVE" (*SE*, pp. 43–4). A drive is a temporally extended and forward-looking mental state that in this case is the empirical manifestation of freedom. But although self-activity or freedom is the essence of the self, it is also only part of the self, and so this drive is only a tendency, something that is potential as well as actual, not fully realized, and therefore the empirical manifestation of freedom must also in some way manifest the incompleteness of freedom at any given time. In his first introduction of the existence of the drive that manifests self-activity in the original "Deduction of the Principle of Morality" itself, Fichte uses this point only to infer that "the drive will be accompanied by a longing" that will be resolved at least to some extent when a "deed is accompanied by a decision" (*SE*, p. 44). But in the fuller discussion in the "Deduction of the Reality and Applicability of the Moral Principle" Fichte clarifies that, since activity requires something that it transforms, freedom must overcome some resistance, and then since both freedom and the resistance that it has to overcome must be empirically manifested in feelings, there must be feelings that have to be resisted as well as the feeling of the longing for the freedom to resist and overcome then. For this reason moral action must take the form of the attempt of moral feeling to overcome or redirect other feelings. Fichte makes these points in the crucial "Proof" and "Corollaries" of this section. First, the key claims of the proof:

> I find myself to be willing only insofar as my activity is supposed to be set in motion by a determinate concept of the same....
>
> Activity cannot be determined by itself, and yet it must be determined if consciousness is to be possible at all. This means nothing else than the following: the activity is to be determined through and by means of its *opposite*...
>
> I cannot however, intellectually intuit, absolutely and by myself, the manner in which I am limited; instead, this is something I only *feel* in sensory experience.... The I is now supposed to be posited as active; and thus it would have to be posited as eliminating and breaking through a manifold of boundaries and resistance, in a succession ...   (*SE*, pp. 88–9)

This argues that activity is made determinate only by overcoming some specific form of resistance, and that I must feel in sensory experience the specific resistance or limits that I have to overcome in my activity as well as feeling, as already argued, the tendency of my activity to overcome them. Fichte reiterates this point in his "Corollaries":

> The I is to be posited as an actual I, but solely in contrast with or in opposition to a Not-I. But there is a Not-I for the I only under the condition that the I acts

efficaciously and feels resistance in its effective operation, which, however, is overcome, since otherwise the I would not be acting efficaciously. Only by means of such resistance does the activity of the I become something that can be sensed and that endures over a period of time, since without such resistance the I's activity would be outside of time, which is something we are not even able to think.   (*SE*, p. 89)

Here Fichte argues that the essential nature of the self and the basis for self-consciousness is not merely the *positing* of a Not-I by the I, as he had in his original presentation of the *Wissenschaftslehre* in 1794, but the *overcoming* of the Not-I by the I, and that both moments, the Not-I and its overcoming, must be *felt* because self-consciousness takes place in time and feeling is the form of the presentation of the moments of self-consciousness in time. But it also should be clear from everything that has preceded the argument that what he is here calling "Not-I" is not something that is simply outside the self, but rather that *in the self* which seems to resist what is essential in the self, its free activity: so the "Not-I" here can only stand for *feelings* that resist the tendency and longing to morality but that can be overcome or redirected under the guidance of the moral law, while the "I" is identified with the self's willing of activity itself as its end. This leads to an empirical model of free, moral action in which feelings resistant to morality must be controlled by the longing to be free and moral in general, which Fichte further amplifies by suggesting that specific feelings resistant to morality must be replaced by others compatible with or hospitable to morality:

What ordinary consciousness tells us therefore is this: in executing our ends, we are bound to a certain order of means. What does this claim mean when one views it from the transcendental viewpoint and when one attends solely to the immanent changes and appearances within the I, in total abstraction from things outside of us?—According to the preliminary elucidations provided above, whenever I perceive I *feel*. "I perceive changes outside of me" means that the state of my feelings has changed within me. "I want to act efficaciously outside of myself" means that I will that the place of one determinate feeling should be occupied by another determinate feeling, which I demand through my concept of an end. "I have become a cause" means that the feeling that is demanded actually does occur. Thus, "I proceed to my end by passing through the means" means that other feelings occur in the interval between the feeling from which I proceed to willing and the feeling demanded by my willing....

Every feeling, however, is an expression of my limitation; and "I possess causality" always means that I expand my limits. Thus what we are claiming is that this expansion can occur only in a certain, progressive series, since we are claiming that our causality is limited to the employment of certain means for accomplishing our end.   (*SE*, pp. 92–3)

Here Fichte suggests that acting is always a temporally extended process, and thus that the act of overcoming resistance that presents itself in the form of feelings must take the form of successively replacing those feelings with others more conducive to the ultimate goal of the action.[36]

The steps in this extended argument are no doubt loose, but its ambitions are interesting. Kant assumed that moral choice, for him the determination of the noumenal will, must have consequences in the empirical world, and he devoted considerable effort in the second and third critiques to justifying our belief in the actuality of the conditions of the possibility of the realization of the ultimate objective of moral choice, namely the highest good, in the natural world. But his account of the mechanisms of human psychology by means of which the moral determination of the will is translated into action in the spatio-temporal realm of nature is sketchy and unargued. In the *Groundwork*, he tended to treat the feeling of respect as an epiphenomenal manifestation of the noumenal determination of the will to be moved by the moral law alone that plays no direct causal role in action (*G*, 4: 401n.). In the *Critique of Practical Reason*, he suggested that the feeling of respect which is itself caused by the moral law and supposedly known a priori to be so does play a causal role in action by striking down feelings of self-conceit (*CPracR*, 5: 73), but he did not offer any argument that this role of the feeling of respect is a *sine qua non* of morally motivated action. In the *Metaphysics of Morals*, published as Fichte was working on *The System of Ethics* and not explicitly referred to in Fichte's work, Kant does argue that the presence of a general moral feeling, conscience, and the more specific feelings of self-esteem and love of one's neighbor are "antecedent predispositions on the side of *feeling*" that are "conditions of receptiveness to the concept of duty" without which we could not be put under obligation," and that although we could not have a duty to somehow get these predispositions if we did not have them at all because in that case the concept of duty could get no purchase on us, we do have a duty to cultivate and strengthen them so that they will be forceful enough to be efficacious when we need them.[37] In a subsequent discussion of the specific feelings of

---

[36] The idea is not that the moral self must overcome nature, including other persons, *outside* of itself; here I agree with Ware and Allen Wood against an interpretation by Michelle Kosch (see Ware 2020, 167–72, referring to Kosch 2015 and Wood 2016, p. 157). It is some feelings within the self that must be overcome by morality, resulting in moral feeling. Ware typically stresses that this is a form of unification rather than opposition within the self, but does say that "we could say that our ultimate goal [in morality] is not one of maximizing control over nature but one of maximizing freedom from obstacles generally, human and nonhuman alike" (p. 172), where those obstacles would include some feelings in oneself that have to be overcome. But for this reason Fichte's moral ideal of "independence and self-sufficiency" must be interpreted carefully: he cannot mean that human beings can or should simply eliminate contra-moral inclinations, as Kant thought that the "Stoic sage" was supposed to do. Neither did Kant think that human beings could or should do this, rather he thought that we might only *wish* we could do so (*G*, 4: 428). A *wish* is precisely something that we might like but cannot rationally will because we cannot bring it about.

[37] Kant, *MM*, Doctrine of Virtue, Introduction, section XII, 6: 399–402.

"*sympathetic joy*" and "*sadness*" or "sympathetic feeling," Kant also says that such feelings are the "means" that nature has afforded us to accomplish our moral goals and that we have a "particular, although only a conditional, duty" to "cultivate the compassionate natural... feelings in us, and to make use of them as so many means to sympathy based on moral principles"[38]—a duty that is conditional, of course, because our duty is not simply to cultivate feelings of sympathy or other moral feelings and then to act on them whenever they happen to present themselves in sufficient strength, but rather to cultivate them so that they will be strong enough for us to act on in those circumstances but only those circumstances where the principle of morality tells us, through the operation of our well-cultivated conscience, that the actions that those feelings prompt us to perform are indeed morally appropriate or mandatory.[39] But Kant does not attempt to embed these eminently reasonable thoughts in any larger theory of human action, let alone to provide a transcendental argument for or deduction of them. That is what Fichte has attempted to do by means of his extended argument that self-consciousness requires a consciousness of free activity, that consciousness of free activity requires a consciousness of both a goal to change reality and the resistance of reality, but especially one's own reality, to that change, that all consciousness requires an empirical manifestation of its essential moments, that we must therefore have feelings that need to be overcome as well as a feeling of our drive or tendency to overcome them, and that finally since action always takes place in temporally extended succession, the act of overcoming feelings that are resistant to morality because of our general feeling or longing for self-activity—morality—must take the form of gradually substituting some specific feelings for non-moral or morally refractory feelings, although apparently Fichte feels no compulsion (pardon the pun) to enumerate them.

Is this really a transcendental argument? There are two assumptions in this argument that might be contested by someone pressing that question. The first would be whether Fichte has genuinely shown the manifestation of moments of self-consciousness in empirical form to be a necessary condition of the possibility of self-consciousness itself, assuming that the strategy of transcendental argumentation is always to argue that its target is a condition of the possibility of self-consciousness itself. His underlying assumption is that we are creatures who are embodied in space and time (see for example *WNM*, pp. 70–1), and that all moments of self-consciousness must present themselves in some spatio-temporal form, indeed some form linked to our possession of bodies. It is not clear that he has given an explicit argument for this assumption. It is also not clear that we can seriously imagine any alternative to this assumption—even "brains in a vat"

---

[38] Kant, *MM*, Doctrine of Virtue, §§34–5, 6: 456–7.

[39] For further discussion of the role of moral feeling in Kant, see Guyer 2008a, chapter 4, and Guyer 2010a and 2010b, both reprinted in Guyer 2016a.

arguments assume that we are at least *body-parts*, namely brains, located in some other bodies, namely vats, and only quibble about whether we can be sure about what sorts of bodies we really have and what surroundings they are really in[40]—and thus it is not clear that any transcendental argument should really be under the burden of proof of showing that we have bodies at all. Perhaps any plausible transcendental argument has to start from the assumption that the conditions of the possibility of self-consciousness must have empirical and therefore bodily manifestations, and the real burden of proof that transcendental arguments should satisfy is only that of showing that specific conditions of the possibility of self-consciousness require specific sorts of bodily functions.[41]

The second objection that could be raised about Fichte's argument would be whether he has really shown that something as specific as *feelings* are a condition of the possibility of the action that is in turn the condition of the possibility of self-consciousness itself. But if feeling is taken in a sufficiently general sense, as a mental state that has some conceptualizable content but also involves some element of bodily awareness, then of course every moment of self-consciousness must for bodily creatures like us be manifested as some form of feeling. The question would then be not whether Fichte has succeeded in showing that self-consciousness depends upon feelings in general, but whether he has succeeded in showing that our self-consciousness as *moral agents*, which is supposed to be the necessary condition of self-consciousness in general, depends specifically on the feelings of a drive to be moral as well as feelings that resist that drive but can at least gradually be overcome by it. Here the first of Fichte's assumptions might seem more contestable than the second: that we have feelings that would incline us to actions contrary to the demands of morality ultimately seems too obvious to need to be proved, and what is interesting is primarily that Fichte has attempted to provide a transcendental proof of the fact that *overcoming* these feelings is always a temporally extended and never completed process. What is less obvious is that Fichte has succeeded in showing that there is a single moral feeling or "longing" that is the start of that process. Nevertheless, it might still be concluded that if certain reasonable assumptions about the burden of proof in transcendental arguments are made, Fichte has shown how some key assumptions of moral psychology might be placed within the framework of a general analysis of the conditions of human action in a way that begins to look like a transcendental deduction of them.

---

[40] For the classical "brain in a vat" argument and its refutation on meaning-theoretic grounds, see Putnam 1979.

[41] As previously noted, Ware takes embodiment, intelligence, and sociality to be "transcendental" conditions of selfhood, but he does not explain in what sense these are genuinely transcendental rather than empirical, causal conditions of selfhood.

7.6. The Problem of Freedom

Fichte seems to have made some advances over Kant in the use of a transcendental method for the deduction of the validity of the moral law and of moral feeling. Has he made a genuine advance on Kant's treatment of the most fundamental problem in his theory of freedom, the apparent contradiction between the claim that the moral law is the causal law of the authentic self and the indisputable reality of immorality?[42] The course of Kant's thought on this problem about freedom from the *Groundwork*, his first work on practical philosophy, to the *Metaphysics of Morals*, his last, is a torturous one: to summarize briefly what we previously discussed,[43] in the *Groundwork* he made the moral law the causal law of the free noumenal self, making it impossible even to conceive how the free agent can choose to violate the moral law and do something immoral; in *Religion within the Boundaries of Mere Reason*, doing in his own terms what Schmid and Reinhold also proposed around the same time, Kant introduced the vital distinction between *Wille* and *Willkühr*, thus separating the will into one faculty that legislates the moral law and another that chooses whether or not to prioritize it over self-love, thus allowing for the possibility of immoral action even though any particular choice to act immorally remains inexplicable; but in the *Metaphysics of Morals*, Kant seemed to remain uncomfortable with this resolution of the problem of the possibility of evil, arguing that "freedom of choice cannot be defined—as some have tried to define it—as the ability to make a choice for or against the law (*libertas indifferentiae*), even though choice as a *phenomenon* provides frequent examples of this in experience,"[44] thereby appearing to take back precisely what he himself had argued in the *Religion*—although, as I suggested, he may only have meant to argue the technical point that a *real* definition of freedom could not be given without inclusion of the freedom to choose for the moral law as its *ratio cognoscendi*, thus using the debate to emphasize his point that we *know* our freedom through our consciousness of the moral law.

It would hardly be surprising that Fichte should attempt to develop a more consistent position on this fundamental issue than he could have found in Kant. But at least at first his transcendental argument that the conception of ourselves as freely self-active agents governed by the self-legislated moral law is a condition of the possibility of consciousness itself seems, like Kant's thought on the issue, to be inexorably torn between the ideas that as free beings we are in fact necessarily governed by the moral law, like a causal law, and that as both natural and rational beings we are necessarily governed by the *ideal* of the moral law but do not

---

[42] George di Giovanni presents Fichte's thought as beginning with his intervention in the debate over the possibility of free immorality among Ulrich, Schmid, Reinhold, and Kant; see di Giovanni 2005, chapter 6.

[43] See also Guyer 2014a, chapter 6.

[44] Kant, *Metaphysics of Morals*, Introduction, section III, 6: 226.

necessarily live up to it. Fichte might ultimately propose a way out of this dilemma, already hinted at in his account of moral feeling, by arguing that recognizing the moral law as an "infinite" ideal that we necessarily strive to fulfill but to which we equally necessarily only asymptotically approach might be sufficient to satisfy the demands of the transcendental theory of self-consciousness without excluding the possibility of immoral actions and even of self-consciousness of them. But such a way out will depend upon the possibility of explaining how transcendental conditions for the possibility of self-consciousness are transformed into a normative ideal for concrete, situated individual human beings.

As Kant's path to his latest treatment of freedom of the will was tortuous—I do not say "final" treatment, because our previous discussion suggest that Kant may never have completely resolved all his concerns about freedom of the will into a stable and coherent position—so was Fichte's thought on this issue by no means free from twists and turns. In his early, Kantian *Critique of All Revelation*, where he had taken a Kantian stance toward the highest good, so did he take a position on freedom of the will similar to that for which Reinhold and Kant were arguing at the same time.[45] Fichte begins his "Theory of the Will" in this work with the statement that "spontaneity produces only forms" (*CR*, p. 14), from which he infers that in at least one way a genuine will necessarily wills the moral law, for that is the only purely formal law of volition. He is happy to present this in the language of Kant's second *Critique*, stating that "it is a *fact of this consciousness* that such an original form of the faculty of desire, and an original faculty of desire itself, actually proclaims itself to consciousness in our mind by means of this form.... By this fact, then, it first becomes certain *that* man has a will" (*CR*, p. 15). In other words, he accepts Kant's equation that a free will is one that wills the moral law (see *CPracR*, 5: 29) along with Kant's position that it is the moral law that is the *ratio cognoscendi* of our spontaneity and not vice versa (5: 47). However, Fichte continues that the spontaneity of our pure will in producing the formal law of morality "does not necessarily effect an actual volition"; to that end a *further* "action of spontaneity in our consciousness is yet required," an exercise of "*freedom of choice (libertas arbitrii)*, given to consciousness empirically in [the] function of choosing" *between* acting in accordance with the moral law and merely gratifying inclination. Fichte continues:

> This freedom is indeed to be distinguished from the absolutely first expression of freedom through the practical law of reason, where freedom does not mean choice at all, since the law allows us no option but rather commands by

---

[45] Just as Kant took up his 1792 article on radical evil into his 1793 *Religion within the Boundaries of Mere Reason*, so did Fichte expand his treatment of free will from the 1792 edition of the *Critique of All Revelation* to the 2nd edition of 1793; see the Editor's Introduction to *CR*, pp. xvi–xvii.

necessity... Without this absolutely first expression of freedom, the second, merely empirical expression could not be saved; it would be a mere illusion...

Nevertheless, "if one conceives the characteristic of *choice* in the concept of freedom... then *moral* necessity can surely not be combined with it" (*CR*, pp. 21–2). In other words, the moral law is a fact of consciousness, as Kant had argued in 1788, and one that is necessary for us to be conscious of our spontaneity at all, but the presentation of the moral law to consciousness is not the same as a decision to act one way or another, and we do not get a full sense of our freedom of choice unless we also recognize our liberty to choose whether or not to conform our conduct to the moral law. This was the same position that Reinhold and Kant himself had reached by 1792. In Fichte's terms, it means that "Pure *volition* is not possible in finite beings," although it is our consciousness of the moral law that "reveals our spiritual nature by its very existence" (p. 23). Of course, our nature is not entirely spiritual.

In the *System of Ethics*, at least a part of Fichte wants to avoid this conclusion. Fichte's attempt to deal with the problem of freedom in the *System of Ethics* goes on for many pages, but throughout the twists and turns of his argument, Fichte seems repeatedly torn between the same two positions between which Kant could never quite decide. On the one hand, Fichte often suggests that the free agent who can fully live up to the demands of morality and the agent who is played upon by natural forces that might appear to be the source for immoral choices are only two ways in which the same self appears, so that there can be no real conflict between them—a position that would be consistent with Fichte's suggestion in *The Vocation of Mankind* that there can be no conflict between the realization of moral objectives and the laws of nature because we are ourselves responsible for nature in general. Thus he writes that "it is always I myself that determines me, and in no way am I determined by the drive," and continues:

> The ground for relating these predicates to one another is the following: although a part of what pertains to me is supposed to be possible only through freedom, and another part of the same is supposed to be independent of freedom, just as freedom is supposed to be independent of it, the substance to which both of these belong is simply one and the same, and is posited as one and the same. The I that feels and the I that thinks, the I that is driven and the I that makes a decision by means of its own free will: these are all the same. (*SE*, p. 104)

This makes it sound as if there could hardly be any conflict between our natural drives and our free will, so that there can be nothing that can stand in the way of complete compliance with morality. As does this passage some pages later:

Are my drive as a natural being and my tendency as a pure spirit two different drives? No, from the transcendental point of view the two are one and the same original drive, which constitutes my being, simply viewed from two different sides. That is to say, I am a subject-object, and my true being consists in the identity and indivisibility of the two. If I view myself as an *object* completely determined by the laws of sensible intuition and discursive thinking, then what is in fact my one and only drive becomes for me my natural drive, because on this view I myself am nature. If I view myself as a *subject*, then this same single drive becomes for me a pure, spiritual drive, or it becomes the law of self-sufficiency. All the phenomena of the I rest solely upon the reciprocal interaction of these two drives, which is, properly speaking, only the reciprocal interaction of *one and the same drive with itself.* (SE, pp. 124–5)

On this account, human action cannot be understood as the product of two genuinely independent forces, natural drives (presumably to satisfy contingent inclinations) on the one hand, and a pure, spiritual drive to be moral on the other hand, either of which drive might but neither of which must dominate the other. The natural and the spiritual or moral drives of the human being are rather one and the same thing seen from two different points of view, so they cannot conflict with one another, and there would be, it seems, no circumstances in which the former could lead to an outcome contrary to what is demanded by the latter.[46]

On the other hand, Fichte also insists that there must be room for moral failure, which can apparently be explained only by the assumption that our natural drives do *not* always coincide with our moral drive and sometimes get the upper hand over the latter. Thus he says that "what drives our nature and determines our physical power need not be only the moral law itself. After all, we are also able to carry out immoral decisions" (SE, p. 75). Thus, "The law reason gives to itself... that is, the moral law, is not a law that it obeys necessarily, since it is directed at freedom" (SE, p. 60). Here Fichte not only maintains that the human agent does not necessarily act in accordance with the moral law, but even suggests that since the moral law is a law that commands freedom or self-activity, it would make no sense to think of it as a law that we are somehow necessitated to follow—the goal that this law commands us to realize would be undermined if we were somehow automatically determined to act in accordance with this law.[47] The moral law commands freedom, but freedom is the capacity to act either for or against the moral law. But if it is possible for us to find it in our nature to make immoral decisions, then all of our natural drives and our pure spiritual drive to be moral cannot simply be the same thing under two descriptions or seen from two points of view: two descriptions of one and the same thing need not mention all the same facts about it, perhaps they need not mention any of the same facts, but they cannot be outright incompatible, for then they cannot be descriptions of the same thing after all.

Sometimes Fichte seems to try to avoid this dilemma by the strategy that Kant had already tried in the third section of the *Groundwork*, that of allowing that there are two potentially conflicting sides to the self, but that only the drive to be moral reflects the "proper" or "authentic" self. Thus Fichte writes:

> the natural drive, understood *as a drive that is determined in a certain precise way*, is *contingent* to the I itself. Viewed from the transcendental standpoint, it is the result of our own limitation. To be sure, it is indeed necessary that we be limited in some way or another, for otherwise no consciousness would be possible. But it is contingent that we be limited *in precisely this way*. In contrast, the pure drive is essential to the I; it is grounded in I-hood as such. For this very reason it is present in all rational beings, and whatever follows from it is valid for all rational beings.—Moreover, the pure drive is a higher drive, one that elevates me above nature with respect to my pure being and demands that I, as an empirical, temporal being, elevate myself above nature.   (*SE*, p. 135)

Fichte argues that a merely natural drive "has no *control* over me, nor is it supposed to have any such control: I am supposed to determine myself utterly independently of the impetus of nature." But the fact that he repeats the words "supposed to" suggests that he does not think it is automatic that the moral law is in control, so that even if the moral law represents the "higher" part of our nature it does not represent the whole of it. Here Fichte does not claim that contingent natural drives and the moral drive are two sides of the same coin, allowing instead that the former might not be controlled by the latter, although they ought to be, because only the latter expresses our "higher" and "essential" self. While leaving room for immorality, this solves the problem of the normativity of morality by fiat, declaring the inalterable formal condition of self-consciousness to be the principle of the "higher" self and downgrading the variable material conditions of self-consciousness, the variable desires that constitute the internal "not-I" to the "I" of the pure will, to lower status. If necessary conditions of self-consciousness are not necessarily always obeyed, then an account of why they *should* be obeyed seems to be owed: the normative question cannot be escaped by a metaphysical sleight of hand.

Further, if free self-activity that is not determined by any merely natural causal processes is supposed to be a condition of the possibility of self-consciousness, then this solution to the dilemma of freedom seems to raise a question about something that has hitherto been taken for granted, namely, how we could even be conscious of merely natural drives that are not under the control of our freely chosen commitment to the moral law as part of our self, even if only a lower or contingent rather than higher and essential part. Fichte needs a solution to this question, because he has reasserted his commitment to the transcendental thesis that freedom is the condition of self-consciousness just a couple of pages previously:

> I, however, am an I solely insofar as I am conscious of myself as an I: that is, as free and self-sufficient. This consciousness of my freedom is a condition of I-hood. . . . a rational being is not possible at all without any consciousness of this freedom, and thus also not possible without the conditions for such freedom, and since one of these conditions is a consciousness of morality, a rational being is also not possible without such consciousness. . . . Here we are claiming only that no human being could be absolutely lacking in *any* moral feeling.   (*SE*, p. 132)

If being conscious of myself as free and self-sufficient is a condition of self-consciousness or "I-hood" itself, it might seem as if I could not even be conscious of a part or aspect of myself that is resistant to morality, thus that the possibility of a non-moral part of myself might be a theoretically possible explanation for my immoral choice but not an explanation for which I could have any evidence. Fichte could avoid this problem, however, by holding that the awareness of *any* freedom, of "*any* moral feeling" as the empirical manifestation of freedom, is sufficient for one to conceive of oneself as a self, rather than that an awareness of the freedom of *each* of one's acts is a necessary condition for the awareness of each of those acts. Indeed, as earlier suggested, perhaps a one-time recognition of the validity of the moral law would be sufficient for self-consciousness even if one then went on, in real time, to repeatedly flout it by acting on the feelings identified with one's "lower" self. This assumption would explain why he is not worried about the possibility that one would be literally unaware or unself-conscious of any of one's natural drives that have not successfully been brought under control of one's rational commitment to the moral law, and is instead concerned only to maintain that as long as one is self-conscious one must be aware of the *call* of the moral law and of the *possibility* of living up to it, thus aware of oneself as *striving* to live up to the moral law. In order to be self-conscious, one must be aware of the moral law and strive to fulfill it, but there is no need for this striving to be fully satisfied, and indeed its complete satisfaction could be indefinitely or "infinitely" remote. This is what Fichte himself presents as the resolution of the dilemma created by his making awareness of freedom the condition of the possibility of self-consciousness:

> The causality of the pure drive must not disappear; for only insofar as I posit such a drive do I posit myself as an I.

We have arrived at a contradiction, which is all the more remarkable since what is contradictory is in this case...a *condition for consciousness.*

How can this contradiction be resolved?...

This can be comprehended only as follows: the intention, the concept that is involved in acting, aims at complete liberation from nature. But it is not as a consequence of our freely designed concept of the action that the action is and remains suitable to the natural drive; instead, this is a consequence of our limitation. The sole determining ground of the matter of our actions is [the goal of] ridding ourselves of our dependence upon nature, regardless of the fact that the independence that is thereby demanded is achieved.... Consequently, the final end of a rational being necessarily lies in infinity; it is certainly not an end that can ever be achieved, but it is one to which a rational being, in consequence of its spiritual nature, is supposed to draw ceaselessly nearer and nearer.   (*SE*, p. 142)[48]

For Fichte, the condition of the possibility of self-consciousness turns out to be an awareness of the necessity of *striving* to fulfill the moral law, not of ever fully succeeding in fulfilling it, but this awareness of striving is then sufficient to spread self-awareness over all of one's self, not just that part of it which is compliant with morality.

Fichte has to give up the claim that all of our natural drives and our pure spiritual drives are exactly the same thing just seen from two different points of view if he is to be able to appeal to a conflict between them in order to explain the possibility of immoral choices. But he does not have to give up the claim that being aware of the moral law is the condition of self-awareness itself if he is willing to allow that, once achieved through awareness of the moral law, self-consciousness can spread itself even to immoral elements of our selves. If it is striving to be moral that makes us aware of ourselves as selves, that is compatible with failure to be fully moral. Here Fichte ends up back in the original position of Reinhold, Kant, and the *Critique of All Revelation.*

Fichte's claim that the final end of a rational being is "infinite" in the sense that it can *never* be fully achieved might seem to be a non sequitur, an inference from the mistaken supposition that an awareness of striving and thus of some opposition that always needs to be overcome is a *necessary* condition of self-awareness rather than an inference from the more plausible premise that even an awareness of striving to fulfill the moral law is a *sufficient* condition of self-consciousness. But, this mistake apart, perhaps he does after all suggest a way between the two

---

[48] This passage does support a more tradition interpretation of Fichte's moral goal as an infinite ideal that can never be fully attained rather than Wood's creative "recursive" conception on which the moral demand can be fully satisfied on one occasion but then arises again on further occasions (a recursion for any individual presumably ended by death).

horns of Kant's dilemma about freedom, and perhaps he does that precisely by keeping his argument a transcendental rather than a metaphysical or transcendent argument. That is, Kant's problem about the possibility of evil arose because he made the claim that the moral law is the causal law of the noumenal self, but Fichte introduces the moral law only as the condition of the possibility of self-consciousness, and this seems compatible with the assumption that we are not moral in every one of our acts, even while we may be fully aware of those acts. So perhaps in this area too Fichte points the way to a successful use of transcendental method in moral philosophy.

However, there would still seem to be one serious objection to the transcendental argument from the fact of our self-consciousness to the fact of our freedom. It would not seem that I could use the fact that self-consciousness implies awareness of my freedom to exclude the possibility that I (or anyone else) lacks freedom in at least some and perhaps morally crucial circumstances, because the connection between self-consciousness and consciousness of freedom could be a merely analytical proposition, sufficient to establish freedom with respect to as much of myself as I am conscious of but not sufficient to establish that there is no unfreedom in myself of which I am not immediately conscious. The proposition might establish that the limits of my self-consciousness are the limits of my freedom, but not that there are no limits to my self-consciousness and thus no limits to my freedom. The strategy of using the non-controversial fact that we are self-conscious to prove the unlimited reality of our freedom might seem as doomed as any other attempt to prove that we have unlimited freedom; it might instead only prove the limits of our self-consciousness.

But this might not be a bad outcome for a transcendental argument from self-consciousness to freedom after all: a Spinozist or a Freudian, for example, holds that one's freedom is limited precisely by the limits of one's self-awareness, and that the connection between freedom and self-awareness does not guarantee the unlimited extent of one's freedom but rather calls for an effort to extend one's self-awareness. I do not think that Fichte intended to reach this conclusion; on the contrary, his transcendental strategy of arguing that the idea of our freedom is the condition of the possibility of self-consciousness itself suggests that he at least started with the intention of proving the unlimited reality of our freedom. But he does seem to have at least backed into the position that our freedom must take the form of an endless striving, not anything that is ever fully realized, and perhaps his own connection between self-consciousness and freedom shows what must be expanded in order to make progress in striving to be free, namely, self-consciousness itself. This would not be a bad moral for a transcendental theory of freedom.

8

Schelling

The Deduction of Evil

8.1. Introduction

Friedrich Wilhelm Joseph Schelling (1775–1854) is not ordinarily thought of as a major moral philosopher.[1] But Schelling engaged moral philosophy, in particular Kant's moral philosophy, twice, and his efforts are worth notice. In the culmination of Schelling's first period of work, the *System of Transcendental Idealism* of 1800, part 4 provides a "System of Practical Philosophy according to the Principles of Transcendental Idealism," in which Schelling attempts to deduce the main features of a moral and political philosophy very much like Kant's. A decade later, in *Philosophical Investigations on the Essence of Human Freedom* (1809), Schelling addresses the age-old issue of theodicy, attempting to reconcile the existence of evil with the existence of God, but in particular tries to deduce the necessity of human evil from the relationship of humans to God. Both of Schelling's ventures into moral philosophy thus have the form of attempting to deduce what Kant was ultimately willing to leave as inscrutable "fact," the normativity of the moral law on the one hand and not merely the possibility but the actuality of human evil on the other. Like Fichte, Schelling attempts to deduce the validity of the moral law as a condition of the possibility of self-consciousness, thus anticipating the later approach of constructivism, and the problems that his deduction faces suggests the problems facing any such approach. His attempt to show that human evil is not merely possible but necessary shows the risk of a priori argumentation on that subject as well.

Schelling's philosophical career was long and complex. His meteoric rise began at the age of 20, by 23 he was a professor at Jena, but at age 34, by then hounded out of Jena after a scandalous marriage and settled into a sinecure in Munich, he

---

[1] For example, he is not discussed in Wood 2010, nor in Irwin 2009 or Skorupski 2021. There is no section on moral philosophy in Bowie 1993. Jaeschke and Arndt 2012 devote fifteen pages to the two phases of Schelling's thought that I will discuss here. These two phases do receive detailed discussion in Kosch 2008, pp. 66–104; see also Kosch 2014. The essays in Höffe and Pieper 1995, are all devoted to Schelling's 1809 essay on *The Essence of Human Freedom*, which will be the topic of the second part of this chapter, but are all in German.

Kant's Impact on Moral Philosophy. Paul Guyer, Oxford University Press. © Paul Guyer 2024.
DOI: 10.1093/oso/9780199592456.003.0009

largely ceased publishing.[2] He did not cease writing or lecturing, however, and, as his posthumous publications indicate, his thought continued to evolve throughout his life, ultimately moving away from his version of transcendental idealism to what he called a "positive philosophy" with a strong emphasis on the historical development of human thought in the form of mythology and religion.[3] I will not attempt to present a complete picture of Schelling's development here, but will focus strictly on his two engagements with Kant's moral philosophy and the lessons they might offer for thinking about Kant rather than about Schelling himself.

The *System of Transcendental Idealism*, which Schelling published at the ripe age of 25, is ordinarily taken to be the culmination of the first phase of his thought, in which he attempted to join "philosophy of nature" with transcendental idealism by combining the view that consciousness evolves out of natural processes with the view that consciousness constructs a representation of both nature and itself. Following this work, Schelling launched what is called his "identity philosophy"; its chief departure from his previous view seems to be that now he regards nature and consciousness as products of a single underlying "absolute" rather than simply of each other. The essay on *The Essence of Human Freedom*, the last work that Schelling would himself publish, comes at the end of the identity philosophy, but replaces the notion of the absolute with a conception of God according to which evil is made possible by God's own complex rather than simple nature and human evil is made necessary by the very difference between mankind and God. Schelling argues that the possibility of evil can be understood only at the cost of a traditional conception of God as omnipotent and entirely benevolent, although Schelling tries to avoid the traditional Christian heterodoxy of Manichaeism by distinguishing between the "ground" of God's existence, which includes evil, and God's existence itself, which does not.[4] Schelling's account of human evil as not merely possible but also necessary not only rejects Kant's position in *Religion within the Boundaries of Mere Reason*, which was heterodox, certainly contrary to the Calvinism of the Prussian ruling house, in its argument that conversion from an evil to a good moral disposition is always within the power of unaided human being, but is itself heterodox in its argument that evil is a necessary feature of the human condition—which after all limits the power of God—even though a kind of *progress* toward the good may also be a necessary feature of the human condition. The fundamental theoretical difference between

---

[2] Schelling broke up the marriage between August Wilhelm and Caroline Schlegel in the period from 1799 to 1803, the Schlegels finally being divorced that year and Caroline free to marry Schelling. They then moved to Würzburg where Schelling took up a professorship and gave the lectures on the philosophy of art that are his most readable work. However, Caroline survived only six years. In 1812, Schelling married a much younger woman, with whom he had six children. For biographical details on Schelling and others in his circle, see Wulf 2022.

[3] See Kosch 2008, pp. 88–9.   [4] See Jaeschke and Arndt 2012, pp. 492–4, and Marquard 1995.

Kant's *Religion* and Schelling's *Essence of Human Freedom* concerns the question whether evil is inscrutable or deducible; the fundamental practical difference concerns the possible completeness of moral conversion. Schelling's position may represent a genuine challenge to Kant's optimism on the latter score.

8.2. The *System of Transcendental Idealism*

In the version of his philosophy that Schelling developed in his first years in Jena, particularly from 1797 to 1800, his transcendental idealism is a complement to his *Naturphilosophie* or philosophy of nature.[5] The philosophy of nature describes the evolution of self-consciousness out of natural forces, while the system of transcendental idealism describes consciousness's construction of its representation of nature and then of itself, in other words, the construction of self-consciousness, the consciousness of consciousness as consciousness. In this regard following Fichte, although he was shortly to break with him,[6] Schelling argues in part 4 of the *System of Transcendental Idealism* that consciousness of having a *will* is a necessary condition of the achievement of self-consciousness, for without consciousness of having a will the (human) subject would in fact have no reason to distinguish itself from its object. Consciousness of having a will in turn requires both a representation of the will as such, or a pure conception of the will, as well as consciousness of *resistance* to the will, which is what marks the difference between the subject and its object. A pure representation of the will is in turn equated with the representation of the will as such as its own *end*, from which Schelling derives the moral law, while the necessity of resistance to the will is equated with the representation of non-moral inclinations, from which Schelling derives the impurity of the human will or the fact that the moral law presents itself to us in the form of the categorical imperative. By means of this argument, Schelling attempts to derive two things that Kant simply took for granted, on the one hand, the validity or binding force of the moral law, which Kant did take for granted in the "fact of reason" version of his moral philosophy in the *Critique of Practical Reason*, and the inevitable presence of inclinations that would if indulged lead us to actions contrary to the moral law, from which Kant derives the fact that the fundamental principle of morality presents itself to us in the form of a categorical imperative constraining us in the face of resistance. Kant always took the existence

---

[5] Some authors prefer to leave *Naturphilosophie* untranslated because in Schelling's hand it is not the name for a general area of philosophy, what we might call philosophy of science, but is the name for a particular theory of nature, one according to which there is a necessary evolution from the simplest forces of attraction and repulsion to self-consciousness as the most evolved phenomenon of nature. For example, in his extended treatment of Schelling in Beiser 2002, Frederick C. Beiser never translates the term.

[6] Kosch discusses Schelling's retentions and departures from Fichte at Kosch 2008, pp. 70–6.

of our potentially contra-moral inclinations for granted. Like Fichte, Schelling thus attempts to derive from the conditions of the possibility of self-consciousness facts about the human condition that Kant took for granted, thereby addressing methodological objections to Kant.

Schelling begins the exposition of his "system of practical philosophy" with a clear statement of what would later be called the distinction between normative ethics and meta-ethics: he says that what he seeks to establish is not a "moral philosophy," that is, a body of specific precepts for conduct, "but rather a transcendental deduction of the thinkability and explicability of moral concepts as such" (STI, p. 155).[7] In its context, this statement signals that Schelling has no intention of departing from the content of Kant's moral philosophy—he is not proposing a new moral philosophy—but that he does aim to provide a transcendental deduction of its central claims, which was precisely what Kant had shied away from in the Critique of Practical Reason. The first proposition in Schelling's series of deductions is then that "the beginning of consciousness is explicable only through a self-determining, or an act of the intelligence upon itself" (STI, p. 155). We may take his point to be that, although in his exposition up to this point of transcendental idealism as a theoretical philosophy he, like Fichte, has been freely speaking of the action or activity of thought in constituting its (representation of its) world, he has not really yet explained how we come to be conscious of thought as an action. To put it another way, while Fichte has been content to postulate "intellectual intuition" as the source of our recognition of the activity of thought itself—an intuition or experience of the activity of the intellect—Schelling thinks that we need to redeem this promissory note with something more concrete. His argument is that the activity of thought is a kind of "self-determination," and that we have our primary experience of or acquaintance with self-determination in the experience of *willing* something: "This self-determining of the intelligence is called *willing*, in the commonest acceptation of the term." So "it is only through the medium of willing that the intelligence becomes an object to itself" (STI, p. 156), that is, not just a source of knowledge but also an object of knowledge, not just consciousness but self-consciousness. This conclusion then requires Schelling to proceed by means of a further analysis of what is involved in becoming conscious of ourselves as willing.

Before we look at the next steps in his argument, we may note that Schelling further signals that he is attempting to provide a transcendental deduction for what Kant had failed to deduce by invoking the term that Kant had made his own, namely "autonomy"; he is attempting to provide the conditions of the possibility of our consciousness of our own autonomy:

---

[7] Translations from *The System of Transcendental Idealism* (STI) are from Schelling 1978. Citations from *Philosophical Investigations into the Essence of Human* Freedom (EHF) are from Schelling 2006.

It is autonomy which is commonly placed at the summit only of practical philosophy, and which, enlarged into the principle of the whole of philosophy, turns out, on elaboration, to be transcendental idealism. The difference between the primordial autonomy, and that which is dealt with by practical philosophy, is simply this: by means of the former the self is absolutely self-determinant, but without being so for itself—the self both gives itself the law and realizes it in one and the same act, wherefore it also fails to distinguish itself as legislative, and discerns the laws in its products, merely, as if in a mirror. By contrast, in practical philosophy, the self as ideal is opposed, not to the real, but to the simultaneously ideal and real, yet for that very reason is no longer ideal, but *idealizing*. But for the same reason, since the simultaneously ideal and real, that is, the producing self is opposed to an idealizing one, the former, in practical philosophy, is no longer intuitant, that is, *devoid of consciousness*, but is consciously productive, or *realizing*.   (*STI*, p. 157)

This makes the general claim that the legislative or autonomous character of the intellect is the basis of all knowledge yet is not itself represented within the framework of ordinary knowledge (it is not so "for itself" in that context),[8] but that it can become explicit in practical philosophy. Schelling's further claim that in the practical sphere the autonomous self is both "idealizing" and "realizing" introduces important themes of his ensuing analysis of willing: willing is "idealizing" in the sense that it holds out before the self the representation of a state of affairs that does not yet but that should exist, and it is "realizing" in that it at least begins the transformation of the current state of affairs into that idealized state of affairs: Schelling will go on to argue, entirely reasonably, and in a way that we might be well advised to consider in interpreting his transcendental idealism as a whole, that willing does not take the form of producing objects out of thin air, but rather "all bringing forth in willing appears only as a forming or shaping of the object" (*STI*, p. 175), that is, working on reality to modify it in the desired direction. His use of the term "idealizing" might also be taken to suggest that this process is never entirely complete, that is, that willing is more than mere wishing (a Kantian point) but neither does it exist only insofar as its goal is fully attained— willing is successful when pre-existing reality is moved in the direction of the goal.

However, the crucial point in Schelling's deduction lies in his argument that for willing to become self-conscious, which is the condition of possibility for the activity of the mind in general to become self-conscious, the will has to become conscious of the difference between itself and any particular object it might have, and that this is possible only through consciousness of the pure form of willing, or the mere form of willing as such—for here is where Schelling derives the

[8] The phrase "for itself" as an expression for self-consciousness would later be adopted by Hegel and by Jean-Paul Sartre.

fundamental principle of morality. There are two phases to Schelling's argument here. First, he argues that willing has to become an object for consciousness in contrast to the particular thing willed, or that "willing" must "become an object for me prior to willing" anything in particular (*STI*, p. 162). This is the source of the requirement that willing must have a pure form, containing no content particular to the individual. Schelling does not explicitly say that this amounts to Kant's formulation that the content of the moral law can only be the requirement that all maxims have the form of law or be universalizable (*G*, 4: 402, 421). But he does say that this entails that the will must be *free*, in the sense of not being determined by (an antecedent desire for) any particular content or object: "Willing itself always remains free, and must so remain, if it is not to cease to be a willing" (*STI*, p. 163). Of course the claim that the will must be free in one sense raises the problem of whether the will must be free in other senses, not just free from determination by one factor (desire for particular objects) but free from all forms of determination. Schelling struggles with this issue both in the remainder of the *System of Transcendental Idealism* and again in the *Essence of Human Freedom*.[9]

But what is important for us now is that from this point Schelling does infer that what morality requires is the restriction of the freedom of each only by the condition that freedom be extended to all. This comes in the second stage of his argument, which turns on the further premise that for willing to become an object to consciousness it has to have an element of *externality*, to be presented to the self as if it came from outside the self and its intelligence, but that the only way it can do this is if it is represented as coming from *another self* or intelligence, if it is present to consciousness in the form of a *demand* or *obligation*. This seems close to Fichte's idea of the "summons"; the idea seems to be that in order to become an *object* for *my* consciousness, I have to represent obligation as coming from outside myself, but in order to represent it *as willing*, I still have to represent it as coming from *some* self or intelligence, so I must represent it as coming from a self or intelligence *other than myself*. As Schelling puts it, continuing a passage previously cited, "willing can become an object for me prior to willing," or perhaps we could add prior to *my* willing, but "This is impossible through my own agency," so it will therefore have to be represented through an act external to *my* intelligence "which can become for it an indirect ground of self-determination, whereby the concept of willing arises for" my own intelligence (*STI*, p. 162). This move, whether sound or not, is what allows Schelling to explain or "deduce" the *imperatival* character of the moral law, but also to introduce the requirement of universal freedom, the ultimate content of the moral law, inferring it not from an antecedent requirement of universalizability but more directly, or in Kant's terms ostensively rather than merely apagogically: in order to represent myself as willing at all, which is

---

[9] See Kosch 2008, pp. 77–80, 90–104.

necessary for my self-consciousness in general, I have to represent at least some other as also willing; but since there is nothing different about the other whom I must represent as willing from any other I might represent, in fact I have to represent *all* others (all others like myself in some relevant regard, presumably, for example in their human form) as also willing, thus represent my willing not as unique but as one that must be made compatible with all others. But since willing has previously been equated with freedom, this means that the fundamental requirement of representing oneself as willing is representing all as equally free. Rather than pausing over, or being sidetracked by, Kant's formula of universal law, Schelling thus directly deduces something coming very close to Kant's formulation of the fundamental principle of morality as that of the (intra- and) interpersonal consistency of the use of freedom. Kant had clearly formulated this in his lectures on ethics, which Schelling could not have heard or seen, and the interpersonal version of it only in his Doctrine of Right, published a few years before Schelling's *System of Transcendental Idealism*. Nevertheless, Schelling appears to have divined the underlying idea of Kant's practical philosophy. In this way his appreciation and appropriation of the fundamental premise of Kant's moral philosophy might have been the deepest to date.

Schelling draws his conclusion in more abstract and more concrete forms. At the most abstract, "The result of our whole enquiry can now be summarized most briefly as follows":

> To achieve the original self-intuition of my own free activity, this latter can be posited only quantitatively, that is, under restrictions; and since the activity is free and conscious, these restrictions are possible only through intelligences outside me, in such a fashion that, in the operations of these intelligences upon me, I discern nothing save the original bounds of my own individuality, and would have to intuit these, even if in fact there were no other intelligences beyond myself. That although other intelligences are posited in me only through negations, I nevertheless must acknowledge them as existing independently of me, will surprise nobody who reflects that this relationship is a completely reciprocal one, and that no rational being can substantiate itself as such, save by the recognition of others as such.   (*STI*, p, 169)

Schelling's use of the term "recognition" in the final sentence of this summary reveals that his deduction of the necessity of restricting our own will by the wills of others in order be able to represent our wills at all has been inspired by Fichte. But in his deduction of a more concrete conception of the demand that we must represent in order to represent ourselves as willing and self-determining, Schelling also uses the Leibnizian language of pre-established harmony,[10] thus indicating

---

[10]   See Kosch 2008, p. 78.

that he thinks that his deduction is not just in the spirit of his immediate predecessor but in the larger tradition of German philosophy of which Kant, who had signaled his own loyalty to the Leibnizian tradition with his conception of morality as requiring the institution an empire of ends, is also clearly a part. Kant's final formulation of the categorical imperative as requiring that "all maxims from one's own lawgiving are to harmonize with a possible kingdom of ends as with a kingdom of nature" (G, 4: 436) itself unmistakably alludes to Leibniz's image of "the harmony pre-established from all times between the realms of nature and of grace,"[11] although on Kant's account it is *we* who must institute the harmony between the realms of nature and grace, not "God as architect and God as monarch."

We cannot follow every twist of Schelling's argument here, but with some elisions it goes thus:

> But now different intelligences can have in common only...forms of restriction...in a general sense; for the latter is precisely that by virtue of which the intelligence exists as a specific individual. Hence it seems that, precisely through...restrictedness, insofar as it is a particular one, all community between intelligences is done away with. However, even through this restriction of individuality, a prestablished harmony can again be conditioned...For whereas the latter...serves to posit something common among intelligences, the... restrictedness, by contrast, serves to posit in every individual something which, precisely for that reason, is negated by all the others, and which they cannot therefore intuit as their own action, but only as other than theirs, that is, as the action of an intelligence outside them.   (*STI*, p. 165)

In other words, in order to represent itself as willing at all, any individual must represent some willing outside itself, and thus restrict its own willing by the willing of another, or of others; but of course for those other wills to be represented as willing, they must also be (represented as) restricting *their* own wills by the wills of others; thus *each* must be (represented as) both restricting and affirming its own will, as being able to act as it will in some regards but also as having to restrict its willing in some regards by the possibility of others affirming their own wills. Each must both be able to exercise its freedom and to limit its freedom by the freedom of others. All of this requires the establishment of a harmony among individual wills, a harmony that cannot be pre-established for us by the action of a benevolent God—at least at this point in Schelling's career, prior to the introduction of his "identity philosophy" or later turns in his development, there is no hint of a divine ground for our own self-determination—but which may be considered pre-

---

[11] Leibniz, *Principles of Nature and Grace*, §15, in Leibniz 1969, p. 640.

established in the sense that each individual must acknowledge the necessity of this form of harmonious restriction as a condition of the possibility of consciousness of any affirmation of his own will and therefore as a condition of the legitimacy of the affirmation of his own will.[12]

Apart from the plausibility of its details, this argument might seem like a blatant inference from an "is" to an "ought," from the conditions of the possibility of our consciousness of ourselves as self-determining intelligences to the acknowledgment of an obligation to respect the capacity of self-determination in each other. But Hume's famous objection to inferring "is" from "ought" in the *Treatise of Human Nature* is not a blanket objection to the general form of any such inference, but rather an objection to attempting to infer an ought from supposed metaphysical necessities apprehended by reason rather than from the facts of human moral sentiments, and would have been so taken by any careful reader of the time;[13] and Schelling is only attempting to locate the right "is" from which to infer the moral "ought," locating it not in some sentiments that already have a moral tone, which would seem circular to him, but in the basic conditions of the possibility of consciousness of ourselves as self-determining intelligences.[14] The real issue would rather be whether Schelling's more abstract or more concrete argument has succeeded in proving that recognition of the will of others and restriction of one's own will by that recognition is really a necessary condition of consciousness of oneself as a self-determining will at all.

Be that as it may, one way in which Schelling attempts to effect the transition from the freedom of the will in the sense of its non-determination by an object other than itself, which has been transmuted into the determination of the will of each by the necessity of acknowledging the existence of the wills of others, into freedom in a libertarian sense, the freedom of the will to obey its own law *or not*, is by an emphasis on the connotation of the term "demand" (*Forderung*). As we saw in Part II, this was a central issue in the reception of Kant's practical philosophy in the 1790s. Schelling writes:

Only through the concept of obligation does the contrast arise between the ideal and the producing self. Now whether the action whereby the required item is realized actually ensues, is uncertain, for the condition of the action that is given (the concept of willing), is a condition thereof as a *free* action; but the condition

---

[12] Kosch thinks that Schelling does "postulate" a divine but never completed harmony among individual human actions in the *System of Transcendental Idealism* (Kosch 2008, p. 78). I am not following her here.

[13] Hume's famous remark is at *Treatise of Human Nature*, book III, part 1, section 1, paragraph 27. For my discussion of this passage and Kant's response to it, see Guyer 2009a; English version in Guyer 2016a.

[14] Kosch also sees Schelling as rejecting a rigid distinction between "is" and "ought," although without mentioning that neither Hume nor Kant accepted a rigid distinction between them either. See Kosch 2008, p. 79.

cannot contradict the conditioned, so that if the former is posited the action would be necessary. Willing itself always remains free, and must so remain, if it is not to cease to be a willing.... And thus we see forthwith a complete removal of the contradiction, whereby the same act of the intelligence had to be both explicable and inexplicable at once. The concept which mediates this contradiction is that of a demand, since by means of the demand the action is *explained, if it takes place*, without it *having* to take place on that account.   (*STI*, p. 163)

Just as Kant had contrasted willing to merely wishing by pointing out that in the case of the former the realization of the intended object must be at least *possible*,[15] so Schelling characterizes willing by insisting that its success must be *possible* but not *necessary*. His remark that a demand explains an action "if it takes place" must then be understood to mean that a (rational) demand for an action explains it in the sense of offering a good *reason* or adequate motivation for it without explaining it through necessary and sufficient conditions that make its occurrence inevitable. It provides a reason for the action without a *causal* explanation of it, at least without a causal explanation that is complete without other conditions, such as that not merely the action but also the *agent* is fully rational.

By these arguments, Schelling has now attempted to derive or deduce the moral law, its imperatival character, and our freedom to obey it or not, all of which the criticism of the previous fifteen years had held to be inadequately grounded by Kant himself. Whether or not we would agree with him, Schelling seems to have thought that his deduction of the first two of these was adequate. He obviously did not intend his verbal derivation of the freedom of the will to be a complete treatment of this issue, since he has more to say on it in the *System of Transcendental Idealism* even before returning to scratch at this wound again in the *Essence of Human Freedom*. In the earlier work, Schelling appeals to a Kantian interpretation of transcendental idealism as distinguishing between how things appear and how they are in themselves in order to solve the problem of the freedom of the will, a distinction that has not previously figured in his exposition of his own version of transcendental idealism, which turns rather on the distinction between the unconscious forces of nature that ultimately generate consciousness and the activity of thought that generates our conscious representations of both nature and ourselves. Schelling is driven to take this Kantian step because he does want to add the libertarian conception of freedom of the will as the freedom to choose between an action and its alternative no matter what has gone before to what might to this point in the argument have been seen as a rationalist conception that locates freedom in the rationality of the will without insisting upon its indeterminacy. He poses the problem as one of finding room for a conception of

---

[15] Andrew Chignell explores the various senses of possibility that might be at stake, not explicitly in the case of willing but in the allied case of hoping, in Chignell 2013.

the "self-acting" self in addition to the "objectively intuitant" self (*STI*, pp. 180–1): the latter may be interpreted as the self insofar as it intuits itself as an object in nature like other objects in nature, thus subject to the laws of nature like anything else, while the former is the self considered as always able to choose between an action and its contrary no matter what the laws of nature might seem to dictate. Schelling formulates the problem of free will as that of showing how these two apparently contradictory conceptions of the will are in fact compatible: "We act freely, and the world"—with everything it contains as world, including the "objectively intuitant" self—"comes to exist independently of us—these two propositions must be synthetically united" (*STI*, p. 182). His strategy is then to propose that the objectively intuitant self is the self considered as it appears, but the freely acting self is the self as it really is.[16] He says, with emphasis, that "*The free-acting and the intuitant selves are . . . different, once we posit that ideal activity which stands opposed to that of production; when we remove it in thought, they are the same*" (*STI*, p. 180). More fully,

> But if we wish to arrive at complete clarity on this matter, we must repeat the reminder, that everything we have so far deduced has had reference only to *appearance*, or was merely a condition under which the self was to appear to itself, and so did not have the same reality as the self itself. What we are just now trying to explain, namely how the self, insofar as it *acts*, can determine something in the self, insofar as it *knows*—this whole opposition between acting and intuiting—undoubtedly also belongs only to the *appearance* of the self, and not to the self proper. The self must *appear* to itself as though something were determined, by its action, within its intuition, or, since it is not conscious of this, within the external world.   (*STI*, p. 181)

This passage suggests that in the end Schelling's argument for a libertarian conception of the free will is the same as Kant's. It also suggests that Schelling, any more than Kant, cannot be interpreting transcendental idealism as, for example, Henry Allison does, by means of what we might call a two-*concept* approach, on which we have one conception of things that includes their spatio-temporality and causal determinism, and another conception of them which omits these features in spite of the fact that they are the necessary conditions of our cognition, or rather precisely to emphasize that these are the necessary conditions of our cognition (what Allison calls "epistemic conditions").[17] For on this interpretation one of our conceptions of objects merely *abstracts from* features of them which the other conception emphasizes, but abstracting from a feature, in this case

---

[16] See also Kosch 2008, p. 79.
[17] See Allison 2004. For my critique of Allison's application of his interpretation of Kant's transcendental idealism to the problem of free will, see Guyer 1992.

causal determinism, does not *change* or *remove it*; thus on the "two-concept" approach, if objects are causally determined under one conception, they are still causally determined, even if the other conception of them omits reference to this fact. Indeed, Schelling's position seems rather to be that the self really is free to choose between any action and its alternative even though it appears otherwise. Thus he ends up stating that the self is "absolutely" free (in the relevant sense) even though it appears determined:

> Since, in the absolute act of the will, the self has as its object only self-determining as such, no deviation from this is possible for the will in its absolute sense; if it can be called free at all, it is thus *absolutely* free, since that which is a command for the will that appears is, for the absolute will, a law that proceeds from the necessity of its own nature. But if the absolute is to appear to itself, it must figure to itself as dependent in its objective upon something else, something alien to it. This dependence, however, does not belong to the absolute itself, but merely to its appearance. (*STI*, p. 190)

This passage seems to state quite clearly that the self, or its will, really is free, in the fullest possible sense, and merely appears to be determined by natural forces alien to it.

This adoption of Kant's position on the freedom of the will, or of this interpretation of Kant's position, creates two problems for Schelling. One is the same problem that Schmid, Reinhold, and Kant himself confronted earlier in the 1790s: if the will is really rational, in Schelling's terms determined by its own pure form, then how, no matter what else may be true of it, could it ever choose to act against rationality, or against the law of its own pure form? But second, Schelling adds something to this already difficult problem: he moves from talking about the will as "absolutely free" to talking about an absolute will, which sounds as if it might be a distinct entity from the wills of everyday life, your will and my will, which may be mere appearances. But if there is a unique thing as the absolute will, then what is its relation to individual wills? And to compound the problem, if there is one absolute will, how is that some everyday wills choose the morally good, but others do not? Mustn't there be freedom in the relation between individual wills and the absolute will, rather than just in the absolute will?

Schelling has no immediate answer to these problems. He will try to deal with them in the *Essence of Human Freedom* a decade later. But before we turn to that, let us note several other points in Schelling's 1800 "system of practical philosophy" in which he attempts to "deduce" aspects of Kant's practical philosophy. As we saw previously, Kant's conception of the highest good and his accompanying doctrine of the postulates of pure practical reason had drawn criticism from the outset: his addition of happiness to the universalizability of maxims as any part of the object of morality was unwarranted, or it even undermined the purity of moral motivation, as Garve had charged, and the postulation of God (the highest original good) and immortality even on merely practical grounds was nothing but wishful thinking, as Thomas Wizenmann had charged.[18] Schelling aims to defend Kant against such charges, at least in a general way, by eliminating the possibility that genuine morality should *not* produce happiness, which he does by another appeal to the distinction between mere appearance and reality that he has already used to defend the freedom of the will.

Schelling formulates the problem of the relation between morality and happiness as that of reconciling the "outward-going activity (the inclination)" of the self, on the one hand, which is the "sole vehicle whereby anything can make its way from the self into the external world," which he also calls the self's "drive," a term that Reinhold had popularized and Schiller and Fichte had adopted from him, and, on the other hand, the "ideal activity" of the self "directed solely to pure self-determination," that is, to its determining itself not to pursue this or that particular object but simply to being a pure will. Schelling then argues that there cannot really be a conflict or even a disparity between these two because the world of particular objects that seem to promise gratification independently of the demands of morality is nothing but a world of appearance, and the only real world is nothing other than that of the pure will itself, a world in which there is no room for a gap to open between the pure will and its realization and thus between pure will and happiness. Schelling writes:

> Assuredly the pure will cannot become an object to the self without at the same time having an external object. But now…this external object actually has no reality *per se*, being simply a medium for the appearance of the pure will, and meant to be nothing else but the expression of that will for the external world. Thus the pure will cannot become an object to itself without identifying the external world with itself. But now when analyzed precisely, the concept of happiness contains no other thought than that of just such an identity between what is independent of willing and the willing itself. Thus happiness, the object of natural inclination, must be merely the appearance of the pure will, that is, be one and the same object as the pure will itself. The two must be absolutely one…
>
> (*STI*, p. 194)

On the one hand, Schelling appeals to a completely common-sensical conception of happiness: it is what arises when one's will is realized, when the objects that one wills to exist do come to be, or, more precisely, to be modified in the particular ways that one wills. On the other hand, Schelling invokes his radical interpretation

---

[18] Concerning the objection by Thomas Wizenmann, who "disputes the authorization to conclude from a need to the objective reality of its object," see *CPracR*, 5: 143n. For discussion of Wizenmann's objection and Kant's response, see Beiser 1987, pp. 109–26.

of transcendental idealism to guarantee that there must be perfect coincidence between the will and its object, and thus happiness: the only object that really exists is pure will, any objects that are subordinated to laws of nature rather than of pure will are mere appearance, and so the pure will must always realize its object because there is no other object than it. Properly understood, happiness is actually identical to morality: "they are both one and the same object, only seen from different sides" (*STI*, p. 194). There is no need for any additional argument to show why happiness should result from morality, nor is there need for any intervention between will and object—such as the action of a benevolent God over an immortal life span for the agent—to make sure that the morality of the agent does produce happiness. Schelling thus uses Kant's transcendental idealism to avoid Kant's doctrine of the postulates of pure practical reason.

We have no record of any response to this argument by Kant, who in his declining health may have been beyond responding to other philosophers by 1800.[19] But from his point of view, this defense of his doctrine of the highest good could hardly have been welcome. To Kant, it would have seemed another version of the Stoic identification of happiness with mere contentment at being virtuous, thus it would remove the contingency of a synthetic connection between doing the right thing for the sake of morality alone and that actually yielding happiness as a natural condition in a natural world that does have its own laws that can only be made necessary by God. By removing God from the linkage between virtue and happiness, this defense would thus undermine Kant's purpose in reconnecting virtue and happiness in the first place, which was precisely to ground the practical argument for the existence of God that he intended to replace the theoretical arguments for divine existence that he had so thoroughly discredited.

The second of these defects in particular might not have seemed much of a loss to the young Schelling, whose philosophy moves between the two poles of nature and self without, apparently, either need or room for God. Shortly after completing the *System of Transcendental Idealism*, however, Schelling began his transition to what he called his "identity philosophy," which differs from his previous philosophy by introducing an "absolute" that underlies both nature and self, including will.[20] This move would take him further from Kant than he had previously gone, because of course for Kant there can be no theoretical cognition of anything absolute or unconditioned. By 1809, Schelling would identify his absolute with God; from a Kantian point of view, that is at least a coherent if not theoretically cognizable or verifiable application of the concept of the

---

[19] Although he did make a reference to the *System of Transcendental Idealism* in the last phase of the notes constituting the so-called *Opus postumum*, drafts for a restatement of his own transcendental idealism that Kant was not able to complete before he died. *Opus postumum*, first fascicle, sheet VII, page 1, 21: 87; translation in Kant 1993, p. 251.

[20] See Bowie 1993, pp. 55–90, and Jaeschke and Arndt 2012, pp. 309–423.

unconditioned. Schelling's task then becomes that of reconciling the possibility of human freedom and freely chosen human evil with the existence of God. This is the issue that Schelling takes up in the *Essence of Human Freedom*. He does not come back to the issue of happiness or of the highest good in that work, so we will drop it from our further discussion of Schelling, with the observation that subsequently Schopenhauer and Nietzsche would take Kant's commitment to the doctrine of the highest good to be a sign of his wishful thinking. After this dismissal the doctrine would not play much of a further role in the general legacy of Kantian ethics although it would continue to be debated in the narrower corridors of Kant scholarship.

Before we turn to the *Essence of Human Freedom*, however, I will make one last point about the *System of Transcendental Idealism*. This is that in this work Schelling also attempts to deduce a philosophy of history, something that Kant had loosely attached to his moral philosophy as a regulative ideal, but that Schelling attempts to connect more tightly to his own version of Kantian ethics. We have not previously encountered responses to Kant's philosophy of history, and it will not be a major theme of this book, but Schelling's attempt at a philosophy of history not only was of importance for his friend and successor Hegel but is interesting enough in its own right to warrant an excursus.[21] Schelling conceptualizes the philosophical problem of history as that of reconciling the contingency of natural events and the necessity of the moral will of human beings.[22] On the one hand, "Not everything that happens is on that account an object of history" (*STI*, p. 199), and a narrative of a mere sequence of apparently contingent events, even if they involve human beings, would not count as a genuine history. On the other hand, "nothing whatever can be an object of history which proceeds according to a determinate mechanism, or whose theory is *a priori* ... Man has a history only because what he will do is incapable of being calculated in advance according to any theory," or, as Schelling memorably says, "Choice is to that extent the goddess of history" (*STI*, p. 200). Schelling does not provide much of an argument for this claim, although we might suppose him to mean that a theory of human conduct on which all its consequences could be known a priori would lay out all those consequences at once, and thus remove time, and with that remove any genuine history. Schelling concludes that genuine history must have a logic, but it can only be that history must embody "the notion of an infinite *tendency to progress*" (*STI*, p. 202) in the moral and political institutions of mankind, which would leave room for contingency or accident in human affairs that transforms mere logic into actual history. Thus it is "the

---

[21] On Kant's philosophy of history, see Yovel 1980; Kleingeld 1995; and the essay collections Höffe 2011 and Wilford and Stoner 2021.

[22] See Kosch 2008, pp. 78–80.

primary characteristic of history ... that it should exhibit a union of freedom and necessity, and be possible through this union alone" (*STI*, p. 203).

However, Schelling's explanation of how this union may be achieved seems rather to undermine it. For he again employs his interpretation of transcendental idealism and ends up arguing that contingency obtains at the level of mere appearance while at the level of genuine reality progress necessarily occurs. Schelling is clearly inspired by Adam Smith's image of an invisible hand producing a common good out of a multitude of actions each of which is aimed only at individual good, but he adds to it a claim of necessity that is missing from Smith's account, and that goes beyond Kant's position that we have to posit the possibility of progress as a regulative ideal for human conduct as well. The Smithian imagery is evident in this passage:

> From the wholly lawless play of freedom, in which every free being indulges on his own behalf, as if there were no other outside him ..., something rational is still to emerge eventually, and this I am obliged to presuppose in every action. Such a thing is inconceivable unless the objective factor in all acting is something communal, whereby all the goals of men are guided to one harmonious whole; and are so guided, that however they may set about things, and however unbridled the exercise of their choice, they yet must go where they did not want to, without, and even against, their own will—

but Schelling makes the difference between his position and that of his predecessors clear when he continues,

> and this owing to a necessity hidden from them, whereby it is determined in advance that by the very lawlessness of their act, and the more lawless it is, the more surely, they bring about a development of the drama which they themselves were powerless to have in view.   (*STI*, p. 207)

As a friend of Hume, Smith could not have claimed that the invisible hand works with inexorable necessity, and Kant too was sufficiently impressed by Hume to be cautious in his assignment of necessity to particular causal laws (see *CPJ*, Introduction, §IV), including those governing human history. But Schelling has no qualms doing this, because he has already reduced the realm of contingency to mere appearance. Thus he can also introduce an "intelligence in itself" which "serves to predetermine once and for all the objective lawfulness of history" (*STI*, p. 208), equate this with an "absolute"—this prior to the full-blown introduction of *the* absolute in his "identity-philosophy" beginning the following year, and then state that "if this absolute is the true ground of harmony between the objective and the subjective in the free action, not only of the individual, but of the entire species, we shall be likeliest to find traces of this eternal and unalterable identity in the lawfulness which runs, like the weaving of an unknown hand, through the free play of choice in history" (*STI*, p. 209).

Now, immediately following this passage, Schelling suggests that "fatalism" is just a matter of perspective, that is, if we focus only on the "*unconscious* or *objective* aspect in all action," we will think that everything in history is "absolutely predetermined," which presumably is also meant to suggest that if we focus on the "conscious" and "subjective" aspects of history, or the gap between intentions and outcomes, the necessary room for contingency and freedom will remain. But this seems to be closing the barn door after the mare has run: he has already made the realization of the pure will's objectives necessary at the noumenal level, just like happiness, indeed the realization of our historical goals no matter how described must be equivalent to happiness on Schelling's conception of the latter, and this means that contingency of outcomes, like freedom of choice itself, can only be a mere appearance. Schelling's reduction of contingency to mere appearance would also be fateful for the philosophy of Hegel.

In the *System of Transcendental Idealism*, Schelling divined the real normative basis of Kantian moral philosophy—the equal value of freedom, or the value of equal freedom—and "deduced" this norm as a condition of the possibility of self-consciousness itself. But by means of his version of transcendental idealism, supposed to provide better arguments for Kant's conceptions of the freedom of the will, the highest good, and historical progress, he in fact only exacerbated the problem that Kant's philosophy had encountered at the outset of the 1790s, the problem that the free will can act *only* in accordance with the moral law, whether we think of its action in historical context or not. Schelling reduced the way out of this problem that Schmid, Reinhold, and Kant himself had all come up with, namely, in Kant's terminology, the distinction between legislative *Wille* and executive *Willkühr*, to a distinction between reality and mere appearance. Our question now is whether Schelling came up with a better solution in the *Essence of Human Freedom*.

8.3. The *Essence of Human Freedom*

Schelling's 1809 *Philosophical Investigations into the Essence of Human Freedom* was the last work he published in his lifetime, and thus the last stage of his work with which most of his contemporaries could be familiar, although he continued to write prolifically for the remaining forty-five years of his life and much of this material was published shortly after his death by his son Karl.[23] The work is often read as Schelling's exercise in theodicy,[24] thus as a response above all to Leibniz's work of that name of 1710. But it is clear that the work is equally a response to

---

[23] See Schelling 1856–61, 1985. [24] See, e.g., the editors' introduction in *EHF*, pp. xi–xv.

Kant's treatment of the human freedom to be evil in his 1793 *Religion within the Boundaries of Mere Reason*, although that work is not a theodicy in any normal sense.[25] If there is a theodicy in Kant, it lies not in his account of radical evil in the *Religion*, but in his doctrine of the postulates of pure practical reason as expounded in the first and second *Critiques*, that is, in the argument that we must believe that the failure of happiness to track virtue that we observe in our natural life spans will be rectified in our immortal life spans, where we have time enough to perfect our virtue, for which God can then provide the appropriate happiness. In my view, Kant's argument in the *Religion* that we are *always* free to convert from evil to good by means of *our own* freedom undercuts his argument for the postulates, above all the postulate of personal immortality.[26] Schelling must have recognized this, and does not take up Kant's doctrine of the postulates in the *Essence of Human Freedom*. What he does do is to attempt to provide what Kant did not provide in the *Religion*, but what some recent commentators have assumed that he did mean to provide,[27] namely not merely an a priori argument for the *possibility* of evil combined with a merely empirical argument for the *actuality* of evil but an a priori argument for the actuality and indeed the *necessity* of human evil. Schelling agrees with Kant in defining human freedom as the capacity to choose good *or evil*, but then argues that the difference between humans and God is marked only and precisely by the fact that humans do exercise this capacity to choose evil. But this theological explanation of the necessity of the evil exercise of the human capacity for evil then raises a question about whether complete conversion from evil to good is ever possible for human beings, an affirmative answer to which had been the chief point of Kant's *Religion*. So while sharing Kant's definition of human freedom, Schelling seems to arrive at a very different conception of its essential limitation.

Before we turn to this central issue, however, we should note that the *Essence of Human Freedom* does employ a very Kantian conception of the goal of morality, thus a Kantian definition of what would constitute both goodness and its opposite, evil. Schelling begins with the general claim that "The thought of making freedom the one and all of philosophy has set the human mind free in general, not merely with respect to itself, and brought about a more forceful change in all divisions of knowledge than any prior revolution" (*EHF*, p. 22). Whatever this may be meant to imply for the case of theoretical cognition, it would also seem to imply that freedom must be the fundamental and foundational notion in practical philosophy as well. As we saw, that was already maintained in the "System of Practical Philosophy" in the *System of Transcendental Idealism*, and in the *Essence of*

---

[25] See Kosch 2008, p. 91. However, Kosch sees Schelling as staying fairly close to Kant's *Religion* in his essay on human freedom (pp. 95–6), whereas I will present him in what follows as departing from Kant on a central point, namely trying to prove the *necessity* of human evil rather than the real *possibility* of overcoming it.

[26] See Guyer 2016b and Guyer 2020a, chapter 4.   [27] E.g., Morgan 2005 and Sussman 2005.

Human Freedom too Schelling conceives of the goal of morality as consisting in each agent acting so as to bring out about maximal equal freedom, and evil as lying in arrogating more freedom for oneself than one is willing to concede to others.

Schelling uses a variety of metaphors to convey this conception of evil, such as "selfhood separating itself from the light," but his more straightforward description is that evil consists in "self-will... striv[ing] to be as a particular will that which it is only through identity with the universal" (*EHF*, p. 33), that is, the will of the agent denying its commonality with all other human wills, thereby arrogating to itself a degree of freedom that it does not share with others. He also says that evil arises when "self-will itself moves from the *centrum* as its place." This might sound as if it confuses evil with good, for one might think that evil consists precisely in always placing oneself at the center of a scope for action or a sphere of privilege and relegating everyone else to the periphery. But what Schelling seems to have in mind is rather that a self-will that moves away from the center

> can no longer bring the forces to unity among themselves as the original will [God] could and, thus, must strive to put together or form its own peculiar life from the forces that have moved apart from one another, an indignant host of desires (since each individual force is also a craving and appetite)... But since there can indeed be no true life like that which could exist only in the original relation, a life emerges which, though individual, is, however, false, a life of mendacity, a growth of restlessness and decay.   (*EHF*, p. 34)

Thus what he seems to mean by the suggestion that it is goodness rather than evil that lies in placing oneself at the center is that by so doing one fully discharges one's own responsibility for harmonizing human activity, for ensuring that each can act freely and openly to realize one's own desires and help others to realize theirs, rather than acting mendaciously to satisfy only one's own, arrogating more freedom to oneself than one allows to others but hiding that one is doing that (which is the only way to get away with it). Of course, in fact, no one person, no matter how noble her actions, can ensure that all human actions or exercise of freedom constitute a harmonious whole, but if *each* agent were to act *as if* it were up to her alone whether humans can exercise their freedom harmoniously, then in fact human freedom would be exercised harmoniously. With these images, Schelling makes it clear that his conception of the fundamental principle of morality is basically the same as Kant's, that is, the harmonious exercise of freedom, and that evil consists in disrupting this harmony by claiming freedom for oneself that one does not extend to others.[28]

---

[28] On this point I agree with Kosch 2008, pp. 99–100, although it seems to me that Kosch undercuts her connection of Schelling with Kant on this point when she argues that Schelling has no "substantive normative ethics" in the essay on human freedom; I take it that his position that evil consists in

The question now is how human evil is possible, indeed why it is even necessary—for Schelling takes the burden of his theodicy to be to show not merely that human evil is compatible with the existence of God but that it is actual and necessary. Schelling formulates his initial question in traditional terms: the challenge for theodicy is posed by the fact that a supposedly benevolent and omnipotent God cannot escape responsibility for evil done by his creatures because that God granted those creatures the freedom that they can then use to do evil. In Schelling's words, "God appears undeniably to share responsibility for evil in so far as permitting an entirely independent being to do evil is surely not much better than to cause it to do so" (*EHF*, p. 23). His first step toward answering this challenge is a radically revisionary conception of God: in spite of God's unitary nature, Schelling distinguishes between "ground" and "existence" within God, a distinction that implies that even within God there must be some kind of progress from evil to good:

> Since nothing is prior to, or outside of, God, he must have the ground of his existence in himself. All philosophies say this; but they speak of this ground as of a mere concept without making it into something real and actual. This ground of his existence, which God has in himself, is not God considered absolutely, that is, in so far as he exists; for it is only the ground of his existence. It [the ground] is *nature*—in God, a being indeed inseparable, yet still distinct, from him. This relation can be considered analogically through that of gravity and light in nature. Gravity precedes light as its ever dark ground, which itself is not *actu*, and flees into the night as the light (that which exists) dawns. Even light does not fully remove the seal under which gravity lies contained. . . . God has in himself an inner ground of his existence that in this respect precedes him in existence; but, precisely in this way, God is again the *prius* of the ground in so far as the ground, even as such, could not exist if God did not exist *actu*.   (*EHF*, pp. 28–9)

Schelling's idea seems to be that God must be conceived as arising from a ground within himself; since God is ultimately supposed to be perfect, the only sense we can make of this is that somehow his perfection arises from his own imperfection, and evil is therefore a necessary part of God himself, even though it is also essential to God—the essence of divine rather than human freedom—that he will transcend his own evil. Such a view might seem to open Schelling up to the charge of Manichaeism, the view that the world is torn between good and evil as

privileging oneself over others is all the basis for normative ethic that is needed, as it is in Kant. Kosch 2014 correctly represents Schelling's substantive ethics as locating evil in privileging oneself over others, and more properly confines the suggestion of a criticism of Kant on the part of Schelling to the point that so doing is a genuine exercise of the power of the will and not a mere "incapacity" (p. 156). Pieper 1995 usefully characterizes Schelling's conception of evil as *Selbstentzweiung* or "self-division," i.e., separating the particular in oneself from the universal that is also in one's self.

two distinct fundamental powers, although given both the obscurity of his book and the larger problems that Germany had to contend with in the immediate aftermath of its defeat by Napoleon, perhaps there were no authorities who could be bothered to censor him for this heterodoxy. Be that as it may, his reconception of God paves the way for his new account of the essence of human freedom: the image of God having been thus remade, humans can also be conceived to contain within themselves the ground of evil as well as good while still being made in the image of God.

The key to Schelling's analysis of human freedom is that there is the same division between "ground" and "existence," imperfection and perfection, evil and good, in the human as there is in God, indeed there must be for humans to be the image of God, but that there *must* also be an enduring imperfection in human beings, some permanence of evil, precisely in order to mark the difference between God and humans, between the essence of divine freedom and the essence of human freedom. Schelling defines human freedom as the "capacity for good and evil" (*EHF*, p. 23), in this regard adopting this position that Schmid and Reinhold had reached and that Kant himself had reached in the *Religion*. But he then goes on to argue on theological grounds that humans do not merely have the *capacity* for evil as well as good but in fact must *do* evil as well as good. In his words,

> The human will is the seed—hidden in eternal yearning—of the God who is present still in the ground only; it is the divine panorama of life, locked up within the depths, which God beheld as he fashioned the will to nature. In him (in man) alone God loved the world, and precisely this likeness of God was possessed by yearning in the *centrum* as it came into opposition with the light. Because he emerges from the Ground (is creaturely), man has in relation to God a relatively independent principle in himself; but because precisely this principle—without it ceasing for that reason to be dark in accordance with its ground—is transfigured in light, there arises in him something higher, *spirit*.... Only in man, therefore, is the word fully proclaimed which in all other things is held back and incomplete.... Were now the identity of both principles in the spirit of man exactly as indissoluble as in God, then there would be no distinction, that is, God as spirit would not be revealed. The same unity that is inseverable in God must therefore be severable in man—and this is the possibility of good and evil.   (*EHF*, pp. 32–3)

But as long as the distinction between ground and existence remains in God he too has at least the possibility of doing evil; the distinctive feature of human beings, what marks the difference between them and God and thereby reveals God to them, is that the distinction between ground and existence, evil and good, is never completely overcome in human beings. Schelling's argument reverses the direction of Descartes's famous argument in the third *Meditation*: there Descartes had argued that humans must have an innate and veridical idea of God in order to recognize their own finitude or imperfection (although he was thinking more of epistemic than moral imperfection), while Schelling argues that humans must have a—veridical—idea of their own—moral—imperfection in order to recognize by contrast the perfection of God. Human evil is the means by which divine existence—in the ordinary sense and in Schelling's special sense of God's full achievement of what is only potential in his own ground—is revealed.

Nothing like this argument is to be found in Kant. Although, as previously mentioned, some interpreters have tried to find in Kant an a priori ground for the occurrence of evil, Kant's actual position is that the *possibility* of evil is analytically contained in the concept of human freedom, the synthetic validity or objective reality of which is proven by our consciousness of our obligation under the moral law; the famous "propensity to evil in human nature" is in fact nothing more than the "subjective ground of the possibility of an inclination (habitual desire, *concupiscentia*), insofar as this possibility is contingent for humanity in general" (*RBMR*, 6: 28); and only an empirical proof of the actual realization of this contingency, that humans exercise their possibility of doing evil, is either necessary or possible, an empirical proof that is amply furnished by the history of human beings in both the "state of nature" and so-called "civilization" (*RMBR*, 6: 33). Even when Kant says that "We can spare ourselves the formal proof that there must be such a corrupt propensity rooted in the human being, in view of the multitude of woeful examples that the experience of human *deeds* parades before us" (6: 32–3), since a propensity is properly a possibility, he is still saying only that we may spare ourselves a formal proof of the *possibility* of human evil, since actuality (the deeds paraded before us) proves possibility. Kant has no interest in arguing for the *necessity* of human evil, although Schelling does.

Further, of course, Kant's point in the *Religion* is that if the possibility of evil is inherent in us because of the very nature of freedom, *then so is the possibility of good*: "it must equally be possible to *overcome* this evil, for it is to be found in the human being as acting freely" (*RBMR*, 6: 37). Indeed, Kant's view is that evil can be overcome by a single act of the free *Willkühr* choosing to subordinate the principle of self-love to the principle of morality rather than vice versa (6: 36). Of course, the act of the free *Willkühr* must be noumenal, and therefore not represented within time; this act cannot be represented as instantaneous or as taking place at a specific moment, for these are temporal determinations. Because this act or "change of heart" must be noumenal, all we can say is that it is the ground of any phenomenal change of heart, however long the latter might take. And because this act is noumenal, it also cannot be evident to a human being that he has actually performed let alone completed this act—he could always be deluding himself, continuing to act out of self-love but outwardly conforming to the moral law because he has come to see that as the most prudent thing to do. It may be evident only to God that a human being has undergone a complete conversion from evil to good. But this *can* be evident to God, on Kant's account, which means that a human being's conversion from evil to good can be complete, or at least entirely whole-hearted: "because of the *disposition* from which it derives and which transcends the senses, we can think of the infinite progression of the good toward conformity to the law as being judged by him who scrutinizes the heart (through his pure intellectual intuition) to be a perfected whole even with respect to the deed (the life conduct). And so notwithstanding his permanent deficiency," that is the epistemological deficiency of the human being with regard to his own underlying moral disposition, "a human being can still expect to be *generally* well-pleasing to God, at whatever point in time his existence be cut short" (*RBMR*, 6: 67). This is just because a human being can make a complete *commitment* to a moral conversion from good to evil even if he cannot know that he has done so.

For Schelling, however, it appears that a human being can at *no* level make more than *progress* toward becoming good, for to do more than that would efface the distinction between human and God. Or at least he cannot do so by his own power, although perhaps God can do it for the human being, by what Kant would have called an act of grace (but rejected): "As man is now, the good as light can be developed only from the dark principle through a divine transformation" (*EHF*, p. 53). The reason for this is that Schelling takes the noumenal character of free choice, which he accepts from Kant, to imply that each human being has only a *single* chance for making a moral choice, and if that cannot be a choice to be perfectly good, as it cannot be if the human is to be at all different from God, then it can only be a choice to be no more than imperfectly good, or always to retain some element of evil; it can at best be a choice of progress toward the good at the level of fundamental disposition, not merely at the level of actions actually performed in a finite life span. In Schelling's hands, Kant's theory of noumenal choice becomes a kind of practical rather than biological preformationism, or fatalism: each human's moral character is determined by a single moral choice somehow made at his creation, indeed the moral choice of all human beings is made at a single moment of creation, and there is only one set of alternatives for that choice, a choice between no progress toward the good and imperfect progress toward the good. In Schelling's version of the creation myth,

> Man is in the initial creation ... an undecided being—which may be portrayed mythically as a condition of innocence that precedes this life and as an initial blessedness. But this decision cannot occur within time; it occurs outside of all time and, hence, together with the first creation (though as a deed distinct from creation). Man, even if born in time, is indeed created into the beginning of the creation (the *centrum*). The act, whereby his life is determined in time, does not

itself belong to time but rather to eternity; it also does not temporally precede life but goes through time (unhampered by it) as an act which is eternal by nature. Through this act the life of man reaches to the beginning of creation...

(*EHF*, p. 51)

Or, "We too assert a predestination but in a completely different sense, namely in this: as man acts here so has he acted from eternity and already in the beginning of creation" (*EHF*, pp. 52–3). And what this single choice can choose is only progress toward good, "toward ever greater increase and toward the final separation of good from evil" (*EHF*, p. 67); but for humans to actually achieve that final separation, whether or not they could know that they have done so, would, again, efface their distinction from God. In a way, Schelling does resolve the problem about freedom that had been bruited since Ulrich: the human being can indeed make only one choice, but that is only a choice of progress toward the good, so its incompleteness leaves room for evil after all.

However, as I already suggested, that humans have only a single opportunity to make their moral choice is not a consequence that Kant draws from his theory of the noumenal location of free choice, nor does it follow from that idea. To be sure, Kant does hold, under the name of "rigorism," that *at any one time* a human being can have only one fundamental maxim (*RBMR*, 6: 23–5)—the options for this choice, either to subordinate self-love to morality or to subordinate morality to self-love, are defined by logic alone—but Kant cannot hold that a human being gets to make this choice only once. On the contrary, his theory clearly implies that a human being can make at least two choices, the (in some sense) initial choice of evil, that is, the choice to subordinate morality to self-love, and then the (in some sense) subsequent choice to reverse one's fundamental maxim and subordinate self-love to morality. That evil is fully imputable and due to a free choice but that any human can convert from evil to good means that each human can make at least two choices. But there is no reason to stop at two, and in fact Kant seems to believe that as long as a person lives she is free and can revise her choice of fundamental moral maxim—a permanent possibility of moral back-sliding is also part of the human condition. All that transcendental idealism implies is that we cannot represent this possibility of multiple choices in our ordinary temporal terms, or more precisely that we cannot take our temporal representation of this possibility of moral choices at face value, although we have no other way of representing it or talking about it. (That is why I said "in some sense" initial and subsequent.) But it would be a fallacy to infer from the non-temporality of moral choice to the conclusion that we only have one crack at it—that would itself be to import our temporal mode of representation into our conception of the noumenal, as Schelling has pretty clearly done in his appropriation of the creation myth. (We will see in a subsequent chapter that Schopenhauer, who in spite of his negative comments about Schelling along with Fichte and Hegel was clearly deeply influenced by the *Essence of Human Freedom*, follows Schelling in committing this fallacy.)

Once again, Schelling has tried to deduce what Kant had merely taken for granted, namely the actuality of human evil. But this deduction has come at great costs. First, it depends upon theological premises of a kind that Kant avoided: Kant's *Religion* shows how to use the central images of Christianity as symbols for central concepts of morality, but Schelling's deduction depends upon taking theological premises literally. Second, Schelling's interpretation of Kant's transcendental idealism as well as his theological derivation of the difference between human beings and God does not allow for a complete moral conversion, instead allowing at most for a single choice of imperfect moral progress. Kant's break with the doctrine of predestination ends up being more radical than Schelling's. Kant may ultimately fall back upon an inscrutable freedom of choice between good and evil, while Schelling's attempt to make human freedom intelligible ends up limiting it to an imperfect choice of the good.

To be sure, Kant's account of the potential of human freedom may seem unduly optimistic, while Schelling's derivation of an imperfect human freedom may seem to yield a result closer to the reality of our moral lives as we experience them. Yet a contemporary reader would probably want to hold that the imperfect character of even the best human beings is contingent, dependent upon nature rather than God or any other necessity, even if well-confirmed. So Schelling's greater realism may come at too high a methodological price for us now.

9

Hegel

The Inescapability of Contingency

9.1. Moral Form and Natural Matter

According to one survey of German idealism, Hegel's *Elements of the Philosophy of Right* (1821), his mature statement of his philosophy of "objective spirit," is

> a treatise in which ethics does not form a special part at all. The question "What should I do?", under which Kant subsumes ethics, is from Hegel's perspective better answered through right, morality, and ethical life [*Sittlichkeit*] than through a separate ethics. For the attempt to answer it without recourse to the particular institutions of ethical life, to family, civil society, and state, remains from Hegel's perspective necessarily fruitless and without consequence. These institutions form the "substantial foundation" of ethical life.[1]

As another commentator puts it, perhaps even more strongly, "Hegel proposes no substantive normative principle from which detailed moral principles must derive, in the manner of a Bentham or Kant. The assumption is that duties emerge immediately from the collectivities, or social wholes, which at any time comprise the state—and which are rational in their time."[2]

These are accurate accounts of how Hegel himself saw things.[3] But from Kant's "perspective," Hegel could have said this only because he did not make Kant's distinction between form and matter, thus between the fundamental principle of morality, or the three formulations of the categorical imperative, as the form of morality, and the matter of morality as the system of juridical and ethical duties that arise for human beings from the application of that fundamental principle to some basic even though only empirically known circumstances of the human condition. For Hegel, if there were to be a general principle of morality in Kant's sense, it would have to emerge from the concrete circumstances of human social

---

[1] Jaeschke and Arndt 2012, p. 645. [2] Skorupski 2021, p. 236.
[3] The literature on Hegel is of course vast. For helpful general surveys of his work, see Taylor 1975; InWood 1983; and Beiser 2005a; in German, Horstmann and Emundts 2002 and Fulda 2003. For a detailed biography, see Pinkard 2000. For discussions of Hegel's approach to moral philosophy and his critique of Kant's, see Walsh 1969; Wood 1990; Knowles 2002; Pippin 2008; Irwin 2009, pp. 200–52; Moyar 2011 and 2021; and Skorupski 2021, pp. 200–97.

Kant's Impact on Moral Philosophy. Paul Guyer, Oxford University Press. © Paul Guyer 2024.
DOI: 10.1093/oso/9780199592456.003.0010

life, but since individual human institutions have their own norms, it would not be necessary to formulate this principle at all. For Kant, our duties and the institutions in which some of them can be realized have to be grounded on the fundamental principle of morality valid for all rational beings, but this approach is anathema to Hegel because Kant's pervasive use of the distinction between form and matter throughout his philosophy is anathema.[4] Indeed, Hegel does not just object to Kant's distinction between form and matter in morality; his most famous objection to Kant is that the categorical imperative is an "empty formalism," and he writes as if Kant had no theory of the actual duties of human beings at all. It is as if Hegel had read only the *Groundwork for the Metaphysics*, the sole objective of which is to "search out and establish" (*aufsuchen und feststellen*) the fundamental principle of morality (*G*, 4: 392), and had never read the later *Metaphysics of Morals*, in which Kant shows how that fundamental principle gives rise to the various classes of duties for human beings.[5]

Kant pictured moral reasoning as the application of a form given by pure practical reason to matter, namely desires or ends suggested by desires, given by sensibility, even before he published his mature, "critical" works in moral philosophy. In one lapidary note from the second half of the 1770s, he stated:

Moral philosophy is the science of ends insofar as they are determined by pure reason. Or of the unity of all ends (that they do not conflict with themselves) of rational beings. The matter of the good is empirical, the form is given *a priori*. Morality is the good from principles of spontaneity. Hence the universality of the good. (Kant, Reflection 6820)[6]

The second and third sentences of this note tells us how the first and last sentences should be understood: Kant's idea is not that pure reason, entirely a priori, spontaneously generates all the ends of moral agents and thereby a complete and universally valid conception of the good, but rather that pure reason spontaneously generates an a priori form that is to be imposed upon the empirically

---

[4] See Guyer 2017. If you like, Hegel is Aristotle to Kant's Plato: like Aristotle, Hegel believes that it makes sense to talk about form only *in re*, as embedded in particular objects, while Kant thinks we can conceive of form apart from matter, although only as an expression of our own forms of cognition, not as existing in some strange immaterial realm. On Hegel's Aristotelianism, see Mure 1940, chapters 1–7, and Beiser 2005a, pp. 210–12.

[5] Although Terry Pinkard asserts that Hegel did study Kant's *Metaphysics of Morals* at the time of its appearance, "and even wrote a commentary during this period on Kant's book, although that manuscript has since been lost" (Pinkard 2000, p. 82). He refers to Karl Rosenkranz's 1844 biography to support this assertion. Dudley Knowles remarkably asserts that appealing to the *Metaphysics of Morals* may "disarm" Hegel's criticism of Kant's formalism but that so doing "diminishes Kant's stature as a moral philosopher" (Knowles 2002, p. 204). This would be so only if one believed that moral philosophy must be a priori at every level, not just the level of fundamental principle.

[6] Kant, Reflection 6820 (1776–8? 1778–9?), Kant 1900–19: 172; translation from Kant 2005, pp. 437–8.

suggested particular ends of all rational beings, or at least all those who can be affected by the actions of any of us, that is, all human beings, in order to organize, select, and constrain such ends, thereby unifying them into a system in which they do not conflict with one another and beyond that promote or help realize one another. Just why pure reason should impose such an a priori form upon the matter that is given to it empirically needs to be explained, to be sure, and in the lectures on ethics that he was giving at the time he penned this note, for which it was probably some preparation, Kant provided that further explanation. But the note by itself suggests that the contrast between empirically suggested ends and an a priori form given by pure reason and to be imposed on this empirical matter by the moral agent lies at the very heart of Kant's entire approach to morality. Insofar as Hegel rejects the very distinction between form and matter, he is bound to talk past Kant, even if there are actually strong substantive affinities between their practical philosophies, in that both reject mere pleasure as the proper end of human beings and thus reject any form of utilitarianism, and instead treat the freedom of individual human beings within their unavoidable social context as the proper topic and goal of morality.[7]

Hegel charged that Kant's categorical imperative is an "empty formalism" that is "indifferent" to its content and therefore compatible with any content from his 1802 essay on *Natural Law*[8] through to the 1821 *Elements of the Philosophy of Right*[9] and beyond, even to his 1827–8 *Lectures on the Philosophy of Spirit*[10] and, implicitly, in the final edition of the *Encyclopedia of Philosophical Sciences* in 1830.[11] For him this was not an isolated objection to Kant's conception of the categorical imperative alone that could be resolved by some technical fix just to that problem.[12] Hegel's objection to the "empty formalism" of the categorical imperative is rather emblematic of his rejection of what he takes to be a fatal flaw in Kant's entire approach to moral philosophy.[13] Indeed, as I suggested, Hegel's objection to an "empty formalism" in Kant's practical philosophy should be seen as part of his critique of Kant's philosophy as a whole, for the distinction between empirical matter and a priori form is as central to Kant's theoretical philosophy as it is to his practical philosophy.[14] Just

---

[7] See, e.g., Skorupski 2021, p. 221.   [8] Hegel 1975.   [9] Hegel 1991.
[10] Hegel 2007, p. 260.   [11] Hegel 1970, §469, pp. 379–80, and §471, pp. 380–1.
[12] See also O'Hagan 1987, p. 136, and Wood 1997, p. 161. A recent article on Hegel's objection proposes precisely to address Hegel's claim as if it were an isolated criticism of Kant's first formulation of the categorical imperative and then canvasses these two (and one more) proposed fix to Kant's purported problem. See Freyenhagen 2012.
[13] Since I first published the material in the present chapter, this point has also been made by García Mills 2017. But García Mills thinks that Kant's distinction between empirically suggested ends as the matter of moral action and the moral law as the form of moral action is more of a problem than I do, and that Hegel's conception of *Sittlichkeit* is a better solution to it than I do.
[14] Sally Sedgwick puts Hegel's general criticism of Kant as an objection to the "externality" of concepts to their objects, when concepts should somehow emerge organically from the experience of their objects; Sedgwick 2012, pp. 137–40. For the most part, though, Sedgwick's work focuses on Hegel's critique of Kant's theoretical philosophy, as does McCumber 2014.

as the latter is built around the distinction between empirically given desires and an a priori form to be imposed on these by pure practical reason, so Kant's theoretical philosophy sees cognition as based upon the imposition upon empirically given sensation of the a priori forms of pure intuition, the a priori forms of pure under- standing or the categories, and the a priori forms of inference and systematization provided by pure reason—and Hegel objects to all of this as much as he objects to the formalism of Kant's practical philosophy. That the "empty formalism" objection to Kant's practical philosophy is rooted in Hegel's fundamental objection to Kant's philosophy in general, its distinction between form and content, is made clear by Hegel's formative essay on "Faith and Knowledge," published in July 1802, a few months before the first part of his essay on "Natural Law" was published in December of that year. This essay begins thus:

> Because the essence of the Kantian philosophy consists in its being critical idealism, it plainly confesses that its principle is subjectivism and formal thinking.... The Kantian philosophy remains entirely within [this] antithesis.... On the contrary, the sole Idea that has reality and true objectivity for philosophy, is the absolute suspendedness of the antithesis. This absolute identity is not a universal subjective postulate never to be realized. It is the only authentic reality. Nor is the cognition of it a [matter of] faith, that is, something beyond all knowledge; it is, rather, philosophy's sole knowledge.[15]

This opening salvo in Hegel's philosophical career also portends objections to Kant's practical philosophy that go beyond the "empty formalism" objection.

Thus, Hegel will further object to Kant's conception of the postulates of pure practical reason, not merely to the idea that they can furnish the basis for a practical faith in the existence of an unconditioned God even in the absence of a sound theoretical argument for that existence but also to the antecedent idea that both the perfection of human virtue and the realization of human happiness must be deferred to the point where only the immortality of the soul and the existence of God can make them possible. For Hegel, concrete ethical life can be and must be achieved only within human history. The present chapter will consider Hegel's objections to Kant's doctrine of the highest good and the postulates of pure practical reason as well as his objections to Kant's conception of the will and its freedom, both of which we have seen to be issues that vexed the reception of Kant's moral philosophy from the outset. But it is Hegel's objection to the "empty formalism" of Kant's fundamental principle of morality that has historically and recently drawn the most attention, so the largest part of the present chapter will be devoted to that topic. We will return to the other topics more briefly after we have

---

[15] Hegel 1977, pp. 67–8.

discussed this issue. Well aware of the dispute between Kant and Schiller on the role of feeling in moral motivation, Hegel also addressed that issue, rejecting any idea of a rigid division between feeling and reason in fully achieved moral motivation while at the same time rejecting any idea, as might be taken to be suggested by the moral sense school of eighteenth-century Britain or by a Fichtean ethics of conscience, that moral judgment could be based on feeling alone. The chapter will conclude with a brief review of Hegel's position on that issue.

Now there can be no question that in theoretical philosophy, Kant held and Hegel recognized that Kant held that the a priori forms of pure intuition, pure understanding, and pure reason could never give us knowledge of objects or ourselves without the empirical input of matter provided by sensibility, and in particular that the most cherished ideas of traditional metaphysics were nothing but empty pretenses to cognitions lying beyond the limits of empirical sensibility, at least as far as strictly theoretical philosophy is concerned. Hegel, like others of his generation following the path blazoned by Salomon Maimon,[16] objected to the idea that empirical sensibility should be considered a source of cognition independent of understanding and reason, although on this point Kant would have regarded his successors as simply relapsing into the "intellectualization" of knowledge that he had already objected to in Leibniz, according to which sense-perception is just an "indistinct" version of what can in principle by represented in purely conception terms (CPuR, A853–4/B881–2); in particular, Hegel objected to Kant's limitation of reason by appeal to the limitations of sensibility. In moral philosophy, Kant also held that real agency requires particular ends empirically suggested by inclination and desire—by our sensible, animal nature—and that the derivation of the actual duties of human beings in a metaphysics of morals can only proceed by the application of the a priori principle of morality valid for any rational being to certain basic but empirically given facts about the human condition. But in this case Hegel's "empty formalism" objection is also a charge of *inconsistency* in Kant's moral philosophy, because Hegel took it to be Kant's ambition in practical philosophy to derive the content of our duties from pure reason, and thus took the alleged fact that the categorical imperative is an empty formalism to show that Kant had failed in his own ambition. However, Kant harbored no such ambition, and was content to let the contents of our duties remain undetermined by and therefore contingent relative to the fundamental principle of morality, which of course was supposed to be derived from pure reason alone. Hegel misunderstood Kant's ambitions in practical philosophy.[17] In

---

[16] See Maimon 2010.

[17] Thus, Kant is already being misrepresented and set up for Hegel's objection in statements such as "Kant was quite clear that ethics, which consists of the laws free agents give to themselves to regulate their behaviour, cannot have its sources in the empirical facts which determine human nature. Such facts are contingent, yet moral laws should be deemed necessary and should constrain all

contemporary terms, Kant looked to the moral law for a "side-constraint" or "second-order" principle for particular maxims of action suggested by our natural inclinations, while Hegel thought that he was attempting but failing at an axiomatic deduction of the full contents of our duties. Moreover, although Hegel himself harbored the ambition of eliminating contingency from his own account of human duties and rights, he failed in his attempt to do so.[18] Thus Hegel's "empty formalism" charge emblematizes not merely a misinterpretation of Kant's ambitions in practical philosophy but also the failure of his own.

To add some detail to these broad claims, this chapter proceeds as follows. First I will argue that Kant's and Hegel's moral philosophies are not just ships passing in the night, like Kantian deontology and utilitarian teleology (at least on standard interpretations, or caricatures, of each); rather, it is worth discussing Hegel's criticisms of Kant's moral philosophy precisely because both moral philosophies are ultimately intended to be founded on the value of human freedom, and to show us the way toward the realization of the human potential for human freedom.[19] At the deepest level Hegel's moral philosophy is in that regard genuinely Kantian. Then I turn to the "empty formalism" objection. Considering this objection against the background of Kant's conception of freedom, I will argue that not only does Kant recognize the ultimate contingency of whether human beings satisfy the demands of morality, but that the entire structure of Kant's metaphysics of morals, both its doctrine of right and its doctrine of virtue, is also intended to show us what room we must allow for the variety and therefore contingency of even morally permissible human desires. Kant's objective is certainly to overcome contingency at the level of the fundamental principle of morality; this is why he rejects utilitarianism in the form with which he was familiar, because the content of the happiness that it proposes to maximize is indeterminate and contingent (G, 4: 417–19). But it is not his goal to eliminate all contingency in the contents of our particular duties, let alone in the contents of our particular actions; his goal is rather precisely to make room for the latter within the general framework of our juridical and ethical obligations. I will then argue that the design of Hegel's philosophy of right, in particular its supersession (*Aufhebung*) of the moments of "abstract right" and "morality" by the institutions

---

rational creatures... Moral laws are not a posteriori, dependent on the facts of human behaviour as we discover them, but a priori, binding us quite independently of our psychological ancestry and personal history... as rational creatures we have the capacity to deploy our faculty of reason to determine the rules which should govern our conduct.... The upshot of this rationalistic orientation is that Kant believes that careful philosophical thought concerning the *form* of a law which inscribes one's duty should determine the *content* of how rational creatures should behave" (Knowles 2005, pp. 200–1). Such statements are true about Kant's conception of the fundamental principle of morality, but are not the whole story of the derivation of human duties, which Kant explicitly says does require empirical information.

[18] See also O'Hagan 1987, p. 157.

[19] In addition to Skorupski 2021, see also Wood 1997, pp. 147–8. For a catalogue of similarities and differences between Kant's and Hegel's conceptions of freedom, see Beiser 2005a, pp. 200–2.

of what he calls "ethical life" (*Sittlichkeit*), is intended precisely to eliminate "externality" and thus contingency from the exercise of human freedom. But I will finally argue that Hegel patently fails to eliminate the specter of contingency from human morality, even in his explication of the highest form of *Sittlichkeit*, namely the function of the state.

9.2. Philosophies of Freedom

The moral philosophies of both Kant and Hegel are founded on the fundamental value of the fullest possible realization of human freedom. But there are also key differences in their conceptions or freedom, or at least differences of emphasis, that emerge in Hegel's "empty formalism" objection.

Hegel's *Elements of the Philosophy of Right* (1821) was the handbook for his lecture course, and corresponds to what he calls "objective spirit" in his larger system of philosophy—the expression of "spirit," which includes human consciousness and thought although it may not be limited to that, in human conduct and institutions.[20] The work is divided into three parts, "Abstract Right," "Morality," and "Ethical Life" (*Sittlichkeit*): the first concerns the expression of individual will in property ownership, the second the morality of individual intentions, and the third the institutions of family, civil society (e.g., the economy), and state within which all human activity takes place, activity of which Abstract Right and Morality are only aspects. The contrast between the organization of Kant's *Metaphysics of Morals* and Hegel's *Philosophy of Right* is striking. Kant begins with the innate right to personal freedom and the innate right to acquire property and contractual obligations, then introduces the state as the mechanism through which that delimited range of rights can be made determinate and secure by the possibility of coercive enforcement through a judicial and penal system;[21] the rights secured by the state then provide the framework within which individuals can pursue their own ends, although constrained also by the non-coercively enforceable ethical obligations to perfect their own natural and moral potential and to promote the happiness of others—the two "ends that are also duties." Hegel reverses Kant's order: for him the freedoms to acquire property and to act responsibly out of one's own intentions can be realized only within the institutions of the family, civil society, and the state. This might just be a difference in the order of exposition, but it reveals the difference between Kant's lean toward

---

[20] I say "although it may not be limited to that" because it is an ongoing topic in Hegel studies whether "spirit" (*Geist*) is just the collective expression of distinctively human mental capacities and accomplishments, or whether human spirit is itself the expression of something divine. Commentators such as Robert Pippin and Terry Pinkard take the former approach, although the latter is more traditional.

[21] For the role of the state in making rights "determinate" and "secure," see Ripstein 2009.

Platonism and Hegel's toward Aristotelianism: for Kant societal arrangements must be grounded on and justified by a fundamental principle of morality. For Hegel, those institutions seem to generate moral principles. Further, the reversal of the order of exposition might also represent a fundamental shift in values: for Kant, the state has only instrumental value, facilitating the individual pursuit of freely chosen ends and the non-compelled assistance of each other's pursuit of ends; for Hegel, the existence of individuals within institutions, ultimately within the state, seems to take on intrinsic value. At some level Hegel recognizes the value of both individual and group—as one commentator puts it, Hegel's conception of freedom

> implies membership of or participation in a whole...But, as Hegel acknowledges in many places, in modern society the Kantian idea of freedom has also become fundamental. I must be in my own right a self-determining agent, a maker of decisions. These two elements of freedom, the element of belonging to a whole...—'objective freedom'—and the element that consists in individual autonomy—'subjective freedom'—are the elements or 'moments' that Hegel thinks have to be somehow reconciled in modern ethical life[.][22]

Yet the structure of Hegel's *Philosophy of Right* can certainly suggest that the value of the freedom of individuals to set and pursue their own ends may end up being subordinated to the value of membership in the various levels of social organization culminating in the state. For Kant the state is the framework within which individuals can be free to set their own ends consistently with each other and to assist each other in the realization of their ends, but its value is instrumental, not intrinsic.

Hegel introduces his philosophy of right with statement that the "The territory [*Boden*] of right is the *realm of spirit* in general and its precise location and point of departure is the *will*; the will is *free*, so that freedom constitutes its substance and vocation [*Bestimmung*] and the system of right is the system of actualized freedom" (*PR*, §4, p. 35).[23] In his characteristic language, he suggests that the goal of spirit in the territory of right as elsewhere is to unify particularity and universality, so that when right is achieved "The will is the unity of both these moments—*particularity* reflected *into itself* and thereby restored to *universality*...*individuality*, the *self-determination* of the 'I', in that it posits itself as the negative of itself, that is, as *determinate* and *limited*, and at the same time remains with itself, that is in its *identity with itself* and universality" (*PR*, §7, p. 41).

---

[22] Skorupski 2021, pp. 220–1.

[23] I have changed the translation of *Boden* from "basis" to "territory" and of *Bestimmung* from "destiny" to "translation" to bring the diction of this passage into closer alignment with standard translations of Kantian terminology, which Hegel is obviously employing here.

The claim that the will must somehow achieve some sort of universality is of course reminiscent of Kant's first formulation of the categorical imperative. Hegel next suggests that in order to achieve this "identity with itself and universality" the will must transcend "the *drives, desires, and inclinations* by which [it] finds itself naturally determined," for these do "not yet have the form of rationality" (*PR*, §11, p. 45). "The freedom of the will, according to this determination, is *arbitrariness*...dependence on an inwardly or externally given content and material...*contingency* in the shape of the will" (*PR*, §15, p. 48). *But this conception of freedom of the will is to be overcome*; in other words, contingency in its material or content needs to be overcome in order to realize freedom of the will and thus right. From the outset of Hegel's theory, Kant's model of applying an a priori form to empirically given matter is under attack. Hegel goes on to describe the will as realizing its freedom when it has *itself* rather than content given from elsewhere—from elsewhere within the agent, or "inwardly," or outside the agent altogether, "outwardly"—as its object: "When the will has universality, or itself as infinite form, as its content, object, and end, it is free not only *in itself* but also *for itself*" (*PR*, §21, p. 52). The will is "completely with itself" only when it "has reference to nothing but itself, so that every relationship of *dependence* on something *other* than itself is thereby eliminated" (*PR*, §23, p. 54). Hegel sums his idea up with what seems his characteristic language of self-reflection, although with a touch of Fichtean diction as well: "The absolute determination or, if one prefers, the absolute drive, of the free spirit is to make its freedom into its object—to make it objective both in the sense that it becomes the rational system of the spirit itself, and in the sense that this system becomes immediate actuality...The abstract Idea of the will is in general *the free will which wills the free will*" (*PR*, §27, p. 57).

These formulations certainly sound like versions of Kant's definition of autonomy as "the will's property of being a law to itself" (*G*, 4: 447). The crucial difference is that while for Kant the idea of complete freedom from determination by "alien causes" is the basis of the *fundamental principle* of morality, for Hegel this conception of autonomy as independence from any role for "alien causes" becomes the *complete* idea of freedom. Kant never conceives of the idea of the free will willing itself as the *whole* of morality. In his lectures on ethics, for example, which were, to be sure, unavailable to Hegel, Kant defines the "essential ends of mankind" as "The conditions under which alone the greatest use of freedom is possible, and under which it can be self-consistent" (*Moral Philosophy Collins*, 27: 346; *LE*, p. 127). The maximally self-consistent and therefore maximal use of freedom is *essential* to morality on Kant's account, but what free agents satisfying this constraint have to do is to impose intra- and interpersonal consistency on their use of their freedom to pursue particular ends. The "essential end" of freedom does not itself determine what those ends are, only the constraint under which they must be pursued. In Kant's mature work, as we saw in Part

I, this thought takes the form that "humanity" must always be treated as an end, never merely as a means, where however "humanity" is the capacity of individuals to set their own ends, "any end[s] whatsoever" (*MM*, DV, Introduction, section VIII, 6: 392); the requirement to treat humanity as an end and never merely as a means, thus not to use others (or even ourselves) merely as means to ends, imposes constraints on what ends we may each set for ourselves, but it is not itself expected to *provide* those ends. (And further, Kant's idea of the highest good as the *complete* object of morality, *combining* virtue and happiness in some form, would make no sense at all if the freedom of the will itself were to be the complete object of morality. We will return to the highest good below.)

Thus Kant is careful to make it clear that the realization of freedom, even the greatest possible use of freedom, does not require the *elimination* of ordinary desires and inclinations, which are given to us empirically, but their *regulation*. He states this succinctly in his lectures, following his promulgation that "The prime rule whereby I am to restrict freedom is the conformity of [my] free behavior to the essential ends of mankind":

> I shall therefore not follow my inclinations, but bring them under a rule. Anyone who allows his person to be governed by his inclinations is acting contrary to the essential end of mankind, for as a free agent he must not be subject to his inclinations, but should determine them through freedom; for if he is free, he must have a rule; and this rule is the essential end of mankind. In animals the inclinations are already determined by subjectively necessitating grounds. . . . Now if man freely follows his inclinations, he is lower even than the animals, for in that case there arises in him a lawlessness that does not exist among them. . . . Animals act according to rules because they are not free. But free beings can act in a regular fashion only insofar as they restrict their freedom by rules. (*Moral Philosophy Collins*, 27: 345; *I.F*, p. 126)

Kant does not say that human beings can and must *eliminate* their inclinations; they must *restrict* action upon them according to rules, or more precisely according to the rule of acting only on such inclinations action upon which is compatible with the greatest possible use of freedom by oneself and others—the greatest possible use of freedom, that is, *in* acting to satisfy inclinations. Without inclinations, there would be nothing for us to act for, nothing for us to use our freedom for. But we must not allow ourselves to be led or driven by our inclinations, as Kant supposes animals are; we must choose which of our inclinations to gratify, and which of theirs to assist others in gratifying. The satisfaction or the maximization of our satisfaction of inclinations is not the *essential* end of morality—that is the preservation and promotion of the freedom of choice of all of us about which inclinations to satisfy, or the satisfaction of which to make into our ends—but it is part and parcel of morality, what will figure as "happiness" in Kant's later characterization of the *complete* good or object of morality (e.g., *CPracR*, 5: 111).

Kant's culminating formulation of the categorical imperative in the *Groundwork*, that all of our maxims must be aimed at transforming the realm of nature into an "empire of ends,"[24] makes the same point. Kant says that we must "abstract from the personal differences of rational beings as well as from the content of their private ends" in order to "think of a whole of all ends in systematic connection (a whole both of rational beings as ends in themselves and of the ends of his own that each may set for himself)" (*G*, 4: 433) and to realize such a state through "*a complete determination of all maxims*" (*G*, 4: 436). If the meaning of the requirement that we *abstract* from "all content of private ends" in morality were that we must *eliminate* all private ends, suggested as they are by inclination, the thought that we would thereby establish "a whole both of rational beings as ends in themselves and of the ends of his own that each may set for himself" would make no sense—there would be no ends of his own for each to set for himself, therefore no ends for anyone, even for the most selfless person who would maximally devote herself to the ends of others. Kant's thought can only be that we need to set aside our own private ends or preferences in deciding to make the moral law and the goal of an empire of ends our "supreme rule," but that what we have then committed ourselves to doing is to permit and promote those of the particular ends of ourselves and others that can be pursued consistently with treating every agent as an end in itself, that is, one who gets to set his own ends, on the basis of his own preferences, as long as those in turn are compatible with the freedom of everyone else to do likewise. The empire of ends is not just a domain of rational *law-givers* but is one of free *end-setters*, who by their mutual commitment to the moral law commit themselves to the conjoint pursuit and promotion of all compatible, freely chosen ends.[25] But no member of the empire of ends can set any ends at all without acting in order to gratify at least some of her inclinations or some of those of others, although a restricted set of them, a set restricted by the requirements of intra- and interpersonal consistency.

Kant's moral philosophy is thus a philosophy of freedom, but at the same time a philosophy of contingency. Indeed, two contingencies are inseparable from Kant's conception of freedom. First, there is ineliminable contingency in Kant's conception of the *content* of particular morally permissible and even the morally mandatory actions of perfecting oneself and promoting the happiness of others: freedom is the essential end of mankind, but freedom is nothing but the capacity of all to set their own ends, subject only to the condition that each do so in a way

---

[24] See Guyer 2022 for my defense of this translation of Kant's phrase *Reich der Zwecke* and a more detailed exposition of the argument of this paragraph.

[25] The interpretation of the members of the empire of ends exclusively as co-legislators of the moral law can be found in many commentators, e.g., Hill 1972; Reath 1997; and Mariña 2021.

consistent with the freedom of all. This restriction may come from pure reason, but the particular ends that can be set even in compliance with it are themselves ultimately suggested only by inclination, by nature, and are thus contingent. Morality is in fact the rule that determines the limits within which the contingency of individual desires may properly be pursued and even promoted. Second, as we saw in Part I, it is a central part of Kant's thought, at least at such decisive moments as the lectures on ethics before the *Groundwork* or the *Religion within the Boundaries of Mere Reason* afterwards if not in the *Groundwork* itself, that contingency in *compliance* with the moral law is ineliminable: the rational agent *should* aim at the greatest possible use of freedom itself, but in the nature of things is also free to undermine this goal, and it can never be explained why any human being uses her freedom to preserve and promote the freedom of all or to destroy or undermine it. Our primary concern here will be with Hegel's response to the first of these contingencies, for Hegel's "empty formalism" objection is nothing less than a rejection of this.

9.3. The Empty Formalism Objection

As already mentioned, Hegel first stated his objection that Kant's categorical imperative is an "empty formalism" in his essay on *The Scientific Ways of Treating Natural Law* of 1802 and reiterated it in the *Phenomenology of the Spirit* (§§429–32, pp. 170–1) before succinctly restating it in his handbook on *The Elements of the Philosophy of Right* of 1821. I will focus on Hegel's presentation of his criticism in the first and the last of these works. In both, Hegel takes it to have been Kant's ambition to derive particular duties from pure reason alone. As we have just seen, this was not Kant's ambition.[26] But as Hegel puts it in *Natural Law*,

> Kant, the man who has expounded this abstraction of the concept in its absolute purity, recognizes full well that practical reason totally renounces the content of law and can do nothing beyond making the *form of fitness* of the will's [*Willkühr*] maxims into supreme law. The maxim of the arbitrary will [*Willkühr*][27] in choosing has a content and includes a specific action, but the pure will [*Wille*] is free from specification. The absolute law of practical reason is to elevate that specification into the form of pure unity ... If the specification can be taken up

[26] See also Geiger 2007, p. 13.
[27] Although *willkürlich* in ordinary usage might well be rendered by "arbitrary," in Kant translations *Willkühr* is never translated as "arbitrary will" but as "elective will" or "power of choice." Using "arbitrary" in translating Hegel, however, does bring out the pejorative implication of his use of the term.

into the form of the pure Concept, if it is not cancelled thereby, then it is justified and has itself become absolute... (*NL*, p. 75)

Or as he says in the *Philosophy of Right*, "the pure and unconditional self-determination of the will as the root of duty...first gained a firm foundation and point of departure in the philosophy of Kant." But, Hegel continues, the form of unity or universality—he uses these terms interchangeably—can be conferred on any content, and thus Kant's formalism is an empty formalism. In *Natural Law*, he makes the argument thus:

> But the content of the maxim remains what it is, a specification or singularity, and the universality conferred on it by its reception into the form is thus a merely analytic unity.... If this formalism is to be able to promulgate a law, some matter, something specific, must be posited to constitute the content of the law. And the form given to this specific matter is unity or universality.... But every specific matter is capable of being clothed with the form of the concept...there is nothing whatever which cannot in this way be made into a moral law. Every specific matter, however, is inherently particular, not universal; the opposite specific thing stands over against it, and it is specific only because there is this specific opposition.... If the one is fixed as absolutely subsistent, then, to be sure, the other cannot be posited. But this other can just as easily be thought and, since the form of thinking is the essence, expressed as an absolute moral law.
>
> (*NL*, pp. 75–7)

That is, it would be a contradiction to assert *p and not-p*, but such a contradiction can be avoided by asserting either only *p* or only *not-p*; the need to avoid contradiction ("unity") does not by itself decide *which* of the two contradictories we should assert or, in the practical case, make into our maxim.

Hegel illustrates this with Kant's example of a maxim to enrich oneself by all safe means, including keeping "a deposit which no one can prove has been made" (*CPracR*, 5: 27). Hegel quotes Kant's statement that "such a principle as a law would destroy itself since the result would be that no deposits would exist" (*CPracR*, 5: 27, cited by Hegel at *NL*, p. 77), but then asks, "Where is the contradiction if there were no deposits?" He takes Kant to be asserting that there would be a contradiction in the non-existence of deposits or of the practice of taking and returning deposits, as such, but denies that there is any such contradiction: "The non-existence of deposits would contradict other specific things," to be sure, "just as the possibility of deposits fits together with other necessary specific things...But other ends and material grounds are not to be invoked: it is the immediate form of the concept which is to settle the rightness of adopting one specific matter or the other. For the form, however, one of the opposed specifics is just as valid as the other" (*NL*, p. 77). That is, each of two contradictories *p* and *not-p* is no doubt connected with other propositions, say *p* with *q* and *not-p* perhaps with *not-q*, and it would therefore be contradictory to assert *p and not-q* or *not-p and q*, but it is no more contradictory to assert *not-p* by itself or along with its accompanying *not-q* than it would be to assert *p* by itself or along with its accompanying *q*, and thus the criterion of "unity" or avoiding contradiction cannot decide between *p* and *not-p*, thus between the (moral) maxim of returning all the deposits that one takes or the (immoral) maxim of keeping deposits when one can get away with it.

Hegel argues in the same way in the *Philosophy of Right*. Here he states that Kant's thought of "infinite autonomy"

> reduces this gain to an *empty formalism*, and moral science to an empty rhetoric of *duty for duty's sake* ... it is impossible to make the transition to the determi- nation of particular duties from the above determination of duty as *absence of contradiction*, which is no different from the specification of *abstract indeterminacy* ... On the contrary, it is possible to justify any wrong or immoral mode of action by this means.—Kant's further form—the capacity of an action to be envisaged as a *universal* maxim— ... does not in itself contain any principle apart from formal identity and ... absence of contradiction ... —The fact that *no property* is present is in itself no more contradictory than is the non-existence of this or that individual people, family, etc. or the complete *absence of human life*. But if it is already established and presupposed that property and human life should exist and be respected, then it is a contradiction to commit theft or murder; a contradiction must be a contradiction with something, that is, with a content which is already fundamentally present as an established principle.
>
> (*PR*, §135, pp. 162–3)

Again the complaint seems to be that while of course it would be a contradiction to assert *p* while denying some necessary condition or consequence of *p* and likewise to assert *not-p* while denying some necessary condition or consequence of *not-p*, it is no more contradictory to assert *p* or endorse the maxim *p* by itself than it would be to assert or endorse *not-p*; but, Hegel alleges, Kant's criterion of non- contradiction as a sufficient condition for morality has the form of requiring that we adopt *p* because *not-p* is somehow contradictory in itself—the absence of property or the absence of human life is somehow self-contradictory—so Kant's test fails.[28]

---

[28] Ido Geiger argues that the thrust of Hegel's "empty formalism" charge is not that Kant's categorical imperative does not yield particular duties, but that it does not provide any motivation for moral action nor provide for the efficacy or realizability of such action; Geiger 2007, pp. 17–29. That interpretation is hard to reconcile with the passage just quoted from Hegel, as well as with Kant's argument that pure practical reason of itself gives rise to the feeling of respect, which is given motivational force in the *Critique of Practical Reason*, and with Kant's doctrine of the postulates of

The obvious response to this objection is that Kant's test does *not* suppose that there is a contradiction *within* any morally mandatory maxim considered by itself, thus that returning deposits or refraining from murder is mandatory not because there is something contradictory *within* the idea of not returning deposits or committing murder by itself, but rather that in the case of an immoral maxim there is a contradiction *between* the idea of acting on that maxim, which is what self-interest proposes, and the *universalization of* that maxim, the possibility of which is what morality demands, and what would follow from that universalization in accordance with the laws of nature. On this account there would be a contradiction between the maxim of enriching oneself by taking deposits that one does not plan to return and the universalization of that policy, which would, in the course of events, undermine the possibility of enriching oneself by taking deposits, or between the maxim of committing murders whenever one wants to and the universalization of that maxim, which would, in the course of affairs, put one's own life and thus one's own ability to commit murders whenever one wants at risk.[29] Kant's claim is not that there is a contradiction within the very concept of any particular immoral deed or maxim, but rather that there is one between the universalization of an immoral maxim and the possibility of one's continuing to act upon it (in the case of what Kant calls a contradiction "in conception") or something else that one necessarily wills (in the case of a contradiction "in willing") (*G*, 4: 424). Hegel seems to have just missed Kant's point.[30]

If Hegel had just missed Kant's point, it might hardly seem worthwhile discussing his charge. But it might be argued that he has not missed Kant's point, for as we have seen he does after all say in the *Philosophy of Right* that "if it is already established and presupposed that property of human life should exist and be respected, then it is a contradiction to commit theft or murder," and this might be interpreted as recognizing that Kant's point is precisely that one cannot coherently will both a maxim and something that will undermine the possibility of acting upon that maxim, namely its own universalization. That interpretation of Hegel's remark might be a stretch. But what is more important is that Hegel could make his real objection to Kant even if he did clearly recognize the structure of Kant's actual argument. For Hegel's real objection appears in the clause that occupies the first elision in my previous quotation from the *Philosophy of Right*, where he says

---

pure practical reason precisely as conditions for the realizability of the complete object of morality. As García Mills 2017 and others argue, Hegel did not find Kant's doctrine of the postulates satisfactory, but that is not to say that he thought that Kant had simply neglected the question of realizability.

[29] For the pioneering analysis of Kant's argument along these lines, see Nell 1975, pp. 59–63; 2nd edition in O'Neill 2013). See also Rawls 2000, pp. 167–70. Wood 1990, chapter 9, points out that Hegel misconstrues the kind of contradiction Kant has in mind, but holds that Kant's test yields only duties of omission, not commission, for which one must turn to the Formula of Humanity (p. 156). Walsh 1975, p. 22, also makes this point, although he thinks that Hegel's criticism of Kant is effective even with regard to negative duties. McCumber 2014 also accepts Hegel's critique of Kant.

[30] See also Irwin 2009, p. 213.

that "One may indeed bring in material *from outside* and thereby arrive at *particular* duties" before continuing "but it is impossible to make the transition to the determination of particular duties from the above determination of duty as *absence of contradiction*" (PR, §135, p. 162). That is, even if Hegel did understand that the contradiction Kant thinks reveals immorality is that between a maxim and the consequences of its universalization, not a contradiction entirely within the immoral maxim or the concept of an immoral deed, he would still object that it is external to the principle of morality and thus arbitrary or contingent with respect to it whether anyone considers acting upon a particular maxim in the first place.[31]

The same conclusion is suggested by Hegel's continuation of his discussion of the "empty formalism" discussion beyond the point in *Natural Law* that we previously reached. It could be argued that there Hegel has indeed recognized precisely the kind of contradiction with which Kant was concerned, when he writes:

> This annihilation of the specific, through its adoption into infinity and universality, is indeed an immediate difficulty for practical legislation. For if the specific thing is such that in itself it expresses the supersession of something specific, then, by the elevation of the supersession to universality or to the state of having been superseded, not only the specific thing which is to be superseded, but the superseding itself, is cancelled. *Thus a maxim referring to such a specific thing, which cancels itself when it is universalized*, would not be capable of being the principle of a universal legislation, and so would be immoral.
>
> (NL, pp. 79–80, emphasis added)

However, the source of Hegel's worry still seems to be that, even on this interpretation of the morally problematic contradiction, the maxim that would be "cancelled" by its own universalization would still be external to the principle or morality or contingent relative to it, that is, not derived from the principle of morality itself. For he subsequently says that "this form," presumably meaning by this the form of the contradiction he has just described, "is precisely what directly cancels the essence of morality, since it makes the morally necessary into something contingent by causing morality to appear in opposition to other matters; *in morality, however, contingency, which coincides with the empirically necessary, is immoral*" (NL, p. 81, emphasis added). Hegel is not objecting that no contradiction can ever be generated between a maxim and its own universalization; he is objecting rather that it is entirely contingent what maxim the Kantian agent proposes to test, so that there is always a residue of contingency within Kantian

---

[31] For discussion of Hegel's view of contingency in general, though not in moral philosophy, see Henrich 1958–9.

morality, even though it is supposed to be an "absolute" or pure, a priori morality. Hegel is arguing that Kantian morality fails on its own terms.

One could question whether Kant's derivation of duties from the categorical imperative is really liable to such a charge of contingency. In the case of perfect, negative duties, the violation of which is condemnable but the fulfillment of which brings no special merit, one might argue that the only relevant contingency would be whether anyone ever contemplates an immoral act such a suicide, murder, or theft, and that in the case where the categorical imperative excludes the permissibility of performing such an act, what it is doing is precisely excluding acting upon a merely contingent desire; but the agent who is *not* tempted by any such desire and thus does not even have to evaluate the permissibility of a proposed maxim is not, after all, subject to any special contingency. And in the case of imperfect, positive duties, such as the development of one's own talents and the promotion the happiness of others (or of all, as Kant ultimately argues; *MM*, DV, §27, 6: 450–1), it could be argued that the perfection of one's own talents is only instrumentally necessary as a means for the fulfillment of other moral duties, which would hardly be contingent, or as means for the promotion of happiness, which turns out to be a necessary end alongside of morality or even as part of morality. However, arguing in this way might be unnecessarily heroic, because Kant's statement, with which we opened, that in morality the form is a priori but the matter is empirical, shows that he never harbored the idea that there is nothing contingent in the derivation of particular duties. Kant's view is that the *fundamental principle of morality* must be pure and a priori, valid independently of any contingent desires or inclinations of particular human beings or even of humankind as a whole, in contrast to other possible rational beings, but it is not his view that there is nothing contingent in the particular duties that human beings have. For example, that human beings have the duty to cultivate their talents, whether for the sake of morality or of happiness, is clearly contingent, because human beings might have been born, like adult insects emerging from their cocoons or foals able to stand up within a few minutes of being dropped, with all their powers fully developed. It is contingent that we are not like that, even though we might find it very difficult to imagine being fundamentally different from how we are. The view that the derivation of duties must be pure and necessary all the way down, with no concession to contingency at any point, is a view that Hegel misattributes to Kant, although it may reflect an ambition that Hegel himself harbors.

In the next section, I will suggest that the entire structure of Kant's final metaphysics of morals is designed to show how morality requires us to *manage* the contingency of our desires, not to eliminate them, and then argue that Hegel's own attempt to show how the contingency that Kantian morality supposedly fails to eliminate can be eliminated in his own account of *Sittlichkeit* in fact fails.

9.4. Managing Contingency

What I mean by claiming that the structure of Kant's metaphysics of morals is intended as a framework for managing the contingency of human desire is this. Kant's metaphysics of morals, like his metaphysics of nature, arises from the application of pure a priori principles, in the case of the metaphysics of morals, to certain fundamental but empirical facts about the human condition, in this case that we are embodied creatures, with bodies that have certain sorts of needs and proclivities, who can move freely on the finite surface of the globe (*MM*, Introduction, 6: 216–17). In this statement, I use the term "metaphysics of morals" in the sense in which Kant uses it in the eponymous work of 1797, where metaphysics of morals "cannot dispense with principles of application, and we shall often have to take as our object the particular *nature* of human beings, which is cognized only by experience, in order to *show* in it what can be inferred from universal moral principles" (*MM*, Introduction, 6: 217) and *not* in the sense in which Kant used the phrase in the *Groundwork*, where he equated metaphysics of morals with "a pure moral philosophy, completely cleansed of everything that may be only empirical and that belongs to anthropology" and based instead "simply in concepts of pure reason" (*G*, 4: 389).[32] One way of characterizing my defense of Kant against Hegel would be to say that Hegel conflates these two different senses in which Kant uses the term "metaphysics of morals," assuming that the derivation of human duties to which Kant refers by his later usage of the phrase is meant to satisfy the constraint of his earlier usage—that is, that the derivation of duties is supposed to be entirely a priori, rather than proceeding by means of applying an a priori principle to certain empirically known facts, or to empirically suggested desires. (Since, like so many after him, Hegel seems to base his impression of Kant's moral philosophy largely on the two foundational works of the 1780s but not on the later *Metaphysics of Morals*, this shortcoming may not be surprising.)

Kant divides the metaphysics of morals in his own later sense into two parts, the doctrine of right and the doctrine of virtue. While he suggests several different criteria for the division, the criterion for the division that he actually carries out is whether or not duties may, from both a physical and a moral point of view, be coercively and collectively enforced through the juridical and penal functions of a state (*MM*, Introduction, 6: 218–19). Whatever satisfies this condition, as it turns out only a subset of our perfect duties to others does, is a duty of right; whatever does not is a duty of virtue.[33] Or more precisely, an ethical duty: at his most careful, Kant states that all duties that can be enforced only by respect for the

---

[32] For more on the multiple senses of Kant's usage of "metaphysics of morals," see Guyer forthcoming (a).

[33] See "Kant's System of Duties" in Guyer 2005, chapter 10, and Guyer 2014a, chapter 7, pp. 276–86.

moral law itself are ethical duties, but that only a subset of those, namely those that involve the promotion of an end, are actual duties of virtue (*MM*, DV, Introduction, section II, 6: 383). Kant then makes it clear that duties of right concern only our obligations in various contexts to leave others as free as we can to *set their own ends*: "What end anyone wants to set for his action is left to his free choice" (*MM*, DV, Introduction, section II, 6: 382). Duties of right thus obligate us to leave others free to set their own ends, so what ends anyone sets and pursues for himself is contingent relative to right, as long as the choice of ends does not improperly encroach on the freedom of others to set *their* own ends—and so on. In "ethics," conversely, "the *concept of duty* will lead to ends and will have to establish *maxims* with respect to ends we *ought* to set ourselves, grounding them in accordance with moral principles" (*MM*, DV, Introduction, section II, 6: 382). Properly speaking, this is true of duties of virtue only, not all ethical duties: the duties not to commit suicide or gluttony, for example, or even the duties not to ridicule or slander others, although they are not to be coercively enforced (for reasons Kant does not spell out) and are for that reason ethical duties rather than duties of right, are duties to treat oneself or others as ends in themselves, but not duties to *promote any particular ends*. There is nothing contingent about them, or not much—it is of course contingent in the grand scheme of things that, for example, our free and rational agency is embodied in the kind of body that can be destroyed by our own acts and can be helped or hindered by what that kind of body consumes. But duties of virtue proper are duties to promote particular ends, "ends that are also duties," namely "*one's own perfection* and *the happiness of others*" (*MM*, DV, Introduction, section VI, 6: 385).

Now, one's own perfection and the happiness of others might sounds like determinate ends, and thus it might seem as if the moral law does directly determine specific duties of virtue for us, leaving no room for contingency. But it should be clear that the concepts of one's own perfection and the happiness of others are abstract, we might say second-order concepts, as is the concept of happiness in general, and still leave what more particular ends we are to set in actually perfecting ourselves or promoting the happiness of others indeterminate and contingent. This is already clear from Kant's treatment of both self-perfection and happiness in the *Groundwork*. There Kant treats self-perfection in the guise of the duty to cultivate one's talents, and says that "as a rational being [one] necessarily wills that all the capacities in him be developed, since they serve him and are given to him for all sorts of possible purposes" (*G*, 4: 423). The phrase "all sorts of possible purposes" makes it clear that the duty to cultivate one's talents does *not* determine what particular ends one should set for oneself, but is necessary precisely because what ends one will want to pursue in life is unforeseeable, and one can best prepare oneself for a wide range of *contingent* possibilities by cultivating broadly serviceable talents; one will thereby maximize one's future freedom of choice of ends. In the "Doctrine of Virtue," Kant divides the duty of self-perfection into two parts, the cultivation of one's *moral* capacities such as conscience and self-knowledge and that of one's *natural* capacities, such as physical strength and dexterity, memory, and reasoning ability. As before, the latter are clearly second-order or general, necessary for all sorts of contingent possible purposes one might adopt or ends one might set during the course of a lifetime. The former are also second-order, in the sense that they will be necessary in whatever occasions for moral choice present themselves to one in the course of one's life—but they do not determine what first-order moral obligations one will have any more than the cultivation of natural capacities determines what first-order ends one will set for oneself, although the *failure* to cultivate talents can *limit* what first-order ends one can set for oneself and thus restrict the range of ends one can freely set for oneself, or the ways in which one can assist others. Thus, both of these "ends that are also duties" leave our *specific* ends in life contingent and leave us free to choose them on contingent grounds, although they are designed precisely to prepare us for dealing with this freedom of choice, and in the case of the cultivation of natural capacities they even maximize our freedom by reducing what would be self-imposed constraints on our free choice of ends in the face of the principle of the *hypothetical* imperative that it is rational to choose an end only when we have suitable means to realize it (*G*, 4: 417).

It is even clearer that happiness—one's own, that of others, or that of all, oneself and others—is a second-order end. This is obvious from the outset of Kant's discussion of happiness in the *Groundwork*: even though happiness may be referred to as if it were a determinate end, "*one* end that can be presupposed as actual in the case of all rational beings," it is actually an "indeterminate concept," referring to a "maximum of well-being in my present condition and in every future condition," or, in the case of universal rather than individual happiness, in the present and future condition of everyone, "all the elements" of which "are without exception empirical, that is, they must be borrowed from experience" (*G*, 4: 415, 418). That is to say, happiness is a second-order concept referring to the satisfaction of a maximally coherent set of one's own first-order ends or those of everyone, *whatever those ends happen to be*—and that of course is precisely why Kant argues in the *Groundwork* that a principle of (maximizing) happiness is too indeterminate to serve as the fundamental principle of morality. It is also why he argues in the *Metaphysics of Morals* that the duty of promoting the happiness of others, once that has been derived as a consequence of the fundamental principle of morality for human beings who naturally desire their own happiness and inevitably hope for the assistance of others in attaining it, a hope they cannot *morally* harbor unless they are willing to assist others in the realization of their happiness as well (*MM*, DV, §27, 4: 450–1), is always a duty to promote their happiness after their *own* conception of it. It must be left "for them to decide what they count as belonging to their happiness" (*MM*, DV, Introduction, section V.B, 6: 388) because happiness is an indeterminate or second-order concept referring to the satisfaction of whatever determinate, first-order desires people happen to have—and have been able to elevate to the status of morally permissible ends insofar as doing so is compatible with their own continued freedom and that of others. Of course, this means that there is a considerable degree of contingency in the contents of any actual conception of happiness. Thus just as the duties of right leave the particular ends that people may rightfully pursue indeterminate and contingent, so in fact do the "ends that are also duties," subject to the constraint of permissibility that also grounds the duties of right. In his doctrine of duties, Kant has made no attempt to eliminate contingency from human conduct, but only limned the constraints within which the inevitably contingent conceptions of individual happiness can be pursued.

By contrast, the project of eliminating rather than merely managing contingency from human conduct is Hegel's, not Kant's. This may seem a surprising claim, because Hegel famously claims that in the "modern state," "Particular interests should certainly not be set aside, let alone suppressed; on the contrary, they should be harmonized with the universal, so that both they themselves and the universal are preserved" (PR, §261, p. 285). That could have been written by Kant, and perhaps it is a piece of good sense that Hegel ultimately cannot resist. But it is not reflective of the program of his philosophy of right. This program is rather expressed in Hegel's introductory statements that "the will, or freedom" must not be "arbitrariness" or "contingency in the shape of the will" (PR, §15, p. 48) but must be entirely "self-determining universality" (PR, §21, p. 52), that in freedom "the will is completely with itself, because it has reference to nothing but itself, so that every relationship of dependence on something other than itself is thereby eliminated" (PR, §23, p. 54). While Kant could be properly described as holding that the determination of the fundamental principle of morality must be an entirely free act of the self-determining will, Hegel's official position at the outset of the Philosophy of Right is that the free will must be entirely self-determining, free from all contingency in the determination of its content as well as its form.

The entire scheme of the Philosophy of Right can be understood as intended to eliminate contingency from human affairs by the institutions of Sittlichkeit or "ethical life" culminating in the modern state. Hegel begins with "abstract right," or what might better be considered an abstract conception of right, one on which property is conceived of as consisting in a direct relation of the individual free will to an object. The problem with this is that it leaves the "coincidence" of anyone's property claims with the property rights of other persons entirely "contingent" and thereby leaves the door wide open to "wrong" and "crime" against them (PR, §82, p. 115).[34] This should then be corrected by the addition

---

[34] The abstract conception of right to which Hegel objects is not Kant's conception of property right, which has the constraint that property claims be subject to an "omnilateral will" built into them (MM,

to abstract right of morality, the conscientious adherence of the individual to universal moral law and aim for universal good, but the problem with this is that morality's conceptions of the law and the good remain abstract, thus still leaving particular duties contingent—this is precisely the point of the "empty formalism" charge, that the moral law in its abstraction is just as compatible with "property and human life" as with the opposite and thus does *not* succeed in eliminating the contingency of abstract right. The institutions of *Sittlichkeit* are then supposed to eliminate the contingency that abstract right and morality, although they are necessary, have left. First, the family is supposed to eliminate the "contingency of merely transient moods" or "subjective and contingent feeling" (*PR*, §176, p. 213) by transforming the relation between man and woman into something unitary and permanent. But even if marriages endure—a point to which I shall shortly return—a family needs resources, which the success of the marriage itself cannot guarantee, and as children grow up and go off, often to start their own families, they need independent resources, and there is always a risk of "arbitrariness and discrimination" (*PR*, §180, p. 215) in the availability of such resources— there might not be enough, some children might inherit but others not, some might be able to establish a career but others not, and so on. The contingencies of family life are then supposed to be rectified by the institutions of civil society— work and "corporations" or economic support-groups of various kinds, and "police" or the provision of public goods such as lighting and bridges (*PR*, §236, p. 262), as well as the "administration of justice." By these means civil society is supposed to ameliorate "contingent arbitrariness and subjective caprice" (*PR*, §185, p. 222), in the most general terms by spreading out risks and increasing resources through public cost-sharing. Yet obviously civil society too can be arbitrary and contingent, affording "a spectacle of extravagance and misery as well as of the physical and ethical corruption common to both." So civil society in turn needs to be regulated by the state (although we would think of "police" or the administration of justice as *part* of the state, Hegel has hived off those functions and seems to be thinking of the state primarily in terms of the legislative and executive functions). The state, Hegel argues, most fully represents the universal and takes account of everyone. Although sometimes the universal seems to take the form of nothing less than a guarantee of "the complete freedom of particularity and the well-being of individuals" (*PR*, §260, p. 283) for Hegel, which would take us back to the Kantian conception of the state, sometimes the state seems to be an "essence" that "realizes itself as a self-sufficient power of which single individuals are only moments" (*PR*, §258, p. 279). This suggests that a state has its own

---

DR, §8, 6: 255–6), but Locke's, on which the constraint to "leave well enough and as good for others" is an external proviso, based in divine command, and to which Kant also objected (§15, 6: 265). See Guyer 1997 and Guyer 2014a, pp. 309–23.

interests rather than just the interest of making the freedom of its citizens to pursue their own lives and their own conceptions of happiness as secure as can be.

But I do not want to press that point. What I do want to argue is that no matter how the function of the state is understood, it is impossible to eliminate contingency from the operation of the state, that is, from the structure and laws of any actual, particular state, a point that Hegel sometimes seems to recognize but sometimes not. For one illustration of this point, let us take the case of marriage. Hegel initially suggests that in order to eliminate contingency from affairs of the heart "marriage should be regarded as indissoluble *in itself*," but then he comes to his senses and recognizes that human affairs are inherently unstable and sometimes a marriage has to be dissolved; yet he then observes that "all legislations must make such dissolution as difficult as possible and uphold the right of ethics against caprice" (*PR*, §163, p. 213). In other words, divorce should be possible but must be regulated by the state. But even if we do not demur at Hegel's claim that the state must make divorce as difficult as possible, surely we must recognize that there is a great deal of contingency in divorce legislation—different states have had and will have different laws about divorce, for example some permitting divorce only for cause and others allowing "no fault" divorce, some allowing only the husband to initiate proceedings, others either spouse, and so on—and even if there were some ideal form of divorce legislation, the granting of divorces and the adjudication of associated matters—alimony, custody, child support, and so on— would still have to be administered by human beings—for example, judges in family court, surrogate court, or orphans court in different US states—and it will simply not be possible to eliminate individual judgment and therefore an element of contingency. Think about the synchronic and diachronic variations in laws regulating marriage—interracial marriage, same-sex marriage, permissible degrees of consanguinity in marriage, morganatic marriage, and so on—and the inescapable contingency of law becomes even more obvious. Law can try to minimize the effects of contingency—that is why there are sentencing guidelines in criminal law, for example, and rules for determining the amounts of damages in tort law—but it cannot eliminate them completely.

More generally, of course, all legislation has to be created as well as administered by human beings, so some element of contingency is ineliminable from every function of the state. Hegel posits both an executive, indeed a monarch, and a legislature—although he gives the monarch a greater role in determining legislation and the legislature a lesser role than we would find in any contemporary constitutional monarchy, let alone a contemporary republic—and here he seems to recognize that there is room for contingency in each. But then he seems to recommend measures that should reduce contingency yet that cannot be expected to eliminate it completely. In the case of the monarch, he argues, both contrary to Kant (see *MM*, DR, note D, 6: 329) and implausibly, that the principle of hereditary monarchy exposes the selection of the monarch to less contingency than election would, but he does not argue that contingency would thereby be completely eliminated (*PR*, §281, p. 323). In the case of the legislature, he argues that its division into two houses, an upper house of hereditary landowners and a lower house of elected delegates, "by creating a plurality of *instances*, not only proves an increased guarantee of mature decisions and *eliminates* the contingent quality which the mood of the moment possesses and which decisions by majority vote may acquire. Above all, it *ensures* that the Estates are less likely to come into direct opposition to the government" (*PR*, §313, p. 351, second and third emphases added). Here Hegel seems to waver between the language of guarantees and that of probability in a single paragraph, but perhaps it would be most charitable to read this passage as saying that the bicameral legislature he proposes reduces the probability of arbitrary and thus contingent legislature without removing it completely.

In any case, whatever Hegel himself may have thought on this point, surely we must recognize that even if the state can or must play a role in correcting contingency in other forms of moral and social regulation, no structure for the state, no matter how wise, can completely eliminate contingency from legislation and administration. For laws must be written and administered by human beings, and human beings, as Kant famously stated, are made out of crooked timber (see IUH, Sixth Proposition, 8: 23, and *RBMR*, 6: 100).[35] For that reason, no doubt, Kant never contemplated the project of eliminating contingency from the content of the moral will that Hegel attributes to him, and Hegel himself would have done better not to undertake any such project, as the conclusion of the *Philosophy of Right* perhaps grudgingly makes clear.

9.5. Hegel's Critique of the Highest Good and the Postulates of Pure Practical Reason

The remaining topics in Hegel's critique of Kant's practical philosophy to be discussed here will be considered in the order in which those topics were introduced in Part I of this work rather than in the order in which Hegel himself expounds them. We can thus begin with his critique of Kant's conception of the highest good and of the associated doctrine of the postulates of pure practical reason. This critique is found in Hegel's seminal *Phenomenology of Spirit* (1807) rather than in his more academic works on practical philosophy such as the early essay on natural law or the later *Philosophy of Right*. We will not attempt to place this critique within the complex argumentation of the whole *Phenomenology*, but will consider it on its own. The gist of Hegel's argument is that Kant's conception

---

[35] For discussion, see Guyer 2009b.

of the highest good represents his attempt to synthesize the demand of morality for attention to duty alone with the natural desire for happiness, but that Kant's deferral of any possible realization of the highest good to a life beyond our natural one and his postulation of the ground of this possibility in a supernatural God represents his failure to realize that rationality, or spirit in Hegel's terminology, must find adequate expression in nature itself.[36] This is a serious objection, but there are two things to say in Kant's defense here. For one, although Kant certainly suggests in the *Critique of Pure Reason* that because of the non-compliance of many people around her with the demands of morality, even a person who is herself virtuous can expect her virtue to be connected to happiness only in "a world that is future" for her (A811/B819), already in the *Critique of Practical Reason*, even though he maintains the postulate of personal immortality, he argues that God must be postulated as a "supreme cause" of *nature* so that we can rationally believe that our efforts at morality will be efficacious *there*, in nature, not in a world that is future for us (*CPracR*, 5: 125). Indeed, already in the essay "On the Idea of a Universal History" from 1784, Kant argues that we must be able to suppose that human happiness will be achieved through human morality in the *history* of the human species, that is, in nature (Eight Proposition, 8: 27), and throughout his works of the 1790s, beginning with the *Critique of the Power of Judgment* and continuing through the pamphlet *Towards Perpetual Peace*, his argument is always that mechanisms *in nature* can be used by the well-intentioned human will—although that is itself "supersensible"—to bring about the highest good *in the world*, the highest good in the world possible through freedom (e.g., *CPuR*, §§84, 87, 5: 435, 450). In this regard Kant was moving in a Hegelian direction before Hegel did.

Alongside this plausible objection, however, Hegel also includes a less persuasive argument that Kant's conception of the highest good is actually self-contradictory, because it postulates the removal of natural resistance to the demands of duty which, on Hegel's reading of Kant, is essential to the nature of duty and virtue. This critique comes in a discussion of "Spirit that is certain of itself" in the final section of the *Phenomenology*, on spirit, but before Hegel has reached the forms of spirit in which it most fully knows itself, namely religion and "absolute knowing," or philosophy itself. More specifically, it is found in a subsection titled "The moral view of the world" (*PS*, §§599–631, pp. 239–51). True to his pose of discussing modes of consciousness and self-consciousness inherent to human thought rather than theories that happen to have been advocated by particular philosophers at particular moments (in this Hegel is adopting the stance that Kant himself took in his critique of traditional meta-physics in the Transcendental Dialectic of the *Critique of Pure Reason*), Hegel does

---

[36] This point is emphasized by Pippin 2008, pp. 100–5.

not mention the name of Kant in this section. But that Kantian moral philosophy is his target is unmistakable from the opening lines of the section. Hegel begins by stating that "Self-consciousness knows duty as absolute essence; it is bound only by duty, and this substance is its own pure consciousness; for it duty cannot acquire the form of something alien" (*PS*, §599, p. 239). The reference to Kant's argument in section I of the *Groundwork* that morally worthy action is motivated by the thought of duty rather than inclination (*G*, 4: 398, 400) and to the opening argument of section III of the same text that the free will "can be efficient independently of alien causes *determining* it" (*G*, 4: 446) could hardly be clearer.[37] But Hegel immediately continues to argue that, although the dutiful will opposes itself to nature, it must also be able to find itself in nature. On the one hand, as Hegel reads Kant, the consciousness of duty "is so completely enclosed within itself, [that] it behaves with perfect freedom and indifference toward [the] otherness" of nature, the realm in which actions have results, including results that make agents or others happy or not, "a *nature* whose laws like its doing belong to itself, as an essence that is unconcerned about moral self-consciousness, just as the latter is unconcerned about it" (*PS*, §599, p. 239). On the other hand, however, not just the "non-moral consciousness" or the human being as a merely natural being that seeks happiness, but even "The moral consciousness cannot renounce happiness and leave this moment out of its absolute purpose" (*PS*, §602, p. 240) or, as Kant, would say, *complete* as well as supreme good (*CPracR*, 5: 110–11). This is because in any action, even one dictated by duty, we are concerned with the realization of the purpose of the action, and, Hegel suggests, "enjoyment" is connected to the "notion" of the "actualization" of such a purpose. Thus, Hegel continues, "the purpose, expressed as the whole with the consciousness of its moments, is that the fulfilled duty be a purely moral action as well as realized *individuality*, and that nature, as the side of *singularity* confronting the abstract purpose, be *one* with this purpose" (*PS*, §602, p. 240). That the attainment of a purpose—any purpose—is accompanied with pleasure or enjoyment is one of Kant's own premises (see *CPJ*, Introduction, section VI, 5: 187), and so Hegel implies that, although for Kant the desire for pleasure is never directly a part of moral motivation, even on Kant's own account there is nevertheless a natural connection between having a purpose, realizing a purpose, and taking pleasure or satisfaction in that; so Kant must after all regard happiness—some sum of satisfaction—as part of the complete good for human beings even as defined by morality[38] (and distinct from the peculiar "contentment" (*Zufriedenheit*) that

---

[37] But see Walker 2022, pp. 67–9 for a clear statement that Kant does not actually say that a moral (that is, morally worthy) action must be motivated by duty *alone*. See also Wood 1990, pp. 146–8, and Irwin 2009, p. 217.

[38] Kenneth Westphal has stressed that this argument is part of Hegel's "naturalistic" response to Kant's "anti-naturalism," i.e., Hegel's rejection of Kant's separation between an internal or noumenal realm of intentions and an external or phenomenal realm of actions. See Westphal 1991, at pp. 140–6.

comes from knowing that one has done the right thing, even when it did not have the desired outcome; cf. *CPracR*, 5: 118). Thus Hegel writes that (even on Kant's own account) "The *Being* that is demanded [by the moral point of view] belongs not to the representation of contingent consciousness, but it lies in the concept of morality itself, whose true concern is the *unity* of the *pure* and the *singular* consciousness; it pertains to the singular consciousness that this unity be *for it* as an actuality, which in the *content* of the purpose is happiness, but in the *form* of the purpose is Being-there [existence] in general" (*PR*, §602, p. 240).

However, as Hegel's use in these passages of the terms "singular" and "singularity," or better "individual" and "individuality," might suggest, he may be taking it to be natural for the individual to be interested in his *own* happiness, and thus giving an individualistic rather than universalist slant to Kant's conception of the highest good. This could lead to an objection like that had been earlier made by Christian Garve, and to which Kant himself had already replied in his 1793 essay on "Theory and Practice," namely that associating virtue with any thought of one's own happiness muddies the purity of moral motivation. But this is not Hegel's objection. Rather, after explaining that in Kant's hands the postulation of the "mediation" or combination of virtue and happiness (the scope of which is not specified), or "the harmony of nature with the moral consciousness," opens up a "whole circle" of other postulates, namely a being as ground of this harmony (God) and "a future infinitely remote" in which consciousness can "bring about this harmony" and continually make progress in morality, he objects that if the harmony that Kant projects "actually came, then the moral consciousness would sublate itself. For *morality* is only moral *consciousness* as the negative essence, and for the pure duty of this essence sensibility has only a *negative* significance" (*PS*, §603, pp. 240–1). That is, Hegel takes it to be essential to Kant's conception of morality as such that it encounter resistance from our sensuous nature, that is, from our natural inclinations, and that moral worth is demonstrated only by maintaining our commitment to morality in the face of such resistance. Thus the very moment in which the goal of harmonizing morality and nature would seem to be achieved would be the moment in which morality disappears, and Kant's conception of the highest good is internally contradictory. On Hegel's account of Kant, "the *completion* of morality *has to be postponed to infinity*" (*PS*, §603, p. 241) not because of the difficulty of achieving full commitment to morality in practice but rather to mask the contradiction inherent in his conception of the relation between morality and happiness, to make it seem as if morality could lead to happiness without undermining the supposition that the "moral consciousness" depends upon conflict with (at least one's own) happiness. As Hegel subsequently says, "If then we allow that this *highest good* is the essence, then consciousness is not in earnest with morality at all. Hence moral action itself drops out, for action takes place only under the presupposition of a negative which is to be sublated by the action." On the assumption that the highest good is essentially what matters, "there is admitted as the essential situation one in which the moral action is superfluous" (*PS*, §620, p. 246).

There are actually several different criticisms here, all of which Kant would have rejected. One is that the morality of the individual exists only in its conflict with contra-moral inclination. To be sure, the possibility of conflict between the demands of morality and of inclination (or self-conceit in the terminology of the *Critique of Practical Reason* or self-love in the terminology of *Religion within the Boundaries of Mere Reason*) is inherent and inescapable in Kant's conception of the human condition, and it is essential to Kant's characterizations of the *categorical imperative* and *virtue* as "the strength of a human being's maxims in fulfilling his duty," even that "Strength of any kind can be *recognized* only by the obstacles it can overcome" (*MM*, DV, Introduction, section IX, 6: 395). But the latter is only an epistemological point, not a point about the essence of virtue, and more generally it is not built into Kant's conception of the fundamental principle of *morality* for *all rational beings* or into the idea of the moral law as the *object* of moral motivation. The possibility or perhaps better the necessity of such a conflict *cannot* be built into Kant's conception of the fundamental principle of morality itself, because that must be valid for all rational beings, and not all rational beings must be conceived to have inclinations contrary to the requirements of morality. The possibility of the morality of God is certainly not conceived as the strength to overcome obstacles or known and measured as such.[39] The possibility of such conflict *is* built into Kant's conceptions of the categorical imperative and of virtue, for the former is by definition the way in which the fundamental principle of morality, a principle of pure reason, presents itself to beings *like us*, in whom "reason solely by itself does not adequately determine the will," beings in whom the will is also "exposed to subjective conditions (certain incentives) that are not always in accord with objective ones" (*G*, 4: 412), and the latter (virtue) is by definition "strength in mastering and overcoming oneself, in regard to the moral disposition" (*Moral Philosophy Collins*, 27: 300) or the "*fortitude*" "to withstand a strong but unjust opponent...with respect to what opposes the moral disposition *within us*" (*MM*, DV, Introduction, section I, 6: 380). So the fundamental principle of morality can indeed present itself to *us* in the form of a categorical imperative only so long as we are capable of having inclinations toward actions (more precisely, toward the adoption of maxims) that would conflict with the demands of the fundamental principle of morality (in the conditions for action in which we find ourselves), and virtue can be manifested only insofar as we can commit ourselves to the fundamental principle of morality in such conditions, that is to say, to the categorical imperative. But this is not to say that *morality* or

---

[39] Thus Irwin writes, "We are not aware of something as duty in opposition to sensuous impulse unless we have impulses that tend to conflict with the moral law. But the holy will observes the moral law for its own sake" (Irwin 2009, p. 219).

what Hegel calls the "moral consciousness" can be manifested only in such circumstances. From Kant's point of view, all that would follow is that upon the completion of progress toward virtue and the ensuing realization of the highest good, should that ever happen, the human being would be transformed into a purely rational being, not that morality itself would disappear—because, again, even purely rational beings are capable of morality even if not of virtue properly defined.

The second objection that is contained in Hegel's remarks is that, if we were successful in our moral efforts, then morality itself would be undermined because there would be no further need for it. This is the claim of an objection Hegel had already made in the essay on natural law, that specific apparently moral maxims turn out to be "self-annihilating," thus that it is not immoral maxims but moral maxims that turn out to be self-contradictory and fail Kant's universalization test. For example, he argues, "The maxim, 'Help the poor,' tested by being elevated into a principle of universal legislation, will prove to be false because it annihilates itself. If the thought is that the poor generally should be helped, then either there are no poor left or there are nothing but poor; in the latter event no one is left to help them" but "In both cases the help" or the possibility of help and thus of moral action "disappears." Yet "If poverty is to remain in order that the duty of helping the poor can be fulfilled, this maintenance of poverty forthwith means that the duty is not fulfilled" (*Natural Law*, p. 80). Hegel tries to construct the practical equivalent of a Cretan liar paradox: if you fulfill the duty, then you cannot fulfill the duty. If we adopted as our maxim to help the poor, then complete success in our efforts to realize that maxim would eliminate poverty, and there would be no further place for morality, at least in that regard.

But this criticism is not compelling. It misconstrues Kant's conception of the nature of a maxim in general, and in particular the nature of the maxims of imperfect duty, such as the maxim to promote the happiness of others, or the adoption of the happiness of others as my end, as Kant puts it in the Doctrine of Virtue of the *Metaphysics of Morals*. A maxim is a conditional, that tells me that in certain circumstances I ought to perform some particular kind of action, or not to do such a thing. For example, the maxim not to commit suicide out of self-love (a maxim of perfect duty) tells me that if I ever, alas, find myself in circumstances where my continued existence promises more pain than pleasure, I must not commit suicide—but if the antecedent of the conditional is not satisfied, then the maxim does not tell me to do anything, in this case to refrain from the proscribed action. The maxim to promote the happiness of others tells me that if I find myself in a situation in which I can promote the happiness of others—by virtue of both their need and my abilities and resources—then I should do so, consistent with the satisfaction of my other relevant duties. Adopting the maxim to alleviate poverty then tells me if I find myself in a situation where there is poverty and I have the resources to alleviate it, then, consistent with my other duties, I should do so. But if the antecedent of the conditional is not satisfied, because there is no poverty, then the maxim does not tell me to do anything—*then and there*. Of course, poverty may always return, and then my maxim, *which remains valid even when there is currently no application for it*, should kick in. Indeed, in real life we would and should suppose that it could always come back, that even equitable economic systems are not self-sustaining, and indeed that taking what steps are necessary to maintain even an already equitable economic system is itself acting on the maxim of combatting poverty—making sure it does not re-emerge would be just as much acting in accordance with the maxim as remedying extant poverty would be. Think of a maxim as in this way like a voluntarily adopted disposition to action: the disposition can remain even when it is not currently active because the conditions for its activation do not obtain.

But there is a serious objection that Hegel could have brought here, namely that it is the idea of *happiness* rather than of *morality* that makes no sense in the conception of the highest good conceived as taking place only in some sort of personal afterlife, because happiness consists in some sum of satisfaction of desires and in that non-natural condition agents will have no such desires—so we have no idea of what could count as happiness in that condition. That said, perhaps there is after all an objection to be made against the very possibility of *morality* in this condition, although not one that Hegel raises, namely that there would in fact be no need for and therefore no possibility of *action* itself in that situation, therefore no possibility of adopting *maxims* of action, the rationality of so doing which always presupposes at least the *possibility* of action, as was assumed in the argument of the previous paragraph, and thus no possibility of moral motivation. If all need for action stemming from desire were to disappear in some ideal condition, no action of any kind would be rational, and the possibility of morality would indeed seem to have disappeared, not because of a lack of resistance to moral action but because of no need for any action. The condition of the highest good, conceived of a state outside of human history, ends up looking like a state of practical entropy.

There is no hint of such a threat in the *Metaphysics of Morals*. Here Kant is constructing a doctrine of duties for human beings in the actual human condition on the basis of a fundamental principle of morality valid for any and all rational beings. In this project, the existence of inclinations that could conflict with the demands of morality is always part of the actual human condition, so there will always be room for virtue, as strength of will in overcoming such inclinations. And there will always be both room for self-improvement and needs of others, both of which will give scope for efforts to fulfill the two ends that are also duties, one's own perfection and the happiness of others. In this final work Kant expresses no supposition that complete harmony between morality and nature can ever be achieved within nature, only progress toward it. But neither does the supposition that such harmony can only be achieved outside of nature, or outside of our natural life span, whether as individuals or a species, make any appearance. Without any assistance from Hegel, the concept of the highest good, although it culminates each of Kant's three critiques, disappears from view altogether. Kant's final position may thus be more "naturalistic" than a fantasy that complete harmony between morality and nature can ever be achieved.

Having said that, we can now turn to Hegel's critique of Kant's treatment of the will.

9.6. Freedom of the Will and the Problem of Evil

Hegel rejects a traditional conception of freedom of the will as liberty of indifference, the freedom to choose between mutually exclusive alternatives without regard to one's prior history.[40] In this, he aligns himself with the position Kant had taken as early as 1755, in his thesis to qualify as a *Privatdozent* in Königsberg, the *New Elucidation of the First Principles of Metaphysical Cognition* in his argument with Christian August Crusius but then rejected in part one of the *Religion* when he firmly separated *Wille*, the source of the moral law, from *Willkühr*, the faculty of choice that can inscrutably choose between good and evil (*New Elucidation*, Proposition IX, 1: 400–5, especially p. 402). Hegel's objection is not directly to the violation of determinism that this position requires, and that Kant had later made possible by his transcendental idealism, but to the very idea that the individual agent has a genuine choice between two exclusive alternatives, which Hegel symbolizes as "+A" and "–A." On Hegel's view, which depends upon his constant tendency to internalize relations into concepts (a pattern of German thought since Leibniz), the choice of +A retains an essential reference to –A, and so the agent cannot really choose between +A and –A after all. As he argues, "We must completely reject that view of freedom whereby freedom is supposedly a choice between opposed entities, so that if +A and –A are given, freedom consists in selecting *either* +A or –A and is absolutely bound to this *either-or*." This is because "As soon as the individual has put himself in the specific position +A, he is equally tied to –A, and –A is something external for him, not in his power" (*Natural Law*, p. 89). The idea that an agent cannot freely choose between some action A and its contrary not-A because "A" appears in both seems particularly lame. An objection that the agent has not herself set the world up so that A and not-A are exclusive alternatives and the only choices open to the agent would be more compelling: we can often wish that the world offered us different possibilities altogether, that we were not sometimes forced to choose between equally unpalatable alternatives, such as "Your money or your life." Being

---

[40] See Pippin 2008, p. 15, and Yeomans 2012, pp. 3–23.

forced to make such a choice is certainly a limitation on our overall freedom. Still, that does not imply that in those unfortunate circumstances the choice between the two unappealing alternatives is not genuinely free. Hegel seems to be demanding freedom from any limitation whatsoever on our options when he writes that freedom would rather lie only in "the negation or ideality of the opposites, as much as of +A as of −A... Something external would *be* for freedom only if freedom were characterized as only +A or only −A. But freedom is just the opposite; nothing is external for it" (*Natural Law*, p. 89).

Thus Hegel arrives at the idea that freedom can only lie in the will choosing something entirely internal to itself. Freedom thus lies in the "identity of the will with itself" (*PR*, §110, p. 138). Or as he puts it in the 1827–8 *Lectures on the Philosophy of Spirit*, "Objective spirit means that the concept [of the will] has only its freedom for its substantial end; this then is rationality." Insofar as it is free, "spirit wills nothing but freedom and has no other end than its freedom" (p. 264). This might sound like a recipe for pure individualism, an agent's concern only with his own freedom, but in Hegel's view such a restriction would be arbitrary, not entailed by the content of the concept of will itself, for concepts are inherently universal even though they must be realized in particulars. Here is where Hegel comes closest to formulating an actual moral principle: the will that does not vainly attempt to choose between alternatives imposed upon it externally and which could never escape from the opposite of what it wants if it attempted to do so, the will that would choose entirely on grounds internal to itself, has no choice but to will the freedom of all; only through such a universal willing can "the universality that is at home with itself, return... out of the externality of nature, and... overcome the externality of nature and... come to itself" (*LPS*, p. 264). By this means "The basis of the will's *existence* is now *subjectivity*, and the will of others is the existence which I give to my end, and which is for me at the same time an other.—The implementation of my end therefore has this identity of my will and the will of others within it—it has a *positive* reference to the will of others" (*PR*, §112, p. 139).

Hegel's starting point in this chain of argument, that the choice of +A cannot escape its opposite −A and thus remains enslaved to external nature, is dubious, but he nevertheless arrives at a conception of freedom that is similar to Kant's conception of autonomy, the will's acting on a law, thus a universal, that it gives to itself, which can be nothing other than the law of the universal validity or possibility of willing.[41] But there are nevertheless key differences between Hegel's treatment of freedom of the will and Kant's. One concerns the possibility of evil. When Kant introduced his conception of autonomy in the *Groundwork* but conjoined it with the assumption that the only free will is a rational or

---

[41] Thus Skorupski states that Hegel "retains the Kantian notion of autonomy" although he "rejects... the supposed deduction" of it "from morality"; Skorupski 2021, p. 285.

autonomous will, he created a fully secularized form of the problem of evil, that of explaining how a rational being could nevertheless violate reason's requirement of universalizability. That is, Kant transfers what was traditionally a problem for the conception of God to the human case.[42] When, like Schmid and Reinhold, Kant separated *Wille*, equivalent to pure practical reason and the source of the moral law, from *Willkühr* as the faculty of choice, he escaped this problem, although at the cost of making the choice between good (subordinating oneself to the moral law) and evil (making an exception from the moral law for oneself), that is, why anyone chooses one way rather than the other, "inscrutable" or inexplicable. Hegel basically accepts Kant's analysis of evil, defining it in his terms as the will letting "its content be determined by...desires etc. in the determination of *contingency* which they have as natural" and hence also letting the will have "the form of particularity...opposed to *universality* as inner objectivity" (*PR*, §139, pp. 167–8). Indeed, to recall the general theme of this chapter, Hegel equates evil with contingency in the determination of the will. But perhaps because of his histor-icized dialectic, that is, his view that the complete form of rationality can only be expressed and realized over time, evil becomes a necessary stage in the develop-ment of the spirit rather than something inscrutable and inexplicable. This might be an advantage over Kant's account, or then again it might seem like an insufferable triumphalism of later stages of civilization over earlier ones—the benighted inhabitants of earlier phases of humanity were doomed to be evil—and an implausible optimism about later stages—as if the relapse into evil were not possible at any point. Kant's inscrutability thesis is at least accompanied with the latter, surely realistic implication. At least in the *Religion*, Kant seems to hold out the moral perfection of humankind as a possibility, not as an historical inevitability.

But as we earlier saw, Hegel seems to avoid leaving even the universalizing will hostage to contingency only by his celebration of the state. That is, while restrict-ing the object of my own will is certainly a form of contingency, since it is contingent that I am who I am, born when and where I was, and that of all the free beings I might make the object of my will it is only myself that I do, making the freedom of others the object of my will along with my own does not release the determination of my will from all contingency as long as what others would freely will and thus what I would will along with them by making them too the objects of my will itself remains contingent. This was precisely the objection that Hegel brought against the "empty formalism" of Kant's categorical imperative when he argued that its application always presupposes something contingent, such as that the practices of making promises or deposits are valuable and should be preserved rather than undermined. Hegel tried to avoid this sort of contingency by making

---

[42] See Insole 2013.

the *state* the ultimate object of the free will, the state as the embodiment of the freedom of all; thus, as he says in the 1827–8 lectures on the philosophy of spirit, "the state is only the mirror image of spirit's freedom, wherein it has its freedom as actual, as a world before itself" (*LPS*, p. 264). This attempts to replace exposing one's own attempt at a universally valid will to the contingency of what others would actually will in the exercise of their own freedom with a state that tells all what to will, invoking the name of universal freedom but in fact denying room for individual freedom.

Hegel tried to avoid this result in the *Philosophy of Right* by the introduction of the sphere of "civil society" between the levels of "morality" and the "state." Civil society, the realm of economic and non-governmental activity, is supposed to afford the individual the possibility of "*determinate particularity*" because while it defines various social roles with their specific obligations and privileges, it also leaves individuals some choice in their entry into one such role or another: "each individual, *by a process of self-determination*, makes himself a member of one of the moments of civil society through his activity, diligence, and skill, and supports himself in this capacity; and only through this mediation with the universal does he simultaneously provide for himself and gain *recognition* in his own representation and in that of others" (*PR*, §207, p. 238, emphasis added). But the question is whether Hegel's model of society does leave adequate room for choice in the selection of roles within civil society and whether even adequate freedom of choice there would do justice to our expectations for individual freedom within the confines of morality's demand to claim as much freedom as we can consistent with allowing and promoting equal freedom for others. Kant's abstract formulation places no further constraint on how that demand might be satisfied within the concrete circumstances of human existence in different times and places; the question is whether Hegel's more concrete approach is not too concrete, whether it allows sufficient room for individual choice and room for choice in a form that applies to a wide range of societies and not just the liberal, constitutional monarchy that he projects in the *Philosophy of Right*.

But that is a question that would take us well beyond Hegel's response to Kant. So instead of pursuing it further, we will now turn to the last aspect of Hegel's response to Kant that we will discuss, although only briefly, namely his treatment of moral feeling.

9.7. Moral Feeling

Like every other German intellectual of his generation, Hegel was certainly well aware of the inconclusive debate between Schiller and Kant that had taken place during his youth, and in fact tries to stake out his own position. As clear a source as any for his views on this issue are the 1827–8 *Lectures on the Philosophy of*

Spirit, even though they come late in Hegel's career and life and more than three decades after the debate between Schiller and Kant. Here Hegel tries to blur the kind of rigid boundary between feeling and reason that he thinks drove the earlier debate. He makes no appeal to Kant's transcendental idealism, which would allow an agent's motivation to be driven entirely by reason at one level, the noumenal, while consisting in feelings, perhaps properly cultivated and restrained feelings, at another, the phenomenal. Instead, Hegel argues that feeling and reason interact at a single level, and that both are necessary for moral motivation. This passage states Hegel's position effectively:

> Duty and right appear as something cold from the perspective of feelings. The heart can indeed constitute a totality against the one-sided understanding, but it is equally one-sided [in its own way]. Whether a content is essential, or right, cannot be decided within the sphere of feeling. Everything willed, in general everything in us must be present in the mode of feeling... But feeling does not exclude having a specific consciousness of what my feeling is and what it is supposed to be. Nor does it exclude that my will is firmly determined and resolved as an insightful will that has insight into right [*or*: concerning the nature of what right and reason are ...] There is more in the heart than the objective [elements of right and duty], namely a particular subjectivity that wants to be comforted and satisfied. However, right and duty require an indifference toward oneself. What is true in these determinations can be determined only from the thinking intelligence. The human being must act from consciousness; and that this content should be true requires that it be grasped in the form of universality, for only thus it is a purified content, a content purified by thought and reflection.
>
> (*LPS*, p. 253)

Hegel's position is straightforward. Everything that human beings think and do has an effect upon their feelings, so there is no prospect of action without feeling. And feeling is not merely epiphenomenal with regard to action, that is, an effect that is not also a cause (as Kant's first discussion of the feeling of respect at *Groundwork* 4: 401n. may suggest); on the contrary, feelings play a causal role in the determination of action (as Kant seems to allow at *Critique of Practical Reason* 5: 75–6). At the same time, moral agents cannot simply act on their untutored feelings, but must consider what is right and wrong and let the results of that consideration penetrate and purify their feelings. But that can indeed happen, thus moral agents do not simply have to act, *per impossibile*, in complete disregard of their feelings; they must purify their feelings and then act with and upon those purified feelings.

This position is a piece of common sense, not dependent upon Hegel's logic, metaphysics, or even the larger argument of the *Philosophy of Right* that freedom of the will can only be achieved and the moral point of view sustained in civil society and the state. It does not seem that different, either, from the position that Kant adopted in his account of the four "aesthetic preconditions of the mind's susceptibility to concepts of duty" in the Introduction to the Doctrine of Virtue in the *Metaphysics of Morals*, several years after his initial skirmish with Schiller, or in his discussion of our imperfect duty to cultivate "sympathetic" feelings in the body of the Doctrine of Virtue (*MM*, DV, §§34–5).[43] But there Kant's moral psychology is still presented against the backdrop of his transcendental idealist theory of freedom of the will, or at least that backdrop has not been renounced. Hegel offers us this piece of sensible moral psychology without the commitment to transcendental idealism—although perhaps his own teleology is meant to offer an alternative kind of guarantee that this happy reconciliation between feeling and reason will be achieved in the fullness of human history, a guarantee that would have its own kind of implausibility. Kant's own teleological view of human history is not evident in the *Metaphysics of Morals*.

In sum, Hegel's response to Kant's moral philosophy is a complex mix of solutions and problems. His conception of freedom as the will being with itself or at home with itself, which in turn requires universality rather than particularity, is clearly inspired by Kant's conception of autonomy. He may go too far in trying to collapse the distinction between the form and matter of such a will, and thus go too far in trying to eliminate the element of contingency in human affairs that Kant's formalist approach recognizes. We might add here that while Hegel's suggestion that the institutions of *Sittlichkeit* culminating in the state will eliminate contingency from duty seems implausible, Kant himself recognizes that individual moral development of course actually takes place within the framework of families, schools, churches, and the state; the function of the moral law is precisely to limit the role that the otherwise entirely contingent expression of self-love might take within these institutions. Turning to the next topic, Hegel may overstate his case in his critique of Kant's conception of the highest good and doctrine of the postulates, but he puts his fingers on some genuine tensions in Kant's position. Hegel's critique of Kant's conception of freedom of the will starts from a tendentious premise, but at least tries to replace Kant's foundation of the possibility of evil in an inscrutable noumenal realm with a dialectical-historical explanation of evil, though that may have its own difficulties. Finally, Hegel's common-sensical account of the relation between moral feeling and reason, independent as it is from his metaphysics and his larger account of spirit, may suggest the wisdom of relieving Kant's account of the "aesthetic preconditions" of the fulfillment of duty from its metaphysical framework as well. Then again, Kant himself may have largely done that in the *Metaphysics of Morals*, a work that seems to have gone AWOL in Hegel's impression of Kant's moral philosophy.

[43] See Guyer 2010b.

10

Herbart and Schopenhauer

The Aestheticization of Morality

10.1. Herbart and the Aestheticization of Morality

This chapter and the next will consider three philosophers who considered freedom to be the foundational value expressed by morality, although they hardly all conceived of freedom in the same way, but who rejected the tight connection between freedom and pure reason, and thus the foundation of morality in reason, that had been drawn by Kant and the succeeding German idealists. Both Johann Friedrich Herbart (1776–1841) and Arthur Schopenhauer (1788–1860) accepted some ideas from Kant but rejected others, particularly in moral philosophy, while Friedrich Nietzsche (1844–1900) generally had nothing good to say about Kant, although I will argue in the next chapter that there are nevertheless some interesting affinities between his thoughts about morality and Kant's. In their general philosophies, that is, their metaphysics and epistemologies, both Schopenhauer and Nietzsche can be understood to some extent as idealists, although that is a polysemous term, and neither is a straightforward idealist in the eighteenth-century sense of the term, that is, someone who asserts that there are only minds, or that all reality is mental. But with that definition in mind, even Kant balked at being classified as an idealist.[1] It is even debatable whether the so-called German idealists themselves, that is, Fichte, Schelling, and Hegel, were actually idealists on that definition. But we do not have to debate that question, for when it came to the fundamental principle of morality Kant was certainly a rationalist, and the others were in their own ways rationalists too, although their conceptions of reason may have differed from Kant's—and the common thread among the philosophers to be discussed now is that none of them thought that morality, or the fundamental principle of morality in case they recognized such a thing, is founded on or derived from pure reason. Among the three philosophers, Schopenhauer's criticisms of Kant were most direct and explicit—his *magnum opus*, the *World as Will and Representation* published at the end of 1818, included a "Critique of the Kantian Philosophy" that comprises about a fifth

---

[1] Kant, *Prol*, §13, note III, 4: 290–4. On the definition of idealism and the question whether Kant's transcendental idealism is actually a form of idealism, see Guyer and Horstmann 2023.

Kant's Impact on Moral Philosophy. Paul Guyer, Oxford University Press. © Paul Guyer 2024.
DOI: 10.1093/oso/9780199592456.003.0011

of the whole book.[2] Neither Herbart nor Nietzsche addressed as many issues in Kant's moral philosophy as Schopenhauer did. But all three, whether gently or harshly, criticized Kant's attempt to establish a morality, let alone a religion, of pure reason.

Herbart grew up in the Westphalian town of Oldenburg, and was already reading Kant as a teenage student at the local *Gymnasium*.[3] He matriculated at the university at Jena in October 1794. Fichte arrived around the same time, and Herbart studied with him, although his doubts about Fichte's idealist *Wissenschaftslehre* began to grow by 1796. In 1797 he went to Bern, Switzerland, as a private tutor, like so many other German intellectuals of his time. He stayed for two years before returning to Oldenburg and then to Bremen until 1802. At that point he finally received his doctorate and habilitation not at Jena but at Göttingen, where he worked as a *Privatdozent* until 1805 and then as a professor *extraordinarius* until 1809, when, five years after the death of Kant, he accepted what had been Kant's chair in Königsberg. He thus served as Kant's successor for almost a quarter-century, before returning to Göttingen, also as an *ordinarius*, in 1833.

Herbart's chief work in moral philosophy, the *Allgemeine praktische Philosophie* ("General Practical Philosophy," although the work has never been translated into English), was published in 1808, thus at the end of his first Göttingen period. It is very different in tone from any of Kant's works in moral philosophy, or even from the works of Fichte and the (not yet published) works of Schelling and Hegel, for all their particular differences with Kant. Frederick Beiser considers the work a philosophical expression of the Romanticism to which Herbart had been exposed in Jena in the 1790s, although he also points out the influence of the Scottish moral-sense school, above all Adam Smith, on Herbart's approach.[4] The basis for this claim is that, certainly contrary to Kant, Herbart argues that morality is founded on taste or aesthetic judgment. What Herbart means by this, however, is quite distinct from what either Kant or the Romantics thought about aesthetic judgment; perhaps what is most distinctive about Herbart's approach is that he founds morality on a series of what he calls "ideals" rather than on any strictly rational principle or principles, and these ideals may well be recommended to us by feelings of approbation rather than by any form of rational inference.

But at least part of what Herbart means by conceiving of moral judgment as a kind of aesthetic judgment is that it is grounded on a felt response to *relations*,

---

[2] Schopenhauer's *World as Will and Representation* was published at the end of 1818, with an 1819 date on it. It was twenty-five years before a 2nd edition was needed; then Schopenhauer added a second volume of additions a hundred pages longer than the first volume, thus reducing the percentage of the work occupied by the "Critique of Kantian Philosophy." See Schopenhauer 2010–18, vol. 1, pp. 441–565.

[3] My biographical information comes from the only monograph on Herbart in English, Beiser 2022.

[4] Beiser 2022, p. 108.

although relations in specific circumstances; the ideals of which he speaks can be thought of as generalizing over types of relations without yielding specific rules for determining right and wrong. To this extent, Herbart might actually share some of the suspicion against general rules that Hegel manifested in arguing that *Sittlichkeit* in its concreteness needs to supersede the empty formalism of Kantian *Moralität*. Further, the relations that Herbart has in mind are relations within or among *wills*. Moral judgment shares with other forms of aesthetic judgment that it is always a response to some sort of relation in some particular instance or context, not to some sort of qualities that can be considered apart from any relation and context, such as specific shapes, colors, and so on; it differs from other aesthetic judgment in that it is always a response to relations within or among wills. The first ideal that Herbart considers is what he calls the "ideal of inner freedom" (*APP*, p. 77), in which there is a harmonious relation between one's will and one's judging (*Beurtheilung*), or between one's will and one's judgment *of oneself*. Here the influence of Adam Smith seems strong: the question is whether one's will, one's desires and intentions, can bear the weight of one's own self-examination. Smith of course attributes self-examination to the "impartial spectator," the man within the breast, while Herbart emphasizes that "The judging and the willing [*das Wollen*] are not two separate, not two different persons, one of which gives the command while the other receives it. It is rather one and the same rational being that wills and that also judges, and wills" (p. 79). Here Herbart does speak of a "rational being" (*Vernunftwesen*), but he does not suggest that such a being has any determinate rule by which to judge the propriety (as Smith would say) of its willing. The lingering influence of Fichte might also be noted here in Herbart's use of the active noun *das Wollen*, "willing," instead of what one might expect, *das Wille* or *die Willkühr*, the "will" or the "faculty of choice." Frederick Beiser associates Herbart's notion of inner freedom with the Stoic as a well as Epicurean ideal of "*ataxia*, tranquility, or peace of mind,"[5] but this might not fit so well with Herbart's Fichtean conception of willing as itself a kind of activity, not a passive state. And Herbart does note that willing ordinarily has consequences, and that these too will enter into one's judging of one's own willing. All of this, it should be noted, is quite abstract. While Kant analyzes the objects of the duty of "self-perfection" into the perfection of one's natural and moral capacities, the former in turn divided into physical capacities, mind, and spirit, the latter into self-knowledge and conscience, although of course those are still fairly general and will mean different things for different people in different circumstances, when it comes to the moral attitude toward oneself Herbart states only this very general ideal of inner freedom as harmony between one's will and one's judgment of oneself. And in fact, Herbart takes pains to distinguish the ideal of inner freedom

---

[5] Beiser 2022, p. 116. On his next page, Beiser notes that willing is an activity for Herbart, although he does not mention Fichte there.

from an ideal of perfection (*Vollkommenheit*), precisely because that risks making inner freedom into too much of an object of direct *desire*. "This error is encountered as soon as the specific difference between taste and desire [*Begehrung*] is lost from view, as soon as that which is not the same is taken as the same" (*APP*, p. 95). Part of Herbart's motivation for classifying moral judgment as aesthetic is to treat it as disinterested, rather than as Kant would, as an interest of reason.

The three remaining ideals that constitute morality for Herbart concern relations among the wills of different persons (*APP*, p. 98), the sphere of morality as generally understood in modern times, the sphere of "what we owe to each other."[6] Under the idea of "benevolence" (*Wohlwollen*) Herbart addresses the relation between one will and one other, in which the first "attaches itself to the foreign will" in the form of intending some good for the other (p. 100). "Justice" (*Recht*) concerns relations among multiple wills "touching upon property and traffic [*Verkehr*]," or trade (p. 108), where however people have primarily their own interests in mind, thus their effects upon others are to some extent unintentional (*absichtloses*), while "fairness" (*Billigkeit*) concerns people's intentional (*absichtliche*) actions affecting each other, and goes beyond matters of property and trade, presumably concerning other rights and obligations, as well. As Herbart puts it, *Billigkeit* concerns the "connection among two [or more] wills insofar as the act of one rational being penetrates through the common medium and interferes with the will of another, so that the other *suffers* from that [or not], and that the intention acting upon him is either welcome or not" (*APP*, pp. 128–9). As in the case of self-regarding inner freedom, Herbart's ideas of benevolence, justice, and fairness are as abstract as possible, and his concern is clearly to demonstrate that they cannot be reduced to specific rules, maxims, or algorithms, but always require taste and judgment for their application. Much of the remainder of his book is then given over to the description of the social institutions within which these ideals may be pursued, such as "just society" (*Rechtsgesellschaft*), the "system of wages," the "system of administration," the "system of culture," and "ensouled society" (family, honor, religion). In these ways Herbart might be thought of as anticipating Hegel's conception of *Sittlichkeit*, or developing in parallel—Hegel developed his concept in Jena manuscripts a few years ahead of Herbart, but did not publish it until his *Philosophy of Right* in 1821, thirteen years after Herbart's book.

Herbart founded his moral philosophy on feelings of approbation toward intra- and interpersonal relations, instead of deriving a fundamental moral feeling—respect—from an antecedently given and formulable moral law. Here there is a fundamental difference with Kant, perhaps one that endures into contemporary moral philosophy. And although Kant did not deny that moral principles need

---

[6] I take this phrase, of course, from Scanlon 1998.

empirical input for their application, that they may not settle casuistical questions for us, and that some degree of judgment is always needed to apply general principles, Herbart stressed that moral ideas are ideals rather than principles much more strongly than Kant. Debate about that point continues into contemporary moral philosophy as well, where "particularism" has some affinity with Herbart's position. So Herbart raised questions about Kant that certainly are worth continuing discussion.

However, Herbart's person and work quickly faded into obscurity—indeed, very few of his books have ever been reprinted, let alone translated into any language other than German. For an anti-Kantian, anti-rationalist philosopher who had much greater influence, whose books have not only been continuously reprinted and widely translated, even all retranslated into English within the last decade or so, we must now turn to the case of Arthur Schopenhauer.

10.2. Schopenhauer: Rationality and the Will

Schopenhauer frequently claimed to be the only true heir to Kant.[7] Indeed, Kant was the only one of his immediate predecessors whom he would acknowledge at all—although he listened to Fichte's lectures in Berlin in 1810–11 and was clearly influenced by Schelling as well, he never had a kind word to say about either. He regarded Kant's argument for transcendental idealism in the "Transcendental Aesthetic" of the *Critique of Pure Reason* as one of the great chapters not merely in that work but in the entire history of philosophy, and patterned his own epistemology and metaphysics on it, following Kant in regarding space, time, and causality as well as other forms of the "principle of sufficient reason" as our own impositions upon a raw experience that is in some way triggered by something that exists independent of those forms and cannot be known by means of them. However, when it came to moral philosophy Schopenhauer vehemently disagreed with Kant. He is perhaps best known, first, for the claim that Kant's conception of the fundamental principle of morality as a categorical imperative is, in spite of Kant's own claim to offer a philosophy of human autonomy, a holdover of theological thinking. More than a century before Elizabeth Anscombe made a similar claim in her 1958 article "Modern Moral Philosophy,"[8] Schopenhauer wrote:

---

[7] Schopenhauer's biography is better known than Herbart's, so I won't repeat it here. For a masterful and detailed biography, see Cartwright 2010. General works on Schopenhauer's philosophy include Gardiner 1963; Hamlyn 1980; Magee 1983; Janaway 1989; Atwell 1995; and Young 2005. Two with a particular focus on Schopenhauer's relation to Kant are Young 1987 and Hannan 2009. Useful collections of papers on Schopenhauer are Janaway 1999; Neill and Janaway 2009; and Norman and Welchman 2023.

[8] Anscombe 1958.

Conceiving ethics in an *imperatival* form, as *doctrine of duty*, and thinking of the moral worth or unworth of human actions as fulfilment or dereliction of *duties*, undeniably stems, together with the *ought*, solely from theological morals and in turn from the Decalogue. Accordingly it rests essentially on the presupposition of the human being's dependence on another will that commands him and announces reward and punishment to him, and cannot be separated from that.

(BM, p. 129)[9]

Schopenhauer's other best-known difference from Kant's moral philosophy is his claim that morality must be founded upon the feeling of compassion for the suffering of others rather than on a requirement that all maxims have the form of universal law. In fact, he sometimes presents this not as an alternative to theological morals altogether, but rather as an alternative theological or at least religious doctrine. He accepts Schiller's (apparent) critique of the (supposedly) Kantian position that "Worth of character is to commence only when someone, without sympathy of the heart, cold and indifferent to the sufferings of others, ... nevertheless displays beneficence merely for the sake of tiresome *duty*," and then continues by opposing a Pauline conception of morality as based upon love to what might be considered a more Mosaic and voluntaristic conception of morality as based upon duties and offices arbitrarily commanded by God:

This assertion, which outrages genuine moral feeling, this apotheosis of unkindness which directly opposes the Christian moral doctrine that places love above all else and allows nothing to count without it (I Corinthians 13, 3), this tactless moral pedantry has been satirized by *Schiller* in two apt epigrams, entitled "Scruples of Conscience and Decision". The immediate occasion for these seems to have been provided by some passages from the *Critique of Practical Reason* that are quite relevant here, such as, e.g.: "The disposition incumbent upon a human being to have in observing the moral law is to do so from *duty*, not from *voluntary liking* nor even from an endeavour that he undertakes *uncommanded*, gladly and of his own accord" [5: 84].—It has to be *commanded*! What a slave-morality! And in the same work [5: 118],...we find that "feelings of compassion and soft-hearted sympathy are themselves burdensome to right-thinking persons, because they bring their well-considered maxims into confusion, and produce the wish to be free from them and subject to lawgiving reason alone". I assert that (unless he has ulterior intentions), what opens the hand of the beneficent agent above...can never be anything other than slavish *fear of gods*...   (*BM*, pp. 136–7)

---

[9] Translation of Arthur Schopenhauer, *Prize Essay on the Basis of Morals*, in Schopenhauer 2009, p. 129. This essay, abbreviated "*BM*," and the companion *Prize Essay on the Freedom of the Will*, abbreviated "*FW*," will both be cited from this volume.

A morality based on feelings of compassion and sympathy, however, is precisely what Schopenhauer himself advocates.

Schopenhauer's repeated accusation that Kantian morality is a "slave-morality"—although it echoes Kant's own accusation that Schiller's thought that we might sometimes have to settle for mere "dignity" (*Würde*) rather than "grace" or graciousness (*Anmut*) is a slavish and "Carthusian" or monkish conception of morality!—must have been deeply influential on Friedrich Nietzsche.[10] I will argue in the next chapter that, even though in the end Nietzsche may have no more time for Schopenhauer's ethics of compassion than for Kant's morality of universal law, his own "transvaluation of values," intended to supersede Kantian morality, is in one way more Kantian than Schopenhauer's ethics of compassion. In this chapter, I will argue that Schopenhauer's own ethics of compassion is not as entirely non-Kantian as he makes it seem, although Schopenhauer's contempt for Kant's late *Metaphysics of Morals* as a work of the latter's "senility" may have masked this fact from him.

But before we can come to any of this, the first point that I want to make is that Schopenhauer's differences from Kant in moral philosophy, his difference on matters of theology and above all on the relation between law and compassion, are not independent of differences in their theoretical philosophies, but are in fact rooted in what is a profound difference between their epistemology and metaphysics in spite of Schopenhauer's admiration for Kant's transcendental idealism. The difference is that, while for Kant we supposedly can have no theoretical knowledge of how things are in themselves independently of how they appear to us, only belief founded on practical grounds or what he later calls "practical-dogmatic cognition" that as we are in ourselves we really are rational or at least free to act in accordance with reason (although, as we saw, in section III of the *Groundwork* Kant came at least dangerously close to arguing that we do have theoretical knowledge of that fact), for Schopenhauer the reality that underlies the appearance of our own rationality and by extension everything else is an entirely non-rational will, and although this will is free in the negative sense of being free from the causal determinism characteristic of the world as it appears, it is not free *to be rational*. Thus a morality reflective of our real nature and circumstances cannot be based on laws or ends of reason, but can at best be based on compassion for the non-rational circumstances of human existence.

That compassion is the only possible basis for morality is also entailed by Schopenhauer's view that no enduring happiness or satisfaction is possible for human beings, those alone among all the living beings of the world who can understand the condition in which all living beings exist, whether they can know this or not, and that what is possible is at most the shorter or longer alleviation of

---

[10] On Schopenhauer's influence on Nietzsche, see the papers collected in Janaway 1998.

suffering. Thus compassion, which leads to the effort to alleviate suffering rather than to promote any positive ends, is the only coherent response to the human condition, and that of any other sentient creatures. But before we can come to the particulars of Schopenhauer's theory of happiness, or more precisely unhappiness, we must first consider the superficial similarity but deeper dissimilarity between Schopenhauer's and Kant's epistemology and metaphysics.

Schopenhauer emphasized the more superficial similarities between his theoretical philosophy and Kant's in his 1813 doctoral dissertation, *On the Fourfold Root of the Principle of Sufficient Reason*, but then revealed the deeper difference between himself and Kant in his *magnum opus*, *The World as Will and Representation*, first published at the end of 1818 (like a new car model, however, dated the following year), and then substantially revised and supplemented later in his life.[11] In the first work, Schopenhauer claims that any form of science is a "*system* of findings, i.e., a unity of connected findings in opposition to a mere aggregate," where the distinction between a system and "a mere aggregate is that each of a science's findings follows from another as its ground" (*FR*, §4, pp. 9–10). His provisional statement of the principle of sufficient reason is *Nihil est sine ratione cur potius sit quam non sit*, "Nothing is without a reason why it is rather than is not" (*FR*, §5, p. 10), and his thesis is that any ground for systematic connection rather than mere aggregation is an instance of sufficient reason. More fully, he asserts:

> *Our cognizing consciousness, appearing as outer and inner sensibility (receptivity), as understanding and reason, divides into subject and object and comprises nothing else. To be object for the subject and to be our representation are the same. All of our representations are objects for the subject, and all objects for the subject are our representations. Now, however, it occurs that all of our representations stand to one another in a connection that is governed by laws and of a form determinable* a priori, *by means of which connection nothing existing of itself and independently, likewise nothing existing in isolation and apart, can be an object for us.* It is this connection that the principle of sufficient reason expresses in its generality.   (*FR*, §16, pp. 30–1; Schopenhauer's emphasis)

This statement combines what Schopenhauer takes to be Kant's transcendental idealism, the position that what we know (our object) is always our own representations, never things as they are in themselves, although there is no reason to doubt that things independent of our representations exist, with his own view that

---

[11] The translations of both *The Fourfold Root of the Principle of Sufficient Reason* ("*FR*") in Schopenhauer 2012 and *The World as Will and Representation* ("*WWR*") in Schopenahuer 2010–18 are based on Schopenhauer's 2nd editions (1847 and 1844 respectively) rather than his slimmer 1st editions. References in *FR* to the later *WWR* are a sure sign that the passages in which they are found come from the 2nd rather than the 1st edition.

all forms of connection among these appearances, the connections that constitute our science or knowledge of them, count as instances of the principle of sufficient reason. In the remainder of the book, he then characterizes four forms or versions of the principle of sufficient reason by means of which we organize our representations into systematic representations of objects.

The order of Schopenhauer's exposition of the forms of the principle of sufficient reason, which Kant himself had argued was valid only as a principle of the possibility of experience (*CPuR*, A200–1/B246), differs from that of Kant's. Kant had expounded first the pure forms of intuition, in the Transcendental Aesthetic, then the "supreme principle of all analytic judgments," the law of non-contradiction, and only then the a priori principles of synthetic judgments, in the Axioms of Intuition, the Anticipations of Perception, and above all the Analogies of Experience, while leaving the fundamental principle of pure practical reason to his works in practical philosophy. Schopenhauer instead begins with causality as the most general principle of empirical knowledge (or synthetic a posteriori judgments), and only then introduces his version of Kant's principle of analytic judgments and then space and time also as versions of the principle of sufficient reason. Finally, he introduces a principle of sufficient reason for willing, but only against the background of his first principle of causality, which means that his account of willing is, at least in *The Fourfold Root*, thoroughly deterministic.

"The first class of possible objects of our faculty of representations is that of *intuitive, complete, empirical* representations" (*FR*, §17, p. 33), and these are organized by the form of causality, which Schopenhauer regards as the self-evident application of the principle of sufficient reason to *change* in time and space, or as the principle of "becoming," even though he has not yet explicitly discussed the more primordial application of the principle of sufficient reason to the delimitation of regions of space and time in what he calls the "principle of the sufficient reason of being" (*FR*, sixth chapter). Beginning with causality, Schopenhauer writes:

> In the present class of objects for the subject, the principle of sufficient reason appears as *the law of causality*, and as such I call it the *principle of sufficient reason of becoming, principium rationis sufficientis fiendi*. All objects that present themselves in the totality of representations that constitutes the complex of empirical reality are, as regards the appearance and disappearance of their states, interconnected through this principle and thus in the direction of the course of time. (*FR*, §20, p. 38)

Deeply influenced by Hume as well as by Kant, although by the content of Hume's conception of causality rather than by his doubts about its foundation in reason, Schopenhauer takes it as self-evident that every change or event in time is grounded or determined by an appropriately contiguous and antecedent one, but moreover that since *each* event in space and time is determined by some other spatially contiguous and temporally antecedent event, in fact *all* events in space and time constitute a system in which each event is fully determined by all that has gone before and adds its effect, although in a way that is in principle entirely foreseeable, to all that comes after. Schopenhauer thus equates the first form of the principle of sufficient reason with the thoroughgoing determinism of the spatio-temporal, empirical world. The principle of ubiquitous causality and the consequent determinism applies not just to inorganic matter, where forms of causality include mechanical, magnetic, electrical, and gravitational forces, and not just to organic life in general, where causality takes the special form of "stimulus," but also to *motives*, which are the causes of "the external actions consciously performed by all animal beings" including human beings (*FR*, §20, pp. 48–9).[12] Motives work through "cognition," or through an agent's representation of the desirability of various outcomes, but that does not exempt them from the principle of causality; it is just the way in which their causality works.

This all-inclusive determinism remains a constant in Schopenhauer's thought and the background of his moral philosophy. Schopenhauer immediately infers from it that the idea *"that two different actions are possible for a given human in a given situation"* is a "complete *absurdity*" (*FR*, §20, p. 50).[13] Even though a human being may have several different motives bearing on the same situation, and think that several different courses of action are possible for him, in fact one of those motives has been determined to be the strongest by the prior history of the individual (and the world) and will in turn determine the action, whether or not that is yet known to the agent. There is no room for freedom even for human beings in the world of appearances except in the Hobbesian, negative sense of an absence of external interference with the action to which an agent is determined by his own history.

Schopenhauer will argue that human beings have a kind of freedom at the level of underlying reality, although his account of this will be very different from Kant's. But that will come up only in *The World as Will and Representation* and the subsequent *Essay on the Freedom of the Will*. Before we turn to those works, we must finish our preliminary account of *The Fourfold Root*. The second version of the principle of sufficient reason that Schopenhauer introduces is the "principle of sufficient reason of knowing," the *principium rationis sufficientis cognoscendi*. This "says that if a judgment would express *knowledge*, it must have a sufficient ground, and on account of this property it receives the predicate *true*" (*FR*, §29, p. 100). Schopenhauer's initial definition of this principle might make it sound as if concerns only analytic truths, for he says that "thinking in the narrower sense"

---

[12] On the naturalistic aspects of Schopenhauer's philosophy, see esp. Young 1987 and Segula 2023.
[13] For discussion of this claim, see Gardiner 1963, pp. 247–63, and Hamlyn 1980. pp. 124–33.

consists "in a combination or separation of two or more concepts under the various restrictions and modifications that logic specifies in the theory of judgments" (*FR*, §30, p. 100). As he continues, however, he makes it clear that judgments can be true for more than purely logical reasons, including but not limited to the law of non-contradiction. They can be true for empirical reasons, when "the judgment itself is *immediately* grounded on experience" (*FR*, §31, p. 102). They can be true for "transcendental" reasons, when they are grounded in "the forms of intuitive empirical cognition, lying in the understanding and pure sensibility as conditions of the possibility of all experience" (*FR*, §32, p. 103) (although the content of this principle of knowing would seem to be coextensive with the preceding "principle of sufficient reason of becoming" and the subsequent "principle of sufficient reason of being"). Finally, they can be true for reasons of "reason" itself, although by this Schopenhauer makes it clear that he means only the principles of ordinary inferential or "mediated cognition" (*FR*, §34, p. 105), and nothing that has any special bearing on practical reason or morality, or any special metaphysical implications at all. As Schopenhauer puts this point in his inimitable style, "If it is...taught that we possess a faculty for cognition which is immediate, material..., and supersensible (i.e., leading beyond all possibility of experience, a faculty expressly intended for metaphysical insight,...and that this faculty comprises *our reason*—then I must be so impolite as to call it a bare-faced lie" (*FR*, §34, p. 109). Reason is simply our capacity for inference, or for constructing syllogisms, and its principle is presumably simply that a valid inference with true premises yields a true conclusion, but it does not introduce any truths of its own. This will be important to keep in mind when we turn to Schopenhauer's attack on the idea that some form of reason, namely pure practical reason, could itself be the source of a substantive moral principle.

The third form of the principle of sufficient reason, to which Schopenhauer gives very little space in *The Fourfold Root* but just because he thinks that Kant has done such a good job in the "Transcendental Aesthetic," is the principle of the sufficient reason of "being," which is that "Space and time are so constituted that all of their parts stand in a relation to one another, so each of them determines and is conditioned by another. In space this relation is called *position*; in time, *succession*" (*FR*, §36, pp. 123–4). Each region of space and duration of time has a location that is uniquely and fully determined by its relation to all other regions and durations, and one might add that each region and duration also has its magnitude determined by the regions and durations surrounding it. Schopenhauer calls this the principle of sufficient reason of "being" because the first thing one must know about an object is where it is in space and time, how much space it takes up and how long it endures—only when one knows this can one go on to ascribe other properties and in particular causal properties to objects. For this reason, one might have thought that Schopenhauer should have stated the principle of sufficient reason of being before that of becoming, as Kant had expounded the pure forms of intuition before the principles of pure understanding including causality. Perhaps Schopenhauer was simply so eager to affirm his commitment to the principle of causality and to determinism that he did not care about this nicety.

Finally, Schopenhauer refers to a fourth version of the principle of sufficient reason, the "law of motivation" (*FR*, §43, p. 136). I say "refers to" rather than "expounds" because Schopenhauer does not quite or fully state the principle, saying just that "It is as inconceivable that there can be an action without a motive as that there can be movement of an inanimate body without a push or pull" (*FR*, §43, p. 137). The principle is probably intended to be something like the Hobbesian principle that action is determined by the *strongest* motive, which Schopenhauer argues at length in the later *Essay on the Freedom of the Will*—and which in the end should be the Lockean point that the true motivation for action is always the strongest aversion to foreseen pain.[14] But the only point that he is really concerned to make in *The Fourfold Root* is that "will" or motivation is just "*causality seen from within*" (*FR*, §43, p. 137). That is, in acting we are aware of our current motives or desires, not their history, and it may seem to us as if something radically different from ordinary causation is going on; but nothing different is going on, our actions are being determined by their antecedents, with our consciousness of our desires or their desirability just being part of the causal mechanism. "This insight," Schopenhauer says in the second-edition version of *The Fourfold Root*, "is the cornerstone of my whole metaphysics" (*FR*, §43, p. 138), and as we shall shortly see it is the cornerstone of his approach to moral philosophy as well.

That reason is just our faculty for truth-preserving but not truth-creating inference and that motivation or will is just causality seen from the inside are two fundamental grounds for Schopenhauer's critique of Kant's ethics. The background to Schopenhauer's criticisms of Kant is his own view that human will is essentially non-rational or even irrational except in the weakest sense, also admitted by Schopenhauer's hero Hume, of enjoying some degree of *instrumental* rationality, that is, an ability to choose reasonable means to ends that are set by something other than reason. Thus the Kantian project, of seeing the moral law as given by pure practical reason, either by pure practical reason itself imposing the requirement of the universalizability of our maxims upon us or by pure practical reason making or recognizing humanity to be an end in itself that can be respected only by adherence to the requirement of universalizability, is basically laughed off by Schopenhauer. And even Schopenhauer's allowance of merely instrumental rationality is limited, because he thinks that what might well be taken as the long-term goal of our instrumental use of reason, namely enduring happiness, is a

---

[14]   See Locke 1975, book II, chapter xxi (2nd edition and following).

hopeless goal for us. His view is that we relentlessly pursue happiness, but are doomed to frustration in this pursuit, and thus that compassion that would prompt efforts to alleviate suffering is the best we can do in morality.

We might, however, conceive of Schopenhauer's argument as proceeding at two levels, an empirical and a metaphysical level, or one level that is independent of his version of transcendental idealism and one that depends upon it.[15] At the latter level, as we will see, he argues that compassion for others and indifference to one's own suffering is a consequence of metaphysical insight, that is, understanding of the superficiality of individuation between different persons and of the underlying real identity of all persons, indeed all existence, as manifestations of a single thing-in-itself. His argument will be that this single thing-in-itself is the very opposite of a rational will, and for this reason he rejects Kant's approach to morality, above all that of the third section of the *Groundwork* which attempts to derive the validity of the moral law for us from our noumenal character as rational wills. Yet insofar as Schopenhauer's own theory has indifference to our own suffering and compassion for the suffering of others deriving at least in part from metaphysical insight, it would seem to be to that extent a theory that grounds morality in reason after all, for what could our capacity for the relevant metaphysical insight be except a kind of reason? Schopenhauer's rejection of reason as the basis for morality might not be as complete as he often likes to make it appear.

What follows will not mirror the order of Schopenhauer's own exposition in *The World as Will and Representation* and the essay on *The Basis of Morality*, but let us consider what can be regarded as Schopenhauer's empirical argument before delving further into his metaphysics. Schopenhauer states his empirical argument concisely in the fourth book of his *magnum opus*, after many pages of metaphysical argument. Or at least this assertion can be considered empirical because its truth does not depend upon Schopenhauer's metaphysics:

> Absolutely every human life flows between willing and attaining. The nature of every desire is pain: attainment quickly gives rise to satiety: the goal was only apparent: possession takes away the stimulus: the desire, the need re-emerges in a new form: if not, then what follows is dreariness, emptiness, boredom, and the struggle against these is just as painful as the struggle against want.

Further,

> The perpetual efforts to banish suffering do nothing more than alter its form. This is originally lack, need, worries over how to sustain life. If (and this is extremely difficult) we are successful in driving out pain in this form, then it

immediately appears in a thousand others, varying, according to age and circumstances, as sex drive, passionate love, envy, jealousy, hatred, anxiety, ambition,
greed, illness, etc., etc. If it ultimately cannot find any other form in which to
appear, then it comes in the sad grey garments of satiety and boredom, and we
then try hard to fend it off. Even if we finally succeed in driving these away, it can
hardly be done without letting the pain back in one of its previous forms and so
beginning the dance all over again; because every human life is thrown back and
forth between pain and boredom.   (*WWR*, fourth book, §57, pp. 340–1)

Damned if we do, damned if we don't. If we fail to satisfy some desire, we are
disappointed, frustrated, or worse, depending on the strength of the desire and the
importance of its satisfaction to our survival. But if we do satisfy the desire, then
there are two possible outcomes: we quickly tire of that satisfaction, and then
formulate another desire, which either painfully goes unsatisfied or even if satisfied quickly pales, leading to yet another desire that will go unsatisfied or else
quickly pale, and so on—or we do not formulate another desire, in which case we
find ourselves in a painful state of tedium.[16] The real point is that there is no
desire, no matter how pressing or apparently important, the satisfaction of which
can bring lasting happiness, and thus lasting happiness itself is not possible, since
happiness would be nothing but the enduring satisfaction of desire. In that case
the best that we can do is to try to alleviate suffering, whether our own or that of
others, perhaps by keeping the interval between desire and satisfaction within
bounds—"For desire and satisfaction to follow each other without too long or too
short an interval in between reduces the suffering caused by both to the smallest
quantity, and constitutes the happiest course through life" (*WWR*, fourth book,
§57, p. 340), which is, however, not a very happy course. For this reason, morality
cannot concern itself with any positive promotion of agents' ends, let alone with
any conception of agents as ends in themselves;[17] at best it can concern itself with
some degree of alleviation of the perpetual suffering that is the human lot (and the
lot of any other creature, at least as long as its consciousness extends beyond a
moment of satisfaction)—at least unless some metaphysical insight allows one or
some to break out of this perpetual cycle of dissatisfaction.

Of course Kant too knew that a life devoted to the pursuit of happiness
promised more frustration than satisfaction; that was part of the reason why he

---

[16] Reginster 2023 is a subtle discussion of this well-known Schopenhauerian trope, arguing that
expectation, frustration, and satiety are not all painful in the same way, indeed that expectation is not
necessarily painful at all; see esp. pp. 27–31. Nevertheless, Reginster does not reject the general outline
of this interpretation of Schopenhauer.

[17] Shapshay 2019 argues that, according to Schopenhauer, "when one looks at the world through the
lens of compassion, one recognizes the inherent moral value of sentient subjects," and attributes to
Schopenhauer a "constructivist" theory that "all value is *constructed* by valuers" who must therefore
themselves have inherent value (p. 140). I find this interpretation difficult to reconcile with
Schopenhauer's position that *nothing* is intrinsically satisfying, as does Reginster 2023, p. 35.

insisted that happiness or its maximization could not be the principle of morality. As early as 1764 or 1765, for example, although Schopenhauer could not have known this, Kant had written in his copy of his early book *Observations on the Feeling of the Beautiful and Sublime* that "It is not compatible with happiness to let the inclinations become excessive, for since there are uncommonly many cases where circumstances are unfavorable for these inclinations, when things are not as desired, they become a source of oppression, misery, and worry, of which the simple person knows nothing."[18] This statement does not go as far as Schopenhauer's: Kant's position is that *excessive* desires all too easily lead to more frustration than satisfaction, while Schopenhauer's is that the attempt to satisfy *any* desires always leads only to frustration. Even so, it is at least in part for this reason that Kant supposes that the immediate object of morality must be something altogether different from happiness; it must be an end set by reason rather than desire, or more precisely by the effect of pure practical reason on the "higher" faculty of desire rather than by inclination on the "lower" faculty of desire. But Schopenhauer's issue with Kant is that he does not recognize any end that might be set or recognized by reason as an alternative to happiness, so morality cannot endorse the pursuit of any positive end, only the alleviation of the suffering inevitably caused by our inexorable pursuit of happiness. (Schopenhauer also thinks that Kant lets happiness as a—hopeless—moral goal return by the back door in his conception of the highest good. We will return to that point.)

Let us now turn to Schopenhauer's grander metaphysics. The gist of Schopenhauer's position is that space, time, and causality, identified in *The Fourfold Root* as two (taking space and time together) of the four principles of sufficient reason and now in *The World as Will and Representation*, are the essential forms of representation of objects and only of our representations of objects, thus of objects as appearances, but that we have another way of approaching objects, beginning with our own bodies, from the inside, as will. In the first book of *The World as Will and Representation*, without adding anything to Kant's arguments for transcendental idealism in the "Transcendental Aesthetic," he states that "we will treat everything merely as representation, as an object for the subject: even the body itself, everyone's point of departure for intuition of the world, is no different from any other real object, and we will treat it too only to the extent that it can be known in cognition, that is, for us it is merely a representation." But he also makes it clear that our cognition (or merely apparent cognition) of ourselves as particular bodies, individuated from others in space and time and standing in deterministic causal relations to all that has come before or will come after in space and time, is an "abstract and one-sided perspective, forcibly separating things that belong together necessarily" (*WWR*, first book, §6, p. 40), and

---

[18] Kant, *Notes in the Observations on the Feeling of the Beautiful and Sublime*, in Kant 2005, p. 7.

that I am conscious of my body "twice over, once as *representation* and once as *will*" (*WWR*, first book, §5, p. 40). Schopenhauer holds that we know ourselves as willing and indeed willing through our own bodies independently of our representation of bodies including our own through the nexus of space, time, and causality, and moreover that in so doing we know not merely our *inner* but our *inmost* nature, our essence. He then argues that since this knowledge of ourselves, but knowledge apart from the ordinary framework of cognition, is our *only* knowledge independent of the spatio-temporal and causal framework of our appearances, it is the only way we can conceive of the inmost essence of *anything*, so any conception of the in-itself that we can have, of the thing in itself behind any appearance, not just the appearance of ourselves, is as will. Will and "this alone gives [one] the key to his own appearance, reveals to him the meaning and shows him the inner workings of his essence, his deeds, his movements" (*WWR*, second book, §18, p. 124), but in addition,

we will go on to use this cognition as a key to the essence of every appearance in nature; and when it comes to objects other than our own body, objects that have not been given to us in this double manner but only as representations in our consciousness, we will judge them on the analogy with our own body, assuming that, since they are on the one hand representations just like the body and are in this respect homogeneous with it, then on the other hand, what remains after disregarding their existence as representation of a subject must have the same inner essence as what we call *will*. After all, what other sort of existence or reality could we attribute to the rest of the corporeal world. Where could we get the elements to construct such a world? We do not know anything—we cannot even think anything—besides will and representation.

(*WWR*, second book, §19, p. 129)

Schopenhauer is careful enough not to commit the outright fallacy of inferring that all things in themselves must be will from the fact that the only one we know is will; he more cautiously says that since it is as will that we know the only thing in itself that we do know that is the only way we can conceive of any thing in itself, so we must conceive of other things at least in analogy with ourselves.[19] Or at least he observes this caution initially; whether he drops it as he continues is another matter. Indeed, we will see in a moment that there is a reason for him to drop it, although that itself might be another fallacy.

But before we turn to that, there is an obvious objection, namely that within Kantian theory we can never *know any* thing in itself, not even our ourselves as things in themselves, so we should not be able to know even that the thing in itself

---

[19] On the need for Schopenhauer to proceed cautiously here, see Janaway 1989, pp. 196–7, and Wicks 2023, pp. 180–2.

in our own case is will. Schopenhauer might seem to overlook this nicety, and thus it might seem as if his generalization of will from the case of our own thing in itself to all others, with whatever qualification he might acknowledge to attend that inference, should never even get off the ground. That we do know our real nature to be will is so fundamental for Schopenhauer that perhaps we should just note this basic divergence from Kant and move on. But it will be more helpful in understanding the real differences between the moral thought of Kant and Schopenhauer to acknowledge that in moral philosophy Kant too allows himself to assert genuine knowledge of our real nature, or what we are in ourselves, as what in later works he calls "practical-dogmatic" knowledge. Although that is a term that Kant introduces in late work such as the drafts for an entry in the essay competition on the question, "What Real Progress has Metaphysics made in Germany since the Times of Leibniz and Wolff?", the assumption itself is evident in such earlier passages as section III of the *Groundwork*, where Kant does not just say that we can *presuppose* or *assume* ourselves to be free (*G*, 4: 448), but rather argues that we "really find" in ourselves "a capacity by which" we distinguish ourselves "from all other things, even from" ourselves "as we are affected by objects, and that is *reason*," and that this is in turn "pure self-activity" or spontaneity, in other words, freedom (*G*, 4: 452). We do not just assume that we are free and rational, in other words, we know it. Since, for Kant, to have a will is to be free and spontaneous, exempt from causal determinism, he is not differing from Schopenhauer in assuming that we do know that our real essence is will. Rather, the difference is that Kant assumes that this will is *rational*, that we know ourselves to be really rational and indeed, at least in the argument of *Groundwork* III, that we know ourselves to have a will by knowing ourselves to be rational. Here is where the key difference with Schopenhauer lies, for as we have already seen Schopenhauer argues on empirical grounds, and as we will shortly see he also argues on a priori or metaphysical grounds, that although there may be a superficial, instrumental rationality to our actions, at the deepest level our will is non-rational or irrational.

Before I come to this point, let me remark on a previous conclusion that Schopenhauer draws and that is crucial for his own moral philosophy. Thus far, although one might have expected that I would refer to *my* will or *her* will or *our wills*, I have been using the indeterminate form "will." This is because even though Schopenhauer thinks that each of us becomes acquainted with will in his or her own case, aware from the inside of how desire leads his or her body to action, because he associates individuation (the "*principium individuationis*" in his preferred phrase) with space and time and thinks of those in turn as the framework for the representation of bodies from the outside, he infers that our ordinary means of individuation do not apply to the in-itself, thus to the will; and from that in turn he infers that there is in fact *one* will underlying all of humanity, indeed all of nature. Although it appears in many different forms, of which human will, or more properly its appearance or "objectification," may be more complex than others in some ways, will is nevertheless just one. Thus Schopenhauer argues that since

> the will as thing in itself lies outside the province of the principle of sufficient reason, and therefore has absolutely no ground; although each of its appearances is entirely subject to the principle of sufficient reason: it is moreover free of all *multiplicity*, notwithstanding its innumerable appearances in time in space. It is itself one, but not in the manner of an object, since an object's unity is known in the manner of an object: nor is it one in the way a concept is, since a concept arises only through abstraction from multiplicity: rather it is one in the sense that it lies outside of time and space, outside the *principium individuationis*, i.e., [outside] the possibility of multiplicity.   (*WWR*, second book, §23, p. 138)

That is, behind the appearances of millions or billions of human beings or other animate or even inanimate beings, there is just one reality, which appears to us through our experience of our bodies and their desires and actions from the inside as will, and which takes on different but still will-like forms in other manifestations. This is not just *qualitative* identity, some commonality of structure or character that "reveals itself just as fully and completely in a *single* oak tree," for example, "as in millions" (*WWR*, second book, §25, p. 153), it is *numerical* identity: at bottom all humans and all beings of whatever kind are one. This will be the metaphysical foundation for Schopenhauer's argument for both the possibility and the necessity of compassion as the basis of morality.

Strictly speaking, Schopenhauer's inference is fallacious: what follows from the (alleged) fact that we cannot apply our ordinary means of individuation to will (or any other characterization of the in-itself) is not that there is just one, but rather that *we have no way of counting* how many there are.[20] For number is not equivalent to spatio-temporal individuation, even though the only kind of units that we humans, representing appearances the way we do, can count are units of space and time, regions of space or periods of time or what fills them. So all that follows is that we have no way of counting things in themselves, not that we can count just one of them. For all we can know, there is a numerically distinct thing in itself associated with each numerically distinct but relatively enduring appearance, such as the body of a human being, or maybe even a numerically distinct one with each time-slice of a human being, say each hour- or minute-long period in the life of a human, or maybe even multiple things in themselves associated with any one

---

[20] Young 2005, p. 182, makes this point, although in a different context, namely in a discussion of Schopenhauer's argument that because the real character of any person is noumenal rather than phenomenal, it must be fixed. Kant's argument in *Religion within the Boundaries of Mere Reason* depends on the falsehood of this claim.

time-slice of a human being. We just have no way of counting. And although Schopenhauer may express some qualification of his inference by saying that the will is not one "in the same way" as the ordinary objects of spatio-temporal representation are, as we will see, his theory of compassion nevertheless places great weight on the assumption that at bottom we—we humans, we beings—are all numerically one.

Schopenhauer draws a second inference that will be vital to his critique of Kant from his metaphysical theory of the will. For it is not only the spatio-temporal framework of ordinary representation that does not apply to the in-itself. In *The Fourfold Root* Schopenhauer had also argued that reason was one of the versions of sufficient reason, and now, in *The World as Will and Representation*, he argues that reason or rationality, even merely instrumental rationality, is also a feature of appearance that does not apply to reality as it is in itself, and thus we cannot suppose that the will, that is, the will at the level of the in-itself, is governed by reason, that its actions or its manifestations in or effects on the spatio-temporal world of actions have reasons or are grounded in reason. In his words, "the will itself, the thing in itself, is groundless, lying outside the province of the principle of sufficient reason." At the superficial level of appearance, "every human being always has purposes and motives guiding his actions, and always knows how to account for his particular deeds," although remember that whatever account a human being gives of his purposes and motives, all of that is causally determined; "but when asked why he wills in general, or why in general he wills to exist, he would not have an answer and in fact the question would make no sense to him; and this is really just an expression of his consciousness that he himself is nothing but will whose willing in general . . . requires a more precise determination through motives only in its particular acts at each point of time." Any particular actions might seem to be willed rationally as a means to some end or purpose, but there is no real reason or ground for willing that purpose; or even if that purpose is itself rationally willed as the means to some further purpose, then there is no rational ground for *that* one. In general, there is no reason for having purposes at all or for willing; we just do it. And thus Schopenhauer reaches the same conclusion he had reached by his empirical argument: "In fact the absence of all goals, of all boundaries, belong to the essence of the will in itself, which is an endless striving" (*WWR*, second book, §29, p. 188). At the empirical level, our willing to realize particular purposes by satisfying particular desires is irrational because whether we realize such particular purposes or not we will always still be dissatisfied. At the metaphysical level, although we seem doomed to continue setting and trying to realize particular ends, only to find ourselves frustrated, there is no ground or reason for the entire enterprise. It just is what we do, severally at the level of appearance but as one at the level of the in-itself. Strictly speaking, the inference that the will in itself has *no* reason for its actions is as fallacious as the inference that there is just one such will; all that should follow from Schopenhauer's application of the multiple forms of the principle of sufficient reason to appearance is that *we have no way of representing* what reasons the will in itself might have for its actions, not that it cannot have any. But once again, Schopenhauer makes the more radical claim.

In this way, starting off from a version of Kant's transcendental idealism, Schopenhauer reaches a conception of the will that is our innermost being that is radically different from Kant's. Schopenhauer confines all manifestations of reason to the phenomenal realm, while for Kant practical reason is our sole source of insight into the noumenal, however qualified the epistemic status of that insight should be; but since the phenomenal realm is also the realm of thoroughgoing determinism, there is no direct connection between reason and freedom for Schopenhauer—or at least so it initially appears. In spite of rejecting Kant's positions on the imperatival character of morality as a product of pure practical reason, on happiness as a possible object of morality, let alone part of its necessary object, and on freedom of the will, Schopenhauer ultimately does derive a certain kind of freedom, freedom negatively conceived as freedom from domination by desire, from his own candidate for metaphysical insight, recognition of the merely phenomenal character of individuation and the ultimate oneness of all being. But before we reach that conclusion, let us examine Schopenhauer's critique of Kant's moral philosophy and his own alternative in more detail.[21]

10.3. Schopenhauer's Critique of Kant's Moral Philosophy and his Alternative

Schopenhauer famously states that "compassion [*Mitleid*] is the real moral incentive" (*BM*, p. 221), more fully that the alleviation of the suffering of others is the ultimate goal of morality and compassion for their suffering leading to action to alleviate it is the highest moral incentive. Among his numerous other criticisms of Kant's moral philosophy Schopenhauer accordingly emphasizes what he takes to be Kant's rejection of compassion as a morally significant incentive, especially in the latter's exposition of the concept of duty in the first section of the *Groundwork for the Metaphysics of Morals* leading to the first formulation of the categorical imperative, and in a related comment in the *Critique of Practical Reason*. Drawing on the *Groundwork*, Schopenhauer writes that, according to Kant,

An action...has genuine moral worth only when it happens exclusively from *duty* and merely for the sake of duty, without any inclination toward it. Worth of character is to commence only when someone, without sympathy of

---

[21] The following two sections are based on Guyer 2012a.

the heart, cold and indifferent to the suffering of others, and *not properly born to be a philanthropist*, nevertheless displays beneficence merely for the sake of tiresome *duty*.[22]

Covering himself with the mantle of Christianity in a way that he does not usually do, as we previously saw, and appealing to Friedrich Schiller's famous lampoon of Kant in the *Xenien*, Schopenhauer continues: "This assertion, which outrages genuine moral feeling, this apotheosis of unkindness which directly opposes the Christian moral doctrine that places love above all else and allows nothing to count without it...this tactless moral pedantry has been satirized by Schiller in two apt epigrams, entitled 'Scruples of Conscience and Decision'."[23] He then quotes from the *Critique of Practical Reason*, "The disposition incumbent upon a human being to have in observing the moral law is to do so from *duty*, not from *voluntary liking* nor even from an endeavor he undertakes *uncommanded*, gladly and of his own accord" (*CPracR*, 5: 84).[24] Then comes his explosion, already quoted, "It has to be *commanded*! What a slave-morality!" (*BM*, §6, p. 137).

But in his last main work in moral philosophy, the *Metaphysics of Morals* of 1797, specifically its Doctrine of Virtue, Kant included "love of human beings" among the four "aesthetic preconditions of the mind's receptivity to the concept of duty" (*MM*, DV, Introduction, section XII, 6: 401–2), and further described "compassionate natural (aesthetic) feelings" as "so many means to sympathy based on moral principles," receptivity to which nature has "implanted in human beings" but which human beings have a duty to "cultivate." The word here translated as "sympathy" is in fact the same word that Schopenhauer uses, namely *Mitleid*, translated as "compassion" (*MM*, DV, §§34–5, 6: 456–7). Thus at least in the *Metaphysics of Morals* Kant recognized the importance of what Schopenhauer claimed he utterly rejected. Now Schopenhauer notoriously thought that all of Kant's work beginning with the second edition of the *Critique of Pure Reason* represented a downhill slide, and that the *Metaphysics of Morals* in particular was a work of Kant's senility. So maybe he just ignored Kant's recognition of "love of human beings" and feelings of "sympathy" in this work. Or even if Schopenhauer did note Kant's recognition of the importance of these feelings, he might well have thought that they represented a substantive departure from Kant's moral theory of the *Groundwork* and second *Critique*, and

---

[22] Schopenhauer cites *G*, 4: 398.

[23] The famous pair of distiches from Schiller is, of course, "Scruples of Conscience: I like to serve my friends, but unfortunately I do it by inclination / And so often I am bothered by the thought that I am not virtuous. / Decision: There is no other way but this! You must seek to despise them / And do with repugnance what duty bids you"; cited from Wood 1999 p. 28.

[24] Schopenhauer has substituted "a human being" and "the moral law" for pronouns in Kant's text, and added the italics.

that, in spite of some late conversion on Kant's part, the author of those earlier works still deserved the excoriation to which he had been subjected.

But Kant's apparent dismissal of compassion, on which Schopenhauer based his criticism of Kant, is only an artifact of his initial statement of the fundamental principle of morality from the concept of duty in the first section of the *Groundwork* on the basis of the example of someone who can do the right thing with moral worth but without a contingent inclination to do it: Kant sets the example up this way so that we can see that the fundamental principle of morality must have nothing to do with inclination and its objects. This is only a preliminary stage even of the argument of the *Groundwork*. Later in the same section of the *Groundwork* and then in the *Critique of Practical Reason* Kant will add that motivation by the moral law *produces* its own feeling, namely the feeling of respect; and finally in the Doctrine of Virtue of the *Metaphysics of Morals* he will argue that naturally occurring feelings of compassion are the *means* that nature has implanted in us to move us from the general commitment to morality to the performance of specific beneficent actions, although they need to be cultivated to be strong enough to do so reliably and may need to be checked by conscience to make sure that they do not lead us to do something that in a particular situation would be morally wrong. Kant's account of the "aesthetic preconditions of the mind's susceptibility to the concept of duty" is an amplification and refinement of his earlier theory of a feeling of respect by treating the particular feelings of love of others—another name for compassion or sympathy—as well as the feeling of self-esteem as the final stage in the etiology of moral actions. Kant seems to have in mind an extended process in which the determination of the will by the moral law—for him, of course, a noumenal matter—leads to the feeling of respect or general "moral feeling," which in turn leads to the cultivation of the natural dispositions to love of others and self-esteem, which in turn can be the proximate causes of morally mandated actions. All of this goes beyond anything said in the *Groundwork*, but is entirely compatible with the suggestion in the *Critique of Practical Reason* that the feeling of respect, although produced by the underlying determination of the will by the moral law, plays a further motivational role in the adoption of particular maxims and thus in the performance of particular actions. In the end, then, Kant as well as Schopenhauer recognizes a necessary role for compassion in moral motivation, although for Kant compassion is not the beginning and end of morality but is part of a complex model of moral motivation that includes a fundamental principle, particular maxims, and properly cultivated feelings.

Obviously there are fundamental differences between the two philosophers' accounts of the origin and function of feelings of compassion or sympathy. First, Schopenhauer is convinced that compassion is not only the necessary but also a completely sufficient incentive for morality, based on his view that there can be no goal for morality other than the alleviation of suffering, while Kant's conception of the goals of morality is more complex, and thus even though he is willing to countenance sympathy as an incentive that is in some way necessary for morality, he could not consider it a complete and sufficient incentive for morality. Second, Schopenhauer's conviction that only compassion can be the incentive for moral-ity, not, as he takes Kant to hold, pure reason, is based on his view, recounted in the previous section, that reason is a superficial feature of human nature, func-tioning at best instrumentally, while for Kant reason is essential to the "authentic being" of humankind. So even if there is a place for sympathy in Kant's complete conception of moral motivation it cannot be to the exclusion of reason, but must be something in some way dependent upon and conditioned by reason. However, while this might suggest that Kant's ethics is to some considerable extent ration-alistic, and Schopenhauer's ethics could not possibly be so, matters are not as simple as this. For in the end, Schopenhauer offers a cognitivist account of the etiology of compassion that sees it as flowing automatically from a metaphysical insight into the superficiality of the numerical distance between persons that simply abolishes any emotional preference for oneself over others, while Kant regards sympathetic feelings for others as an independent yet natural endowment of human beings that needs to be cultivated and also possibly constrained under the guidance of reason, but that does not simply flow automatically from reason. Kant's account of the role of sympathetic feeling in virtue thus manifests a more complex and arguably more plausible view of human nature than Schopenhauer's.

Schopenhauer's ethics is based on the premises that there is no such thing as pure practical reason, only instrumental or prudential reason, thus that there are no ends of reason but only ends set by feeling, and further that there is no positive happiness available to human beings, only the alleviation of pain, whether that is merely the pain of boredom or something worse. From these premises it follows that pure reason can set no moral ends for human beings. Only the feeling of compassion can motivate the alleviation of pain. Because Schopenhauer does not recognize pure practical reason, he rejects Kant's conception of the fundamental principle of morality as a principle valid for all rational beings as well as his conception of the categorical imperative as the way in which our own pure practical reason presents this principle to the other, sensible aspect of our being. He therefore also rejects Kant's specific conception of duties to oneself, which can make sense only if we have a twofold self, in which our own rational self can put our sensible self under obligation (*MM, DV*, §3, 6: 418). It is because of his rejection of pure practical reason as a source of obligation within ourselves that Schopenhauer can make sense of Kant's ethics of obligation only as a holdover of divine command ethics, in which we are put under obligation by an external power, in spite of Kant's own explicit rejection of theological ethics (*CPracR*, 5: 40–1, *Moral Philosophy Collins*, 27: 255 and 277–8, and *Moral Philosophy Mrongovius II*, 27: 1425–6). Like Schopenhauer, David Hume had also held that practical reason is only instrumental reason, in the service of ends set by feeling, and if he did not go so far as thinking of happiness as consisting only in the alleviation of suffering nevertheless he did think of "tranquillity" as the one of the highest goals of morality, thereby elevating freedom from importunate desires above any more positive goals of morality. But Schopenhauer departs from Hume in conceiving of the feeling of compassion as flowing directly from metaphysical insight into the underlying unity of all being, an insight that one might well think can in the end be assigned only to pure *theoretical* reason. Because of its metaphysical foundation in his own version of transcendental idealism, Schopenhauer's ethics of compassion can thus hardly be considered a strictly empiricist theory.

As we saw, Schopenhauer's charge that there is no such thing as pure practical reason is deeply rooted in his entire philosophical outlook going back to *The Fourfold Root of the Principle of Sufficient Reason*,[1] in which he argued that practical reason is just another one of the forms of the principle of sufficient reason that we impose upon appearance, and that it is never pure because it needs the material of appearance to have any determinate content. Schopenhauer's conception of practical reason as merely instrumental, as merely reflection on how best to achieve one's ends whatever they might be, manifests itself in his critique of Kant's moral philosophy and in the exposition of his own. In the essay on the *Basis of Morals*, Schopenhauer argues against the idea that being moral can be equated with being rational precisely because rationality can be put to the service of the ends of an agent whatever they may be. In contrast to Kant's equation of pure rationality and morality, Schopenhauer argues that rationality is concerned only with "*relations of causality*," which means that it tells us only about means to ends, and does not set ends itself:

> In all ages, by contrast, that human being has been called *rational* who does not allow himself to be guided by *intuitive* impressions, but rather by *thoughts and concepts*, and who as a result always sets to work reflectively, consistently and thoughtfully. Such action is everywhere called *rational action*. But this is no way implies righteousness and loving kindness. Rather, one can set to work extremely rationally, that is, reflectively, thoughtfully, consistently, in a planned and methodical way, yet be following the most self-interested, most unjust and even the wickedest of maxims. That is why before Kant it never occurred to any human being to identify acting justly, virtuously and nobly with *acting rationally*: instead they distinguished the two entirely and kept them apart.   (*BM*, §6, p. 151)

Rationality is just the methodical discovery of causal connections and the application of the resultant knowledge to the pursuit of an agent's ends; whatever the latter may be, they are not determined by reason. They must be determined by feeling, and thus the difference between a virtuous agent and one who is not is not

326 KANT'S IMPACT ON MORAL PHILOSOPHY

a difference in their rationality, but a difference in their feelings, the former being determined by the feeling of compassion for others and the latter either by feelings of self-love or even outright malice toward others.[25] Thus Schopenhauer opposes Kant on the basis of a conception of reason and of the relation between reason and feeling that is identical to that of Hume. However, Schopenhauer also sees compassion as the feeling that flows from the most adequate insight into the underlying unity of all reality, and that can be considered as a foundation of morality in pure theoretical rather than practical insight in a way that has no parallel in Hume's strictly empiricist approach to ethics.

But let us leave Schopenhauer's metaphysics for the moment and instead further explore the implications of Schopenhauer's rejection of a Kantian conception of pure practical reason. One implication is that, since in Schopenhauer's view pure practical reason's provision of the fundamental principle of morality is a sham, Kant's derivation of more particular forms of duty from this principle is also a sham, indeed that Kant's derivation of duties inescapably turns on a hidden commitment to egoism or self-love. Schopenhauer's general claim that any morality other than his own is really a form of egoism, with reason merely serving self-interest, is manifest in *The World as Will and Representation*, where he writes that "a morality that *does* motivate can do so only by influencing self-love" (*WWR*, §66, p. 394), and where in the "Critique of the Kantian Philosophy" he writes that Kant's requirement to act only on universalizable maxims is still a principle founded on egoism, although on the egoism of everyone, not just one's own: "my goal becomes the well-being of everyone, without distinction, instead of my own well-being. But it is still a question of well-being. I then discover that everyone can be equally well off only when each person makes other people's egoism the limit of his own" (*WWR*, p. 555). In the *Basis of Morality*, Schopenhauer goes even further in his argument that for Kant "the canonical rule of human acting remains simply egoism, under the guidance of the law of motivation, i.e., the wholly empirical and egoistic motives of each occasion determining the acting of a human being in every individual case" (BM, §6, p. 144). Specifically, Schopenhauer analyzes Kant's applications of the requirement of universalizability as turning upon our wish to avoid undesirable consequences *for ourselves* of the universalization of our proposed paths of actions. When we reflect upon the consequences of the universalization of our proposed maxims of making false promises or being indifferent to the needs of others, we realize that this would have untoward consequences for ourselves, that we would "rashly...sanction a law that is unfair to ourselves!" In such cases "the maxim of self-interest would

---

[25] For this distinction, see Schopenhauer, *BM*, §14, pp. 190–7, on "Anti-moral incentives," esp. p. 194, where Schopenhauer distinguishes the maxim of "the most extreme egoism," "Help no one; rather harm everyone if it brings you advantage," from the maxim of "malice," "Harm everyone to the extent that you can."

conflict with itself," and supposed moral obligation would rest "upon a presupposed *reciprocity*, and consequently" would be "thoroughly egoistic" (*BM*, §7, p. 157). However, a charitable interpretation of Kant's derivation of specific kinds of duties from the categorical imperative's requirement that we act only on universalizable maxims would rather be that *prudence* does not always require us to consider what would follow from the universalization of our proposed maxims, but requires us to consider that only if the universalization of our maxim would actually follow from our acting on it; we only raise the question of what would follow from the universalization of our maxims in *every* case of proposed action because of a purely *moral* motivation, although our reflection on the *consequences* of the considered universalization of our maxim can then take prudential considerations into account.[26] But because he rejects any conception of pure practical reason, Schopenhauer can make no sense of the idea that the demand to universalize our maxims in the first place flows from pure practical reason rather than from prudential reason; he can understand the procedure of first universalizing our maxim and then sees what follows only as prudential and egoistic from the outset.

A second implication of Schopenhauer's rejection of any conception of pure practical reason is his view that Kant's ethics is really theological, simply the traditional ethics of divine command in fancy new dress.[27] Schopenhauer's claim that "Conceiving ethics in an *imperative* form, as *doctrine of duty* ... undeniably stems ... solely from theological morals" (*BM*, §4, p. 129) has already been quoted. A specific piece of evidence that Schopenhauer offers for this charge is that Kant expresses imperatives in the archaic form "*du sollt*" ("Thou shalt") rather than in the modern form "*du sollst*" (You should") (*BM*, §4, p. 127).[28] But the deeper reason for Schopenhauer's charge must be that, since he rejects the idea of pure practical reason, he cannot recognize any authority *internal* to the human being from which a command, specifically a command for the human being to override his own inclinations if necessary to comply with the demands of morality, could arise. An ethics of imperatives, Schopenhauer holds, requires an "authority" from which commands can issue,[29] but if there is no authority within a human being from which the categorical imperative can issue, it can only rest "on the presupposition of the human being's dependence on another will that commands him and announces reward and punishment to him, and cannot be separated from that" (*BM*, §4, p. 129). Further, Schopenhauer's charge that Kant's ethics is theological is intertwined with his charge that, in spite of its appearance,

---

[26] For a clear interpretation of Kant's universalization argument along these lines, see O'Neill 2013 (originally 1975), chapter 5.

[27] In addition to Anscombe 1958, see also Janaway's introduction to *BM*, p. xxx.

[28] On this point see Janaway's note a on p. 127, and Cartwright 1999, pp. 256-7.

[29] This is a supposition that goes back to the widely influential writings of Samuel Pufendorf from the late seventeenth century, e.g., Pufendorf 2003, book I, chapter II, paragraph IV, p. 43, and Pufendorf 2009, book I, definition XIII, pp. 202-28.

Kant's ethics is egoistic: the motivation to *obey* divine commands can only be the thoroughly egoistic motivation to avoid punishments and earn rewards. This charge is made against Kant in spite of the fact that such a conception of moral motivation had been denounced as "mercenary" since Shaftesbury's *Moralists* in 1709,[30] and that Kant himself thoroughly rejected such a conception of moral motivation, arguing in his lectures on ethics:

> if we are to abide by the moral law out of fear of God's punishment and power, and this because it has no ground other than that God has commanded it, then we do so not from duty and obligation, but from fear and terror, though that does not better the heart. If, however, the act has arisen from an inner principle, and if I do it, and do it gladly, because it is absolutely good in itself, then it is truly pleasing in the sight of God.   (*Moral Philosophy Collins*, 27: 1426)

To be sure, Schopenhauer could not have heard or read Kant's lectures. But he thinks that Kant cannot escape theological morality precisely because he rejects the idea that there is any pure practical reason in the human being that could serve as such an "inner principle."

For the same reason, Schopenhauer rejects the Kantian conception of duties to the self. Kant himself had made it clear that the idea of duties to oneself, of putting oneself under an obligation, would be a contradiction were it not for the difference between the human being as a "sensible being" and as an "intelligible being," which is in turn qualified "not merely as a being that has reason, since reason as a theoretical faculty could well be an attribute of a living corporeal being," and is thus only a being with pure *practical* reason and the freedom to act in accordance therewith (*MM*, DV, §§1–3, 6: 417–18). Schopenhauer accepts Kant's distinction between the sensible appearance of the human being and the reality that underlies it, but does not consider that underlying reality "intelligible" or rational. Therefore he cannot make sense of the idea of that "intelligible" but internal being giving commands to its own "sensible" appearance. For him, Kant's duties to self can be nothing but "partly prudential rules, partly dietetic prescriptions, neither of which belong in morals proper" (*BM*, §5, p. 132).

Above all, Schopenhauer's rejection of Kant's conception of pure practical reason means that he has no room for the idea of such pure reason setting moral ends. This means that he can recognize no end for human beings except the pursuit of happiness. But happiness in turn he interprets as nothing but the alleviation of suffering, the remission of pain, with nothing more positive than that to be set as the goal or object of morality, and the alleviation of pain is the

---

[30] See *The Moralists*, part II, section III, in Shaftesbury 1999, vol. 2, pp. 45–6. It is striking here that Shaftesbury refers to the "slavish Spirit" of a morality based on fear of punishment and hope of reward; both Kant, as we have already seen, and Nietzsche, as we will subsequently see, took up that terminology.

most to which the feeling of compassion can move us. Kant's conception of the highest good, including the positive happiness of all, as the object of morality is not open to him. Schopenhauer expounds his view about happiness at length in *The World as Will and Representation*, and then presupposes it in *On the Basis of Morals*. His view that happiness lies only in the alleviation of suffering might look as if it is founded on a conception of pleasure according to which pleasure can consist only in the removal of an antecedent pain, not just in the obvious case in which, for example, a violent bodily pain is remitted, but in every case in which an antecedent desire is satisfied, because an unsatisfied desire is itself a pain. Thus, "All satisfaction, or what is generally called happiness, is actually and essentially only ever *negative* and absolutely never positive. It is not something primordial that comes to us from out of itself, it must always be the satisfaction of some desire" (*WWR*, §58, p. 345). However, there is more to Schopenhauer's view than this, because he holds not just that satisfaction always presupposes an antecedent pain, but that the attempt to produce positive happiness is doomed: either the antecedent pain is not successfully removed, in which case of course it just endures; or the apparent desire that was successfully satisfied was not the real source of the pain, which persists even after what was supposed to alleviate it has been accomplished; or neither of these is the case, because even if the desire was correctly identified and successfully satisfied, the inevitable result of satisfying a desire is then boredom, itself another form of pain, and so pain returns. In Schopenhauer's words, "The nature of every desire is pain: attainment quickly gives rise to satiety: the goal was only apparent: possession takes away the stimulus: the desire, the need re-emerges in a new form: if not, then what follows is dreariness, emptiness, boredom, and the struggle against these is just as painful as the struggle against want" (*WWR*, §57, p. 340). In other words: you can't win: there is no enduring pleasure whether you succeed in satisfying any particular desire or not. This is the real reason why happiness cannot be something positive: there is no end the realization of which can produce enduring satisfaction. The best that human beings can hope for is release from pain, but in the form of repeated intermissions in their pain, because since satiety itself is a pain, there is nothing that can count as the permanent removal of pain—except for death, which however human beings inevitably put off as long as they can because the underlying reality of will manifests itself as will to life.[31]

So the best that one can hope to do for others is to alleviate their suffering, where however that means to be engaged in an ongoing project of producing intermissions in their suffering, because anything that might look like a permanent end to suffering would just be another form of suffering, namely boredom.

---

[31] Again, for a sophisticated treatment of these issues, see Reginster 2023.

For this reason too Kant's conception of the highest good or *summum bonum*, for Kant "universal happiness," understood as maximal realization of ends, "combined with and in conformity with the purest morality throughout the world" (*TP*, 8: 279), indeed the result of the purest morality under ideal conditions (*CPuR*, A809/B837), has to be rewritten as the negative ideal of the complete remission of pain:

> if we would like to retain an old expression out of habit, giving it honorary or *emeritus* status, as it were, we might figuratively call the complete self-abolition and negation of the will, the true absence of the will, the only thing that can staunch and appease the impulses of the will forever, the only thing that can give everlasting contentment, the only thing that can redeem the world... —we might call this the absolute good, the *summum bonum*. (*WWR*, §65, p. 389)

But just as, at least on his initial account, Kant's positively conceived highest good can never actually be realized, or at least cannot be realized within the natural life span of human individuals or the human species and must instead be deferred to a life that is "future for us" (*CPuR*, A811/B839), so too Schopenhauer's negatively conceived *summum bonum* must also remain a mere ideal: the highest good would be to alleviate all suffering, but that is not something we can accomplish within the natural life of any beings, because the complete alleviation of suffering would itself be a form of suffering, namely boredom terminated only by death.

Schopenhauer's negative conception of happiness as only the alleviation of suffering leads to his conclusion that the highest moral incentive must be compassion, the feeling that prompts one to attempt to alleviate the suffering of others. Thus he draws the conclusion in *The World as Will and Representation*:

> The only thing that goodness, love and nobility can do for other people is alleviate their suffering, and consequently the only thing that can ever move them to perform good deeds and works of charity is the *cognition of other people's suffering*, which is immediately intelligible from one's own suffering and the two are considered the same. From this, however, it follows that the nature of pure love (αγαπη, *caritas*) is compassion—compassion that alleviates the suffering that belongs to every unsatisfied desire, be it great or small.

And he continues,

> Thus, we will not hesitate to contradict *Kant* directly, who would only acknowledge true goodness and virtue as such when they emerge from abstract reflection, and in fact from the concept of duty and the categorical imperative, and who describes the feeling of compassion as a weakness, absolute not as a virtue.
>
> (*WWR*, §67, p. 402)

Schopenhauer's charge that Kant considers compassion a weakness is certainly not correct. What we must consider first, however, is his suggestion that he opposes Kant's derivation of goodness and virtue from "abstract reflection." This charge is problematic, because as the previous sentence makes clear, for Schopenhauer, compassion, although it is a feeling, also flows from cognition, here the cognition of other people's suffering. What Schopenhauer really objects to is Kant's claim that virtue emerges from "the concept of duty and the categorical imperative," in other words, from pure *practical* reason, while his own view is in fact that cognition, although a feeling and motivating only insofar as it is a feeling, emerges from pure *theoretical* reason. The cognition in question is the insight that there is no difference between oneself and others: not merely no difference in *kind*, each being an instance of the same kind and worthy of whatever treatment every other of the same kind is worth, even oneself, but rather no difference in *number*, each apparently distinct individual in fact being a manifestation of one and the same underlying reality. This is the essence of Schopenhauer's version of transcendental idealism—although, as already suggested, it rests on a fallacy to which Kant himself did not succumb, namely the fallacy of inferring that because our normal, spatio-temporal system of individuation does not apply to underlying reality, there is in fact just *one* underlying reality, rather than an *indeterminable* and *inaccessible* number of underlying reality or realities, or even more precisely a number that cannot be determined by *theoretical* means—and it is the metaphysical basis of Schopenhauer's ethics. His view is that each of us should do whatever he can to alleviate the suffering of others because there is ultimately no numerical difference between oneself and others, and the insight that this is so will produce the feeling of compassion that prompts individuals—who differ from each other only at the empirical level, at the level of appearance—to attempt to do this. Of course Schopenhauer may now be hoist by his own petard, for this doctrine could itself be regarded as a form of egoism: one cares about others only because one regards them as part of oneself.[32]

Be that as it may, Schopenhauer appeals to this metaphysical insight as the ultimate source of the motivation to be just to others—which he interprets as inflicting no harm on them in order to alleviate one's own suffering, now counting persons in the ordinary, phenomenal way—as well as to be virtuous or good to them—which he interprets as the attempt to alleviate the suffering they will inevitably experience, if not from one's own injustice to them then from a myriad of other sources. Thus he writes first:

---

[32] See, e.g., Young 2005, pp. 182–3. The obvious response to the objection is that once someone has attained to Schopenhauer's metaphysical insight, they no longer consider *themself* a *self* in any meaningful sense. E.g., Janaway 1989, pp. 281–2; Atwell 1995, p. 156.

> [F]or someone who is just, the *principium individuationis* is no longer the absolute barrier that it is for someone evil, he does not affirm the appearance of his own will alone and negate all others; ... other people are not just masks for him, entities whose essence is entirely different from his own. Instead, he shows in his way of acting that he *recognizes* his own essence (namely the will to life as thing in itself) in foreign appearances that are given to him as mere representations, and thus rediscovers himself in these other appearances to a certain extent, namely that of doing no wrong, i.e., failing to cause harm. (*WWR*, §66, p. 397)

Schopenhauer emphasizes that justice is based on recognition, a term that wears its cognitive import on its face.[33] He then continues that "positive benevolence" also follows from metaphysical insight, namely "seeing through" the *principium individuationis* of spatio-temporal difference:

> We have found that voluntary justice has its most intimate beginnings in our ability to see through the *principium individuationis* up to a point, while an unjust person remains completely trapped in this principle. This ability to see through the *principium individuationis* can take place not only up to the point required for justice, but to a greater extent as well, and this leads to positive benevolence and beneficence, to loving kindness.

The person who "*makes less of a distinction than is usually made between himself and others*," which for Schopenhauer is something that follows from theoretical insight into the fact that at the deepest level of reality there *is* no distinction between oneself and others, is someone whom the "*principium individuationis, the form of appearance, no longer has*... quite so tightly in its grip; the suffering he sees in others affects him almost as much as his own, so he tries to establish an equilibrium between the two, giving up pleasures and undertaking renunciations to alleviate other people's suffering" (*WWR*, §66, pp. 398–9). Here Schopenhauer correctly infers that if the metaphysical insight on which compassion rests is that we who differ at the level of appearance are all one at the level of ultimate reality, then what follows is not that we should attempt to alleviate only the suffering of *others*, but rather that we should attempt to alleviate the suffering of *all*, ourselves as well as others. As Kant says in his account of the duty to promote the more positively conceived happiness of others, "all *others* with the exception of myself would not be *all*" (*MM*, DV, §27, 6: 451).

In *The Basis of Morals*, Schopenhauer attempted to expound his ethics without direct appeal to his metaphysics, having construed the challenge of the Danish

---

[33] Thus the concept of recognition is central not only to the practical philosophies of Fichte and Hegel, as recent writers such as Ludwig Siep and Axel Honneth have stressed, but to that of their opponent Schopenhauer as well. See Siep 1979 and Honneth 1995.

Academy of Sciences for whose competition he was (unsuccessfully) writing as that of providing an empirical basis for morals, but in two final sections he nevertheless reiterates his conception of theoretical insight into the unitary nature of all being as the basis for the feeling of compassion that he had propounded in *The World as Will and Representation*. He sums up the main argument of the work by saying that it is "from a wholly immediate sympathy with the well-being and woe of others, whose source we have recognized as compassion, that the virtues of justice and loving kindness come"—justice consisting in self-restraint from harming others for one's own benefit, and loving kindness consisting in trying to alleviate the suffering of others. Compassion is a feeling, but it comes from a cognitive state: "if we go back to what is essential in such a character, we find it undeniably in *his making less of a distinction than everyone else between himself and others*" (*BM*, §22, p. 249). For the main purposes of the essay, Schopenhauer was content to leave this cognitive condition or achievement itself unexplained. However, making less of a distinction between self and others than everyone else does is entailed by theoretical insight into the ultimate nature of reality, because the distinction between persons is only an artifact of appearance and at the deepest level of being there is no numerical difference between persons. Schopenhauer writes:

> If *anything at all* is indubitably true among the insights that *Kant's* admirable profundity gave the world, it is the *Transcendental Aesthetic*, in other words the doctrine of the ideality of space and time. It is so clearly grounded that it has not been possible to raise so much as an apparent objection against it.... But if *time* and *space* [are] foreign to the thing in itself, i.e., the true essence of the world, then necessarily *plurality* is foreign to it also: consequently in the countless appearances of this world of the senses it can really be only one, and only the one and identical essence can manifest itself in all of these.   (*BM*, §22, p. 251)

Moreover, Schopenhauer claims, this insight is not limited to Kant or those who correctly understand Kant: it is age-old wisdom, expressed millennia before Kant in the Vedas, and again in John Scotus Eriugena, the Sufis, and Giordano Bruno (*BM*, §22, p. 252).

As already argued, Schopenhauer is wrong about what follows from transcendental idealism: if space and time are features of mere appearance, not of reality, it does not follow that plurality is foreign to reality, only that our ordinary way of representing and determining plurality is inapplicable to reality.[34] And Kant himself never supposed that the singularity of ultimate reality followed from

---

[34] This is so even if Adolf Trendelenburg's famous objection is rejected that it does not follow from the fact that we have a priori representations of space and time that space and time are not in some sense also properties of things in themselves. For even if it is accepted that things in themselves are not

transcendental idealism, for he always assumed that there is a plurality of numerically distinct moral agents, at the level of both appearances and things in themselves, even if he never explained how we can know that there are multiple noumenal agents. But Schopenhauer does assume that both transcendental idealism and the wisdom of the ages imply that there is no real numerical distinction between what appear to be numerically different agents at the level of appearance, and that this insight immediately leads to the feeling of compassion.

> "My true, inner essence exists in every living thing as immediately as it reveals itself in my self-consciousness to myself alone."—It is this knowledge, for which the standing expression in Sanskrit is the formula *tat-twam asi*, i.e., "You are that", that erupts as *compassion*, upon which, therefore, rests all genuine, i.e., disinterested virtue, and whose real expression is every good deed. It is this knowledge, ultimately, that every appeal to leniency, to loving kindness, to mercy in place of right, conforms with: for such an appeal is a reminder of the respect in which we are all one and the same being. (*BM*, §22, p. 254)

Schopenhauer's claim is thus that the feeling of compassion follows inevitably from theoretical insight into the unitary character of reality. He does not say that *only* those with such theoretical insight are compassionate, although he has suggested that even at the empirical level the feeling of compassion is connected at least with a refusal to insist upon the reality of numerical difference between persons (or indeed between persons and the rest of nature). But neither does he seem to think that there are numerous compassionate persons while there are only a few with the genuine metaphysical insight from which compassion necessarily erupts. Rather, the entire structure of *The World as Will and Representation*, beginning with Schopenhauer's version of transcendental idealism and ending with his ethics of compassion, suggests that theoretical insight into the metaphysics that he takes himself to share with Kant, the Vedas, and other wisdom through the ages, is indeed the only path to genuine compassion.

10.4. Kant, Reason, and Sympathy

Kant would not have been without resources to respond to Schopenhauer. Like others before him, beginning at least with Schiller's jest in *Xenien*, Schopenhauer takes Kant's examples of dutiful, morally worthy conduct in the first section of the *Groundwork* to mean that Kant recognizes no place for feelings, a fortiori for the

---

spatio-temporal, there still might be some way, perforce unknown to us, in which they are plural rather than singular. For discussion of Trendelenburg's objection, see Kemp Smith, 1923, pp. 113–14; Paton 1936, vol. 1, pp. 164–84; and Guyer 1987, pp. 362–9.

feeling of compassion, in moral motivation, that he holds that morally worthy action must be motivated by pure practical reason *instead* of by compassion. As an interpretation of Kant's complete model of moral motivation, this is wrong for two reasons. First, as already noted, the examples in *Groundwork* I play a heuristic role: what Kant is doing is contrasting *imagined* agents motivated by feeling or inclination *alone* with imagined agents motivated by pure practical reason *alone*, arguing that the latter and not the former demonstrate genuine moral worth, and from that concluding that the fundamental *principle* of morality, which obviously must be open to the morally worthy agent to act upon, cannot be grounded in feeling but must instead be derived from pure practical reason.[35] But the *Groundwork*, aimed at clarifying and securing the fundamental principle of morality (G, 4: 392), was never intended to be a complete description of the moral psychology of the virtuous human being, and its argument in section I does not mean that there is no place for feelings such as compassion in the *complete* mental state of morally motivated *real* agents. Kant ultimately shows what that place is in the Doctrine of Virtue of the *Metaphysics of Morals*.

But second, what is not always kept in mind, in *Groundwork* I Kant is arguing from the point of view of *common sense*, and thus accepting a contrast between feeling and reason as mutually exclusive motivational alternatives that may not in fact be part of his *own* complete theory of motivation. In fact, Kant has not yet introduced his transcendental idealist distinction between phenomenal and noumenal in *Groundwork* I, and thus cannot yet introduce his own view that the determination of the will ("elective" will or the faculty of choice, that is, *Willkühr*) at the *noumenal* level can have a variety of manifestations at the phenomenal level, not limited to the exercise of reason at the phenomenal level but also including the modification or even creation of feelings at the phenomenal level. Thus, in Kant's own eventual view reason and feeling need not be mutually exclusive alternatives: the presence or cultivation of feelings like compassion, at the phenomenal level, could itself be a manifestation of reason, operating at the noumenal level. If this is so, then the distance between Schopenhauer and Kant might not be as great as the former assumes: for Schopenhauer, compassion is a consequence of insight into noumenal reality, while for Kant morally appropriate feelings of compassion may be the product of the noumenal determination of the will by reason. To be sure, differences between the two remain. Schopenhauer attributes compassion *wholly* to theoretical insight, and to insight into the noumenal that itself apparently occurs at the phenomenal level, while for Kant it is pure practical reason, working at the noumenal level, that effects the feeling of sympathy. Further, Kant does not

---

[35] For an interpretation of Kant's examples in *Groundwork* I that makes clear that Kant is contrasting two imagined cases of motivation to elucidate the character of the fundamental principle of morality, see Barbara Herman, "On the Value of Acting from the Motive of Duty" (originally 1981), in Herman 1993, pp. 1–22, at pp. 19–21.

in the end claim that compassionate feeling is wholly *produced* by reason or the will determined by reason, but rather holds that compassionate feeling is an endowment of *nature* that must be both *cultivated* and *conditioned* under the guidance of reason—thus, in Kant's ultimate view, feelings of sympathy are actually *affected* rather than *effected* by pure practical reason. This may be a more realistic picture of the possibilities for human moral motivation than Schopenhauer's.

This last point, however, also suggests that the relation between the common-sense model of the relation between reason and feeling and Kant's model is complex, and indeed Kant may not always manage his own model correctly. The common-sense model is that reason and feeling are simply alternatives. Kant's model is that at the phenomenal level both reason and feeling may be the product of the noumenal determination of the will by the moral law, and so in that case there need not be a necessary conflict between phenomenal reason and feeling, two products of a common, intelligible cause. However, sometimes Kant does lapse into treating reason and feeling as independent factors that always have the potential to conflict; he does this, for example, in the second part of section III of the *Groundwork*, even after he has just introduced transcendental idealism with its thesis that the whole empirical character of a human being is a product of his intelligible choice.[36] In the end, I suggest, we may interpret Kant as creating a model on which reason and compassionate feeling, although two different factors in human nature at the phenomenal level, cooperate in the virtuous agent, at the behest of the noumenal determination of the will by pure practical reason—and although for Kant no human being is ever completely virtuous, this should not be chalked up to irremediable conflict between reason and feeling at the phenomenal level, but to incomplete commitment to the moral law at the noumenal level.[37]

In the present section, I will first return to Kant's use of the examples of motivation in *Groundwork* I, and then sketch the course of his progress toward his model of cooperation between phenomenal reason and compassionate feeling in the Doctrine of Virtue of the *Metaphysics of Morals*. Schopenhauer focuses on Kant's example of the philanthropist (*BM*, §6, pp. 136–7), so we can do the same. The example comes in the course of Kant's analysis of the concept of duty, "which contains that of a good will though under certain subjective limitations and hin-drances" (*G*, 4: 397), a concept that is supposed to be a piece of common sense the analysis of which will lead to a first formulation of the categorical imperative.[38]

---

[36] Thus, contrast *Groundwork* 4: 453–4 with the immediately preceding 4: 451–2. For further discussion of this issue, see Guyer 2007c.

[37] See esp. Kant's remark in his reply to Schiller's *Anmut und Würde* in *Religion within the Boundaries of Mere Reason*, 6: 24–5n.

[38] I say "first formulation" in a dual sense: the analysis of the concept of duty will lead to the initial formulation of the categorical imperative in section I of the *Groundwork*, but this initial formulation will be the same as the first of the five different formulations of the categorical imperative that Kant then enumerates in section II. For discussion of the five formulations, see Paton 1947, book III, pp. 129–98, and the large literature that Paton's analysis has spawned, e.g., Guyer 1995.

The overall argument is simply that, since duty can be fulfilled without any inclination to do so, the fundamental principle of morality can directly concern neither
inclination nor any object of inclination, thus it cannot be a material principle (as
Kant puts the same point in the *Critique of Practical Reason*, 5: 21–2), rather it can
only be a formal principle, the sole candidate for which is "*I ought never to act except
in such a way that I could also will that my maxim should become a universal law*"
(*G*, 4: 402). In discussing the duty of beneficence in particular, which in the
confirmation of Kant's formulations of the categorical imperative in *Groundwork*
II will function as the example of one of the four main classes of duty, namely
imperfect duty to others (*G*, 4: 421n., 423, and 430), Kant asks us to imagine "souls so
sympathetically [*theilnehmend*] attuned that, without any other motive of vanity or
self-interest they find an inner satisfaction in spreading joy around them and can
take delight in the satisfaction of others insofar as it is their own work." He says that
the actions of such souls are to be encouraged because, after all, they do conform to
duty. Nevertheless, their actions lack "moral worth," because "their maxim lacks
moral content, namely that of doing such actions not from inclination but *from
duty*." By contrast, the beneficent action of a philanthropist, *formerly* motivated by
the sort of sympathetic feeling Kant has described, but *now* "overclouded by his own
grief, which has extinguished all sympathy with the fate of others," thus *now*
unmoved by the troubles of his others because of his own, who *now* "tears himself
out of this deadly insensibility" and "does the action without any inclination, simply
from duty,... first has its genuine moral worth" (*G*, 4: 398). Schopenhauer interprets
this example as saying that "Worth of character is to commence only when someone,
without sympathy of the heart, cold and indifferent to the sufferings of others, and
not properly born to be a philanthropist, nevertheless displays beneficence merely for
the sake of tiresome *duty*" (*BM*, §6, pp. 136–7). But Kant is specifically contrasting a
person motivated *solely* by feeling, although in fact the complex feeling or
complex of feelings containing both sympathy toward others and desire for
self-gratification or self-congratulation, and one motivated *solely* by principle,
or even contrasting one and the same person formerly motivated by sympathy
and now motivated by principle, and saying that in *this* kind of case moral worth
is found in the latter rather than the former case—and so the principle of
morality must be one that can be acted on out of duty rather than inclination.
He is not yet considering the possibility that someone might have or have
cultivated sympathy *because* of his conception of duty or his moral principle,
let alone denying that possibility or its desirability as a complete model of human
virtue. At this point he is only offering a thought-experiment to reveal a necessary
feature of the fundamental principle of morality, not yet describing the complete
mental state of virtuous agents in real life.[39]

---

[39] My point is not, as is sometimes argued, that the action of the morally worthy agent may be
overdetermined, determined by *both* inclination and duty, but rather that the cultivated state of

Further, notice that Kant has not said that the person whose action first has moral worth when, because of his conception of duty, he tears himself out of the deadly insensibility to the troubles of others into which his own troubles have cast him, was "not properly born to be a philanthropist," as Schopenhauer would have it. On the contrary, such a person *was* born to be a philanthropist, but, deprived of his natural tendency to beneficence by some great personal misfortune, will now be able to be beneficent only if he can instead turn to the concept of and commitment to duty. Kant does continue his discussion of the motivation for beneficence by saying that "if nature had put little sympathy in the heart of this or that man"—*but note that now Kant is not talking about the same man, but introducing a new thought-experiment*—"if nature had not properly fashioned such a man (who would not in truth be its worst product) for a philanthropist, would he not still find within himself a source from which to give himself a far higher worth than a mere good-natured temperament might have? By all means!" (*G*, 4: 398). *Now* Kant is considering the case of someone "not properly born to be a philanthropist," and arguing that such a person could nevertheless find within himself a source of moral worth, and one "far higher" than mere "good-natured temperament," i.e., mere natural feeling or inclination. But he also says of such an imagined person only that he would *not* be the *worst* product of nature; he does not say he would be the *best*. But again, Kant is just not yet considering the possibility that sympathetic feelings might in some sense be *produced* or *strengthened* by commitment to duty, so he can hardly be saying that an agent with no sympathetic feelings at all is better than one who has some.

So let us now turn to the development of Kant's own complete model of moral motivation and the place of feelings of sympathy or compassion in it. In the *Groundwork*, Kant begins to develop this model at the penultimate stage of his analysis of the concept of duty, just before he draws from his analysis his first formulation of the categorical imperative. At this step he makes the claim that, since "an action from duty is to put aside entirely the influence of inclination and with it every object of the will... there is left for the will nothing that could determine it except objectively the *law* and subjectively *pure respect* for this practical law" (*G*, 4: 400–1). In this statement "pure respect" might mean nothing but the determination of the will to affirm the moral law, whatever the phenomenological character of that determination might be, if indeed it has any phenomenal character at all. However, in the footnote attached to the following paragraph, Kant explicitly calls respect a *feeling*. It is not a feeling "*received* by means of influence [*Einfluß*],"[40]

---

sympathetic feeling is itself a (phenomenal) product or effect of an underlying commitment to and determination of the will by the moral law (which determination may be considered noumenal if one wishes to remain within the framework of Kant's transcendental idealism).

[40] Perhaps "influx" would be a better translation of *Einfluß* than "influence": Kant's point is that this feeling is internally generated rather than a mere response to something external. "Influx" was a term used in earlier eighteenth-century debates about the mind–body relationship, familiar to Kant from his student days at Königsberg.

however, but "a feeling *self-wrought* [*sebtstgewirktes*, or "self-effected"] by means of a concept of reason and therefore specifically different from all feelings of the first kind, which can be reduced to inclination or fear" (*G*, 4: 401n.)—that is, positive feelings of attraction toward an action or negative feelings of aversion. So moral motivation does involve a feeling in some way. However, this feeling, supposed to follow from rather than preceding an exercise of reason, seems intended to differ from any feeling of sympathy, which would be a form of inclination, and certainly differs from any feeling of self-gratification at the thought of doing something beneficent for someone else, the distinctively non-moral motivation that Kant attributed to the philanthropist prior to becoming overwhelmed by his own troubles in his earlier example. So Kant does seem to allow a role for feeling in moral motivation, though not for a feeling of compassion. The character of the role he allows for the feeling of respect is also obscure, and this role may be merely epiphenomenal, not causal: Kant states that "respect . . . signifies merely conscious-ness of the *subordination* of my will to a law without the mediation of other influences on my sense." This may suggest that the feeling of respect is the form that my awareness of the determination of my will by the moral law takes, but that this feeling plays no role in my actually performing the morally requisite action.

Kant continues to distinguish the feeling of respect from any ordinary inclina-tion in the *Critique of Practical Reason*, but grants it a causal rather than merely epiphenomenal role in the performance of morally worthy action, at least at the phenomenal level. As he had previously described respect as a feeling "self-wrought by means of a rational concept," Kant now describes respect as "sup-plied" or "effected" by the "moral law in itself," and he rejects "any other incentive (such as that of advantage)" that might "so much as *cooperate* alongside the moral law." But he also calls respect itself an "incentive" (*Triebfeder*), which suggests that it does have some causal role to play in the production of action and is not merely the form that our awareness of our motivation by the moral law takes. He then describes this role. Respect is a feeling that involves both pain, at the striking down of self-conceit, which is the elevation of self-love into a principle of action, by the moral law, as well as pleasure at the recognition that it is our own power of reason that requires this infringement upon self-conceit (*CPracR*, 5: 72–4). Further, he states that by means of this complex feeling of respect "the representation of the moral law deprives self-love of its influence and self-conceit of its illusion, and thereby the hindrance to pure practical reason is lessened and the representation of the superiority of its objective law to the impulses of sensibility is produced and hence, by removal of the counterweight, the relative weightiness of the law (with regard to a will affected by impulses) in the judgment of reason" is also produced (*CPracR*, 5: 75–6). This suggests that the feeling of respect plays a causal role in the performance of morally worthy actions because it is what outweighs other feelings that might lead to improper actions and is to that extent the cause of proper ones. This could be reconciled with Kant's initial claim that "What is essential to any moral worth of action is *that the moral law determine the will immediately*" (*CPracR*, 5: 71) by supposing that cognizance of the moral law determines the will, or leads to the *intention* to perform the right action (at the noumenal level, on Kant's theory of free will), but that such determination of the will leads to *action* (at the phenomenal level) *through* the production of producing the feeling of respect that outweighs other feelings that would otherwise prompt other actions. So the feeling of respect would then have a mediate but causal and not merely an epiphenomenal role in the production of morally worthy action. However, although Kant has now clearly allowed a causal role for feeling, namely the feeling of respect, in the performance of morally worthy action, this feeling continues to be distinguished from all other feelings or inclinations, and thus it seems to remain the case that there is no place for feelings of compassion in Kant's account of such action. Schopenhauer's objection still seems to be in order.

In the Doctrine of Virtue of the *Metaphysics of Morals*, however, Kant suggests an even more complex model of the etiology of morally worthy action, and one that does seem to allow a distinct place for feelings of compassion.[41] In the Introduction to the Doctrine of Virtue, Kant enumerates four "aesthetic precon-ditions of the mind's receptivity to concepts of duty" (*MM* DV, Introduction, section XII, 6: 399). Kant's term "aesthetic preconditions" as well as the term translated as "mind," namely *Gemüth*, make it clear that Kant is discussing elements in the empirical or phenomenal etiology of virtuous action; this empir-ical theory of virtuous action can be reconciled with his transcendental idealist theory of moral motivation by regarding everything he is about to describe as the effect of the noumenal determination of the will immediately by the moral law (or that theory could now just be ignored). The four "aesthetic preconditions" are "moral feeling," "conscience," "love of human beings," and "respect" (6: 399–403). There are two key terminological departures here from Kant's earlier usage of terms: by "respect" he now means specifically "self-esteem" or "respect for [one's] own being" (6: 402–3), not respect for the moral law itself, while what Kant had previously called respect, namely respect for the moral law itself, is now called "moral feeling," "the susceptibility to feel pleasure or displeasure merely from being aware that our actions are consistent with or contrary to the law of duty" (6: 399).[42] It should also be noted that conscience does not seem to be a feeling, like moral feeling, love for humanity, or self-esteem, but rather something more like the empirical manifestation of "practical reason holding the human being's duty before him for his acquittal or condemnation in every case that comes under a law" (6: 400). Conscience, in other words, is the empirical disposition to

---

[41] As previously noted, I have discussed this model more fully in Guyer 2010b. See also chapter 3.3 above.

[42] However, it may be noted that in the *Critique of Practical Reason* Kant has already called respect by the alternative name "moral feeling" at least once; see 5: 76.

ask about a prospective action whether it is consistent or not with the moral law.[43] Kant says that each of these, the three feelings of moral feeling, love for humanity, and self-esteem, and the empirical disposition of conscience, are "natural predis- positions of the mind" to *have* which "cannot be considered a duty" because it is rather "by virtue of them that" human beings "can be put under obligation" (6: 399). So they are natural endowments, *not* "self-wrought" by means of a rational concept, although Kant goes on to say that "Consciousness of them is not of empirical origin," but can "only follow from consciousness of a moral law, as the effect this has on the mind." However, he says of each of the aesthetic preconditions that it can and must be *cultivated* and *strengthened*. In the first case of moral feeling, Kant says that it can be cultivated and strengthened "through wonder at its inscrutable source" (6: 400), while in the other cases Kant says merely that they must be cultivated and strengthened.

I have suggested the following interpretation of these claims. All four aesthetic preconditions are natural endowments of human beings—present, to be sure, alongside other natural endowments, other particular inclinations as well as the general tendency that Kant calls self-love, which disposes one to gratify these inclinations—which are not themselves due to pure practical reason. But through contemplation of the moral law, humans can be led to take steps to cultivate and strengthen moral feeling, the general empirical predisposition to act in accordance with the moral law, and then through cultivated and strengthened moral feeling can in turn be led to cultivate and strengthen the more specific dispositions of conscience, love of others, and self-esteem. Conscience, again, would be the disposition to raise the question of whether a particular proposed action (or its maxim) is consistent with morality, while love of others and self-esteem would be specific feelings that would prompt the performance of actions fulfilling our duties to others and self respectively, in particular the imperfect duties of virtue to others and self, when so doing has passed the test of conscience. On this model, moral feeling would be the general disposition to cultivate and act upon the more particular feelings of love of others and self-esteem, just as self-love is the general disposition to cultivate and act upon other sorts of inclinations, while conscience would be the empirical disposition to test even maxims suggested by the well- cultivated feelings of love of others and self-esteem (as well as maxims suggested by inclinations) for moral permissibility or necessity.

To turn back to Schopenhauer, we can see that this model does not merely allow a place for the feeling of love of others, which certainly sounds similar to what Schopenhauer calls "loving kindness," in moral motivation. Rather, for Kant this feeling is an indispensable moment in the fulfillment of duties of virtue to others, namely the proximate cause of the performance of such actions, although

---

[43] One might well think that conscience is *accompanied* by feelings, e.g., feelings of unease at ignoring its voice or of satisfaction at hearkening to it; but Kant does not say this.

the cultivated condition of this feeling is itself the effect of a complicated and by no means purely cognitive process. Finally, Kant adds to this model feelings of sympathy (*Mitleid*, which is again the same that is rendered as "compassion" in Schopenhauer translations). These are mentioned in Kant's discussion of "duties of love" to others (*MM DV*, §29, 6:452) in part II of the Doctrine of Virtue, which also considers "duties of respect" to others; and since Kant's original discussion of "love of human beings" in the Introduction to the Doctrine of Virtue had made only the negative point that the feeling of love may succeed rather than precede the willing of beneficent acts to others (*MM DV*, Introduction, section XII, 6: 401–2), perhaps the subsequent discussion of sympathetic feelings should count as his positive discussion of the feeling of love. After all, Schopenhauer used "compassion" and "loving kindness" as synonyms, so Kant may also have used "love of human beings" and "sympathy" as synonyms. In any case, what Kant argues is that feelings of sympathy, "feelings of pleasure or displeasure (which are therefore to be called 'aesthetic') at another's state of joy or pain (shared feeling, sympathetic feeling)," are feelings "receptivity" to which "nature has already implanted in human beings"; that they are "means to promoting active and rational benevolence" toward others; and that we have "an indirect" "though only a conditional duty" "to cultivate the compassionate natural (aesthetic) feelings in us, and to make use of them as so many means to sympathy based on moral principles and the feeling appropriate to them" (*MM DV*, §§34–5, 6: 456–7). These claims may be understood as follows. First, whatever the story about the relation between the noumenal determination of our will and the phenomenal etiology of moral action may be, at the empirical level we find in ourselves a natural susceptibility to sympathy that is arises independently of reason but is amenable to being acted upon by reason in at least two ways: it can be cultivated and strengthened at the behest of reason, and it can impel us to action by serving as a means to promoting "active and rational benevolence." But further, Kant's dual qualification of benevolence, that it be both active and rational, as well as his further comment that we have only a "conditional" duty to use our susceptibility to sympathy as a means to action, implies that our action upon our cultivated and strengthened feelings of sympathy, although it may often or perhaps even almost always be morally appropriate, is not automatically so, and must always remain conditional upon the consistency of the proposed action with the principle of morality (that it be permissible or mandatory under that law). For it is easy to construct cases in which acting upon sympathy would lead to an impermissible action: Barbara Herman's example of someone prompted by sympathy to help another struggling with a heavy package when to do so would actually be to aid and abet a theft[44] is one such case. Sympathetic feelings are needed to perform

---

[44] See Herman 1993, pp. 4–5.

beneficent actions: they are the proximate cause of such actions, what intervenes between one's general commitment to the principle of morality, one's recognition that beneficence is a duty that flows from this general commitment, one's recognition of a situation as one in which one could help, on the one hand, and the actual performance of a beneficent action, on the other. But what these feelings prompt one to do in any particular circumstances might always need to be checked against the requirements of morality to make sure that what they would lead one to do is in fact the right thing to do in those circumstances. (In Herman's example, the right thing to do would be to call the police, not to help, although for Herman it would be "rules of moral salience" rather than conscience that would tell us that.) That is why the duty to act upon these feelings is conditional. Another way to put this point would be to say that these feelings can be acted upon only when they pass the muster of conscience—that is why Kant includes conscience along with feelings of love or sympathy (as well as self-esteem) among the "aesthetic preconditions" of "susceptibility to concepts of duty." Conscience is what prompts us to check whether the action to which feelings of sympathy prompt us is in fact morally correct by testing the maxim on which we would be acting if we were to act as prompted; this is the form that checking whether in our present circumstances action upon ordinary inclinations would be morally permissible would take in the Kantian framework.

Thus, for Kant, compassion has to be accompanied by conscience. We might now expound Kant's whole final model of moral motivation by saying that our general commitment to morality, which is made effective, at least at the phenomenal level, though moral feeling, the heir to his earlier feeling of respect, is what leads us to cultivate and strengthen conscience on the one hand and the particular feelings of love or sympathy for others (and self-esteem) on the other. Conscience and the feelings of sympathy (and self-esteem) must then work in cooperation, the feelings prompting us to particular actions but conscience prompting us to check whether those actions are in fact morally correct.

In conclusion, Schopenhauer's idea is that compassion automatically flows or "erupts" from theoretical insight into the unity of all being. Kant does not make the mistake of inferring from the transcendental ideality of space and time to the unity of all being, rather simply presupposing that even at the noumenal level there is a plurality of moral agents, so this supposed theoretical insight is not part of his model of human motivation at all—Kant always supposes that there is a genuine plurality of moral agents, and that any one human agent is interacting with other human agents. Instead, Kant supposes that the moral law flows from pure practical reason, a faculty that Schopenhauer in turn denied, and then that our commitment to the moral law can and should lead us to cultivate and strengthen but also control our natural disposition toward sympathy. There are two key points to Kant's model. First, sympathy, although it is something to which we have a natural susceptibility, must be cultivated and strengthened—it does *not* flow directly from cognition. Second, sympathy, although necessary for benevolent action, must also be controlled by reason and its recognition of the moral law—for sympathy and morality can always come apart, sympathy prompting us to a particular action which is in fact inconsistent with morality. While there can be no doubt that compassion is a fundamental virtue of human beings that may better deserve the overemphasis that Schopenhauer gives it rather than the late and passing notice that Kant gives it, Kant's view that sympathy is a natural susceptibility of human beings that we have to work to strengthen seems more realistic than Schopenhauer's view that compassion flows automatically from metaphysical insight, and Kant's view that sympathy and morality may come apart, thus that the promptings of sympathy may always need correction by conscience, seems a salutary correction to Schopenhauer's romantic idea that compassion alone is a sufficient condition for human virtue.

11

Nietzsche's Transvaluation of Kantian Values

Schopenhauer's metaphysical masterpiece was largely ignored for the first quarter-century of its existence, and in 1840 his essay on *The Basis of Morality* was denied the prize for which it was submitted to the Danish Academy of Sciences even though it was the only entry in their contest! (Schopenhauer's evident disrespect for other philosophers, as well as his misjudgment in relegating the metaphysical foundations of his moral philosophy to the final sections of the work despite this being what the Academy was most interested in, seem to have been among the reasons for this decision.) But in the second half of the nineteenth century, especially after his death in 1860, Schopenhauer became an immensely popular and influential philosopher. Philosophers of all stripes took his views seriously, and his work influenced creative types in other fields as well, from Richard Wagner to Thomas Mann. Among those influenced by Schopenhauer, Friedrich Nietzsche (1844–1900) straddles the boundaries between "philosopher" and other "creative types." (Indeed, Nietzsche tried his hand at both poetry and musical composition, without notable success in either medium.) Specifically, it was the influence of Schopenhauer that turned Nietzsche away from being a classical philologist, even though his first, most deeply Schopenhauerian book, *The Birth of Tragedy* of 1872, was still presented as if it were a work of classical philology. Following Schopenhauer, Nietzsche offered many criticisms of Kant's moral philosophy, which he associated with the "Socratic" rationalism that he despised. At the same time, one of the boldest claims in Nietzsche's "transvaluation of all values" was that the morality of Christianity—which, as we have seen, even Schopenhauer did not entirely reject—was a "slave morality," and as we have seen, even though Schopenhauer accused Kant of promulgating a "slavish morality," Kant himself had argued against a slavish conception of the moral law as a burden and of virtue as monkish; David Hume had also attacked what he called "monkish virtues," and at the very beginning of the eighteenth century Shaftesbury had already called any morality based on fear of punishment and hope of reward as "mercenary" and "slavish." So the description of at least certain conceptions of morality and its requirements as "slavish" was not unique to Nietzsche, although the slur may not have meant the same thing to everyone who used it.

Kant's Impact on Moral Philosophy. Paul Guyer, Oxford University Press. © Paul Guyer 2024.
DOI: 10.1093/oso/9780199592456.003.0012

Different as their views are in so many respects, both Kant and Nietzsche take a certain kind of self-affirmation rather than self-abnegation to be central to morality. Further, although Nietzsche objects to Kant's categorical imperative on the ground that it subjects everyone to the same laws and values, properly understood Kant's moral philosophy is based on the ideal of the maximally consistent use of freedom on which each gets to set his or her own ends to the greatest extent compatible with others doing so as well. Kant's ideal thus leaves room for, indeed prizes, the expression of individual freedom in a way that is not entirely remote from Nietzsche's transvaluation of values. While Nietzsche clearly rejects Kant's conception of moral law as universally valid, indeed in the double sense of binding on every human being and being applicable to well-defined or definable action-types, Nietzsche's positive conception of the value of the "noble" or "sovereign individual" may be closer than he realized to Kant's conception of humanity as the capacity to set one's own ends. As Kevin Hill has put it, Nietzsche committed "to the Enlightenment's valorization of human freedom and autonomy while abandoning its egalitarianism."[1] But if something along these lines is right, then Nietzsche's failure to recognize the space for his own view within Kant's framework may be another instance of thinking that Kant cared about law—universalizability—for its own sake, rather than as the means to freedom, although in Kant's case equal freedom for all and not maximal freedom for some.[2]

Let us consider these two themes in turn. Nietzsche's objection to "slave morality" and his recommendation of the replacement of it together with a morality for "nobles" at the cost of the slaves who are incapable of it is a prominent theme in the two books on morality of his maturity, *Beyond Good*

---

[1] Hill 2003, p. 231.

[2] It should not be surprising that Nietzsche did not understand Kant's moral philosophy very well, and therefore did not recognize what he shared with Kant as well as where he differed: his knowledge of Kant seems to have been very much secondhand, acquired from his reading of Schopenhauer, F. A. Lange's *History of Materialism*, originally published in 1865, thus during Nietzsche's first year at university (Lange 1925), and then from further works by neo-Kantians beginning with Kuno Fischer. Hill 2003, p. 20, and Young 2010, p. 89, claim that Nietzsche made a close study of Kant's *Critique of the Power of Judgment* in 1868–9, and Hill further claims that he made a close study of Kant's *Critique of Practical Reason* in the 1880s, when he was writing the books we will focus on in this chapter. However, Bailey 2013 p. 147, reports that all of the passages from Kant that Nietzsche cites are to be found in the secondary sources that he is known to have read, and that there is no other evidence that he ever read Kant firsthand. Nietzsche's utter neglect of Kant's conception of artistic genius (*CPJ*, §§46–9) when he accuses Kant along with Schopenhauer of having offered an aesthetics of the "spectator" only, not of the artist (*GM*, III §6, p. 74) does strongly suggest that he had *not* made a careful study of the third *Critique*.

The literature on Nietzsche is vast. The most recent, highly detailed biography is Young 2010. Modern Anglophone scholarship begins with Kaufmann 1968 (1950) and Danto 1965; subsequent valuable works on Nietzsche's philosophy as a whole include Schacht 1983, Nehamas 1985, Clark 1990, and Richardson 1996; useful multiauthor collections covering a wide range of topics include Magnus and Higgins 1996; Ansell Pearson 2006; and Richardson and Gemes 2013. Monographs on Nietzsche's views about morality, typically in the form of commentaries on *On the Genealogy of Morality*, include Leiter 2002, Janaway 2007, and Reginster 2021; collections of essays on Nietzsche and morality include Leiter and Sinhababu 2007, Gemes and May 2009, and May 2011. Hill 2003 is devoted entirely to Nietzsche's relation to Kant.

and Evil (1886) and *On the Genealogy of Morality* (1887).[3] Nietzsche takes slave morality to have been invented by the Jews, presumably during their long periods of Babylonian and then Roman suppression, and then carried on by the offspring of Judaism, namely Christianity. In one of his most often quoted passages, Nietzsche writes:

> It was the Jews who, rejecting the aristocratic value equation (good = noble = powerful = beautiful = happy = blessed) ventured, with awe-inspiring consistency, to bring about a reversal and held it in the teeth of the most unfathomable hatred (the hatred of the powerless), saying: "Only those who suffer are good, only the poor, the powerless, the lowly are good; the suffering, the deprived, the sick, the ugly, are the only pious people, the only ones saved, salvation is for them alone, whereas you rich, the noble and powerful, you are eternally wicked, cruel, lustful, insatiate, godless, you will also be eternally wretched, cursed and damned!"... We know *who* became heir to this Jewish revaluation.
>
> (*GM*, I §7, p. 17)

He interprets it as a strategy aimed at transforming ("transvaluing") the misery of those in a position of weakness into a strength or virtue by transforming their contemptible self-abnegation before more powerful human rulers into an admirable self-abnegation before a God who demands precisely that. This might seem to be a strategy aimed at benefitting the oppressed, but at the same time it also benefits a priestly class that takes on much of the trappings of an oppressive nobility itself: "If the highest caste is at the same time the *clerical* caste and therefore chooses a title for its overall description which calls its priestly function to mind, this does not yet constitute an exception to the rule that the concept of political superiority always resolves itself into the concept of psychological superiority" (*GM*, I §6, p. 15)—or perhaps vice versa.[4]

It might be difficult to produce much historical evidence that Jews conceived of themselves in such terms even during the Babylonian exile or under Roman rule; perhaps it would be easier to pin such an attitude on early Christianity. But the point of Nietzsche's "genealogy" is not historical accuracy, but to highlight what he takes to be harmful to human flourishing in the moral conceptions prevailing in his own time. His diagnosis of the latter might be trenchant even if his historiography is fanciful, and conversely contemporary morality might be sound even if its historical origins were flawed—people can believe the right thing for the wrong reasons.[5] Nevertheless, Nietzsche clearly believed that the contemporary version of

---

[3] Although Van Tongeren 2006, p. 396, suggests that Nietzsche rather proposes a fruitful struggle between these two (and possibly more) moralities.

[4] On the nobility of the priestly class, see Anderson 2011.

[5] For a similar point, see Irwin 2009, pp. 353–5.

Judeo-Christian morality was harmful to human flourishing, or at least the flourishing of those most capable of flourishing, and for that reason contemptible. And since Nietzsche clearly imbibed much of his attitude toward Kant from Schopenhauer, and the latter, as we saw, accused Kant of deriving his categorical imperative from theological assumptions, Nietzsche too associated Kant with the morality of Christianity, although he was much more interested in criticizing Christianity itself than "the stiff but demure tartuffery used by the old Kant to lure us along the clandestine, dialectical path that leads the way (or rather: astray) to his 'categorical imperative'," a "spectacle" that "provides no small amusement for discriminating spectators, like us, who keep a close eye on the cunning tricks of the old moralists and preachers of morals" (*BGE*, §5, p. 8).[6]

Nietzsche contrasts "slave morality" to "master morality" or the morality of the "noble" in the final section of *Beyond Good and Evil*, "What is Noble?," and then expands upon this theme in *On the Genealogy of Morality*, although in the latter he refers to "the noble" but not "slave morality" (e.g., *GM*, I §11, p. 22). In *Beyond Good and Evil*, he characterizes the "noble type of person" as the one "who feels that *he* determines values, he does not need anyone's approval, he judges that 'what is harmful to me is harmful in itself,' he knows that he is the one who gives honor to things in the first place, he *creates values*"; who enjoys "the feeling of fullness, of power that wants to overflow, the happiness associated with a high state of tension, the consciousness of a wealth that wants to make gifts and give away"; and who "honors the powerful as well as those who have power over themselves." Such a character "helps the unfortunate too, although not (or hardly ever) out of pity, but rather more out of an impulse generated by the over-abundance of power." Thus the noble might actually help the less fortunate in some way or another, but not as an act grudgingly self-imposed because *due* to them, but as a natural consequence of his own well-being. "The noble and brave types of people who think this way are furthest removed from a morality that sees precisely pity, actions for others, and *désintéressement* as emblematic of morality." This is an important point, because it might seem that Nietzsche's "nobles" require "slaves" for the exercise of their nobility, as the master in Hegel's "master-slave" dialectic requires a slave to be a master. This does not seem right, although Rolf-Peter Horstmann's note that "there seems to be no reason to think that Nietzsche would not allow in principle that each of us could be transformed into a 'free spirit,' i.e., a person who has the capacity and strength to create and stick to the 'right' values" may go too far in the opposite direction;[7] Nietzsche does seem to believe that some people are simply more naturally fitted to be moral than

---

[6] Nietzsche uses the word "tartuffery" repeatedly in both *Beyond Good and Evil* and *On the Genealogy of Morality*, a term connoting religious hypocrisy that was current in English even before Molière named his hypocrite "Tartuffe" in his eponymous play of 1664.

[7] *BGE*, Introduction, p. xvii note.

others.[8] Alexander Nehamas seems to land in the right place when he argues that, at least in the 1880s, beginning with the book *Daybreak* (1881), "Nietzsche no longer denies that moral motives and moral actions exist," that "he considers moral action unegoistic, but he no longer conceives of it as particularly other regarding."[9] The noble does not act for his own sake *in contrast* to the sake of others, he is in a way beyond petty selfishness, but neither does he act simply for the sake of others, or because others are in need. The noble has some great project of his own; if that turns out to benefit others, fine, but if not, also fine.[10]

Be all that as it may, slave morality is the natural expression of "people who were violated, oppressed, suffering, unfree, exhausted, and unsure of themselves."[11] Such people would inevitably form "A pessimistic suspicion of the whole condition of humanity...perhaps a condemnation of humanity along with its condition. The slave's gaze resents the virtues of the powerful. It is skeptical and distrustful, it has a *subtle* mistrust of all the 'good' that is honored there," even a distrust of the "happiness" of the noble as not "genuine."

> Conversely, qualities that serve to alleviate existence for suffering people are pulled out and flooded with light: pity, the obliging, helpful hand, the warm heart, patience, industriousness, humility, and friendliness receive full honors here, – since these are the most useful qualities and practically the only way of holding up under the pressure of existence. Slave morality is essentially a morality of utility [*Nützlichkeits-Moral*]. Here we have the point of origin for that famous opposition between "good" and "*evil*" [*böse*], as contrasted to the nobles' opposition between good and *bad* (*schlecht*).
>
> (*BGE*, "What is Noble," §260, pp. 154–6)

In this seminal passage, Nietzsche explicitly mentions neither Christianity nor Kant, indeed his central argument that the attempt of the weak to transform their own need for pity and succor into a virtue by celebrating pity and succor aimed at others is really just hypocrisy or tartuffery, a sly stratagem to get help for themselves by pretending to care about others, seems aimed as much at English utilitarianism as at anything else. This is suggested not only by his use of the term "*Nützlichkeits-Moral*" in the present passage as by repeated references to utilitarianism elsewhere in *Beyond Good and Evil* and explicit references to John Stuart

---

[8] See, e.g., Gemes 2009, p. 46: Nietzsche's "positive, and more profound and original, objective is to offer his readers the challenging notion that agency free will [as Gemes calls it], genuine autonomy, and hence existence as an individual and self, is possible for *some*" (emphasis added). Bailey 2013 argues that Nietzsche recognizes degrees of worth in different persons based on their degree of agency. Huddleston 2019 argues that creative persons may work toward the creation of a culture that makes life livable for other members of their society, although he does not argue that they are or need be motivated by the intention to do so.

[9] Nehamas 1985, p. 204.   [10] See also Reginster 2007.

[11] On slave morality, see Leiter 2002, pp. 202–8; Wallace 2007; Reginster 2021, pp. 78–83.

Mill and Herbert Spencer a few pages before (*BGE*, "Peoples and Fatherlands," §253, p. 144). But in *On the Genealogy of Morality*," Nietzsche associates slave morality much more explicitly with Christianity and suggests that as an apologist for Christianity Kant is an apologist for the slave morality as well. As far as Nietzsche is concerned, British consequentialism and German deontology are both expressions of slave morality.[12]

Nietzsche begins *On the Genealogy of Morality* with the suggestion that Schopenhauer's morality of compassion was also unable to escape the grip of Christianity. In confronting Schopenhauer, he says in the Preface, "I dealt especially with the value of the 'unegoistic', the instincts of compassion, self-denial, self-sacrifice which Schopenhauer had for so long gilded, deified, and transcendentalized until he was finally left with them as those 'values as such' on the basis of which he *said 'no'* to life and to himself as well" (*GM*, Preface, §5, p. 7). Here Nietzsche is turning the table that Schopenhauer turned on Kant back upon himself, suggesting that Schopenhauer's morality too retains a theological element ("deified"). But his main concern in this work is to expand upon his view that the slave morality of self-abnegation and pity, really the morality of self-pity, is the essence of Christianity, still at work in the morality of Kant at least as much in that of Schopenhauer (even though on his view of Kant, taken over from Schopenhauer, Kant has a "low opinion of compassion"), and what needs to be "transvalued" in his own post-Christian morality of the nobles, which can be compared to the pre- or non-Christian moralities of the Roman, Arabian, Germanic, Japanese nobility, Homeric heroes, Scandinavian Vikings, who in this regard "are all alike," even though for Nietzsche no two things or states of affairs are ever exactly the same and there can be no simple return to any earlier historical stage (*GM*, First Essay, §11, p. 23; the quotation about Kant's opinion of compassion is still from *GM*, Preface, §5, p. 7; Schopenhauer's opinion that Kant has a "low opinion of compassion" has been contested in the previous chapter).[13] Nietzsche's notorious ascription of the origin of slave morality to Judaism has already been quoted (*GM*, I §7, pp. 17–18). Quite apart from the question about how well this comports with other things that Nietzsche said about the Jews, for example, his expressed contempt for the anti-Semitism of contemporary Germany (*GM*, III §26, p. 117), where anti-Semitism surged as soon as Bismarck included equal civil rights for Jews as part of German unification,[14] there is a question here about whether this is an accurate reading of historical Judaism or a projection back onto it of the sensibility of Christianity, or some particular later version of Christianity. (For that matter, there is also a question

---

[12] I owe this point to Alexander Nehamas.

[13] On what we might call, to use, perhaps ironically, a term from contemporary meta-ethics, Nietzsche's historical "particularism," see Nehamas 2017.

[14] See, e.g., Aly 2014.

about how accurate Nietzsche's account of non-Christian nobility, for example the Homeric conception, is.[15]) But there can be no mistaking Nietzsche's attitude toward Christianity itself: it transforms the noble virtue of self-affirmation into the slavish virtue of self-abnegation and self-abasement, resulting from a *ressentiment* that "itself turns creative and gives birth to values: the *ressentiment* of those beings who, denied the proper response of action, compensate for it only with imaginary revenge" against the nobles, denying them entrance to heaven.[16] "Whereas all noble morality grows out of a triumphant saying 'yes' to itself, slave morality says 'no' on principle to everything that is 'outside', 'other', 'non-self': and *this* 'no' is its creative deed" (*GM*, I §10, p. 20).

How is the existence of such a negative morality compatible with Nietzsche's underlying conception of a "will to power," which is his transformation of Schopenhauer's conception of the will as the in-itself into a conception of a drive to the exercise of power in every living being, or, what is relevant, in every human being? The obvious answer is that the promise to oneself of happiness in an afterlife as recompense for misery in this life and the attempted denial of that happiness to the actual nobles is the only expression of the will to power possible for people in the circumstances of Nietzschean slaves. The will to power is not identical with a will to life, or self-preservation, because powerful nobles may well risk their lives in the pursuit of what they see as even greater ideals and thus greater expressions of their power.[17] But for the slaves or the weak who can neither save their own lives nor risk them in pursuit of any greater goal, the illusion of an eternal life may be the only form in which they can express their own will to power. Of course, the exploitation of Christianity for the self-aggrandizement of a priestly class would be a more obvious expression of the will to power on the part of the people who can make it into that class.

Once it has become widespread and culturally entrenched, how can the slavish mind-set of Christianity possibly be overcome? Given Nietzsche's general denial

---

[15] A major theme of the treatment of Nietzsche in Irwin 2009 is that Nietzsche's characterization of Homeric nobility is misleading, and that at least some degree of direct regard for others was part of Homeric nobility and common morality in the classical period as well—Achilles is an exceptional character precisely because of his purely selfish rage against Hector, and Plato's Callicles (and Glaucon and Adeimantus in book 1 of the *Republic*) are arguing against common Greek morality, not from a standpoint within it; see pp. 334–45.

[16] Nietzsche always uses the French word *ressentiment* instead of any comparable German word (e.g., *Entrüstung*), and both translators and commentators, from Kaufmann in 1950 to Reginster in 2021, follow him in this practice. But I have not seen any discussion of why he uses this French word and treats it as a foreign word; perhaps it is to intimate that *ressentiment* is optional, that is, perhaps natural for people in certain circumstances but not necessary or inevitable? On Nietzsche's account of *ressentiment*, see in addition to Wallace 2007 and Reginster 2021, Solomon 1996 and Poellner 2011.

[17] See Hill 2003, pp. 211–12. From his own point of view, Kant also recognized that it is not life as such that is of unconditional value, but rather to live life "throughout as a human, not, that is, in a state of well-being, but so that one does not dishonor humankind" (*Moral Philosophy Collins*, 27: 342; of course, even had he been a Kant scholar, Nietzsche could not have known this passage in his time). This is the view that would later be expressed as the thesis that a good will is the only thing of unconditional value.

352 KANT'S IMPACT ON MORAL PHILOSOPHY

of a libertarian and Kantian conception of free will, namely that anyone is always free to choose and do one thing even if their entire history would seem to have condemned them to the contrary, the answer to this can also be only that this will naturally happen as the expression of the will to power of some noble individuals: "It is just as absurd to ask strength *not* to express itself as strength, not to be a desire to overthrow, crush, become master, to be a thirst for enemies, resistance and triumph, as it is to ask weakness to express itself as strength" (*GM*, I §13, p. 26). Indeed, Nietzsche thinks that the idea of free will itself is an invention of slave morality, the fantasy that the *choice* of self-abnegation is always within one's own power even if nothing else is:

> This type of man *needs* to believe in an unbiased "subject" with freedom of choice, because he has an instinct of self-preservation and self-affirmation in which every lie is sanctified. The reason the subject (or, as we more colloquially say, *the soul*) has been, until now, the best doctrine on earth, is perhaps because it facilitated that sublime self-deception whereby the majority of the dying, the weak and the oppressed of every kind could construe weakness itself as freedom, and their particular mode of existence as an *accomplishment*.   (*GM*, I §13, p. 27)

The nobles, however, do have a kind of freedom, indeed are defined as a type by a kind of freedom, namely the freedom to set and pursue their own ends regardless of the opinions and preferences of the weak, even regardless of the costs of their actions to the weak if the pursuit of their own goals turns out to have such costs, but this is a freedom of *action*, not a mythical freedom of *choice*. For Nietzsche, the latter is as much a myth as "the Kantian 'thing-in-itself'": the "strong person" has "the *freedom* to manifest strength or not," as circumstances warrant, but there is no "substratum" of free will beyond his action: "there is no 'being' behind the doing, its effect and what becomes of it; 'the doer' is invented as an afterthought,— the doing is everything" (*GM*, I §13, p. 26).[18]

So Nietzsche clearly rejects Kant's metaphysics of transcendental idealism and along with that his commitment to the freedom of the will.[19] Nietzsche recurs to this point much later in *On the Genealogy of Morality*, in the remarkable comment that "even in the Kantian concept of 'the intelligible character of things', something of this lewd aescetic conflict still lingers, which likes to set reason against reason: 'intelligible character' means, in Kant, a sort of quality of things about which all that the intellect can comprehend is that is, for the intellect— *completely intelligible*" (*GM*, III §12, p. 87). Since for Kant "intelligible character"

---

[18] The literature on Nietzsche's attitude towards freedom of the will is enormous. For a start, see Schacht 1983, pp. 296–316; Leiter 2002, pp. 87–101; Leiter 2009; Leiter 2011; Gemes 2009; Pippin 2009; Richardson 2009.

[19] Risse 2007 argues that for Nietzsche Kant's transcendental idealist defense of free will is part and parcel of his defense of Christianity.

is determined by the completely free choice of the noumenal will, Nietzsche is criticizing Kant's doctrine of free will by saying that it is unintelligible (which, in a certain way, Kant himself never denied). But what is surprising about this passage is its description of Kant's doctrine as "lewd asceticism." This might be a subtle reference to the fact that for Kant it is only the absolute freedom or spontaneity of the noumenal will that allows us to liberate ourselves from domination by our inclinations, the promptings of mere nature, and his view, as expressed in the *Groundwork*, that it is *only* by liberating ourselves from such inclinations that we can express our "proper" or "authentic" selves (*G*, 4: 457). But imputing such subtlety to Nietzsche might presume a closer acquaintance with Kant's texts than he actually had; it would probably be best just to take the remark as an expression of Nietzsche's general view that Kant, like Schopenhauer (with whom the term "asceticism" is most naturally associated; *WWR*, book 4), is, in spite of some effort on his part to break with Christianity, still largely an apologist for its morality. This is suggested in another of Nietzsche's remarks about Kant, in this case in the Second Essay of *On the Genealogy of Morality*. Here Nietzsche is animadverting against the Christian conception of justice as another manifestation of slave morality, and associates Kant with it:

> In *this* sphere of legal obligations, then, the moral conceptual world of 'debt', 'conscience', 'duty', 'sacred duty', has its breeding ground—all began with a thorough and prolonged bloodletting, like the beginning of all great things on earth. And may we not add that this world has really never quite lost a certain odour of blood and torture? (not even with old Kant: the categorical imperative smells of cruelty...)   (*GM*, II §5, p. 41)

Here Nietzsche is associating the conception of justice as revenge, as the coerced repayment of debt ("an eye for an eye"), with the slave morality of *ressentiment*, and associating Kant with this conception of morality—not entirely unreasonably, to be sure, since Kant himself does invoke the "law of retribution (*ius talionis*)" (*MM*, DR, General Remark following §49, E, 6: 332) in his account of legal punishment (although in what role is debatable).[20]

There can be no doubt of Nietzsche's association of Kant with the morality of self-abnegation or asceticism. Nor can there be any doubt of at least some tendency in that direction on Kant's own part, for Kant does at least once say

---

[20] The traditional interpretation has been that Kant holds a retributivist theory of punishment, that is, that the point of punishment is retribution. More recently, some have argued that Kant holds a deterrent theory of punishment (see esp. *Moral Philosophy Collins*, 27: 286) but uses the *ius talionis* to determine the appropriate amount of punishment; see esp.y Hill 2000, pp. 173–99. Sometimes, however, Kant clearly gets caught up in the enthusiasm for retribution that underlies so much popular sentiment about punishment even today, e.g., in his notorious insistence that even if a society is dissolving every last criminal must be punished (*MM*, DR, General Remark E, 6: 333).

that "it must be the universal wish of every rational being to be altogether free from" "inclinations themselves, as sources of needs" (*G*, 4: 428). But Kant himself also rejects a "slavish" conception of morality, and his attitude toward our natural tendencies is more complex than a remark like this might suggest. Before we turn to Kant's possible response to Nietzsche, however, let us complete our account of Nietzsche's attempted critique of Kant by considering more of his view about the categorical imperative. His remark that the categorical imperative smacks of torture and revenge may seem stretched, but other remarks suggest a more straightforward objection to it, namely, an objection to the validity of any completely universal law for human conduct. This can reflect his general view that no two states of affairs, whether the states of any person's mind, let alone those of different persons, or the situations in which they find themselves, are ever exactly the same.[21]

Nietzsche does not refer to the categorical imperative at all in *Beyond Good and Evil*, and beyond the suggestion in *On the Genealogy of Morality* that it has never quite lost its odor of blood and torture, he otherwise only once hints that he himself will hearken to an "enigmatic" but "oh-so-anti-Kantian" categorical imperative, without spelling out its content (*GM*, Preface, §3, p. 5). We have to turn to other, earlier works of Nietzsche to find any more sustained critique of Kant's version of the categorical imperative. One criticism that Nietzsche makes in the still early *Human, All Too Human* is clearly misguided. Here he writes:

> The...morality, namely Kant's, [that] demanded of the individual actions which one desired of all men: that was a very naïve thing; as if everyone knew without further ado what mode of action would benefit the whole of mankind, that is, what actions at all are desirable; it is a theory like that of free trade, presupposing that universal harmony *must* result of itself in accordance with innate laws of progress. Perhaps some future survey of the requirements of mankind will show that it is absolutely not desirable that all men should act in the same way, but rather that in the interest of ecumenical goals whole tracts of mankind ought to have special, perhaps under certain circumstances even evil tasks imposed upon them. (*HATH*, vol. 1, §25, p. 25)

It was the core of Kant's argument against a moral principle advocating the maximization of happiness—that is, against the early form of utilitarianism that he was familiar with from Francis Hutcheson—that happiness, whether individual or collective, is too indeterminate a goal to furnish a moral principle (although he would later readmit first individual, subsequently collective happiness into the "object" of morality through the concept of the highest good, to which Nietzsche

---

[21] See Nehamas 1986 and, again, 2017.

might well have objected). In other words, Kant rejected precisely the assumption that everyone could know "without further ado what mode of action would benefit the whole of mankind," at least if "benefit" is taken to mean "maximize the happiness of," and argued for the formal criteria of acting only on universalizable maxims or always treating humanity as an end and never merely as a means precisely in order to avoid the impossible calculation of maximal utility.[22]

A second passage in *Human, All Too Human* suggests that, in spite of its pretense to universality, the categorical imperative, or more precisely, since there really is no single categorical imperative, the concept of the categorical imperative, is really used just to lend dignity to the norms of particular communities and their cultures:

> To be moral, to act in accordance with custom, to be ethical means to practise obedience to a law or tradition established from of old.... He is called "good" who does what is customary as if by nature, as a result of a long inheritance, that is to say easily and gladly, and this is so whatever what is customary may be (exacts revenge, for example, when exacting revenge is part of good custom...)...To be evil is "not to act in accordance with custom", to practise things not sanctioned by custom, to resist tradition...How the tradition has *arisen* is here a matter of indifference,[23]—and has in any event nothing to with good and evil or with any kind of immanent categorical imperative;—

Here Nietzsche adds a footnote observing, innocuously enough, that "Kant considered the categorical imperative...to derive from the nature of rationality," but then continues:

> it is above all directed at the preservation of a *community*, a people; every superstitious usage which has arisen on the basis of some chance event mistakenly interpreted enforces a tradition which it is in accordance with custom to follow; for to sever oneself from it is dangerous, and even more injurious to the *community* than it is to the individual...
>
> (*HATH*, vol. 1, "Of the History of the Moral Sensations," §96, p. 51)

Here Nietzsche is arguing that the invocation of a purportedly completely universal categorical imperative is in fact nothing more than a cover for the norms of

---

[22] This in turn suggests that the happiness of all required in the highest good cannot be the object of a calculation separate from consideration of what morality as such requires, but can only be something ideally to be achieved through complete conformity with the requirements of morality; for this reason, Lewis White Beck's position that the highest good does not actually add to the requirements of morality, as against John Silber's position that it does, must be correct. See Beck 1960 and Silber 1963.

[23] This admission is striking, because it might undermine Nietzsche's entire methodology of "genealogy"!

a particular community, an attempt to lend such norms even more force than they already have by calling those who adhere to them "good" and those who flaunt them "evil," and thus an attempt to suppress rather than encourage individuality. Thus the invocation of "the" categorical imperative stands in the way of what Nietzsche favors, the development of the "free spirits" who will later become his "nobles" rather than "slaves." The free spirits are precisely those who can break free of the customary norms of their group, which are in fact grounded not in pure reason as Kant supposed but in mere tradition originating in some historical accident or other.

> He is called a free spirit who thinks differently from what, on the basis of his origin, his class and profession, or on the basis of the dominant views of the age, would have been expected of him. He is the exception, the fettered spirits are the rule; the latter reproach him that his free principles either originate in a desire to shock and offend or eventuate in free actions, that is to say actions incompatible with sound morals.... [W]hat characterizes the free spirit is not that his opinions are the more correct but that he has liberated himself from tradition, whether the outcome has been successful or a failure. As a rule, though, he will nonetheless have truth on his side, or at least the spirit of inquiry after truth: he demands reasons, the rest demand faith.
>
> (*HATH*, vol. 1, "Tokens of Higher and Lower Culture," §225, p. 108)

This passage may show more deference to the ideal of truth than Nietzsche later allows, when he argues in *Beyond Good and Evil* that the unconditional value of truth and knowledge is a "prejudice" of philosophers and all that matters is whether "a judgment preserves and promotes life" (*BGE*, "Of the Prejudices of Philosophers," §4, p. 7; Nietzsche says of the "unconditional belief or conviction" that truth and *trust* is always more valuable than falsehood and distrust "could never have originated if truth *and* untruth had constantly made it clear that they were both useful, as they are"; *GS*, §344, p. 201. This suggests Nietzsche's well-known view that sometimes belief in something false can be useful, but also the deeper point that *distrust* of what is too readily presented as *received* truth is often valuable). But the ideal of the free spirit clearly pervades all of Nietzsche's subsequent philosophy, whether under that name or under others, such as that of the noble, the *Übermensch*, and the like, and Nietzsche clearly sees the universalistic pretenses of the categorical imperative as only an obstacle to the development of free spirits.

A passage in Nietzsche's next major book, *The Gay Science* (1882), also suggests that the appeal to the categorical imperative is nothing but a cover or prop, although now a support for those who are almost but not quite free spirits, who do have a revolutionary idea but not enough confidence *in themselves* and in the validity of their idea *for themselves* to put it forth without the claim to universal validity. In a paragraph on "unconditional duties" he writes that

All persons who feel that they need the strongest words and sounds, the most eloquent gestures and postures, in order to be effective *at all*—revolutionary politicians, socialists, preachers of repentance with or without Christianity, all of whom refuse to accept semi-successes: they all speak of "duties" and indeed always of duties with an unconditional character...So they reach for moral philosophies that preach some categorical imperative...Because they want the unconditional confidence of others, they first need unconditional confidence in themselves on the basis of some ultimate, indisputable and inherently sublime commandment, and they want to feel like and pass themselves off as its servants and instruments....Whoever feels his dignity violated by the thought of being the *instrument* of a prince or party or sect or even a financial power—say, as the descendant of an old, proud family—but still wants to or must be this instrument before himself and before the public, needs poignant [*pathetische*] principles that can be mouthed at any time, principles of an unconditional "ought" to which one may openly submit and be seen to have submitted without shame.

(GS, §15, pp. 32–3)

"*Pathetische*," somewhat oddly translated as "poignant," suggests that the appeal to a categorical imperative relies on pathos in its audience to buck up the one who invokes it, but also that there is something pathetic about this appeal: to appeal to a categorical imperative means that the appellant does not quite have the courage of his convictions, is not enough of a free spirit to say openly that this is what *he* believes whether others like it or not, so he tries to shame them into agreeing with him with this instrument. This is clearly not a noble trait. Of course, it might well be objected that not every appeal to *a* categorical imperative invokes *the* categorical imperative, the genuine article, so it might well be true that the name of the categorical imperative is often exploited for the psychological purpose that Nietzsche alleges without that entailing the spuriousness of the genuine article.

But another passage in *The Gay Science* clearly shows that Nietzsche means something stronger, that the very concept of a categorical imperative is doomed because what it presupposes, that different situations are sufficiently similar to make the kind of generalization he supposes it to demand, is impossible. In part of this lengthy passage,[24] Nietzsche argues:

No one who judges, "in this case everyone would have to act like this" has yet taken five steps towards self-knowledge. For he would then know that there neither are nor can be actions that are all the same; that every act ever performed was done in an altogether unique and unrepeatable way, and that this will be equally true of every future act; that all prescriptions of action (even the most

[24] Also cited in Hill 2003, pp. 207–8.

inward and subtle rules of all moralities so far) relate only to their rough exterior; that these prescriptions may yield an appearance of sameness, *but only just an appearance*; that as one observes or recollects *any* action, it is and remains impenetrable; that our opinions about "good" and "noble" and "great" can never be *proven true* by our actions because every act is unknowable . . . Let us therefore *limit* ourselves to the purification of our opinions and value judgments and to the *creation of tables of what is good that are new and all our own*: let us stop brooding over the "moral value of our actions"!   (*GS*, §335, p. 189)

Here Nietzsche runs together two points, one of which Kant actually endorses but the other of which points to a genuine issue about the application of the categorical imperative. What Kant could endorse without reservation is Nietzsche's second point, that we are confined to judging the "exterior" of actions, not only those of others but even our own, while their interior remains hidden from us, and that thus we ought to confine ourselves to figuring out what would really be right to do—creating the tables of what is good, in Nietzsche's words—and stop brooding over our real motivation, thus over own moral worth. Kant frequently makes the same point: our real motivation, what fundamental maxim, whether that of morality or of self-love, we are really committed to remains hidden from us, both because of our empirical psychology and because, at least for him, of the noumenal location of our real choice. Even in his fullest discussions of conscience, Kant never suggests that we spend our time trying to figure out whether we are morally worthy, but rather that we should expend the utmost effort trying to figure out what the right thing *to do* is (*MM*, DV, §§13–14; *Moral Philosophy Collins*, 27: 351–7; *Metaphysics of Morals Vigilantius*, 27: 613–19). Our real moral worth will consist just in our commitment to doing that.

Nietzsche's first point, that the categorical imperative is impossible, thus there can be no genuinely universalizable principles or in Kant's terms maxims, because no two circumstances are ever exactly the same, is more problematic. It might seem that to insist upon this would simply be to deny the possibility of action on principles, including Nietzsche's own, and indeed of conceptual thought altogether. Of course no two real objects are ever exactly alike in every conceivable detail, nor are any two circumstances for action exactly alike—that is what we learned from Leibniz's principle of the identity of indiscernibles, and that Kant would have known as well as Nietzsche did. But even supposing that to be true does not undermine the impossibility of concepts on Kant's account, because they are formed by picking out relevant similarities among objects and ignoring their differences, and he would certainly claim that it does not undermine the possibility of forming universalizable maxims, grounded upon concepts of relatively similar situations. However, the ease of determining what *count* as relevant similarities among situations for action and therefore what count as the right maxims for moral evaluation has long been recognized as a genuine difficulty in applying Kant's formulation of the categorical imperative as the requirement that we act only on universalizable maxims—tailoring maxims to particular circumstances seems to threaten the value of the universalizability test.[25] This is one among many reasons why the best approach to moral philosophy may be through Kant's second and third formulations of the categorical imperative, that is, through the ideas that humanity in any person ought to be treated always as an end and never merely as a means and that all our maxims ought to be collectively aimed at the transformation of the kingdom of nature into an empire of ends—for these are *ideals*, not putative *decision-procedures*. But neither Nietzsche nor in this regard his master Schopenhauer ever think of Kant's categorical imperative as anything other than the demand for readily universalizable maxims of action.

Be that as it may, the part of the passage from the *Gay Science* quoted thus far is preceded by a more interesting part.[26] Here Nietzsche writes:

> And now don't bring up the categorical imperative, my friend! The term tickles my ear and makes me laugh despite your very serious presence. I am reminded of old Kant, who helped himself to the "thing in itself"—another very ridiculous thing!—and was punished for this when the "categorical imperative" crept into his heart and made him stray back to "God", "soul", "freedom", "immortality", like a fox who strays back into his cage. Yet it had been *his* strength and cleverness that had broken open the cage! What? You admire the categorical imperative within you? This "firmness" of your so-called moral judgement? This absoluteness of the feeling, "here everyone must judge as I do"? Rather admire your *selfishness* here. For it selfish to consider one's own judgment a universal law, and this selfishness is blind, petty, and simple because it shows that you haven't yet discovered yourself or created for yourself an ideal of your very own—for this could never be someone else's, let alone everyone's, everyone's!
>
> (*GS*, book 4, §335, pp. 188–9)

Only after the last exclamation remark does Nietzsche invoke the principle of the identity of indiscernibles. But his preceding point is independent of any such metaphysics. His objection to the categorical imperative is essentially just that it is incompatible with the development of individuality, or with the recognition of individuality as a valid ideal—perhaps not one that everyone can achieve, but one that free spirits or nobles must aim at—"must" at least in the sense that they inevitably *do*, whether or not from Nietzsche's point of view it is permissible to say that they *ought* to.

The real meaning of Kant's assertion that the humanity in every person must always be treated as an end and never merely as a means is that each of us must

---

[25] See the extensive literature beginning with Singer 1961. See chapter 14 below.
[26] This part is elided in the quotation from the passage in Hill 2003.

allow all of us to set his or her own ends, to form his or her own ideals for life and action, subject to the constraint that each of us set ends only that are compatible with all of us setting our own ends. Nietzsche's conception of the free spirits recognizes the value of *their* setting their own ends, but he does seem to insist that nobles need not recognize the value of slaves setting their own ends, even if they could do it, and indeed that nobles may use slaves as mere means to their own ends if necessary. Before we consider this issue, however, let us first consider whether Nietzsche's critique of slave morality is in fact a critique of Kantian morality. As I earlier noted, Kant himself objects to "slavish" morality, as Hume before him had objected to "monkish virtues,"[27] so there may actually be some overlap between their positions on this point. But is any resemblance between their positions more than verbal and merely apparent?

Kant himself objected to a "slavish" conception of morality. To be sure, in making this objection he had in mind something somewhat different from Nietzsche's objection. He was far from condemning Christian morality wholesale; on the contrary, his *Religion within the Boundaries of Mere Reason* was intended to reconstruct Christian morality, or more precisely to demonstrate that some central tenets of Christianity, such as its conception of the both human and divine Christ and a proper understanding of grace, are apt, or even the best, symbols of central tenets of the morality of pure practical reason, such as its thought that in spite of our sensible nature and its inclinations we also have pure reason as the source of the moral law and the freedom to choose to make that law our fundamental maxim no matter what. But Kant did object to any thought that morality requires self-abnegation, any form of self-flagellation whether metaphorical or literal, total suppression of our natural impulses. He did think that morality requires striking down *self-conceit*, that is, making self-love into one's supreme principle, but not that it requires the elimination of self-love from its proper place (in this regard his position is comparable to that of Joseph Butler, who thought that a deficiency of self-love was just as much a moral problem as a deficiency in love of others),[28] and thus a certain kind of self-affirmation. The Kantian morally worthy person may not be identical to the Nietzschean free spirit or noble, but he is far from an ascetic, at least in any normal sense—she is certainly not a Schopenhauerian ascetic, who renounces all desire as the only way to avoid suffering.

There are two aspects to Kant's argument in the *Religion* that might be mentioned in this context. The first is his explicit rejection of a slavish acceptance of morality in the footnote added to part 1 of the book in which he engages with Friedrich Schiller's recently published essay on "Grace and Dignity" (*Anmut und Würde*) (see Chapter 3 above). Kant takes Schiller to be arguing that moral actions

---

[27] Hume 1998, section 9, paragraph 3, p. 73.
[28] Butler 2017, e.g., Preface, pp. 7–9; Sermons I–III, pp. 17–37.

should ideally be performed with grace, that is, with a complete harmony between our intentions and all aspects of our actions—for Schiller, action is graceful when there is no conflict between their voluntary and their involuntary components, which would indicate a hidden reservation about the action—but that we might sometimes have to settle for dignity, that is, performing an action out of principle even when the effort of overcoming resistance remains visible in our conduct. Kant takes this to be a criticism of his moral theory, when in fact Schiller probably intended it to be an affirmation of Kant's moral theory, with his criticism aimed only at Kant's aesthetic theory, specifically at Kant's conception of the "ideal of beauty" (*CPJ*, §17), which implausibly takes the fixed form of a beautiful human countenance rather than the graceful movement of a human being as evidence of his or her moral commitment.[29] Failing to see that, Kant responds to Schiller by insisting that any sign of merely grudging acceptance of the moral law, any sign of resistance to it, shows that the agent is not really fully committed to the moral law, has not really made it his or her fundamental maxim, even though so doing is always within his or her power—the core claim of *Religion*. Thus it is actually Kant who adopts the position often attributed to Schiller, namely that it is always possible for us to perform our duty gracefully, rather than the more realistic Schiller himself. Kant puts his response this way:

> Now, if we ask, "What is the *aesthetic* constitution, the *temperament* so to speak *of virtue*: is it courageous and hence *joyous*, or weighed down by fear and dejected?" an answer is hardly necessary. The latter slavish frame of mind can never be found without a hidden *hatred* of the law, whereas a heart joyous in the *compliance* with its duty (not just complacency in the *recognition* of it) is the sign of genuineness in virtuous disposition, even where *piety* is concerned, which does not consist in the self-torment of a remorseful sinner (a torment which is very ambiguous, and usually only an inward reproach for having offended against prudence), but in the firm resolve to improve in the future. This resolve, encouraged by good progress, must needs effect a joyous frame of mind, without which one is never certain of having *gained* also a *love* for the good, i.e., of having incorporated the good into one's maxim. (*RBMR*, 6: 24n.)

In other words, the truly virtuous agent performs her duty happily, not grudgingly, thus *without resentment*. Kant does not use Nietzsche's word *ressentiment*, but it seems natural to equate his conception of a slavish frame of mind with one that accepts the moral law only with resentment at the necessity of striking down self-conceit, and likewise to equate his conception of a joyous frame of mind with one that fully identifies itself with its duty with no hidden reserve

---

[29] For this approach to Schiller's essay, see Guyer 2007b. See also chapter 6 above.

of resentment. This seems at least part of what Nietzsche has in mind with his own conception of nobility.

Nevertheless, Nietzsche's conception of the *ressentiment* of slave morality certainly involves more than Kant's conception of a slavish or resentful frame of mind in the performance of duty. Kant's conception of resentment has nothing to do with the specific *content* of morality, but Nietzsche's conception of *ressentiment* has everything to do with the content of morality: his central claim is that the slave morality of Christianity has tried to transform the negative qualities of weakness and self-abasement into positive virtues, and that this transvaluation of values must itself be transvalued. It is on this ground that the larger debate between Kant and Nietzsche must be judged. Before we turn to that, however, we can note a second theme in part 1 of Kant's *Religion* that bears on the question of whether Kantian morality itself demands that we suppress our own nature, more precisely whether our rational nature must suppress our sensible nature, thus whether it is on Nietzsche's terms a slavish morality of self-abnegation. What I have in mind here is Kant's argument that the "predisposition to animality" in the human being, which consists of the threefold drives for "self-preservation," for "the propagation of the species through the sexual drive" and the "preservation of the offspring thereby begotten," and for "community with other human beings, i.e., the social drive" (*RBMR*, 6: 26), are not themselves sources of or forces for evil, but are in fact "predispositions *to the good*," "original" dispositions belonging to "the possibility of human nature" (6: 28). That is, they are means through which the end set for us by nature *and approved by morality* (that is, our own reason), namely, the perfection of the human species itself, can be achieved, although only if they are governed by the fundamental decision to subordinate self-love to morality when they conflict rather than to subordinate morality to self-love (which would be self-conceit). If these natural predispositions are governed by self-conceit rather than by morality, then they degenerate into "the *bestial vices of gluttony, lust and wild lawlessness* (in relation to other human beings)" (6: 26). But if they do, that is not the fault of nature, but of our own free will: for Kant, the choice whether to have natural, healthy self-love remain within the confines of morality or to let it degenerate into bestiality is always ours, always "a deed of freedom (for otherwise the use or abuse of the human being's power of choice with respect to the moral law could not be imputed to him, nor could the good or evil in him be called 'moral')" (6: 21).

Exactly at this point, of course, there is an insuperable difference between Kant and Nietzsche: Kant is committed to the absolutely free choice of human beings between good and evil, while Nietzsche has no truck with the idea of free will.[30] For Nietzsche,

---

[30] Among the sources on this topic already cited, Gemes 2009 is an attempt to make space for some conception of free will by rejecting "deserts free will," i.e., a libertarian conception of free will as a

The *causa sui* is the best self-contradiction that has ever been conceived, a type of logical rape and abomination. But humanity's excessive pride has got itself profoundly and horribly entangled with precisely this piece of nonsense. The longing for "freedom of the will" in the superlative metaphysical sense (which, unfortunately, still rules in the heads of the half-educated), the longing to bear the entire and ultimate responsibility for your actions yourself and to relieve God, world, ancestors, chance, and society of the burden—all this means nothing less than being that very *causa sui*, and, with a courage greater than Münchhausen's, pulling yourself by the hair from the swamp of nothingness up into existence. . . . in real life it is only a matter of *strong* and *weak* wills.

(Nietzsche, *BGE*, "On the Prejudices of Philosophers," §21, p. 21)

Free spirits are free in that they can and do liberate themselves from the constraints of prejudice and custom in their societies, but they are not free to *choose* whether or not to do so; it is just their nature to do so, as it is the nature of the slavish to be slavish. Some people have strong wills and can seek power directly, some have weak wills and can seek power only through the subterfuges of slave morality, but in either case that is a matter of nature, not of choice. Of course, that being so, one might well ask why Nietzsche bothers to write: won't the nobles be nobles and the weak be weak quite apart from whatever he says? Well, even the strong might not always realize their own strength, or realize that the slave morality valorized by their society is not inevitable, and Nietzsche's writings might be liberating for them, if not for everyone. Indeed, to think that all potential nobles will become actual nobles entirely independently from Nietzsche's unmasking of the slave morality around them would be fatalism, not determinism. But then again, Nietzsche is also suspicious of determinism, a doctrine that may be used to justify inaction and thus the status quo as much as it is used for anything else. If anything, he wants to claim that he has no use for either free will or determinism—as opposed to Kant, who had use for both, one at the noumenal level and the other at the phenomenal level. Of course, we have already seen what use Nietzsche had for Kant's notion of the thing in itself, and thus for the distinction between the noumenal and the phenomenal—namely, none at all.

Let us turn now to Nietzsche's second main objection to Kant, that the categorical imperative tries to impose a single model of conduct on to everyone, when free spirits must be free to follow their own ideals (let's not say *choose*). This is a part of Nietzsche's perspectivism, which is not solely an epistemological doctrine, holding that beliefs are always adopted from some point of view or other, but also a practical doctrine, holding that the principles that are best for

---

condition of responsibility or imputability, and "agency free will." Of course Nietzsche recognizes freedom in the sense of non-domination by others: that is certainly one thing that distinguishes nobles from slaves.

people in some circumstances are not necessarily the best for those in different circumstances—what we might call Nietzsche's particularism, his way of applying the Leibnizian principle of the identity of indiscernibles and therefore the difference of discernibles, has both theoretical and practical consequences. Can Kant accept any form of perspectivism with regard to values rather than knowledge? Here it might seem as if the answer should be simple: the advocate of the categorical imperative could hardly accept any such thing. But I will argue that here too Kant's position is complex, and that a thesis about the ineliminable variety of individual human ends that might capture at least a part of perspectivist thought about values is absolutely fundamental to Kant's moral philosophy.[31]

Kant obviously held that there is a single categorical imperative valid for all human beings, indeed for all conceivable rational beings. He argues that the mere concept of a categorical imperative itself implies that there can only be a single such principle. Since by definition such an "imperative contains, beyond the law, only the necessity that the maxim be in conformity with the law, while the law contains no condition to which it would be limited, nothing is left with which the maxim of action is to conform but the universality of a law as such," and "There is, therefore, only a single categorical imperative ...: *act only in accordance with that maxim through which you can at the same time will that it become a universal law*" (*G*, 4: 420–1). Kant's concept of a single categorical imperative necessarily valid for all rational beings obviously drove Nietzsche into a rage. But was that a blind rage, that is, did it prevent Nietzsche from seeing that Kant accepted at least part of what Nietzsche himself was after when he claimed that "each one of us should devise *his own* virtue"? It did, for Kant grounded this first formulation of the categorical imperative upon the premise that each one of us must respect the free and rational agency of every other, thus respect the ends that each of us freely sets for him- or herself, and therefore even promote the happiness of each after his or her own conception—to the extent, of course, that so doing is consistent with continuing to respect the free and rational agency of everyone else (*G*, 4: 428). Kant interpreted this to require each of us to respect the freedom of all to set their own ends and even to entail and imperfect duty, a duty of wide latitude, to promote the diversity of values and ways of life chosen by our fellows—again, of course, subject to the condition that those diverse values and way of life include recognition of the freedom of others to choose their own values and ways of life, with only ends that would violate this condition counting as "impermissible." Of course Kant recognized that no one person can promote even the permissible ends of everyone else, thus that we each have to limit our assistance of others in some way, and allowed that we have to limit that assistance of others to their pursuit

---

[31] Nietzsche's perspectivism is of course a huge topic of discussion. In addition to Nehamas 1985 *passim*, see also Clark 1990 and Anderson 2005, 2018; Gemes 2013 argues for a psychological rather than epistemological interpretation.

of ends that are not merely permissible but of which we ourselves approve. Nevertheless, he is emphatic that "It is for them to decide what they count as belonging to their happiness" but it is not up to me to decide what should make them happy, within the limits of permissibility (*MM*, DV, Introduction, Section V.B, 6: 388). To this extent, Kant's insistence upon a single categorical imperative as our most general moral principle is meant to promote the possibility of the realization of a diversity of more concrete values and ways of life. It might sound paradoxical, but in this way the categorical imperative is intended as an anti-perspectivist foundation for a perspectivism of values. If the ground of a possible categorical imperative is the humanity in each of us, defined as the "capacity to set oneself an end—any end whatsoever" (*MM* DV, Introduction, section VIII, 6: 392), then the inference to be drawn from these premises is that to respect rational being in ourselves and others is not merely to respect everyone *as* ends in themselves, but also to respect everyone's own choice *of* their particular ends. Kant makes this clear in his political as well as his foundational moral writings. For example, in the 1793 essay on "Theory and Practice" he writes that "No one can coerce me to be happy in his way (as he thinks of the welfare of other human beings); instead, each may seek his happiness in the way that seems good to him, provided he does not infringe upon the freedom of others to strive for a like end" (*TP*, 8: 290). Since it is their capacity for freedom that makes others into objects of duty for us and it is their exercise of freedom that must be preserved and promoted, to attempt to promote their happiness after any conception of it other than their own would be to undermine precisely what gives us an obligation to promote it in the first place.

However, even were Nietzsche to concede that Kant, like himself, recognizes the value of people setting their own ends rather than having ends imposed upon them, he would still object to Kant's further formulations of the categorical imperative. One objection would be to Kant's apparent insistence that we have a duty to promote the permissible happiness of others, after their conception of it, but no duty to promote *our own* happiness; another objection could be that our duty to promote the happiness after their own conception of it is apparently unlimited, regardless of our own valuation of their values. The second point is easily met: Kant limits the claims of others upon me in saying that "it is open to me to refuse them many things that *they* think will make them happy but I do not, as long as they have no right to demand them from me as what is theirs" (6: 388). The last clause means that if I owe something to somebody as a matter of right, that is, on Kant's scheme, property right, for example if I owe something in repayment of a debt or fulfillment of a contract, then I have no ground to withhold it from its rightful owner regardless of my conception of the prudence or wisdom of the end to which he will use it, that is, the conception of happiness he will use it to serve. But in other cases, I may well be permitted to use my own disapproval of another's chosen values as a ground for withholding my assistance from him: after all, the duty of beneficence is an imperfect duty, and there will be many others with whose ends I am more comfortable for me to help instead, and others more comfortable than I am with the ends of the one whom I choose not to help who can help him instead of me. The imperfect duty of beneficence is not a duty to help everyone else in the world all the time, and there will be many circumstances in which I can use my own discomfort with another's conception of his own happiness as a ground for saving my beneficence for another occasion and another recipient, although no doubt there will also be some where I cannot allow myself this luxury.

The more difficult objection would seem to be Kant's position that it is only the happiness of *others* that is a duty that is also an end, not *one's own* happiness: surely a morality that does not value one's own values cannot count as even a modified form of value-perspectivism. Here I think one must say that Kant's bark is ultimately worse than his bite. His argument for recognizing only the happiness of others and not one's own as an end that is also a duty is that, first, while anything that "everyone already wants unavoidably, of his own accord, does not come under the concept of *duty*, which is *constraint* to an end adopted reluctantly," and, second, "*his own happiness* is an end that every human being has (by virtue of the impulses of his nature)," so that "it is self-contradictory to say that he is *under obligation* to promote his own happiness" (*MM*, DV, Introduction, section IV, 6: 386). This argument is clearly unsound: whatever one might think of its first premise, that is, the conception of duty—about which Nietzsche would not think much—the second is clearly false. If we mean by happiness anything more than momentary gratification of a current desire, then there are all sorts of situations in which our immediate impulse is not to our own happiness in any extended sense, and in which we might have to constrain ourselves—even if no one else has a right to do so—to pursue our long-term happiness rather than our momentary gratification. Moreover, Kant ultimately, even if only grudgingly, seems to recognize this. While he initially rejects "an alleged *obligation* to attend to my *own* (natural) happiness" as any excuse for failing to promote the happiness of others, and allows only an indirect duty to promote my own happiness insofar as that is necessary to remove temptations that might tempt me to do evil (6: 388), he subsequently concedes that I must recognize my own happiness as well as that of others as a legitimate object of benevolence, "since all *others* with the exception of myself would not be *all*," so that in order for the maxim of benevolence to "have within it the universality of a law...the law making benevolence a duty will include myself, as an object of benevolence, in the command of practical reason" (*MM*, DV, §27, 6: 451). One might argue that Kant is here saying only that I must will that *others* should promote my happiness by being benevolent to me, not that *I* have any duty to promote my own happiness. But it seems a little hard to see why I should think that others can have an obligation to do something for me which I have no obligation to do for myself, namely, promote my own happiness.

In any case, whether Kant clearly realizes it or not, the underlying obligation to treat humanity *in my own person* as well as that of others as an end and never merely a means would appear to give rise to an obligation to respect and promote *my own* freely chosen ends as well as those of others. That would seem a sufficient basis for the conclusion that each one of us has a duty to promote both his own happiness and that of others, but the happiness of each after his own conception. And that, in turn, could suggest that each one of us has not merely a duty to respect the freely chosen conceptions of happiness of others, but also even the duty to choose *freely* his or her own conception of happiness in the exercise of his or her humanity. But this is, of course, where Nietzsche would make his deepest objection. First, he would not share Kant's conviction that everyone does have equal humanity, or equal agency, or an equal ability to set his or her own ends. Some persons are naturally stronger than others, that is, naturally better at setting and pursuing their own ends. In his view, some persons just are strong, others just are "weaklings" (e.g., *GM*, I §15, p. 29). From his point of view, Kant's premise that "their nature" "marks out" *every* person as an end and not just a means (*G*, 4: 429) is just false, just a fabrication *of the weak*. And then, since Kant's claim that we each have a duty to treat the humanity of all as an end in itself is based on that factual premise, Nietzsche would have no ground to accept Kant's assertion of such a duty. He would not recognize any basis for such a duty either in a conception of pure reason as itself demanding universality or in an alleged fact of equal humanity. Thus, in principle Nietzsche should share the value that Kant, in his terms, places on agents getting to set their own ends, but in practice he sees no ground for attributing this capacity to all and therefore attributing equal, let alone unconditional value to all. The overlap between Kant's space for perspectivism within his universalistic framework and Nietzsche's version of a perspectivism of values without such a framework is very far from complete.

PART IV

THE ANGLOPHONE RECEPTION:
IDEALISM PRO AND CON

12

Kant and Anglophone Idealism

Bradley to Paton

The movement commonly called British idealism flourished above all in the three decades from around 1870 to 1900, or from around the time of the death of John Stuart Mill to the triumphant critique of Francis Herbert Bradley's version of this approach by G. E. Moore and Bertrand Russell around the turn of the century. Of course the established proponents of the school did not simply retire or die all at once in 1900, and important chairs in England and especially Scotland continued to be held by figures associated with the movement to one degree or another for decades longer, for example by Robin George Collingwood in Oxford and Norman Kemp Smith in Edinburgh into the 1940s. The movement should also not be called just "British" idealism, since there were major proponents of idealism in the United States as well, above all Josiah Royce, who taught at Harvard from 1883 until his death in 1916, surviving attack by the American "New Realists" by at least several years. The movement is also often called British (and American) Neo-Hegelianism, but that is too restrictive. I will call it "Anglophone idealism" in this chapter.

Anglophone idealism is often considered as much a moralistic social movement as a development in academic metaphysics. Bradley held a non-teaching fellowship at Merton College, and his influence, based entirely on his publications, was confined to academics. But T. H. Green, at Balliol College, was a popular lecturer who influenced a generation of Britons in public life, and many other members of the school whom we will not be able to consider here, such as Bernard Bosanquet[1] and Henry Jones,[2] also wrote and taught for a broad audience, and indeed were often directly involved in public affairs.[3] But the academic and the public sides of Anglophone idealism came together in moral philosophy. In moral philosophy, all of the leading proponents of this movement—who for our purposes will include

---

[1] Bernard Bosanquet's chief works bearing on moral philosophy and its implications are Bosanquet 1894, 1912, 1913.

[2] See Jones 1909 and Jones 1910. See also Boucher 2009.

[3] For a general history of British (not Anglophone) idealism that covers all these figures and more, see Mander 2011. Mander's sequel, Mander 2016, narrows his topic to moral philosophy, but broadens its scope to include discussion of Royce. For an essay on Bradley, Green, and Bosanquet, see Vincent 2014; for essays on a wider range of the British idealists, see Sweet 2009. On the social role of the British idealists, esp. Green, see Vincento 2014, pp. 435–7; Skorupski 2021, pp. 41–2; and Vincent and Plant 1984.

Kant's Impact on Moral Philosophy. Paul Guyer, Oxford University Press. © Paul Guyer 2024.
DOI: 10.1093/oso/9780199592456.003.0013

not only Bradley, Green, and Royce but also the Scotsman Edward Caird, who first held the chair of moral philosophy at Glasgow and then succeeded Benjamin Jowett as Master of Balliol at Oxford, as well as Herbert James Paton, another Scotsman who held the chair in moral philosophy at Oxford a generation later— took seriously the charge that Kant's categorical imperative is an "empty formalism." In this they may have been influenced by Hegel, although as we have seen it is a mistake to associate that charge uniquely with Hegel, since the objection had been made against Kant all the way back to Pistorius's 1786 review of the *Groundwork*. But more positively, while all of these authors appropriated ideas and approaches from Hegel in addition to the "empty formalism" charge, they are equally well seen as developing Kantian approaches to moral philosophy. This is particularly clear in the case of Caird, whose monumental study of *The Critical Philosophy of Kant* presents Kant's successive formulations of the categorical imperative in section II of the *Groundwork* as his own progress toward overcoming the empty formalism charge. But as we will see, there are importantly Kantian aspects to the moral philosophies of Green, Royce, and Paton as well. In general, the Anglophone idealists, while beginning with the worry about empty formalism, developed a conception of morality as the coherent and harmonious expression of the social nature of human beings that can be regarded as a development of Kant's "fruitful concept" of the empire of ends (G, 4: 433). This the true even in the case of Bradley, although he presented himself as resolutely anti-Kantian, as well as of the others, who were generally less polemical than Bradley and evinced high esteem for Kant.[4]

12.1. Bradley

Francis Herbert Bradley (1846–1924) was elected to a fellowship at Merton College after completing his undergraduate studies at University College, Oxford. The Merton fellowship, which required no teaching, was terminable only upon marriage, and Bradley retained it for the duration of his life. Apparently spending vacations in France with his mistress was not considered to violate the terms of the fellowship. After an early essay on "The Presuppositions of Critical History" (1874), Bradley published *Ethical Studies* in 1876. A second edition with some additional, unfinished notes was posthumously published in 1927. The work was influential throughout Bradley's lifetime and beyond. His

---

[4] Robert Stern presents Green and Bradley as trying to defend versions of perfectionism (Green "capacity-based perfectionism" and Bradley "holistic perfectionism") against Kant's critique of perfectionism (Stern 2017). I have argued that, in spite of his criticisms of the particular form that perfectionism takes in Wolff and Baumgarten, Kant's own moral philosophy can be considered as an alternative form of perfectionism (Guyer 2011a); in what follows I will be arguing that Green and Bradley are best seen as fleshing out Kant's perfectionism rather than simply adding it to his position.

other chief works were *The Principles* of Logic (1888) and *Appearance and Reality* (1893, with an important appendix added to the second edition of 1897). As already mentioned, Bradley's work came under heavy attack by the young G. E. Moore and Bertrand Russell just before the turn of the twentieth century, thus Anglophone "analytic" philosophy can be considered to have been launched with the critique of Bradley. The central idea of *Appearance and Reality*, that reality as such—everything that is—can contain no contradictions—nothing can both be and not be—is a metaphysical implication of any logic, and hard to dispute. Bradley's further inference that any representation of reality that contains any contradictions—as so many of ours do—can only be appearance, not a representation of reality as it really is, is also hard to dispute. Some of the further inferences that Bradley draws are highly disputable, but they are not our concern here.[5]

Bradley's *Ethical Studies* was published almost two decades before *Appearance and Reality*, and however much of his later metaphysics Bradley might already have had in mind, the earlier work does not overtly depend upon it.[6] Or, perhaps better, the arguments of *Ethical Studies* and *Appearance and Reality* differ in a subtle but important way. The argument of the later work is that the only reality is the necessarily consistent universe as a whole, but that any and every representation of it available to us is partial and in some way inconsistent. The argument of the earlier work is that, while the moral goal of each of us is self-realization, this is not the realization of apparently individualistic and potentially conflicting selves, but of our selves as part of a single, consistent whole, ultimately all of humanity.[7] In this case a completely consistent whole is not a mere metaphysical posit that cannot figure directly in any particular quotidian or scientific representation of reality, but the concrete object of the moral endeavor of each and all of us. As far as Kant is concerned, Bradley conceives of his fundamental moral principle that any of us can achieve self-realization only as part of the larger self consisting of all of us as a criticism of and alternative to what he regards as Kant's essential individualism. But if we conceive of the ultimate end of Kantian morality as the self-consistent exercise of the freedom of each and all of us, or the setting of ends by each of us in a way consistent with an empireof ends of all of us, the difference between Kant's moral vision and Bradley's may not be so great as Bradley thought: Kant never loses sight of the fact that each of us is a separate moral agent who is responsible for his own choices, but always sees the only possible criterion of

---

[5] For brief discussions of Bradley's metaphysics, see Mander 2011, pp. 104–19, and Mander 2020, chapter 12; for more extensive treatments, Mander 1994 and Allard 2005. For an account of Russell's critique of Bradley's metaphysics, see Hylton 1990.

[6] Andrew Vincent, however, characterizes the argumentation in *Ethical Studies* as "provisional," in anticipation of the subsequent work in metaphysics; Vincent 2014, p. 424. On Bradley's moral philosophy more generally, see Irwin 2009, pp. 536–80; Keene 2009; Mander 2011, 181–94; Mander 2016, pp. 158–60.

[7] For a similar interpretation, see Mander 2011, pp. 184–6, 189–90.

moral choice as the intra- and interpersonally consistent use of freedom by all of us, and, though it took some time for Kant to become clear about this, the only possible object of morality as the highest good including the happiness for all that would result from this choice although it is not anyone's immediate motivation.

Bradley's method in *Ethical Studies* supports the view that there must be something of enduring value in Kant's moral philosophy (perhaps even more than Bradley recognizes), for the method itself is Hegelian to the extent of finding some aspect of truth, although only partially understood, in every position preceding his own.[8] The work begins with critiques of "The Vulgar Notion of Responsibility,"[9] of the equally vulgar question "Why Should I Be Moral?,"[10] a vulgar form of hedonism which takes *my own* pleasure as an adequate end for my action, and finally of the supposedly Kantian notion that "Duty for Duty's Sake" is an adequate conception of morally apposite motivation and action, before proceeding to develop its own more adequate conception of morality in the progression from "My Station and Its Duties"[11] (only the first, preliminary rather than final statement of Bradley's moral ideal, as is often thought) through "Ideal Morality" to a concluding supersession (or *Aufhebung*) of an absolute contrast between "Selfishness and Self-Sacrifice." (Although the titles I have quoted names each of the book's seven "essays," it is clearly not a book of separate essays, but a continuous argument.) In the first essay, Bradley argues that both a libertarian conception of freedom of the will and the supposition that determinism is incompatible with freedom depend upon an abstract, atomistic conception of the self and of its separate acts; a fuller, more adequate conception of the self will recognize that later acts are not separate from earlier ones, like individual marbles in a bag of them or individual grapes in a bunch (*ES*, p. 37), thus either simply undetermined by them or simply determined by them, and will not separate the self from its world, but will instead see character as expressed in action as a continuing development continuous with a larger world (see especially *ES*, pp. 50–5, one of the notes prepared for the second edition). Bradley's discussion of responsibility thus prepares the way for the enlarged view of self that is the central idea of his moral philosophy.

The second essay argues that to look outside of morality for a reason to be moral is another error of abstraction, presuming a separation between the self that is to be moral and its states (e.g., pleasure). Instead, Bradley argues, to be moral is just to realize the self, so there can be no question why the self should be moral; but still we must find out what it means to "find and possess ourselves as a whole"

---

[8] Mander 2011, p. 182, refers to the "explicitly dialectical" method of *Ethical Studies*. Irwin says that Bradley "is similar to Hegel...in so far as he expounds his position, including his conception of self-realization, dialectically. We start from a rough conception, and consider various attempts to articulate it..."; Irwin 2009, p. 547. Vincent 2014, p. 424, refers to Bradley's method as "dialectical," and to *Ethical Studies* as more Hegelian than Bradley's other works.

[9] Discussed at Irwin 2009, pp. 540–3.   [10] Discussed at Irwin 2009, pp. 544–7.

[11] Discussed at Irwin 2009, 567–70.

(*ES*, p. 73). The third essay, a powerful critique of utilitarianism,[12] argues that the realization of the self cannot be an "abstract end," and that the idea of "the greatest amount of pleasure," whether of oneself or of everyone, is precisely an "abstract end, and ... altogether unrealizable" (*ES*, p. 125). The most obvious meaning of this is that to separate pleasure as its product from any specific conception of activity is a false abstraction: pleasure is not some discrete feeling separable from the activity that produces it and fungible, equally well produced in some other way. But even more important is Bradley's claim that the idea of myself as existing independently of its activities but also independent from other selves is also a false abstraction. Thus the idea of a sum of pleasure for myself independent of the activities that produces it but also the idea of a sum of pleasure of all independent of the concrete relations among all are both false abstractions. Instead, Bradley suggests, "if my self which I aim at is the realization in me of a moral world which is a system of selves, an organism in which I am a member, and in whose life I live—then I cannot aim at my own well-being without aiming at that of others" (*ES*, p. 116). This states the thesis that Bradley will more fully develop in the final three essays of the book. But first comes his reduction of Kant's moral philosophy to the idea that duty must be performed for the sake of duty, and his argument that this too is a false abstraction.[13]

More precisely, Bradley begins Essay IV with the claim that, while the error of hedonism and utilitarianism was to identify the self or selves with its "particular feelings," and thus to make the goal of morality simply "the maximum number of particular feelings," Kant's error "is the opposite, since for mere particular [he] substitutes mere universal; we have not to do with feelings, as this and that, but with a form which is thought of as not this or that" (*ES*, p. 142). From this opening sally we can see that his critique of Kant is a version of the empty formalism charge.[14] To be sure, Kant's conception of the good will advances beyond hedonism by not separating the end of moral action from the self, and not making "an ultimate end of anything except myself." Thus "the end falls not outside the self of the doer, nor further outside of his activity," and this is what is right in Kant's insistence that the good will and not anything to be effected through it is the only unconditional good (*ES*, p, 143). But the conception of the good will is still too abstract, telling us only "*that* will is the end" but not "*what* will is the end," that is, what in particular the good will is to will. Kant's conception of the good will is also right insofar as it gets us past sheer individualism: "It is not an end for me without being one also for you, or for you and me and not for a third person ... [it] is not the particular will of particular men ... It is the same for you and me ... thus

[12] See Irwin 2009, pp. 558–61, and Vincent 2014, p. 426.
[13] Irwin 2009 discusses Bradley's critique of Kant at pp. 561–5; see also Vincent 2014, p. 426.
[14] Mander appears to accept Hegel's and Bradley's versions of the "empty objection" without demur; Mander 2011, p. 187. I have of course raised doubts already about the justice of this objection. Irwin criticizes Bradley's version of the empty formalism charge; Irwin 2009, pp. 562–5.

objective and universal" (*ES*, p. 144). But this still does not tell us what in particular to will, either for ourselves or for others. Kant's good will "is the will which is determined by the form only, which realizes itself as the bare form of the will." Of course (Kant recognizes) that as a mere form, the good will has to be filled, and on this approach all that is available to fill it is "an 'empirical' nature, a series of particular states of the 'this me', a mass of desires, aversions, inclinations, passions, pleasures, and pains, what we may call a sensuous self" (*ES*, p. 145), some of which will be selected as compatible with the formality of the good will and others not. But on Bradley's account, this means that the Kantian self is bifurcated into two, an empirical self and "the self which is formal will," and these "elements are antithetical the one to the other" (*ES*, p. 146). This is implicit in Kant's terms "ought" and "duty," which connote one self forcing itself upon the recalcitrant other. Thus this is what is implied by Kant's idea of duty for duty's sake (*ES*, p. 147). There is no adequate account of self-realization to be found down this path.

Bradley finds the theory that acting morally is doing for duty's sake even worse off than has thus far been suggested. To will is necessarily to will *something*, and "To realize means to translate an ideal content into existence, whether it be the existence of a series of events in time only, as in mere psychical acts, or existence both in space and time, as is the case in all outward acts" (*ES*, p. 149). "To act you must will something, and something definite." Thus "To will in general is impossible, and to will in particular is never to will nothing but a form" (*ES*, p. 153). But the idea that the good will wills only itself thus denies the very concept of a will; it contradicts itself, the cardinal sin. Even the explication of willing the good will by avoiding contradiction is "useless," for a contradictory will must contradict something willed, or a non-contradictory will not contradict anything willed; but the idea of a purely formal will denies that there is anything in particular that must not be contradicted. Thus, if "What duty for duty's sake really does is first to posit a determination, such as property, love, courage, &c, and then to say that whatever contradicts these is wrong" (*ES*, p. 156), it may be gaining the necessary content, determinacy, content, or particularity, but only at the cost of undermining its formality. Thus the very idea of "a formal will is self-contradictory" (*ES*, p. 154). This is Bradley's version of the empty formalism charge. As we saw, however, Kant's own application of the requirement to avoid contradiction applies to the conjunction of a *proposed* maxim and its universalization, so it is not liable to this objection. Kant does not *presuppose* some antecedently given good and then tell us not to undermine it; he tells us to consider our own possible maxim and ask whether we could universalize it without undermining it.[15]

---

[15] Irwin does not offer this defense of Kant against Bradley. He rather emphasizes that Kant's approach requires not simply rejection of self-contradiction as such, which is meaningless without something that must not be contradicted, and then argues that "a rational agent as such chooses something more definite than mere consistency in choosing. A rational agent as such chooses to treat

Bradley's own conclusion is that "'duty for duty's sake' says only, 'do the right for the sake of the right', it does not tell us what right is" (*ES*, p. 159). To tell us what right is, he thinks that we need the substantive account of self-realization that is begun, although not completed, in the next essay, on "My Station and Its Duties." The basis of Bradley's positive argument is that what morality requires is self-determination, but that the self is "neither a collection of particular feelings," as is assumed on the hedonistic, utilitarian approach to morality, "nor an abstract universal," as is assumed on the theory that morality simply requires the performance of duty for duty's sake (*ES*, p. 161). Instead, the approach that supersedes these holds that a self is properly a part of a larger social organism, a "moral organism," and that "the self-realization of the whole body" of such an organism "is the self-realization of each member, because the member can not find the function, which makes him himself, apart from the whole to which he belongs. To be himself he must go beyond himself, to live his life he must live a life which is not *merely* his own, but which, none the less, but on the contrary all the more, is intensely and emphatically his own individuality" (*ES*, pp. 162–3). Thus individuals realize themselves by wholeheartedly fulfilling their positions—"stations"—within their society. Not only are the characters of individuals formed by the societies into which they are born and the particulars of their situations—every individual is "born in a family,...lives in a certain society, in a certain state" (*ES*, p. 173)—but their duty is to play their part in the ongoing existence and life of this whole or these concentric, smaller (family) and larger (state) circles. Abstracting for a moment from the various levels of society intermediate between family and state (what is now, following Hegel, often called "civil society"), Bradley states that "we must say that a man's life with its moral duties is in the main filled up by his station in that system of wholes which the state is, and that this, partly by its laws and institutions, and still more by its spirit, gives him the life which he does and ought to live" (*ES*, p. 174).

But the words "in the main" are important in Bradley's dialectical method of exposition, for, forestalling the kind of objection that is often brought against Hegel's apparently complete subsumption of individual freedom into the life of family, civil society, and state in his *Philosophy of Right*, Bradley places two kinds of constraint on the model he has just sketched.[16] First. he argues that morality cannot simply require total identification with the communities into which one is

---

rational agents as ends in themselves rather than simply as means"; Irwin 2009, p. 563. I certainly do not disagree with this, but it needs to be spelled out. I spell it out by equating free rational agency with setting ends freely, and inferring that what Kant requires is consistency with the recognition that all persons have such agency, thus making each choice in a way that is consistent with the possibility of the exercise of free choice by all rational agents, or, of course, all rational agents who might be affected by our own choice.

[16] See Vincent 2014, p. 427, although he puts the point by saying that "the station thesis fails to account for everyday moral struggles, particularly within the individual and between the individual and the community."

born and of which one finds oneself a part, because the communities of which anyone is a member "may be in a confused or rotten condition, so that in it right and might do not always go together" (*ES*, pp. 203–4), in which case the duty of the individual might be to transform his society rather than simply maintain it. Second, Bradley argues that an individual may have other duties, perhaps higher duties, than those to any particular society, to a community that is not "a visible community at all" (*ES*, p. 204). As he develops this objection, Bradley argues that an individual may have duties of self-perfection that do not directly impact or benefit others, such as the duty to pursue an art or science, and that such duties are fully part of morality, which might conflict with other moral duties, as duties can, but which are none the less genuinely moral duties.[17]

Bradley amplifies the first constraint in a variety of ways: even the best community can in fact assure correspondence between the interests of the individual and of the whole only "in the gross," not "in every single detail," and ultimately the larger community may require the sacrifice of the individual in a way that can never be convincingly described as fully in the interest of the individual even on the most elevated conception of individual identity. Nevertheless, individuals must reflect on the position of their communities in history, and realize that development is required and try to move that along; and people must also consider what Bradley calls "cosmopolitan community," and not only develop a "notion of goodness not of any particular time and country" but also reach out beyond their own communities to other human beings in practice (*ES*, pp. 204–5). Second, Bradley argues that "the content of the ideal self does not fall wholly within any community, is in short *not* merely the ideal of a perfect social being. The making myself perfect does not always directly involve relation to others." Specifically, "The production of truth and beauty (together with what is called 'culture') may be recognized as a duty; and it will be very hard to reduce it in all cases to a duty of any station that I can see" or a direct duty to benefit others (*ES*, p. 205). Bradley will have none of what we might call a Pufendorfian argument that the function of duties to oneself is always that of improving one's ability to serve others;[18] in fact, he is agreeing with Kant that there are direct and not merely instrumental duties of self-perfection. Kant characterizes such duties as duties to perfect one's own faculties or capacities, not just one's moral capacities but one's physical and mental capacities more generally. Bradley puts them in terms of pursuing objects, such as truth, beauty, and culture, but that will of course require the development of the same faculties Kant had in mind. Either way, the underlying assumption is that the duty to perfect or "realize" humanity in one's own person or that of any other, as Kant puts it, certainly includes duties to directly or indirectly benefit others, but also includes the duty to realize one's own

---

[17] See Mander 2011, pp. 190–1.   [18] See Pufendorf 2003, book I, chapter V, paragraph I, p. 70.

potential in ways that may not directly benefit anyone else. The conclusion of the essay on "My Station and Its Duties" thus brings Bradley's position closer to Kant's final position than may initially have seemed possible, and closer than Bradley himself may have acknowledged.

In the following essay of *Ethical Studies*, on "Ideal Morality," Bradley recognizes that there can be conflict between the duty to pursue a personal end like an art or science and duties to benefit others. Such conflicts are not contests "between the claims of morality and of something else not morality," but rather collisions of duty within morality like any other collisions of duties (*ES*, p. 225). Anticipating the position more recently called "particularism,"[19] Bradley argues that morality does not provide any rules or algorithms for the resolution of such collisions: "The difficulties of collisions are not scientific problems; they arise from the complexity of individual cases, and this can be dealt with solely by practical insight, not by abstract conceptions and discursive reasoning" (*ES*, p. 225). In other words, dealing with collisions of duties always requires judgment by individuals about the particular circumstances confronting them. In this, Bradley might seem to disagree with Kant, whose distinction between perfect and imperfect duties might be thought to resolve all such collisions by means of lexical ordering: perfect duties seem always to trump imperfect duties, thus you cannot murder someone to get a cadaver for your anatomical drawing practice, nor can you take the money that you need to repay debt to buy art supplies for yourself; and even within the sphere of imperfect duties, it might seem that there is a clear lexical ordering, with duties to your children trumping all others, duties to your more extended family trumping obligations to strangers, and so on. Kant does famously assert that there can be no collisions of duty, only conflicting grounds of obligation, thus implying that in any case there is always one and only one thing that it is right to do (see Kant, *MM*, Introduction, section III, 6: 224). But he does not actually demonstrate that there can never be conflicts among perfect duties, or that imperfect duties are sufficiently well-defined to ensure that they can always be lexically ordered; after all, they are imperfect precisely because judgment is necessary to determine when, how, and how far they can be fulfilled. On this issue, Bradley's position, although not explicitly formulated as a criticism of Kant, may be wiser than Kant's.

But the larger point of the chapter on "Ideal Morality" can be seen as a major concession to Kant. For what Bradley argues is that "the greater part" of one's "better self" consists in one's "loyally, and according to the spirit, performing his duties and filling his place as the member of a family, society, and the state" (*ES*, p. 220), or willing to fulfill one's various duties, other-regarding and self-regarding as they may be, as parts of what it is to strive for a good will as such.

---

[19] Associated especially with the work of Jonathan Dancy, e.g. Dancy 2004.

Morality then will be the realization of the self as the good will. It is not self-realization from all points of view, though all self-realization can be looked at from this one point of view; for all of it involves will, and so far as the will is good, so far is the realization moral. Strictly speaking and in the proper sense, morality is self-realization within the sphere of the personal will. We see this plainly in art and science, for there we have moral excellence, and that excellence does not lie in mere skill or mere success, but in single-mindedness and devotion to what seems best as against what we merely happen to like.... From the highest point of view you judge [a] man moral not so far as he has succeeded outwardly, but so far as he has identified his will with the universal, whether that will has properly externalized itself or not. (*ES*, pp. 228–9)

Thus, Bradley reaches the Kantian starting-point, "Nothing... is good but a good will." But his interpretation of this is not what Kant initially means by it, but more like what he means when his formulations of the categorical imperative culminate in the Formula of the Empire of Ends: "The end for morals is not the mere existence of any sort of ideal indifferently, but it is the realization of an ideal will in my will. The end is the ideal willed by me, the willing of the ideal in and by my will, and hence an ideal will" (*ES*, p. 230). Only the individual can will, even if what he wills is to be part of something larger than himself. And without the will to be moral, what seems like outward success in the fulfillment of duties counts for nothing moral—this is of course pure Kant—while with such a will, failures to fulfill specific duties or to resolve collisions of duties in a way that others or even oneself subsequently might think best are not moral failures. Even when we have no mechanical way of resolving conflicts of duties, morality is always within our reach if we have a good will. Thus, in spite of his initial argument that the notion of duty for duty's sake is an empty formalism, and must be supplemented by a substantive conception of self-realization, Bradley ends up affirming Kant's position that when it comes to moral appraisal, a good will is both the necessary and the sufficient condition of moral goodness.

It remains unclear just how much of a concession to Kant Bradley thought that he was making in his theory of self-realization and his argument that a good will is the essence of personal morality. In a footnote to the chapter on "Duty for Duty's Sake" (a note already present in the first edition), he had acknowledged that the model of duty for duty's sake that he was there attacking is "not a statement of the Kantian view," which is "far wider," but, he had continued, "and at the same time more confused" (*ES*, p. 148). That does not suggest that he was preparing the way for an ultimate reconciliation with Kant. But other British idealists, for all the Hegelian aspects of their thought, did think that there were deep affinities between their moral thought and that of Kant. T. H, Green thought that his version of perfectionism was Kantian as well as Hegelian, and Edward Caird thought that Kant himself had overcome the empty formalism of his first formulation of the categorical imperative by the second and third formulations, the third especially— that of the empire of ends—making way for an organic conception of the larger whole to which individuals belong (even if, as Bradley has argued, the duties connected with membership in an empire of ends cannot be reduced to other-regarding duties, not to hurt or to benefit others). So let us now turn to those authors.

12.2. Green

Thomas Hill Green (1836–82) was six years older than Bradley. Green had made his mark in 1874, with a lengthy critique of empiricism as the introduction to an edition of the works of Hume. But the work for which he is now best known, the *Prolegomena to Ethics*, was published only posthumously in 1883, based on lectures that Green had given as Oxford Whyte's Professor of Moral Philosophy, the chair he held from 1878 to his premature death in 1882. Both the lectures and the publication thus succeeded the younger Bradley's *Ethical Studies*, and for that reason it makes sense to consider Green's response to Kant's moral philosophy after Bradley's rather than before. This also makes sense because, while Bradley considered the idealist ethics of individual self-realization as part of a larger whole as a critique of Kant, Green was clearer that this approach was rather a develop-ment of at least one aspect of Kant's own moral philosophy. Henry Sidgwick went so far as to state that Green is—"avowedly"—"a disciple of Kant." And Terence Irwin writes in turn that "it is reasonable to regard Green as basically a Kantian; this is how Sidgwick interprets both his metaphysics and his ethics."[20]

While Bradley published *Ethical Studies* before publishing his metaphysics in *Appearance and Reality* and presented his position as a dialectical development of common ethical intuitions rather than as depending upon metaphysical founda-tions, Green's *Prolegomena to Ethics* contains its own prolegomena, two initial books on the "Metaphysics of Knowledge" and "The Will" that prepare the way for two further books on "The Moral Ideal" and the "Practical Value" of this ideal. Under the rubric of the "Metaphysics of Knowledge" (book 1), Green argues that all knowledge of nature is itself non-natural, an "eternal consciousness" in which natural, biological human beings participate or which each partially realizes but which cannot be fully realized in any one individual and cannot even be reduced to a collection of the individual consciousnesses that exist at any one time or that

---

[20] Sidgwick 1902, p. 15; Irwin 2009, p. 582. See also Vincent 2014, p. 428. On the moral philosophy of Green, see Lamont 1934; Irwin 1984 and Irwin 2009, pp. 581–624; Thomas 1987; Dimova-Cookson 2001; Brink 2003; papers by David Brink, Skorupski, Irwin, and Andrew Vincent in Dimova-Cookson and Mander 2006; Simonhy 2009; Mander 2011, pp. 195–208, and Mander 2016, pp. 155–65; and Skorupski 2021, pp. 440–58. Irwin 2009 discusses Green's proximity to Kant at pp. 581–2, 597–602, and 622–4.

have existed up to any one time.[21] This metaphysical conception prepares the way for a moral conception of individual human beings as realizing themselves only as part of a larger community, but one which is never fully realized and thus always leaves room for moral progress. Green's argument begins with a premise explicitly inspired by Kant, which is the gist of his critique of empiricism, namely that consciousness does not consist of immediately given data or simple ideas, but of relations among data that must be constituted by mind. In particular, an individual, Green supposes, does not conflate experience or knowledge with whatever limited subset of possible relations among objects she might herself actually recognize, but instead "conceives a single and unalterable order of relations determining them, with which its temporary presentation, as each experience occurs, of the relations determining it may be contrasted" (PE, p. 17). In Green's view, "experience, in the sense of a consciousness of events as a related series—and in no other sense can it help to account for the knowledge of an order of nature—cannot be explained by any natural history, properly so called" (PE, p. 23), because no event in the series of natural causes and events can count as a representation of the relation of cause and effect that binds that series together.[22] (As Kant and Hume actually share the premise that the relation of necessary connection is never directly given among our impressions of objects, so on this point Green's thought too is not as different from that of his bête noire Hume as might initially appear.) Green further argues that experience or consciousness of relations cannot be equated with "the incidents of an individual life which is but for a day," and must "rather...be sought in the unity of its object as presented to all men, and in the continuity of all experience in regard to that object" (PE, p. 53). And "all" cannot mean "all who currently exist" or "all who have existed until now," because surely the reality of objects is not confined to the present or the past plus the immediate present. Objects and therefore the collective consciousness that constitutes them must be something that transcends the past and present and carries on into the future, as far as we can imagine. This is what Green calls the "eternal consciousness," or "eternally complete consciousness" (PE, p. 77).[23]

Green does not want to call this consciousness "supernatural" because that would be "misleading," suggesting "a relation between it and nature of a kind which has really no place except *within* nature." He presumably means that we would be tempted to model the relation between natural and supernatural on a relation like that between microscopic and macroscopic or between physical and chemical within nature (PE, p. 61). A "relation which...exists only in the medium of consciousness, only between certain objects as they are for consciousness,

---

[21] There is a good summary of Green's metaphysical presuppositions at Vincent 2014, p. 429.

[22] On this as the key premise of Green's opposition to naturalism, see Skorupski 2021, p. 445.

[23] As Irwin 2009 puts it, "The relevant self-conscious subject cannot be you or me, since the world is independent of finite substances"; p. 583. See also Nicholson 2006.

cannot be a relation between consciousness and anything else" (*PE*, p. 69). Instead, he says, "We are most safe in calling it spiritual, because...we are warranted in thinking of it as a self-distinguishing consciousness" (*PE*, p. 61), a consciousness that distinguishes itself from nature. At the same time, Green does not want to deny that human beings are finite, mortal, biological organisms: writing after Darwin, after all, he has no intention of reviving a pre-modern conception of personal immortality. Instead, he proposes, the individual acquisition of knowledge "can only be explained by supposing that in the growth of our [individual] experience, in the process of our learning to know the world, an animal organism, which has its history in time, gradually becomes the vehicle of an eternally complete consciousness" (*PE*, p. 77). The eternal consciousness is "realised or communicated to us" as individuals "through modification of the animal organism," which thereby comes into relation "with the relations, characteristic of knowledge, into which time does not enter, which are not in becoming, but are once and for all what they are" (*PE*, p. 78). But the knowledge of any particular person or people is precisely always in becoming and not yet once and for all everything it might be.

This is the metaphysical model of the relation between the individual and the human entirety that Green will transpose from a theoretical into a practical key as the foundation of his ethics. But before he does that, he also exploits his conception of the non-natural and spiritual to make room for a conception of freedom of the will. Insofar as human consciousness is "the self-realisation or reproduction...through processes...empirically conditioned, of an eternal consciousness" that does not exist "in time but" is "the condition of there being an order in time," it is not determined *by* that order. "In virtue of his character as knowing, therefore, we are entitled to say that man is, according to a certain well-defined meaning of the term, a 'free cause'" (*PE*, p. 85). We might think of Green as relying on a negative definition of freedom, as freedom from determination by natural, temporal causality, trusting that the reader will not annoyingly ask for a more positive or direct conception of what this freedom is like apart from the specification of its ideal object or goal, to be supplied in due course. Indeed, Green relieves himself of any burden of explaining the nature of freedom precisely by means of his distinction between the natural and the non-natural: any explanation of how freedom works would be an explanation of "Why any detail of the world is what is...by reference to other details which determine it," which is precisely what freedom precludes. "Why the whole should be what it is, why the mind which the world implies should exhibit itself in a world at all, why it should make certain processes of that world organic to a reproduction of itself under limitations which the use of such organics involves—these are questions which, owing perhaps to those very limitations, we are equally unable to avoid asking and to answer" (*PE*, p. 93). In other words, freedom is necessarily inexplicable. Green does not want to take over Kant's distinction, or an interpretation of Kant's distinction, between noumena and phenomena as two different sets of objects or realms of being, but he does want to exploit Kant's view that freedom positively conceived is inscrutable, or perhaps that freedom cannot be positively conceived except by the moral law or ideal that, it will subsequently be shown, it aims to realize.

In spite of such a limitation, Green quickly generalizes his account from one of freedom in cognition to freedom in action more generally, stating that "Human action is only explicable by the action of an eternal consciousness, which uses them"—"all the processes of brain and nerve and tissue, all the functions of life and sense, organic to this activity (even though they, as in the thinking man, cannot, for reasons given, properly be held to be merely natural)"—"as its organ and reproduces itself through them" (PE, p. 93). The key to Green's distinction between the theoretical and the practical is a Kantian distinction between knowledge as the realization of what it *is* and action as aiming at what *ought to be*, now applied within the domain of "wants" itself. The "animal system is not organic merely to feeling of the kind just spoken of as receptive, to *impressions*, according to the natural meaning of that term, conveyed by the nerves of the several senses," but it "is organic also to *wants*, and to impulses for the satisfaction of those wants, which may be in many cases occasioned by impressions of the kind mentioned, but which constitute quite a different function of the animal system" (PE, p. 97): that is, there are empirical, immediately given wants or desires, just as there are empirically given impressions or sensations. But just as the latter do not by themselves constitute knowledge, but rather constitute knowledge only when they are taken up into a system of relations that only the eternal consciousness can constitute, so does there "supervene...upon the succession of wants a consciousness—not a succession—of wanted objects," a "consciousness which yields...the conception of something that *should be* as distinct from that which *is*, a world of practice as distinct from that world of experience" (PE, p. 99). In the first instance, this might just be an individual's conception of some satisfiable set of his own wants (a conception that invariably turns out to be one of a satisfiable subset of one's own wants, since even one's own wants will include mutually exclusive ones), but ultimately it will be a conception of what should be that transcends individual desires.

Here lies the basis for the polemic that Green, like Bradley, conducted with utilitarianism, and that leads instead to an ethics of self-realization, but realization of an extended self.[24] For just as genuine knowledge of the world is not merely a chain or sum of impressions, so a genuine conception of what should be cannot be a conception of the satisfaction of a mere summation of particular wants or desires. Green's argument can be reduced to two main steps. First, he argues that the individual strives for satisfaction of more than just a sum of desires; he strives to realize a unified or coherent self that has desires. But second, the

---

[24] See Irwin 2009, pp. 593–7; Mander 2011, pp. 201–8; and Mander 2016, pp. 158–61.

coherence or unity at which the individual aims is not just coherence among his own desires, or even among a larger domain including not just desires but also his knowledge, his capacities, and so on; rather, the individual aims, at least insofar as he forms a coherent conception of consciously aiming at all, at "the perfection of human life" in general, "some organization of society in which the individual is a perfectly adjusted means to an end which he is not in himself," or not *merely* in himself (*PE*, p. 207). The first stage of this argument is still made in book 2, on the will, where Green argues that, just as experience is not merely the passive receipt of impressions, but a coherent relation among impressions which must be "enacted," or which can only be produced by the activity of a mind, so must the object of the will be not merely the gratification of whatever desires happen to come along, but rather "the direction of a self-conscious subject to the realisation of an idea" (*PE*, p. 172), namely the idea of a unified subject itself. Green sums up the first stage of his argument thus:

> If it is a genuine definition that we want of what is common to all acts of willing, we must say that such an act is one in which a self-conscious individual directs himself to the realisation of some idea, as to an object in which for the time he seeks self-satisfaction. Such being an act of willing, the will in actuality must be the self-conscious individual as so directing himself, while the will in possibility, or as a faculty, will be the self-conscious individual as capable of directing himself.   (*PE*, p. 174)

This is a highly formal or abstract account of willing: it aims at "self-satisfaction," or as Green will subsequently characterize it, a state in which a self-conscious self can "rest," can be content, in other words, need not further will. To flesh out this abstract idea without lapsing into utilitarianism—equating self-satisfaction with the satisfaction of a maximally compossible set of passively received desires—is the challenge for Green (or, although he does not mention this, lapsing into Schopenhauer's asceticism). His basic strategy for accomplishing this is to see the individual as finding self-satisfaction or "rest" not in the mere satisfaction of his own desires but in his contribution to the establishment of an enduring human community that satisfies all: "In the broad result it is not hard to understand how man has bettered himself through institutions and habits which tend to make the welfare of all the welfare of each, and through the arts which make nature, both as used and as contemplated, the friend of man" (*PE*, p. 197). This simple statement makes two distinct claims: that self-satisfaction depends on the satisfaction of more than one's individual self, and that self-satisfaction requires more than just welfare, more than just the satisfaction of obvious physical and emotional needs, but includes the development of the arts through which nature is "contemplated" as well as "used," that is, the development of the whole range of human capacities or potential, not just the human capacities that can be used as means to secure adequate food, shelter, sex, and so on. (To continue the contrast with Schopenhauer, Green's model of supra-individual satisfaction is analogous to the underlying metaphysics of Schopenhauer's ethics of compassion, but Green believes that individuals can contribute more to the whole than the mere temporary alleviation of suffering.)

The claim that individuals can and should contribute to the satisfaction of a larger whole than themselves depends on Green's metaphysics as unfolded in his epistemological prolegomenon, that is, his theory of the individual human organism as a genuine self only insofar as it is part of a larger community. Green makes this clear:

> We saw reason to hold that the existence of one connected world, which is the presupposition of knowledge, implies the action of one self-conditioning and self-determining mind; and that, as our knowledge, so our moral activity was only explicable on supposition of a certain reproduction of itself, on the part of this eternal mind, as the self of man—'a reproduction of itself to which it makes the processes of animal life organic, and which is qualified and limited by the nature of those processes, but which is so far essentially a reproduction of the one supreme subject, implied in the existence of the world, that the product carries with it under all its limitations and qualifications the characteristic of being an object to itself.'   (*PE*, p. 198, quoting from an earlier passage in the work, p. 110)

The second part of Green's claim, that satisfaction for all of us, not just for our biologically individual and separate selves, will be found only in the development of all our capacities, not just practical but also theoretical (and, as Bradley had argued, even aesthetic), comes simply from generalization of what ordinary human beings want to what the comprehensive supra-individual collectivity of human beings or the eternal consciousness must want. As the individual reflects on himself he realizes that he wants more than satisfaction of merely natural desires—"It is in virtue of this self-objectifying principle that he is determined, not simply by natural wants according to natural laws, but by the thought of himself as existing under certain conditions, and as having ends that may be attained and capabilities that may be realised under those conditions" (*PE*, p. 199)—and then he realizes that the larger self of which his biological organism is only a part, or which his biological organism only partially realizes, must want the development of all these capacities for all human beings, not just for his own biological organism or any other particular biological organism.

Green does not want to end up arguing that individual human beings are ultimately to be superseded or sacrificed by something other than human beings; so having stated his conception of the moral ideal in these abstract terms, he turns around and makes it clear that what he means is that human beings are not truly satisfied or "at rest" with the satisfaction of merely self-regarding desires. Rather,

"They are interested in each other *as persons* in so far as each, being aware that another presents his own self-satisfaction to himself as an object, finds satisfaction for himself in procuring or witnessing the self satisfaction of the other. Society is founded on such mutual interest" (*PE*, p. 218). This line could have been written by a sentimentalist such as Adam Smith. Perhaps to avoid the collapse of his position into an empirically based sentimentalism, Green adds that "the converse is equally true, that only through society . . . is personality actualised" (*PE*, p. 218). His claim is not merely that as a matter of fact human beings are satisfied with the satisfaction of other human beings, but that human personality is developed only in society, so it could not be otherwise than that human beings need others to be satisfied in order to be satisfied themselves: it is an essential rather than accidental feature of human psychology. But also, like the Bradley who moves beyond the standpoint of "My Station and Its Duties," Green does not want to accept that human beings should merely accept the mores of their current society because that society fixes the limits of their personality. Rather, human "self-objectifying" self-consciousness includes the capacity to envision a better society than anyone's current society, a society in which more human capacities rather than fewer are developed by more rather than fewer people. For example, a member of Victorian society (like himself) is capable of realizing that it is not yet a satisfactory society, one with which anyone should rest content, because such a society has not yet "reached a stage in which the proper and equal sacredness of all women, as self-determining and self-respecting persons, could be understood" (*PE*, p. 316). Green's vision of the social identity of individuals allows for criticism of contemporary society because the society that constitutes the identity of individuals is possible as much as actual—this was implicit in his original definition of will, and how he negotiates the transition from the natural to the normative.

So far this account of Green's moral philosophy has said nothing of Kant, and indeed an explicit treatment of Kant that may have been part of Green's intention for the work (see *PE*, p. 177) was not included in the material that he left behind (see *PE*, Preface, p. cxvi). But that he conceived of his own view as a development from Kant's rather than an outright rejection of it becomes apparent at various points. For example, following the plea for the recognition of the full personality of women that has just been quoted, Green continues by arguing that a society in which women are not extended equal respect and equal rights with men is one "not in a state in which the principle that humanity in the person of every one is to be treated always as an end, never merely as a means, could be apprehended in its full universality; and it is this principle alone, however it may be stated, which affords a rational ground for the obligation to chastity as we understand it" (*PE*, p. 316). Although Green does not adequately explain why only chastity—presumably he means chastity outside of marriage, since he raises no objection to marriage and was himself married—rather than their genuinely free consent to any sexual interaction should be the necessary condition for treating women as ends and not merely as means, any more than Kant himself successfully explains the derivation of some of his own strictures on sexual activity from his general principles, the allusion to Kant's Formula of Humanity and a recognition of it as the basis of a Kantian approach to moral philosophy in general is unmistakable.[25] More fully, the following passage makes clear that Green considers his own position a version of Kant's; as the center point of the central chapter on "The Characteristics of the Moral Ideal" in the central book on "The Moral Ideal and Moral Progress," this might even be regarded as the central passage of the entire *Prolegomena to Ethics*:

> If there is a progress in the history of men it must be towards an end consisting in a state of being which is not itself a series in time, but is both comprehended eternally in the eternal mind and is intrinsically, or in itself, eternal. Further: although any other capacity may be of a kind which, having done its work in contributing to the attainment of such a state of being, passes away in the process of its attainment—as the particular capacities of myriads of animals, their function fulfilled, pass away every hour—yet a capacity consisting in a self-conscious personality cannot be supposed so to pass away. It partakes of the nature of the eternal. It is not itself a series in time; for the series of time exists for it. We cannot believe in there being a real fulfilment of such a capacity in an end which should involve its extinction, because the conviction of there being an end in which our capacities are fulfilled is founded on our self-conscious personality—on the idea of an absolute value in a spirit which we ourselves are. And for the same reason we cannot believe that the capacities of men—capacities illustrated to us by the actual institutions of society, though they could not be so illustrated if we had not an independent idea of them—can be really fulfilled in a state of things in which any rational man should be treated as a means, and not as in himself an end. On the whole, our conclusion must be that, great as are the difficulties which beset the idea of human development when applied to the facts of life, we do not escape them but empty the idea of any real meaning, if we suppose the end of the development to be one in the attainment of which persons—agents who are ends to themselves—are extinguished, or one which is other than a state of self-conscious being, or one in which that reconciliation of the claims of persons, as each at once a means to the good of others and an end to himself, already partially achieved in the higher forms of human society, is otherwise than completed. (*PE*, p. 217)

Two important things happen in this passage. For one, Green makes it plain, in a way that Bradley did not, that his perfectionist or self-realization conception of

---

[25] "Green's concentration on the Formula of Humanity departs from Hegel and Bradley"; Irwin 2009, p. 599.

morality can be regarded as an extension of Kantian morality, in which the Formula of Humanity's requirement that each, oneself and others, always be treated as an end and never merely as a means, is the foundation of morality, and that the Empire of Ends, a condition in which each is treated as an end and *therefore* the particular ends of each are also treated as ends for all, the condition realized if indeed each is really at once a means to the good of others and an end to himself, is the moral ideal, the object of the will that properly follows from its commitment to the Formula of Humanity.[26] But the first part of this passage also suggests that Green is worrying about Kant's doctrine of the Postulates of Pure Practical Reason, in particular trying to avoid any objection that the possibility of morality might be supposed to rest on a primitive conception of personal immortality. Instead, Green is trying to argue that his own conception of individual consciousness as always a part and participant in eternal consciousness, which does not exist in (unnaturally) extended time but is rather the condition of the possibility of the consciousness of time itself, already supplies the proper subject of morality as well as of experience and knowledge. On such an approach, the idea of personal immortality does not have to be added on to the basic principles of Kantian morality. Rather, the idea that the full range of human capacities can only be realized in something larger than any individual is part of the doctrine from the start. And "can only" includes "can": that is, any condition of rationality according to which it is rational to strive for the full realization of human capacities if there is adequate reason to believe that such realization is possible is satisfied by the theory from the outset. Human consciousness, even when considered only from a theoretical standpoint, has already included the idea of an eternal consciousness; this has been present in the moral theory throughout, and therefore need not be regarded as an arbitrary addition to the moral theory.[27]

---

[26] Irwin argues for the superiority of Kant over Green when he writes that "Green and Bradley say too little about how morality allows me to recognize my ends in the ends of others", while "according to a Kantian conception, morality does not require the subordination of myself to a larger whole; it involves my acceptance of principles that I can see are appropriate to rational agents who deserve to be recognized as such. In so far as I regard other people as ends, I regard their ends as my ends"; Irwin 2009, pp. 622–3. This seems unfair to Green, whose whole argument is that individual self-realization is possible only as part of the self-realization of humanity as a whole; it is correct that a Kantian conception does not require the *subordination* of the individual to a larger whole, and also correct to imply that the larger whole—in Kant's terms, the empire of ends—does not have any ends of its own beyond the ends of individuals. It should be stressed that Kant's conception of the relation of individuals to the whole is that of membership on equal terms: at law each should have as much freedom to set her own ends as anyone else, and in ethics the ends of each are as worthy of promotion as the ends of any other, subject to the requirement of mutual compatibility. Skorupski implies this point about Kant when he writes that "the ethical notion of *impartiality* does not play the foundational role for [Green] that it plays for Kant and Mill. Instead, the important notion [for Green] is that of the *common good*"; Skorupski 2021, p. 449.

[27] So Irwin's statement that "Green inherits from Kant the difficulty of explaining the connexion between regarding oneself as an end and regarding rational agency in general as an end" (Irwin 2009, p. 599) is also a little misleading: for Green, this is a problem resolved by his metaphysics of the self

It seems clear that in this passage Green is not only acknowledging the Kantian inspiration of his normative moral theory but also implying that his own meta-physics, also Kantian in its starting-point although going beyond Kant in its argument that eternal consciousness (and not just unity of apperception) is the condition of the possibility of experience itself, solves one of the traditional problems with Kantian moral philosophy, namely the problematic pretensions of the doctrine of the postulates. But let us now try to compensate for the fact that Green did not live to write the explicit response to Kant that he intended to include in the *Prolegomena* by looking at his actual lectures on Kant, which were also included in his posthumous *Works*.

The material on Kant printed in the second posthumous volume of Green's work (1886) comes from courses given at various dates, the material on the *Critique of Pure Reason* stemming from lectures he gave while still a tutor at Balliol, around 1874–5, while the material on Kant's moral philosophy comes from the lectures he gave as White's Professor, thus from 1878 on. (In this material Green used translations from T. K. Abbott, which appeared in 1879.) Green's approach to Kant is far more sympathetic than Bradley's was: his aim is to show that apparent objections to Kant, in the first instance to his theory of freedom of the will and above all the charge of empty formalism against the categorical imperative, can be resolved, and indeed resolved by a conception of the perfection of the self as object of the will to be found in both Kant and Green's own philosophy. His interpretation of Kant culminates in the claim that the self that is the object of the free and autonomous will can only be the self as a member of the *Reich der Zwecke* or, as he translates it, following Abbott, the "kingdom of ends" (*LK*, p. 146). But this is to imply that Kant ultimately had the same idea as Green himself, namely that the foundation of morality is that the identity of the individual human agent is constituted only along with its membership in the eternal community of humans, or to imply that Green's own idea is an interpre-tation of Kant's.

Green's lectures (or at least the posthumously published version of them) start with Kant's treatment of freedom of the will, although it might seem as if this is an issue that could have followed the discussion of the normative concepts of Kant's moral philosophy that comes only later. But the idea that Green sees as central to the success of Kant's theory of free will is also the basis for both Kant's and his own normative moral philosophy, so it makes sense for him to have started where he did. This is the idea of the self as a unity constituted by our own power of reason as the object of willing, rather than mere desires. This idea of the object of willing explains how there can be free will that falls short of truly moral willing, because

before he even begins discussing ethics, while for Kant the key to moral philosophy is not to regard "rational agency in general as an end" but to regard free rational agency *in all its instances* as an end for all rational agents.

the idea of self that is the object of an agent's will might not yet be the perfected idea of the self as part of the empire of ends. But this idea of the object of willing also provides the foundation for Kant's and Green's normative ethics, namely the idea of the perfected self.[28]

Green is actually concerned with two potential problems in Kant's theory of free will, first that the noumenal will that is the locus for freedom as opposed to the causally determined phenomenal actions of an agent might be located in an ontologically mysterious realm behind the screen of the phenomenal world, and second that, however that metaphysical issue might be resolved, the only free self must be the truly autonomous or morally perfected self, so that there can be no possibility of free yet immoral action—in other words, the problem first identified by Ulrich in 1788 (and to receive renewed attention in an article by Henry Sidgwick published in *Mind* two years after Green's lectures, better remembered than Ulrich's earlier objection).[29] Green's solution to the first threat is to argue that the proper locus of responsibility is the *character* of the agent, which cannot be identified with any of its particular acts at particular places and times, and is always a manifestation of the agent's faculty of reason, however ill or well developed, but is also not located in some mysterious realm outside of space and time. According to Green, Kant "did not mean that the same man had two characters, but that one and the same character (in the ordinary sense of the word), i.e. series of acts (inner as well as outer), was related at once to an intelligible cause consisting in reason, and to a series of empirical causes consisting of other phenomena" (*LK*, p. 101). The gist of his approach, in other words, is that we can accept the Kantian idea that willing is founded in the exercise of reason without committing ourselves to the existence of a separate realm of noumena, which no post-Kantian idealist wants to do. In his interpretation of Kant's practical as well as his theoretical philosophy, Green wants to argue for the intellectual constitution of the world of objects, in the first case the constitution of mere sensations into a world of objective experience that does exist and in the second case the constitution of desires into an objective world that ought to exist, without insisting upon a dualistic ontology of phenomena and noumena. As W. J. Mander puts this point in his discussion of Green, "so the issues of whether or not there is a prior cause or of what kind it may be, fall away as beside the point—we move out of the realm of causal explanation altogether."[30]

Whether Green could succeed in thus defanging Kant's ontology may be open to question. But his solution to the problem of the possibility of free yet immoral action may be less controversial. Like Sidgwick a few years later, Green argues that

[28] On Kant's moral philosophy as a form of perfectionism in spite of his specific criticism of Wolff's and Baumgarten's version of perfectionism, see Guyer 2011a.

[29] Henry Sidgwick, "The Kantian Conception of Free Will," *Mind* 13 (1888), reprinted in Sidgwick 1907, pp. 511–16.

[30] Mander 2011, p. 197.

there are two senses of freedom in Kant, in his terms a "formal" sense in which freedom is the ability to either perform or refrain from a given action and another sense, substantive rather than formal, in which freedom is "autonomy in Kant's sense (as = a state in which [an agent] is determined by a conception of himself as giver of universal law)" (*LK*, p. 109). Green argues that the paradox that if freedom is equated with autonomy than a "vicious act is not free" can be avoided by recognizing that Kant uses freedom in two different senses:

> Was Kant's view that, although the vicious act is not free, yet a man is free to do it or not to do it; that he freely submits to the loss of freedom, the bondage of heteronomy? In such a view, freedom is used in two senses. The submission could not be said to be rationally determined in Kant's sense; therefore the man does not *freely* submit in this sense of freedom; whereas the loss of freedom to which the vicious man submits is the loss of it in the sense of rational determination. I think there is this double meaning of freedom in Kant.   (*LK*, pp. 107–8)

(Sidgwick would subsequently distinguish these two senses of freedom as "Neutral or Moral" freedom, that is, slightly misleadingly, the ability to choose either what is morally right or not which makes one a subject of moral evaluation in general, and "Good or Rational" freedom, that is, the exercise of freedom in accordance with impartial reason which makes one subject to moral commendation in particular.[31]) For Green, both the virtuous and vicious exercise of freedom in the first sense can count as exercises of freedom because willing is never simply acting on impulse, rather even the vicious agent has as his object not just the satisfaction of some particular desire but the realization of a certain conception of his self, just not as advanced or perfected a conception of self as the virtuous agent has. Making a conception of oneself the object of will is the essence of freedom in the sense of a capacity: "A man not merely acts so as to satisfy himself (probably he does not so act), but his act is determined by the idea of himself as the object for the sake of which the act is done, and for that reason he imputes it to himself, and is *in this sense* really free" (*LK*, pp. 108–9); but this conception of himself need not be the conception of himself as a giver of universal law along with others in an empire of ends, and thus it is possible to act freely yet viciously, as well as to act freely and virtuously. In acting freely, one does not simply seek to gratify some impulse or desire, but rather evinces a conception of oneself as the kind of person who thinks that such a desire should be gratified. Yet one might still have a selfish

---

[31] Sidgwick, "Kantian Conception of Free Will," p. 512. In his *Lectures on Green*, Sidgwick states that in the *Prolegomena* Green tried to avoid the danger of confusion between the two senses of freedom by using the term only in the sense of what Sidgwick calls neutral freedom (Sidgwick 1902, pp. 15–16). He obviously did not have in mind Green's discussion in his lectures on Kant of the two senses of freedom; Green's *Collected Works* containing the lectures were published from 1885 to 1888, the year in which Sidgwick published his article, but Sidgwick could well not yet have read them when he wrote his piece.

conception of the self to be realized, one that ignores others or pits itself against them, or conversely, one might have a conception of oneself as part of the kingdom of ends, with particular desires to be gratified only insofar as they fit into that larger conception of self. Green writes, "It is through reason that man conceives himself as the object of his actions, but the reason is imperfectly communicated to him so far as he has no true conception of what the self is which he seeks to satisfy." *This* freedom, not yet autonomy, is nevertheless "the condition of autonomy" (*LK*, p. 109). Green's solution to the problem of free yet vicious action might be thought to be a kind of intellectualism or Socratism: an agent is free insofar as he acts, through his reason, in accordance with a conception of himself as the object to be realized, but he may have a truer or false conception of that self that is to be realized.

The idea of the object of the will as a conception of the self is also the basis of Green's approach to the other traditional problem for Kant's moral philosophy that he takes up, namely the threat that the categorical imperative is merely an empty formalism. Green does not mention the name of Hegel, let alone that of Pistorious, as the originator of this charge, but he does indicate that he is concerned with what "the exponents of Kant call 'duty for duty's sake'" (*LK*, p. 111). As we saw, that was the rubric under which Bradley discussed the empty formalism objection, so there seems little room for doubt that this is what Green is worried about.[32] His response is that "the universal practical law on which Kant insists is unintelligible except as implying an object unconditionally good to which it is relative. It has no content, it prescribes nothing, except what is relative to this object" (*LK*, p. 111); but it does have such an object, characterized first as the good will, then as humanity as an end in itself, and finally as the empire of ends in which humanity is recognized and treated as an end in itself in all humans. The key to this solution, Green argues, is that

> when Kant excludes all reference to an object, of which the reality is desired, from the law of which the mere idea determines the good will, he means all reference to an object *other than of which* the presentation *ipso facto* consists the moral law. That in that law, the willing obedience to which characterises a good will, there is implied some reference to an object, and that this object moves the will in the right sort of obedience to the law, appears from his account of man as an absolute end, on which he founds the second statement of the categorical imperative.   (*LK*, p. 131)

Green does not cite a Kantian text in support of this interpretation, but he easily could have: Kant himself asserts that "Practical principles are *formal* if they

---

[32] See also Mander 2011, p. 203.

abstract from all subjective ends, whereas they are *material* if they have put these, and consequently certain incentives, as their basis" just before he introduces his Formula of Humanity as the "ground of a possible categorical imperative" (*G*, 4: 428), and thus implies that the principle always to treat humanity, whether in one's own person or that of any other, as an end and never merely as a means, *is a formal principle*. Green is accepting an interpretation of Kant's formulations of the categorical imperative on which to act only on maxims that could also be willed as universal laws is the same as to act on the principle that *everyone* must be treated as an end in him- or herself, and on which the establishment of an empire of ends is simply the consequence of actually adhering to such a principle.

This resolution of the charge of empty formalism and the implicit identification of the foundation of Kant's moral philosophy with that of Green's own is accomplished in several steps. First, Green invokes his conception of self-consciousness, as the basis for the constitution of the object of both experience and will, in particular in the moral case, as "the presentation of self as an end or as that to which all ends are relative, carr[ying] with it a distinction between that which is good as satisfying a present want, and that which is good for me on the whole; in other words, that capacity for determination by the conception of the desirable, as other than determination by desire, which may become determination by the consciousness of law" (*LK*, pp. 136–7). This is the translation of his earlier account of Kantian formal or neutral freedom as still requiring some conception of the self into his own preferred language of self-consciousness as constituted and as in the practical case constituting the object of the will itself. He then argues that the only adequate conception of the self is that which sees the self as part of the larger human whole, and that Kant has recognized precisely this point in his own concept of the empire of ends:

> Now the self, the fuller satisfaction of which is presented as thus absolutely desirable, is from the first a self "existing in manifold relations to nature and other persons," and "these relations form the reality of the self." Thus the conception of a self to be satisfied necessarily carries with it the conception of this object "as common to himself with others." Such a conception in its most primitive form is the germ of what Kant calls a "Reich der Zwecke," a "kingdom of ends." (*LK*, p. 146)

The last quoted phrases are Kant's, of course; the previously quoted phrases do not appear to be from Kant, so insofar as they are being quoted, they would seem to be quoted from elsewhere in Green himself. In other words, Green is here asserting the basic equivalence of Kant's moral philosophy, above all its resource for rebutting the charge of empty formalism—that its conception of the self as the object of the will is formal but by no means empty, precisely because it is universalistic rather than subjectivistic, or selfish—and his own.

In this last quote, Green says that Kant provides only the "most primitive form" of the adequate idea of the self as the object of the moral will. It is certainly true that in neither the *Groundwork* nor the *Critique of Practical Reason*, Green's two primary texts in his lectures on Kant's moral philosophy (as in so many courses on Kant's moral philosophy since), does Kant spell out in any detail what it means to treat either oneself or others as ends and never merely as means. Kant does do this in the *Metaphysics of Morals*: In the "Doctrine of Virtue," he argues precisely that what treating oneself as an end requires is self-perfection, while in the "Doctrine of Virtue" and the "Doctrine of Right" together he argues that, since one cannot perfect another in the place of the other doing it herself, what treating the other as an end requires is, first, allowing the other the maximal amount of freedom to set her own ends and thus to perfect herself consistent with allowing an equal amount of freedom for all, and then actually promoting the happiness of others—that is, assisting them in the realization of their own ends—to the extent that so doing is consistent with fulfilling all of one's other duties both to them, the others, and to oneself. Green does not discuss Kant's own interpretation of what it is to treat oneself and others as absolute ends in his lectures on Kant, nor does he draw any explicit connection between his own account of self-perfection and Kant's interpretation of treating humanity always as an end in the *Prolegomena to Ethics*. Perhaps he would have done so had he lived to finish the *Prolegomena* instead of just leaving us his unconnected notes for that book and for the lectures on Kant. But even lacking such a detailed translation between Kant's theory and his own, there can be no doubt that Green has made it clear in the lectures that he thinks that Kant solves the empty formalism problem in a way that points to his own moral theory.

Before leaving Green, we may well ask whether his development of Kant can count as a defense and as an improvement. Henry Sidgwick, for one, certainly did not find Green's version of Kantian freedom an improvement: in particular, he did not see how an account of freedom as striving to realize a conception of oneself, whether a less or more adequate one, as also a form of neutral or moral freedom could be right, because it is in no way incompatible with determinism. In Sidgwick's words, "Green's use of the terms 'freedom' (cf. 'free effort to better himself") and 'self-determination' is misleading: since any particular man's effort to better himself, as its force depends on any moment on his particular past, is not 'free' or 'self-determined' in the only important sense."[33] More importantly, Sidgwick argues that Green's conception of the good as "full realisation" of the true capabilities of a human self might be question-begging, that is, might work only insofar as it presupposes a *moral* conception of the self. As Sidgwick puts it, Green's answer to the question, "What will afford an abiding satisfaction of an abiding self?...takes various forms, not easily made consistent, and contains,

---

[33] Sidgwick 1902, p. 22.

obscurely combined, wider and narrower views of man's true good. It is realisation or full realisation (1) sometimes of capabilities, and (2) sometimes of *moral* capability."[34] Unless some conception of moral capability or of the perfection of a moral self is presupposed, then, so Sidgwick supposes, Green has no basis for ruling out the perfection of capabilities for "the voluptuary's life" as an adequate instantiation of self-perfection. But if he is to rule that out, he must be relying on something other than the sheer idea of perfection itself.

Of course Green did think he had something more to fall back on than the mere conception of self-realization or perfection, namely his social conception of the real identity of any self. Sidgwick was hostile to Green's metaphysics, and spends several pages mercilessly criticizing Green's conception of "eternal consciousness" and idea of individual participation therein.[35] But the real question would be whether Kant himself had an adequate argument that pure reason tells us that our true or in Kant's own word "proper" (*eigentliche*) self (*G*, 4: 457) can find its full identity only in an empire of ends, and is obligated to find such an identity. Henry Sidgwick could not have thought so, since the conclusion of his *Methods of Ethics* is precisely that reason itself cannot decide between a self-regarding, prudential conception of rationality and a universalizing conception—this is what he calls "an ultimate and fundamental contradiction in our apparent intuitions of what is Reasonable in conduct"[36]—and thus that only an intuition or moral sentiment can decide the question for any individual. Since reason itself is ambiguous, reason itself cannot tell us what it is to be fully reasonable. The real question between Sidgwick on the one hand and Green and before him Kant on the other is then whether a social interpretation of the "proper self" is sufficiently persuasive to overcome Sidgwick's paradox.

This question can hardly be answered by a single, knock-down argument, but, if at all, only by seeing how the Kantian conception of the proper self has been fully developed throughout its history. So let us leave it hanging for now, and turn to the next of the Anglophone idealist interpreters of Kant to be considered here, namely Edward Caird.

12.3. Caird

The name of Edward Caird will be less well-remembered than those of either Bradley or Green.[37] Caird (1835–1908) was a Scot, educated at Glasgow and

---

[34] Sidgwick 1902, pp. 46–7.   [35] Sidgwick 1902, pp. 49–59.

[36] Sidgwick, *ME*, p. 508. Jens Timmermann has argued that Sidgwick's "dualism of practical reason" is certainly not Kantian, because for Kant, if pure practical reason has spoken against some action that one might have wanted to do for the sake of one's happiness, then reason has *nothing* to say in behalf of that action; Timmermann 2022, pp. 133–4.

[37] Mander 2011 discusses Caird at pp. 208–18. See also MacEwen 2009.

St Andrews and then, like Adam Smith a century earlier, as a Snell Exhibitioner at Balliol College, Oxford, which he entered in 1860 and from which he received his BA in 1863.[38] His first round of undergraduate studies having been frequently interrupted by illness, he was already 25 when he started at Balliol, and his companions were more the younger fellows rather than the other students, including among the former Green, Caird's senior by only one year. Making up for lost time, however, Caird was shortly appointed to the chair of moral philosophy at Glasgow, which he held from 1866 until 1893; he then returned to Oxford to serve as Master of Balliol until 1907. His oldest brother John Caird (1820–98), the leading liberalizing theologian of nineteenth-century Scotland, was Professor of Divinity at Glasgow and Principal of the university from 1873 to 1898, thus during much of John's tenure there. Like his brother John, Edward was a prolific publisher, although his only systematic works in moral philosophy were a work on *Ethical Philosophy*,[39] published the year he started as professor at Glasgow, and his posthumously published lectures.[40] He published a shorter work on Kant in 1877[41] and then in 1889 a monumental study of *The Critical Philosophy of Immanuel Kant*, in two volumes totaling 1,300 pages.[42] His other works included a monograph on Hegel[43] and several volumes on the family business of religion.[44] The influence of Hegel can be detected in Caird's approach to Kant's theoretical philosophy, in which he emphasizes not the dualism between intuition and concepts, between self and objects, but rather the way in which empirical consciousness of self and empirical consciousness of objects are intertwined for Kant. A remark such as this sums up this aspect of Caird's interpretation: "It is only as self-consciousness involves or includes the consciousness of objects that it can be the source of any ideal of knowledge to which that consciousness does not conform, and if in this way it transcends the empirical consciousness, it must be capable of transforming it" (*CPK*, 2. 153).[45] In his approach to Kant's moral philosophy, Hegel's influence is most apparent in Caird's application of a dialectical method to the interpretation of the relation among the formulations of the categorical imperative. This interpretation, which may be regarded as the centerpiece of Caird's pages on Kant's moral philosophy, is a far more sympathetic response to the "empty formalism" charge than Hegel himself provided: Caird's leading idea is that the sequence of formulations of the categorical imperative from the Formula of Universal Law through the Formula of Humanity to the Formula of the Empire of Ends is a progressive, dialectically unfolding exposition of Kant's vision of the essence of morality as consisting in the contribution of each to a community of agents, each of whom is treated as an end in himself, a vision

---

[38] Details on Caird's education may be found in Jones and Muirhead 1921.
[39] Caird 1866.   [40] Caird 2008.   [41] Caird 1877.   [42] Caird 1889.
[43] Caird 1883.   [44] Caird 1893 and Caird 1904.
[45] For further discussion of Caird's interpretation of Kant's theoretical philosophy, see Guyer 2015b, at pp. 129–37.

that thus brings Caird's approach to Kant and to moral philosophy itself into proximity to the social conception of self-realization by which Bradley thought that he distinguished himself from Kant but by which Green thought that he acknowledged his own proximity to Kant.[46]

In Caird's view, the basis of Kant's moral philosophy is that the idea(s) of pure reason that can only be conceived but not known in the theoretical case furnish the proper ideal for us to try to realize in practice: "the ideal object I think (i.e., the object which is thought as conforming to the pure unity of self-consciousness) becomes itself the principle to which I seek to bring the known world into conformity; in other words, it is set before me as an end I seek to realise" (CPK, 2. 160). In other words, Caird's view is that for Kant it is not conformity to law as such that is the fundamental goal of morality, but the realization of an ideal, or the transformation of the "known" or natural world into conformity with that ideal, for which conformity to law is a means. In particular, the *unity* of the self is not just a theoretical datum but a practical goal: Caird sees Kant's theoretical and practical philosophies as unified by the fact that the unity of consciousness itself is, first, not merely a theoretical or epistemic given but an epistemic ideal, but, second, also the fundamental goal of action. By means of our reason we seek to make the world into a fit object for a unified self-consciousness.

> Perhaps we may say—though Kant does not say it in so many words—that *just because reason cannot find its ideal realised in the world, it seeks to realise that ideal for itself.* The formal or analytical unity of self-consciousness thus brings with it a motive to action, an idea of reason by which it determines itself. In its practical use reason does not simply give rise to an idea to which, or by which, we may direct our empirical synthesis: it does not simply make a demand which it waits for experience to fulfill so far as it may. It makes a demand, in the first instance, only upon itself. Hence, it is in this case free to develop its ideal without let or hindrance, and to represent to itself a world conformable thereto—a world organised in conformity with the unity of self-consciousness.   (CPK, 2. 164–5)

With this approach, Caird attempts to obviate any need to ask why we should be moral, or to provide any separate ground for accepting the dictates of pure practical reason: it is part of what it is to aim at a unified consciousness at all that we also seek to transform the world into conformity with a practical ideal of unity.[47] The challenge for Caird is then to show that the condition for unity of

---

[46] Mander also emphasizes that Caird's interpretation of Kant's moral philosophy takes the form of a dialectic culminating in the empire of ends formulation of the categorical imperative; Mander 2011, pp. 216–18.

[47] Caird's view might be seen as an anticipation of the kind of constructivist approach promoted by Christine Korsgaard in Korsgaard 2009, esp. chapters 6–7. But he makes it clear that a unified self is not simply *given* by the fact of our agency but its *goal.*

consciousness is in fact the realization of the empire of ends, that is, an *interpersonal* ideal—which is of course what the other idealists we have considered were also trying to argue. As he himself puts it,

> Kant is interested (1) to purify the moral consciousness from all empirical elements which can only determine it in so far as it is not determined by itself, and (2) to develop the content of this pure ideal consciousness as affording a principle of complete determination for the self, which (3) involves that it should furnish a determination for the empirical consciousness and the empirical world. And the essential difficulty of his whole view of the moral life lies in the reconciliation of the first of these points with the third; of the negative moment of thought, by which the pure idea of the moral law is first reached, with the positive way in which its content is developed...   (*CPK*, 2. 167–8)

Note that Caird does not say that Kant is interested in purifying the moral consciousness from all empirical elements as such, but only in purifying it from empirical elements that would determine it in lieu of the moral consciousness determining itself. This is compatible with requiring the moral consciousness to determine itself by a pure, self-given principle, but one that allows in empirical elements as subordinate to that principle, indeed which cannot lead to particular actions without such empirical elements, just as a priori principles of cognition do not actually give rise to cognitions without empirical intuitions.

Caird then takes up this challenge in his central chapter on "The Formulation of the Moral Law." This chapter is particularly marked by Caird's method of proceeding from more abstract to more concrete, which his biographers Jones and Muirhead described in Hegelian terms: "Caird sought the truth that lay hidden in the doctrines he deemed erroneous, and treated the errors themselves as truth in the making, abstract statements summoning forth their opposites, and pointing towards a unity beneath the opposition."[48] Caird begins by attributing to Kant the thought that the self can constitute its identity as a self through adherence to a universal law through which it can overcome being passively determined by mere impulses, understood as stimuli external to the real identity of the self. In Caird's words, "if we conceive *ourselves*, our ego, as determined by such affections as motives, or, in other words, if we conceive ourselves as active in view of them, it cannot be simply because we are conscious through inner sense that such stimuli affect our sensibility" (*CPK*, 2. 183). He continues, "the self can will itself as universal, and this, as against all particular desires, will constitute its determination of itself" (*CPK*, 2. 186). In other words, acting in accordance with a universal law is the only way in which to truly act as a self at all; anything less is simply to be

---

[48] Jones and Muirhead 1921, pp. 35–6.

acted upon by stimuli external to the proper self. But this thought, Caird argues, seems open to the objection of empty formalism, which he ascribes to Hegel's 1802 essay on natural law and presents in Hegel's form, namely that "if we abstract from everything but itself, we can universalise *any* particular rule without contradiction," thus "that out of the abstract idea of law, or, in other words, out of the idea of self-consistency, no particular rules or laws of actions can be developed. Until some particular line of action has been suggested *with* which we are to be consistent, we cannot say what self-consistency means"; for example, "Universal stealing" may indeed be "self-contradictory, but only because it presupposes that right of property which at the same time it denies" (*CPK*, 2. 186–7). Caird's argument, however, is that this objection seems compelling only because Kant is using a "method of abstraction," starting off with a simple contrast between self and non-self, and thus starting off with his most abstract formulation of the categorical imperative, "really treating one aspect of the moral life as if it were a complete account of it" (*CPK*, 2. 207). As Kant fleshes out his conception of selfhood through the subsequent formulations of the categorical imperative, he will also, according to Caird, flesh out his conception of the moral ideal in a way that circumvents the empty formalism charge. He also holds that his interpretation will undermine the charge of rigorism (though he does not use this term), the objection that Kant is mindlessly committed to absolute rules such as "Thou shalt not steal" or "Thou shalt not kill" without any qualification (e.g., "Thou shalt not kill except in self-defense"), which are not appropriate in every situation and which can even come into conflict with each other: his claim is that this problem can be avoided once it is seen that "the true moral vindication of each particular interest cannot be found by elevating it into something universal and absolute, but only in determining its position in relation to the others in a complete system of morality," in which "property, life, freedom, the welfare of the individual, and of the family, must each in its turn become an end of the one moral life which manifests itself in them all, and each in its turn must be reduced into a means to the rest" (*CPK*, 2. 189). This is what, Caird holds, the Formula of the Empireingdom of Ends, reached through the Formula of Humanity as an End in Itself, allows. As he puts it, "Kant himself has supplied us with all the ideas needed for his own correction, for, in the three formulae in which he expresses the moral law, he first carries us beyond the idea of self-consistency to the idea of consistency with the self, and from that to the idea of a kingdom of ends" (*CPK*, 2. 207).

The advance first to Kant's second formulation and then from the second to the third takes place by means of two iterations of the characteristically British idealist idea of an organic whole (an idea that would remain central to the *Principia Ethica* of the supposed critic of British idealism, G. E. Moore, in 1903).[49] For Caird, the

---

[49] Moore 1993, e.g., pp. 263–4.

idea that humanity must be an end in itself is the idea that the self must be so regarded, and what it is to regard the self as an end in itself is to recognize that "each element of life should be regarded merely as an element, which owes its value to its place in an organic whole determined by one principle" (*CPK*, 2. 215). The agent who recognizes this will not simply act on impulse nor simply elevate the idea of following one particular kind of impulse into an absolute law; he will act only in ways consistent with pursuing a unified life, life as an organic whole. This thought is necessary in particular to explain the contradiction supposedly involved in violations of imperfect duties, what Kant called the contradiction in willing rather than contradiction in conception (*G*, 4: 424): the contradiction in, say, neglecting one's talents, is a contradiction between that path of (in)action and the idea of one's life as an organic whole, and as an end in that way, the realization of which will certainly require the cultivation of (at least some) talents (see *CPK*, 2. 220). Further, insofar as the agent is thereby freed from determination exclusively by particular desires, he will achieve an impartial will, and will not be "biassed by the particular character of his own desires to give their objects an undue importance in the order of ends"; instead, "his own individual existence" will stand "before him as an object like other existences" (*CPK*, 2. 214). This already suggests that the use of reason involved in seeing the whole of one's own life as an end makes it clear that other lives have the same status.

The second application of the idea of a human life as an organic whole comes in the transition from the Formula of Humanity to that of the Empire of Ends. Here we have not just an abstract recognition that the status of one's life as an end in itself is no different than that of anyone else's, but a positive recognition that each human is what he or she is only as part of the larger whole of humanity, and thus that action in consistency with the idea of oneself as an end involves action in consistency with the idea of all as part of an end in itself. "The idea of a kingdom of ends . . . involves nothing less than the organic unity of rational beings as such. It involves that the rational nature of man is not only a common element in them, but a principle which determines their particular natures in relation to each other, and so fits them, by virtue of their reciprocally complementary characteristics, to be members in one social organism" (*CPK*, 2. 225). Caird thus interprets Kant's concept of the realm of ends in terms of the idea that any self is what it is only as part of the larger society extending to all of humanity that we have found in Bradley and Green. To be sure, Caird argues, and fairly enough, that Kant does not work this idea out in very much detail, and that he would have to give up his initial commitment to "the negative relation of the universal to the particulars" (*CPK*, 2. 226) in order to do so, that is, that he would have to moderate his initial contrast between the form of law and any end or matter in order to more clearly recognize that the whole human community as one social organism is an end in itself. More generally, Kant would have to be clearer about the intimate relation between the a priori and the empirical, form and matter, law and the cases to which it is to be applied: "this idea of a kingdom of ends, or, more generally, the idea of a realised good, is impossible *even as an Idea* except by the recognition of a relation between the empirical and the ideal, which Kant does not recognise" (*CPK*, 2. 227). So Kant, in Caird's view, is a Moses who cannot quite cross the River Jordan, but he is looking in the right direction, at the idealist conception of the individual as what he or she is only as part of a social whole, indeed *the* social whole, and as an end in him- or herself only insofar as the latter is also an end in itself.

Having addressed two of what we have seen to have been the main stumbling-blocks to acceptance of Kantian morality since its earliest reception, namely doubt that the categorical imperative is really derivable from pure reason and the charge of empty formalism, Caird goes on to consider the three further chief issues in the reception of Kantian morality—the problem of free will, the problem of moral feeling, and the problem of the highest good—before turning to the details of Kant's doctrines of right and virtue. Caird tries to resolve the first of these issues essentially along the same lines as his Balliol friend Green, thus by arguing that free action is self-conscious action, but that self-consciousness is only gradually achieved, that is, real humans only gradually come to recognize that their true identity can be realized only as part of the whole of humanity, so that there are actions that are free insofar as they aim at self-realization but morally faulty insofar as they aim at a not yet perfected conception of self-realization. As he puts it, free immorality "can exist for a spiritual being only as a consequence of its imperfect development, i.e., of the fact that in it self-consciousness is inadequate to its own idea, or, in other words, that it is a self-consciousness which is in process of growth. For such a self-consciousness the world," particularly the world of other human beings, "may be an external and resistant sphere of action, just because the content of self-consciousness in its case is not adequate to the form" (*CPK*, 2. 262). Whether this resolution of the paradox of free immorality does sufficient justice to our intuitions about responsibility or imputation which drive this paradox may be just as much a question in the case of Caird as in that of Green. Although he refers only to recent "intellectualists" such as Christine Korsgaard and Andrews Reath, not to Caird or other idealists, Jens Timmermann has recently and vigorously argued that such an approach fails to acknowledge that we can know perfectly well what is the right thing to do (through the application of the categorical imperative by our *Wille*) and know-ingly choose not to do it (through our power of choice, or *Willkühr*).[50]

Caird's discussion of the possibility of moral feeling in Kant is brief but interesting. He focuses on the feeling of respect ("reverence" as he calls it), and his claim is that Kant's assumption that pure reason can and must affect our sensibility to produce such a feeling can seem gratuitous, given Kant's initial

---

[50] Timmermann 2022, chapters 6–7.

commitment to an abstract conception of the moral law, which can seem utterly remote from feeling of any kind. "As ... with Kant the law remains abstract, and so opposed to the matter which alone can realise or particularise it, so the feeling which arises from a consciousness of the law cannot become, in the full sense of the word, positive" (CPK, 2. 281). However, as before he argues that the spirit of Kant is better than much of the letter, and that in spite of his abstractions Kant does recognize a "gradual process by which the content of desire is brought into harmony with the principle of morality" (CPK, 2. 282) and a "*progressus ad infinitum*" toward an "ultimate unity between the natural and the spiritual, in spite of the antagonism into which they are brought" at the stage of moral development that Kant typically assumes (CPK, 2. 283). In other words, while Kant typically presents the feeling of respect as a feeling of conflict between our frustration at having to subordinate our self-conceit to the moral law and our satisfaction that we are giving that law to ourselves, Caird subtly changes this into the possibility of progress from an experience in which frustration may dominate to one in which satisfaction does. This may seem a hopeful way of transforming what for Kant is an abstract relation between noumenal reason and phenomenal sensibility into a process within the psychological development of a self in which both reason and sensibility are empirically present.

Finally, Caird celebrates the conception of the highest good as Kant's own supersession of the abstract opposition between morality and happiness with which he begins his exposition of his moral philosophy in the *Groundwork* and the Analytic of the *Critique of Practical Reason*. That is, although Kant initially insists that morality and happiness have nothing to do with each other, his concept of the highest good expresses the fact that he has had to "retrace the steps whereby he had first separated the spiritual from the natural world" and that he has been forced, "in spite of his conception of the moral law as a merely formal requirement of universality ... to typify the realisation of the moral law by a natural system which in all its particularity is governed by that law" (CPK, 2. 290). Indeed, on Caird's interpretation the concept of the highest good represents Kant's movement towards overcoming two dualities: first, that between the form of moral law in the individual, which seems to have nothing to do with his own happiness, and the matter of his desires, which seems to have everything to do with happiness, and that between what may be expected to be realized in an individual human life span and what could be realized only in more than that. Caird's suggestion is that Kant is on the right path to overcoming the former dualism by his conception that "the inherent opposition of the terms brought together"—moral obligation and happiness—"can be conceived to be attained only by a *progressus ad infinitum*" (CPK, 2. 302), but that he essentially takes an easy way out by postulating personal immortality and a God who will make good in the afterlife of the worthy individual the unjust unhappiness he may have suffered in his natural life. For Caird, it is a mistake to separate virtue and its reward when "just *through* this relation" of any stage of the virtuous life "to the whole, it is in a sense complete in itself" (*CPK*, 2. 307); even more so is it a mistake to locate the reconciliation of the worthiness to be happy with happiness in an individual afterlife when in fact it is to be found in "the realisation of a kingdom of ends," which is possible and in progress on earth insofar as people are acting morally. Again Caird sees Kant as a Moses who points the way toward but cannot quite step into the promised land of the empire of ends:

> In this last movement of Idealism, however, Kant refuses to follow it; for, by him, the antagonism of universal and particular is stated in such a way as to involve, not merely that in our particular experience there is never a final realisation of the universal, but in the sense that in it there cannot be a realisation of the universal at all . . . Now, this gulf is fixed between the universal and the particular by Kant's imperfect view of the universal, which for him has not contents. Yet, even while he so conceived it, he was obliged by the very nature of the universal to postulate the possibility of transcending the division he had made . . . But, if we take from his theory the idea of an irreconcilable opposition of particular and universal, and substitute for it the idea of the universal as synthetic, no objection can be taken to the definition of the religious consciousness as a faith of reason; the *Summum Bonum* is never realised as a matter of sight, just because it is always realising itself.   (*CPK*, 2. 313–14)

That is, once we relax the rigid distinction between universal and particular, form and matter, and thus between morality and happiness, a relaxation to which Kant himself pointed the way with his concept of the empire of ends—after all, "a whole both of rational beings as ends in themselves *and of the ends of his own that each may set himself*" (*G*, 4: 433, emphasis added)—then we will not need to defer the realization of the highest good to an afterlife where it will be produced by the grace of a divinity, but will realize that it is always being produced by our own moral actions themselves.

How much *faith* may be required to envision *this* possibility may remain a question, however. It might be that moral effort is fully rational as long as we have no good reason to think that it must be doomed to failure, and no stronger theoretical commitment than that is required. It might also be argued that in writings of the 1790s, such as the *Critique of the Power of Judgment*, the essay on "Theory and Practice," and *Towards Perpetual Peace*, Kant was himself in the process of replacing his initial conception of the highest good as something to be achieved in the afterlife of individual agents with something to be realized in the eventual history of the human species, which would be much closer to Caird's preferred view. With these caveats, however, we will let Edward Caird's attempt to let the spirit of Kant triumph over at least some of his letters stand, and turn to the sole American Kantian idealist to be considered here, namely Josiah Royce.

12.4. Royce

It might seem surprising to characterize Royce as an idealist Kantian, since his form of confident idealism seems closer to the absolute idealism of Hegel than to the limitations inherent in Kant's transcendental idealism. But in coining this phrase, I am thinking primarily of Royce's chief contribution to moral philosophy, his *Philosophy of Loyalty* of 1908.[51] What I argue here is just that Royce's conception of loyalty is an imaginative reconstruction of Kant's conception of an empire of ends that can stand on its own without much of the machinery of Kant's transcendental idealism, including his transcendental idealist theory of freedom of the will.

Josiah Royce (1855–1916) was the leading voice for idealism in the United States in his time. He was the son of English parents, but he grew up in the California gold rush town of Grass Valley, where his unsuccessful businessman father and school-teacher mother tried to piece together a living.[52] He then attended the new University of California at Berkeley and was one of the earliest PhDs at the equally new Johns Hopkins University; his supporters there made it possible him to study in Germany as well, where he listened to Hermann Rudolf Lotze among others. He then languished for several years teaching English back at Berkeley before William James discovered him and brought him to Harvard, where he started as a fill-in instructor and then spent the rest of his career as the complement to James in the first Golden Age of Harvard philosophy.[53] This path from frontier obscurity to the heart of American academia gave him a strong sense of the dependence of any individual on the support of others, which expressed itself in his commitment to the idea of community. He did not argue, as did Bradley and Green—the latter of whom certainly influenced him, and with the former of whom he argued in his *magnum opus*, his Gifford Lectures on *The World and the Individual* of 1899–1901[54]—that the identity of the individual self is literally constituted by a larger society, but he had a firm conviction of the dependence of the individual on society in a myriad of ways and of the corresponding obligation of the individual to contribute to society. This commitment to the idea of community is most evident in Royce's late works, *The Philosophy of Loyalty* from 1908 and *The Problem of Christianity* from 1913.[55] The former is a straightforward work of moral and social philosophy presented without much in the way of metaphysical presuppositions. The latter, Royce's last major work although he published several more books before his premature death three years later, is a remarkable work, Royce's answer to Kant's *Religion within the*

---

[51] Royce 1995.
[52] Royce never forgot his California roots, and published a remarkable work of history, highly critical of the American expropriation of California from Mexico, Royce 1886. For Royce's biography, see Kuklick 1972.
[53] See Kuklick 1977.   [54] Royce 1899, 1901.   [55] Royce 2001.

Boundaries of Mere Reason, in which the author first presents his philosophy of loyalty as an interpretation of Pauline Christianity and then, in its second half, under the influence of Charles Sanders Peirce, recasts his earlier argument that the always incomplete individual search for and apprehension of knowledge can only be understood as an attempt to participate in a larger understanding of the world (his "argument from error") as an argument that reality just is the interpretation of its collective experience that humankind would ideally or in principle achieve.[56] Here a conception of the community, in the form of a community of interpretation, becomes the key to Royce's theoretical philosophy, just as a conception of a community of social causes becomes the key to his practical philosophy.

In earlier works such as *The Spirit of Modern Philosophy* (1892)[57] and his *Lectures on Modern Idealism* delivered in 1906 although published only posthumously in 1919,[58] Royce had displayed his profound learning and the origins of his own eclectic form of idealism in Kant, Schelling, Hegel, and Schopenhauer. *The Philosophy of Loyalty* and *The Problem of Christianity* are written without much historical reference, except for the references to Pauline Christianity and Peirce in the latter work, which however Royce certainly does *not* present as his own version of Kant's rational reconstruction of the core ideas of Christianity. But virtually the only historical philosopher mentioned in *The Philosophy of Loyalty* is Kant, and while Royce presents his central idea as a corrective to the narrow conception of autonomy that he there ascribes to Kant, his conception of loyalty can in fact be construed as a successor to Kantian morality or a more generous interpretation of it in which the idea of the empire of ends is its centerpiece.[59]

Royce presents the problem to be solved by his conception of loyalty as at least in part a problem presented by Kant's conception of autonomy. This is because Royce, as many more recent writers have also done, conceives of autonomy as the expression of individual choice or will: he takes the core idea of Kant's conception to be that the individual agent must make his moral choices for and by himself. As Royce puts it,

> If you want to find out, then, what is right and what is good for you, bring your own will to self-consciousness. Your duty is what you yourself will to do in so far as you clearly discover who you are and what your place in the world is. This is, indeed, a first principle of all ethical inquiry. Kant called it the Principle of the Autonomy or self-direction of the rational will of each moral being.   (PL, 14)

However, Royce sees this conception of the good will as the autonomous will as incomplete, offering no solution to the problem also faced by utilitarianism,

---

[56] On Royce and Peirce, see Oppenheim 2005 and Parker 2008.
[57] Royce 1892.   [58] Royce 1919.
[59] Mander compares Royce's conception of loyalty more generally to Kant's categorical imperative; Mander 2016, p. 150. See also Foust 2012.

namely that without some form of external constraint the will bent on self-realization will in fact just be seeking to satisfy a haphazard and ultimate conflicting congeries of desires, "merely brooding over my natural desires or ... following my momentary caprices" (*PL*, p. 14). (Royce also brings his argument to bear on Nietzsche's conception of self-realization, which he argues suffers from the same defect as both utilitarianism and the simplified conception of individual autonomy that he is attacking; see *PL*, 39–41.) The idea that the pursuit of pleasure itself might be a unifying, coherent goal that could constitute the object of a unified self-consciousness is deceptive, Royce argues, here tacitly adopting the argument that Kant himself makes in section II of the *Groundwork* and in the Analytic of the *Critique of Practical Reason*, because "the desire to escape from pain and to get pleasure ... simply gives back again, under new names, that chaos of conflicting passions and interests which constitutes, apart from training, my natural life" (*PL*, 15): the commitment to pursuing pleasure and avoiding pain sounds like a coherent goal, but in fact it is nothing but a second-order desire to satisfy all one's desires and avoid their frustration, the coherence or otherwise of which is entirely dependent on whether those first-order desires happen to be compatible or not. Of course here we may remember Schopenhauer as well. This problem of an incoherent set of desires and consequently an incoherent will can be avoided only by a "social order," but then again not just by any social order in which we happen to "grow up," for without further constraint "social training too" just "gives us a mass of varying plans of life,—plans that are not utterly chaotic, indeed, but imperfectly ordered" (*PL*, p. 15). The solution to this dilemma, Royce argues, is what he calls loyalty, namely, attachment to a cause which, "for the first,"

> seems to the loyal person to be larger than his private self, and so to be, in some respect external to his purely individual will. This cause must, in the second place, unite him with other persons by some social tie such as a personal friendship, or his family, or the state may, in a given case, represent. The cause, therefore, to which the loyal man is devoted, is something that appears to him to be at once personal (since it concerns both himself and other people), and impersonal, or rather, if regarded from a purely human point of view, super-personal, because it links several human selves, perhaps a vast number of selves, into some higher social unity. (*PL*, 25)

Commitment or loyalty to a cause is supposed to give an individual a plan of life, thus a way of transcending the problem of incoherent desires:

> A loyal man is one who has found, and who sees, neither mere individual fellow-men to be loved or hated, nor mere convention nor customs, nor laws to be obeyed, but some social cause, or social system of causes, so well knit, and to him, so fascinating, and withal so kindly in its appeal to his natural self-will, that he

says to his cause: "Thy will is mine and mine is thine. In thee I do not lose but find myself, living intensely in proportion as I live for thee." If one could find such a cause, and hold it for his lifetime before his mind, clearly observing it, passionately loving it, and yet calmly understanding it, and steadily and practically serving it, he would have one plan of life, and this plan of life would be his own plan, his own will set before him, expressing all that his self-will has ever sought. Yet this plan would also be a plan of obedience, because it would mean living for the cause.   (PL, 22)

The idea is that attachment to a cause is a product of individual choice, thus satisfying the demand for autonomy as Royce is construing it, yet it is one that gives direction and coherence to an individual life, thus overcoming the problem of autonomy as Royce construes it.

But this position is open to the obvious objection that, even if loyalty to some social cause or other can give direction to an individual life and free it from the chaos of conflicting personal desires, *social causes* themselves can be contingent and conflicting. Kant illustrated the merely apparent coherence of the pursuit of mere desire-satisfaction with the example of the Habsburg emperor Charles V and the French king Francis I, who seemed to be in unison insofar as they both wanted the same thing, but unfortunately were in conflict because they both wanted something they could not both have, namely, sole rule of Milan (*CPracR*, 5: 28) and beyond that of the throne of the Holy Roman Empire itself. Now just imagine loyal supporters of the two rulers: each supporter will be attached to a cause greater than himself, namely the welfare of the House of Habsburg on the one hand or of the House of Valois on the other, and of course these houses, thus these causes can, and did, come into conflict with each other, introducing chaos into the lives of many of their followers, indeed chaos beyond what those individual followers could have caused for themselves. Loyalty to a cause thus hardly seems the solution to the supposed problem of autonomy when the causes themselves can so readily conflict.

Of course Royce could hardly fail to be aware of such an obvious objection; he clearly states it himself when he writes "Now, it is obvious that nobody can be equally and directly loyal to all of the countless actual social causes that exist. It is obvious also that many causes which conform to our general definition of a possible cause may appear to any given person to be hateful and evil causes, to which he is justly opposed" (*PL*, 51). Royce's solution to this next dilemma is what he calls "loyalty to loyalty" (*PL*, 56). Here his idea is that the only causes that really transcend the supposed confines of individualistic autonomy are those which, even if *different* from other causes, are *compatible* with the loyal commitment of other people to other causes, and which thus allow for more rather than less loyalty in the world as a whole. The idea is that, in addition to being loyal to some particular cause that gives his life coherence, the moral individual is also loyal to the possibility of loyalty as such, thus to the possibility of other people pursuing other causes, different from but compatible with his own cause and with the yet other causes of yet others, and that this gives the loyal life even further direction and coherence. As Royce expresses his idea in the form of a moral principle,

> In so far as lies in your power, so choose your cause and so serve it, that, by reason of your choice and of your service, there shall be more loyalty in the world rather than less. And, in fact, so choose and so serve your individual cause as to secure thereby the greatest possible increase of loyalty among men. More briefly: *In choosing and in serving the cause to which you are to be loyal, be, in any case, loyal to loyalty.* (PL, 57)

If this principle, expressed here in consequentialist, maximizing form, is adopted, then "The choice of any cause will in consequence be such as to avoid unnecessary conflict with the causes of others" (PL, 63). An inveterate synthesizer, Royce was no doubt interested in showing how his position appropriated the truth in utilitarianism as well as in Kantianism.

Royce concludes his chapter on "Loyalty to Loyalty" by arguing that it gives rise to a familiar set of duties to self and others. First, it gives rise to "duties to myself... precisely in so far as I have the duty to be actively loyal at all. For loyalty needs not only a willing, but also an effective servant. My duty to myself is, then, the duty to provide my cause with one who is strong enough and skilful enough to be effective according to my own natural powers. The care of health, self-cultivation, self-control, spiritual power..." (PL, 67). If loyalty to loyalty is the overarching principle of duty, then one has the subsidiary duty to develop one's own capacities and resources for advancing one's own cause and, as appropriate, the causes of others, or at least the commitment of others and their capacities to serve their own causes, even when those causes are different from one's own. Second, Royce argues that the idea of loyalty to loyalty also gives rise to individual rights, namely "my right to protect my service, to maintain my office, and to keep my own [property] merely in order that I may use my own as the cause commands" (PL, 68). These rights are actually correlatives to the obligations on others under the principle of loyalty to loyalty to respect and promote my commitment to my own cause, even when it is different from theirs. Finally, the duty of loyalty to loyalty gives rise to two classes of duties to others, "duties to my neighbors," corresponding to their duty to recognize my rights to advance my cause and my duty to develop my resources for advancing my cause. These are the duties to others of justice and benevolence, on the one hand the duty of "fidelity to human ties in so far as they are ties," "the more formal and abstract side of loyal life," and, on the other hand, concern for the welfare of others, "in so far as, if you help [them] to a more efficient life, you make [them] better able to be loyal" (PL, 68–9). In other words, insofar as you must be loyal to loyalty you have a negative duty not to interfere with the pursuit of their causes by others as long as they are themselves also loyal to loyalty and thus pursue causes different from but compatible with your own, and you also have a positive duty to assist them in pursuing their own causes more effectively, insofar of course as doing so is compatible with your effective pursuit of your own causes(s).

It should by now be apparent that Royce's idea of loyalty to loyalty is not a corrective to Kantian morality but an interpretation of its central idea of the empire of ends, the systematic whole in which each is an end in himself and in which the particular ends that each chooses are ends for all insofar as those choices are also compatible with the idea of an empire of ends. For what Royce means by a choice of cause is the same as or at least an example of what Kant means by an end set in accordance with reason, that is, not a mere desire but a desire elevated into an end in virtue of its accordance with rationality itself, or with the requirement of the universalizability of maxims, thus in virtue of its compatibility with one's own other choices and with the free choices of others. And Kant himself closely identifies his actual principle of autonomy with his principle of the empire of ends, alternating between them as apparently equipollent versions of the third formulation of the categorical imperative (G, 4: 432–3, 436–7). Acting autonomously is in fact acting not merely in accordance with one's own will, but willing in accordance with reason, thus in a way that could be universally legislative for all; and the outcome of everyone acting autonomously would be the realization of an empire of ends. Loyalty to loyalty would be acting both in service of a cause that one has chosen for oneself—one's own end—but also in accordance with a universalizable ideal, namely autonomy for all, thus the pursuit of causes as ends by others as well as by oneself. Royce's idea of loyalty to loyalty thus brings the Kantian ideas of autonomy and the empire of ends "closer to intuition," as Kant had argued that those conceptions themselves bring the abstract idea of a categorical imperative "closer to intuition" (G, 4: 436).

What Royce adds to his conception of loyalty in *The Problem of Christianity* is the argument that loyalty to loyalty is not only aimed *at* a universal community but can only be achieved *by means of* a community with a universalistic ethos, represented in Christian historiography by the Pauline church (since Jesus did not himself found a church). The only reference to Kant in this work is in its second, theoretical half, in a chapter on "Perception, Conception, and Interpretation" (PC, 278–9). This is the part of the work in which, inspired by Peirce, Royce transforms his idealism from a conception of individual thought against the background of the thought of the absolute to a model of reality as the interpretation of experience to which humankind collectively approaches. In the first part of the work, however, Royce argues that Christianity's three central concepts of original sin, grace, and atonement can be interpreted as symbols for what he calls "the moral burden of the individual," "community" as the only means to overcoming that burden, and the recognition that past deeds cannot be undone but that acknowledgment of that fact can lead to better conduct in the future on the part of the original agent or others. Royce's conception of the moral burden of the individual is clearly indebted to Kant's image of the "unsocial sociability" of humankind as well as to Hegel's presentation of the struggle for recognition in the form of the master-slave dialectic in *The Phenomenology of Spirit*. Royce argues that our very self-consciousness arises from both our recognition by others and our need to distinguish ourselves from others. Some of the disharmonies of human life "result merely from the mutual misunderstandings of men," but deeper than that a human being comes to self-consciousness as a moral being only "through the spiritual warfare of mutual observation, of mutual criticism, of rivalry" (*PC*, 111): it is only from the opposition of others to our will that we come to have a distinct sense of self at all, but the object of the will must become cooperation with rather than opposition to those very same others. Royce's argument is then that it is only "the social will, in its corporate capacity, the will of the community, [that] forms its codes, its customary laws; and attempts to teach each of us how he ought to deal with his neighbors so as to promote the general social harmony" (*PC*, 112). This is his version of the role for the "invisible church" in establishing the "ethico-civil condition" that Kant expounds in part 3 of the *Religion*. Finally, Royce's secularized interpretation of atonement addresses the same issue that Kant addresses in part 2 of the *Religion*, namely, that the past cannot literally be undone even after the moral conversion of the individual, that there is a debt that somehow must be paid. Here the difference is that, while Kant focuses on the negative side of this issue, arguing that it is precisely the painfulness of the conversion to the new, morally better man that pays the debt of the old, morally worse man (*RBMR*, 6: 73–4), Royce focuses on the positive, arguing that, even though the past cannot be undone, it can be a spur to make the world better in the future. Royce construes what Kant called evil in the form of betrayal or disloyalty to a freely chosen cause, and then argues that recognition of the impossibility of changing the past can nevertheless lead to new, creative forms of action in behalf of the betrayed cause that actually make the world a better place, a fuller realization of that cause, than it would have been had the breach of loyalty never taken place. His reinterpretation of atonement is that "*The world, as transformed by this creative deed, is better than it would have been had all else remained the same, but had that deed of treason not been done at all*" (*PC*, 180).

This solution is different and more optimistic than Kant's. But perhaps the most striking part of Royce's model of atonement for disloyalty is his recognition that the possibility of disloyalty is part and parcel of the fact that loyalty itself is a product of freedom. If loyalty is the product of a truly free choice, then of course there must also be a possibility of a free choice of disloyalty—that is what it means for the choice of loyalty to be free in the first place. In Royce's words:

All the highest forms of the unity of the spirit, in our human world, constantly depend, for their very existence, upon the renewed free choices, the sustained loyalty, of the members of communities. Hence the very best that we know, namely, the loyal brotherhood of the faithful who choose to keep their faith,— this best of all human goods, I say,—is simply inseparable from countless possibilities of the worst of human tragedies,—the tragedy of broken faith.... this fact is due not to the natural perversity of men, nor to the mere weakness of those who love and trust. This fact is due to something which, without any metaphysical theory, we ordinarily call man's freedom of choice.   (PC, 176–7)

Royce is not interested in explaining the possibility of freedom by appeal to anything like Kant's transcendental idealism; he takes the possibility of freedom for granted, and is bent only on showing that it includes the possibility of both original sin and atonement, though atonement achieved only the communal transformation of the world and not by individuals *per impossibile* changing the past. But that the possibility of evil is part and parcel of the possibility of doing good and conversely that the possibility of reform toward goodness is part and parcel of the possibility of evil is precisely what Kant meant by calling evil "radical," rooted in freedom itself. On this point, as in his conception of loyalty to loyalty itself, Royce is working within a Kantian framework, and adopting Kant's 1792 conception of the complete freedom of *Willkühr* as the response to the problem of determinism raised by Ulrich.

Even more bluntly than did Kant himself, Royce concludes his reinterpretation of Christianity by arguing for the transcendence of any form of historical, sectarian Christianity. *The Problem of Christianity* ends with the following plea:

Look forward to the human and visible triumph of no form of the Christian church. Still less look to any sect, new or old, as the conqueror. Henceforth view the religious ideal as one which, in the future, is to be won, if not at all, by methods distinctively analogous to the methods which now prevail in the science of nature... what I mean is that since the office of religion is to aim towards the creation on earth of the Beloved community, the future task of religion is the task of inventing and applying the arts which shall win men over to unity, and which shall overcome their original hatefulness by the gracious love, not of mere individuals, but of communities.... Judge every social device, every proposed reform, every national and local enterprise by the one test: *Does this help towards the coming of the universal community.* If you have a church, judge your own church by this standard.... To do that, however, does not mean that you shall either conform to the church as it is, or found new sects.... We can look forward, then, to no final form, either of Christianity or of any other special religion. But we can look forward to a time when the work and the insight of religion can become as progressive as is now the work of science.   (PC, 404–5)

The answer to the "problem" of Christianity, in other words, is the supersession of Christianity by social and political work towards a universal community here on earth, in the natural lifetime of humankind. Royce in early twentieth-century Cambridge and Boston, even in early twentieth-century Oxford where *The Problem of Christianity* was first presented as lectures, could afford to be blunter about his secular version of faith than Kant was able to be in 1792. But it might also be argued that the secularization of Kant's conception of the highest good in the 1790s had already become evident to discerning readers of the third *Critique*, with its stripped-down regulative deism, which limited the idea of God to that of an author of nature in which human freedom can be realized and silently eliminated all ideas of personal immortality and divine reward for virtue,[60] and that Royce's faith in the coming of the universal community without the trappings of historical and sectarian Christianity was his interpretation of Kant's own reinterpretation of his earlier conception of the highest good, or was at least very much in the spirit of the latter. On this point too then Royce's own moral philosophy can be regarded as another version of Anglophone idealism's appropriation of Kant's moral philosophy.

Idealism in American largely ran its course with Royce; his approach to philosophy was already under attack by self-designated "New Realists" before his death in 1916, before he reached 61. Idealism in some form lasted longer in Britain, in spite of the attacks of Moore and Russell in Cambridge at the turn of the century and of John Cook Wilson's form of realism at Oxford in the next few decades; some figures influential at Oxford into the 1920s and 1930s, such as H. W. B. Joseph and R. G. Collingwood, remained sympathetic to some aspects of idealism. Idealism as metaphysics or theoretical philosophy was completely erased at Oxford only after World War II. The chair in moral philosophy, however, remained in the hands of a philosopher deeply influenced by both Kant and the idealist tradition in ethics until 1952, namely H. J. Paton, so this chapter will conclude with a look at his own contribution to moral philosophy (as opposed to his significant contributions to Kant scholarship).

12.5. Paton

Herbert James Paton (1887–1969) is remembered chiefly as a Kant scholar. *Kant's Metaphysic of Experience*, published in two volumes in 1936, is a detailed commentary on the *Critique of Pure Reason* through the Transcendental Analytic, of particular note as the first English-language work to make extensive use of Kant's notes on metaphysics, as recently edited in volumes 17 and 18 of the *Akademie*

---

[60] See esp. Guyer 2020a, chapter 4.

edition by Erich Adickes and published in 1926 and 1928. After World War II, Paton published a translation of Kant's *Groundwork for the Metaphysics of Morals*, titled *The Moral Law*, and then a commentary on the *Groundwork*, titled *The Categorical Imperative*.[61] Paton's translation was the basis for the translation by his student Mary Gregor, posthumously published in 1996 in her volume *Practical Philosophy* in *The Cambridge Edition of the Works of Immanuel Kant*, which was in turn revised by Jens Timmerman in 2011; so Paton's remains the basis for the main line of translations of the *Groundwork* into English. His commentary on the *Groundwork*, meanwhile, framed a discussion of the number of and relations among the formulations of the categorical imperative in section II of the *Groundwork* that has continued ever since.

But before turning to Kant scholarship, in 1927 Paton had published his own moral theory in *The Good Will*. Although this is not an historical work, Paton does acknowledge Plato and Kant as his polestars in moral theory. He clearly has in mind Plato's theory of the just soul as part of the just state in the *Republic* and Kant's image of the empire of ends in the culminating formulation of the categorical imperative. The work can be regarded as an interpretation of these ideas, particularly the latter, in terms borrowed from the coherence conception of truth that dominated British idealism. Paton's thought is that the moral will aims at intra- and interpersonal coherence in practice or action, just as the coherence of thought among the multi-generational community of inquirers is the aim for theory or knowledge. *The Good Will* can thus be regarded as a final flowering of the moral tradition of British idealism.[62] Although Paton nowhere mentions the name of Josiah Royce, he drafted the book during a 1926 sabbatical at the University of Southern California supported by the Laura Spelman Rockefeller Memorial, a philanthropic enterprise of John D. Rockefeller in honor of his deceased wife. As previously mentioned, Royce had been a native Californian and an early graduate of the first University of California campus at Berkeley before heading east to Johns Hopkins and eventually Harvard, and if Paton had not previously been familiar with Royce's work he certainly could have heard of him during his California stay. Be that as it may, there are pronounced affinities between Royce's conception of loyalties to diverse particular communities unified by loyalty to the idea of loyalty itself and Paton's conception of the goal of morality as the overall coherence of the coherent wills of all rational beings and their various societies intermediate between individuals and all rational beings.

But of course Royce and Paton shared the common heritage of Anglophone idealism, so there is no need to claim a direct, unacknowledged influence of the former on the latter. Paton was Scottish born, and took his first degree at Glasgow in 1908, where the idealist Henry Jones set the tone of the department. Following

---

[61] Paton 1947.   [62] And is so treated in a rare discussion in Mander 2016, pp. 151–4.

in the distinguished footsteps of Adam Smith and the idealist philosophers Edward Caird and J. H. Muirhead, Paton then went to Balliol College, Oxford, where he took firsts in classical moderations in 1909 and *litterae humaniores* in 1911. His tutor was J. A. Smith, another idealist, who introduced him to the philosophy of Benedetto Croce. He was elected a fellow of Queen's College and served there until 1927, including a stint as dean, although his term there was interrupted by World War I, when he served in Admiralty intelligence alongside his close contemporary R. G. Collingwood. In 1927 he returned to Glasgow as Professor of Logic and Rhetoric, and then in 1937 was called back to Oxford as White's Professor of Moral Philosophy. Again his tenure at Oxford was interrupted by war: during World War II he worked part-time in the Foreign Office. Apart from philosophy his passion was politics and international affairs, and he served on the executive committee of the League of Nations Union until the League was superseded by the United Nations. He returned to Scotland after his retirement from Oxford, and was active in the reform of St Andrews University. His last book, *The Claim of Scotland* (1968), was an argument for greater Scottish autonomy within the United Kingdom, although not for Scottish independence.

Paton's adherence to the most fundamental ideas of British idealism as it flourished in Scotland and at Oxford is evident in *The Good Will*, which begins with a vigorous polemic against the founding document of twentieth-century Cambridge philosophy, the 1903 *Principia Ethica* of G. E. Moore; a second edition of *Principia Ethica* was published in 1922, which might be why Paton felt compelled to respond to it a few years later.[63] The central idea of Moore's work is that morality is founded in the intrinsic and indefinable goodness of certain states of affairs—above all, beauty and friendship, or aesthetic experience and the experience of friendship—and that what is right to do or what ought to be done is to maximize those states of affairs; Moore's position was a form of utilitarianism grounded on an objectivist ontology. Tacitly following Kant's insistence in the *Critique of Practical Reason* that the moral law's determination of what is right is antecedent to any determination of what is good, Paton argued that the good is just the object of the will, specifically that what is morally good is the object of the good will, and that the good will is that which aims, ultimately consciously or intentionally, at the greatest possible intra- and interpersonal coherence; the good is then just whatever objects of will are compatible with the good will so understood.[64] Paton understood this conception of the good will as the analogue of the idealist conception of the aim of knowledge: knowledge aims at coherence of belief, and morality aims at the coherence of will.

---

[63] See Moore 1993.

[64] As Mander puts it, for Paton "goodness belongs to willing which is 'coherent with itself'" (Mander 2016, p. 152), but this coherence must be understood both intra- and interpersonally—each will and all wills must be coherent.

Moore's *Principia Ethica* offers more argument against hedonism, whether in egoistic or universalistic thus utilitarian form, than against a Kantian moral philosophy. Its primary targets are thus Mill and Sidgwick rather than Kant, although Moore does have some objections against Kant in his critique of "metaphysical" rather than "naturalistic" ethics. Paton's polemic against Moore does not concern Moore's interpretation or critique of Kant, however. We will return to Moore's earlier critique of Kant's theory of freedom in the next chapter, but our discussion of Moore here will be confined to the points to which Paton objected. Moore's approach to ethics in *Principia* was really part of the polemic against idealism, above all the idealism of F. H. Bradley, which he and Bertrand Russell had led in the decade of the 1890s, and Paton's response to Moore's position in *Principia* is in turn grounded in a philosophical position that is generally idealistic although certainly not specifically Bradleian. In particular, Moore's position in ethics is grounded in the kind of logical atomism that he and Russell opposed to the idealist view that reality is best understood as a system of relations within a single whole or all that can only be captured cognitively through the apprehension of coherence. In the case of ethics that means, at least in Paton's hands, that morality, which concerns intention and action rather than knowledge, mandates intentional effort to pursue the ideal of intra- and interpersonal coherence in willing. Specifically, Moore held—here in implicit polemic with Kant—that the recognition of the good must precede the determination of what is right, or what ought to be done, and that goodness itself is something simple, intrinsic, and unanalyzable that cannot be defined by anything else, that is, by analysis into the properties of anything else, whether the latter be thought to exist naturally or metaphysically, sensibly or supersensibly. To think otherwise is to commit what Moore called the "naturalistic fallacy," regardless of whether the properties into which goodness is falsely analyzed be natural in the ordinary sense—objects of the natural sciences—or metaphysical.[65] (In a new preface that Moore drafted for a second edition of *Principia* in 1922 but decided not to publish, he admitted that the "naturalistic fallacy" is not a fallacy in the ordinary sense of a violation of the rules of inference, but just a confusion about what sort of property goodness is or what sort of predicate "good" is—in Kant's terms, more like a substantive paralogism than a formally invalid inference.[66]) The point of all this for Moore is really just to establish that what is good is not the subject of any analytical judgment, but only of a synthetic judgment or judgments, which can in turn be known to be true not through logic, any natural science, or any metaphysical theory, but only by "intuition."[67] He also puts this point by claiming that the first principles of ethics, as first principles, cannot be derived from anything else; they just have to be recognized as self-evidently true. After his elaborate argument that the

---

[65] On the "naturalistic fallacy," see Sinclair 2019.   [66] See Moore 1993, pp. 16–20.
[67] Moore 1993, Preface to the 1st edition, pp. 34–5; §6, pp. 58–9.

intrinsically good is *not* pleasure—an argument weakened by the absence of any attempt to define pleasure—his "intuition" tells him that "By far the most valuable things, which we know or can imagine, are certain states of consciousness, which may be roughly described as the pleasures of human intercourse and the enjoyment of beautiful objects."[68] This is the statement that made *Principia Ethica* the bible for the literary and artistic movement that has come to be known as "Bloomsbury," most enduringly represented by the novels of Virginia Woolf and E. M. Forster and the art theory of Clive Bell, the quondam husband of Virginia's sister Vanessa—the plea of Margaret Schlegel, the protagonist of Forster's novel *Howards End*, namely "Only connect!," epitomizes the substance of Moore's ethics.[69] (Forster would surely have known Moore personally through the Cambridge "Apostles," the intellectual nursery for at least the male members of Bloomsbury.)

Paton objects to both the methodological or meta-ethical and the substantive claims of Moore, and argues instead for a conception of the moral ideal that, as I said, can be considered as an interpretation of Kant's empire of ends as well as of Socrates's image of justice in the *Republic*. Paton's meta-ethical objections to Moore include an objection to Moore's anti-Kantian strategy of deriving the right or what we ought to do from an antecedent determination of what is substantively good, such as aesthetic experience or the experience of friendship. Instead, he holds, everything good is the object of the will, and what is morally good is the object of the moral will: thus, how we ought to will must be determined first, and that then determines what is good, or, to put it in other terms, the determination of what constitutes the good will must be the starting-point of ethics, and any other kinds of (moral) goods can be determined only as the objects of the good will in these circumstances or those. In Paton's view, in general "the goodness of things seems to be relative to their purpose, and purpose seems to imply some kind of will, it seems to demand a person who has [a] purpose.... All this would mean that the goodness of things [is] dependent upon will" (*GW*, p. 24), and consequently the moral goodness of anything else dependent upon a morally good will, the characterization of which is thus the fundamental task of moral philosophy. Second, Paton objects to Moore's appeal to self-evident intuitions: with Moore in mind, he refers to those

> who affirm without shame or subterfuge that values must be apprehended in [a] purely intuitive way. The result is obvious. They can only assert dogmatically that they know what goodness is, and that this thing, that thing, and the other thing, are good in themselves. The cynical observer can hardly fail to suggest that there is a curious resemblance between what they happen to like and what they assert

[68] Moore 1993, §113, p. 237.   [69] Foster 1910, p. 227.

to be absolutely good. They seem to be imposing their own purely subjective preferences on all other men. (GW, pp. 24–5)

As a Scot in very English Oxford for much of his career, Paton apparently always maintained cordial and correct relationships with his colleagues, but was not especially "clubable" like Moore in the Apostles, and while Moore might have been found in an art gallery in his spare time, Paton was more likely to spend his on a tennis court. Perhaps the experience of being something of an outsider allowed him to recognize that what for Moore were self-evident, intuited, synthetic truths about what is ultimately good were just personal preferences.[70] In general, Paton agrees with Moore that there can be no direct proof of moral first principles by straightforward deduction from something else, in which case of course they would not be first principles, but, in the idealist traditions, he holds that ethical principles can and must be validated by their coherence with our overall conception and knowledge of reality.

Finally—and here we move from meta-ethics to substantive moral philosophy—Paton objects to Moore's conception of the good as simple and undefinable. For him, as an heir to the idealist tradition, there are no simples but everything is connected to everything else, and goodness can never be an intrinsic property of something simple but can only consist in the coherence of something complex, or in the coherence of something complex within itself and within ever-larger contexts—ultimately, in the coherence of any individual human will both within itself and with the community of all rational beings. In the spirit of Bradley, what Paton objects to is Moore's method of abstraction, his attempt to isolate goodness from everything else instead of finding it precisely in the coherence of everything. "Mr. Moore, in his passion for the objectivity of goodness, seeks to divorce it altogether from human nature and human will" (GW, p. 120). This leads Paton to a moral position in the spirit of Bradley, Green, and Royce: "To find a moral good and evil we must pass beyond the isolated and abstract individual, and ultimately to an all-inclusive society of all reasonable beings" (GW, p. 27). "In the special case of goodness, that self or will is coherent and good which wills the momentary actions as part of an all-inclusive whole of coherent willing, and, in willing the part, wills the whole" (GW, p. 28). Of course, both forms of coherence can only ever be ideals, or regulative principles, goals that we strive to achieve in our finite lifetimes and in our finite interactions with the small part of the rest of humanity, let alone of all possible rational beings, with whom any one of us ever actually interacts. Paton can put this point in fancy terms: "willing—and indeed all spiritual activity—is not immediate but self-mediating and self-transcendent, that it is in short a spiritual activity and not a thing" (GW, p. 121).

---

[70] See W. H. Walsh's memorial notice, Walsh 1972, at p. 296.

But this is only his use of idealist language to insist that goodness cannot consist in some simple relationship between a will and an object that is intrinsically good, which can be considered out of its larger context, indeed as it were out of time itself. Rather it consists in the temporally extended relationship of one act of willing in an individual to the other actual and possible acts of willing of that individual and to the actual and possible wills of other human beings, indeed of other reasonable beings if there are any besides humans (not an issue to which Paton wishes to devote much ink).

The fundamental principle of Paton's normative ethics is thus that "Good and evil arise in so far as the one will can be divided against itself." The divided will is evil; "The good will overcomes this division or antagonism or incoherence, and is the synthesis of differences in one coherent whole" (GW, p. 122).[71] Meta-ethically, this is not to be the deliverance of some sort of pure intuition, but is to be grounded "on the basis of a reasonably critical common sense, in the light of which action itself usually takes place" (GW, p. 78). This could make it sound as if Paton's model is his Glasgow predecessor Thomas Reid rather than Kant; but of course Kant himself purported to argue from "common rational moral cognition" in section I of the Groundwork (G, 4: 393) and even maintained, whether credibly or not, that the metaphysical argument of section III, from the "self-activity" of the noumenal self to its autonomy and therefore subjection to the moral law, is based on a distinction between phenomena and noumena evident to "the commonest understanding" (G, 4: 450). Paton is not following Kant in appealing to any distinction between phenomena and noumena, but is proposing to ground the argument for his conception of good will on a persuasive definition of reason, reasonableness, or rationality—in this he is preparing the way for the "constructivist" approach to Kantian moral philosophy that we will examine in the final chapter of this book.[72] His task is to argue that the ideal of reasonableness that sets coherence in the individual will as the task of each individual also sets the coherence of individual wills with each other as the task of each individual, to the extent that working towards that goal is in the power of each. How does reason demand that the "policy" or coherent life of each—it would imply too much foresight to call this "life-plan"—become part of the "social will" that comprehends individual families and associations up to the level of individual states and then beyond that to humanity as a whole?

---

[71] Paton 1927, p. 122.

[72] But unlike John Rawls later, Paton makes no distinction between reasonableness and rationality. For Rawls the former is the recognition that like cases should be treated alike, and is the source of morality; the latter is the application of means-end reasoning to one's own advantage. For Paton, means-end reasoning is part of reason as such, though drawing on factual knowledge of the world (GW, p. 92), but only part of reason or reasonableness, which sets the goal of coherence among volitions, actions, and the facts of the world in which they take place.

In part Paton repeats the traditional argument going back to Hobbes that prudence requires coherence between the individual will or policy and that of increasingly broader societies:

> By some kink or flaw or passion we may try to shut ourselves into ourselves and to satisfy only what are called the self-regarding instincts, but there is in this nothing reasonable and a life of this kind is patently straitened and impoverished. We should merely impoverish and straiten our lives still more, if we attempted to satisfy even the self-regarding instincts in complete isolation from other men. There may indeed be times when we can secure food and wealth and safety by being entirely indifferent to others, but generally speaking the exact reverse of this is truth. It is well to recognize at this level that the satisfaction of instinct may bring us into conflict with others, but we must recognise also, not only that some instincts are directed to the interests of others, but that all instincts may be, and some must be, satisfied in cooperation with others ... Whatever be the case with animals, human beings definitely, and apart from any theories, like to eat and drink in company, to make and spend money in cooperation with others, to share with others in the joys of creation, in the pains and fears of combat, in the excitement of triumphs won and of perils escaped.   (GW, pp. 231–2)

One might think here of the observation of another Scot, this time David Hume, that the human being is "the creature of the universe, who has the most ardent desire of society," so that "We can form no wish, which has not a reference to society" and "Every pleasure languishes when enjoy'd apart from company."[73] This was Hume's way of stating the ancient argument that in fact human self-interest and interest in the well-being of others typically coincide. Or as Paton puts the point, in words that could easily have come from Hume or from that other Scot, Adam Smith, "Not only do we enter into the worlds of art and thought and action through our sympathy and cooperation with others, but our enjoyment is intensified, and our consciousness of value increased, because we can share in these worlds with others and others can share with us" (GW, p. 299). But of course for Hume this was an empirically founded generalization, and as Kant objected no genuinely universal and necessary principle can be empirically grounded: in the case of aesthetics a mere "tendency" towards "sociability" and the "empirical interest in the beautiful" grounded upon it is not enough to ground the judgment that an object is truly beautiful, but such a judgment must have some sort of a priori foundation (CPJ, §41, 5: 296–7); and the same is true in moral philosophy. That self-interest and interest in others coincide most of the time is not good enough; and Paton too recognizes that morality cannot be merely a matter of

---

[73] Hume, T, book II, part II, section 5, paragraph 15; vol. 1, p. 234.

social instincts. That we are born into families and rely upon families and larger communities is certainly a fact, and takes us some of the way to the formation of a will that is concerned with its coherence with the wills of others in such groups as well as with its more internal coherence, but this alone cannot take us all the way to the moral or good will (*GW*, pp. 239–40). Nor will the fact that we all (supposedly) recognize the necessity of following the rules of the state for our "security and for the satisfaction of our economic needs" and treat the obligations of the state as if they were "already absolute," unlike the rules of, say, cricket, which we recognize to be a game "which we may share in or not, more or less as we please" (*GW*, p. 287). For no state represents the interests of all of humanity, but that is the object of morality. To be sure, Paton observes, in most cases morality will make no greater demand on individuals than that they play by the rules of their families, their businesses or professions, and their states, and most of the time most people can do this without special effort (*GW*, p. 292)—in practice, morality is not always demanding—but it is always possible that it might demand more than this. What is the basis of this demand?

The answer to this question seems to be Paton's allegiance to the idealist ideal of coherence. The final book of *The Good Will* starts with a renewed emphasis on coherence as the goal of thought as well as action, goals that he takes to be self-evident, and to be more fully realized the wider their scope. Thus "We recognise the truth of our thinking by its coherence with the thinking of ourselves and others ... we have in our living and growing thinking, in our science and history and philosophy, a body of truth which lives through the principle of coherence" (*GW*, p. 316). Similarly, "we judge our actions by their coherence with the actions of those who are making a serious effort to will coherently with all good men." The ideal of the good will is, in a way, circular: to have a good will is to will coherently with other people of good will. But this is a virtuous circle; whether in the case of truth coherence is what it consists in or is just our best criterion for what truth actually consists in, correspondence between belief and fact, in the case of action coherence among wills, the condition in which each can pursue his or her own policy or life insofar as it is consistent with and conducive to the successful pursuit of their policies by others, is goodness, or the goodness of will, itself. There is no need to worry about "cheap scepticism" here, according to Paton (*GW*, p. 244). Ultimately, Paton takes it to be self-evident that to aim at coherence not only within one's own will but with the will of in principle all others is what it is to have a good will. Like Moore, the principle of morality must ultimately be founded on a self-evident recognition that might just as well be called an intuition as anything else. The difference, it can be said on Paton's behalf, is that Paton's preference for coherence in willing is entrenched in a larger ideal of coherence in human thought and action generally, whereas Moore's preferences for the enjoyment of beauty and the friendship of others have to stand on their own as, so to speak, atoms of goodness.

In his otherwise judicious assessment of Paton's strengths and weaknesses as both a Kant scholar and a philosopher in his own right, W. H. Walsh objected that Paton failed to answer "the question what more there is to a good will besides its coherence.... In general, the weakness of his ethical theory lies in failure to deal adequately with the objective side of value: he is so anxious to connect goodness with willing that he forgets that a will must have a content as well as a form. No doubt devotion to the common Idealist slogan about the inseparability of form and content, subject and object, helped to conceal this important truth from him."[74] This misses the point of Paton's conception of coherence and of Kant's idea of the empire of ends, of which Paton's moral ideal can be considered an interpretation. Kant defines the empire of ends as "a whole both of rational beings as ends in themselves and of the ends of his own that each may set himself" (G, 4: 433); the point is that morality does *not* directly dictate the ends that each may set for him- or herself, or the content of individual wills, but requires only that each be left as free to set his or her own ends, whatever they might be, as is compatible with all being equally free, and then that people help others in the pursuit of their permissible needs when they can, within the framework of their other duties. Kantian morality is concerned with the formal requirements of action, at several levels, rather than with trying to specify some first-order ends as valid and mandatory for everyone; the "ends that are also duties," self-perfection and the happiness of others, are still second-order, formal ends. That is what Moore, for example, got wrong with his insistence that aesthetic experience and the enjoyment of friendship are the ultimate goods for everyone, but what Paton got right. And in making his objection to Paton, Walsh may have revealed that he was more of a Hegelian idealist than Paton was, that is, that it was he who wanted to collapse or at least disregard the distinction between form and content, as opposed to recognizing that this distinction is essential to morality—that leaving each as free to set his or her own ends—whether pushpin or poetry, as Jeremy Bentham famously put it—as is compatible with all being equally free.

To conclude this discussion of *The Good Will*, I return to my opening suggestion of a connection even if not one of actual influence between Paton and Royce. Royce's version of the empire of ends was the idea that morality requires loyalty not only to specific causes, but also to the ideal of loyalty itself—that the moral person recognizes the value of loyalties other than her own, and works toward a world in which different loyalties may be possible, not identical to each other but in some way compatible with each other. Paton also puts his moral ideal in terms of loyalty, suggesting that perhaps he did imbibe Royce while he was in California:

---

[74] Walsh 1972, p. 298.

We might describe the principle of coherence as a principle of loyalty or even of love. But it is not a blind loyalty or a mere personal love. It is loyalty to a society of persons as animated by the spirit of loyalty or love itself. The good man has loyalty, and in a sense love, for those with whom he collaborates; his will is set on working with them, but it may be that he has to cease working with them and even to oppose them, if this is necessary for the coherence of the whole. In this he is not disloyal but more loyal... (*GW*, p. 345)

A person of good will shows her loyalty in the first instance by collaborating with and promoting the aims of specific societies—family, school, business, church, state—with which she identifies; but those loyalties are constrained by her loyalty to the idea of the coherence of human wills or the wills of all reasonable beings in general; specific loyalties are always conditional upon this fundamental loyalty. It is hard to imagine that Paton's expression of his point in these Roycean terms was entirely coincidental; but even if it was that only confirms that this was a reasonable way for both Paton and Royce to interpret the Kantian ideal of the empire of ends.

In sum, the moral philosophies of Bradley, Green, Caird, Royce, and Paton all culminate in interpretations of Kant's conception of the empire of ends. Since Kant himself regarded this as the culminating formulation of the categorical imperative, the ideal for the "complete determination" of all maxims (*G*, 4: 437), the Anglophone idealists, in spite of their supposedly Hegelian loyalties, deeply and beneficially imbibed the spirit of Kant's moral philosophy. We will now turn to look at a series of British philosophers, from Henry Sidgwick to Bernard Williams, who distanced themselves from Kant wholly or in good part.

13

Kant in Cambridge

Sidgwick and Moore

13.1. John Stuart Mill

It is common now to oppose Kantianism to utilitarianism or more generally consequentialism as the two main modern approaches to moral philosophy. Some add "virtue ethics" as a third, equally independent and important approach,[1] although a Kantian would argue that a virtuous person, the fundamental concept in virtue ethics, cannot be defined except as one committed (with the "strength of will") to the performance of right actions, and a utilitarian would argue that a virtuous person cannot be defined except as one committed to the pursuit of good actions, in the form of those with the best consequences foreseeable to the agent. Thus both Kantians and consequentialists would regard virtue ethics as an approach to ethics that is dependent upon their own rather than equally fundamental to it. Another alternative to Kantianism on the one hand and consequentialism on the other hand has been "particularism," the view that moral judgments are not based on general principles, whether Kantian or consequentialist in character, but are self-standing responses to particular situations, with general principles merely summaries of such responses. This position has recently been represented by Jonathan Dancy,[2] but could be traced back to Adam Smith's account of the role of general rules in ethics.[3] An intermediate connection is the "intuitionism" of the early twentieth century, represented by H. A. Prichard, and W. D. Ross, who argued for the immediate perception of multiple moral rules or duties at a level of generality between moral judgments about particular situations and actions and a fundamental, universally valid principle of the type sought by both Kantians and consequentialists. This chapter will focus on the apparent conflict between Kantian and utilitarian moral philosophy, as presented by Henry Sidgwick and G. E. Moore. The following chapter will focus on the conflict between Kant and the "intuitionist" "deontologists" Prichard and Ross, who argued that we intuit a number of distinct "*prima facie*" duties rather than a single fundamental principle, whether Kantian or consequentialist, and the account of the "limits" of moral philosophy offered by Bernard Williams, who

---

[1] See, e.g., Baron et al. 1997.   [2] Dancy 2004.
[3] See Smith 1976, part III, chapter IV, esp. pp. 159–60.

Kant's Impact on Moral Philosophy. Paul Guyer, Oxford University Press. © Paul Guyer 2024.
DOI: 10.1093/oso/9780199592456.003.0014

declared a pox on the houses of both Kantianism and consequentialism in favor of a different form of individualism, that is, for the position that putative moral duties do not always override the identity-defining projects of individuals. Elizabeth Anscombe criticized both consequentialism (this name was her coinage) and Kantian moral philosophy, and she will also be briefly discussed. The chapter after that will concern the attempt by a number of writers both British and American, namely Richard Hare, Kurt Baier (an adoptive American), Marcus Singer, and finally Derek Parfit, to argue that Kantianism and utilitarianism have similar normative implications. The final chapters of this Part and of the whole book examine the "constructivist" approach to Kant's moral philosophy initiated by John Rawls and pursued by many of his students, foremost among them Thomas Nagel, Onora O'Neill, Christine Korsgaard, and Adrian Piper.

I start with Sidgwick because a confrontation with Kant was not a large part of the agenda of the first great nineteenth-century utilitarian, John Stuart Mill. Mill's empiricist, inductivist approach to the principles of natural science, mathematics, and even logic in his *System of Logic*, first published in 1843, is certainly directed in a general way against the a priori approach to these issues that he associated with Kant and other German philosophers. But he does not seem to have been closely engaged with Kant or his successors, certainly in his formative years. In a letter to Auguste Comte, he wrote about them:

> I cannot perhaps give you a very decided opinion, having myself read neither Kant nor Hegel, nor any other chiefs of this school. I have known them only from their English and French interpreters. This philosophy, for me, has been very useful. It has corrected the exclusively analytic aspect of my thought, as nourished by Bentham and French philosophers of the eighteenth century.

He adds here that he found the idea of historical development in the Germans, particularly Hegel, helpful, but continues:

> When I later attempted to read some German philosophical works, I found that I already possessed all that was useful to me, and the rest was tedious to the point where I could not continue the reading.[4]

So Mill certainly attributed no formative role in the development of his own thought, whether in the way of influence or of opposition, to German philosophy in general or to Kant in particular.[5] This seems to be as true for moral philosophy

---

[4] Mill 1956–91, vol. 13, p. 576, cited from Rosen 2022, p. 109.
[5] The exception to this would be the influence of Wilhelm von Humboldt's *On the Limits of State Power* on Mill's *On Liberty*.

as for theoretical philosophy. In his central text in moral philosophy, *Utilitarianism* (1863), Mill has only this to say about Kant:

> This remarkable man, whose system of thought will long remain one of the landmarks in the history of philosophical speculation, does, in the [*Groundwork for the Metaphysics of Morals*], lay down an universal first principle as the origin and ground of moral obligation; it is this:—"So act, that the rule on which thou actest would admit of being adopted as a law by all rational beings." But when he begins to deduce from this precept any of the actual duties of morality, he fails, almost grotesquely, to show that there would be any contradiction, any logical (not to say) physical impossibility, in the adoption by all rational beings of the most outrageously immoral rules of conduct. All he shows is that the *consequences* of their universal adoption would be such as no one would choose to incur.[6]

Thus Mill joins a long line of critics from Schopenhauer to Parfit arguing that Kant's fundamental principle of morality is just consequentialism in disguise. His version of the objection is perhaps closest to Schopenhauer's, and is open to the same response: Yes, in working out whether we could act on a maxim while also willing it to be a universal law of nature, that is, willing that everyone else also actually act upon it, we consider what the consequences of the latter would be for the former, that is, whether we could indeed act upon our proposed maxim if everyone else did so as well. This is the intellectual test that in recent years Onora O'Neill and John Rawls have called the "CI-procedure."[7] But the difference between Kant's use of consequences and the standard consequentialist test of proposed maxims of action (as Kant would put it) or actions (as consequentialists would put it) is obvious: to apply the test, the consequentialist asks whether the *actually* expected consequences of the action, as best they can be foreseen, would constitute the best possible outcome (e.g., greatest possible happiness for all affected) in the situation at hand, while Kant's test asks the agent whether the *hypothetical* consequences of his proposed maxim, that is, what would follow *if* everyone else also acted on it, would be *consistent* with his own proposal to act on the maxim; and on Kant's approach, the reason *why* the moral agent must ask this question is not because he is—immediately and directly—concerned with the actual consequences of his action—although in the end the agent cannot help but be concerned with universal happiness as well as with rightness, which is why only the highest good is the *complete object* although not *supreme principle* of morality (*CPracR*, 5: 110–11)—but because the agent must ask after the universalizability of his maxims to assess whether his maxims would treat the humanity

---

in every rational being or person, himself and all others, as an end and never merely as a means (G, 4: 428–9). Asking about the hypothetical consequences of the universalization of a proposed maxim is only a step in asking about the universalizability of the maxim, not a question about the actual consequences of the maxim, and that is in turn only a step toward asking whether the maxim of one's proposed action treats everyone as an end, not merely a means, and could thereby serve as part of the legislation for an empire of ends.

A serious engagement with Kant's moral philosophy awaited the next great British utilitarian, Henry Sidgwick. Before we turn to Sidgwick, however, let me suggest that at the deepest level of his thought Mill seems to have understood Kant and learned from him much better than he realized. For *On Liberty* is just as much a Kantian work as *Utilitarianism* is supposed to be anti-Kantian. In his recent book on the "progressive," "humanist" Mill, Philip Kitcher shows that "*On Liberty* emphasizes a fundamental freedom, grounded in the ability to choose the pattern of your own life, and to pursue it as you think best"—*yet*, "Everyone should have this freedom."[8] Kitcher also argues that Mill's great tract on *The Subjection of Women* is premised on the recognition that "when basic physical needs are satisfied, 'freedom is the first and strongest want of human nature'."[9] Mill reconciles this recognition of the fundamental value of freedom with his utilitarianism simply by supposing that it is the satisfaction of this first and strongest want of human nature in all that will produce the greatest happiness in all. Now, Kitcher does not association Mill's recognition that freedom is the first and strongest want of all human beings with Kant; he says rather that Mill "makes the notion of autonomous choice (derived from the German thinker Wilhelm von Humboldt) central to the good life. People should decide what is most important for them. The life you live should be your own."[10] Kitcher is referring to von Humboldt's essay on the *Limits of State Action*, written in 1791–2 but published only posthumously in 1852[11]—but thus right in the middle of Mill's mature work. I have not discussed von Humboldt's work in this book because it more properly belongs to a work on Kant's specifically political rather than general moral philosophy. But what inspired von Humboldt? Surely nothing other than Kant's moral ideal of the value of equal freedom. In learning from von Humboldt, and reworking the utilitarianism that he learned from Jeremy Bentham and his father James Mill, John Stuart Mill was learning from Kant.

The greatest follower of John Stuart Mill was Henry Sidgwick. But Mill's failure to acknowledge the Kantian source for his own doctrine of liberty may have had the effect of masking the importance of the value of liberty from Sidgwick. Or so I shall now argue.[12]

---

[8] Kitcher 2023, p. 18.   [9] Kitcher 2023, p. 110.   [10] Kitcher 2023, p. 24.
[11] See von Humboldt 1969, p. vii.   [12] In what follows I draw on Guyer 2020b.

13.2. Sidgwick

Henry Sidgwick (1838–1900) tried to steer a path between the empirically based utilitarianism of Jeremy Bentham and John Stuart Mill and the idealism of many of his later Victorian contemporaries, above all his Rugby School and Cambridge classmate Thomas Hill Green.[13] That is to say, Sidgwick wanted to argue for utilitarianism, but on the basis of self-evident axioms rather than empirical generalizations, thus on the basis of "non-natural" premises cognized a priori. In this he influenced George Edward Moore (1873–1958), who commenced twentieth-century British ethics and meta-ethics with his *Principia Ethica* in 1903, and attended at least one of Sidgwick's courses at Cambridge as well as hearing him at meetings of the Cambridge Apostles, of which both were members. But in this meta-ethical approach if not in his utilitarian conclusion Sidgwick himself acknowledged the influence of Kant. Indeed, in the first edition of *Methods of Ethics*, the *magnum opus* first published in 1874 but which Sidgwick revised through the sixth edition, posthumously published in 1902, Sidgwick wrote that Kant as well as Samuel Clarke were "the two thinkers who in modern times have most earnestly maintained the strictly scientific character of ethical principles," by which he meant their self-evident, a priori character.[14] But Sidgwick also criticized Kant on several points. If he is remembered by contemporary Kant scholars at all, it is for the critique of what he thought were the confusions of Kant's treatment of freedom, first published in *Mind* in 1888 and then reprinted as an appendix to the final editions of *Methods of Ethics*. Because he was so dismissive of Kant's treatment of freedom, specifically of freedom of the *will*, I will argue, he did not recognize Kant's treatment of freedom of *choice and action* as the foundation of morality, although as we have seen this was a foundation somewhat disguised by Kant in the *Groundwork* under the guise of "humanity," and clearer in other sources such as the lectures on ethics to which Sidgwick had no access. Rather, Sidgwick identified Kant's concept of humanity strictly with rationality, not free choice and action, and did not see how that could provide an informative end for morality, or conception of the good; he thought the maximization of happiness was a more plausible candidate for that role. But Kant's treatment of happiness as the indirect object of morality, the ideal

---

[13] The literature on Sidgwick is vast, although little of it directly concerns his relation to Kant. For intellectual biography, see Schultz 2004 and Schultz 2017, chapter 4. The first extended treatment of Sidgwick's moral philosophy was Broad 1930, chapter 6, which comprises half of the book (pp. 143–256). Schneewind 1977 is a detailed analysis of Sidgwick's philosophical context as well as of his arguments. Other useful works on Sidgwick include Irwin 2009, pp. 426–535; Phillips 2011 and 2022; De Lazari-Radek and Singer 2014; Hurka 2014, chapters 5 and 7; Crisp 2015; and the essays collected in Harrison 2001, and Paytas and Henning 2020. Schultz 2014, De Lazari-Radek 2017, and Skorupski 2021, pp. 458–81, are helpful brief treatments of Sidgwick, the first including an extensive bibliography.

[14] Sidgwick, *ME*, 1st edition, p. 357, cited in Schneewind 1977, p. 291.

consequence of treating all persons as ends in themselves in virtue of their humanity, has advantages over Sidgwick's direct appeal to happiness, particularly, I will suggest, in dealing with the inability to resolve the "dualism of practical reason" that in Sidgwick's eyes ultimately doomed his own project of arguing for utilitarianism. Finally, Sidgwick was critical of Kant's doctrine of the postulates of pure practical reason, that is, of Kant's acceptance of belief in the existence of God and the personal immortality of human beings on practical rather than theoretical grounds. Indeed, Sidgwick spent much time in the examination of "parapsychology"—claims to communication with the spirits of the dead and that sort of thing—in the search for empirical evidence of immortality, and honestly concluded that no such evidence was forthcoming, and therefore no empirical evidence for the postulate of immortality. On this issue Sidgwick insisted upon an empiricist rather than a priori method. Yet he also concluded that the dualism of practical reason could not be resolved without the postulate of the existence of a benevolent author of the universe, and thus conceded the necessity if not the plausibility of Kant's postulate of the existence of God.[15]

Some lecture notes included by his editor E. E. Constance Jones in the Preface to the sixth edition of *Methods of Ethics* sum up Sidgwick's criticism of Kant's position on free will:

> Kant's resting of morality on Freedom ... involves the fundamental confusion of using "freedom" in two distinct senses—"freedom" that is realised only when we do right, when reason triumphs over inclination, and "freedom" that is realised equally when we choose to do wrong, and which is apparently implied in the notion of ill-desert.   (*ME*, p. xvii)

This criticism and the prominence that it has since been given are puzzling. The criticism itself is puzzling, because as we have seen this objection was raised early and Kant seems to have made precisely the distinction that Sidgwick wants at least by the time of the 1793 *Religion within the Boundaries of Mere Reason*, to which Sidgwick does not refer.[16] Kant did not make this distinction in Sidgwick's words, of course, but made it in the form of his distinction between *Wille* and *Willkühr* in the *Religion* and then the *Metaphysics of Morals*, and, more importantly, substantively in the form of his insistence upon our radical freedom to choose whether or not to subordinate self-love to the moral law. And the prominence given to this criticism by Sidgwick may also seem puzzling because the issue of free will does

---

[15] On this issue, see e.g., Schultz 2017, pp. 276–301 and Phillips 2022, pp. 215–20.

[16] Perhaps because this late work of Kant's was not widely known in the English-speaking world until the 1934 translation by Theodore M. Greene and Hoyt H. Hudson, Kant 1960. There was in fact a much earlier complete translation, by Semple in 1838, but that could well have faded from memory by Sidgwick's time. For further information on the translations, see George di Giovanni's "Translator's Introduction" in Kant 1996b, at pp. 50–4.

not itself seem central to the argument of *The Methods of Ethics*, being the explicit subject of only one of thirty-five chapters—although in this chapter Sidgwick does give an exceptionally lucid statement of the position that determinism is the presupposition of all explanations of human action, yet that it is irrelevant to the practical task of decision-making and also irrelevant to our practices of holding people responsible and punishing them for their violations as long as we do not accept a retributive theory of punishment (*ME*, pp. 70–2).[17]

However, a general discomfort with Kant's position on freedom is central to one of the main arguments of *Methods*, namely discomfort with Kant's attempt to derive our determinate duties from freedom of choice—the freedom of each human being to set and pursue her own ends—as the foundational *value* from which our more determinate duties can be derived, including what Kant calls the imperfect duty to promote the happiness of others and what Sidgwick calls the duty of "Rational Benevolence." There are two central debates in *The Methods of Ethics*, one between "philosophical intuitionism," which insists upon the self-evident fundamentality of certain duties—in this regard what we now call "deontology"[18]—and utilitarianism, the view that the greatest possible happiness of sentient beings is the fundamental good and defines what is right, and one between utilitarianism or "universalistic hedonism" and what Sidgwick calls "rational egoism" or "egoistic hedonism," the view that it is self-evidently rational for each agent to pursue *his or her* own happiness even if that conflicts with the pursuit of universal happiness, which it sometimes even if not always does. Kant is Sidgwick's poster boy for "philosophical intuitionsm," and the heart of the debate is the question whether Kant or utilitarianism succeeds in deriving a duty of benevolence with sufficient determinacy to resolve any moral conflicts within the practice of benevolence or between the practice of benevolence and the other fundamental requirement of morality, namely justice, which Sidgwick holds to be a *sine qua non* of any adequate "method of ethics." Sidgwick's position is that Kant's treatment of this duty is a failure that can only be remedied by appeal to the utilitarian principle that "the conduct which, under any given circumstances, is objectively right, is that which will produce the greatest amount of happiness on the whole; that is, taking into account all whose happiness is affected by this conduct" (*ME*, p. 411). Of course, this is a direct rejection of what Kant himself intended as the alternative to the form of utilitarianism with which he was

---

[17] On the relevance of Sidgwick's discussion of freedom of the will to the larger argument of *Methods*, see Schneewind 1977, pp. 207–12, and Nagano-Okuno 2020. For a brief treatment, see Phillips 2022, pp. 53–7.

[18] This term was apparently originally coined by Jeremy Bentham; see Richardson 2006. It was given wide currency, in the adjectival form "deontological," by C. D. Broad in Broad 1930, at pp. 162–4, and has since become a retrospective characterization of Kant's approach of putting the determination of the "right" before that of the "good." Broad contrasted deontological theories to "teleological" theories, including utilitarianism; G. E. M. Anscombe later replaced Broad's "teleological" with "consequentialist," which has now become standard; see Phillips 2022, p. 62, referring to Anscombe 1958.

familiar, that represented for example by Francis Hutcheson, for Sidgwick's claim is that only utilitarianism can give *determinate* duties while Kant's criticism was precisely that the concept of happiness is too *indeterminate* to give rise to a determinate specification of our duties. In Kant's words, "Happiness is such an indeterminate concept that, although every human being wishes to obtain this, he can still never say determinately and consistently with himself what he really wishes and wills.... One cannot therefore act on determinate principles for the sake of being happy, but only on empirical counsels... which experience teaches are most conducive to well-being on the average" (G, 4: 418). Sidgwick rejects Kant's worry and claims to have bettered him on the question of the duty of benevolence—although Sidgwick's ultimate concession that he cannot provide a rational ground for deciding between universalistic and egoistic hedonism, that is, between utilitarianism and rational egoism, should certainly cast doubt on his claim to have shown that utilitarianism is superior to Kantianism.

   I will return briefly to the problem of resolving what Sidgwick called the "dualism of the practical reason" at the end of this discussion. But my project here is not to try to establish whether Sidgwick's utilitarian principle does yield the determinacy of duties that he thought was lacking in previous accounts of benevolence including Kant's. I will not be asking whether Sidgwick establishes that meaningful quantifications of happiness and therefore comparisons of quantities of happiness, whether diachronic intrapersonal, synchronic interpersonal, or diachronic interpersonal, are really possible, or even whether Sidgwick actually succeeds in deriving maximizing utilitarianism from his premises.[19] I will argue only that Kant has a more plausible derivation of the duty of benevolence than Sidgwick recognizes. This is not, however, a direct derivation from the value of happiness, but an indirect derivation that goes through the value of freedom, the foundation of Kant's approach to moral philosophy to which Sidgwick seems to have been blind. Perhaps the confusion of some of Kant's treatments of the freedom of the will in the works prior to the *Religion* blinded Sidgwick to Kant's treatment of freedom of choice as the fundamental moral norm and value, which can be separated from the metaphysical question of whether human wills are always free to choose to do what is right. Or maybe he could never really question the view of happiness as a meaningful account of the fundamental value for human beings that he inherited from Bentham, Mill, and many others

---

[19] Schneewind saw no problem in Sidgwick's derivation of the requirement to maximize (aggregate) happiness (Schneewind 1977, pp. 307–8). Irwin argues that Sidgwick does not succeed in deriving maximizing utilitarianism from the maxims of justice, prudence, and benevolence recognized by previous intuitionists but only from his metaphysical assumption that all individuals are only parts of a single larger whole (thus Sidgwick's ethics turns out to be a rationalist version of Schopenhauer's, or closer to the moral philosophies of Bradley and Green than is usually thought), and that both maximization and any distributive constraint on aggregate happiness require additional principles to the goodness of happiness as such, thereby undermining Sidgwick's attempt to provide a single foundational principle for utilitarianism (Irwin 2009, pp. 509–10, 515–18).

in the British tradition, and for that reason never really gave Kant's radical alternative a chance.

The fundamental issue between Sidgwick and Kant is to some extent obscured by the facts that Kant's account of the duty of benevolence is only part of his larger system of duties, as Sidgwick himself recognized, and, as Terence Irwin has argued, Sidgwick's utilitarian principle itself functions only within a larger account of duty that also shares elements with Kant's own wider scheme. Sidgwick does not reject Kant's system of duties as a whole, although he does criticize some aspects of the system beside the duty of benevolence, nor does he in fact attempt to replace it entirely and solely with the utilitarian principle. Rather, he does leave in place central features of the common-sense morality that he took Kant to have attempted to formalize, although his project is to justify them on utilitarian grounds. So we have to consider Sidgwick's critique of Kant's treatment of the positive duty of benevolence, which reveals his failure to appreciate that Kant was attempting to derive even this duty to promote happiness not from the value of happiness as such but from the value of freedom, in the larger context of Sidgwick's argument.

Sidgwick considers three "methods of ethics," namely "egoistic hedonism," "intuitionism," and "universalistic hedonism," or for short "egoism," "intuitionism," and "utilitarianism." By a "method of ethics" Sidgwick means "any rational procedure by which we determine what individual human beings 'ought'—or what it is 'right' for them—to do, or to seek to realize by voluntary action" (*ME*, p. 1), or a normative principle or set of principles about what we ought to do rather than an epistemological or meta-ethical principle about how we know what we ought to do. But while egoistic and universalistic hedonism do sound like normative positions, commanding either the pursuit of one's own happiness or the pursuit of the happiness of all as the basis of all duty, to more recent ears intuitionism sounds like a meta-ethical rather than normative method of ethics, that is, it would seem to concern the basis on which duty is known rather than the content of duty, namely by intuition or perception rather than by induction, inference, or some other method.[20] But Sidgwick considers that a variety of "intuitions"—about individual situations and proposed courses of action within them, perceived by "perceptional intuitionism";[21] about moral rules of "common

---

[20] "Philosophical intuitionism" is contrasted to "common sense intuitionism," which refers to the common-sense assumption that multiple deontological principles are simply given, as in, for example, the Ten Commandments; philosophical intuitionism is essentially the effort to reduce common-sense intuitionism to a single principle not necessarily cast in everyday language—thus, Kant's categorical imperative. Sidgwick's discussion is confused by his use of "intuitionism" to connote both positions on the normative *contents* of morality ("methods of ethics") and a meta-ethical position about the *source* of morality ("first principles"); see Phillips 2022, pp. 59–65. Hurka 2014, pp. 112–22, focuses on Sidgwick's intuitionism as a meta-ethical position. In the end, Sidgwick's meta-ethical position is that *any* plausible ethical theory must have some self-evident foundation, thus meta-ethically even utilitarianism is a form of intuitionism.

[21] This is what Jonathan Dancy has revived under the name of "particularism"; see Dancy 1993 and 2004.

sense," recognized by "dogmatic intuitionism"; or about genuine philosophical principles, recognized by "philosophical intuitionism"—are supposed to yield normative principles distinct from those of either egoistic or universalistic hedonism, so that intuitionism can be considered a distinctive ethical as well as meta-ethical method.[22] Egoistic hedonism is initially dismissed as too patently in conflict with our pre-theoretical beliefs about and right and wrong to be a contender as a genuine method of ethics, although it will come back to haunt Sidgwick in the form of the supposed dualism of practical reason; but the first debate of the book is between common-sense or dogmatic intuitionism and utilitarianism. Sidgwick's meta-ethical argument is that both Kantianism and utilitarianism need at least one intuition for their foundation, and so in its meta-ethical sense intuitionism cannot be dismissed, but that utilitarianism does a better job than Kantianism of saving what is true in the normative content of common-sense or dogmatic intuitionism and in particular a better job of resolving the conflicts of duties that arise on common-sense intuitions. Kant himself certainly thought precisely the opposite: in his own view his approach to morality—whether it emphasizes the universalibility constraint on permissible maxims or the status of persons as ends and never merely as means—avoids the indeterminacy of any conception of happiness, whether personal or interpersonal, that plagues utilitarianism. This is the main issue between them. (Sidgwick himself dispatched what is now supposed to be the third main method of ethics, "virtue ethics" before it ever got off the ground, with the statement that the "so-called Virtues which can be thought to be essentially and always such … as Wisdom, Universal Benevolence, and (in a sense) Justice … manifestly involve [a] notion of Good, supposed already determinate"; *ME*, pp. 392–3. Kant would have said that the identification of such virtues depends upon an antecedent conception of what is right rather than what is good, but would have agreed that any definition of the virtues in virtue ethics is parasitic on a more fundamental principle of morality. So virtue ethics is not an issue between Sidgwick and Kant.[23]) To put the main point another way, since Sidgwick largely accepts the duties of justice and prudence as formulated in both common-sense and philosophical intuitionism, including Kant's, the real debate between him and Kant concerns, again, the duty of benevolence.

Sidgwick sets the terms of this debate by proposing criteria for a successful method of ethics that any rational person would be hard-pressed to deny; they could be taken as criterial of rationality itself.[24] Were Sidgwick's criteria quoted without citation one might easily imagine that they came from Descartes's *Rules*

---

[22] For further discussion of this issue, see De Lazari-Radek and Singer 2014, p. 68, and Crisp 2020.

[23] Phillips 2022, p. 149, suggests that Sidgwick does not address what is now called virtue ethics. I think what I have just cited says all that needs to be said on the subject.

[24] David Philipps calls Sidgwick's primary mode of argumentation "criterial"; see Phillips 2011, pp. 63–76, and Phillips 2022, pp. 100–4.

for the Direction of the Mind, Spinoza's *Emendation of the Intellect*, or Locke's *Conduct of the Understanding*. Sidgwick's four conditions on any "reasoning" that would "lead us cogently to trustworthy conclusions" are (i) "The terms of the proposition must be clear and precise" (here Sidgwick himself mentions Descartes as a predecessor); (ii) "The self-evidence of the proposition must be ascertained by careful reflection," not asserted on the basis of "mere impressions or impulses" nor "mere opinions, to which the familiarity that comes from frequent hearing and repetition often gives a false appearance of self-evidence"; (iii) "The propositions accepted as self-evident must be mutually consistent"; and (iv) "Since it is implied in the very notion of Truth that it is essentially the same for all minds, the denial by another of a proposition that I have affirmed has a tendency to impair our confidence in its validity," thus "the absence of...disagreement must remain an indispensable negative condition of the certainty of our judgments" (*ME*, pp. 338–42).[25] From the last two requirements in particular Sidgwick infers the requirement of *determinacy*: any successful moral principle must exclude contradiction among particular judgments about duty within any one agent's set of moral judgments and between the moral judgments or judgment sets of different agents. If competing claims to duty do present themselves in either of these cases, there must be a way of resolving the apparent conflict. Sidgwick's general claim is that "we have no means of reducing" such a conflict "to a common standard, except by the application of the Utilitarian—or some similar—method" (*ME*, p. 342)—although in his view there is no other, "similar" method that can do this job. Kant would not disagree with Sidgwick's conditions: he too insists that any genuine practical law must be truly universal (and therefore necessary), and that there can be no unresolved conflicts of duty.[26] The difference between them is rather that Sidgwick denies that Kant's fundamental principle of morality can satisfy this requirement, while Kant denies that any conception of happiness, thus, *avant la lettre*, Sidgwick's method of utilitarianism, could satisfy the requirement.

But there is also an area of agreement between Sidgwick and Kant.[27] This is as follows. Sidgwick takes the lesson of common-sense intuitionism to be that there are three fundamental moral obligations, more basic than a variety of other duties

---

[25] De Lazari-Radek and Singer discuss these four criteria under the rubric "Sidgwick on Justifying Ethical Principles" (2014, pp. 90–2). I would rather think that the role of these criteria is to determine whether a proposed method of ethics is even a candidate for success, leaving the further question of the justification of any method of ethics that might pass this test open. This might better fit the structure of Sidgwick's overall argument as it evolves through the several editions of his work: in the earlier editions, the argument is that only utilitarianism can pass the test provided by the criteria, so no further question of justification need be broached; in the later editions, Sidgwick acknowledges that utilitarianism itself must rest on some fundamental justificatory intuition; see Preface to the 6th edition, pp. xx–xxi (of the 7th). See also Schneewind 1977, ch. 10, pp. 286–9; Hurka 2014, pp. 112–17; Schultz 2014, pp. 469–70 and Schultz 2017, pp. 255–6; and De Lazeri-Radek 2017, pp. 512–14.

[26] On the universality of any genuine practical law, see *CPracR*, 5: 19, and *MM* DV, Introduction, section VI, 6: 389; on the impossibility of a conflict of duties, see *MM*, Introduction, section III, 6: 224.

[27] See also Schneewind 1977, p. 286.

(or virtues) that common-sense recognizes, such as truthfulness, courage, and humility, namely the obligations to adhere to justice, prudence, and benevolence. Sidgwick takes Kant's form of philosophical intuitionism to replicate the principle of justice with the universal law formulation of the categorical imperative, which implies the negative (and perfect) duty not to harm the external freedom of others, and to be a basically adequate account of the common-sense duty of justice. (Sidgwick touches upon Kant's category of perfect duty to self, such as the duty to refrain from suicide from self-love, as part of common-sense intuitionism, but does not mention it in connection with Kant himself; see *ME*, pp. 327–8.) Sidgwick is less receptive to Kant's account of the two general imperfect duties, the duties to promote one's own perfection and the happiness of others. He objects to Kant's claim that there is no direct duty to promote one's own happiness, which Kant supposes everyone naturally seeks without constraint. This is why Kant designates self-perfection rather than prudence as the general form of imperfect duty to oneself. But Sidgwick does not see his disagreement with Kant about prudence as very deep (see also *OHP*, p. 276). His deep disagreement is rather that Kant does not have a cogent method of deriving the duty to promote the happiness of others, for two reasons. First, he thinks that Kant's attempt to derive such a duty from the requirement to universalize one's own maxim of seeking help from others to promote one's own happiness depends upon a contingent assumption that not everyone will make ("an empirical proposition which Kant cannot know *a priori*"; *ME*, p. 389).[28] Second, he thinks that Kant's requirement always to treat rational beings as ends rather than means has nothing to do with happiness at all: "the subjective ends of other men which Benevolence directs us to take as our own ends, would seem, according to Kant's own view, to depend upon and correspond to their *non-rational* impulses—their empirical desires and aversions" (*ME*, p. 390), not their *rational* nature. I will be questioning precisely this objection below. But first, a brief account of Sidgwick's own attempt to reconstruct the common-sense duties more successfully than he thinks that Kant managed to do.

Sidgwick accepts as self-evident the following two principles. The first is that "it cannot be right for A to treat B in a manner in which it would be wrong for B to treat A, merely on the ground that they are two different individuals, and without there being any difference between the natures or circumstances of the two which can be stated as a reasonable ground for differences of treatment." He regards this statement of the traditional canon of rationality that like cases be treated alike as equivalent to Kant's requirement of the universalizability of maxims. The second is that "the mere difference of priority and posteriority in time is not a reasonable ground for having more regard to the consciousness of one moment [than] to that

---

[28] See also Hurka 2014, p. 277.

of another" or, in the form in which this principle "practically presents itself to most men," "a smaller present good is not to be preferred to a greater future good (allowing for difference of certainty)" (that is, allowing a discount for the uncertainty of one's continued existence or capacity to enjoy the good at issue at any particular time in the future), which is the principle of prudence and at least part of one's own practical rationality that ought to be perfected by Kant's lights (*ME*, pp. 380–1). But as Sidgwick says, explicitly about the first of these principles but in effect about both, such principles "manifestly" do "not give complete guidance." The first principle merely throws "a definite *onus probandi* on the man who applies to another a treatment of which he would complain if applied to himself," but does not establish that this burden of proof cannot be satisfied (*ME*, p. 380); the second principle is not specific enough about what sorts of present and future goods can be compared to each other. But above all, these two principles do not establish that one has any positive duties to increase the good of others in any form, that is, they do not establish a principle of benevolence. The first is a negative principle, telling you not to treat one person differently from another, including not treating others differently from yourself, but does not tell you in positive terms what you owe to anyone, yourself or others;[29] the second principle patently applies only to oneself.

However, Sidgwick does believe that careful reflection leads to a reliable account of positive duties of benevolence to others.[30] His argument proceeds from the further, supposedly also self-evident principles that "the good of any one individual is of no more importance, from the point of view (if I may say so) of the Universe, than the good of any other," and further that "as a rational being I am bound to aim at good generally—so far as it is attainable by my efforts,—not merely at a particular part of it." These two principles together imply that each is to aim at the good of all, that is, "From these two rational intuitions we may deduce, as a necessary inference, the maxim of Benevolence in an abstract form: viz. that each one is morally bound to regard the good of any other individual as much as his own." From this it follows in turn that one is morally right to aim at one's own good only insofar as it is considered a part of the aggregate that is the general good, and as no more an important part than any other. Of course, this principle is to be applied in light of any "special grounds for believing that more good is likely to be realised in the one case than in the other" (*ME*, p. 382), that is, some reason to believe that one can make a greater contribution to the aggregate general good by contributing to one's own good or that of those nearer to oneself rather than to that of those who are more remote, or absence of reason to believe

---

[29] Thus Sidgwick's criticism is a predecessor of Allen Wood's argument that Kant's Formula of Universal Law can give rise only to duties of omission, not to duties of commission; see Wood 1999, pp. 100–2, 109.

[30] See De Lazari-Radek and Singer 2014, pp. 119–20.

that one can effectively contribute to the good of those who are more remote. But this qualification does not address what Sidgwick takes to be the basic problem with this common-sense but abstract principle of benevolence, namely that its conception of the "good" is too indeterminate to allow for any determinate comparisons between what one might do for oneself and what one might do for others, or to resolve the kinds of conflicts that by Sidgwick's lights a successful method of ethics must be able to do. Here is where he then in effect compares Kant's philosophical method to his own, and argues that Kant does not have a cogent and determinate way of making this common-sensical principle of benevolence sufficiently determinate but that he, Sidgwick, does, namely the principle of utilitarianism, which calls for comparisons of *happiness* rather than the more abstract "good" that will be sufficiently determinate to resolve potential conflicts of duties. Thus, while Sidgwick interprets Kant as accepting Rational Benevolence from common sense, he takes issue with Kant's account of the grounds of this principle, as well as with Kant's view that the duty to promote happiness is constrained by other duties. As we shall see, these disagreements arise ultimately from Sidgwick's and Kant's divergent views on the value of freedom and its foundational relation to the basic principle of morality.

Sidgwick's criticisms of Kant are not confined to his treatment of benevolence, or as Kant puts it the imperfect duty to promote the happiness of others (*G*, 4: 430; *MM*, DV, Introduction, sections IV, V.B, 6: 385–8). Sidgwick also objects to Kant's version of the first of the self-evident intuitions of common-sense morality, essentially, reason's demand that like cases be treated alike. It would be more precise to say that Sidgwick's most challenging objection to Kant is his objection to Kant's treatment of the duty of benevolence, and that this is where Sidgwick's view that Kant does not have a clear conception of freedom is going to be most costly, either to Kant or to Sidgwick himself. So let us look first at Sidgwick's other objections to Kant and then return to his objection to Kant's account of the duty of benevolence. After that we can consider Sidgwick's attempt to resolve his problem with the dualism of practical reason by means of empirical evidence for something like Kant's postulates of pure practical reason.

(i) Sidgwick brings up Kant in his first discussion of the "intuitionist" principle, which however he also accepts himself, that "We cannot judge an action to be right for A and wrong for B, unless we can find in the nature or circumstances of the two some difference which we can regard as a reasonable ground for difference in their duties" (*ME*, p. 209).[31] He says that applying this test to one's proposed actions "will often disperse the false appearance of rightness which our strong inclination has given to it," and to that extent it is valuable—a good way of stepping back from impetuousness, one might suggest. But he thinks that Kant

---

[31] On Sidgwick's several formulations of this principle, see Schneewind 1977, pp. 291–3.

went too far when he "held that all particular rules of duty can be deduced" from his version of this principle, what is now generally called the Formula of Universal Law, namely "the one fundamental rule 'Act as if the maxim of thy action were to become by thy will a universal law of nature.'" Sidgwick actually has two different criticisms to make here. First, he claims that "this appears to me an error analogous to that of supposing that Formal Logic supplies a complete criterion of truth" (*ME*, pp. 209–10). This could be taken to mean that Kant's formula of universal law supplies only a necessary but not a sufficient condition of duty, that is, that any proposed course of action that fails this test is morally wrong, but the principle is not by itself sufficient to determine everything that is morally obligatory. It would be surprising for Kant to have made such a blunder, since he himself had argued that satisfaction of the formal principle of *theoretical* judgment, namely the principle of non-contradiction, is a necessary but not a sufficient condition of truth, and he should have seen the parallel (*CPuR*, A151/B190). Yet Kant does seem to suggest that all classes of our duty can be derived from the Formula of Universal Law alone, for example, when he illustrates it in the *Groundwork* (4: 422–3). Some commentators have suggested that Kant did not intend the Formula of Universal Law to ground all human duties, but rather intended it to function only as part of a complex categorical imperative, a system of laws, also including the Formula of Humanity, from which latter only our positive duties to self and others can be derived.[32] Sidgwick will object to Kant's attempt to derive such duties from the concept of humanity, or as he puts, rational being, and one might take this objection, what I am regarding as his main objection to Kant, to moot the question of whether Kant really thought he could derive all our duties from the Formula of Universal Law alone.

The deeper answer to Sidgwick's objection is that in the case of neither the Formula of Universal Law nor the Formula of Humanity does Kant actually think a formal principle by itself suffices to derive the particular duties of human beings. Rather, in his actual system of duties in the *Metaphysics of Morals*, as opposed to his merely illustrative suggestion of such a system in the *Groundwork,* Kant makes it clear that the particular duties of human beings can be derived from the formal principles of morality valid for and binding upon any and all rational beings only with the addition of certain fundamental facts about human nature and the human condition, for example that human beings are embodied and share the finite surface of a terraqueous globe (*MM*, Introduction, 6: 217). Kant's view is that the derivation of the *fundamental principle* of morality must be a priori, or in the terms of the first *Critique* purely or "absolutely" a priori (*CPuR*, B2–3), but he does not think that the derivation of particular duties is entirely a priori any more than he thinks that particular truths of natural science or ordinary experience are known entirely a priori.

---

[32] See Wood 2006.

However, Sidgwick makes a second objection to Kant's Formula of Universal Law, namely, that it does not exclude any possible maxim, thus does not even act as a necessary condition or constraint on proposed maxims of actions. This is also a criticism that has been made many times since:[33]

> I conceive that all (or almost all persons) who act conscientiously could sincerely will the maxims on which they act to be universally adopted: while at the same time we continually find such persons in thoroughly conscientious disagreement as to what each ought to do in a given set of circumstances.   (ME, p. 210)

—in other words, the sincere Nazi is perfectly happy to universalize his maxim to kill as many Jews as possible, thus that everyone should aim to kill as many Jews as possible.[34] Of course the conclusion that this maxim is morally acceptable, let alone obligatory, is blatantly contrary to every pre-theoretical moral judgment of any reasonable person, and the conflict between the Nazi who believes this and the Jew who believes the opposite is precisely the sort of conflict that a successful method of ethics is supposed to avoid.

The response to Sidgwick's criticism is as well-known as the criticism itself: it gets the Nazi's maxim wrong. The principle he is really prepared to act upon is the principle to kill as many of his enemies as possible, for that is the principle on which he would act if his enemies happened to be someone other than Jews (for example, just Slavs, or Roma, or homosexuals, who were "enemies" of the Nazis and would have been even if Jews had not been); and the Nazi *cannot* coherently universalize his maxim if that is what it really is, for willing that others who might have *him* as their enemy kill as many of their enemies as possible, thus kill *him* if they can, would undermine his intention to kill as many of *his* enemies as possible (or, if not that, then it would conflict with his general intention to maintain the conditions of his rational willing).[35] Of course, this response depends upon the assumption that we are able to identify an agent's actual or "sincere" maxim, and that is an issue in the face of Kant's recognition that the true motives of others or even ourselves are often inscrutable.[36] I will not attempt to decide here whether that is really an objection to Kant's account of the fundamental principle of morality, given that his primary concern is not our tendency to make moral

---

[33] E.g., Singer 1961 and O'Neill 1975/2013, chapters 2 and 5.

[34] For an illuminating discussion of the uniqueness of the Nazi attack upon the Jews within their larger pattern of genocide and within instances of genocide more generally, see Evans 2015, pp. 365–89.

[35] For discussion of precisely what sort of contradiction might be involved in a maxim of murder, see Herman 1993, chapter 6 ("Murder and Mayhem").

[36] As Hurka puts it, "This objection forgets that a Kantian maxim is a mental state of intending that for any person in particular circumstances has a specific content" (Hurka 2014, p. 276). To use the categorical imperative as a test for the rightness of *other* people's intentions, one would need adequate access to such mental states, and that might be a problem. However, Kant intends the categorical imperative to serve primarily as a test for *one's own* proposed maxims, and in this case there should be less of an issue about epistemic access to one's own maxims—although according to Kant's

assessments of each other or even of our own past actions, but to correctly identify and firmly establish the principle that we should use in reasoning about what we should do going forward—what maxims we should accept for ourselves. Rather, the point I want to make here is that Sidgwick's failure to anticipate this obvious response is part of his more general failure to appreciate that Kant does have a coherent conception of freedom and its potential as a normative principle for moral philosophy. For we could say that the agent who attempts to act on a non-universalizable maxim is one who either simply ignores the freedom of others, that is, is willing to privilege his own freedom over that of any one whom he sees as conflicting with it, or else effectively wills to undermine his own freedom, by willing that others should freely adopt a maxim that could destroy his own freedom, as the maxim that everyone should try to kill his enemies would. Kant's supposition that there can be no conflict of duties, understood to apply both intrapersonally and interpersonally, entails that in every situation there is some course of action or restraint from action available that will preserve the freedom of all involved, thus either one's present self and one's future self, or one's own self and other selves. The willingness to universalize any old maxim violates the maximal preservation of freedom, and should be rejected for that reason.

(ii) Sidgwick's next objection to Kant is to his view that "a good will is the only absolute and unconditional Good" (*ME*, p. 222), which Sidgwick interprets as the view that a morally good agent must not be moved by "the emotion of affection, but merely [by] the resolution to benefit" (or, presumably, to fulfill some other class of duty, such as not to harm oneself or others), "which alone has 'true moral worth'." In other words, Sidgwick raises the objection to Kant's apparent model of moral motivation that as we saw had been raised since the earliest reception of Kant's moral theory. Sidgwick does not think that he actually has to appeal to any special utilitarian principles to reject Kant's apparent view, for he thinks that "Common Sense" itself will answer the question "whether an act is virtuous in proportion as it was done from regard for duty or virtue ... in the negative: for the degree in which an act deserves praise as courageous, loyal or patriotic does not seem to be reduced by its being shown that the predominant motive to the act was natural affection and not love of virtue as such" (*ME*, p. 223). Rather, Sidgwick supposes, a good part of virtue will consist in the cultivation of natural affections to courage, loyalty, patriotism, and so on, and more generally virtue will consist in the settled disposition to such affections and action upon them and not in regard to duty as "the ultimate spring of action" (*ME*, pp. 223–4). Here Sidgwick could argue that Kant's position is in conflict with both common sense and with

---

transcendental idealism there is an insuperable epistemological problem about knowledge of one's own *fundamental* maxim. But that would be an issue only for (one's own) assessment of one's *moral worth*, not for the rightness of particular intended maxims.

utilitarianism, for insisting that people focus on duty as such will not be as efficacious a source of happiness as cultivating the emotions of affection.

The obvious response to Sidgwick's objection, as I have argued in response to earlier versions of it, is that he has misconstrued the strategy of the first section of the *Groundwork*.[37] Kant is not there providing his full account of the psychology or phenomenology of morally worthy action, but is conducting a thought-experiment aimed at elucidating a key feature of the fundamental principle of morality, one that Kant even thinks will suffice to identify it. That is, Kant opposes two kinds of stick-figures, one the agent who is motivated to perform morally correct actions solely by inclination, even of an ordinarily beneficial kind, but who for that reason cannot be counted upon to act correctly should that inclination disappear, as inclinations often do, the other one who is motivated to act solely by regard to duty, and who can therefore do what is right even in the complete absence of inclination (*G*, 4: 397–8). Kant infers from the mere conceivability of the latter figure that the principle of duty cannot be derived from inclination or from the objects of inclination—thus from any conception of happiness as the gratification of some sum of inclinations (*G*, 4: 418)—but can only concern the form of our maxims, namely their universalizability (*G*, 4: 402)—form being the only alternative to matter in Kant's view, and universality being the only alternative to particularity in maxims that would be patently immoral. But once the moral law has been thus derived from the thought-experiment, the work of that experiment has been done, and Kant can in due course provide a fuller and more realistic phenomenology of moral motivation, which is that a human being expresses or exercises her commitment to fulfilling her duty precisely by cultivating and strengthening a variety of "aesthetic preconditions of the mind's susceptibility to concepts of duty," or natural affections or feelings that can, at the empirical level where human action takes place, prompt one to morally correct action and can be acted upon in cases where conscience determines that the action so prompted is in fact morally correct (*MM*, DV, Introduction, section XII, 6: 399–403). Thus, Kant does not merely "relax" the "rigidity" of his conception of virtue or moral worth in order to allow for the cultivation of and action upon such feelings as "Gratitude," as Sidgwick thinks (*ME*, p. 223). Rather, he supposes that cultivation of and action upon moral feelings of several kinds—love of others, sympathy, gratitude, self-esteem—are the "means" that nature has afforded us "to promoting active and rational benevolence" or other duties (*MM*, DV, §34, 6: 456), the normal means *through which* we express and exercise our underlying regard to duty, as beings whose fundamental choice of maxim takes places at the noumenal level but must be expressed at the phenomenal level, through the feelings characteristic of that level.

---

[37] For a fuller version of what follows, see Guyer 2010b.

Now we could suggest that Sidgwick exaggerated the difference between Kant on the one hand and both common sense and himself on the other just because of his over-reliance on the *Groundwork* and corresponding neglect of a late section in the second half of the later *Metaphysics of Morals*. But the root of Sidgwick's failure to appreciate Kant's real position on the relation between moral feeling, regard for duty, and moral worth lies in his general view that Kant's position on freedom is a morass of confusion—his easy rejection of Kant's treatment of freedom of the will as a tissue of confusion hurts him here. For to appreciate Kant's actual position, one has to be ready to accept Kant's position that a morally worthy regard for duty can be expressed through the cultivation of and action upon moral feelings, which Kant himself models as a relation between the noumenal and the phenomenal: the underlying regard to duty, or as Kant puts it in *Religion within the Boundaries of Mere Reason*, the choice of the fundamental maxim to subordinate self-love to morality (*RBMR*, 6: 35–6), is conceived of as a noumenally free choice, while the cultivation of moral feelings and actions prompted by them is conceived of as something taking place at the phenomenal level, grounded in some way in what has transpired at the noumenal level but not literally caused by a choice at that level for the simple reason that causation is a relation between two temporally successive states of affairs and choices at the noumenal level are supposedly not temporal and therefore do not have determinate positions in time. Of course Sidgwick is not friendly to the metaphysics of transcendental idealism, as is clear from his posthumously published *Lectures on the Philosophy of Kant* (*LPK*, lectures II and III); indeed, few are unless they water it down into a distinction between two "viewpoints" or ways of conceiving of objects.[38] But one does not have to take all of Kant's transcendental idealist model of free will on board in order to appreciate this conception of the relation between underlying commitment to principle and cultivation and action on moral feelings. However one understands responsibility for choice of fundamental principles, one can still hold that one's fundamental moral commitments are not expressed by an immediate causation of action by principles, as if one had to think of those principles just before acting and act directly and only out of them. Rather, they can be expressed through the cultivation of feelings that can then be allowed and counted upon to prompt actions in appropriate circumstances. (We will return to this point in the next chapter in discussing the well-known objection of Bernard Williams that Kant's model of moral motivation requires "one thought too many.")

(iii) Sidgwick's discomfort with Kant's conception of freedom also underlies his objection to Kant's doctrine that the perfection of others, specifically the

---

[38] Notably Graham Bird, in Bird 1962 and Bird 2006, and Henry Allison, in Allison 1983. Kant's resolution of the problem of free will is a notorious stumbling block to their approach to transcendental idealism, since *abstracting* away from determinism in our *conception* of things as they are in themselves would not change the fact that things in themselves *are* deterministic, if they are. See Guyer 1992.

perfection of their virtue, cannot be a duty for me, leaving only their happiness as an end that is also a duty regarding others. This is half of the basis for Kant's argument that the two ends that are also duties are my own perfection and the happiness of others, the other half of the argument being that my own happiness cannot be a duty for me because I naturally desire it and never have to constrain myself to pursue it by regard for duty (*MM*, DV, Introduction, sections IV and V.B)—a lame argument, to be sure, because of course my immediate desires can get in the way of my interest in my own long-term satisfaction, or my short-term conception of my happiness can get in the way of my long-term conception of it. I might have to force myself to act in the interest of my long-term happiness on the basis of rationality, which seems a lot like acting out of duty, although the response to this might be that in this case there is really nothing to prevent me from simply changing my conception of my long-term happiness. But Sidgwick's concern is with the other half of the argument, based on Kant's assumption that one person cannot promote another's self-perfection. What Kant has in mind is *moral* self-perfection, and his assumption is that one's moral self-perfection can only ever be the product of one's own free choice to make the moral law one's fundamental maxim. Sidgwick recognizes that Kant's argument is that "my neighbor's Virtue or Perfection cannot be an end to me, because it depends upon the free exercise of his own volition, which I cannot help or hinder." Yet he takes it to be "undeniable that we can cultivate virtue in others: and indeed such cultivation is clearly the object not only of education, but of a large part of social action, especially of our expression of praise and blame" (*ME*, p. 240).

Kant certainly does suppose that moral education is a central part of education.[39] But a careful reading of his treatment of moral education in both his critical works and his lectures on pedagogy shows that in his view it is above all demonstration by example to the pupils that they really do have the freedom to live up to the moral law, with such examples making their freedom more graphic to them than the philosopher's "ought implies can" ever can. Moral education consists in putting before children examples of honest people, to whom they can compare themselves, who choose to do what is right in spite of promises of great rewards for not doing so or threats of punishment for doing so. The example of such people, such as the unnamed man who refused to calumniate Anne Boleyn in spite of Henry VIII's threats (Kant is thought to refer to the courtier Henry Norris, who was accused of adultery with her but insisted upon her innocence, and paid for this with his life) brings home to the learners the "power over the human heart" that a pure morality can have, that is, the fact of their own freedom (*CPracR*, 5: 156).[40] The freedom the fact of which is thus brought home, however, is the freedom

---

[39] See his *Lectures on Pedagogy*, trans. Robert Louden in Kant 2007, e.g., 9: 447, 450, 453–5, 464, 475, 480–6, 486–93.

[40] For fuller discussion, see Guyer 2011b.

of each to make one's own choices, including the freedom to make the moral law one's fundamental maxim. In Kant's view, moral education reinforces the individual's recognition of her own freedom rather than in any way diminishing it.

More generally, Kant holds that natural processes can develop abilities of the phenomenal self that can be used for good purposes if the individual so chooses, but cannot by themselves substitute for the free choice of right over wrong by the noumenal self; that is why "discipline" can be an "ultimate end" of nature in human development but the freedom to use that discipline on behalf of the good remains "a supersensible faculty" (*CPJ*, §§83–4, 5: 432, 435). So for Kant there remains a dividing line between everything that anyone can do to help anyone else use their freedom correctly and the choice of the other to so use their freedom. Once again, Sidgwick rejects Kant's noumenal account of freedom of the will, and there is no such barrier for him; virtue must be a phenomenal characteristic of phenomenal selves achieved by natural causes, because there are no others, and there can be no rigid separation between what one person can do to contribute to another's virtue and what the other must do. How much one person can contribute to the development of virtue in others must be an empirical question. But even without acceptance of Kant's noumenal theory of free will, it seems plausible to suppose with Kant that moral education can inculcate in its recipients the recognition, first, that the freedom of choice of each is equally valuable, and second that they may well be freer than they think and can always at least try to do the right thing. But such education cannot in any straightforward way make people even try to do the right thing. You do not need to accept Kant's transcendental idealist defense of free will to acknowledge that when it comes to moral education you can lead the horse—the human pupil, that is—to water, but you cannot make him drink. Of course you can help others see both what it would be to be virtuous and that they are as capable of it as anyone else, but you cannot be virtuous for someone else.

(iv) The previous two issues turn on Sidgwick's rejection of Kant's approach to freedom of the will. But the most important of his objections to Kant turns instead on his rejection of Kant's view of freedom of choice as the foundational value on which all of morality can be built. More precisely, the interpretation that Sidgwick gives to Kant's foundational conception of humanity as the sole unconditional end in itself shows that he does not recognize that for Kant this is an expression of the idea that freedom itself is the foundational value of morality, and the objections that Sidgwick makes to Kant's use of this idea turn on the interpretation that he places upon it.[41]

---

[41] In a brief but suggestive paper, Onora O'Neill argued that "The lingering sadness of so many passages in *The Methods of Ethics* reflects Sidgwick's dispassionate and stoical refusal to assert claims that cannot be supported by reasons and his view that practical reason supplies no more than universal generalisations and instrumental rationality," thus that "Although his discussion of practical reason is

The crucial encounter with Kant comes in the chapter on "Philosophical Intuitionism," the penultimate chapter of book 3 of *The Methods of Ethics*. Here Sidgwick offers a brief review of the history of "philosophical intuitionism" including Socrates, Plato and Aristotle, the Stoics, the English rationalist Samuel Clarke, and finally Kant. His discussion of Kant begins with the remark that "Among later moralists, Kant is especially noted for his rigour in separating the purely rational element of the moral code: and his ethical view also appears to me to coincide to a considerable extent, if not completely, with that set forth in the preceding section" (*ME*, p. 385). By that Sidgwick means that Kant's accounts of justice and the prudential side of self-perfection coincide with the accounts of those obligations developed by common-sense intuitionism and accepted by Sidgwick himself, although in due course to be underwritten by utilitarianism. But his issue is now with the positive side of Kant's argument that "the only real ultimate" and positive end that we have with regard to others "is the object of Rational Benevolence as commonly conceived—the happiness of other men." He claims that "Kant's conclusion appears to agree to a great extent with the view of the duty of Rational Benevolence that I have given:—although I am not altogether able to assent to the arguments by which Kant arrives at his conclusion" (*ME*, p. 386). He considers two arguments that Kant offers for this duty, and finds them both wanting.

The first argument is that which Kant states in his illustration of the Formula of Universal Law in the *Groundwork* and repeats in the Doctrine of Virtue of the *Metaphysics of Morals*, namely, as Sidgwick puts it, "We...necessarily constitute ourselves an end for others, and claim that they shall contribute to our happiness; and so, according to Kant's fundamental principle," namely, the requirement that moral maxims be universalizable, "we must recognize the duty of making their happiness our end" (*ME*, p. 389). In Kant's terms, the will of someone who decided to universalize the maxim of not helping others in need when he could "would conflict with itself, since many cases could occur in which one would need the love and sympathy of others and in which, by such a law of nature arisen from his own will, he would rob himself of all hope of the assistance he wishes for himself" (*G*, 4: 423). Sidgwick's objection to this is that the assumption "that every man in need wishes for the aid of others is an empirical proposition which Kant cannot know *a priori*," for "We can certainly conceive of a man in whom the spirit of independence and the distaste for

often conducted in Kant's terminology, it is profoundly unlike Kant's"; O'Neill 2001, at p. 88. I agree with this assessment of the failure of Sidgwick's critique of Kant, but O'Neill does not say (in this piece) what more should be included in a proper (and properly Kantian) account of practical reason. My suggestion in what follows is that it is the element of the freedom to choose one's own ends for action subject to the rest of the constraints of practical reason, which is to say precisely "universal generalisation and instrumental rationality."

incurring obligations would be so strong that he would choose to endure any privations rather than receive aid from others."[42] Here we could again counter that, as Kant makes clear in the *Metaphysics of Morals*, while the *fundamental principle* of morality, the derivation of which he calls "metaphysics of morals" *in the Groundwork* (see G, 4: 390), must be universal and necessary, valid for all rational beings, and thus knowable entirely a priori, the *derivation of particular duties* for human beings, what he calls "metaphysics of morals" *in the work of that title*, is not and cannot be entirely independent of empirically known *facts* about human nature (*MM*, Introduction, 6: 217). The mere fact that we can *conceive* of a person who is always willing to forego the assistance of others in the achievement of his own ends and the attainment of the happiness that this constitutes is of no philosophical significance, for the empirical fact that no one can reasonably count on always being able to achieve all his ends by his own means and on remaining content with that restriction *is* properly used in deriving the duties of human beings from the universal moral principles valid for all rational beings even if some overly self-confident individual fails to realize this. The problem for this confident individual might not be exactly the same as that for the Nazi, who by universalizing his own maxim to kill his enemies whenever he can wills his own destruction, but is rather that by universalizing a maxim of non-assistance he misunderstands the real conditions of human willing—that *no one* can ever *count on* achieving their goals entirely by their own efforts—and thereby contradicts the possibility of his own rational willing under all humanly possible circumstances. And were it to be countered that for some independence from assistance by others is simply more important than any other particular goal, Kant could reply that this is an unrealistic picture of human nature, which is entirely properly considered in the derivation of the duties of human beings although not in the derivation of the fundamental principle of morality valid for all rational beings.

We might also say that no one who takes proper account of the point of view of *others* could reasonably impute to *all* others such an unconcern or distaste for assistance even if that trait were powerful in himself. He would have no reason to think that all others resembled him in this regard, and further could coherently adopt a maxim of helping others *who want help* when he can even if he reasonably thought there were some others who would never want help. This would be a perfectly reasonable restriction on his maxim of beneficence, for since no one is ever going to be able to help everyone else who might need help, anyone is going to have to find some principles by which to limit his beneficence. But this brings us to the question of what is involved in properly treating others as ends in themselves and never merely as means to one's own ends, and this is the issue in

---

[42] This passage is also cited in Hurka 2014, p. 277.

Sidgwick's objection to Kant's second, "apparently different line of argument" for "Rational Benevolence." Here Sidgwick has in mind Kant's argument for and application of the principle that humanity is always to be treated as an end in itself, never merely as a means. As Sidgwick puts it, Kant

> lays down that, as all action of rational beings is done for some end, there must be some absolute end, corresponding to the absolute rule before given, that imposes on our maxims the form of universal law. This absolute end, prescribed by Reason necessarily and *a priori* for all rational beings as such, can be nothing but Reason itself, or the Universe of Rationals; for what the rule inculcates is, in fact, that we should act as rational units in a universe of rational beings...
>
> (*ME*, pp. 389–90)

—that is, treat others as "rational units" just as much as I treat myself as such. "Now, says Kant," Sidgwick continues, "as long as I confine myself to mere non-interference with others, I do not positively make humanity my end" (see *G*, 4: 430); rather, "Virtue is exhibited and consists in the effort to realise the end of Reason in opposition to mere selfish impulses." Sidgwick's objection to Kant then turns on his interpretation of "Reason itself" as the absolute end of all moral actions: it is not clear what it would be to make this an end of action, but it is clear that such an end must have nothing to do with ordinary desires and therefore with happiness, the fulfillment of desires, the end of the duty of benevolence as ordinarily conceived, and of course as conceived in utilitarianism. In Sidgwick's words,

> The conception of "humanity as an end in itself" is perplexing: because by an End we commonly mean something to be realised, whereas "humanity" is, as Kant says, "a self-subsistent end": moreover, there seems to be a sort of paralogism in the deduction of the principle of Benevolence by means of this conception. For the humanity which Kant maintains to be an end in itself is Man (or the aggregate of men) *in so far as rational*. But the subjective ends of other men, which Benevolence directs us to take as our own ends, would seem, according to Kant's own view, to depend upon and correspond to their *non-rational* impulses—their empirical desires and aversions. It is hard to see why, if man *as a rational being* is an absolute end to other rational beings, they must therefore adopt his subjective aims as determined by his non-rational impulses.
>
> (*ME*, p. 390)

We can set aside Sidgwick's worry that as a "self-subsistent end" reason is not even the sort of thing that can be promoted by actions; if, as on his own account, virtue is the sort of thing that one person can cultivate in others, then it would seem as if reason or rationality would be too, precisely the sort of thing that can be promoted or "realised" through education.[43] Let us focus instead on the "paralogism" that Sidgwick insists undercuts Kant's argument from "Reason itself" as the absolute end of morality to "Benevolence." This objection assumes that reason has nothing to do with the satisfaction of "empirical desires and aversions" but that the happiness that is the object of benevolence consists in the satisfaction of such desires and aversions. Thus, Sidgwick assumes, benevolence can consist only in helping others satisfy their desires and aversions to the extent that one can. This diagnosis depends on interpreting "humanity as an end in itself" as pure rationality and on taking such rationality to have nothing to do with empirical desires and aversions.

However, Kant himself suggests a very different interpretation of the idea of humanity as an end in itself. In the Doctrine of Virtue of the *Metaphysics of Morals*, he defines humanity as that "by which ... alone [one] is capable of setting himself ends" (Introduction, section V.A, 6: 387), or as "the capacity to set oneself an end—any end whatsoever" (section VIII, 6: 392). Kant does not suggest that humanity has nothing to do with particular ends, rather he defines it as the capacity to *set* oneself particular ends. If ends can be set on the basis of empirical desires or aversions, or not set without some such desires or aversions, then it is connected rather than disconnected to such desires and aversions, and, insofar as happiness consists of the satisfaction of desires and aversions, humanity is connected to that too. To be sure, setting an end is not just *having* an empirical desire or aversion, but results from using reason to make the satisfaction of a desire or aversion into the object or goal of an action or maxim of actions, by judging first that satisfaction of such an empirical inclination is consistent with empirical practical reason (prudence) but also, at least optimally, with the fundamental principle of morality and the general system of duties that follows from it under the circumstances of human existence or even required by this. This is why Kant describes the "empire of ends" the effort to realize which is prescribed by his final formulation of the categorical imperative in the *Groundwork* as "a whole of all ends in systematic connection (a whole both of rational beings as ends in themselves and of the ends of his own that each may set for himself)" (*G*, 4: 433): what it is to treat another rational being as an end in itself is to treat the particular ends that *it* sets for itself as also ends for *oneself*, as long as that is consistent with treating *everyone*, including of course oneself, as an end in him- or herself. The particular ends that each sets for him- or herself originate with natural desires and aversions,

---

[43]   This is a quick argument that reason or rationality is the kind of thing that can be adopted as an end to be promoted, not merely not acted against; to be sure, Kant does not suggest that anyone has a duty to produce *rationals* or rational *beings* in the sense of procreating. He does not even argue that marriage is morally undertaken only with the goal of procreation, although he does argue that sexual intercourse is moral only within marriage. See *MM*, DR, §24, 6: 277: "The end of begetting and brining up children may be an end of nature ... but it is not *requisite* for human beings who marry to make this their end in order for their union to be compatible with rights, for otherwise marriage would be dissolved when procreation ceases."

although those do not become ends until they pass through the screens of both prudential and, again optimally, pure practical reason.[44]

Several things follow from the assumption that humanity really is the capacity to transform empirical desires and aversions into ends through the exercise of reason. One will be that reason's own requirement of universalizability—that like cases be treated alike—be applied, and thus that in setting one's own ends one must take account of others' ends as well. Perhaps this will be enough to get the duty of "Rational Benevolence" off the ground. But if it is not enough by itself, perhaps it will be when supplemented with a further canon of practical rationality, the complement of what Kant makes explicit as the principle of hypothetical imperatives: that is that if one wills the end, one must also will some adequate means to it (G, 4: 417); the complement of this is that one cannot rationally set an end for oneself if one does not reasonably believe oneself to have some adequate means to realize it. This principle, valid for pure as well as empirical practical reason, then suggests that if one is to make the humanity of all and not just of oneself an end, one must be prepared to make means available to others, when and insofar as one can, for the realization of their ends, that is, to make it possible for them reasonably to set those ends for themselves. One thereby makes available means to their happiness, not because happiness is itself the foundational value of morality, but because all humans getting to rationally set their own ends is, and happiness is the natural outcome of being able to set and realize one's ends.

Another way of putting this point is to say that humanity consists in the *freedom* of human beings to set their own ends, but that this freedom is restricted when people are deprived of means to ends they could otherwise rationally set for themselves, and conversely that this freedom is promoted and extended when means are afforded to people that allow them to set ends for themselves that they otherwise could not. This is the way in which taking freedom, in the sense of the ability to set and pursue ends rationally, can function as a foundational value for the derivation of the duties, in particular the duty of benevolence. The connection to happiness would not be explicit in the concept of humanity, but would follow from the assumption that happiness consists simply in the realization of ends or follows from it.

The response to Sidgwick would thus be that a proper understanding of Kant's conception of humanity as not just "Reason itself" but as the capacity to set ends for oneself in a rational way does, when subjected to the requirement of univer-salizability, give rise to the duty of "Rational Benevolence." Of course it would take more than I have said here to show that this derivation of the duty of benevolence gives rise to no more conflicts than does Sidgwick's utilitarian goal of the greatest

---

[44] I am putting the point this way because I do not want to fall back into the trap of assuming that all use of practical reason is the moral use of reason, which would leave Kant with the problem of explaining the possibility of free but immoral action discussed in Chapter 3 above.

aggregate happiness, or conversely that Sidgwick's principle of happiness gives rise to no fewer conflicts than Kant's principle that humanity as the capacity of each to set and pursue his own ends must always treated as an end and never merely as a means in one's own person and that of every other. All I will suggest here on this score is that one way in which Kant reduces conflicts among duties is by suggesting that perfect duties not to destroy others or their freedom always take priority over promoting or enhancing the scope of their agency, that is, satisfaction of perfect duties not to harm takes priority over imperfect duties to benefit. The same sort of principle is surely built into Sidgwick's method of ethics, which recognizes the principle of justice before it recognizes the principle of rational benevolence, and presumably prioritizes the former over the latter. To be sure, that leaves open that even when the satisfaction of perfect duties such as justice is presupposed there may still be competing demands for anyone's benevolence that cannot be mechanically resolved, for example, between benevolence toward one's parents on the one hand or one's children on the other, or between benevolence toward the small number of one's own children and the larger number of the children of some community beyond one's own family. It is not clear that Kant's derivation of the duty of benevolence provides a mechanical method for the resolution of such conflicts. But I think it is safe to say that Sidgwick would have had to have gone a lot further in the exposition of his utilitarianism to guarantee that his method could resolve such conflicts any better than "philosophical intuitionism" as represented by Kant.

(v) Finally, a few words about Sidgwick's "dualism of the practical reason." After his long attempt to show that utilitarianism or universalistic hedonism is more successful than even the best version of philosophical intuitionism, that is, Kant's, at reconstructing the ethics of common sense—putting that upon a secure foundation and revising it where necessary—Sidgwick returns to the subject of egoism, and concedes that he has not succeeded in showing that egoistic hedonism is any less rational than universalistic hedonism. He famously concludes *The Methods of Ethics* by stating that there may be an "ultimate and fundamental contradiction in our apparent intuitions of what is Reasonable in conduct," namely between the intuition that it is always reasonable to seek one's own greatest happiness and always reasonable to seek the greatest happiness of all without special regard to one's own happiness, or between "self-interest" and "duty" (*ME*, p. 508). He supposes that any contradiction between duty and self-interest would be avoided if "there actually is a Supreme Being who will adequately reward me for obeying those rules of duty, or punish me for violating them," or if, "omitting the strictly theological element of the proposition," I may just find "in my moral consciousness, any intuition, claiming to be clear and certain, that the performance of duty will be adequately rewarded and its violation punished. I feel indeed a desire, apparently inseparable from the moral sentiments, that this result may be realised not only in my own case but universally." Sidgwick obviously has in mind here something like Kant's postulates of pure practical reason, although Kant insisted upon both the existence of God and personal immortality (at least in his initial presentation of the doctrine of the postulates in the first *Critique*) as conditions for the possibility of the highest good as a conjunction of virtue and happiness—duty and self-interest—in which we can believe on practical rather than theoretical grounds, in Sidgwick's terms as "inseparable from the moral sentiments." But Sidgwick was not friendly to Kant's postulates—in his *Lectures on the Philosophy of Kant*, he says that they "illustrate well both the ingenuity of Kant and what I may perhaps be allowed to call his *naïveté*" (*LPK*, Lecture I, p. 19). He has no disposition to solve the dualism of practical reason on Kant's grounds. We would not accept a mere "strong disposition to accept" an otherwise unsupported premise in order to solve an apparent contradiction in the domain of natural science, but would regard relying on a mere predisposition as "opening the door to universal scepticism," and he argues that we should hold to the same standard in the case of ethics (*ME*, p. 509). We need not just a predisposition but scientifically acceptable evidence that there is no ultimate contradiction between duty and self-interest. Indeed, in the first edition of *The Methods of Arguments* Sidgwick had concluded even more strongly that

> without a hypothesis [*verifiable*] by experience reconciling the Individual with the Universal Reason, without a belief, in some form or other, that the moral order which we see imperfectly realized in this actual world is yet actually perfect...the Cosmos of Duty is thus really reduced to a Chaos: and the prolonged effort of the human intellect to frame a perfect ideal of rational conduct is seen to have been foredoomed to inevitable failure.[45]

If the postulates of pure practical reason cannot be accepted on the basis of mere predisposition or any other non-empirical grounds, Sidgwick suggests, the coherence of reason and thus the rationality of utilitarianism, the best version of morality, can be saved only by empirical evidence for them.

There is debate whether the dualism of practical reason should be a genuine problem for Sidgwick. Irwin has argued that it should not be, because by Sidgwick's own lights if the axioms from which he has worked lead to a contradiction they cannot be genuine axioms in the first place.[46] Schneewind, however, has argued that the dualism is a genuine problem for Sidgwick, because even if there is no immediately obvious, verbal contradiction between the two claims that self-interest is an ultimate principle of action and duty is an ultimate principle of action, if they lead to contradictions in any particular case, then they are still

---

[45] Sidgwick 1874, p. 473, cited from Schneewind 1977, p. 352.   [46] Irwin 2009, p. 528.

contradictory.[47] Schneewind's argument seems correct, but it is not my task to determine here whether Sidgwick is really subject to the dualism of practical reason that would in his own eyes undermine his entire project. He himself thought that he was, that only empirical evidence for personal immortality would resolve the issue, and that even after many years of "psychical research" no such evidence was forthcoming.[48] The case for empirical evidence for the existence of God was no better.

Kant too obviously thought that his own account of morality was in trouble without the postulates, although he precluded the possibility of empirical evidence for their truth from the outset (and thereby saved himself from Sidgwick's years of hopeless "psychical research"). But need he have thought so? Irwin suggests that if "we accept a non-hedonistic account of a person's good, we have a better prospect of showing that morality promotes it."[49] He suggests that Kant's position that "morality requires treatment of persons as ends, not merely as means" will avoid the problem, because when we see "the importance of treating oneself as an end in relation to particular passions . . . we can also see the importance of treating oneself as an end in relation to other people."[50] I do not find this self-explanatory, to put it mildly. An explanation of why treating oneself as an end must always be compatible with rather than contradictory to treating all others as ends remains required. However, if we think of the supreme end of morality not as happiness but as treating the humanity in every person, in the form of their freedom of choice, as Sidgwick did not, then a solution suggests itself. For while there can certainly be irresolvable conflicts between the conditions for the happiness of different individuals—in Kant's example, the French King Francis I and the Holy Roman Emperor Charles V both wanted Milan, but they could not both have it, and so could not both be happy (*CPracR*, 5: 28)—if the end of each is the freedom of choice of all, there is always a non-contradictory solution to such a conflict: each can freely choose to refrain from something that might make them happy, thereby treating the freedom of each as an end in itself even if the happiness of both cannot be realized. Unlimited happiness for each is not the end of morality; the exercise of freedom by each in a way consistent with the equal freedom of others is, and there is always at least one solution to that problem. In Kant's terms, the happiness that is part of the complete good for human beings is the greatest happiness for all, considered collectively and in conjunction with, indeed as the product of, the purest morality throughout the world—not the greatest happiness imaginable for each, considered in isolation (*TP*, 8: 279). There is no ineliminable contradiction in this conception of collective happiness; and in Kant's example, the two rulers both forgoing Milan might have comprised the greatest happiness possible for them collectively, with neither getting Milan but neither suffering the even greater

---

[47] Schneewind 1977, pp. 373–4. See also Phillips 2022, pp. 220–30.
[48] See Schultz 2017, pp. 276–301.   [49] Irwin 2009, p. 529.   [50] Irwin 2009, pp. 530–1.

pain of envy of the other if he had gotten it. (And both agreeing to let the citizens of Milan freely decide their own fate would have been an even greater contribution to the greatest happiness possible for all!) Kant's theory of freedom as the foundational moral value might have avoided Sidgwick's dualism of practical reason.[51]

In sum, Kant has a better argument for the duty of benevolence than Sidgwick allows; his account of freedom of the will is not always plagued with the ambiguity that Sidgwick alleges; and he may have a better solution to the supposed dualism of practical reason than Sidgwick himself. We can turn now from Sidgwick to his successor as the leading light in moral philosophy at Cambridge in the first years of the twentieth century, his student Moore. Kant does not play as big a part in Moore's presentation of his own position in moral philosophy as he does for Sidgwick, but Moore developed a more trenchant critique of Kant on freedom of the will than Sidgwick had, and also, surprisingly, uses Kant as one example of the supposed "naturalistic fallacy" in moral philosophy.

13.3. Moore

George Edward Moore (1873–1958) was a bit of a patricide: he was a Cambridge student of J. McT. E. McTaggart as well as of Henry Sidgwick, but made his reputation as a young man with an attack on the theoretical philosophy of British idealism—although here he took as his explicit target F. H. Bradley's version of idealism rather than McTaggart's, which in any case was not fully published until well after Moore's attack[52]—and with the ethics and meta-ethics expounded in his pretentiously entitled *Principia Ethica* of 1903, which adopts some of the meta-ethical spirit of Sidgwick's *Methods* but unmistakably differs from his teacher in its substantive account of the good. Kant is only a minor target in *Principia Ethica*, but Moore had actually won his postgraduate fellowship at Trinity College with a dissertation on Kant, and one of his earliest publications was a critique of Kant's theory of freedom of the will, published in *Mind* in 1898. This article has not been noted in Kant scholarship in recent decades, but it is worth discussion because it is an insightful, one might daresay conclusive criticism of Kant's transcendental idealist rescue of a libertarian conception of freedom of the will. But as we will see from a look at *Principia Ethica*, Moore's sound criticism of the Kant's metaphysics of the free will may have led him to throw out the baby with the bath-water, that is, to dismiss as well Kant's theory of freedom of choice and action as the fundamental value in morality. This dismissive attitude may be something Moore

---

[51] Paytas 2020 argues against both Kant and Sidgwick that the Stoic view that the world is just can be defended.

[52] See Guyer and Horstmann 2023, pp. 150–8, and Baldwin 1990, chapter I.

learned from Sidgwick, and whether through Sidgwick or Moore it was deeply influential on the subsequent British reception of Kant's moral philosophy. We will see this in the next chapter.

We begin, then, with Moore's 1898 article "Freedom." Moore starts by stating that the article "is selected from a much longer essay on Kant's notion of Freedom," and expresses the hope to enlarge that in turn into a treatise on the whole of Kant's "Ethical Philosophy."[53] In the end he did not do so, but at this early point in his career he clearly was not only interested in but also influenced by Kant. He was clearly attracted to transcendental idealism's insistence on the ultimate unreality of time—although in this he could have been influenced by Bradley as well as by his tutor McTaggart, whose most famous article would argue, a decade later, for the unreality of a "past, present, and future" representation of time ("A-series") as opposed to a tenseless system of dates ("B-series")[54]—as well as by Kant, and, like Sidgwick, he was generally influenced by Kant's insistence that the most fundamental principle of ethics should be a priori, or in his own terms "non-natural." We will come back to that issue when we turn to *Principia Ethica*. Here, however, the point to note is that Moore's rejection of Kant's transcendental idealist theory of freedom is not based on an objection to transcendental idealism itself, although soon enough Moore would reject that and opt for an extreme form of realism, in which not only objects but also concepts, properties, and propositions are all realities that exist independent of our consciousness or cognition of them. His objection is rather that Kant's idea of human wills as multiple sources of agency that, as noumenal, are free from determinism just does not make any sense. It is not that the ultimate timelessness of reality makes no sense, but that the idea of timeless *activity* makes no sense: the concept of activity is essentially temporal, it is the concept of bringing about a state of affairs at one time that did not exist at another. (I put it in this general way because in context one activity might be understood as bringing something into existence that did not previously exist but another as putting out of existence something that previously did, e.g. bringing a human life into existence or destroying one.) In Moore's words,

> That time itself cannot be conceived to be fundamentally real is always admitted by Kant himself, and indeed he has attempted a proof of it. How far his proof is satisfactory, and whether, if unsatisfactory, any other proof is forthcoming, is too large a question to be fully discussed here. I can only state that the arguments by which Mr. Bradley has endeavoured to prove the unreality of Time appear to me perfectly conclusive. The question which remains, then, is whether we cannot conceive a timeless activity; for it is to such that Kant must be referring us, for justification of the notion of 'pure Will'. That such a notion is very difficult to

---

[53] Moore 1898, 179.   [54] McTaggart 1908.

maintain appears plainly enough ... It is a notion which would seem to rest on a combination of the notion of causal dependence between things in time, with that of logical dependence. Both are necessary connexions, but in the one case between things, in the other between concepts.[55]

This is interesting. Moore does not just put the idea of timeless activity, the idea of initiating a change that yet does not take place in time, in an unflattering light, although he does do that, and does it as well as anyone has since. He also offers an error-theory for this error: Kant has confused the conceptual relation of one thing being a ground—or reason—for another with the idea of one thing being a cause for another; the relation of ground and consequence, for example between concepts or propositions, can be timeless, but the idea of one thing changing another just cannot be. This is not to deny, Moore makes clear, that understanding something as a reason for doing something else cannot be a cause of the latter; on the contrary, this is perfectly possible, but in this case it is the temporal event of taking something as a reason for doing something that leads to an action in time, and this is not a timeless kind of action or agency. Or as Moore puts it,

> Kant has therefore confused the purely natural process of human volition, with the transcendental aspect of it, which alone entitles us to ascribe to man "practical freedom"; and it is solely on this confusion that the special place he assigns to man as a "free" agent seems to be based. It is true that the content of the idea, which acts as a cause in volition, is different from the content of any other natural cause; but that content is merely the form of the cause, and difference of form is something which in no way renders one natural cause more or less of a cause than any other.[56]

That is, it is true that humans have reason, thus can recognize reasons, or ground-and-consequence relations, and act upon them, and in that regard they differ from other beings in nature and have a different kind of agency, and it is true that ground-and-consequence relations, or one thing being a reason for another, are not intrinsically temporal relations; but this does not mean that the process of a human being recognizing and acting upon a reason is not something that takes place in time—and in accord with the same sort of laws, or determinism, as any other kinds of causation in nature. Thus Moore goes beyond just asserting that the idea of activity that is not temporal makes no sense, as many others certainly have since he wrote; he explains that while something being a reason may not be a temporal relation, someone acting upon a reason is.

[55] Moore 1898, p. 202.   [56] Moore 1898, p. 201.

This criticism seems to cut the transcendental idealist theory of freedom of the will off at the knees before it even gets going, or at least puts a heavy burden upon Kant of explaining how we can understand something as an *act* even though we cannot represent it in *our* usual temporal form. Still, this objection might be open to the objection that, even though time is only our own form of intuition for representing change, including intentional activity, and therefore we cannot represent noumenal change in temporal form, this does not imply that there can be no change and activity at the noumenal level; it implies only that we have no way of representing that, but can still conceive of its possibility. But Moore also has another line of criticism worthy of note. This is that if reason and whatever the freedom of reason is supposed to be is understood as the noumenal ground of *any* reality, it must be understood as the noumenal ground of *all* reality—we have no basis on which to divide noumenal reality up into discrete parts.

> And indeed, it must be admitted that there is no longer any reason for connecting the "Intelligible character" with the psychological character which distinguishes one individual from another. The "Intelligible Character" is the one sufficient reason of all phenomena, whether processes of inanimate nature, or human actions. It is not proved that it is individualised in a multiplicity of souls; and it is certain that in any case it is the same in each.[57]

This is subtly different from the criticism going back to Ulrich and revived by Sidgwick that if the free, noumenal will is essentially rational and to be rational is to be moral, then there is no way to explain how a free agent can be immoral. It is the different criticism that there is no way to explain why one phenomenal agent should act differently from any other, whether either acts morally or immorally, if the noumenal ground of all is one and the same. This objection would hold whether the noumenal ground is supposed to be essentially rational, as it is by Kant, or essentially irrational, as it is by Schopenhauer (whom Moore mentions in passing in this article). Moore also notes that Kant helps himself to the idea that human beings know their noumenal and not just phenomenal character by "mere apperception," not just in section III of the *Groundwork* but actually in the *Critique of Pure Reason* itself, and to the conclusion that human beings thereby actually know their free and rational nature. This should not be possible within the epistemological constraints of transcendental idealism. But even if this epistemological presumption is allowed to pass, it will still remain that all human beings thereby know themselves to have one and the same will—the same, that is, both quantitatively and qualitatively—and then there can be no explanation of the

---

[57] Moore 1898, p. 184.

differences among individual wills and, one might add, of individual responsibility for those differences. This is an interesting criticism, although it too is open to the objection that, while our spatio-temporal forms of intuition are our only ways of individuating objects, and we cannot use them to individuate noumena, this does not imply that noumena *are* all one and not individuated although in some way that we cannot represent. To assume that because space and time apply only to phenomena there can therefore *be* only one noumenon is fallacious, indeed a fallacy of which Schopenhauer was guilty although Kant himself was not.

These responses to Moore's objections may seem a stretch; be that as it may, his objections sufficed for Moore, and for this reason he made no attempt to defend the transcendental idealist theory of the free will, or indeed to defend any libertarian conception of freedom of the will. Thus in his 1912 textbook *Ethics* he follows the traditional British defense of compatibilism, as pioneered by Hobbes, Locke, and Hume, arguing that human freedom can be understood as the freedom to perform or refrain from an action if one so chooses, but not as freedom to choose one way rather than another regardless of antecedent circumstances, or to choose either one way or another even if all the initial conditions remain exactly the same.[58] Indeed, it has remained characteristic of the Anglophone revival of attraction to "Kantian" ethics since the mid-twentieth century that few have attempted to revive or reconstruct Kant's transcendental idealist defense of freedom of the will. But later "Kantians" have attempted to save the baby of Kant's normative ethics in some form from the bath-water of his metaphysics of free will. In Moore's case, his well-grounded antipathy to Kant's theory of the freedom of the will may be connected to his rejection of Kant's normative ethics as well in *Principia Ethica*.

To be sure, Kant is not the major target of *Principia Ethica*. If anything, that is Sidgwick, although Moore's relationship to him might be called that of love-hate. In the most general terms, Sidgwick's method in *The Method of Ethics* is intuitionist, although his normative ethics is not what he calls intuitionism; his intuition of certain fundamental principles of reason and justice was supposed to lead to universalistic hedonism, although in the end he conceded that he could not eliminate rational egoism as a species of rationality. Moore also argues that ethics must be founded on a fundamental intuition of what is good, but famously asserts that the good is not pleasure in general, rather "By far the most valuable things, which we know or can imagine, are certain states of consciousness, which may be roughly described as the pleasures of human intercourse and the enjoyment of beautiful objects"[59]—although he adds that his intuition is that the

---

[58] See Moore 1912. Moore mentions Locke and Hume at 1898, p. 189, where they are described as having done "some service to the question, inasmuch as their treatment of it is a protest against the freedom 'to do, if I choose,' with 'freedom to choose'."

[59] Moore 1993, p. 237.

"organic wholes" consisting of the experience of human intercourse plus the reality of a worthy partner or the experience of beauty occasioned by an objectively beautiful object are more valuable than the experience alone.[60] This argument comes in his concluding chapter on "The Ideal," that is, the ideally good. But this conclusion is not presented as an alternative to Kant's moral philosophy, in either its conception of what is right or obligatory or in its conception of what is good. Moore deals with Kant before he gets to this point in his exposition.

He begins this exposition with the assumption that moral philosophy must begin with an account of the good, not of the right; doing what is right will simply be maximizing the good (and Moore does not worry about issues of distribution, i.e., *whose* good? mine? yours? everyone's?). He notoriously argues that the good is an indefinable, non-natural property; we simply know what "good" means, thus we cannot determine what is actually good from any definition of "good" but must discover the truth of a synthetic proposition that such-and-such is good. After these meta-ethical moves in his chapter 1, Moore then argues in chapters 2 and 3 that the synthetic proposition needed cannot be furnished by any "naturalistic ethics" such as the evolutionary ethics of Herbert Spencer or by the "hedonism" of John Stuart Mill and Sidgwick. Mill's mistake is simply to confuse the desirable with what is desired,[61] which violates the sort of objectivity or realism at which Moore aims, while Sidgwick commits two fundamental errors, in Moore's view. First, he fails to recognize that, for example, "it is better that [a] beautiful world should exist, than … one that is ugly" "quite apart from any possible contemplation by human beings."[62] Second, and more important, he fails to recognize that an "organic whole" such as the combination of a beautiful world with human contemplation of it is more valuable not only than the existence of a beautiful world by itself but also than the experience of other kinds of human pleasure. A "pleasurable contemplation of Beauty certainly has an immeasurably greater value than mere Consciousness of Pleasure."[63] Sidgwick's error, in view of what Moore's intuitions tell him, is actually twofold: he fails to recognize that an organic whole consisting of experience plus its proper object is always more valuable than experience alone, but he also admits into his entirely generic account of pleasurable experience as the good, whether that of an individual in the case of rational egoism or of all sentient beings in the case of universalistic hedonism, all sorts of pleasures that are less valuable than those of the experience of human intercourse and beautiful objects. As Mill objected to Bentham, Moore is objecting to Sidgwick that he makes no distinction between the value of pushpin and the value of poetry. (This of course endeared Moore to the Bloomsbury circle.)

---

[60] On Moore versus Sidgwick on the nature of the good, see Hurka 2014, pp. 194–204.
[61] Moore 1993, p. 119.   [62] Moore 1993, p. 135.   [63] Moore 1993, p. 145.

Moore makes no appeal to Kant's own argument against the kind of utilitarianism with which he was familiar that any conception of happiness is too indeterminate, changeable, and, in a multi-person case, potentially conflicted to serve as the foundation of moral philosophy, although he could have done so. Rather, he attacks Kant in his chapter 4, which argues that "Metaphysical Ethics," although a priori, also cannot furnish the necessary synthetic proposition about what is actually good. Attempts to derive what is good from metaphysics, Moore states,

> have a merit, not possessed by Naturalism, in recognising that for perfect goodness much more is required than any quantity of what exists here and now or can be inferred as likely to exist in the future. And moreover it is quite possible that their assertions should be true, if we only understand them to assert that something which is real possesses all the characteristics necessary for perfect goodness.

In other words, metaphysical approaches to ethics properly aim at a priori knowledge of what is necessarily good, not empirical knowledge of what is perforce only contingently good, here or there but not everywhere and always. However, metaphysical ethics still makes what Moore regards as the fundamental error in ethical method, namely attempting to derive the synthetic proposition that something in particular is good from a definition, in this case of some metaphysical definition:

> They also imply... that this ethical proposition *follows* from some proposition which is metaphysical: that the question "What is real?" has some logical bearing upon the question "What is good?" It was for this reason that I described "Metaphysical Ethics" in Chapter II as based upon the naturalistic fallacy. To hold that from any propositions asserting "Reality is of this nature" we can infer, or obtain confirmation for, any proposition asserting "This is good in itself" is to commit the naturalistic fallacy. And that a knowledge of what is real supplies reasons for holding certain things to be good in themselves is either implied or expressly asserted by all those who define the Supreme Good in metaphysical terms.[64]

It seems odd of Moore to call the purported fallacy of metaphysical ethics a "naturalistic" fallacy, since metaphysics is defined by its appeal to non-natural rather than empirical sources of insight.[65] If Moore wanted to subsume the fallacy of both naturalistic and metaphysical ethics under a single rubric, perhaps he

---

[64] Moore 1993, pp. 164–5.   [65] For a similar point, see Hurka 2014, pp. 93–4.

would have done better to call it the "derivational fallacy" or something along those lines. Terminology aside, his real point is that, just as an ought cannot be derived from an is, so what is good cannot be derived from any statement of fact, whether natural or metaphysical, but can only be known be an intuition.

In any case, Moore's specific charge against Kant is that he attempts to derive his account of the good from a metaphysical conception of the will, and that this cannot be done. Moore objects in two ways to Kant's identification of "what ought to be with the law according to which a Free or Pure Will *must* act." His first objection is that if a pure will must act, that is necessarily acts, in a certain way, in accordance with a certain law, then it makes no sense to think of that law as a "separate standard" or norm for that will.[66] It just is how a pure will operates, and if we are not ourselves pure wills, it is not clear why what is in any case not actually a norm for a pure will should be a norm for us, impure wills that we are. Alternatively, if we want to say that the necessary character of a pure will should be a norm for us impure wills, then we need to know that the pure will is a good will. This cannot be known from the definition of a pure will—that would be an example of the naturalistic fallacy in Moore's view. There needs to be an independent basis for judging the pure will to be a good will. This argument has the same form as what Moore next states, namely that it is a fallacy for Kant to suppose "that 'This ought to be' means 'This is commanded'," "by some real supersensible authority." Perhaps what ought to be is commanded by some real supersensible authority, whether God or, as in Kant's fundamental view, our own reason, but it is not the fact of its being commanded—or willed—that makes what is commanded obligatory, but an independent standard of goodness, which applies either to the authority that commands or to what it commands. "It is only if it be itself so good, that it commands and enforces only what is good, that it can be a source of moral obligation."[67] That the will, whether pure or otherwise, wills something is not what makes it good; either the will must be independently good and recognizable as such, or what it wills must be so. The "assertion 'This is good' is *not* identical with the assertion 'This is willed,' either by a supersensible will, or otherwise, nor with any other proposition"; a fundamental intuition of what is good is needed.

It is ironic that Moore made this objection to Kant, since it is very much the objection that Kant made to divine-command ethics in many places, and indeed the objection that enlightened thinkers have always made to divine-command ethics, beginning with Socrates's objection to Euthyphro and including those two lodestars of the Enlightenment in Britain and Germany, Shaftesbury and Wolff.[68] It may be a sound objection to divine-command ethics, or to any version of the

---

[66] Moore 1993, p. 177.   [67] Moore 1993, pp. 178–9.

[68] For Shaftesbury, see *Inquiry concerning Virtue or Merit*, in Shaftesbury 1999, vol. 1; for Wolff, his rectoral address on the *Moral Philosophy of the Chinese*, Wolff 1985.

thought that something is good, or obligatory, just because it is willed by something or someone. But it is not clear that this is a fair objection to bring against what Kant is actually doing with his notion of the good will. Kant begins section I of the *Groundwork*, of course, with the claim that a good will is the only thing that is unconditionally and absolutely good, good independently of what state of affair it actually brings about or even is intended to bring about, and without which nothing else is necessarily good. But it must always be kept in mind that this claim is only the starting point of Kant's "transition" from "common" to "philosophical" knowledge of morals, and is used by Kant only to ground his argument that the motivation for a morally good act has nothing to do with ordinary inclination and that therefore the fundamental principle of morality has nothing to do with the satisfaction of inclination, that is, happiness. In this way having nothing to do with the material of our intentions, that is, the objects of desire, Kant infers, the fundamental principle of morality can instead concern only the form of our intentions, that is, with our maxims, requiring that they have the form of a possible law, or universalizability. But Kant does not say that this is what *makes* the moral law true or *explains* either the rightness of the moral law itself or the goodness of the good will. On the contrary, once having arrived at the formulation of the same requirement of universalizability in the second section of the *Groundwork*, in a transition from "popular" moral philosophy to a genuine "metaphysics of morals," where "transition from" now means "replacement by," Kant states that this version of the categorical imperative needs a "ground" of its possibility, i.e., an explanation, and he then states that this lies in the fact that humans and in general all rational beings are marked out *by their nature* as ends in themselves, not to be used merely as means (*G*, 4: 428–9). This is a fact about wills, a synthetic proposition rather than a mere analysis, and apparently known by something much like a pure intuition—just as Moore demands.

Further, when Kant makes it clear that by rational being or humanity, that is, rational being as instantiated in human beings, he means that capacity of human beings to set their own ends (*MM*, DV, Introduction, 6: 387, 392), he makes it clear that what he means is that it is the capacity to set our own ends that itself must always be treated as an end, not merely as a means—not merely as a means to our own pleasure, whether the means be our own capacity to set ends or someone else's. In other words, Kant's position is that will, in the sense of *Willkühr*, the capacity of choice or the capacity to set ends (thus not, or not just, *Wille*, which is identical to pure practical reason and issues the moral law, but makes no decisions at all; see *MM*, Introduction, 6: 226–7) is supremely valuable, the "inner worth of the world" as he puts it in his lectures on ethics (*Moral Philosophy Collins*, 27: 344)—which, to be sure, Moore could not have known— and is never to be treated as a mere means to something else. This is a synthetic, not analytic proposition asserting the goodness of the will, as Moore desires. And at least in some places, such as the lectures on ethics from the 1770s and the exposition of the second formulation of the categorical imperative in the *Groundwork*, Kant treats much as the object of a Moorean intuition. Elsewhere, I have argued, Kant suggests an argument, but one derived from the nature of reason, not the nature of the will, namely, that it is a contradiction to deny that something that obviously has a will of its own does have a will of its own, which is what we do, he implies, if we treat it as if it did not.[69] If it be considered a metaphysical fact that human beings each have wills of their own, then this may be considered a metaphysical argument, but it is not one that attempts to derive the moral law from a definition of will, but from the fact that humans have wills. It is at the very least a different argument than the one that Moore criticizes.

Moore makes one last objection to Kant's moral philosophy in *Principia Ethica*. This objection has nothing to do with the naturalistic fallacy. It is rather the objection that by characterizing virtue as rendering us *worthy* of happiness in his account of the highest good, Kant "is in flagrant contradiction with the view, which he implies and which is associated with his name, that a Good Will is the only thing having intrinsic value," thus that Kant is, "inconsistently, an Eudaemonist or Hedonist," at least in part.[70] This can be regarded as Moore's version of the objection going back to Christian Garve that Kant's conception of the highest good undermines the supposed purity of his moral philosophy. Moore's specific objection is that Kant is treating *both* the good will and happiness as having intrinsic value, and that this contradicts Kant's claim that the good will is the only thing with intrinsic value. Strictly speaking, this objection fails, because Kant does not claim that the good will is the only thing with intrinsic value, but that it is the only thing with *unconditional* or *absolute* value.[71] Kant allows that happiness has *intrinsic* value, at least in the sense of not being valued as a means to anything other than itself or needing an explanation or ground of its value, but claims that in the eyes of "impartial reason" anyone's happiness must be *conditioned* by their virtue, or is approved of only if it is accompanied by virtue. Thus happiness does not have *unconditional* value. Perhaps Moore meant to include being unconditioned, or possessing its value always and regardless of anything else, in his conception of intrinsic value; but at the very least he owed us an explicit assertion and defense of that assumption. On his own terms, Kant is not guilty of self-contradiction here.

To be sure, Moore's objection does remind us of a more general one to Kant's theory of the highest good, or at least some of his presentations of it, namely that he does not explain *why* virtue should make one who achieves it worthy of happiness. Kant's claim, in the *Critique of Practical Reason*, that virtue is the only unconditional good, that happiness is an intrinsic and conditional good, and that the *complete* human good therefore consists of both virtue and happiness,

---

[69] See Guyer 2019.　　[70] Moore 1993, pp. 223–4.
[71] On this distinction, see Langton 2007.

may make sense, but he never explicitly explains why virtue should automatically make anyone worthy of happy. Perhaps he thinks that this just follows from the fact that the absence of virtue is felt, or judged in the eyes of "impartial reason," to make anyone unworthy of happiness. But he certainly owed us more of an explanation of his claim than he offered.

Let us now turn to some successors of Moore, the group of philosophers who were willing to call themselves intuitionists. These are chiefly H. A. Prichard, David Ross, and C. D. Broad. They share the meta-ethical assumption of Moore and Sidgwick that the fundamental principles of morality are known by some sort of pure intuition, but differ from both in their normative ethics, holding that morality begins not with intuitions about what states of affairs are good, thus with any form of consequentialism, but with intuitions about what sorts of actions are right, obligations, or duties. For this reason they have been called, starting with Broad himself, deontologists rather than teleologists, and in this regard they are closer to Kant than Moore or Sidgwick was. But they differ fundamentally from Kant in holding that there are multiple fundamental duties and thus principles of morality, not derivable from a single principle, rather than a single principle of morality which, with the input of certain empirical facts about the human conditions but not any additional principles of duty, ground the duties that we have. Kant's assumption, that there must be such a principle—and indeed Sidgwick's assumption as well that there must be a single principle of morality in order to resolve potential conflicts between competing claims of duty—is in fact what Prichard called the basic "mistake" of moral philosophy. We will then consider Bernard Williams's rejection of Kant on the basis of a different kind of moral pluralism, one that recognizes not a plurality of duties rather than a single principle of duty, but a plurality of personal projects that are not automatically overridden by moral obligations.

14

Kant in Oxford

Prichard and Ross to Anscombe and Williams

14.1. The Oxford Intuitionists Prichard, Ross, and Anscombe; Broad at Cambridge

We begin this chapter with a group of philosophers who, unlike Sidgwick and Moore, agreed with Kant in commencing moral philosophy from a conception of duty or obligation, not from a conception of the good—thus, deontologists rather than teleologists. But they disagreed with Kant in insisting upon a plurality of duties, not reducible to a single underlying obligation, and not automatically excluding the possibility of irremediable conflicts of duties (*MM*, Introduction, 6: 224). I discuss these philosophers in chronological order, thus Prichard, Ross, Broad, and Anscombe. I include Anscombe among the Oxford intuitionists because she wrote her most famous paper in ethics while she was at Oxford, before becoming Professor of Philosophy at Cambridge, as well as because of affinities between her views in that paper and the views of Prichard and Ross.

14.1.1. H. A. Prichard

Harold Arthur Prichard (1871–1947) was a lifelong teacher at Oxford and White's Professor of Moral Philosophy from 1928 to 1937. A student of John Cook Wilson, the first prominent Oxonian to combat the idealism of the generation of T. H. Green, F. H. Bradley, and Edward Caird, he carried on the battle. He was not a prolific writer, but practiced a close style of argument with attention to ordinary usage that strongly influenced the next generation of Oxford philosophers including Gilbert Ryle, J. L. Austin, and H. L. A. Hart. In the education of such figures he played a role similar to that of Moore at Cambridge, and his realist approach to philosophy, including his intuitionist approach in meta-ethics, was not entirely dissimilar to that of Moore, although Prichard used this method to advocate a pluralist deontology—that we immediately recognize a variety of duties not derivable from or reducible to a single overarching principle—rather than Moore's sort of consequentialism, which found the right in the maximization of the good and in particular, as we saw, in a highly aestheticized conception of the good as the maximization of the enjoyment of human intercourse and the

Kant's Impact on Moral Philosophy. Paul Guyer, Oxford University Press. © Paul Guyer 2024.
DOI: 10.1093/oso/9780199592456.003.0015

experience of beauty. That moral philosophy can and must find such a single principle and derive more particular rules of duty from it is what Prichard regarded as the fundamental mistake of moral philosophy, as he argued in his best known and most influential paper, "Does Moral Philosophy Rest on a Mistake?" (1912).[1] Kant, of course, would be primary target for anyone concerned to deny that all duties or classes of duties must in some form be derivable from a single fundamental principle of morality, although the major point that Prichard explicitly makes against Kant in this essay is that Kant's attempt to derive our duties from the intrinsic goodness of the good will alone is doomed because "in reality the rightness or wrongness of an act has nothing to do with any question of motives at all."[2] On Prichard's view, the rightness of an action is different from and must be determined antecedently to the "intrinsic goodness of an action," which does lie "solely in its motive."[3] We will come back to this point, and its subsequent development by David Ross, Prichard's colleague and editor, shortly. But first we should note that the importance of Kant to Prichard is also evident in "Duty and Interest," his 1929 inaugural lecture as White's Professor, which he concludes by stating that although Kant's "moral philosophy is of course open to many obvious criticism[s, n]evertheless he always strikes me as having, far more than any other philosopher, the root of the matter in him," namely in his insistence on having "nothing to do either with the idea that the rightness of action depends on its being for our own good, or with the idea that we think of it as so depending, or with the idea that desire for our own good is our only motive."[4] In Prichard's view, the form that the mistake of moral philosophy took prior to Kant, a mistake far more pernicious than any of Kant's, was its attempt to portray morality as always a form of enlightened self-interest. Prichard also wrote a commentary on the *Groundwork for the Metaphysics of Morals,* posthumously published only in the 2002 *Moral Writings* in twenty-six pages. Because of its very recent posthumous publication, this commentary could not have been influential on the subsequent British reception of Kantian moral philosophy, except in the case of those who might have heard him present similar views in classes.

The only book that Prichard published in his lifetime was also on Kant, although in fact on Kant's theoretical philosophy, titled *Kant's Theory of Knowledge.*[5] "This book," he states, "is an attempt to think out the nature and tenability of Kant's transcendental idealism, an attempt animated by the conviction that even the elucidation of Kant's meaning, apart from any criticism, is impossible without a discussion on their own merits of the main issues which he

---

[1] Prichard 1912, reprinted in Prichard 1949, cited here from the most recent edition, *Moral Writings,* edited by Jim McAdam (Oxford Clarendon Press, 2002), pp. 7–20.
[2] Prichard 2002, p. 11.   [3] Prichard 2002, p. 14.
[4] Prichard 2002, pp. 21–49, at pp. 48–9.   [5] Prichard 1909.

raises."[6] The emphasis in this sentence should be on "tenability": Prichard's approach to Kant is primarily a criticism from the standpoint of his own meta-physical and epistemological realism. Prichard's criticism of the argument of the *Critique* is summed up in his final "Note on the Refutation of Idealism," namely "that Kant, without realizing what he is doing, really abandons the view that objects in space are phenomena, and uses an argument the very nature of which implies that these objects are things in themselves"[7]—as well it should.[8] His view is that Kant successfully shows that "the consciousness of my successive states must be a *thing* external to me in opposition to the representation of a thing external to me, and a thing external to me in opposition to a thing [internal] to me can only be a thing in itself,"[9] but that Kant is mistaken in thinking that he can reconcile this conclusion with continued adherence to transcendental idealism as the doctrine that space (and time) and everything in it are mere representations, not things in themselves. Thus when Kant argues that "external appearance is really immediate," he must be arguing that we immediately experience things that exist independently of our representations of them, not merely our own representa-tions. So understood,

the *Refutation* may be considered to suggest the proper refutation of Descartes . . . . Descartes' position is precisely an inversion of the truth . . . our consciousness of the world, so far from being an uncertain inference from the consciousness of our successive states is in reality a presupposition of the latter consciousness, in that this latter consciousness only arises through reflection upon the former . . . therefore Descartes' admission of the validity of self-consciousness implicitly involves the admission *a fortiori* of the validity of our consciousness of the world.[10]

"Consciousness of the world": Prichard's view is that we are directly or immedi-ately conscious of things independent from ourselves and our representations of them, and moreover that through this consciousness we know both that these objects exist and what at least some of their properties are. He does not give any attention to Kant's attempt, especially in the *Prolegomena to Any Future Metaphysics*, to defend the position that we can know *that* things exist independ-ently of our representation even though we know them only *as* we represent them,

---

[6] Prichard 1909, p. iii.   [7] Prichard 1909, p. 321.

[8] See my own treatment of the Refutation of Idealism, Guyer 1983, and, expanded from that, Guyer 1987, part IV. Although I used a lot of material from Kant's *Handschriftliche Nachlass* that Prichard did not use in 1909, my conclusion was partly similar to his, a point I neglected to mention in 1983, although differing on whether the Refutation is compatible with transcendental idealism properly understood.

[9] Prichard 1909, p. 323. Prichard's text actually repeats "external," but that makes no sense, so surely he intended "internal" where I have inserted it.

[10] Prichard 1909, pp. 323–4.

thus we do not know anything more about *what* they are other than that they exist and are in some way the ground (though not literally the cause) of our representations of them (*Prol*, §13, note III, 4: 286). No doubt he would not have been impressed by Kant's attempt to have his cake and eat it too, but he does not even give it a run for its money.[11] However, what is important for us is Prichard's own conviction that we can have immediate knowledge of objective facts, and his importation of this view into moral philosophy in the form of the position that we have immediate knowledge that certain kinds of actions are right and obligatory, others not, and that we do not need to derive such knowledge from any higher principle.

The fundamental mistake of moral philosophy, according to Prichard, is thinking that what is right has to be derived from some account of the good, rather than being immediately known as right. The account of goodness has taken either of two forms in the first instance, in fact, direct or indirect versions of Sidgwick's rational egoism, namely, one's own happiness is supposed to be self-evidently good, or something else "realized in or by the action" is supposed to be good.[12] "Plato, Butler, Hutcheson, Paley, Mill, each in his own way seeks at bottom to convince the individual that he ought to act in so-called moral ways by showing that to do will really be for his happiness";[13] to this list might be added Hobbes, some strands in his opponent Cumberland, and many others. Hume's view might be more complex, namely that it is always *someone's* happiness—agreeableness—that is the ultimate object of morality, but that sympathy can allow us to enjoy the happiness of others without denying its primary status as their happiness, not our own; this view might be considered to straddle the boundary between rational egoism and universalistic hedonism. Alternatively, one might think, like Kant, that right actions are those which have as their end not happiness but something else, namely something "intrinsically good," which could then take either of two forms: "They are either actions in which the agent did what did because he thought that he ought to do it, or actions of which the motive was a desire prompted by some good emotion, such as gratitude, affection, family feeling, or public spirit, the most prominent of such desires in books on Moral Philosophy being ascribed to what is vaguely called benevolence."[14] But since Kant will not allow mere desires any moral significance, whether as good in themselves or as right, he must hold that intrinsically good actions are those in which the agent did what he did because he thought that he ought to do it. Against this Prichard brings what is basically Hume's objection to the idea that "the first virtuous motive, which bestows a merit on any action, can...be a regard to the virtue of that

---

[11] This is my point of disagreement with Prichard's assessment of the Refutation.

[12] On Prichard's interpretation of even Butler and Sidgwick as egoists, see Hurka 2014, p. 134.

[13] Prichard 2002, p. 8.   [14] Prichard 2002, p. 11.

action":[15] the criterion of merit—either goodness or rightness—must be independent of "regard to the virtue of the action" in order for the virtuous motivation to know what to aim at; virtuous motivation might be glossed as "I want to do the right thing" or "the best thing," but neither of those tells me what the right or best thing is. So Prichard infers that "in reality the rightness or wrongness of an act has nothing to do with any question of motives at all."[16] Doing an action out of a certain kind of motivation may be what makes it good—the position that Ross will develop—but it is not what makes it right. The "intrinsic goodness of an action lies solely in its motive," Prichard is prepared to say, but "the rightness of a right action lies solely in the origination in which the act consists."[17] The latter statement is not very clear, because "origination" might sound a lot like "motivation," but what Prichard means is that attempting to bring out about certain sorts of states of affairs is intrinsically right and immediately recognized as such. "The sense of obligation to do, or of the rightness of an action of a particular kind is absolutely underivative or immediate."[18] Our "sense that we ought to pay our debts or tell the truth" does not arise "from our recognition that in doing so we should be originating something good," for example something that would increase the happiness of the recipient of such an action. Rather, we simply "recognize, for instance, that [the] performance of a service to X, who has done us a service, just in virtue of its being the performance of a service to one who has rendered a service to the would-be agent, ought to be done by us."[19] That is, we simply know that we ought to, or that it is right to, repay debts, whether of gratitude or otherwise, to tell the truth, and so on—although of course it is part of Prichard's point that there is no principled way to spell out the "and so on." "This apprehension is immediate, in precisely the sense in which a mathematical apprehension is immediate, e.g. the apprehension that this three-sided figure, in virtue of its being [such], must have three angles."[20] Prichard's choice of a mathematical example to illustrate his point that the epistemology of judgments of right is the same as that of other cognition, is not meant to suggest that moral judgment is a priori as contrasted to empirical or a posteriori, whether synthetic a priori as mathematical judgment would be for Kant or analytic a priori as it would be, for example, for Bertrand Russell. It is just meant to assert that the knowledge of what is right is immediate and self-evident, thus in no need of derivation from any single, higher principle. That is the gist of Prichard's intuitionism.

Whether this intuitionism has any merit on its own, it cannot be said that Prichard, whether in the 1912 essay or in the later manuscript on the *Groundwork*, where he repeats the basic objection that Kant's "principle, so far from being a

[15] David Hume, *T*, book III, part 2, section 1, paragraph 4 Hume, vol. 1, p. 307.
[16] Prichard 2002, p. 11.   [17] Prichard 2002, p. 14.   [18] Prichard 2002, p. 12.
[19] Prichard 2002, p. 13.   [20] Prichard 2002, p. 13.

principle from which particular duties can be *derived*, will *presuppose* them,"[21] displayed any subtle understanding of Kant's own argument about the good will. As I have previously suggested, section I of the *Groundwork*, the only place where Kant begins his attempt to clarify the content of the moral law from the concept of the good will and an account of good, or in the human case, dutiful motivation, is only meant as an introductory "transition" from "common rational cognition" of morals and not as his fundamental and final, philosophical argument, which comes in section II of the *Groundwork*. And what the argument of *Groundwork* I is supposed to show is that if, as we are all supposed to know, a good will is not one that is motivated by any mere inclination or any mere object of inclination, moral maxims must be characterized by something else, namely their form, having the form of a law, or being universalizable. Or so Kant quickly infers in *Groundwork* I (4: 399–401); in section II he actually says that for a principle not to be formal is just for it not to be based on something entirely subjective, like inclination: "Practical principles are *formal* if they abstract from all subjective ends, whereas they are *material* if they have put these, and consequently certain incentives, at their basis" (*G*, 4: 428). This leaves the way open for Kant to analyze the requirement of formality by that of universalizability, as he did in the first section of the *Groundwork* but also does in his argument in section II that "when I think of a *categorical* imperative in general I know at once what it contains," namely simply the requirement that our maxims conform to "the universality of a law" (*G*, 4: 421), but also to hold that an objective rather than subjective *end* may satisfy the requirement of formality, thus that a good will—were Kant to return to that concept in *Groundwork* II, which he does not—may be displayed by aiming at an objective rather than subjective end rather than—or in addition to—by acting on a universalizable rather than non-universalizable maxim. The only objective end, Kant will of course argue, is humanity itself, or rational being more generally although we know it only in its human form, and any maxim that makes this its end, Kant assumes, will also be universalizable.

Kant's formulation of the requirement of universalizability suggests that this is not intended to be a *sufficient* condition for the derivation of duties; after all, it has to be *applied* to maxims, and these presumably have to be suggested from some other source. In the *Metaphysics of Morals*, the idea of humanity as an end in itself will be broken down into the two ends that are also duties, self-perfection and the happiness of others. The idea of humanity as an objective end might seem a better candidate for a sufficient condition of rightness, but Prichard is not much impressed with this idea, and does not give it much of a hearing; nor does he consider the two ends that are also duties of the *Metaphysics of Morals*. He does not mention humanity as an end in itself at all in his 1912 essay, but he does bring

[21] Prichard, "Kant's *Fundamental Principles of the Metaphysics of Morals*," in Prichard 2002, pp. 50–76, at p. 57.

it up in his manuscript commentary. He brings it up, however, only quickly to dismiss it. He starts by describing Kant as merely adding "a second . . . criterion of moral principles," not, as Kant himself says, a *ground* for any possible categorical imperative (*G*, 4: 428). He then describes Kant's idea as "that man's rational nature gives an absolute value to his personality, i.e. a goodness which is that of being a means or instrument to something else but which is intrinsic and constitutes the man, in Kant's language, an end in himself," supposed to be a fact that then "justifies the principle 'So act as to treat humanity whether in thine own person, or in that of any other, in every case as an end, and never as a means only'."[22] This account of the fact from which Kant begins and the formulation of the categorical imperative which he derives from it is certainly correct, as far as it goes, and expresses a recognition that Kant *does* think that a normative "ought" can be derived from an "is," a fact about the essence or as Kant later says "proper self" (*G*, 4: 457) of human beings, *in some way*. Prichard is still on the right track when he argues further that the idea of what it is to treat a person as an end in itself cannot be understood on any ordinary model of an end for action, namely a state of affairs to be brought about by the action or an object to be produced, "for neither a person nor even his rational nature can strictly be an end,"[23] that is, a state of affairs to be brought about, a criticism that many have repeated since. So in his view the real force of Kant's Formula of Humanity must lie in its second half, that is, the imperative *not* to treat a person, whether another or oneself, simply as a means to some end of one's own, presumably a non-moral end, an end suggested merely by inclination. However, Prichard then argues that what it is not to treat someone else as a mere means is not to treat that person in a way that violates "certain claims on us, i.e. rights against us, which we ought to respect, in virtue of which we ought to act towards him in certain ways, whether it suits us or not," and that what it is not to treat oneself as a mere means is not to violate certain obligations concerning the use of one's own capacities that one has. In both cases, Prichard maintains, the principle of Formula of Humanity, "so far from being a principle from which particular duties can be *derived*, will *presuppose* them. . . . we cannot by applying it *discover* particular duties . . . on the contrary any application of it *presupposes* an independent knowledge of them."[24] In other words, not to treat a person as a mere means is not to violate any antecedent obligations that one has to such a person, whether another or oneself, and the second formulation of the categorical imperative tells us nothing more than this, which we already know but can apply only on the basis of antecedent knowledge of our obligations—which of course, in Prichard's view, can be given only by immediate intuitions such as that we should repay our debts, tell the truth, or, in

[22] Prichard 2002, p. 56.   [23] Prichard 2002, p. 56.   [24] Prichard 2002, p. 57.

the case of duties to ourselves, not neglect or abuse our natural capacities, whether mental or physical.

In making this criticism, Prichard makes no reference to Kant's definition of humanity in the Introduction to the Doctrine of Virtue of the *Metaphysics of Morals* as the capacity of a human being to set its own ends. In view of the status of this text as a commentary on the *Groundwork* alone, indeed one that was not published and therefore perhaps not polished by Prichard, this hermeneutical lapse might be forgiven. But neither does Prichard refer to Kant's statement within the *Groundwork* that "Rational nature is distinguished from the rest of nature by this, that it sets itself an end" (*G*, 4: 437), a statement which, since by "humanity" Kant clearly means in the *Groundwork* just rational nature insofar as it is instantiated in human beings, might be thought to define what he means in the imperative always to treat humanity as an end and never merely as a means. This imperative does have content of its own, namely that one must not treat the capacity to set ends whether in oneself or others as a mere means to something else, for example, one's own mere pleasure. Kant clearly does think that this requirement does give rise to specific duties in the actual, empirical circumstances of human existence, the very same duties derived from the more obviously formalistic requirement that our maxims be universalizable, a point which he makes in the four examples that follow each of the first two formulations of the categorical imperative, the Formulas of Universal Law and Humanity in the *Groundwork*, and which he makes even better in the subsequent *Metaphysics of Morals*. Again, the latter text is not part of Prichard's brief in his draft commentary, but knowledge of it might have tempered his confidence in his criticisms of the *Groundwork*.

Prichard is guilty of the same omission in his criticism of Kant's final formulation of the categorical imperative. He reports this formula, usually called the Formula of Autonomy, as that "The third criterion is based on the idea that a moral principle is something which a man in virtue of his rational nature *imposes on himself and all other men*."[25] His interpretation that the moral principle is something that each human being imposes on him- or herself is unexceptionable, but his implication that we also impose it on *each other* is problematic, and seems to violate what Prichard does regard as the point of the third formulation, namely that it brings out that the moral law is not heteronomous, that is, imposed on us by any external authority, but is autonomous, which presumably means precisely that it is imposed on each of us by his or her own "proper self," namely his or her own reason. As we will see in a moment, the idea of the autonomy of the moral law is actually the target of Prichard's most characteristic criticism of Kant, but first a word on his omission of a proper understanding of Kant's concept of humanity

---

[25] Prichard 2002, p. 57.

from what is in fact Kant's final formulation of the categorical imperative, the Formula of the Empire of Ends. Prichard follows Kant in stating merely that the Formula of Autonomy gives rise "to the idea that the moral beings form a *kingdom of ends*, i.e. a democracy of rational beings who impose on themselves and others, as subjects, a common system of law."[26] This is correct so far as it mirrors Kant's statement that "By an empire I understand a systematic union of various rational beings under common laws," and this is a statement that could be open to Prichard's criticism that such a notion presupposes antecedent knowledge of what the laws are, that it simply tells us that each of us should treat everyone in accordance with moral laws but cannot tell us what those laws are, something that only intuition can do. However, it neglects the genuine content in Kant's subsequent statement that "since laws determine ends in terms of their universal validity, if we abstract from all the content of their private ends we shall be able to think of a whole of all ends in systematic connection (a whole both of rational beings as ends in themselves and of the ends of his own that each may set himself), that is, an empire of ends" (*G*, 4: 433). This definition of the empire of ends is not entirely easy to parse, but what the parenthesis suggests is that, while the necessary universality of genuine law requires that we ignore merely personal inclinations or preferences, our own or those of others, in the formulation and acceptance of our general principles, the point of those laws is precisely to allow individuals to set their own ends, in the exercise of their own humanity, insofar as the pursuit of such ends can be joined in "systematic connection," that is, to the extent that each person's determination and pursuit of her own ends is compatible with every person's determination and pursuit of her own ends. Determining just what the constraints of such a "systematic connection" are may not always be easy—if it were, there would never even be the appearance of moral dilemma—but the idea is hardly vacuous.

Now back to Prichard's larger criticism of Kant's idea of autonomy: "The view... that we impose moral principles on ourselves is mistaken." It is a truism, Prichard suggests, that "it is *we* who *recognize* moral principles," but "though this recognition is *our* act and an act of our own rational nature, we do not *invent* the principles, as the legislator invents laws. We *find* them." Indeed, "This is perhaps the fundamental mistake in speaking of moral *laws*. While a law is always the invention, though not the arbitrary invention of a human being, a moral principle is not invented at all."[27] In other words, the elementary mistake of Kant's moral philosophy, to go back to Prichard's 1912 term, is not merely that there is a single moral law, but that the principle(s) of morality should be compared to law at all.[28] A law is the product of a human act of legislation, but for Prichard a duty is an objective fact, simply recognized by creatures like us in an act of immediate

---

[26] Prichard 2002, p. 57.   [27] Prichard 2002, pp. 57–8.   [28] See also Hurka 2014, p. 274.

intuition, like many other objective facts, such as those of mathematics. Recognition is an act of a rational being, but so far as Prichard is concerned what is recognized is not in any way the *product* of rationality. This simply gives no hearing to Kant's position that the moral law is in some way, although not of course a mere "invention," a product of our own reason. For Kant, the larger point of course is that the moral law is a product of *our* reason, not of something else, not even the reason of God, should there be such a thing—Kant's emphasis, so to speak, is not on "invention" or "product," but on "ours." Prichard is rather indifferent to this larger issue, however, in his distaste for the idea that any kind of laws are the product of thought rather than objective realities that are simply intuited. This distaste is evident in Prichard's approach to Kant's theory of knowledge as well: "The fundamental objection to this account of knowledge seems so obvious as to be hardly worth stating; it is of course that knowing and making are not the same. The very nature of knowing presupposes that the thing known is already made, or, to speak more accurately, already exists. In other words, knowing is essentially the discovery of what already is."[29]

For all of Prichard's appreciation of Kant's separation of duty from any personal interest in happiness, the incommensurability of their basic philosophical attitudes could hardly be clearer. Although the places where this basic difference in approaches is particularly clear include the unpublished commentary on the *Groundwork* and the 1909 book on Kant's theoretical philosophy that was not reprinted for many decades,[30] Prichard's objectivist approach to moral philosophy and the criticism of Kant on this basis was either influential on or representative of British attitudes to Kant's ethics for several generations, and it would be many decades before a "constructivist" interpretation rather than "realist" reinterpretation of Kant's approach would actually become the default position in Anglophone interpretation of Kantian ethics.[31]

14.1.2. W. D. Ross

There are other points worth discussing in Prichard's commentary on the *Groundwork*, but at this point let us turn to Kant in the work of William David, subsequently Sir David Ross (1877–1971), another in the long line of Scottish philosophers who revivified philosophy at Oxford. Ross had a distinguished career: he was a Fellow at Merton College from 1900 until 1945, the deputy to the White's Professor from 1923 to 1928 when he chose not to stand for election to

---

[29] Prichard 1909, p. 235.
[30] Lewis White Beck included it in a "collection of eleven of the most important books on Kant's philosophy reprinted" in 1976, but how much influence Prichard's book had even then is dubious.
[31] See the final chapter on Rawlsian "constructivism."

the chair, in favor of Prichard, and instead became Provost of Oriel College from 1928 until 1947, Vice-Chancellor of the University of Oxford from 1941 to 1944, thus during World War II, and fulfilled other positions of public service during World War I and later.[32] He was more a scholar of Aristotle than Kant, although his final book was his own commentary on Kant's *Groundwork*, titled *Kant's Ethical Theory* although it concerns only the *Groundwork*.[33] Ross published two substantial works on moral philosophy in general, *The Right and the Good* in 1930 and *The Foundations of Ethics*, based on his 1935–6 Gifford Lectures, in 1939.[34] In spite of his publication of these two substantial books on ethics rather than a few articles, Ross's approach can be considered an expansion and refinement of Prichard's. The intuitionist thesis that we have immediate acquaintance with a multiplicity of duties, rather than producing a fundamental principle of morality by our own reason, is prevalent throughout his work, and permeates his commentary on the *Groundwork*.

Like Prichard, Ross thinks that Kant is correct to locate the goodness of an action in its motivation of respect for duty rather than self-interest. On this point, he expresses his admiration for Kant at least as strongly as Prichard had: "Kant's principle is of vital importance as stating the spirit of morally good action—that morally good action is action in which one does not assert for oneself a privileged position of exemption from ordinary moral rules." But also like Prichard, Ross insists that Kant's insight into the motivation that constitutes the moral goodness of action "will not tell us in particular what we ought to do," that is, the good does not determine what is right, but presupposes an account of the right.[35] Or as he puts the point in *The Right and the Good*,

> Moral goodness is quite distinct from and independent of rightness, which...
> belongs to acts *not* in virtue of the motives they proceed from, but in virtue of the
> nature of what is done. Thus a morally good action need not be the doing of a
> right action, and the doing of a right action need not be a morally good action.
> The ethical theories that stress the thing done and those that stress the motive
> from which it is done both have some justification, ... but the two types of theory
> have been at cross-purposes, because they have failed to notice that they are
> talking about different things. Thus Kant has tried to deduce from his conception
> of the nature of a morally good action rules as to what types of act are right.[36]

But in Ross's view that is a confusion. Ross further follows Prichard in rejecting the idea that what is right or obligatory can be reduced to or derived from a single principle, and also in rejecting the characterization of the purported single

---

[32] For more details, see Hurka 2014, pp. 18–19.   [33] Ross 1954.
[34] Both published by the Clarendon Press, Oxford.   [35] Ross 1954, p. 45.
[36] Ross 1930, p. 156.

principle of morality as a law, because he agrees with Prichard that a law is imposed by an authority but that is not the way to think about either a principle or principles of morality: "We are unable, then, to say that morality is essentially something imposed by any will, and it seems best to say that here the analogy between morality and law breaks down, and therefore to avoid the phrase 'moral law' and speak simply of duty or the right."[37]

In the statement of his own moral theory, Ross goes beyond Prichard in offering not merely several examples of immediately intuited duties or obligations that need no foundation but rather a fuller although still open-ended list, namely the duties of fidelity to commitments, gratitude, distributive justice, beneficence, self-improvement, and the more stringent duty of non-maleficence or not injuring others.[38] He famously characterizes all of these as *"prima facie"* duties, meaning that in particular situations they can conflict with each other in such a way that only one rather than another can be fulfilled. It has been suggested that they would better be called *"pro tanto"* duties, because in such situations the duty that cannot be fulfilled then and there is not a merely apparent duty that turns out not to be a duty at all, which is what *"prima facie"* would imply, but rather it remains a genuine duty which cannot be satisfied then and there but will have to be satisfied or at least recognized and honored at some other time in some other way.[39] That is, not keeping a promise to have lunch with a friend because one had to stop on the way to help accident victims does not simply wipe out all obligation to the friend, but means that one should find some reasonable way to make it up to the friend, whatever that might turn out to be—perhaps a mere explanation will do, perhaps something more will be needed (for example, not only rescheduling the lunch but picking up the tab instead of splitting it). It is indeed part of Ross's picture that the *prima facie* principles of morality cannot be applied mechanically, but must be weighed in view of particular circumstances; in this regard his position is the forerunner of what has more recently come to be known as "particularism." Kant himself expresses a similar point, although Ross does not cite him in this regard, when he argues that there can be no conflicting obligations but only conflicting "grounds of obligation" with only one actual obligation in the case of such a conflict (*MM*, Introduction, 6: 224). However, Kant seems to assume that there will always be an obvious solution to such conflicts—that "the stronger *ground of obligation* prevails (*fortio obligandi ratio vincit*)"—and that the other ground of obligation does not actually give rise to an obligation in such a circumstance, nor does he suggest that one still has some sort of obligation to satisfy the weaker ground of obligation. So perhaps his account comes closer to

---

[37] Ross 1954, p. 26. See Hurka 2014, p. 274.   [38] Ross 1930, p. 21.
[39] See Kagan 1989, p. 17n. Barbara Herman has made a similar point, although not with reference to Ross. See Herman, "Obligation and Performance," originally in Amélie Rorty and Owen Flanagan (eds), *Identity, Character, and Morality* (Cambridge, MA: MIT Press, 1990), reprinted in Herman 1993, pp. 158–83.

being a genuine theory of *prima facie* rather than *pro tanto* duty, not what Ross himself meant by *prima facie* duty, and maybe Ross did well after all not to cite Kant in this context.

However, although Ross clearly follows Prichard's general line both in his criticism of Kant and in his own moral theory, his commentary on the *Groundwork* is more detailed and makes several valuable points in defense as well as in criticism of Kant. The first point that I will mention is his subtle treatment of the classical objection, going back to Schiller's satirical poem, "that for Kant an action is not good if it is done gladly, without difficulty—with the paradoxical consequence that the existence of a kindly natural disposition or the formation of good habits makes actions less good."[40] In Ross's view, "Kant is far from insisting, as he has often been charged with insisting, that there is a natural opposition between sense of duty and inclination; what he does insist on is that there is a complete difference between the two."[41] That is, the presence of an inclination in favor of an action (let's assume for the sake of simplicity that it is in fact a right action) does not render the action other than morally good; it is rather irrelevant to the question of whether the action is actually done out of a sense of duty. A right action done only from an inclination is still a right and dutiful action, just not a morally good one, which is of course what Kant himself holds. More importantly, perhaps, Ross notes that "the human will is *always* subject to subjective restrictions and hindrances" arising from inclination, but this only means that a human will is never "a holy will," "divine or angelic," not that it is never a good will.[42] The character of the human will is always to be accompanied by inclination, whether selfish or generous; what makes a human will a good will is that it acts out of a sense of a duty independently of either sort of inclination. In particular, Ross holds, although he does not think Kant was adequately clear about this, "that the sense of duty may be equally strong in two acts, in one of which there is, and in the other there is not, a co-operating morally indifferent motive, and that in that case the two actions are equally good."[43] Kant's treatment of the relation between the sense of duty and other inclination needs some fine-tuning, Ross thinks, but he does not follow Prichard in thinking that Kant simply ignores natural inclinations and that he should have celebrated those alone and not a separate and perhaps mythical "sense of duty."

Second, Ross gives a good statement of what is a genuine problem in the application of the first formulation of the categorical imperative, the requirement of the universalizability of one's maxims, and which has come to be widely recognized as a problem, namely the problem of the specificity of an agent's maxim and determining consequently what maxim an agent is proposing to act upon. As Ross puts it, "Any individual act," but here we could add any specific

---

[40] Ross 1954, p. 14.   [41] Ross 1954, p. 17.
[42] Ross 1954, p. 14.   [43] Ross 1954, pp. 17–18.

maxim of action, "is an instance of a class of acts," or class of maxims, "which is a species of a wider class of acts which is a species of a still wider class; we can set no limit to the degree of specification which may intervene between the *summum genus* 'act' and the individual act" or maxim.[44] For example, a proposed action might be described as just a lie but also more specifically "under the sub-species 'lies told to murderous persons'" or more generally "under the genus 'statements'," and the results of universalizing a proposed maxim of action might seem acceptable under one of these classifications of the action but not under another. In Ross's view, "Kant pitches, arbitrarily, on the middle one of these classes, and since acts of this class are generally wrong, and are indeed always prima facie wrong, he says that the particular lie is wrong," when he or anyone might well have come to a different conclusion about the universalizability of the more specific and restricted maxim to tell lies only to murderous persons when doing so might thwart their murderous intentions. "The test of universalizability applied at one level of abstractness condemns the act; applied at another level of abstractness it justifies it"; and this is a problem, Ross argues, because "the principle itself does not indicate at what level of abstractness it is to be applied."[45] Ross concludes from this that the "whole method of abstraction, if relied upon, when used alone, to answer for us the question 'What ought I to do?', is a mistake," and of course recommends that we rely instead on his substantive principles of prima facie duty and our ability to weight them properly in cases of conflict. But here perhaps he gives up on Kant too soon, and an alternative treatment of this issue would be to say that we have to test our proposed maxims of action at all levels of abstraction, and that if they pass the test of universalizability at none then they are impermissible but if they pass at one then they are permissible at precisely that level of abstraction. In other words, telling lies without further specification is impermissible, but telling lies to thwart the intentions of murderous persons is permissible. Of course, testing all the maxims at all levels of abstraction that could apply to a particular action is not actually possible, whether at the time of action or at any time, and so the requirement of the categorical imperative understood in this way could only be a regulative ideal. Kant does not suggest this qualification, at least in the *Groundwork*, but it might not be an unrealistic appraisal of what is morally possible in the actual circumstances of human life.

Third, Ross's treatment of the Formula of Humanity as an End in Itself is not uncritical but it is more sympathetic than Prichard's. First, Ross asserts that the "notion of self-subsisting ends is nothing but an embarrassment to Kant," but that Kant is not wrong when "he interprets 'treating [humans] as ends merely as not interfering with them." Like Prichard, he assumes "that just means recognizing their rights,"[46] and thus presupposes some antecedent determination of human

---

[44] Ross 1954, p. 32.   [45] Ross 1954, p. 33.   [46] Ross 1954, p. 51.

rights, which of course will come only from intuition of our prima facie duties. By introducing the idea of non-interference he at least leaves open that this is itself a substantive constraint on our actions that might give rise to some account of our duties. But further, Ross is not as hostile to the idea of humanity as an end in itself as first appears. While he insists that it makes no sense to think of human beings as such as ends in themselves, he does concede that "If there is something that has absolute value, there must be a duty to conserve this and to promote it to the best of one's ability." And he continues, "Now there is such a thing, viz., good will, and it exists either actually or potentially in every man; therefore in all our actions we must treat neither ourselves nor others as mere possible enjoyers of pleasure, but as beings in whom good will may be and should be conserved and promoted." On this point, he claims, "In spite of great obscurity of expression, Kant's thought here is profoundly true."[47] Even if it makes no sense to think of humans (or other beings, or other rational beings) as self-subsisting ends, it does make sense to think of the preservation and promotion of some actual or potential property of such beings as a genuine end of action. It may be controversial whether humanity as an end in this sense should be identified with the good will, or whether that which is to be treated and properly so as an end can be humanity in the more general sense of Kant's definition of it as simply the capacity of a person to set her own ends; in more recent commentary, Richard Dean and Henry Allison have defended the first position, and I have defended the latter.[48]

Finally, Ross makes an important point about section III of the *Groundwork*. Kant's transcendental idealist defense of free will might well have been consigned to the dustbin of history by Moore's 1898 article on "Freedom," and Ross makes no attempt to revive Kant's metaphysics. "The whole doctrine of noumena and phenomena has been found by critics to be one of the most puzzling and unsatisfactory parts of Kant's metaphysics."[49] Like Moore, he emphasizes that Kant's assumption that the noumenal is the ground of the phenomenal "gives no account of moral conflict."[50] But Ross does think that, even though Kant is wrong to ascribe the motivation or the decision to act on the moral law to a timeless noumenal self,

> He is perhaps right in a sense in thinking of the awareness of duty as something that does not arise at this or that moment and then disappear. From the time at which we have achieved sufficient maturity to recognize that there is such a thing as duty, the recognition of it may be present in the background of consciousness, when it is not in the foreground, throughout our waking lives, or the greater part of them.[51]

---

[47] Ross 1954, p. 52.
[48] See Dean, 2006; Allison 2011, esp. pp. 213–18, and Guyer 2016a, esp. chapter 4, "Freedom and the Essential Ends of Mankind," and chapter 6, "Setting and Pursuing Ends: Internal and External Freedom."
[49] Ross 1954, p. 77.   [50] Ross 1954, p. 81.   [51] Ross 1954, p. 80.

Motivation by the sense of or respect for duty is not to be confused with an efficient cause operating at a specific moment, although, in Ross's view, it will need to be accompanied by further awareness, such as that in a specific circumstance some specific action is what duty requires, in order to become effective. We will see the importance of Ross's translation of Kant's noumenal motivation by the moral law into a background rather than momentary attribute of ordinary, empirical human beings when we turn to Bernard Williams's famous "one thought too many" objection. Further, Ross suggests that, if not identical to this, Kant's distinction between our phenomenal and noumenal selves and wills can be transformed into a "different double membership," namely between our faculty of reason and our faculty of desire (in Kant's view, our lower faculty of desire). "We are thus in a sense members of two worlds, not of a world of noumena and of a world of phenomena, but of two worlds equally real, the world of rational beings and the world of animals; and the moral life is a result of the tension between the tendencies arising in us from this double membership."[52] Surely Kant is right to see our nature as divided in this way and the tensions of our moral life as arising from this dualism, even if he places an untenable metaphysical interpretation on it in the hope of defending the indefensible belief that we are always free to do what is right no matter what our previous history and present condition.

14.1.3. C. D. Broad

All of his criticisms aside, Ross thus defends Kant's most basic insights, that morality sometimes requires us to ignore or override our natural interest in our own happiness and that our own nature sometimes makes this hard or maybe even impossible. A subsequent British critic of Kant who was not so happy with the first of these conclusions was Bernard Williams. But before turning to him, let's take a brief look at a third intuitionist, namely Charlie Dunbar Broad (1887–1971), associated with Cambridge rather than Oxford. Broad studied at Trinity College and held a fellowship there beginning in 1911, but also held positions at St Andrews and Bristol before holding a sequence of university positions at Cambridge, culminating in the Knightsbridge Professorship of Moral Philosophy from 1933 to 1953. He published across a wide range of subjects from history of philosophy to contemporary philosophy of science, and also carried on his predecessor Sidgwick's critical "psychical research." Sidgwick receives the lengthiest discussion in Broad's major publication in moral philosophy, *Five Types of Ethical Theory* from 1930—thus the same year as Ross's *The Right and Good*—but Kant also gets a chapter. Broad takes a slightly more nuanced approach to Kant than his Oxford contemporaries did. He starts off

---

[52] Ross 1954, pp. 85–6.

with the criticism that Kant's initial claim that "Nothing is intrinsically good but a good will" proves "only that a good will is a *necessary constituent* of any whole which is intrinsically good";[53] here Broad's language reflects the influence of Moore at Cambridge. He describes Kant as holding that "a right action is one that is done from a sense of duty,"[54] and it looks as if he is going to make the same criticism as the Oxford intuitionists, namely that while this may be a proper account of *good* action, it does not offer but must presuppose a criterion of *right* action, with good action then being more complex, namely right action done from a sense of duty. However, Broad then seems friendlier to Kant when he interprets Kant's categorical imperative as the requirement that "A principle of conduct is right if and only if it would be accepted on its own merits by any rational being, no matter what his special tastes and inclinations might be. It must therefore be a principle which is acceptable to rational beings simply because of its intrinsic form, and not because it is a rule for gaining some desired end"; in introducing this characterization of the categorical imperative Broad makes the useful point that "It would be better to call it the 'Supreme Principle of Categorical Imperatives'. For it is a second-order principle which states the necessary and sufficient conditions that must be fulfilled by any first-order principle if the latter is to be a categorical imperative and action determined by it is to be morally right"[55] (although Broad does not mention this, what Kant refers to as "the hypothetical imperative," "Whoever wills the end also wills (insofar as reason has decisive influence on his actions) the indispensably necessary means to it that are within his power," should also be called the second-order principle of first-order hypothetical imperatives) (G, 4: 417). Here Broad seems to differ from the Oxonians in recognizing the value of the principle of categorical imperatives: he defends it from the objection that is "'empty', 'sterile', and 'merely formal'" on the ground that it should not be expected to generate substantive duties all by itself, any more than the rules for valid syllogisms furnish particular valid syllogisms all by themselves; rather "The business of ethics is to provide a test for rules of conduct, just as it is the business of logic to provide a test for arguments."[56] He seems prepared to concede that Kant's principle of categorical imperatives does do this in requiring that "Any action which, in a given situation, is right or wrong at all would be right or wrong for *any* rational being whatever in that situation, no matter what his special tastes and inclinations might be,"[57] thereby rejecting any proposed action—or as we would now say, maxim—that does not satisfy this requirement. Here it looks as if Broad is prepared to concede that the categorical imperative is an adequate criterion of rightness. However, he then retrenches and rejoins his Oxford colleagues by insisting that "one can no more infer that a rational being would recognise any principle as right than that it would recognise

---

[53] Broad 1930, p. 117.   [54] Broad 1930, p. 116.   [55] Broad 1930, pp. 120–1.
[56] Broad 1930, pp. 122–3.   [57] Broad 1930, p. 124.

any end as desirable,"[58] and argues that if it is true that any rational being would accept a particular (first-order) imperative, that is "because of its special content, and not because of any peculiarity of its form." Using one of Ross's examples, Broad continues, "I think that the principle that gratitude is due to our benefactors is a plausible example of such a principle. Now, if this would be accepted by any rational being who understood the meaning of the terms 'gratitude' and 'bene-factor', it is because there is an intrinsic relation of *fittingness* between the former kind of emotion and the latter kind of object."[59] Presumably such a relation can be known to us and known only by an immediate intuition, and thus Broad ends up in the same place as the Oxonians—although it might be suggested that his language is deeply Cantabrigian, going back not merely to Moore but to the Cambridge Platonists such as Ralph Cudworth and Samuel Clarke, who spoke precisely in terms of the "eternal verity" of relations of "fittingness." Whether in Oxford or Cambridge form, the British resistance to the sufficiency of Kant's Formula of Universal Law to determine our duties has deep roots. In the end, Broad concedes that "The only importance of Kant's criterion is as a means of avoiding personal bias."[60]

Even this accomplishment would not seem that important to Bernard Williams, who resisted both utilitarian and Kantian approaches to moral philosophy precisely on the ground that neither allows sufficient room for personal preference in the conduct of one's life.

14.1.4. G. E. M. Anscombe

Before we turn to Williams, however, a brief word about another philosopher who attacked both Kantianism and consequentialism, whether in the style of Sidgwick or of Moore, would be in order. I refer to G. E. M. (Gertrud Elizabeth Margaret) Anscombe (1919–2001). Anscombe took her first degree at Somerville College, Oxford, and was then a postgraduate at Cambridge, where she went to study with Ludwig Wittgenstein. She then returned to a fellowship at Somerville and then again to Cambridge to serve as Professor of Philosophy from 1970 to 1986. She was thus one of those few people who studied and taught at both Oxford and Cambridge; Bernard Williams would be another. Anscombe is known for her translation of Wittgenstein's *Philosophical Investigations* (1953) and of other of his posthumous works as well as for her commentary on his *Tractatus Logio-Philosophicus*, and indeed she ended up buried next to Wittgenstein. In ethics, her most famous works were the monograph *Intention* (1957)[61] and the paper "Modern Moral Philosophy" (1958).[62] The title of this paper is reminiscent of

---

[58] Broad 1930, p. 127.   [59] Broad 1930, p. 128.   [60] Broad 1930, p. 131.
[61] Anscombe 1957.   [62] Anscombe 1958.

Prichard's "Does Modern Moral Philosophy Rest on a Mistake?," but the mistake that Anscombe alleges against all modern moral philosophy both from the time of Butler and Kant and that of Mill and Sidgwick through her contemporaries is even more fundamental than that which Prichard alleged, and includes Prichard along with everyone else: her claim is that the concept of the *morally* obligatory and wrong and the language of "ought" (as opposed to that of what is *legally* right, wrong, or obligatory) makes no sense apart from the theological ethics of divine command of which it was, in her view, originally a part.[63] She alleges this charge against both Kant and the utilitarians, or as she calls them, consequentialists. Kant cannot escape from this charge, in her view, because his attempt to save the traditional concept of obligation by introducing the idea of "legislating for oneself" is absurd, as if it were a vote by oneself in which one always votes 1-0 for the right course of action.[64] In the single paragraph in which she dismisses Kant, she gives no hearing to his view that it is one's reason that commands imperatives to one's impulsive nature (in the terminology of Ross, for example), and makes no attempt to show that *this* idea is absurd—although Schopenhauer had attempted to do precisely that, more than a century earlier, by undermining the idea of rationality itself. Against consequentialism, Anscombe repeats her charge that the idea of moral obligation makes no sense outside of a theological context but also that the idea of calculating all the consequences of an action in order to hold a person responsible for them is absurd. In spite of her blanket accusations against all moral philosophy, Anscombe in fact holds a position that is not very different from that of Prichard and Ross: "It would be a great improvement if, instead of 'morally wrong,' one always named a genus such as 'untruthful,' 'unchaste,' 'unjust.' We should no longer ask whether doing something was 'wrong,' passing directly from some description of an action to this notion; we should ask whether, e.g., it was unjust; and the answer would sometimes be clear at once."[65] For example. "It is possible, if one is allowed to proceed just by giving examples, to distinguish between the intrinsically unjust, and what is unjust given the circumstances."[66] Here she is making a distinction between what is unjust no matter what and what is unjust in certain circumstances but might be permissible in others, but the point is that she assumes that certain things *are* intrinsically unjust (or unchaste, and so on), and that we simply know that, and also that we simply know that something else that might be unjust in certain circumstances is permissible in others. Here her meta-ethical—metaphysical and epistemological—assumptions are no differ- ent from those of Prichard and Ross, indeed she might be taken to be offering an interpretation or at most a refinement of Ross's conception of prima facie duties.[67]

---

[63] Anscombe 1958, pp. 5–6.   [64] Anscombe 1958, p. 2.   [65] Anscombe 1958, p. 9.
[66] Anscombe 1958 p. 15.
[67] On Anscombe (and Philippa Foot) as opponents of Richard Hare, see Mac Cumhaill and Wiseman 2022. Foot will be discussed in the last section of this chapter, and Hare in the next chapter.

14.2. Bernard Williams on Moral Obligations
and Personal Projects

Bernard Williams offered a far more sustained attack on both Kantian and utilitarian ethics and a more radical alternative than Anscombe. In some ways he continued the British tradition, which might be called one of pluralistic deontology, of recognizing a variety of particular sorts of duty without supposing that they can be derived from a single underlying fundamental principle of morality—indeed, he preferred the term "ethics," understood as if it is a plural term, to the singular "morality," which he took to connote being based upon such a single, foundational principle. For this reason Williams has been classified by one writer as an "anti-theorist" in moral philosophy.[68] But he did not suppose that ethics was comprised solely of duties; rather, a classicist by training (having been a brilliant student of the ancients at Balliol College, Oxford), Williams remained true to his roots by advocating that the study recently known as morality would be better replaced—or reconstructed—as the study of satisfying ways to live.[69] Part of what would constitute a satisfying way of life would be the fulfillment of obligations, both those voluntarily undertaken by individuals and those imposed by their society, but another part would be the pursuit of individual projects or goals, and the former would not automatically outweigh the latter—that's why his second collection of papers, and most important collection in ethics, was illustrated with a painting by Paul Gauguin, who abandoned his family and other obligations to go paint in Tahiti, and who, at least given how his painting turned out, can be considered to have been right to have done so.[70] Here Williams is clearly departing from the deontologists of the previous generation, who did not suggest that individual projects such as that of Gauguin might be judged to be of equal or even greater value than the fulfillment of obligations. This might be regarded as Williams's advocacy of individualism. Williams also departed from the previous Oxford and Cambridge deontologists in his meta-ethics as well as his ethics: he did not hold that duties had some kind of realist basis and were known by some kind of intuition; he held that norms of obligation were constituted by particular cultures or societies at particular times and places, and were transmitted to members of those cultures by ordinary means of acculturation and known to members of other societies—e.g., historians and sociologists—by ordinary, empirical methods of investigation. He considered himself to be a moral objectivist but not a moral realist who would hold that moral values had some kind of foundation external to human attitudes about them. And while the social nature of ethical

---

[68] See Robertson 2017.

[69] This can be taken as the defining feature of ancient ethics as opposed to modern moral philosophy; e.g., see Cooper 2012.

[70] Williams 1982; the case of Gauguin is discussed in the title paper, "Moral Luck," pp. 20–39.

norms makes them cognizable by both members of a culture and outsiders, they also limit the possibility of moral judgment: members of a contemporary Western society, for example, can understand the ethics of "a Greek Bronze Age chief, or a mediaeval Samurai," but since "the outlooks that go with those...are not real options for us," that is, late twentieth- or early twenty-first-century Anglo-Americans or Western Europeans, it does not make sense for us to condemn the former for actions or attitudes that seem wrong to us now and indeed are wrong for us now. This is what Williams calls the "truth in relativism."[71] Thus Williams embedded the deontological pluralism of his predecessors in an historically contextualist as well as individualistic framework that they had not employed.[72]

The big fish that Williams went after were not the pluralist deontologists such as Prichard, Ross, Broad, and Anscombe, but the two mains forms of "morality," that is, theories deriving all duties from a single fundamental principle of morality, namely utilitarianism on the one hand and Kantian morality on the other. Utilitarianism was the major target of several of Williams's earlier books, including *Morality* (1972) and *Utilitarianism: For and Against* (1973), while Kant and Kantianism were added to his targets in "Persons, Character and Morality" (1976) and his *magnum opus, Ethics and the Limits of Philosophy* (1985).[73] Williams objected to utilitarianism that it made no room for personal integrity—while standard utilitarianism would tell an innocent bystander offered the chance to save nineteen captives by shooting the twentieth when the officer in charge would otherwise shoot all twenty, that violates the integrity of the bystander who has nothing against any of the captives—and that it also downgraded personal goals or projects by allowing an individual to pursue them only when so doing is the best contribution the individual can make to the greatest good for the greatest number. But of course it is Williams's objections to Kant and Kantianism that concern us here. His objections are that Kantianism leaves no room for individualism, but above all that it makes no room for properly internal motivation. Both of these points can be framed in terms of Williams's distinction between "internal" and "external" reasons. Internal reasons are reasons for action included within an individual's own psychology of preferences and desires, her "subjective motivational set," containing "such things as dispositions of evaluation, patterns of emotional reaction, personal loyalties, and various projects, as they may be abstractly called, embodying commitments of the agent," while external reasons

---

[71] Williams, "The Truth in Relativism," 1982, pp. 132–43, at p. 140.

[72] One Oxford philosopher of the earlier generation whom Williams did admire was R. G. Collingwood, who could have been a source for Williams's historicism; see "An Essay on Collingwood," published only posthumously in Williams 2006. Collingwood condemned the "realists" including Prichard and Moore as "minute philosophers" in his polemical but fascinating *Autobiography* of 1939.

[73] Williams 1972; Smart and Williams 1973; Williams 1976b; Williams 1985.

would concern rules or norms that supposedly apply to and bind an agent regardless of what is in her subjective motivational set.[74] More precisely, external reason *statements* concern such norms, for Williams's conclusion is that there are no such things as external reasons: supposed norms do not give individuals reasons to act at all unless there is something, some preference or feeling, in the agent's subjective motivational set that can actually move them to action. "No external reason statement could *by itself* offer an explanation of anyone's action."[75] Of course Williams does not mean to deny that *reasoning* can affect and alter one's subjective motivational set: causal reasoning revealing that *C* is the only or most effective means to realize *E* can give one a reason—that is, a desire— to bring about *C* *if* one already has some desire for *E*, or deliberation about some alternative possible *E*s might lead one to realize that one is a better fit with one's subjective motivational set than the other and thereby create a desire for it. Nevertheless, in the case of a supposed purely external reason, "*ex hypothesi*, there is no motivation for the agent to deliberate *from*, to reach [a] new motivation."[76] Williams is clearly taking the side of Hume, who holds that reason *by itself* provides no motivation for action, although it can instruct us about the best means to ends of action for which we already have some motivation, in the form of "sentiment."[77] But, Williams holds, an external reason theorist who holds that an agent can acquire a motivation simply because he thinks there is an external reason to do some action, "even though, before, he neither had a motive to" do it, "nor any motive related to" doing it, is deluded.[78] And this applies to Kant, Williams believes: the idea that consciousness of the moral law, the para- digmatic external reason, could create a motivation for acting in accordance with it, in the form of the feeling of respect, is "bluff"[79] or bunk. Rather, "practical deliberation is first-personal, radically so, and involves an *I* that must be more intimately the *I* of my desires than [Kant's] account allows."[80]

But this charge neglects Kant's account of the *feeling* of respect, at least in its most fully developed form. While in the *Groundwork* Kant might have suggested that the feeling of respect is entirely epiphenomenal, merely an empirical expres- sion of some noumenal determination of the will by the moral law alone and directly (*G*, 4: 401n.), by the time he wrote the *Metaphysics of Morals* he held that, at least at the phenomenal level, the determination of the will—here *Willkühr*, or faculty of particular choice, rather than *Wille*, the source of the moral law (see *MM*, Introduction, section III, 6: 226)—"proceeds **from the representation of a possible action to** the deed through the feeling of pleasure or displeasure" (*MM*, DV, Introduction, section IIa, 6: 399), or more precisely, through the feeling of respect or "moral feeling," which is actually a combination of feelings of

---

[74] Williams 1980, pp. 102, 105.   [75] Williams 1980, p. 106.   [76] Williams 1980, p. 109.
[77] Hume, *T*, III.i.1, paragraph 12, vol. 1, pp. 295–6.   [78] Williams 1980, p. 109.
[79] Williams 1980, p. 111.   [80] Williams 1985, p. 67.

pleasure *and* displeasure (see *CPracR*, 5: 73–5). More fully, Kant argues that moral feeling or respect in the general sense, conscience as the disposition to hold one's proposed or past actions up to the court of morality, and the more specific feelings of love for others and respect in the special sense of respect for oneself or self-esteem (*MM*, DV, Introduction, section XII, 6: 399–402), must all have some natural basis or "susceptibility," precisely because they cannot be summoned up from nothing by pure reason—just as Williams supposes—and must also be cultivated or strengthened by various practices (see also *MM* DV, §§34–5, on the necessity of cultivating and strengthening naturally based feelings of sympathy) so as to be strong enough to be effective when needed, or, in terms of the second *Critique*, to outweigh other inclinations when that is (morally) necessary (*CPracR*, 5: 76). Kant does not suppose that the moral law, as an "external reason," could lead to action without appropriate items in an agent's subjective motivational set; for Kant, however, the human subjective motivational set—generally—includes predispositions or susceptibilities that can, with proper development, make the moral law into an internal rather than external reason. Now, Kant's claim that we can know a priori that the moral law must produce the feeling of respect (*CPracR*, 5: 73) can certainly be questioned, and his claims that we (all) have predispositions to the "aesthetic preconditions of the mind's susceptibility to the concept of duty" (*MM*, DV, Introduction, section XII, 6: 399), and that there are effective means to cultivating and strengthening them, should perhaps best be taken as empirical claims. There could then be an empirical issue between Kant and Williams as to who has the more empirically adequate account of what is actually in the typical human subjective motivational set. But Kant's account, taken as an empirical account, certainly deserves more of a hearing than Williams gives it.

Simon Robertson observes that "The backdrop to [Williams's] criticisms is an enduring commitment to the idea that an adequate picture of ethical life must be phenomenologically and psychologically realistic,"[81] but another of Williams's criticisms of Kant's account of moral motivation arises not from thinking that Kant is never interested in the phenomenology of morally worthy motivation, but from thinking that Kant is doing moral phenomenology at a moment when he is not. I have in mind Williams's well-known adoption of Charles Fried's earlier criticism that Kant attributes "one thought too many" to the morally motivated agent, or an agent with an estimable good will. The charge is that, according to Kant, in order to act with a good will, the agent has to act out of an immediate, conscious awareness of the moral law and the permissibility of his action under that law. For example, faced with the choice of saving either his wife or a stranger in a shipwreck where he cannot save both, in order to act with a good will the

---

[81] Robertson 2017, pp. 684–5.

agent must first consider whether the moral law allows him to give the preference to saving his wife—test the maxim of saving his wife rather than a stranger in such a situation—and only then (try to) save his wife. This "construction provides the agent with one thought too many: it might have been hoped by some (for instance, by his wife), that his motivating thought, fully spelled out, would be the thought that it was his wife, not that it was his wife and that in situations of this kind it is permissible to save one's wife."[82] But to ascribe such a view to Kant is simply to confuse the thought-experiment that Kant uses to identify the fundamental principle of morality in section I of the *Groundwork* with his actual psychology and phenomenology of morally worthy actions, which as already suggested is developed and/or presented only in the Doctrine of Virtue of the *Metaphysics of Morals*, a dozen years later, and which suggests that the proximate cause of morally worthy action is precisely properly cultivated feeling *conditioned* by the constraint of the moral law but not necessarily arising from immediate, present consciousness of that law. In *Groundwork* I, Kant is conducting a thought-experiment aimed only at identifying the moral law by describing two stick-figures, one moved solely by feeling and the other solely by principle (actually, these may be two different stages in the life of one stick-figure, the formerly benevolent but subsequently emotionally indifferent philanthropist); his point is that the latter can be esteemed while the former is not, merely encouraged, and thus that the content of the moral law cannot directly concern our feelings, but must instead be a formal constraint on particular maxims, namely that they themselves have the form of a law, or be universalizable (*G*, 4: 399–401). But this is not to say that Kant thinks that in real life morally worthy agents act without feeling; the whole point of cultivating moral feeling and the other "aesthetic preconditions" of duty as described in the Doctrine of Virtue is so that a morally worthy agent will be able to act from them when the time comes.

One key point in a response to the "one thought too many" objection is that Kant intends the categorical imperative to function as a limiting condition on the adoption of individual maxims. This point has been stressed by Barbara Herman, but is made by Kant himself.[83] Kant himself uses the term "limiting condition" (*einschränkende Bedingung*) (*G*, 4: 431), although he applies it to the "matter" or content of the categorical imperative, namely the status of humanity as an end in itself, rather than to its form, namely universalizability: but since he takes the former to imply the latter, this means that the requirement of universalizability is to function as a limiting condition on our choice of maxims. Kant makes no suggestion that one has to consciously think of a "limiting condition" at the moment of action in order to be acting with due regard to it.Indeed, if one thinks

---

[82] Williams 1976b, p. 18.
[83] Herman 1981, reprinted in Herman 1993, pp. 1–22, at pp. 14–15, and "The Practice of Moral Judgment," in Herman 1993, pp. 73–93, at pp. 74–5.

of maxims as principles of action which an agent has developed and entrenched over time, as it makes sense to think of them, rather than as being chosen anew at the moment of every action, then a mature agent will typically have taken due regard of the categorical imperative itself, as the limiting condition on all her more particular maxims, or as her "fundamental maxims" in the language of the *Religion*, and on that basis engaged in a lifelong project of cultivating her natural susceptibilities to the concept of a duty. Such an agent will perforce have paid her necessary dues to the categorical imperative long before the moment of any particular action, not at that moment. And of course on Kant's own official, transcendental idealist theory of free will, the choice of fundamental maxim is a *noumenal* act, or "act," not associated with any particular moment in phenomenal time, nor *ever* directly accessible to the agent or to any other human being. In his view that the only good will is one that acts *from* the moral law rather than from mere inclination or feeling, Kant is decidedly *not* engaging in phenomenology, and a phenomenological criticism such as that of Fried and Williams is irrelevant. When Kant does engage in moral phenomenology, as in the Doctrine of Virtue, then he makes it clear that morally worthy action is proximately caused by feelings such as those of love of others, self-esteem, gratitude, and sympathy, which have been strengthened and cultivated out of an agent's underlying or overarching commitment to morality; and that is certainly a long-term process, not something that takes place at the moment of action. Even without Kant's transcendental idealism, the distinction between an agent's long-term commitments and feelings strengthened by those, on the one hand, and the agent's thoughts at the moment of some particular action, is entirely reasonable.

The larger issue between Williams and Kant, however, is whether Kant has any successful derivation of his single fundamental principle of morality from some conception of pure reason and whether his principle allows adequate room for individual preferences and projects. Williams's central engagement with Kant in *Ethics and the Limits of Philosophy* is found in chapter 4, "Foundations: Practical Reason." Here he considers Kant's attempt to formulate and establish "general and formal principles to regulate the shape of relations between rational agents" starting "from a very abstract conception of rational agency."[84] Even this opening characterization of Kant's projects shows the distance between Williams and Kant: Williams refers to "general and formal principles" when, of course, Kant is aiming at a single fundamental principle of morality, although one that presents itself in several different formulations; and, unless one's relation to oneself is supposed to count as a relation "between rational beings," Williams, like many recent moral philosophers, is neglecting the category of duties to oneself, which for Kant was not merely important but, he sometimes says, of primary importance, as

---

[84] Williams 1985, p. 54.

fulfillment of duty to self is the condition of the possibility of the fulfillment of any other kind of duty—a position that makes sense once we see that Kant includes the perfection of one's moral capacities as part of the fundamental positive duty to self, namely self-perfection (see *MM*, DV, §§13–15). Indeed, since for Kant the essence of duty to self is duty to the humanity in one's own person (*G*, 4: 428–9) or in oneself, as contrasted to the merely animal in oneself, and not a relation to any other rational being, Williams's neglect (or rejection) of this category of duty can be seen as part of his general refusal to take seriously Kant's idea of duty in general as the duty to treat humanity as an end and never merely as a means. His criticisms of Kant's attempt to ground the principle(s) of morality from a very abstract conception of rational agency are based largely on what Kant considers to be the mere form rather than the matter of the categorical imperative (see *G*, 4: 436).

Williams's critique of Kant proceeds in two stages. First, he expounds and then criticizes an argument that he considers to be in the spirit of Kant but to be "simpler and more concrete than Kant's" actual argument. He finds a version of this argument in Alan Gewirth's 1977 book *Reason and Morality*,[85] but his criticism of the argument is prescient, because the argument is very much what Christine Korsgaard (at the start of her career a junior colleague of Gewirth at the University of Chicago) would ascribe to Kant himself in 1986, and what Allen Wood would also ascribe to Kant a decade later.[86] The heart of the argument, as Williams presents it, is this: "As rational agents ... we want ... freedom, though that does not mean limitless freedom,"[87] because, as Williams has argued over several preceding pages, as rational agents we recognize that our freedom must be exercised in and therefore constrained by various natural laws, so that, even not yet taking account of the actions of other persons that might impinge upon our own freedom of action, we cannot rationally will everything that we might want.[88] Then, Williams asks,

> Does this commit us to thinking that our freedom is a good and that it is a good thing for us to be free? One path leading to this conclusion would be to say that when an agent wants various particular outcomes, he must think that those various outcomes are good. Then he would be bound to think that his freedom was a good thing, since it was involved in securing those outcomes.[89]

To make this into an argument for the moral law, in its form that one should act only on universalizable maxims, two steps are actually required. First, one must argue that, because one freely chooses particular goods, one must think that one's freedom to choose is also a good thing, indeed, an unconditionally or absolutely

---

[85] Gewirth 1977.   [86] Korsgaard 1986 and Wood 1999.
[87] Williams 1985, p. 58.   [88] Williams 1985, pp. 56–7.   [89] Williams 1985, p. 58.

good thing. But second, because one must think one's own freedom is a good thing, one must think that everyone else's freedom is an equally good thing, and so exercise one's own freedom only in ways compatible with the freedom of everyone else—that is, act only on maxims that could also be willed by all, thus as universal laws. But Williams finds problems at both stages of the argument. First, "In any ordinary understanding of *good*, surely, an extra step is taken if you go from saying that you want something or have decided to pursue it to saying that it is good, or (more to the point) that it is good that I have it."[90] In particular, it does not follow from the fact that I freely choose something, as a good, that my freedom itself is a good thing. Even supposing that "I must regard my own freedom as a good ... I must not be misled into thinking that my freedom constitutes good, period. This would be so only if it were a good, period, that I should be a rational agent, and there is no reason why others should assent to that."[91] Second, even if I could infer that my freedom is a good, I would also have to be able to infer from the fact that my freedom or rational agency is a good then that of others is equally so, so that "if in my case rational agency alone is the ground of a right to noninterference, then it must be so in the case of other people."[92] Williams does not actually object to this second step, because he correctly sees that if I think freedom is *objectively* good in my own case, then it is objectively good and worthy of respect wherever it occurs. But he thinks that "the argument must go wrong when I first assert my supposed right,"[93] that is, when I assert that I (and anyone) have a right to freedom because my freedom (and anyone's) is an objectively good thing.

Williams then turns to what he thinks is a better characterization of Kant's own project, which starts not "from what rational agents need" but what from in Kant's "view rational agents essentially *were*" (*sic*: surely this should be "are"). As Williams sees it, Kant "thought that the moral agent was, in a sense, a rational agent and no more," in particular, "a 'noumenal' self, outside time and causality, and thus distinct from the concrete, empirically determined person that one usually takes oneself to be." Such an argument would present "great difficulties and obscurities," Williams says,[94] although he does not spell these out; they would certainly include the classical difficulty of how such a noumenal self could do anything *other* than choose to be moral. Stepping back from the "more extravagant metaphysical luggage of the noumenal self," Williams then considers the flesh-and-blood human being who would want to act in accordance with the idea of a purely rational self. Bypassing the question of why an ordinary human being should, let alone must want to act in accordance with such a metaphysical idea, Williams focuses on what he takes to be the failure of Kant's ideal "to apply to practical deliberation, and to impose a necessary impartiality on it, because

---

[90] Williams 1985, p. 58.   [91] Williams 1985, p. 59.   [92] Williams 1985, p. 60.
[93] Williams 1985, p. 60.   [94] Williams 1985, p. 64.

practical deliberation is first-personal, radically so, and involves an *I* that must be more intimately the *I* of my desires than this account allows."[95]

But this objection misses the mark. One way of answering it is to emphasize that Kant invokes the noumenal self, paradigmatically in the *Religion*, to explain the moral agent's choice of *fundamental maxim*—in the form given to this choice in the *Religion*, whether to subordinate morality to self-love or self-love to morality (*RBMR*, 6: 35–6)—and not to explain the whole choice of an actual agent. Kant never imagines a human being choosing an action with no inputs other than his fundamental maxim, (supposedly) chosen by his noumenal self; he imagines an individual choosing more particular maxims in light of his choice of fundamental maxim on the one hand and his circumstances, including his desires, plans, previous choices about which of his talents to develop, etc.—in other words, everything in the "intimate *I*" that Williams thinks that Kant neglects.

Another way of putting the response to the objection is to say that Williams never takes seriously Kant's conception of humanity, or, we might say, of rational *agency*. Kant makes it clear that humanity is not simply rationality in the abstract, but in the first instance the capacity to *set ends*. Perhaps this should be understood as the capacity to set ends in a rational way, but Kant's only explicit definitions of humanity—in the Introduction to the Doctrine of Virtue in the *Metaphysics of Morals*—emphasize that it is "the capacity to set oneself an end—any end whatsoever" (*MM*, DV, Introductions, section VIII, 6: 392; compare section V.A, 6: 387). What it is to treat humanity as an end *in one's own person and that of every other*, as Kant's second formulation of the categorical imperative in the *Groundwork* requires (4: 428), is then to find a way to set one's own ends in a way that is fully compatible with the capacity of each and every other human being to set her own ends (and with one's own continuing capacity to do so), *but there is no other constraint on the ends that one may set in the exercise of one's humanity*. Kant's conception of humanity, as opposed to Williams's incomplete conception of Kant's conception of rationality, presupposes that one will set oneself *particular* ends and that there is no other constraint on this selection than the one just described. Kant's conception of humanity, or rational agency, is not one that ignores the human capacity and need to pursue particular ends, suggested by the "intimate *I*" of each; rather it provides the framework within which each may morally do so.

14.3. Morality as a System of Hypothetical Imperatives: Philippa Foot and John McDowell

Another of the "anti-theorists," as Simon Robertson calls them, makes explicit a point that is implicit in Williams's critique of Kant. In her well-known article from

---

[95] Williams 1985, p. 67.

1972, "Morality as a System of Hypothetical Imperatives," Philippa Foot argues for two claims.[96] First, she argues that none of the various verbal forms that categorical imperatives might take, whether grammatically imperatival ("You must φ") or descriptive ("φ-ing must be done"), proves that what is so commanded is actually binding, mandatory, or overrides all other courses of action possible in the relevant circumstances. Her argument for this is a comparison of moral categorical imperatives with similarly formulated categorical imperatives in law and etiquette: "Contracts must be fulfilled" or "Invitations in the third-person must be answered in the third-person"[97] have the same form as moral imperatives, but no one believes that they are really categorical in the sense of demanding obedience no matter what, in particular no matter whether the addressee cares to avoid a penal or social consequence. So it cannot be inferred from the form of moral commands that they are really categorical, either. "The conclusion we should draw is that moral judgments have no better claim to be categorical imperatives than do statements about matters of etiquette. People may indeed follow either morality or etiquette without asking why they should do so, but equally well they may not."[98] Second, however, all these sorts of commands may be regarded as what Kant classifies as hypothetical imperatives, because they all bind agents, when they do, only if the agents have certain relevant desires. Just as, in Kant's example, a hypothetical imperative like "If you want to poison someone, you should use arsenic" applies to someone only if he wants to poison someone else, and indeed binds him if arsenic is the only poison available, so the force of the commands of etiquette and morality depend upon desires to be socially adept or moral, although the demands of morality may seem more binding than those of etiquette because of the way we have been brought up. "But are we then to say that there is nothing behind the idea that moral judgments are categorical imperatives but the relative stringency of our moral teaching? I believe that this may have more to do with the matter than the defenders of the categorical imperative would like to admit."[99] The force of the supposedly categorical imperative or imperatives of morality actually rests only on the strength of our feelings of their stringency, or our desires, and this implies that they can be outweighed by other, non-moral desires. This is what I mean by saying that Foot makes explicit what is implicit in Williams, or more accurately, perhaps, that Foot's meta-ethical argument implies an ethical conclusion that Williams asserts explicitly while not explicitly making Foot's meta-ethical argument.

Even within the domain of morality, although it might be limited by non-moral desires, Foot suggests the kind of pluralist deontology that Williams also inherited from the earlier generation such as Prichard, Ross, and Broad, namely that there are variety of duties not reducible to or grounded on any singular

---

[96] Foot 1972.   [97] Foot 1972, p. 308.   [98] Foot 1972, p. 312.   [99] Foot 1972, p. 310.

formula—although she puts this more in terms of virtues than of duties, a charter member as she was of virtue ethics as an alternative to both Kantianism and utilitarianism. Criticizing Kant's "thesis that a truly moral man acts 'out of respect for the moral law'" in the third and final stage of her paper, she asks the rhetorical questions "what reason could there be for refusing to call a man a just man if he acted justly because he loved truth and liberty, and wanted every man to be treated with a certain minimum respect? And why should the truly honest man not follow honesty for the sake of the good that honest dealings bring to men?"[100] Obviously it is supposed to be self-evident that certain goods, virtues, and wants or desires for them obtain and do not need any further more abstract and singular motivation such as respect for the moral law.

That Foot herself was still working well within the paradigm of ordinary language philosophy is revealed by the fact that she simply assumes that Kant was inferring the categorical status of moral demands from the categorical nature of the language in which they are expressed, rather than the other way around, and that Kant can thus be defeated simply by showing that there are other sorts of demands that are expressed in categorical language but are obviously not genuinely categorical. But while Kant sometimes appeals to what is commonly said to introduce a philosophical point, as when he appeals to how we talk about the beautiful versus how we talk about the agreeable to explicate his philosophical claim that judgments of taste claim subjective universal validity (*CPJ*, §7), he never intends such appeals to be sufficient *arguments* for his theses. For that he needs, and attempts to offer, philosophical argumentation from what he takes to be non-linguistic premises, for example from claims about the nature of perceptions, imagination, understanding, or reason. In the moral case, of course, he intends to base his conclusions on indubitable facts about reason in its application to action. To be sure, his argument may nevertheless be unsound. In a non-linguistic moment, Foot asserts that "The fact is that the man who rejects morality because he sees no reason to obey its rules can be convicted of villainy but not of inconsistency. Nor will his action necessarily be irrational."[101] But Foot does not examine Kant's own attempts to demonstrate the inconsistency or inconsistencies in immoral action, or examine any more general conception of rationality in order to sustain her claim that villainy may be unappealing, even more unappealing than breaches of etiquette, but it is not irrational. Her objection to Kant is, at the least, unproven.

In another well-known paper, John McDowell responded to Foot's article. He agreed, however, that "one need not manifest irrationality in failing to see that one has reason to act as morality requires," so he shares Foot's opposition to Kant's fundamental project. He questions, however, "whether it follows that moral

---

[100] Foot 1972, p. 314.   [101] Foot 1972, p. 310.

requirements are only hypothetical imperatives."[102] His argument with Foot, however, is only with her Humean model of the role of desire in hypothetical imperatives, that is, her assumption that motivation consists in the presence of a desire combined with a belief that performing some particular action or kind of action is the way to satisfy that desire. McDowell's chief point is that "desire need not function as an independent component in the explanation" of an action, "needed in order to account for the capacity of the cited reason to influence the agents will"; in his view, an "agent's conception of the situation, properly understood, suffices to show us the favourable light in which his action appeared to him,"[103] and no separate, antecedent desire is needed to explain the agent's behavior. Ascribing a desire to the agent is just another way of saying that a certain situation presented itself to him as favoring a certain kind of action. But this just means that McDowell is not any happier with the Kantian model of hypothetical imperatives, and thus with the explication of morality as a system of hypothetical imperatives, than Foot was with the Kantian model of morality as categorical. It is hardly a defense of the Kantian claim that morality is categorical, binding, and overriding.

An Oxonian who was friendlier to Kant, at least in the sense of holding that once we have "climbed the mountain" of both utilitarianism and Kantianism we will see that they have arrived at the same summit, was Derek Parfit. But Parfit's project was actually part of a lineage of attempts to narrow the gap between Kantianism and utilitarianism by a number of philosophers including Richard Hare, Kurt Baier, and Marcus Singer. In the next chapter we will look at those philosophers before returning to Parfit's project.

---

[102] McDowell 1978, at p. 13.   [103] McDowell 1978, p. 16.

PART V

THE ANGLOPHONE RECEPTION: CONSEQUENTIALISM AND CONSTRUCTIVISM

15

Combining Kant and Consequentialism

Hare to Parfit

15.1. Introduction

The reception of Kant's moral philosophy has been divided from the outset between those who find the gist of it in Kant's conception of moral *law*, or in the idea that the requirement of the universalizability of maxims is not just a necessary but also the sufficient condition for both the determination and the establishment of all our moral duties, and those who find the core of Kant's moral philosophy in his idea of humanity as the *freedom* of each human being to set his or her own ends, with the task of morality being then to determine the conditions under which the maximum freedom of each can be reconciled with the equal freedom of all, the Formula of Universal Law in turn being intended as a method for accomplishing this goal. In this final part of this book, treating the non-idealist response to Kant in both Britain and the United States in the twentieth century, I initially intended to treat the British part of this response in one chapter and the American part in another. Each of these chapters has now been divided for reasons of length, in the first case into the two chapters preceding this and in the second into this and the two following chapters. But more importantly, the division between British and American responses turned out to be simplistic. While George Bernard Shaw is alleged to have said that Britain and the US are two countries separated by a common language,[1] the boundary between British and American philosophy in the post-World War II period has sometimes reflected that aphorism but has never been completely impermeable. In particular, I had originally intended to complete this book with a discussion of Derek Parfit's 2011 *magnum opus*, *On What Matters*, and his attempt in that work to demonstrate that Kantianism and utilitarianism are "climbing the same mountain" or two sides of the same coin (Parfit 2011–17). But while in many ways Parfit (1942–2017), a graduate of Eton and Balliol and a lifelong Fellow of All Souls' College at Oxford,[2] could hardly have been more British, he also turned from his original subject of

---

[1] Interview with Shaw by George Mallory, *Christian Science Monitor*, September 1942.

[2] Although his position there was not initially permanent and, as his biographer David Edmonds reports, it was only the threat of losing it that induced him to publish his first book, *Reasons and Persons* (Parfit 1984) and thereby gain tenure, which he then held until retirement. See Edmonds 2023, chapters 11–12.

Kant's Impact on Moral Philosophy. Paul Guyer, Oxford University Press. © Paul Guyer 2024.
DOI: 10.1093/oso/9780199592456.003.0016

modern history to philosophy while visiting classes at NYU, Columbia, and
Harvard on a Harkness Fellowship; he later had extended appointments at
Harvard, Rutgers, and NYU for much of his career, and had as many American
colleagues and students as British; so he was intellectually at home in the US as
much as in Britain. So my next thought was to postpone discussion of Parfit's
work from the end of the previous chapter until the conclusion of a final one on
Rawls and some of his students, thereby fulfilling my own prenatal name for this
project, "From Pistorius to Parfit." But then I came to see Parfit's project as the
continuation of one that had begun before John Rawls's use of what he called the
"Kantian interpretation" as the foundation of the political philosophy of *A Theory
of Justice*[3] in 1971 and the more general "Kantian constructivism" in moral
philosophy developed by Rawls himself and the many philosophers influenced
by him in the following decades.[4] This is the project of combining a Kantian
insistence on universalizability as in some form a defining feature of morality with
some form of consequentialism that we find in R. M. (Richard Mervyn) Hare
(1919–2002), Kurt Baier (1917–2010), and Marcus G. Singer (1926–2016). These
philosophers comprise an Anglophone but geopolitically diverse group: Hare was
thoroughly English, White's Professor of Moral Philosophy at Oxford, although
he taught for some post-retirement years at the University of Florida; Baier was a
Viennese lawyer who fled to England after the *Anschluss* of Austria by Nazi
Germany in 1938 but was then interned by the British in Australia, where upon
release he earned BA and MA degrees at the University of Melbourne and then
returned to Oxford for a D.Phil., but after several years back at Melbourne and
then the Australian National University spent most of his teaching career at the
University of Pittsburgh; and Singer was a New York Jew who earned his BA at the
University of Illinois and his Ph.D. at Cornell and spent his entire career teaching
at the University of Wisconsin, as American a story as can be. But they were all
tied together by an attempt to combine some form of Kantian universalism with
some form of consequentialism, the project that Parfit continued or resumed. All
of these philosophers displayed little friendliness toward Kant's idea of humanity
as an end in itself and the "ground of a possible categorical imperative"
(*Groundwork*, 4: 428). Rather, they focused on the requirement of universalizability. They can be described as attempting to ground morality on the nature of
rationality as such, obviously a Kantian project, but as conceiving of reason in
material terms as responsiveness to reasons rather than in more formal terms as
the avoidance of contradiction—although this aspect of rationality plays a major
role in Singer's defense of the categorical imperative as a paradigm of what he calls
the generalization principle, the most spirited defense of Kant's own moral
philosophy among these philosophers. What can be called the realism about

[3] Rawls 1971, §40 (revised edition), pp. 221–7.   [4] The key texts here are Rawls 1980 and 1989.

reasons that is common to these philosophers is also a central aspect of T. M. Scanlon's "contractualism," although he has generally distanced his approach from Kantianism more than these philosophers or than Rawls himself. So he will not be a major figure in the story that follows. David Cummiskey's "Kantian Consequentialism" differs from these projects, although it is the only one to use such a name, by deriving a form of consequentialism from the Formula of Humanity as an End in Itself, thus from a mandate for preserving and promoting the conditions for the exercise of rational agency, rather than from universalizability alone (Cummiskey 1996). In this way his approach comes closest to my own.

In the present chapter, I will focus on Hare, Baier, Singer, Cummiskey, and Parfit, in a roughly chronological order. I will discuss the work of Hare first: although the book on which I will concentrate, *Freedom and Reason*, appeared only in 1963, after the works of Baier and Singer that I will discuss, it drew upon the general approach to moral theory laid down in Hare's 1952 book *The Language of Morals*, so he gets to go first. Then I will discuss Baier's *The Moral Point of View*, which appeared in 1959, followed by Singer's *Generalization in Ethics*, from 1961. Then, after a comment on Cummiskey, and skipping half a century, during which the approach of "Kantian constructivism" inspired by Rawls came to the fore, I will turn to Parfit's attempt to demonstrate that consequentialism and Kantianism (as well as the "contractualism" of T. M. Scanlon) yield the same normative results in spite of their different foundations and meta-ethics. In the remaining two chapters, I will first travel back in time to discuss Rawls and then move forward with a discussion of several other versions of the "Kantian constructivism" that he inspired, including those of Thomas Nagel (*avant la lettre*), Onora O'Neill, Christine Korsgaard, and Adrian Piper.

As suggested, all of the philosophers to be discussed in this chapter accept a requirement of universalizability or generalization, as Singer calls it, as essential to morality, and recognize this requirement as Kantian in spirit, although only Singer is willing to defend Kant's own formulation of the universalizability requirement in much of its detail. But all also think that the formal requirement of universalizability needs to be combined with some material consideration, to use Kant's own terminology, in order to yield determinate duties. All thus think that the Kantian universalizability requirement has to be combined with some form of consequentialism, although they differ on whether this should be called utilitarianism: as already mentioned, Parfit as the latest member of the group thinks that Kantianism and utilitarianism are two routes for reaching the same mountaintop, so that they are compatible and complementary, perhaps ultimately interdependent, while Singer discredits traditional utilitarianism on Kantian grounds. But all think that universalization has to take into account the consequences of proposed actions—as indeed did Kant himself, although in his view the relevant factor is the relationship between an agent's actual proposed action or maxim of action and its consequences in a *possible* world in which his maxim is universalized, not the likely consequences of his action in the *actual* world, and the consequences in that possible world that are to be considered are those for the possibility of the agent's acting on the proposed maxim, or for the agent's rational agency in general, not those for the happiness of the agent or anyone else. Further, the Kantian agent's reason for considering the results of the universalization of his maxim in such a possible world is not a prudential concern for the actual consequences of his action in the real world, but a purely moral concern with the consequences of the possible universalization of his maxim, that is, with a question asked on moral rather than prudential grounds. That the requirement of universalization is moral rather than prudential is a common theme in the moral philosophies to be examined in this section, although they tend to treat this requirement as the foundation of morality rather than as the consequence of something even more fundamental, namely the status of humanity as an end in itself. The rejection of this foundation for morality is a fundamental difference between these philosophers and Kant, and between them and Rawls, at least the Rawls of *A Theory of Justice*, as well.

15.2. Hare

Hare's work in the 1950s and 1960s was part of the ordinary-language approach to philosophy characteristic of the Oxford of that period, what we might call J. L. Austin's version of the linguistic turn in philosophy rather than Ludwig Wittgenstein's Cambridge version, and he presented the requirement of universalizability as the meta-ethical implication of moral language.[5] Hare called his meta-ethical position "universal prescriptivism": his argument is that all imperatives are prescriptive in their force (in what Austin might have called their perlocutionary force, H. P. Grice their pragmatic force)[6] rather than descriptive; descriptive language describes facts, but does not tell anyone what to do, even if the facts described are relevant to what someone should do, while imperatives tell someone what they should do, or what they must do. This is of course Hume's distinction between "is" and "ought" in linguistic terms (*LM*, p. 29), and Hare played a large role in elevating the non-derivability of "ought" from "is" into a dogma of the 1950s and 1960s. Hare then argues that moral imperatives are universally prescriptive, that is, they commend, or command, a course of action, or non-action (a prohibition), to anyone in a certain kind of situation. Such imperatival force need not be reflected in the surface syntax of a moral statement:

---

[5] For a collection of essays on the work of Hare by leading contemporaries, see Seanor and Fotion 1988.

[6] See Austin 1955 and Grice 1989.

"No smoking!" on a sign communicates to anyone who understands it that they must not smoke in that location just as well as "You [or 'You all'] must not smoke [or 'are not permitted to smoke'] here" would do (*LM*, pp. 175–9). The use of the word "ought" can express imperatival force, as in "You ought not to smoke here," but is not necessary for that purpose, as a sentence in apparently descriptive form such as "Smoking is not permitted here" could have the same force. Likewise the word "right" in a sentence that looks like a description can in fact communicate an imperative: "It is not right to smoke here" or "You have no right to smoke here" can communicate the same content as "You ought not to smoke here" or "You must not smoke here." So "ought" and "right" are frequently used to communicate prescriptions, or imperatives, and are typical moral language. But they need not be moral, they might be used to make merely prudential recommendations, and might be addressed to a specific person or specific persons: "You ought to comb your hair," for example, would not be addressed to everyone, or even to everyone who has hair, but perhaps only to a group or a single person looking to make a good impression; "You ought to save for retirement" or "You must save more for retirement" would not be addressed to everyone, but perhaps only to those with no independent wealth but with a good enough income to be able to afford to set some aside, and who also have a reasonable expectation of living past some expected retirement age (for example, you would not say it to a squadron of fighter pilots about to take off for a mission over heavily defended enemy territory). Thus there may be singular imperatives or prescriptions, but moral imperatives, whether expressed in syntactically imperatival form or not, are universal in their address, addressed to all humans, not just one or just those in some small, particular class, such as all those who can but also need to save for retirement, or all those with hair who also need to make a good impression on someone else who cares about the appearance of the former. Thus "universal prescriptivism": a course of action is commanded—or prohibited—for all. To be sure, even a moral command might address only people in particular circumstances: in one way, a command or imperative like "Never make a promise you do not intend to keep" is directed only at people contemplating making a promise; but anyone might find herself in that situation, not just, for example, someone with messy hair or adequate income to set some aside for retirement but with no inherited wealth. In that way, moral commands are universal.

In *The Language of Morals*, Hare described his analysis as a matter of logic rather than, say, linguistic convention; he moved easily from talk of grammar to talk of logic (e.g., *LM*, pp. 64, 92). Indeed, Hare says that "the basis of Hume's celebrated observation on the impossibility of deducing an 'ought'-proposition from a series of 'is'-propositions" is a "logical rule," and that Kant's rejection of "heteronomy"—any attempt to derive a moral principle from something non-moral, such as mere inclinations or desires—"also rested" on the "logical rule" that "*No imperative conclusion can be validly drawn from a set of premises which does not contain at least one imperative*" (*LM*, pp. 28–9). Hare was not trying to present morality as a matter of mere linguistic convention. But by calling his analysis of the force of moral judgments and moral terms a matter of logic, he was trying to suggest that his characterization of the force of such language is fundamental, in no more need of some further foundation than is logic itself. Comprehension and facilitation of his view might be motivated or encouraged by examples from ordinary life and discourse, but that should not be understood as a deductive argument for universal prescriptivism from some more fundamental premise or premises, factual or moral (although, as with other parts of logic, it might be necessary to show that the logic of moral judgment is consistent or free of self-contradiction; see *LM*, chapter 2, "Imperatives and Logic"). That the Kantian requirement of universalizability might itself be derived from something even more fundamental, such as the status of humanity as an end in itself, is no part of Hare's view.

The title of Hare's second book, *Freedom and Reason*, can be interpreted to reveal several of his basic assumptions. By "Reason" he means *reasoning*, thus by moral reason moral reasoning, and by "Freedom" he means the human ability to engage in moral reasoning, not freedom of the will in any metaphysical sense. He also does not consider freedom as a value, let alone an intrinsic and/or fundamental value, so he does not present the universalization prescribed by moral terms according to his analysis in *The Language of Morals* as a means to the realization of freedom. In spite of his insistence on universalizability, therefore, he does not reproduce the Kantian structure according to which the status of humanity as an end in itself is the *ground* of a possible categorical imperative (*G*, 4: 428) and the requirement of the universalizability of maxims the *means* by which it may be insured that agents are acting only on maxims that treat humanity always as an end and never as a means. Instead, Hare argues from his prescriptive universalism to a form of utilitarianism.

His argument is that universal prescriptivism is itself a strictly meta-ethical position, which does not by itself imply a theory of value or of the good, but which sets the framework for moral reasoning, which in application turns on utilitarian considerations, but yields a form of utilitarianism in which the usual distributive concerns are already resolved by that framework. This passage demonstrates the structure of his overall theory:

> Ethical theory, which determines the meanings and functions of the moral words, and thus the "rules" of the moral "game", provides only a clarification of the conceptual framework within which moral reasoning takes place; it is therefore ... neutral as between different moral opinions....
>
> The rules of moral reasoning are, basically, two, corresponding to the two features of moral judgment which I argued for ..., prescriptivity and universalizability. When we are trying, in a concrete case, to decide what we ought to do,

what we are looking for...is an action to which we can commit ourselves (prescriptivity) but which we are at the same time prepared to accept as exemplifying a principle of action to be prescribed to others in like circumstances (universalizability). If, when we consider some proposed action, we find that, when universalized, it yields prescriptions which we cannot accept, we reject this action as a solution to our moral problem—if we cannot universalize the prescription, it cannot become an "ought". (FR, pp. 89–90)

The crucial second step in moral reasoning then becomes determining whether the consequences of a proposed action, were the action to be universalized, that is, performed by everyone, would be acceptable *to the agent proposing the action*, where "acceptable" means simply in accord with the agent's preferences in general. A "provisional or suggested moral principle [is] rejected because one of its particular consequences"—at least one, that is—"proved unacceptable" to the agent considering the action. Hare dresses up his account of such reasoning by analogizing it to the formation of a scientific hypothesis and then undertaking experiments designed to falsify it; here he cites Karl Popper's model of "conjecture and refutation" (FR, pp. 91–2; see Popper 1961 and 1963). But the idea is simple, as Hare's example shows: in considering whether to (seek to) put another into debtors' prison for not paying back a debt, I ask myself how I would like it if everyone did this, thus whether another would have me put into prison if I could not pay back my debt to him? Before considering the universalization of my proposed action, I might be "*inclined* to do this, or *want*...to do it," but my stronger preference would of course be to stay out of prison than to see someone else in prison, so the consequences of universalizing my proposed course of action would become unacceptable to me, that is, contrary to my preferences or inclinations all things considered (FR, pp. 90–1). Or as Hare puts it, the "necessary ingredients" in moral reasoning are "logic (in the shape of universalizability and prescriptivity), the facts, and the inclinations or interests of the people concerned" (FR, p. 94). The last ingredient needs explication: the inclinations or interests of other people may determine how they would respond to the universalization of one's proposed action, which becomes part of the consequences of one's proposed action, but it is one's own inclinations or interests that determine whether one is willing to accept the consequences of one's proposed action, including those arising from the inclinations of others. This is of course a radical difference with Kant, for whom the test of universalization is not compatibility with one's own inclinations, but with one's own rational agency and ultimately that of everyone.

If everyone were to make their moral decisions in the way proposed by Hare, the result would be a kind of utilitarianism with a built-in distributive constraint: everyone would maximize the satisfaction of their own preferences, or act to produce the consequences most acceptable to themselves, consistent with the ability of everyone else to do the same. In that way, the result would be a version of the greatest average utility, although it would certainly not be permissible to increase the average level of utility by, for example, simply reducing the number of agents while holding the total amount of utility constant, presumably because no one involved would find that strategy acceptable. The approach is like Kant's in that it is not merely prudential: an agent does not consider the consequences of universalizing a proposed course of action because he believes that his acting in the way proposed would as a matter of fact lead everyone else to act that way too, and thus actually bring about the consequence that he would find unacceptable. Rather, the agent considers how he *would* like it *if* everyone did what he is considering because the "logic" of morality, universal prescriptivism, requires him to ask this question. In this regard Hare's position is like Kant's, but the difference remains that Hare's agent asks just whether he would like the consequences of such universalization, not whether they would be compatible with his own free agency and that of others.

Thus Hare was right to emphasize the affinity of his view to utilitarianism rather than to Kant. As he put it, the "standpoint" to which agents are brought by "the requirement of universalizability" has "some affinities with traditional utilitarianism." He sees traditional utilitarianism as resting on the principle "Everybody to count for one, nobody for more than one" (*FR*, p. 118),[7] applied to the "consideration of the substantial inclinations and interests that people actually have." This conception of utilitarianism has some distributive constraint built in: in any case in which a resource is to be divided, the default position is that because each person counts the same, each should receive the same share of the good; if the good is to be divided otherwise, then "there must be something about [the] case to make this difference, for otherwise we are making different moral judgments about similar cases," and that is what is prohibited by the requirement of universalizability (*FR*, p. 119)—or, we might suggest, any conception of rationality. However, Hare recognizes that there are problems with straightforward utilitarianism: "the problem of the commensurability of desires, inclinations, &c." (*FR*, p. 119); "the choice between the equal but very incomplete satisfaction of a number of people's desires, and the more complete satisfaction of the desires of most of them, purchased at the cost of the complete frustration of the desires of a few"; "the vexed problem about *higher* and *lower desires*" (*FR*, p. 121); and most generally, whether "an account couched in terms of desires or interests could be easily translated into one in terms of pleasure or happiness," as used in traditional presentations of utilitarianism (*FR*, p. 122). Nevertheless, in Hare's view utilitarianism is a useful model for moral *reasoning*, his topic in *Freedom and Reason*: "It is in the endeavour to find lines of conduct which we can prescribe universally in a given situation that we find ourselves bound to give equal weight to the desires of

---

[7] Here Hare is quoting Mill, *Utilitarianism*, chapter 5, who was in turn quoting Bentham.

all parties (the foundation of distributive justice); and this, in turn, leads to such views as that we should seek to maximize satisfactions.... what I shall have to do, in order to answer this question, is to put myself imaginatively in the place of the other parties ... and ask the same sort of questions as we made the creditor ask when he had imagined himself in the situation of his debtor," that is, how would he like it if what he proposed to do to the other were done to him? (FR, p. 123). We might put Hare's position by saying that utilitarianism is a method of moral reasoning rather than a decision-procedure. Then, Hare concludes, "the principle of universalizability could generate, by means of such arguments as we have been considering, and given the other necessary conditions, a system of morality of which both Kant and the utilitarians could approve—Kant of its form, and the utilitarians of its content" (FR, p. 124). This is crediting Kant with far more tolerance for reasoning on the basis of inclination or preference than he actually had.

Having said this, however, Hare also makes clear that he does not think that utilitarianism, even in his form, is a complete system of morality: it can, "in principle, cover only a part of morality, albeit a very important part" (FR, p. 119). The other part of morality consists in what Hare calls "ideals," ideals of "human excellence" (FR, p. 147), and his claim is that these need not be universalizable. How much one wants to develop one's own excellence in some way or other, or to help others develop theirs, whether one wants to devote oneself to public service or private prosperity—these are not matters that generalize. Rather, Hare supposes, "These questions are very like aesthetic ones. It is as if a man were regarding his own life and character as a work of art, and asking how it should be completed"—not everyone will give the same answer, nor is there any reason why everyone should.[8] To be sure, ideals can be pushed to the point of "fanaticism," the condition in which one favors one's own ideal over the universalizable aspect of morality, but "liberalism" is the correct stance toward ideals: "In saying that the liberal respects the ideals of others we mean that he thinks it wrong to interfere with other people's pursuits of their ideals just because they are different from his own" (FR, p. 178)—but only of course if they too are respecting the same constraint. Hare concludes that "It is part of the liberal's ideal that a good society, whatever else it is, is one in which the ideals and interests of all are given equal consideration. It is, to use Kantian language, a kingdom of ends in which all are, at least potentially, legislating members" (FR, p. 179). To continue with Kantian language, Hare's ideals seem to subsume Kant's imperfect duties, which allow each individual latitude in the choice of how and when best to fulfill them—the Kantian duty of self-perfection allows latitude in the choice of which of one's gifts and

---

[8] Hare's idea of considering one's life as if it were a work of art is striking. Usually this idea is found in a different tradition, namely the Nietzschean tradition, which John Rawls classified as "perfectionist." For an example of the Nietzschean approach, see Nehamas 1983 and 2000.

potential talents to develop, the Kantian duties of mutual aid and beneficence require choice in when and how best to deploy one's own resources in behalf of others, and so on. Universalizability is a necessary but not sufficient condition for determining how best to fulfill one's imperfect duties, and Hare recognizes that in stating that liberal morality requires both the utilitarian approach to people's interests and the more loosely defined respect for their ideals.

Nevertheless, Hare's position differs, radically, from Kant's in that, once universalization over people's interests and liberalism with respect to their ideals are seen as required by the "logic" of moral language, nothing more than agents' preferences need be considered. Hare himself must surely have meant to signal a difference with Kant in treating preferences, even preferences for ideals, as nothing but inclinations. Hare does regard "the distinction between deontological and teleological theories [as] a false one," because "It is not possible to distinguish between a moral judgement made on the ground of the effects of an action, and one made on the ground of the character of the action itself" (*FR*, p. 124). But he makes no suggestion that the dual requirements of universalizability and respect for ideals are themselves both expressions of or grounded in some higher value or good, such as that of humanity as an end in itself, understood as the freedom of each to set her own ends. He does not argue that acting only in universalizable ways is a way of ensuring that one's own free choice does not compromise the free choice of others, or that respecting the ideals of others is a way to recognize their freedom to determine their own ideals, nor that the liberal constraint on expression of ideals is a way of recognizing the equal freedom of all. He just supposes that the requirement of universalization comes from the meaning or "logic" of moral language, requiring no further explanation, and that ideals are expressions of individual preference that do not have to be universalized as long as others are allowed their own ideals and they in turn allow yet others their own preferences in ideals as well. In the end, nothing but agents' interests and inclinations, including their inclinations toward ideals, need be considered. Inclinations, screened by the logic of moral terms, become the basic moral reasons on Hare's account. And inclination is the only basis for the addition of "ideals" to Hare's account; there is no recognition of a *duty* of self-perfection, even one where mere preference might be allowed some role in determining in what particular way any agent can best fulfill this duty. Hare's model is one on which the constraint of universalizability is supposed to *permit* some room for personal ideals, but not one where formulating and achieving personal ideals would actually be part of the duty of self-perfection as it is for Kant.

So Hare's approach to moral philosophy accepts some aspects of Kant's own approach, but not his attempt to replace mere inclination or preference satisfaction as the substantive content of morality with a conception of the intrinsic and unconditional value of rational agency as such. Let's see now how and if so then to what extent that changes among the other philosophers who were interested in bridging the gap between Kantianism and utilitarianism, namely Kurt Baier and Derek Parfit. Marcus Singer, whose main work intervenes chronologically between those of Baier and Parfit, certainly did not present his own approach to generalization as a rapprochement with utilitarianism, but we will see in due course how Kantian his foundation for his own approach ultimately is; and David Cummiskey, although, as already mentioned, he is more explicit in calling his position a form of "Kantian consequentialism" than any of others were, does assign a value to rational agency as such that a philosopher such as Hare did not.

15.3. Baier

Kurt Baier's first and most influential book, *The Moral Point of View*, was published in 1959; a much later book, *The Rational and the Moral Order: The Social Roots of Rationality and Morality* (Baier 1995), reveals the gist of the argument of the earlier book by its subtitle and expands and refines its approach, but appearing after American moral philosophy had already been dominated by Rawls and his school, did not enjoy as wide a reception as the earlier book had.[9] Baier's original work is another attempt to reconcile Kantianism and consequentialism, although he is careful to distinguish his consequentialism from traditional utilitarianism, defined by the requirement to optimize benefits or produce the greatest good for the greatest number. Baier's approach rather identifies the fundamental rules of morality with necessary conditions for the preservation of human society, pretty much the same across all human societies in spite of many dissimilarities of circumstances and culture reflected in some of the less fundamental moral rules of particular societies. Tthe substance of this view is set within the formal framework of the "moral point of view" and "moral reasons," according to which, in case of conflict, the interests of the whole always override particular interests of individuals. Baier holds that Kant more or less correctly characterized the moral point of view and the weight of moral reasons, although he was mistaken to think that formal considerations alone could yield the substance of morality. As he puts it, "a morality based on the categorical imperative" *alone* "is useless for it rejects as immoral only self-contradictory and self-frustrating maxims," which in Baier's view would make up only a very small part of even the moral rules that are absolutely necessary for the preservation of any society. In other words, Baier's attitude toward Kant is a form of the traditional objection that the categorical imperative is an "empty formalism": Baier's view is that Kant was correct in his conception of the good will as requiring action on principle, ready to override an agent's selfish interests, but wrong to think that only the categorical

---

[9] Schneewind 1996, is a volume of essays on Baier's work.

imperative could provide the necessary principles. Only the interests of any society as a whole can provide the substantive principles that can and must override the interests of an individual when necessary.

Many interesting details aside, then, Baier's position consists of two main parts, a Kantian characterization of the moral point of view as the formal constraint on moral reasons, and a social theory of the substance of moral reasons. This social theory substitutes for the value of humanity or rational agency as an end in itself in Kant's theory. The consequentialist substance of the theory is announced in Baier's preface. A moral agent can be trivially defined as "a person who is already determined to do whatever is morally right and to refrain from doing whatever is morally wrong," but, Baier continues,

> If my case is to be more than an empty definition of "moral agent," I must mention a reason why any and every agent *should be* a moral and not an immoral agent, why everybody should do what has the weight of moral reasons behind it and refrain from doing what has the weight of moral reasons against it. The reason is that a general acceptance of a system of merely self-interested reasons would lead to conditions of life well described by Hobbes as "poor, nasty, brutish, and short." These unattractive living conditions can be improved by the general adoption of a system of reasoning in which reasons of self-interest are overruled, roughly speaking, when following them would tend to harm others. Such reasons are what we call "moral reasons," and we rightly regard them as overruling reasons of self-interest, because the acceptance of self-interested reasons as overruling moral ones would lead to the undesirable state of affairs described by Hobbes. This is the reason why moral reasons must be regarded as superior to self-interested reasons and why everyone has an excellent reason for so regarding them.   (*MPV*, pp. vi–vii)

We might regard Baier's position as combining a Kantian meta-ethics with a Hobbesian normative ethics: the analysis of the concepts of moral reasons and the moral point of view yield the result that morality consists in acting on general principles, that is, principles concerning the effect of one's own actions on everyone else, that can override one's own particular interests in case of unavoidable conflict, while the factual account of what rules are actually necessary for the preservation of society provide the substance of those principles.

Baier defines several central moral concepts in terms of the moral point of view: thus, "our moral convictions are true if they can be seen to be required *from the moral point of view*," and "A person is of good will if he adopts the moral point of view as supreme, as overriding all other points of view" (*MPV*, pp. 184–5). So the basic meta-ethical work in his theory has to be done by his account of the moral point of view itself. The function of the moral point of view is to serve as "a court of appeal for conflicts of interest." "Hence," Baier notes, "it cannot (logically) be identical with the point of view of self-interest," for that is just one party to the conflicts which the moral point of view has to resolve; hence, he adds, Sidgwick was "wrong in thinking that consistent egoism is one of the 'legitimate methods of ethics'" (*MPV*, p. 190). Rather, the moral point of view is defined by the two formal considerations of (i) acting "on principle and not merely on rules of thumb designed to promote one's aim" (p. 191), and (ii) acting on principles "considered as being acted on *by everyone*" and as "*meant for everybody*" (p. 195). According to Baier, Kant grasped (i) "even if only obscurely": he saw that "adopting the moral point of view involves acting on principle" and "involves conforming to rules even when doing so is unpleasant, painful, costly, or ruinous to oneself," for "a moral agent ought not to make exceptions in his own favor." But he was wrong to interpret this to mean "that moral rules are absolute inflexible and without exceptions," like "Thou shalt not kill" or "Thou shalt not lie" (p. 191). Or, more precisely, Kant failed to note that many rules, legal rules but moral rules as well, are simply more complex and detailed than that. The "exceptions" to a no-parking rule like "except in front of a parking meter" or "except on Sunday mornings and after 8 P.M. every day" are not actually exceptions to the rule but just clauses of the rule more fully stated, i.e., "There is to be no parking on city streets except in front of a (properly paid) parking meter and between 8 P.M. and 7 A.M." (p. 192). Likewise, "We can say that a man does not know fully our moral rule 'Thou shalt not kill" if he does not know that it "*has several recognized exceptions*, among them 'in self-defense'" (p 193), or similarly, we could say that the proper rule concerning lying is not simply "Thou shalt not lie" but "Thou shalt not lie except in order to protect an innocent person from a crime" (and any other exceptions that could pass the test of universalization). Genuine moral rules do need to be precisely formulated, but once they are then they can serve, as Kant thought, as principles to which no exceptions can be made on grounds of self-interest.

Baier then continues to condition (ii) of the moral point of view: Moral rules are thought of as acted upon *by everyone* and as meant *for everyone*. This in turn means, first, that they must not be "self-frustrating," or as "frustrated as soon as everybody acts on them"; they must not be "self-defeating." A rule would be self-defeating if its point would be defeated as soon as a person lets it be known that he has adopted it, for example the principle "Give a promise even when you know or think that you can never keep it, or when you don't intend to keep it"—whatever the fate of the practice of promising as a whole might be, no one would accept *your* promise if they knew that was *your* maxim. Second, it means that moral rules must not be "morally impossible," or could not even be thought, such as the rule "Always assert what you think not to be the case," a moral equivalent of the principle of the Cretan liar (*MPV*, pp. 196–7). Baier holds that all these "clarify some valuable remarks contained in Kant's doctrine of the categorical imperative" (p. 199)—presumably he has in mind Kant's distinction between the "contradiction in conception" and "contradiction in willing" applications of the categorical imperative (*G*, 4: 424). Still, they are only formal constraints; they do not tell us what the content of the fundamental principles of morality should actually be:

> The conditions so far mentioned are merely formal. They exclude certain sorts of rules as not coming up to the formal requirements. But moral rules should also have a certain sort of content. Observation of these rules should be *for the good of everyone.* (p. 200)

Here is where Baier's version of consequentialism enters his argument.

The substance of morality is then, according to Baier, constituted by the fundamental principle "it is in the interest of everyone alike if everyone alike should be allowed to pursue his own interest provided this does not adversely affect someone else's interests," as for example "Killing someone in the pursuit of my interests would interfere with his" (*MPV*, p. 202). Baier emphasizes that this does not amount to traditional utilitarianism: "It does not follow from this, however, that it is wrong not to promote the greatest good of the greatest number, or not to promote the greatest amount of good in the world. Deontologists and utilitarians alike make the mistake of thinking that it is one, or the only one, of our moral duties 'to do the optimific act'" (p. 203). Baier's view is that the fundamental principle or principles of morality are what is required to preserve society, not everything that might be done to make it better or best—an open-ended goal that can in any case never be achieved. This does not mean that moral rules are strictly negative prohibitions, like "Thou shalt not kill except in self-defense" or "Thou shalt not lie except to protect the innocent from crime"; the preservation of society might require that we positively benefit others in particular circumstances, to save them from destitution or destruction. Thus "We are morally required to do good," but "only to those who are actually in need of our assistance" (p. 203), where "actually in need" must be a more restrictive condition than "would in some way benefit from" or "like" our assistance. The general aim of the preservation of society can be specified in terms of the basic functions of society:

> Not the least important contribution which the existence of a society makes to the life that is worth living is the provision of established patterns of behavior giving everyone confidence and security. It provides institutions and definite rules for the realization of the most fundamental human needs and desires. It makes arrangements about mating and the rearing of children, about the ways individual members of the society may use their talents to make a living, and the like. (*MPV*, p. 253)

There will certainly be many prohibitions among the rules necessary to preserve these functions and institutions of a society: "society has to prohibit those courses of action which, because of the particular nature of the social framework, would be harmful if everyone or even if only a few people entered on them" (p. 255). Logically, perhaps any prohibition can also be stated positively ("Thou shalt never do φ" might convert to "Thou shalt always do some non-φ"), but some of the rules necessary to preserve a society, at least some particular society, might be substantively positive ("Everyone who is able must help with the harvest," although that is still formally convertible to a prohibition: "No one who is able may refrain from helping with the harvest"). But even those rules would fall short of requiring that everyone always act so as to produce the greatest good for the greatest number available to them, or so Baier is clearly thinking.

Baier concludes with some discussion of Hume as well as further discussion of Kant. (He does not observe that his distinction between rules necessary for the preservation of (a) society on the one hand and conduct on the other that might be optimific but is not morally requisite closely parallels Adam Smith's distinction between justice which is necessary precisely for the preservation of society, breaches of which are therefore appropriately punished, and beneficence, which improves society and is to be praised and encouraged but failures of which are not appropriately punished.[10]) In his concluding discussion of Kant, he argues, inter-estingly, that Kant's hypothetical imperatives should not be counted as impera-tives at all; they are really just statements of facts, about means to ends, that someone deliberating a particular action needs to know: Kant "fails to distinguish conditional recommendations from mere statements of necessary connections," what he calls hypothetical imperatives being merely the latter (*MPV*, p. 283). But his main response to Kant remains that although Kant correctly captures the general and overriding character of moral reasons and principles through his conceptions of the categorical imperative and the good will, he still succumbs to the "empty formalism" objection, failing to recognize that while in a few cases the necessity of avoiding self-contradictory, self-frustrating, or self-defeating actions might yield moral principles, in most cases the further consideration of the necessary conditions for the possibility of society will have to be invoked. It is notable, however, that Baier always formulates possible moral conflicts as conflicts between the *interests* of individuals and the *interests* of all, and formulates the formal principle of morality, as we have seen, as "it is in the interest of everyone alike if everyone alike should be allowed to pursue his own interest provided this does not adversely affect someone else's interests" (*MPV*, p. 202). Baier does not define what he means by "interest," but there is no reason to think that he does not just mean preferences, desires, or inclinations, as did Hare. Baier never refers to Kant's concept of humanity as an end in itself or to his interpretation of humanity as the capacity of human beings to set their own ends, and he dismisses Kant's premise that the fundamental principle or principles of morality must be valid for

---

[10] See Smith, *TMS*, part II, section II, chapter 3, pp. 85–91.

all rational beings, not just human beings (p. 182). Baier takes the preservation of society, as we saw, to require the general protection of what he takes to be certain basic human interests, such as in earning a living, mating and procreating, and so on, but he does not see the human capacity to set their own ends or *determine their own interests* as that which is to be preserved and promoted by morality. If humanity so understood is thought to be a possible ground for the categorical imperative, or for the moral point of view, then Baier misses the opportunity to provide such a foundation for the moral point of view, and leaves his account to rest instead on human interests without further explanation or evaluation. The requirement that each person's pursuit of her own interests not conflict with everyone else's similar pursuit is left to stand on its own.

Marcus Singer's account of generalization in ethics, which appeared two years after Baier's book and to which we now turn, explicitly discusses Kant's concept of humanity as an end in itself, but is not very friendly toward it. However, Singer does provide a vigorous and perhaps unsurpassed defense of Kant's formulation and application of the categorical imperative in the form of the requirement of universalizability.

15.4. Singer

Marcus Singer's 1961 book *Generalization in Ethics*, based on his 1952 Cornell Ph.D. dissertation, was widely noticed at the time of its publication, but was eclipsed by the Rawlsian revival of Kantian ethics, beginning with Thomas Nagel's *The Possibility of Altruism* in 1970 and then Rawls's own *Theory of Justice* in 1971. This was unfortunate, for whatever the merits of the approach to Kant of Rawls himself and of those influenced by him, Singer's work included a sustained and vigorous defense of the conception and application of the categorical imperative that remains as useful as anything published since. The book was both rigorously argued and deeply informed about the history of the objections to Kant's moral philosophy but also about the history of moral philosophy generally. It merits the continued attention of any student of Kant's and Kantian moral philosophy.

Singer paid such attention to the categorical imperative because he regarded it as closely connected to his own conception of the validity of the "generalization argument" in moral philosophy, or as an anticipation of it that needs only to be stripped of a few bells and whistles—such as Kant's notion of testing whether a maxim can be willed if universalized rather than simply whether an intended action could be generalized—in order to be seen as the best anticipation of his own generalization argument in the history of ethics. (Singer uses "ethics" in the general sense as equivalent to morality itself, not in Kant's special sense as one of the two branches of morality, alongside right or justice. For convenience, I will follow Singer's usage in this section even though in general I have tried to avoid it.) We can consider later the differences as well as the similarities between the approaches of Kant and Singer, but first we should examine the two main stages of Singer's work, his exposition of his own approach and then his defense of Kant's categorical imperative. This examination should be preceded with a remark on Singer's conception of his methodology in ethics, namely that the basic method of ethics is not the *justification* of a or the fundamental principle of ethics from some indubitable premise or premises, but the *defense* of a generally recognized principle of ethics and conception of moral arguments from as many objections as possible. As he makes this point explicit, late in the book, "what is relevant here," or, he might have said, what has been relevant, "is not so much a justification in the sense of a demonstration, or a deduction from self-evident principles, as a *defense*. This involves the elimination of misunderstandings, the meeting of difficulties, and the answering of objections, and this is a procedure I have in fact followed" (*GE*, p. 336), indeed, he might have added, in the justification of both his own approach and Kant's categorical imperative. For this accurately describes his approach to the categorical imperative as a model of moral argument, particularly in its first formulation as the Formula of Universal Law. However, it might also be said here that Singer's approach limits his defense of what I have taken throughout to be another and even more basic feature of Kant's moral philosophy, namely his appeal to the status of humanity as an end in itself as the *ground* of a possible categorical imperative. Singer considers Kant's conception of humanity only as another possible version of the rule for moral judgment, and finds that it does not add anything to the requirement of universalizability; indeed, he thinks, *it* is open to the objection that it is an "empty formalism" in a way that he argues that the requirement of universalizability is not (*GE*, p. 235). He has no interest in the potential of humanity as an end in itself as the ground of a possible categorical imperative because of his view that the basic principle of ethics needs only a defense, not a deduction. This approach, which he shares with Hare and Baier, may be a significant limitation of Singer's defense of Kant.

We will return to that issue later. For now, we can start with a brief account of Singer's own model of generalization in ethics. As he sees it, there are three basic components to moral reasoning, that is, the process of judging actions, in the first instance judging an agent's own proposed action, namely the "generalization argument," the "generalization principle," and the "principle of consequences." The generalization argument is the basic form of moral reasoning: it begins with the question about a proposed or completed action, "What would happen if everyone did that?," which may then lead to the realization that "If everyone did that, the consequences would be disastrous" or not, and from thence to the conclusion that the proposed action is prohibited or permitted (*GE*, p. 3). Slightly more formally,

> The generalization argument has the general form: "If everyone were to do *x*, the consequences would be disastrous (or undesirable); therefore no one ought to do *x*." It will be convenient to refer to any particular argument of this or some equivalent form as an instance, or application, of the generalization argument. Any actual instance of this argument may of course appear with many variations of wording. One might merely ask the question, "What would happen if everyone did that?" or "How would you like it if everyone did that?"   (*GE*, p. 61)

Kant's requirement of universalizability is basically one variant wording for starting a generalization argument, although in Singer's view it needs to be pruned of some unnecessary excrescence.

However, the inference from the second stage of a generalization argument to its conclusion, that is, from "it would be disastrous if everyone were to do *x*" to "*x* is prohibited" or "No one may do *x*," might seem fallacious: perhaps the disastrous results of everyone doing *x* could be averted merely if *not everyone* did *x*, that is, if *some* people but *not all* did *x* or were permitted to do *x*. For example, the disastrous effects of no one voting might be averted if some percentage of the electorate between none and all voted (as actually happens, of course), and so no particular person might be under any obligation to vote (*GE*, pp. 74–5). This is where the generalization principle comes in. The generalization argument (or generalization arguments) involve "an inference from 'some' to 'all'"—from "some must not do *x*" to "all must not do *x*" or "no one may do *x*"—that would ordinarily be fallacious.

> It is true that the generalization argument involves an inference from "not everyone has the right" to "no one has the right," from "it would not be right for everyone" to "it would not be right for anyone." This inference, however, is mediated, and therefore qualified, by the principle that *what is right (or wrong) for one person must be right (or wrong) for any similar person in similar circumstances*. For obvious reasons I shall refer to this principle as the "generalization *principle*," even though it has traditionally been known as the principle of fairness or justice or impartiality.   (*GE*, p. 5)

Or as Singer also states the generalization principle, "*If not everyone ought to act or be treated in a certain way, then no one ought to act or be treated in that way without a reason*" (p. 31). Now, as Singer's use of the synonyms "fairness," "justice," and "impartiality" suggest, the generalization principle does not solve the logical fallacy in the generalization argument with a strictly logical principle. It is a substantive, normative principle: that in any form of *inquiry* like cases should be treated alike may be a theoretical principle, but that in any form of *action* like cases should be treated alike is a practical principle. That this principle is needed to make generalization arguments work shows that it is the fundamental principle of ethics. As such, it is subject to Singer's method of defense rather than deduction: "The generalization principle is not likely to be regarded as fallacious. Yet it has frequently been regarded as vacuous and hence devoid of significant application. This is also not so, and the best way of showing this is by showing how it can be significantly and usefully applied" (p. 5). Much of Singer's book is devoted to doing precisely that.

The "principle of consequences" is also necessary to make generalization arguments work. Singer's introduction of this principle is perhaps confusing. He first states it as that "If the consequences of A's doing x would be undesirable, then A ought not to do x" (GE, p. 63), or more precisely as "(1) If the consequences of A's doing x would be undesirable, then A ought not to do x *without a reason or justification*" (p. 65). However, what makes it prohibited for A to do or omit x is not that the consequences of A's doing or omitting x would be undesirable; what would make it prohibited for A to do or omit x would be that the consequences of *everyone* doing or omitting x would be undesirable, so what is required for generalization arguments is the principle that "(2) If the consequences of every- one's doing x would be undesirable, then not everyone ought to do x" (p. 65). Singer characterizes (2) as itself the generalization of (1), but it seems like a separate principle. It is then what needs the generalization principle in order to complete a generalization argument: If the consequences of everyone doing or omitting x would be undesirable, then not everyone ought to do or omit x will imply that no one should do or omit x only if it is also true that if not everyone ought to act or be treated in a certain way then no one ought to act or be treated in that way. In this way a sound generalization argument requires both the principle of consequences in its generalized form (2) and the generalization principle.

It can hardly fail to be noticed that Singer's principle of consequences and thus his model of generalization arguments turn on the *undesirability* of the conse- quences of the generalization of a proposed action. This raises the question of undesirability *to whom* (an individual agent or everyone?) but also the question of whether such arguments propose a straightforward conception of desire, for example interests or inclinations as in the theories of Hare and Baier. Oddly, Singer does not directly address the first question; presumably he simply takes it to be obvious—perhaps as another application of the underlying ideal of fairness or impartiality—that it is of course undesirability to everyone, or to anyone, but not just the agent, that is decisive. It will be noticeable, however, that in his treatment of Kant's categorical imperative his main difference with Kant is to diminish the idea that the possibility of *willing* is a separate and fundamental moral criterion; in his view, Kant is also just concerned with the desirability of the consequences of universalizing a proposed course of action. So let's see if Singer can defend that position.

Singer defends the categorical imperative from various standard criticisms in his chapter 8, then argues that it is really his own requirement that actions be generalizable in chapter 9. Since many of the standard objections to the categorical imperative turn on issues about what maxim an agent should be taken to be acting upon, while Singer argues that the role of Kantian maxims is only to describe properly the actions that agents should be able to universalize and that once that is recognized the difference between Kant's position and his own largely disappears, it will make sense to consider that point first and then turn back to some of the more specific defenses of Kant's version of the universalization test.

In chapter 9, Singer considers only the first formulation of the categorical imperative, the Formula of Universal Law, which he cites in chapter 8 only in its own first formulation, and in an archaic translation, as "Act only that maxim whereby thou canst at the same time will that it should become a universal law" (*GE*, p. 217). His claim is that the references to both maxims and willing in this formulation are otiose, and that in application—the title of chapter 9 in which he makes this argument is "The Application of the Categorical Imperative"—Kant's arguments turn on one of two results: *actions* fail the test of universalizability either if they would be impossible *to perform* if, *per impossibile*, they were universalized, or if they would be possible to perform but would produce disastrous consequences. In the first case, of course, actions cannot be willed if they cannot be performed at all, but that they would then be impossible to will does not need to be explicitly added. In the second case, no rational agent would knowingly perform an action with disastrous consequences, so of course no rational agent would knowingly will to perform such an action, but again the latter does not need to be explicitly added. These two cases cover the cases that Kant distinguishes, namely the case of the contradiction "in conception" and the contradiction "in willing" (*G*, 4: 424), but in Singer's view the impossibility of willing derives from the impossibility of acting, rather than vice versa, so does not need to be explicitly mentioned. The reference to maxims is also unnecessary in Singer's view because a maxim merely properly describes an intended action. For Kant, "To say that someone is acting on a certain maxim is to imply (if not to say) that he is acting for a certain purpose, or with a certain end in view, or with a certain intent; and to specify the maxim is to specify the purpose or intent of the action, as well as something of its circumstances" (*GE*, p. 244). But in that case, "to specify the maxim of an action is really to specify more clearly the nature of the action." Singer continues that "Just as the same kind of action can be performed in different contexts or circumstances, it can be performed on different maxims or for different purposes; and, similarly, its morality—whether it is right or wrong—can depend on its maxim" (*GE*, p. 245). But his point is the converse: the morality of the maxim depends on whether the action as properly described by the maxim can be universalized at all or if so then without disastrous consequences. Thus there needs to be no special role for maxims, just properly described actions. For example (my example), to adopt the maxim "Kill another only if attacked and if that is the only available means of defense" would just mean to perform or try to perform only a certain kind of action, namely killing another only if attacked and only if that is the only means of self-defense. That kind of action is what would have to be able to pass the universalizability test, and the maxim just describes it properly.

Supposing that at least with regard to maxims the difference between Kant's formulation of the universalizability test and Singer's is only verbal, let's turn to Singer's reinterpretation of Kant's distinction between the two ways to fail the test, by a contradiction in conception or a contradiction in willing. His first argument is that what Kant considers a contradiction in conception upon universalization— the standard example being that making a false promise would become a contradiction if everyone were (known) to make false promises, because then making any kind of promise would become impossible—can be understood as an *action* that would become impossible if universalized; of course it would then also be impossible to *will* such an action, but that goes without saying. Or, take the case of someone intending to steal, that is, to make someone else's property his own by unauthorized expropriation, to describe it in the necessary detail; this would become impossible because if it were universalized there would be no such thing as property, as opposed to mere momentary physical possession, at all, and therefore no one could steal property and make it his own property. As Singer puts it:

> It could not be willed to be a universal law that everyone could steal whenever he wished to, for if everyone stole whenever he wished to, or took for his own anything he happened to want, there would be no property and hence nothing to steal—there would be nothing he could call his own. Stealing presupposes that there is such a thing as property—and this presupposes some measure of stability in society. Someone who wishes to steal something presumably wishes to keep it as his property; but if everyone were to act in this way no one would be able to keep anything as his property, and hence there would in effect be no such thing as property. Not only would the purposes of one's act be defeated if everyone were to do the same, but not everyone *could* act in the way in question. To put it another way, if everyone were to act in this way, no one would be able to.
>
> (*GE*, pp. 252–3)

The point is that, if one's intended impermissible act were to be universalized, that act would become impossible, and therefore of course it could not be rationally or coherently willed. That follows from its impossibility, but neither the contradiction in willing, therefore willing itself, nor the maxim of the action need to be explicitly mentioned.

In this context, Singer conclusively refutes the notorious objections of Mill and Hegel. First he cites Mill, who asserted that Kant "fails, almost grotesquely, to show that there would be any contradiction, any logical (not to say physical) impossibility, in the adoption by all rational beings of the most outrageously immoral rules of conduct. All he shows is that the *consequences* of their universal adoption would be such as no one would choose to incur" (*GE*, pp. 250–1).[11] No: Singer's analysis shows that Kant is correct in arguing that there would be an impossibility in certain kinds of actions if they were, *per impossibile*, universalized, and the question of the choiceworthiness of the consequences of such actions under that condition cannot even be raised. To be sure, this actually calls for a refinement of Singer's own initial statement of the form of the generalization argument. It cannot be stated as just "the fact that the consequences of *everyone's* acting in a certain way would be undesirable, provides a good reason for concluding that it is wrong for *anyone* to act in that way" (p. 4); the form of the argument must be stated more fully as that "everyone's acting in a certain way, if even possible, would be disastrous, provides a good reason for concluding that it is wrong for anyone to act that way" by means of the generalization principle. This principle then involves several canons of rationality: that the action would be impossible if universalized can be considered a metaphysical fact, but that it is irrational to attempt the impossible is a canon of rationality; then in the case in which the action would be possible but its results would be disastrous, the necessary generalization principle, that if it would be wrong for everyone to perform an action than it would be wrong for anyone to do it unless there is some relevant difference between the circumstances of that person and those of others, can also be considered a canon of rationality.

We can return to the case in which an action would be possible even if universalized but its consequences disastrous—Singer's version of Kant's contradiction in willing criterion—shortly, but first let's examine his response to Hegel. Hegel's charge, as Singer quotes it from *The Philosophy of Right*, is that Kant's "criterion of non-contradiction is productive of nothing, since where there is nothing, there can be no contradiction either.... The absence of property contains in itself just as little contradiction as the nonexistence of this or that family, etc., or the death of the whole human race." It is only if it is "presupposed that property and human life are to exist and be respected" that "it is then a contradiction to commit theft or murder" (*GE*, p. 251).[12] This is the same as Hegel's earlier version of the "empty formalism" objection in the essay on natural law: the universalizability test of the categorical imperative is an empty formalism because it does not produce any contradiction unless some antecedent condition, in particular an antecedent conception of a good that should not be contradicted, is presupposed. In Singer's view, "this objection of Hegel's is almost incredibly simple-minded. For it entirely ignores the fact that the maxim of an action, which is what the

---

[11] Singer is citing from Mill, *Utilitarianism*, chapter I, paragraph 4; in Mill 1956–91, vol. 10, p. 207. See chapter 13.1 above.
[12] Singer cites Hegel 1942, addition to paragraph 135, p. 254.

categorical imperative is designed to test, is itself a 'determinate principle of conduct' and 'already possesses a content'" (pp. 251–2). That is, Hegel fails to see that the test is not "supposed to be applied in a vacuum"—it is the agent's own maxim that already presupposes the institution of property, for example, when he proposes to expropriate the property of another as his own, and that the universalization of the agent's maxim would contradict or nullify his own maxim by making the action he proposes impossible. "Kant never says that the 'absence of property contains in itself' a contradiction," or that "the existence of property is a logical necessity" (p. 252); he argues rather that it is presupposed or necessitated by the agent's own maxim but contradicted by the (morally necessary) universalization of that maxim. Hegel just misses the self-undermining, self-defeating, or self-frustrating nature of the agent's willing both an (impermissible) maxim and the (morally necessary) universalization of the maxim. Now, to be consistent with his own more refined critique of Kant, that he needs neither the notion of a maxim nor that of willing, Singer should have stated this riposte to Hegel without referring to either maxims or willing. But presumably this would easily be done by saying that Hegel failed to see that, in the kind of contradiction in conception cases to which he was objecting, the contradiction is simply between the possibility of the agent's *intended action* and the consequences of the (morally necessary) generalization or universalization of that action: under the latter condition, the action simply cannot be done, so of course it is irrational to attempt it. That the proper description of the intended action can be put in the form of a maxim is not the point on which the generalization argument turns, and that an agent cannot will an action that would be impossible (under the morally necessary condition of universalization) is a consequence of its impossibility as long as the agent is rational at all, so does not need to be separately mentioned.

Whether or not we agree that Kant's references to maxims and willing are otiose, Singer's argument that both Mill and Hegel failed to understand the self-defeating character of actions that would fail Kant's Formula of Universal Law and his own generalization argument is certainly correct. So let's now turn from his version of the contradiction in conception case of the universalizability test to the contradiction in willing case, that is, Kant's analysis of the basis for imperfect duties such as those of self-perfection and mutual assistance, as Kant describes imperfect duties to others in the *Groundwork*—his general characterization of the imperfect duties to others as that of promoting their *happiness* may fall afoul of Singer's criticism of utilitarianism, to which we can return after the present point. According to Kant "the impossibility of *willing* that everyone act in a certain way, without it being impossible for everyone to *act* in that way," is the ground for the immorality of failing to develop one's own talents or to aid others in their moments of need. But according to Singer, Kant's application of this test depends on his assumption that "there are certain essential ends of humanity, or certain essential (or necessary) ends of purposes of nature" for human beings, "certain ends that every rational person, in virtue of his rationality, would necessarily 'will,' certain purposes that every rational being necessarily has" (*GE*, p. 260). Here is where Singer's aversion to Kant's concept of humanity as an end in itself kicks in: he finds Kant's conception of "necessary ends" or "*nature's purposes* for humanity in our own person" obscure, and thinks that "Kant's notion of essential purposes is...simply a particular and not very plausible view of the proper standard for determining [the] consequences [of everyone acting in a certain way] to be undesirable" (*GE*, p. 261); in other words, he thinks that Kant is clumsily applying his own generalization argument-form. Or so he initially states. In fact, his subsequent exposition suggests that perhaps Kant's idea of a contradiction in willing is not so clumsy after all; in particular, Kant's appeal to what can be willed is not otiose.

Singer considers two kinds of cases. First, although this seems more relevant to perfect duty than to imperfect duty, he argues that no one could willingly be raped (or be subjected to other kinds of assault or violence), because rape is by definition to suffer sexual action against one's will, so one could not will to be raped—that would be to both will and not will the same thing, a contradiction. But this does not yield an objection to rape just because of undesirable consequences. It may be impossible to will to be raped, but of course it is not impossible to rape contrary to the will of the victim; the impermissibility of raping must therefore depend upon the inviolability of the will of others, or their need to be able to will whatever it is that you will to do or to happen to them. It seems hard to eliminate the inviolability of will from this argument; the violation of the will of the victim is what makes rape so heinous, not just the consequences, such as that the victim did not enjoy it. Contrary to what defense lawyers or conservative politicians might suggest, whether or not the victim enjoyed the rape is simply irrelevant to the crime.

The second kind of case that Singer considers, more properly a case of Kant's imperfect duty to others, is that of the person confident of his own strength and resources who does not want to help others because he thinks he will never need help himself. Singer's analysis is that the person who considers the maxim "No one need ever help anyone who is in need of help" cannot universalize this maxim, "for even though [he is] not now (let us suppose) in need of help of any sort, it is possible that a situation will arise in which" he is. He would certainly "have no control over this." "But if [he] should ever be in a situation in which [he does] need help (and the fact that [he is] not now is irrelevant), [he] would have willed... *that everyone who is not in such a situation* need not help" him— and "he could not be willing not to be helped" if he should ever be in a situation in which he needs help (*GE*, pp. 269–70). "No one," he continues, "no matter how wealthy, strong, or self-sufficient, can so order and determine things as never to be in need of help of any kind or degree. Hence no one, no matter how wealthy, strong, or self-sufficient, could be willing for other to ignore his need *when he is* in need of help" (*GE*, p. 270). This argument does turn on "undesirable

consequences": that no one need help him is the consequence of the universalization of the self-sufficient man's maxim not to help others in need no matter how
dire that need might be. (Of course someone might help him even though no one
need help him, but he could hardly count on this possibility.) Perhaps this can be
restated without explicit appeal to a maxim, in terms rather of the consequences of
the universalization of the man's intended action. But it is harder to see how it can
work without an appeal to the character or conditions of rational willing: Singer
may be trying to make it appear to be an *impossibility* of acting in a way that if
universalized would block the availability of help for oneself. But unlike the case of
willing one's own rape, there is no impossibility in this; it would just be the height
of irrationality, or stupidity, something that one could will but could not rationally
will. Some notion of what rational beings can rationally will does seem necessary
here; then the principle of consequences would apply, for the consequences of the
universalization of one's proposed action, or maxim (take your choice) would be,
not impossible, but irrational.

Like others in the group of philosophers we are now discussing, Singer was
dismissive of Kant's conception of humanity as an end in itself. He claimed that
Kant's principle of humanity (which he refers to as "personality," even though
Kant means something different by that, at least in *Religion*, namely the ability of
human beings to be moral, not just to set their own ends; see *RBMR*, 6: 27-8) is
itself too "formal" and empty. It is not a criterion at all, for just what it would
require in a particular situation is indeterminate until it has been determined
whose ends are to count as "rational" (*GE*, pp. 235–6). But in fact Kant's
conception of humanity and its status as a morally necessary end in itself does
give a criterion for specifying what is disastrously undesirable, or for distinguishing between what it is irrational for anyone to will and what is merely undesirable
for any or everyone. If the duty to treat humanity as an end and never merely as a
means is understood as comprising the duty to preserve the capacity to set ends
rather than to destroy or compromise it and the duty to promote this capacity by
enhancing the means available to agents and thereby the ends they can rationally
set for themselves, then the idea of humanity as an end in itself does distinguish
between consequences of the universalization of maxims or actions that are
merely undesirable and those that are incompatible with or disastrous for rational
willing. If the universalization of a proposed course of action would destroy,
compromise, or fail to promote the ability to set ends, that is one thing, and
that is why such an action cannot be morally willed; if it would just be undesirable
or unpleasant to oneself or others in some way but would not destroy, compromise, or fail to enhance the ability of oneself or others to set their own ends, then
the action may be morally permissible even if unadvisable in some other way.
Kant's notion of humanity as an end in itself may be just what is needed to spell
out what constitutes rational or irrational willing in the cases in which willing the
conjunction of one's action and its universalization is simply impossible.

Before we turn, more briefly, to some features of Singer's defense rather than restatement of the categorical imperative, let's turn, also briefly, to his treatment of utilitarianism, for this also bears on the case of Kant's imperfect duties. Singer's position is a form of consequentialism rather than utilitarianism. But this is not for the usual reason for distinguishing between these two types of position, that classical utilitarianism prescribes the maximization of *pleasure* while consequentialism may prescribe some more general form of *preference-satisfaction*. His argument is rather that the proscription of actions that if universalized would have disastrous consequences does not entail the prescription of whatever actions would always have the best or optimific consequences. (In this his position is similar to that of Baier.) In his terms, the truth of the principle of consequences plus the generalization principle, thus that it is wrong for anyone to do what would have undesirable consequences if everyone did it unless there is some reason for distinguishing between the special circumstances of someone and those of everyone else, does not entail that "If the consequences of A's doing *x* would be desirable, then it is A's duty to do *x*" (*GE*, p. 180). It does not follow from the fact that everyone doing *x*, which A is considering, would be disastrous, that anyone, including A, let alone everyone, has the duty to do something that would make anyone or everyone happier, or optimize their situation in some way. All that follows is that neither A nor anyone else has the right to do anything that would make anyone's situation disastrous—where presumably that means at least worse off than they actually are, or maybe a lot worse off than they actually are, but not merely worse off than they might be but are not. This is not to say that the principle of consequences gives rise only to duties that are "merely negative," or prohibitions, or "that there are no actions that one ought to *do* but only actions that one ought *not* to do." For example, that one cannot choose never to help others means that one may sometimes have the duty to help them, even "that a person may have the duty to sacrifice his time, his convenience, his interest, or even his life in order to save the life or protect the interests of another." Of course, then the issue is to specify when and how much a person must sacrifice in order to avoid dereliction of the duty not to never help—the traditional issue concerning Kant's imperfect duties.[13] For Singer, the answer to this question is provided by the principle of consequences, not the obverse of the principle: one has a duty to help "if the consequences of not doing so would be undesirable," but not "if the consequences of not doing so would not be undesirable." (GE, p. 187). But this is still highly indeterminate: undesirable to whom, and how undesirable? He cannot mean undesirable just to the agent, because then even a small cost to the agent could outweigh a very large benefit to others. But even if the criterion is undesirable to all, then a clear criterion between truly disastrous and merely unpleasant

---

[13] See Cummiskey 1996, pp. 109–13.

consequences will still be needed, or else a standard problem for the aggregation of costs and benefits in traditional utilitarianism will arise after all: an aggregation of very small desirabilities to many potential beneficiaries could outweigh a very large sacrifice by the agent.

Singer's claim that the principle of consequences does not entail its converse seems correct, but any suggestion that the principle of consequences itself suffices to make positive duties such as the duty of mutual aid determinate seems less convincing. The success of Singer's critique of utilitarianism is not our problem, however. Our question is rather how well his attempt to reconstruct Kant's imperfect duties on the basis of his generalization argument including the principles of consequences works. Our brief detour through his critique of utilitarianism suggests that a more informative standard than mere undesirability or even disaster may be needed to determine the positive consequences of negatively phrased duties such as not to neglect the development of one's own potential or not to assist others. My suggestion would be that a more favorable attitude toward Kant's conception of humanity might help, in particular that a distinction between helping others toward their happiness in any way and to any degree on the one hand and, on the other, helping them preserve and promote their free agency in the sense of their ability to set their own ends might help, or, in one's own case (although neither Singer nor the others under discussion here are very friendly towards Kant's category of duties to self), that a distinction between promoting any of one's own ends and developing one's capacity to set one's own ends might help. Of course, in either case the determination of whether a course of action would really promote the capacity of others or oneself to set ends, or would only benefit in some other way, will not be a priori or mechanical, rather it will be empirical and still require judgment. Still, this criterion may be more informative and more determinate than the test of just avoiding consequences that are undesirable or disastrous.

Application of the proposed criterion might well require revision of Kant's own treatment in the *Metaphysics of Morals* of the imperfect duty—an end that is also a duty—to promote the happiness of others. This is a more general duty than the duty of assistance or mutual aid offered as the example of imperfect duties to others in Kant's fourfold division of duties in the *Groundwork*, which is meant to illustrate and confirm the applicability of the categorical imperative. Kant is careful in his initial introduction of that duty to include some restriction on the duty to make the happiness of others our own end: he limits our obligation to promote the happiness of others by helping them to realize their ends to their *permissible* ends, that is, the ones that themselves pass moral scrutiny, and he also says that "it is open to me to refuse them many things that *they* think will make them happy but that I do not, as long as they have no right to demand them from me as what is theirs," (*MM*, DV, Introduction, section V.B, 6: 388), that is, no perfect or inviolable right to property. In the latter case, if I owe someone something, I am obliged to give it to them, regardless of whether I think that will actually benefit them; but otherwise, in view of the fact that many more claims on my beneficence will typically exist than I could possibly ever satisfy, I may and must use my own judgment in deciding whom to help and how. But the duty to promote the happiness of others still remains highly indeterminate. If instead of arguing simply that I have a duty, although qualified in this way, to promote the happiness of others, Kant had argued that I have a duty to promote the *humanity* of others, as he suggests in the *Groundwork* (4: 430), that is, their ability to set their own ends, or in more contemporary language perhaps a duty to promote their free agency, he might have offered a more determinate criterion for determining the scope of our imperfect duty to others. Similarly, if the category of duty to self is to be recognized, the criterion of cultivating those of our potential capacities and talents that bear on our ability rationally to set our own ends might be more informative than one of simply cultivating our potential talents whatever they might be. But we will have to leave this issue with these hints.

Instead, let's turn now to Singer's defense of the categorical imperative from two main kinds of objection, for this remains of enduring value. In chapter 8, Singer focuses on the objection to Kant's "rigorism," the objection that Kant's ethics issues not a single categorical imperative but "'categorical imperatives,' which take no account of individual situations, personal differences, or extenuating circumstances"—imperatives such as "Never lie" or "Never kill another human being," which lead to such counterintuitive imperatives as "Never lie even to a would-be murderer in order to save the life of an innocent person"—in this case, indeed, a demand that seems to honor one intuitive duty (never lie) only at the cost of another (do not allow innocent people to be killed). Singer's response is that such rigorism (even though Kant does occasionally suggest it himself) "has no essential connection with the categorical imperative, since it is actually inconsistent with it" (*GE*, p. 218). The nature of Singer's answer is already suggested by the example I have given: *the* categorical imperative is just the general requirement that one act only in ways that pass the test of generalization, and the argument is then that the generalization of overly general rules like "Never kill another human being" would have disastrous consequences, but the generalization of more restrictive rules as "Never kill another human being except to save the life of an innocent person from one who is not" and "Never kill another human being except in self-defense" would pass the test. Or take the case of a maxim or practice of making lying promises: "Kant has shown that it is generally wrong (and surely this is enough). He has not shown that *no matter what the circumstances*, the supposition that everyone could make a lying promise in those circumstances would have" the disastrous consequence of destroying the practice of promising, which is not merely generally useful but necessary for a proposed action of an agent. In cases in which "*the reasons in terms of which the rule is established are the very same reasons which, in certain circumstances, would suffice to override it*" (*GE*, p. 231), those sorts of circumstances just have to be included in the proper statement of a proposed course of action or practice—in Kant's preferred term, although not Singer's, a proposed maxim—in order for it to be usefully submitted to the test of generalization.

Properly formulating the maxim or description of the action to be submitted to that test is also the basis of Singer's response to the objection that he considers in chapter 9, namely that the application of the categorical imperative yields "examples of maxims of actions (a) that can be universalized, and yet are wrong, or (b) cannot be universalized, and yet are not wrong"—that is, false positives and false negatives (*GE*, p. 239). Singer's argument is that, when it seems as if a maxim cannot be universalized and yet acting on it would not be wrong, that is because the maxim is too generally formulated, and when it seems that the maxim could be universalized yet acting on it would be wrong, that is because the maxim is too particularly formulated. An overly particularized maxim is one like "I will not repay my roommate if I owe him exactly $9.81 and if he is exactly __ years old and I weigh exactly __ pounds"[14] could be generalized without destruction of the practice of lending money to one's roommate and thereby frustrating the original purpose of the debtor. But of course that is not his real maxim, which is something more like "I will not repay my debt to my roommate if I think I can get away with it," and the (known) generalization of that maxim would have disastrous consequences for the would-be borrower. Conversely, the case of lying promises offers an illustration of the second point: "Lying merely for one's own convenience and lying in order to save the life of some innocent person are two different sorts of actions, actions whose maxims are quite different" (*GE*, p. 247), and while the excessively general maxim "Never lie" should not pass the generalization test precisely because it includes cases like lying merely for one's own convenience, the maxim "Lie only if necessary to save the life of an innocent person" would pass the test, that is, its generalization would not have disastrous consequences, and so is permissible or perhaps even obligatory. Thus the most general maxim about lying that would pass the test would be something like "Never lie except to save the life of an innocent person and...," adding in other specific kinds or maxims of lying that would also pass the test.

About the objections that the categorical imperative yields false positive and false negatives, Singer's conclusion is:

> There is some notion afoot that the determination of the maxim on which someone is acting is an arbitrary matter. But while it may be a difficult matter to formulate the maxim of an action, just as it may be a difficult matter to

---

[14] Singer 1961, p. 297.

determine just what sort of an action it is, it is not an arbitrary one. One cannot change the maxim on which one has acted, any more than one can change the circumstances and purposes of the maxim on which one has acted. In particular, it is not open to one to formulate the maxim of his action in such a way that it could (logically) apply only to him in just these circumstances. For everyone else can do the same, and thus the argument can be reiterated for every maxim of the same type. And in practice the type is not very difficult to determine.

(*GE*, pp. 296–7)

Reiterability is a crucial part of the generalization test. If anyone could lie to save an innocent life in the specified kind of circumstances, that maxim passes the test; if not everyone could refuse to pay back their debts on entirely arbitrary grounds, that maxim fails the test.

I believe that Singer's strategy for refuting these kinds of objections remains sound, and has not been superseded. Before skipping ahead half a century and turning to the last of the philosophers attempting to reconcile Kantianism with some form of consequentialism that I will consider, namely Derek Parfit, I will briefly comment on David Cummiskey's "Kantian Consequentialism" of 1996.

15.5. Cummiskey

David Cummisky's project was to show that "Kant's main argument is consistent with consequentialism and provides a compelling justification for a new form of Kantian consequentialism" (Cummiskey 1996, p. vii). The reason that he calls his position, which he presents more as a philosophical reconstruction rather than historical interpretation of Kant's own, a version of consequentialism rather than, say, a reconciliation of consequentialism and deontology, is that he does not think that Kant's division between perfect and imperfect duties is hard-and-fast, thus Kant's perfect duties are not unconditional deontological constraints on the pursuit and the promotion of the good, nor are Kant's imperfect duties always less than completely stringent—in a situation in which one is the only person who could render aid to another person in truly dire straits, the duty to aid, ordinarily considered an imperfect duty and therefore of wide latitude, is just as stringent as a perfect duty such as the duty not to destroy or defraud another person. That one duty may typically be expressed as a prescription and the other as a proscription, or as a duty of commission rather than omission, is insignificant, since the linguistic forms of prescriptions and proscriptions are typically convertible (Commiskey 1996, pp. 105–23). Kant's theory fundamentally requires the promotion of the good, with its apparently deontological constraints being required to ensure that the good is maximally well distributed among all human beings, therefore the theory is essentially a form of consequentialism.

But the difference between "Kantian consequentialism" and any traditional form of utilitarianism is that the good that is to be promoted is not happiness or preference-satisfaction, or at least not directly. Rather, "Kantian consequentialism...constrains the maximization of happiness with a principle that requires one to maximally promote the conditions necessary for autonomous rational agency.... preserving, developing, and exercising our rational capacities is more important than maximizing happiness" (p. 4). In other words, rational agency, that is, humanity insofar as it is instantiated in human beings and comprised by various rational capacities, is the good that is to be maximized as the proper consequence of morally permissible and/or mandatory action. Kantian consequentialism thus does not focus on the hypothetical consequences of the universalization of proposed maxims that may properly be considered on any interpretation of Kant's application of the categorical imperative, but on the consequence of the universalization of agent's maxims for the preservation and promotion of rational agency or humanity—and not just any agent's *own* humanity, but "rational agency as such," as Cummiskey often writes, that is, rational agency in potentially all of its instances accessible to us. This is a fundamental difference between Cummiskey's "Kantian consequentialism" and the other attempts to reconcile Kantianism and consequentialism that we have considered in this chapter, which focus on the satisfaction of inclinations or interests, whether individual or social, or the avoidance of "disastrous" consequences, as in Singer's version.

This naturally raises the question of how Cummiskey, or Cummiskey's Kant, is supposed to argue that rational agency as such is the value to be maximized in Kantian consequentialism. He first argues, as others such as Allen Wood also did, that Kant's Formula of Universal Law is not sufficient to yield positive duties such as the duties of self-perfection and of aid to others. He particularly dislikes Kant's use of a generalization argument (e.g., *MM*, DV, §27) to argue for the imperfect duty of aiding others, since in his view it really is contingent whether anyone rightly thinks he will ever need aid from others and therefore should generalize a maxim to provide it if needed (Cummiskey 1996, pp. 107–8). The vulnerability of human capacities for rational agency would provide a more direct argument for this duty, if indeed rational agency as such can be shown to be a necessary end for human beings. I would argue here that the vulnerability of our capacities for rational agency, vulnerability to ill health, ill will, inadequate resources, and so on, is also a contingent and only empirically known matter, but I would not worry about this, since Kant makes it clear that the derivation of *all* human duties depends upon the addition of certain basic but still contingent and only empirically known facts about human nature to the fundamental principle of morality that is valid for all rational beings (*MM*, Introduction 6: 217). The important question is rather how is the status of rational agency as such as the necessary aim of a Kantian consequentialism to be defended?

Cummiskey's initial move is to argue that since all willing involves some end, willing in accordance with a necessary law must depend upon willing a necessary end (Cummiskey 1996, p. 56). If this were Kant's whole argument, however, it would be fallacious: if the fundamental principle of morality, for example in the form of the Formula of Universal Law, were already established, it would require that *any* permissible end pass the test, but not that there be *one* necessary end. But Cummiskey's position is rather that the categorical imperative *presupposes* an end-in-itself for its own justification (p. 63), and that this is the role of rational agency as such. He then proceeds along the line laid out by Christine Korsgaard in her 1986 paper "Kant's Formula of Humanity," reprinted in her book *Creating the Kingdom of Ends* in the same year as Cummiskey's own book appeared (Korsgaard 1996a), and which Allen Wood would also adopt three years after Cummiskey's book (Wood 1999). This is the "regress" argument, which Cummiskey also calls a "transcendental" argument (p. 68), that the "full justification" for any action "requires that at some point there is an unconditioned condition of value. Only something that is unconditionally valuable can provide an unconditional, sufficient, determining ground for action. . . . Kant's approach is part of the tradition that assumes that infinite chains and circular chains of justification are unacceptable" (pp. 64–5). The first move of this argument is thus that ascribing even conditional value to any particular end and therefore action requires that its value derive from something of unconditional value, something that must be an end-in-itself. The next move is that, since any particular end set by a rational agent will be of only contingent value, the only candidate left for the unconditionally valuable end-in-itself "must be rational nature itself. Rational nature, the power of rational choice, is the unconditioned condition of all value" (p. 73). The final step is to make clear that this is not just *one's own* rational nature or agency, but anyone's and everyone's:

> Now, if rational nature has the power to confer value, it has this power whether it is my rational nature or anyone else's. Or to put the point differently, if I believe that my rationally chosen ends provide reasons for action, then so too must I recognize the rationally chosen ends of others as reasons for action. If I must think of my rational nature as an end-in-itself, then I must also think of rational nature as such as an end-in-itself. (p. 73)

Rational nature as such or in general, that is, in all its instantiations accessible to us, is the ultimate end to be preserved and promoted, thus to be preserved from harm and promoted in various ways. That is what constitutes Kantian consequentialism. Of course, applying this abstract goal in practice will involve all sorts of trade-offs: sometimes I will have to forego some goal of my own for the sake of other goals of my own, sometimes I will have to forego some goal of my own for the sake of some goal of others, sometimes I will have to forego the promotion of some goal of others for the sake of some goal of my own, and so on. But the key point is that such trade-offs, if one wants to call them that, will always be trade-offs within the overall goal of the preservation and promotion of rational agency as such, not trade-offs between that goal and some other, deontological constraints. In that sense Kantian consequentialism remains consequentialism, not some hybrid between deontology and consequentialism.

Cummiskey's emphasis on the primacy of rational agency as the end-in-itself is certainly compatible with my own approach to Kant's moral philosophy, although I prefer to emphasize the less abstract idea of the freedom to set our own ends that Kant suggests in the early lectures on ethics and the late *Metaphysics of Morals* rather than the more abstract idea of rational agency as such. I am less enthusiastic about reliance on the regress argument also favored by Korsgaard and Wood, as it seems to depend upon the permissibility of simply stopping a potential regress from something merely contingent to something that exists necessarily in practical reasoning, when Kant disallows any such move in theoretical reasoning. I also think that Cummiskey falls into the common trap of treating *setting* one's own ends and having the means to successfully *pursue* them as two different elements of rational agency as such, when I think that having (or believing that one has) adequate means to an end is a necessary condition for rationally setting that end in the first place; thus widening the range of one's possible means to possible ends through both self-perfection and assistance from (and to) other is not a separate condition only for the successful pursuit of ends, but for maximizing the range of ends that one may rationally set in the first place (and *mutatis mutandis*, that others may set for themselves). But these reservations aside, Cummiskey's "Kantian consequentialism" is worth remembering because it places more distance between Kant's moral philosophy and the assimilations of it to more ordinary utilitarianism that we encountered in Hare, Baier, and Marcus Singer.

Now let us see how the most recent rapprochement of Kantianism and utilitarianism, that attempted by Derek Parfit, fares, and especially what role the value of humanity itself might play on his account.

15.6. Parfit

Kant was not a strong presence in Derek Parfit's first book, *Reasons and Persons* (1984). That book focused above all on the moral implications of personal identity: what kind of interest can one have about the well-being of future persons whose identity is not yet established, or even one's own future self? Kant comes to the fore in Parfit's second work, the monumental *On What Matters* published in two volumes in 2011, with a third volume following in 2017, the year of Parfit's death. The first two volumes use the format of Tanner Lectures, in which comments by a number of distinguished colleagues accompany the lead author's own lectures, although in this case the material is greatly expanded: Parfit's lectures, originally delivered at Berkeley in 2002, are expanded into a first volume of 450 pages, with the commentaries by Susan Wolf, Allen Wood, Barbara Herman, and T. M. Scanlon in the second volume then followed by another 600 pages of response from Parfit! Volume 3 then comprises Parfit's responses to a baker's dozen of further papers by a group of distinguished philosophers assembled by Peter Singer, also published in 2017 (Singer 2017).[15] All of that material can hardly be discussed here. But Parfit begins *On What Matters* by asserting that "Kant is the greatest moral philosopher since the ancient Greeks," although he immediately adds that "Sidgwick's *Methods [of Ethics]* is, I believe, the best book on ethics ever written." That conjunction puts his project in a nutshell: he aims to show that Kant's basic insight in moral philosophy is not merely compatible with a form of consequentialism, namely, rule-utilitarianism, but, properly understood, leads to it. Both are "climbing the same mountain." Parfit thus revives the project of Hare, Baier, and Singer that we have discussed in this chapter, although he refers to none of their works, published half a century before his own. Only that aspect of Parfit's project will be discussed here.

More precisely, Parfit aims to show that three approaches to the fundamental principle of morality rather than two land at the same place: his version of Kant's approach, which he calls "Kantian Contractualism," and which states that "Everyone ought to follow the principles whose universal acceptance everyone could rationally will or choose"; an alternative version of "contractualism" which he derives from T. M. Scanlon, and which states that "everyone ought to follow the principles that no one could *reasonably reject*"; and his version of rule-utilitarianism, that "Everyone ought to follow the principles whose universal acceptance would make things go best" (Parfit 2011, vol. 1, pp. 21, 23). The conclusion of his entire argument is thus what he calls the "Triple Theory": "An act is wrong just when such acts are disallowed by the principles that are optimific, uniquely universally willable, and not reasonably rejectable" (Parfit 2011, vol. 1, p. 25). The difference between what Parfit calls Kantian contractualism and Scanlonian contractualism is subtle, even elusive: presumably the difference is that even if everyone *could* reasonably will the acceptance of some principle, someone might *also* have some reason to reject the principle; and indeed Parfit, who might go down as the greatest inventor of puzzle-cases in the history of philosophy, does construct cases in which an agent might have sufficient reasons to choose either of two mutually exclusive alternatives—e.g., to save the life of another at the cost of one of her own limbs, but alternatively to save her own limb

---

[15] The volume edited by Peter Singer contains responses to *On What Matters* to date. Edmonds 2023 is a biography with brief accounts of Parfit's main ideas. Chappell 2021 is a brief survey of Parfit's work, with more emphasis on issues from *Reasons and Persons* than those from *On What Matters*. Dancy 1997, is a collection of essays on *Reasons and Persons*; Kirchin 2017, a collection on *On What Matters*. McMahan forthcoming, is a collection on all of Parfit's work.

at the cost of the life of another—with no decisive reason to choose between them. In such cases, agents *could* reasonably reject a principle that they *could also* will to be universally accepted, such as "Everyone should choose to save a life at the cost of the loss of one of their own limbs."[16] However, I am not going to worry about this difference, and will focus on the main thrust of Parfit's argument, from "Kantian Contractualism" to "Kantian Rule Consequentialism." For that will suffice to make my chief point, which I share with Husain Sarkar in his closely argued *Kant and Parfit* (Sarkar 2018), that Parfit is able to get his utilitarian conclusion from Kant by making utilitarian assumptions from the outset of his argument. Indeed, Sarkar has argued the point so thoroughly that my treatment of Parfit here can be briefer than his many hundreds of pages might seem to require.

Parfit's own initial summary of his crowning argument can serve to identify the crux of his argument. In his words:

According to one version of

Rule Consequentialism: Everyone ought to follow the principles whose universal acceptance would make things go best.

Such principles we can call optimific.

Kantians could argue:

Everyone ought to follow the principles whose universal acceptance everyone could rationally will, or choose.

Everyone could rationally choose whatever they would have sufficient reasons to choose.

There are some optimific principles.

These are the principles that everyone would have the strongest impartial reasons to choose.

No one's impartial reasons to choose these principles would be decisively outweighed by any relevant conflicting reasons.

Therefore

Everyone would have sufficient reasons to choose these optimific principles.

There are no other significantly non-optimific principles everyone would have sufficient reason to choose.

Therefore

It is only these optimific principles that everyone would have sufficient reasons to choose.

---

[16] For fine-grained discussion of the difference, see Scanlon 2011.

Therefore

Everyone ought to follow these principles.

This argument's first premise is the Kantian Contractualist Formula. The argument is valid, and its other premises are true. So this Kantian Formula requires us to follow these Rule Consequentialist principles.

(Parfit 2011, vol. 1, pp. 23–4)

Granting Parfit's claim that the argument is valid, the question of whether it soundly yields a Kantian conclusion, thus whether Kantianism entails a form of utilitarianism, turns on (i) the interpretation of Kant's categorical imperative as the premise "Everyone ought to follow the principles whose universal acceptance everyone could rationally will, or choose" and (ii) the premise that the determinants of what anyone can rationally choose are the "strongest impartial reasons," which are equivalent to "optimific principles." Parfit covers a lot of ground to get to his formulation (i), and that needs some discussion; but obviously the main potential difference with Kant will be in premise (ii).

Parfit's premise (i) suggests that he must begin his appropriation of Kant from the idea of universalizability, as do the others discussed in this chapter. In fact, unlike the others, he begins with an interpretation of Kant's requirement that humanity always be treated as an end and never merely as a means, namely a requirement of consent to how one is treated. Parfit treats this as the first implication of Kant's "best-loved principle, often called *the Formula of Humanity*: We must treat all rational beings, or persons, never merely as a means, but always as ends" (Parfit 2011, vol. 1, p. 177). He interprets this in turn as "It is wrong to treat anyone in any way to which this person could not rationally consent" (Parfit 2011, vol. 1, p. 181). He raises the question of whether Kant has actual or only possible consent in mind, and correctly argues that it is the latter, citing Kant's statement that a wrongly treated person "could not possibly agree to my way of treating him." Many passages from Kant's moral and also from his political philosophy support this interpretation, including Kant's interpretation of the social contract as an idea that tests the legitimacy of legislation rather than a requirement for the actual consent of the governed (*MM* DR, §47, 6: 315–16). What is more of an issue is Parfit's account of what could make consent itself rational. After considering a variety of possible interpretations of the principles and counter-examples to them, his usual method, Parfit arrives first at the formulation that "It is wrong for us to treat people in any way to which they would not have sufficient reasons to consent, except when, to avoid such an act, we would have to bear too great a burden" (Parfit 1911, vol. 1, p. 210). As Sarkar argues throughout his book, consequentialism already seems to be baked into this formulation: the reasons that anyone could have to consent or not to a way of being treated, or the reasons that an agent could have to treat another in a certain way and that the patient could have for consenting to that way of being treated or not, are reasons of well-being; the rider that the weight of the burden that the proposed course of action would place on the agent needs to be compared to the burden that would be placed on the patient makes that clear. To avoid an immediate collapse into consequentialism, Parfit turns to the second component of the humanity formula—that is, what is required in order to treat someone as an end, and not merely not to treat her merely as a means, which might be satisfied by her possible rational consent. He says that "Some acts are wrong even though everyone could rationally consent to them." This requires at least one principle other than possible consent, and so Parfit turns to the second part of Kant's formula to see if he can find the additional principle there. This is the idea of treating persons as ends in themselves, or having respect for their dignity as rational beings. But here his claim is that this is not an informative concept, or that the idea of treating persons with respect is parasitic on some antecedent conception of what it is to treat them morally: "to decide whether some act would be ... incompatible with respect for persons, we would first have to decide whether this act would be wrong" (Parfit 2011, vol. 1, p. 234). His initial formulation of the consent principle can be fleshed out with the idea of treating people as ends rather than merely as means, but if the idea of treating persons with respect as ends is parasitic on the idea of treating them morally, this addition comes down to "We do *not* treat someone merely as a means, nor are we even close to doing that, if either (1) our treatment of this person is governed in a sufficiently important way by some relevant moral belief, or (2) we do or would relevantly choose to bear some great burden for this person's sake" (Parfit 2011, vol. 1, p. 227). Part (2) of this test again measures consequences; part (1) leaves open whether "relevant moral beliefs" are themselves consequentialist in nature, or whether there is still some non-consequentialist test for "moral beliefs." This question remains open at the end of Parfit's discussion of "Kantian dignity," where he states that "When Kant claims that all rational beings have the kind of value that he calls dignity, he does not mean that all rational beings are good"; he "means that all rational beings have a kind of value that is to be respected, since these beings ought to be treated only in certain ways" (Parfit 2011, vol. 1, p. 243; see also vol. 2, pp. 156–68, his reply to Wood 2011). Respect is to be defined by the ways in which rational beings ought to be treated, rather than vice versa; so the question remains whether that can be determined on other than consequentialist grounds.

After a discussion of Kant's concept of the highest good, to which I will return, Parfit turns to Kant's conception of universalizability. He does not mention Kant's claim that the status of humanity as an end in itself is supposed to be the *ground* of a possible categorical imperative (*G*, 4: 428), that is, that it is supposed to be reason for the requirement that we act only on universalizable maxims, but the connection between universalizability and the requirement of possible consent, the part of Kant's Formula of Humanity that Parfit finds useful, is obvious: if we can act towards anyone and everyone only in ways to which they could consent, then our maxims must be universalizable, that is, acceptable by everyone else. Parfit is not much impressed by Kant's argument, which so many others have found to be his best argument from the categorical imperative, namely that some maxims are impermissible because their universalization would make it impossible for agents considering them to accomplish what they propose to do by means of them (or example, to acquire money by false promises when the universalization of their maxim would make promises and therefore acquiring money by false promises impossible). He prefers the interpretation that "We could not rationally choose or will it to be true that some maxim is a universal law if we are aware of facts that give us clearly decisive reasons not to make this choice" (Parfit 2011, vol. 1, p. 285). Making what we want to do impossible would certainly be one "decisive reason" not to choose to act on a maxim the universal acceptance of which would have that result, but that is only one case; Parfit's notion of "decisive reasons" is much broader. More generally, what he considers decisive reasons seem to be consequentialist: thus, a significant benefit to others or a widespread positive effect on well-being could be a decisive reason; but so could be saving one's own life. But, as Barbara Herman points out, the aim of preserving and promoting rational agency or the conditions for rational willing in oneself and others is *not* anything that Parfit considers a reason, let alone an overriding reason, for the adoption of a principle.[17]

Like Marcus Singer, Parfit is also not friendly to Kant's idea of maxims; he thinks that it is hard to determine someone's maxim, that maxims might after all be sufficiently particular to avoid untoward consequences from their generaliza-tion, and so on. Instead, he argues that what is to be subjected to the universal-izability test is "the morally relevant description of my [proposed] act." For example, it may be "irrelevant that I am stealing from someone who is a woman, and who is wearing white and eating strawberries. The relevant facts may be that I am stealing from someone who is no richer than me, merely for my own amusement. In applying" the universalizability test to such revised descrip-tions of the "morally relevant facts" in any particular case, "we should ask whether I could rationally will it to be true that everyone acts in this way, and that everyone believes such acts to be permitted. If the answer is No...these revised formulas would rightly condemn my act" (Parfit 2011, vol. 1, p. 297). In other words, the ultimate test of morality is simply "What if Everyone Did That?," applied to the "morally relevant description" of a proposed act (vol. 1, p. 300).

The question remains, though, what determines "moral relevance"? Parfit's example suggests consequentialist reasons: that the victim of a proposed theft would be no richer than the potential thief suggests that how much harm the theft

[17] Herman 2011, e.g., pp. 85–6.

would do to the victim compared to how much benefit it would do to the perpetrator is a morally relevant consideration. In general, Parfit assumes that the facts to be considered relevant in answering "What if everyone did that questions?" concern costs and benefits to agents and patients. This is clear in the case of what Kant classifies as the imperfect duty to others, namely beneficence or the promotion of their happiness (like the other authors considered in this chapter, Parfit has no use for the idea of duties to oneself): the limitation to such an imperfect duty is that, "if everyone promoted the happiness of others at a greater cost to their own happiness, everyone would lose more happiness than they gained" (Parfit 2011, vol. 1, p. 307)—it is the net amount of happiness that would follow from the universalization of one's proposed act that determines what is morally permitted or required. And in many of the cases that Parfit considers, such as whether one has an obligation or whether it is even permissible to save the life of another at the cost of a limb of one's own, the magnitude of the benefits and harms to the parties involved is always the relevant factor.

This not only grants a large role to consequentialist reasoning in Parfit's version of Kantianism, which has come down to the requirement to ask "What if Everyone Did That?," but also leads to indeterminacies parallel to those of Henry Sidgwick's famous "Dualism of the Practical Reason," although it was a hope of Parfit's project to avoid that. Could everyone have decisive reason to accept the principle always to save the life of another (or more than one other) at the cost of one's own limb? Yes, people could rationally will that, thinking of the widespread salvation of life that might follow and the great benefit that would be to many people. But could everyone have decisive reason to accept the principle always to save a limb of one's own (though maybe not just a pinkie, or a scratch on a pinkie) even at the cost of the life of another, or maybe even more than one other? Yes, everyone could have reason to accept that principle also, given the tremendous compromise of one's own life plans and happiness that the cost of a limb or, in Parfit's most macabre case, the loss of both hands by a young and promising cellist in order to save the life of another, might produce. Given how difficult it is to actually make determinate comparisons of costs and benefits, consequentialism seems invariably to leave some dilemmas unresolved.[18]

Now, that Parfit's reconstruction of Kant's universalizability test depends upon consequentialist considerations at some point in its application may not be in and of itself an objection to his project, as Husain Sarkar seems to assume throughout his book. The crucial difference between Kant's role for consequentialist considerations and any traditional form of consequentialism is where the

---

[18] Allen Wood objects vigorously to Parfit's use of such thought-experiments, arguing that true morality would consist in taking proactive steps to avoid such situations in the first place: e.g., morality should focus on building earthquake-proof structures in the first place, not on the question of whether rescuers should save this person's legs or hands at the cost of that person's life; Wood 2011, pp. 66–82. Parfit does not address this complaint in his response to Wood.

consequentialist considerations enter into the argument. In Kant's version of morality, one does not raise the question whether a maxim can be universalized out of prudential concern about the consequences of one's actual action; one asks whether one's maxim could be universalized because that is a demand of pure practical reason, however that is to be understood, and then asks what would the consequences of one's action be in the possible world in which it was universalized. Even if the consequences of one's actions would be beneficial to oneself or even to others in the actual world if one's maxim were not in fact universalized, the fact the consequences of one's maxim would be self-frustrating or deleterious to others in the possible world in which it was, contrary to fact, universalized would be morally decisive because morality, not prudence, requires one to ask how things would go in such a possible world. Ordinary consequentialism requires one to ask about the consequences of one's action in the actual world, not in a possible but, because of the nature of pure practical reason, morally relevant other world.[19]

But one could put to Parfit the question whether a more generous attitude towards Kant's Formula of Humanity, more particularly to his idea of rational beings or more precisely rational *agents* as ends in themselves, could in fact resolve some of the dilemmas that Parfit's approach leaves unresolved. The striking thing about Parfit's approach is that it leaves Sidgwick's dualism of practical reason unresolved, that he constructs so many cases in which one could permissibly choose either one's own well-being or the life of others because everyone could permissibly choose either way. If one thinks Kant's idea of rational agency or humanity as the capacity to set one's own ends—and Parfit does think that this is what Kant at least sometimes means by humanity, although he thinks that Kant also sometimes means by it the capacity to be moral (Parfit 2011, vol. 1, p. 242, and vol. 2, pp. 162–4)—has some content and is not just dependent upon an anteced-ent conception of what is morally permissible or requisite, one could resolve at least some of Parfit's cases. In particular, if one thinks that Kant's conception yields a lexical ordering of obligations—first preserve the existence of beings capable of setting their own ends (insofar as that is compatible with the existence of other such agents, thus the likes of Hitler and Stalin fall outside of this protection—for Parfit's worry about them, see vol. 2, p. 160), next preserve their general capacity to set ends (with the minimal restrictions necessary to preserve that capacity in others as well), next preserve their opportunity to exercise that capacity on particular occasions (compatible with satisfaction of the first two constraints), finally promote or enhance their capacity to set their own ends (compatible with satisfaction of the first three constraints), then one might have

---

[19] In the course of his response to Herman, Parfit makes a similar point in a comment on Schopenhauer's objection that Kant's reasoning is in fact merely prudential (Parfit 2011, vol. 2, p. 186).

ways of resolving some of Parfit's dilemmas that are more decisive than the vaguer conception of facts about well-being to which he appeals, and the difficulty in comparing differential effects on the well-being of different parties that plagues Parfit's approach might be ameliorated. I certainly admit that Kant hardly makes such a lexical ordering of duties concerning humanity as the ability to set ends explicit, but I have argued that Kant hints at such an ordering in his remarks about the relation between perfect and imperfect duties and in the sequence of his illustrations of the application of the first two formulations of the categorical imperative in the *Groundwork*; the idea there is that the sequence of duties not to commit suicide (preserve the existence of a rational being), not to commit fraud (preserve the ability of others to exercise their freedom to set their own ends), and to enhance one's own abilities and promote the happiness of others can be construed as a lexical ordering.[20] In particular, the development of one's own talents can be seen as necessary to enhance the means available to oneself, which in turn broadens the range of ends one can rationally set for oneself, since one cannot rationally set an end for which one has no means; enhancing one's own abilities also broadens the range of ways in which one could rationally choose to help others. And if promoting the happiness of others is understood as taking place by affording them means to realize their own ends—since one does not directly inject happiness into others, but can afford them or help them obtain means to their ends—then that too can be understood within the framework of this lexical ordering.[21]

This reference to happiness can bring us back to Parfit's discussion of Kant's conception of the highest good. Parfit's treatment of the highest good is striking in two ways. On the one hand, he uses Kant's claim that the highest good (or "greatest good," as Parfit calls it) is the object of the command "Everyone ought always to strive to promote a world of universal virtue and deserved happiness" (Parfit 2011, vol. 1, p. 245) as a key step in his program to demonstrate that Kantianism actually leads to rule-consequentialism or -utilitarianism. For he spends the first of the two sections that he devotes to the highest good arguing that Kant was reasonable to suppose that we can each make the greatest contribution to the happiness of all by following general rules rather than by trying to calculate the effects of particular actions: he cites Kant's statement that "a lie... always harms another, even if not another individual, nevertheless humanity in general, inasmuch as it makes the source of right unstable,"[22] which demonstrates Kant's recognition that the contribution of an act to the general happiness is to be determined by the effect of a general rule like "Do not lie" or the "whole scheme" of conduct of which a particular action is a part to happiness, not by trying to calculate the effects of lying or telling the truth in a particular circumstance (Parfit

---

[20] See Guyer 2005b, section 3, esp. pp. 256–7, and Guyer 2007c, esp. pp. 93–5.
[21] See Guyer 2016c.   [22] From Kant's essay "On a Supposed Right to Lie," 8: 426.

2011, vol. 1, p. 255). Parfit suggests that Kant shares this reasoning with Hume and also with Sidgwick, who argued similarly a century later (vol. 1, p. 251). What is striking, however, is that Parfit does not do much to explore how happiness in any form, whether one's own or that of all, has suddenly entered into Kant's conception of the complete *object* or goal of morality. He starts the section by writing "The Highest or Greatest Good, Kant claims, would be a world in which everyone was both wholly virtuous, or morally good, and had all of the happiness that their virtue would make them deserve" (vol. 1, p. 244), and leaves this claim unquestioned. He thus seems to accept what Kant himself sometimes seems to suggest, as in the *Critique of Practical Reason*, that virtue and happiness are two separate things, one the moral end of individual human beings and the other—in the form of their *own* happiness—their natural end, and that an "impartial reason" requires an external connection between them, namely that someone who is virtuous deserves to be happy (*CPracR*, 5: 110). He does not consider whether there might be a more internal or intimate connection between virtue and happiness. But, although not in the opening move of the Dialectic of Pure Practical Reason in the second *Critique*, Kant does suggest an internal connection between the virtue of each and the happiness of all. One path from the first to the second is through the universalizability requirement: everyone naturally wishes for their own happiness and for assistance from others in attaining it, but no one can morally make it their maxim to pursue their own happiness including seeking help from others when necessary except by universalizing this maxim, thus being prepared to help others attain their happiness when they can—and if everyone were to adopt this universalized maxim, that would of course tend to produce the greatest happiness for all that is possible by human efforts. Kant suggests this argument in his first exposition of the fourth example of the application of the categorical imperative in the *Groundwork* (4: 423) and in his proof that the end of promoting the happiness of others is also a duty in the Doctrine of Virtue of the *Metaphysics of Morals* (§27, 6: 451). To be sure, the happiness of *others* that each has the duty to promote according to the latter argument might seem to fall short of the happiness of *all* that is supposed to be included in the highest good, because, as Kant famously argues in the Doctrine of Virtue, it is not a duty to promote one's *own* happiness since one already *naturally* desires that; but of course, if *everyone* were promoting the happiness of others to the greatest extent humanly possible, then *others* would be promoting *anyone's own*, so *collectively all* would be promoting the happiness of *all*. This is thus one argument by which Kant demonstrates that even though happiness, especially one's own happiness, cannot be the morally worthy *motive* for persons with good will, the happiness of all is nevertheless a necessary component of the complete *object* of morality.

The other kind of argument at which Kant at least hints is an argument from the status of humanity as an end in itself: if treating others as ends in themselves includes making their ends one's own, or promoting them insofar as one can (consistent of course with one's necessary respect for the humanity in oneself), *and if happiness consists in nothing but the realization of one's ends*, then treating others as ends in themselves includes promoting their happiness, to be sure not directly by simply gratifying their wishes but by helping them achieve their own ends themselves. Kant at least hints at such an argument in the *Groundwork*'s fourth illustration of the application of the second formulation of the categorical imperative, the Formula of Humanity as an End in Itself, when he states that "there is still only a negative and not a positive agreement with *humanity as an end in itself* unless everyone also tries, as far as he can, to further the ends of others" (4: 430). By means of these arguments, stated or hinted, Kant goes further than merely suggesting that "impartial reason" holds that virtuous persons *deserve* happiness, and rather explains why virtue directly *requires* the promotion of happiness. Parfit's overall argument would surely have been strengthened by attention to these Kantian arguments; his argument that Kant recognized that we can each best promote the happiness of all by following general rules rather than by attempting to calculate the costs and benefits of particular actions could then have followed this vital preliminary.[23]

However, starting off from what might seem like Kant's own unmotivated insistence that virtuous people deserve to be happy, Parfit does make an important point about desert. He considers Kant's suggestion that "It would be best... if everyone's degree of happiness was *in proportion* to their degree of virtue, or worthiness to be happy," and the interpretation of this by "some writers" to mean that "of the worlds that are not ideal," that is, in which everyone is not maximally virtuous, "the best would be those in which this *proportionality condition* would be met" (Parfit 2011, vol. 1, p. 245)—that is, in which those who are virtuous are rewarded with happiness, to a degree proportionate to their degree of virtue, but those who are vicious are punished with unhappiness, to a degree proportionate to their degree of vice. He says that this cannot have been Kant's view, because this condition could be satisfied by worlds in which there was a great deal of vice as long as there was also a great deal of unhappiness, and surely such "worlds would clearly be much worse than worlds in which everyone had slightly less or slightly more happiness than they deserved." Here Parfit is clearly attributing purely consequentialist reasoning to Kant, and this might be questioned. However, he is on safer ground when he says that "claims about desert," specifically negative claims, "cannot be plausibly derived from, or claimed to be supported by, Kant's other formulas," and that "Nor does Kant try to support these claims in these ways." Further, he suggests, "Kant came close to seeing that" (Parfit 2011, vol. 1, p. 257). His argument for that, in the next section, is essentially that Kant is a

---

[23] Parfit's brief appendix G, "Kant's Claims about the Good (Parfit 2011, vol. 2, pp. 272–7, discusses what he takes to be problems with Kant's attempt to distinguish well-being from the morally good, but does not further address Kant's argument for the *highest* good.

determinist about human choices and actions, at the phenomenal level, and that this is not compatible with holding that those who commit vicious acts *deserve* to be punished. From this Parfit infers, as well as affirming in his own voice, that "We can deserve many things, such as gratitude, praise, and the kind of blame that is merely moral dispraise. But no one could deserve to be less happy.... If Kant had seen that no one could deserve to suffer, or to be less happy, his ideal would still have been a world in which we were all virtuous and happy" (Parfit 2011, vol. 1, p. 272). But Parfit could also have considered that in his own discussions of punishment, although Kant does say that malefactors *deserve* their punishment, he never says that the *purpose* of punishment is to inflict unhappiness on them, or to bring their level of happiness down to the level of their vice. And in his deepest statement about punishment, in the *Lectures on Ethics*, Kant states that "All the punishments of princes and governments are pragmatic," either "*correctivae* ... imposed in order to improve the criminal," or "*exemplares* ... given as an example to others," thus rehabilitative and/or deterrent, "the purpose being either to correct or to present an example to others," and suggests that retributive punishment is none of our business, at least not our collective business (*Moral Philosophy Collins*, 27: 286). In general, Kant's moral philosophy is oriented prospectively, on how we ought to act, and not retrospectively, concerned with judgments about how we have acted. Precisely because our truest motivations are hidden from us, indeed necessarily so because, at least in Kant's view, our choice of fundamental maxims takes place at the noumenal level, that kind of moral judgment and any retribution is best left to God, "who scrutinizes the heart" (*RBMR*, 6: 67). For this reason, inflicting unhappiness on wrong-doers because they deserve it is not a task for human beings and not any part of the highest good that is *humanly* possible, or the complete object of *human* morality. On this point Parfit is on firm Kantian grounds although he does not spell them out.

There is much more that could be said about Parfit's vast work. But at this point we will turn from the attempt to demonstrate the affinity between Kant and utilitarianism or consequentialism to the other main approach to Kant in recent Anglophone, especially American, moral philosophy, the "constructivist" interpretation pioneered and inspired by John Rawls. This movement has assumed the more traditional position that Kant's moral philosophy was strictly opposed to utilitarianism, thus that a contemporary "Kantian ethics" can be a fundamental alternative to utilitarianism.

16

Kantian Constructivism I

Rawls

16.1. Rawls's Kantian Constructivism

"Kantian constructivism" is a term that John Rawls introduced in his 1980 John
Dewey Lectures at Columbia University, published that year in the *Journal of
Philosophy* under the title "Kantian Constructivism in Moral Theory." In spite of
the generality of "moral theory," however, Rawls's brief in these lectures was to
explicate the Kantian character of the argument for the *political* philosophy,
specifically the principles of justice, that he had expounded in his *magnum opus*
of 1971, *A Theory of Justice.* In that work he had already made clear that he
accepted a "Kantian interpretation" of his argument for his two principles of
"justice as fairness." (*TJ*, §40, pp. 221–7). In subsequent work, especially the 1985
paper "Justice as Fairness: Political Not Metaphysical" (Rawls 1985) and then his
1993 book *Political Liberalism,* Rawls argued that citizens' conception of themselves as "free and equal persons," which he had presented as the foundation of
their acceptance of the principles of justice as fairness in the "Kantian
Interpretation" in *A Theory of Justice*, need not and should not be construed as
grounded in a "comprehensive moral view" of a religious or metaphysical nature,
for there would never be unanimity about any such view in a modern, religiously
and philosophically pluralistic democracy. Instead, he argued the principles of
justice could and should be grounded in their self-conception as free and equal
persons that citizens of a democracy could be expected to share regardless of
differences in their comprehensive moral views (and with that he abjured any
ambition of providing principles of justice that would be accepted in *all* possible
societies). In two other texts from the 1980s and 1990s, however, Rawls offered a
"constructivist" interpretation of Kant's own *moral* philosophy (*not*, except for a
few brief allusions, Kant's *political* philosophy), and presented this interpretation
in such a friendly way as to suggest that his own comprehensive *moral* view
was in fact Kantian constructivism. These texts are "Themes in Kant's Moral
Philosophy," presented at a Stanford University Centennial Conference in 1987
and then published in the volume of papers from that conference in 1989 (*TKMP*),
and the ten lectures on Kant in his *Lectures on the History of Moral Philosophy*,
edited by Barbara Herman and published in 2000, but based on notes from the
final version of Rawls's course on the history of moral philosophy delivered, prior

Kant's Impact on Moral Philosophy. Paul Guyer, Oxford University Press. © Paul Guyer 2024.
DOI: 10.1093/oso/9780199592456.003.0017

to his retirement from Harvard, in 1991 (*LHMP*). In these texts Rawls shows how Kant's categorical imperative, as the most general and fundamental moral principle for human beings, which gives rise to the two sets of duties that Kant classifies as the coercively enforceable duties of right and the non-coercively enforceable ethical duties, including the specific duties of virtue to promote one's own perfection and the happiness of others, could be itself be derived from the conception of oneself and others as free and equal persons. After a brief review of Rawls's derivation of the principles of justice and fairness from the self-conception of free and equal persons in *A Theory of Justice* and "Kantian Constructivism," my primary focus in this chapter will be on Rawls's reconstruction of Kant's moral philosophy under the aegis of "Kantian constructivism," with an eye to both what he accepts from Kant and what he rejects in this reconstruction. Both what he accepts from Kant and what he rejects presumably reflect Rawls's own comprehensive moral view.

In both "Kantian Constructivism" as a theory of justice and Kantian constructivism as a comprehensive moral view, Rawls makes it clear that the term "constructivism" applies to the derivation of political or more generally moral principles *from* the conception of free and equal persons, *not* to the conception of free and equal persons itself as the starting-point of political philosophy or moral philosophy generally. Many of Rawls's students, however, from his earliest students at Harvard such as Thomas Nagel, Thomas Scanlon, and Onora O'Neill to later students such as Christine Korsgaard and Adrian Piper, attempted to develop "Kantian" moral philosophies that were to be constructivist all the way down, that is, which were *not* to start from an overtly *moral* concept such as that of free and equal persons, but from an even more minimal concept, such as the concept of a person as such or of rationality, or practical rationality, as such, or, in O'Neill's case, just from the concept of *multiple* persons who have to reason together.[1] Such starting-points could be considered metaphysical or logical, although to be sure not religious. In particular, we can see Nagel (who published *The Possibility of Altruism*, based on his Harvard dissertation, in 1970, the year before *A Theory of Justice*) as well as Korsgaard as attempting to derive morality from a metaphysical but not moral conception of persons as such, while O'Neill (who published *Acting on Principle*, based on her dissertation, in 1975, thus after *A Theory of Justice* but well before those texts of Rawls directly devoted to Kant), Scanlon, and Piper can be seen as attempting to derive morality from a non-metaphysical conception of

---

[1] Sharon Street has made a similar distinction between "restricted constructivist views" and "unrestricted or metaethical constructivist views." The former are intended to give an account of the normative force of some particular principle or principles "*within* substantive normative ethics," the latter "seek to give an account of what it is for *any* normative claim to be true." Street classifies Rawls's theory of justice without qualification in the former category, thus in any of its versions it is according to her only a restricted constructivism, presupposing some non-constructivist foundation. See Street 2010, pp. 367–9. For O'Neill's approach, see O'Neill 2003, esp. pp. 357–61, and O'Neill 2015a.

rationality, or perhaps better *reasoning,* as such. I will discuss the views of most of these philosophers in the following, final chapter. Throughout this discussion, my sympathy will be with Rawls himself, that is, with the view that while Kant's own *derivation* of duties can be usefully characterized as constructivist, and that there is much to be said for such an approach to the derivation of duties, this derivation has to begin with a moral conception of persons, not a purely metaphysical one or a purely logical conception of reasoning. I will argue that this is particularly clear in the attempt of O'Neill to derive morality from a model of reasoning: it works only because the model of reasoning at issue is itself subject to moral constraints from the outset. In words borrowed from Anthony Simon Laden, these constructions from the character of reasoning itself work only because, like Rawls's own versions of constructivism, they are ways "of doing moral and political philosophy that [are] moral all the way down,"[2] not built upon normatively neutral, metaphysical foundations.

This is not the place for an extensive discussion of Rawls's political philosophy or of the relations between that and Kant's *political* philosophy.[3] My concern will be Rawls's presentation of his theory of justice in the guise of "Kantian constructivism" and then his "constructivist" interpretation of Kant's own *moral* philosophy, which I take it he does endorse, as reconstructed, as his own comprehensive moral view, even if this is not supposed to be required as the necessary foundation of his Kantian constructivism in political philosophy. Rawls might make Kant's *political* philosophy seem prominent in his own approach to the subject when he states very early in *A Theory of Justice* that "The Main Idea of the Theory of Justice" is "to present a conception of justice which generalizes and carries to a higher level of abstraction the familiar theory of the social contract as found, say, in Locke, Rousseau, and Kant." "In order to do this," he continues,

> we are not to think of the original contract as one to enter a particular society or to set up a particular form of government. Rather, the guiding idea is that the principles of justice for the basic structure of society are the object of the original agreement. They are the principles that free and rational persons concerned to further their own interests would accept in an initial position of equality as defining the fundamental terms of their association. These principles are to regulate all

---

[2] Laden 2014, p. 65.

[3] For my discussions of Rawls's political philosophy and its relation to Kant's own, see Guyer 1997, Guyer 1998a, Guyer 2014b, and Guyer 2018a. Discussions of Rawls's political philosophy in its own right are far too numerous to list here, but Freeman 2007 is an indispensable starting-point. See also Maffettone 2011 and Taylor 2011, as well as the collections Freeman 2003, Mandle and Reidy 2014, and Brooks and Nussbaum 2015. Two books by political theorists on the development of *A Theory of Justice* and more broadly of the development of Rawls's views in post-World War II political thought are Gališanka 2019 and Forrester 2019, respectively. Howard Williams will discuss the legacy of Kant's political philosophy up through Rawls in his volume in the present series.

further agreements; they specify the kinds of social cooperation that can be entered into and the forms of government that can be established. This way of regarding the principles of justice I shall call justice as fairness.   (*TJ*, p. 10)

This passage introduces one key aspect of the extended argument for two principles of justice that Rawls is about to launch, but also leaves one key aspect unmentioned. The passage makes clear that Rawls's idea of the social contract is hypothetical: a government does not derive its legitimacy from an actual agreement made and renewed in real time by real people,[4] but from its satisfaction of the general principles of justice that *would* be agreed to by free and rational, that is, self-interested but hypothetical persons in a hypothetical "original position" of equality. In this position, as the argument is developed, their equality would be modeled or operationalized by a "veil of ignorance" that would deprive them of information about their specific resources and needs, so that even out of mere self-interest they would agree to the principles that would best advantage anyone, even those who, when the veil was lifted, might turn out to be the most needy and least advantaged. This is because for all that the parties know behind the veil of ignorance, any of them could be in that position and find herself in it once the veil is lifted, so everyone should, as a matter of pure self-interest, agree to such principles, on what Rawls calls the "maximin" principle of rationality, that is, the principle of maximizing the worst possible outcome for oneself (*TJ*, §26, pp. 130–9). Rawls's argument is then that the principles that would be agreed to under such conditions—that is to say, in such a thought-experiment—would be his two principles of justice, namely, in the form in which Rawls first introduces them,

First: each person is to have an equal right to the most extensive scheme of equal basic liberties compatible with a similar scheme of liberties for others,

and,

Second: social and economic inequalities are to be arranged so that they are both (a) reasonably expected to be to everyone's advantage, and (b) attached to positions and offices open to all.   (*TJ*, §11, p. 53)

Rawls spells out the concept of basic liberties employed in the first principle by means of a list of more specific civil and political liberties or rights, including the rights to vote and hold office, freedom of speech and assembly, liberty of conscience and freedom of thought, freedom of the person, and the right to hold personal property. "The second principle applies ... to the distribution of income

---

[4] For a view of this sort, at least of the American constitutional polity, see Tuck 2016.

and wealth and to the design of organizations that make use of differences in authority and responsibility" (p. 53). The two principles are "lexically" ordered, as Rawls says, so satisfaction of the first principle is the highest priority of a just society, and the application of the second principle is to be limited by the requirements of the first; satisfaction of the first principle is never traded off for increased satisfaction of the second. Rawls interprets the second principle as the "difference principle," that is, the principle that only those inequalities are to be permitted that would most benefit the *least* well-off, or make the most difference to them, or, as it can also be put, inequalities will be permitted only when any alternative distribution of resources would actually make the least well-off even worse off. Or, "an equal distribution is to be preferred" unless there is an unequal distribution that makes "both persons... (limiting ourselves to the two-person case for simplicity)" or all parties to the agreement about the basic structure of society in the original position "better off." (*TJ*, §13, pp. 65–6). A good deal of the argumentation of part I of *A Theory of Justice* is fairly technical argument that this is indeed what rational persons would prefer under the veil of ignorance, addressed to the large body of economists and social scientists who are constitutionally disposed, we might say, to utilitarianism.[5]

However, the emphasis on "free and rational," that is to say, self-interested bargainers, in Rawls's opening statement, can be misleading, and indeed did mislead some critics, who asked why would such persons agree to bargain under a veil of ignorance that is not present in real life? The answer, as Rawls makes clear in the following pages, is that the design of the constraints on the bargaining that is to take place among the hypothetical persons in the original position, summed up by the idea of the veil of ignorance, itself derives from the *moral* constraints on their choice of political principles or principles of justice that *are* accepted by *real* people, who in Rawls's terminology are "reasonable" and not just "rational" or self-interested. Rawls first emphasizes the hypothetical rather than historical nature of the agreement reached in the original position as a social contract: "The original position is not, of course, thought of as an actual historical state of affairs, much less as a primitive condition of culture. It is understood as a purely hypothetical situation characterized so as to lead to a certain conception of justice." He then explains what he means by the veil of ignorance that is supposed to ensure fairness in this bargaining situation: "Among the essential features of this situation is that no one knows his place in society, his class position or social status, nor does any one know his fortune in the distribution of natural asserts and abilities, his intelligence, strength, and the like... their conceptions of the good or their special psychological propensities." That is, no one knows what particular kind of life she would like to lead or what her material resources and psychological

5 See Laden 2014, p. 67.

strengths and weaknesses actually are. All of this "ensures that no one is advantaged or disadvantaged in the choice of principles by the outcome of natural chance or the contingency of social circumstances." Thus, "Since all are similarly situated and no one is able to design principles to favor his particular condition, the principles of justice are the result of a fair agreement or bargain" (*TJ*, §3, p. 11). However, what takes some more pages to emerge is that the reason why *real* people should and would actually accept the principles of justice that emerge from this thought-experiment is that real people have a sense of justice or fairness; real people are reasonable as well as rational, that is, they are moved by the idea of fairness, by the idea that they are morally equal, as well as by self-interest, indeed they regard fairness as properly constraining self-interest, and thus they are willing to accept the principles that apply their sense of fairness to the basic structure of society or fundamental rules of social interaction and cooperation even at the cost of limiting the satisfaction of their own interests by the two principles. The purely rational, self-interested parties in Rawls's original position are hypothetical; the reason why real people accept the principles that emerge from the original position is that they are reasonable, or moral, as well as rational.

> One should not be misled, then, by the somewhat unusual conditions which characterize the original position. The idea here is simply to make vivid to ourselves the restrictions that it seems reasonable to impose on arguments for the principles of justice, and therefore on these principles themselves. Thus it seems reasonable and generally acceptable that no one should be advantaged or disadvantaged by natural fortune or social circumstances in the choice of principles.   (*TJ*, §4, p. 16)

Again,

> It seems reasonable to suppose that the parties in the original position are equal. That is, all have the same rights in the procedure for choosing principles; each can make proposals, submit reasons for their acceptance, and so on. Obviously the purpose of these conditions is to represent equality between human beings as moral persons, as creatures having a conception of their good and capable of a sense of justice.   (*TJ*, §4, p. 17)

The reason why *we* should and would accept the results of the principles agreed to in the hypothetical original position is that *we are such moral persons*, each having a conception of our own good but also each having a sense of justice.

Rawls will frequently refer to these two abilities, our ability to form (and revise) a conception of our own good and our sense of justice, as the two "moral powers" of human beings. In Kant's own terminology in *Religion within the Boundaries of*

Mere Reason,[6] these would be the human predispositions to rationality or human-ity on the one hand, the ability to set our own ends, and morality or personality on the other hand, the ability to be moved by the moral law not only when it is consistent with our self-interest but even when it is not (*RBMR*, 6: 26–7). For Kant, our fundamental choice in life is whether we will put personality or morality ahead of self-interest or mere rationality, or vice versa, that is, "*which of the two [one] makes the condition of the other*" (*RBMR*, 6: 35–6). Rawls seems to assume that at least in the choice of principles of justice for the basic structure of society, human beings are disposed to rank being reasonable over being rational, being moral over being merely self-interested. *Within* the thought-experiment of the original position, the hypothetical bargainers representing us are supposed to be moved only by rational self-interest, but Rawls sets the thought-experiment up the way that he does because he supposed that we real people are reasonable as well as rational, and indeed rank being reasonable even more highly than being rational. Rawls's distinction between the moral reasoning of real people and the self-interested reasoning of the hypothetical figures within the original position can be taken to be his version of the distinction between the moral principle of universalization and the application of consequentialist reasoning subsequent to the application of that principle which I have proposed in defense of Kant, for example from Schopenhauer's objection that Kant's reasoning is just consequen-tialist. To be sure, while Kant supposed that real people are always aware of the moral law and moved by it to some degree, he also recognized that they can, indeed often do, subordinate morality to self-interest (this is what Kant calls "radical evil"; *RBMR*, 6: 32–9); and Rawls does not assume any more than Kant did that real people will always act on the principles of justice without the prod of coercion through the judicial and penal powers of government, or even with them.

Rawls has an elaborate account of his methodology, turning on the idea that the principles of justice as he formulates and refine them represent a "reflective equilibrium" between our basic moral beliefs or "intuitions" and the detailed reasoning about equal liberty and advantage that takes place in the original position.[7] Rawls's methodology is thus grounded in empiricism, while in the *Critique of Practical Reason* Kant proposes to uncover the fundamental principle of morality by a priori cognition of the "fact of reason" *CPracR*, 5: 30). Nevertheless, just as Kant claims that with his formulation of the fundamental principle of morality as the categorical imperative he is only articulating the

---

[6] The *Religion* does not figure prominently in Rawls's presentation of Kant, but see section 16.2.4 below. As far as I can recall Rawls does not notice the similarity between his two "moral powers" and Kant's two natural predispositions to the good.

[7] See *TJ*, §4, pp. 15–19. In his later paper and lectures on Kant, Rawls will replace the language of reflective equilibrium with that of a "coherentist" theory of justification and objectivity rather than truth. For discussion of Rawls's views about methodology, see Scanlon 2003 and Irwin 2009, pp. 897–906.

implicit form of everyday moral reasoning rather than introducing some hitherto unknown innovation,[8] so Rawls claims that with his principles of justice he is only working out the implication for the political sphere of our basic self-conception as free and equal persons.

This is what Rawls then argues in the keystone section of A *Theory of Justice* titled "The Kantian Interpretation of Justice as Fairness." Rawls begins this section with the remark that "there is a Kantian interpretation of the conception of justice" from which follows "the principle of equal liberty and the meaning of the priority of the rights that it defines" even over the second principle of justice, the principle of equal opportunity and the difference principle (*TJ*, §40, p. 221). There are two things to note about this statement. For one, it suggests that there may be a Kantian argument for only the first principle of justice, the principle of equal (maximal) liberty for all. However, since, as I have argued elsewhere, Kant's analysis of the necessary conditions for the rightful acquisition of private property also entails a moral constraint of fairness on such property, a Kantian interpretation of justice as fairness should include some version of Rawls's second principle of justice.[9] Second, Rawls says that there is *a* Kantian interpretation of his argument for the first principle. It has been argued that Rawls was implying that it was possible to interpret his argument in a Kantian way, but also "that it was possible, and even perfectly legitimate, to interpret his theory of justice in another, non-Kantian way," namely as an argument against utilitarianism in the sphere of justice (the original home of utilitarianism in Hume and Bentham, to be sure) on premises that utilitarians would accept.[10] This would suggest that Rawls's 1980 presentation of his theory of justice as "Kantian Constructivism" represented a narrowing of his view from 1971, which would in turn suggest a zig-zag pattern of intellectual development, in which in 1971 Rawls held that it was possible to reach the principles of justice from several different moral theories, then in 1980 held that his position was essentially Kantian, then in 1993, in *Political Liberalism*, held that the principles of justice were the content of an "overlapping consensus" possible among people with different "comprehensive moral views," thus implicitly restoring the indefinite article "a" for the Kantian interpretation of justice as fairness in the 1999 revision of A *Theory of Justice*, perhaps with any further tergiversation prevented only by Rawls's death in 2002! I take the "Kantian Interpretation" to be Rawls's own understanding of the foundation of justice as fairness in 1971, I doubt whether there was any substantive change in his view of the moral foundation of the principles of justice, or at least of the first principle to which he actually refers, between 1971 and 1980, and so I will proceed as if

---

[8] See esp. *G*, section I, 4: 403–4, and *CPracR*, 5: 29, 5: 36, and esp. the footnote at 5: 9: "But who would even want to introduce a new principle of all morality and, as it were, first invent it? Just as if, before him, the world had been ignorant of what duty is or in thoroughgoing error about it."
[9] See again Guyer 1997 and 1998a.   [10] Krasnoff 2014, p. 73.

"Kantian Constructivism" just explicates the thought Rawls had already suggested in §40 of *Theory*. Be that as it may, the more interesting question might be whether Rawls's "political liberalism" really eschews a Kantian foundation in favor of a merely "overlapping consensus" among radically different "comprehensive moral views." My guess is that Rawls's own reconstruction of Kant's moral philosophy without the metaphysical commitments of the postulates of immortality and God and without the noumenal metaphysics of free will in his paper "Themes in Kant's Moral Philosophy" presented in 1987 and then in his lectures on Kant meant that he always regarded those beliefs in immortality and the existence of God as representative of a controversial comprehensive moral view that need not be accepted in a pluralistic democracy and that he himself did not accept, but that he always held to the Kantian interpretation of the principles of justice as a justification that could be shared among people even with different "comprehensive moral views" and thus as a common moral foundation that would be accepted by anyone in a democratic society.[11] But I will come back to that; first, we must consider the Kantian interpretation as presented in 1971 and "Kantian Constructivism" as presented in 1980.

Rawls's claim is that "The original position may be viewed...as a procedural interpretation of Kant's conception of autonomy and the categorical imperative within the framework of an empirical theory"of "the elementary facts about persons and their place in nature"(*TJ*, §40, p. 226). This suggests that at least in *A Theory of Justice* Rawls was prepared to accept a Kantian moral foundation for the principles of justice; the question is whether he ever really gave that up, or only wanted to argue later that the principles could be justified even to those who refused to accept Rawls's own, basically correct Kantianism. Rawls then presents the relevant aspects of Kant's moral theory in three steps that parallel his own reasoning to the principles of justice. "For one thing, he begins with the idea that moral principles are the object of rational choice.... Moral philosophy becomes the study of the conception and outcome of a suitably defined rational decision" (*TJ*, §40, p. 221). Here the emphasis is on a purely rational decision procedure, although employed under suitable conditions. Taken by itself, this would suggest that both Kant's moral theory and Rawls's theory of justice are meant to be grounded on a conception of *rationality* as such, and as we will see some

---

[11] I am thus sympathetic to Irwin's argument that, while *A Theory of Justice* was Rawls's attempt to ground political philosophy in moral philosophy, his later work culminating in *Political Liberalism* was intended as political philosophy only, expounded without its moral foundation but not implying any change in Rawls's moral philosophy. See Irwin 2009, pp. 956–9. In contrast, O'Neill 2003 holds that as Rawls's "work developed he...changed his views of the range of ethical principles that can be constructed, of the justification of [the original position] itself, and of the audiences who can be given reasons to accept OP. Broadly speaking, he [took] an increasingly refined and restricted view of all three" (p. 349), in other words, he addressed his later argument only to those who happened to share the "overlapping consensus" on democratic principles, not all human beings as such. As we will see, O'Neill proposes an unrestricted moral constructivism that addresses all human beings. We will return to the issue between Rawls and O'Neill.

subsequent versions of constructivism, such as that of Onora O'Neill, attempt to derive the fundamental principle of morality from such a basis, that is, a conception of rationality alone. However, Rawls makes it clear that in Kant's view as well as his own, that is only part of the basis for morality or justice: in the sentence that comes between the two just quoted, he adds that for Kant moral principles "define the moral law that men can rationally will to govern their conduct *in an ethical commonwealth*" (emphasis added), and the conception of an ethical commonwealth already includes normative constraints in addition to whatever might be thought to be the constraints inherent in rationality as such, such as the avoidance of contradiction or the "slender basis" that moral principles be "general and universal." (The term "ethical commonwealth" echoes Kant's term "ethical community" in part 3 of Kant's *Religion*, which connotes not just the formal structure of an empire of ends but also a membership of real people actually disposed to support each other in their effort to be moral; *RBMR*, 6: 95–6.) Rather, for Rawls this second requirement, that the concept of rationality is to be applied along with the idea of an ethical commonwealth, has "immediate consequences": "For once we think of moral principles as legislation for a kingdom of ends" (which Rawls is assuming is the same as an ethical commonwealth, although as just suggested for Kant the latter term might include the former but means more) "it is clear that these principles must not only be acceptable to all but public as well." Applying the latter constraint to the design of the original position and the first constraint, of rationality as such, in the form of practical rationality, to the decision-making of the bargaining parties within the original position is what, in Rawls's view, will yield the two principles of justice. But Rawls is also concerned throughout *A Theory of Justice* with the motivation of real people to accept and maintain the principles of justice arrived at through the thought-experiment of bargaining in the original position, and to this end he emphasizes that "Kant supposes that [his] moral legislation is to be agreed to under conditions that characterize men as free and equal rational beings" (*TJ*, §40, p. 221), or that "a person is acting autonomously when the principles of his action are chosen by him as the most adequate possible expression of his nature as a free and equal rational being" (p. 222). Indeed he supposes that for Kant if someone "desires above all else to realize" "his true self" "by expressing it in his actions" "then he will choose to act from principles that manifest his nature as a free and equal rational being" (p. 224). This is the third step—for Kant and Rawls persons are assumed to *want* to express their nature as free and equal persons in their moral and political principles, respectively, and the way they can and must do so is by subscribing to Kant's categorical imperative in the one case or Rawls's principles of justice in the other.[12] Of course, neither Rawls nor Kant (at least, as we saw, by 1792) assumes that this

---

[12] Irwin's fundamental objection to Rawls's "Kantian interpretation" and thus to Rawls's own moral philosophy, which he takes to be expressed in the "Kantian interpretation," is that it is founded on a

desire is always the most effective in any person; otherwise departures from morality or justice would be impossible, which they obviously are not.

In the present section of *A Theory of Justice*, Rawls uses the idea of wanting to *express* one's nature as a free and equal person to respond to Sidgwick's famous objection to Kant's theory of free will.[13] He puts Sidgwick's objection thus:

> [O]n Kant's view the lives of the saint and the scoundrel are equally the outcome of a free choice (on the part of the noumenal self) and equally the subject of causal laws (as a phenomenal self). [But] Kant never explains why the scoundrel does not express in a bad life his characteristic and freely chosen selfhood in the same way that a saint expresses his characteristic and freely chosen selfhood in a good one.   (*TJ*, §40, p. 224)

The objection is that if a phenomenal life fully expresses an agent's noumenal choice of fundamental maxim, as according to Kant it must (*CPracR*, 5: 99–100), then either the noumenal self, as fully rational, can choose as its fundamental maxim only the moral law, in which case no one could be a phenomenal scoundrel at all, or else, as fully free, the noumenal self can choose either the maxim of morality or that of self-love, in which case a phenomenal scoundrel expresses his noumenal choice and character as fully as a phenomenal saint does. Rawls's way out of this dilemma is to hold that noumenal selves are free but have "a desire to express their nature as rational and equal members of the intelligible realm" in the phenomenal realm, which they do by deciding "which principles when consciously followed and acted upon in everyday life will best manifest this freedom in their community, most fully reveal their independence from natural contingencies and social accident"—in other words, they will reason as in the original position—*but*, since this is a *desire*, real people apparently do not necessarily *act* upon it. This is neither of the two alternatives that Kant's premises in the *Groundwork* and *Critique of Practical Reason* allow, although Kant himself does sometimes hint at such a position, as when he represents pure reason and our sensible nature as contending forces (e.g., *G*, 4: 454). And it may be what Kant's ultimate distinction between *Wille* and *Willkühr*, between pure reason as the source of the moral law and our freedom to choose whether or not to make the moral law our fundamental maxim, amounts to, although for Kant that must still be a distinction at the noumenal level in order to ensure complete freedom for *Willkühr* to decide one way or the other. Rawls certainly does not commit himself to that: although he is willing to let Kant's ascription of the moral law, i.e., *Wille*, to

---

contingent *desire* to express our nature as free and equal beings rather than upon something necessary, as he takes to be the case in Aristotelian naturalism or the idealist morality of Bradley and Green. See Irwin 2009, pp. 945–8, 953–6, 960–1.

[13] See Chapter 9 above.

a noumenal self pass, he does not defend Kant's noumenal account of choice or *Willkühr*, thus does not assert our complete freedom to choose morality over immorality regardless of any prior history. Since Kant's assurance on this matter is indefensible, Rawls's position, even if partly implicit, seems to be only one that is philosophically plausible.

In his later writings and lectures on Kant Rawls locates human freedom in freedom of *reasoning* without even asking whether humans are always free to make their reasoning efficacious in their actions. But for now I want to turn to a different feature of Rawls's "Kantian interpretation." He supposes that his argument "adds the feature that the principles chosen are to apply to the basic structure of society" and that the expression of the nature of people "as free and equal rational beings" through his principles of justice is "subject to the general conditions of human life" are *differences* between his argument for the principles of justice from the original position and Kant's moral theory. In particular, although I did not previously mention this point, he takes the reasoning in the original position to assume that all parties need and want certain "primary goods," "things that it is rational to want whatever else one wants," thus things that anyone will want whatever their particular position in society turns out to be when the veil of ignorance is lifted, that is, in real life—"social goods" such "rights, liberties, and opportunities," and some level of "income and wealth," as well as "natural goods" that are not created by society but certainly influenced by it, "such as health and vigor, intelligence and imagination." (*TJ*, §11, p. 54). Terence Irwin initially interprets the Rawlsian primary goods to be necessary for the *effective realization* of individuals' conceptions of the good, whatever those might turn out to be, while I would argue that, since agents cannot rationally set ends for which they do not believe themselves to have adequate means, primary goods are necessary to maximize the possibility of free choice of conceptions of the good in the first place.[14] Either way, Rawls takes it to be a matter of empirically known fact that these resources are necessary for the realization of conceptions of the good in actual human life but are also limited in the actual circumstances of human life, and he takes it that such empirical facts can play no role in Kant's moral theory. He must be supposing that Kant's moral theory is intended to be entirely a priori.

But this is false. Kant's position in the *Metaphysics of Morals* is unequivocally that the *fundamental principle* of morality must be and is known a priori to be valid for all rational beings, but that the derivation of the actual duties of right and ethics of human beings very much depends on the application of this fundamental principle to the particular nature and circumstances of actual human life, which

---

[14] See Irwin 2009, p. 936. Irwin comes closer to my position when he writes that according to the 2nd edition of *A Theory of Justice*, "We recognize that the primary goods are resources for affirming our freedom and equality in the choice of ways of life" (p. 951). My way of putting this point is that for Kant a moral distribution of means is one that makes possible the maximal but still equal freedom of all to set their own ends.

can be known only empirically. As I have repeatedly stressed, Kant states that "a metaphysics of morals cannot dispense with principles of application, and we shall often have to take as our object the particular *nature* of human beings, which is cognized only by experience, in order to *show* in it what can be inferred from universal moral principles. But this will in no way detract from the purity of these principles" (*MM*, Introduction, 6: 217). The empirically known facts about human life include that we are embodied, need to use external objects to sustain our lives and realize our goals, and all live on the finite surface of a globe any point of which can be reached from any other, so that competition for land and all the resources that depend on it is always possible, and also that we all have the potential for various intellectual and physical as well as moral capabilities, but that these need to be cultivated and even then we may need assistance from each other in order to realize our goals. The application of the fundamental principle of morality in light of the former facts is what gives rise to the duties of justice, and the application of that principle in light of the latter facts is what gives rise to ethical duties, including the duties of virtue to promote our own perfection and the happiness of others. Contrary to Rawls, there is no daylight between himself and Kant on the necessity of some empirical assumptions for the application of the fundamental principle of morality, specifically for the derivation of duties of right, in Kant's terms, or principles of justice, in Rawls's. Rawls surely could have made that clear had he made more use of Kant's Doctrine of Right than he ever did.

That being said, let us now turn from the "Kantian interpretation" of *A Theory of Justice* to Rawls's designation of his approach to political philosophy as "Kantian Constructivism." The Dewey lectures given under that name in 1980 were preceded by a paper titled "A Kantian Conception of Equality" in 1975. Here Rawls premises that "any conception of justice expresses a conception of the person, of the relations between persons, and of the general structure and ends of social cooperation" (Rawls 1975, p. 254). He then states that a "Kantian conception of equality" presupposes that "a well-ordered society" is to be "effectively regulated by a public conception of justice," that is, one accepted by all its members and known by each to be accepted by all, and that "the members of a well-ordered society are, and view themselves, as free and equal moral persons." The definition of free and equal moral persons is that upon reaching the age of reason (unspecified), (i) "each has, and views the others as having, a realized sense of justice," that (ii) "each have, and view themselves as having, a right to equal respect and consideration in determining the principles by which the basic arrangements of their society are to be regulated," and (iii), "Finally, we express their being free by stipulating that they each have, and view themselves as having, fundamental aims and higher-order interests (a conception of their good," which they are free to pursue as they see best within the limits following from (i) and (ii). (i) and (ii) define the "moral power" that Rawls typically refers to as the sense of justice, and (iii) the power that he defines, as he does here, as being able to form one's own conception of one's good, in my own terminology, to set their own ends. He further adds that free and equal persons not only "conceive of themselves as capable of revising and altering [their] final ends" but also "give priority to preserving their liberty in this regard" (Rawls 1975, p. 255, see also p. 260). Introducing a theme that he will increasingly emphasize in subsequent writings, but that those who have studied Rawls's biography have established was a central part of his thought even since college, and certainly since his return from combat in the Pacific in World War II, he modestly remarks that "It is perhaps useful to observe that the notion of a well-ordered society is an extension of the idea of religious toleration" (Rawls 1975, p. 256).[15] After explaining how free and equal persons in a well-ordered society would choose the two principles of justice, and how the placeholder of "equal basic liberties" in the first principle is to be filled in by "a list of liberties" including "freedom of thought and liberty of conscience, freedom of the person and political liberty" (p. 259), while the conception of advantage employed in the second principle, the difference principle that only those inequalities that most improve the situation of the least advantaged are just, has to be spelled out with a conception of "social primary goods" (p. 260). Rawls explains what makes this conception of justice Kantian.

Rawls highlights two points: first, that "the notion of a well-ordered society" can be regarded "as an interpretation of the idea of a kingdom of ends[16] thought of as a human society under circumstances of justice," and second, that there is room in his account of justice for an application of Kant's distinction between "positive and negative freedom" (Rawls 1975, p. 264). Kant himself defined the empire of ends as "a whole of all ends in systematic connection (a whole both of rational beings as ends in themselves and of the ends of his own that each may set himself)" (G, 4: 433); Rawls does not spell out the comparison between his own conception of a well-ordered society and Kant's idea of the empire of ends, but it seems natural to read his conception of persons pursuing their own conceptions of the good within the limits determined by the principles of justice deriving from their sense of justice as his equivalent for Kant's idea of rational beings setting

---

[15] See Freeman 2007, pp. 8–12, and Reidy 2014.

[16] This is how Rawls translates Kant's expressions *Reich der Zwecke* in this essay. Later he will translate it as "realm of ends." The latter might seem preferable, because it does not connote that there is a single ruler of a systematic connection of free and equal persons; no doubt in early, Norman-influenced English, "realm" did mean the domain of a king, as in modern French *royaume*, but in contemporary English it does not so obviously have that connotation. Thus H. J. Paton preferred "realm" to "kingdom" (Paton 1947, p. 188). However, in political and historical contexts *Reich* is usually translated as "empire," of course, and I have come to prefer this translation on the ground that an empire is a union of sovereignties, with an emperor as overlord but as the lord over units that do not lose all their own sovereignty. In Kant's conception of the empire of ends, individual persons are autonomous agents with only the moral law itself over them all, although apart from the moral law itself only "a completely independent being, without needs and with unlimited resources adequate to his will," i.e., God, could be thought of as an actual sovereign for the empire of ends. But Kant increasingly comes to conceive of God as an "idea," not a "substance" (e.g., *OP*, 21: 32–7).

ends of their own within the limits set by their regard for all such beings as ends in themselves. In his subsequent discussions of the empire of ends, Rawls will typically stress that it is a legislative framework more than he will stress that individuals may pursue their own ends within the limits of that framework (that is, their permissible ends), indeed that individuals should assist each other in their pursuits of their ends (although even then the empire of ends on Kant's account does not quite amount to the ethical community, where individuals assist each other in the pursuit of virtue, not just of freely set particular and permissible ends); but his conception of the empire of ends as an image of a well-regulated society for persons with the two moral powers ought to make the latter seem as important as the former.

Rawls's second point is that Kant's distinction between negative and positive freedom applies to his own conception of justice. In fact, Kant does not speak of negative and positive freedoms, but of negative and positive *conceptions* of freedom. The negative conception of freedom is that of the freedom of the determination of the will from "alien causes," the positive conception is that of the determination of the will by a law that it gives itself, but in fact these two conceptions are co-extensive: the will can achieve freedom from determination by alien causes only by determining itself in accordance with a law that it gives itself, namely the moral law (*G*, 4: 446–7). Still, Rawls's interpretation can be reconciled with Kant's actual distinction. Rawls equates negative freedom with the limitation on information imposed by the veil of ignorance, and positive freedom with the parties in the original position, thus behind the veil of ignorance, conceiving of themselves "as free and equal moral persons . . . in their adoption of the conception of justice" and applying this conception of themselves and their principles of justice "to the controlling institutional subject," i.e., the basic structure of society or the state (Rawls 1975, p. 265). To be sure, it is actual people who must preserve and promote their freedom, so Rawls's idea can only be that when real people accept the principles of justice that follow from the imposition of the veil of ignorance in the thought-experiment of the original position that liberates them from determining their choice of principles solely by their actual, contingent advantages and disadvantages, thus from what in Kant's terms are "alien causes," factors extraneous to actual people's conception of themselves as free and equal moral persons. It is their self-conception as free and equal persons that requires real people to include of the veil of ignorance in the ground-rules of the original position and to accept the principles at which the hypothetical people in the thought-experiment arrive. Thus, in spite of Rawls's divergence from Kant's terminology, his negative and positive freedoms are also co-extensive: the positive self-conception of free and equal moral persons is what requires them to impose the veil of ignorance on the original position and by that means to liberate themselves from the contingencies of their particular circumstances in their adoption or acceptance of the principles of justice.

In this essay, Rawls did not yet use the expression "Kantian constructivism." That awaited his 1980 Dewey lectures, presented under that title at Columbia University and published in Columbia's *Journal of Philosophy* later that year. Here Rawls explicitly presents "justice as fairness" as a "Kantian variant" of a more general notion of "constructivism," and says that he is doing so in order "to consider certain aspects of the conception of justice as fairness which I have not previously emphasized and to set out more clearly the Kantian roots of that conception" (Rawls 1980, p. 303). He does not suggest that he is introducing any substantive departures from *A Theory of Justice*, and he does suggest that the theory of justice is essentially Kantian, not merely that it might be given *a* Kantian interpretation alongside other possible interpretations. He then says:

> What distinguishes the Kantian form of constructivism is essentially this: it specifies a particular conception of the person as an element in a reasonable procedure of construction, the outcome of which determines the content of the first principles of justice. Expressed another way: this kind of view sets up a certain procedure of construction which answers to certain reasonable requirements, and within this procedure persons characterized as rational agents of construction specify, through their agreements, the first principles of justice....
>
> The leading idea is to establish a suitable connection between a particular conception of the person and first principles of justice, by means of a principle of construction.   (Rawls 1980, p. 304)

There is nothing new in this description of the strategy developed at length in *A Theory of Justice* and summarized in the essay on "A Kantian Conception of Equality" except for the words "constructivism" and "construction" themselves, and Rawls does not unpack the significance of these terms until the last of his three lectures.

There Rawls presents constructivism as a method of ethics overlooked by Henry Sidgwick but to be contrasted to rational intuitionism (although for Sidgwick the term "methods of ethics" refers primarily to the three different normative approaches of intuitionism, rational egoism, and universalistic hedonism, while Rawls's constructivism connotes in the first instance a meta-ethical method, which however has normative implications). The fundamental difference between Sidgwick's and indeed all forms of rational intuitionism, on the one hand, and constructivism, on the other, is that while Sidgwick and other rational intuitionists (where this term now connotes Sidgwick's meta-ethics) start "with the idea of a method of ethics as a method specified by certain first principles," which must be regarded simply as given, by "intuition," constructivism starts with a "conception of the person and the social role of morality as main parts of a moral doctrine" (Rawls 1980, p. 341). Kantian constructivism, which is in fact "the leading historical example of a constructivist doctrine" (p. 342), would then be the variant of constructivism that starts with a Kantian conception of the person. In more detail, rational intuitionism presupposes that "the basic moral concepts of the right and the good ... are not analyzable in terms of nonmoral concepts," and, second, that "first principles of morals (whether one or many), when correctly stated, are self-evident propositions about what kinds of consideration are good grounds for applying ... the ... basic moral concepts" (p. 32), while Kantian constructivism presupposes no self-evident *principles*, but starts from a conception of the person, or from "notions which characterize persons as reasonable and rational and which are incorporated into the way in which, as such persons, they represent to themselves their free and equal moral personality. Put another way, first principles of justice must issue from a conception of the person through a suitable representation of that conception as illustrated by the procedure of construction in justice as fairness" (p. 346)—which is of course nothing but the argument that real reasonable as well as rational persons would accept the principles of justice arrived at in the thought-experiment of the original position with the veil of ignorance, and that the two principles of the greatest possible scheme of equal basic liberties and equality of opportunity plus the difference principle are those principles. Constructivism means that basic principles such as the principles of justice are not "self-evident" and "intuited," but are reached by argument from premises derived from the conception of ourselves as free and equal persons (and then applied in the further construction of the constitution and legislation of particular polities in their particular circumstances). Rawls then continues to argue that the objectivity of the results of construction should not be understood on the model of truth as the correspondence of belief to an independent realm of facts, but on the model of argument by shared rules from a shared starting-point, thus that "objectivity is not given 'by the point of view of the universe,' to use Sidgwick's phrase," but "is to be understood by reference to a suitably constructed social point of view, an example of which is the framework provided by the procedure of the original position" (p. 356). For Rawls moral objectivity does not require an ontology of moral facts other than what reasonable and rational people think.

It should be obvious that, although constructivism does not begin from self-evident, intuited moral principles, neither does it begin with a morally neutral conception of the person. It begins with a morally laden conception of the person, which is assumed to be shared among normal people but is not itself constructed or derived from anything else. For Rawls, constructivism merely makes clear what is implicit in a conception of oneself and others as free and equal persons, with the two moral powers, that is already shared—a moral conception of the person. A "Kantian conception of justice tries to dispel ... conflict between the different understandings of freedom and equality by asking: which traditionally recognized principles of freedom and equality, or which natural variations thereof, would free and equal moral persons themselves agree upon, if they were fairly represented solely as such persons and thought of themselves as citizens living a complete life in an ongoing society?" (Rawls 1980, p. 305). Or, even more fully,

> To justify a Kantian conception within a democratic society is not merely to reason correctly from given premises, or even from publicly shared and mutually recognized premises. The real task is to discover and formulate the deeper bases of agreement which one hopes are embedded in common sense, or even to originate and fashion starting points for common understanding by expressing in a new form the convictions found in the historical tradition by connecting them with a wide range of people's considered convictions: those which stand up to critical reflection.... a Kantian doctrine joins the content of justice with a certain conception of the person; and this conception regards persons as both free and equal, as capable of acting both reasonably and rationally, and therefore as capable of taking part in social cooperation among persons so conceived. In addressing the public culture of a democratic society, Kantian constructivism hopes to invoke a conception of the person implicitly affirmed in that culture, or else one that would prove acceptable to citizens once it was properly presented and explained. (Rawls 1980, p. 306)

By the "content of justice" Rawls means the two principles of justice, the principles of equal basic liberties on the one hand and of equality of opportunity plus the difference principle of the other. By calling these "deeper bases of agreement" he means that they are the basis for the more particular laws and institutions establishing rights and determining the rules for the distribution of resources in particular societies. By arguing that Kantian constructivism "joins the content of justice with a certain conception of the person" he means that these basic principles can be shown to be those that would be accepted by persons who conceive of themselves as both rational, that is, interested in effectively realizing their own conceptions of the good, but also as reasonable, that is, recognizing the equal validity of the claims of all to be able to realize their own conceptions of the good. The two moral powers, the capacity to formulate one's own conception of the good and the sense of justice, which Rawls foregrounds in these lectures (p. 312), correspond to rationality and reasonableness.

Rawls spends the remainder of the first two lectures spelling out the chain of reasoning from this self-conception of free and equal persons to the original position to the two principles of justice, with no significant departure from the argumentation of *A Theory of Justice*, but with special emphasis on the connection between freedom and the two moral powers: one aspect of freedom is that "citizens think of themselves"—that is to say, each thinks of both himself and others—"as self-originating sources of valid claims," and, "as free persons, citizens recognize one another as having the moral power to have a conception of the good" (Rawls 1980, pp. 330-1). Once again, citizens think of themselves and of others as having the two moral powers of rationality and reasonableness. The crucial point in all of this, however, is Rawls's reference to the hope that the deeper bases of agreement are "embedded in common sense" combined with the suggestion that common sense actually consists in "the convictions found in the historical tradition," or the "considered convictions," "those which stand up to critical reflection," of people in a historical tradition. The self-conception of citizens in a democratic culture as free and equal moral persons is itself an historical artifact, not a necessary truth of some kind that can be known entirely a priori. On this point, there is of course a significant difference between Rawls and Kant: it is important to Kant to show that the categorical imperative as he clarifies it is implicit in "common rational moral cognition" (*G*, 4: 393, 404), but he also insists that the categorical imperative is synthetic a priori, necessarily valid for all human beings, indeed all rational beings, not just those in a particular culture at a particular historical moment. The political content of "Kantian Constructivism" does not differ from that of *A Theory of Justice* on the one hand or of *Political Liberalism* on the other, although the later work presents this content not as the expression of a trans-cultural human desire to express our nature as free and equal beings but only as an "overlapping consensus" that can be reached in the "political culture of a democratic society...always marked by a diversity of opposing and irreconcilable religious, philosophical, and moral doctrines" (Rawls 1993, pp. 3–4).

Thus the question how limited, how culturally relative, the conception of the self as a free and equal moral person among others really is becomes the fundamental question for Rawls's political philosophy. One might argue that such a self-conception is really widespread among human beings, tacitly if not explicitly accepted by anyone who does not believe that slavery is morally acceptable or that their god orders them to slay anyone who does not worship the same way they do. That is too broad a question to tackle here. Instead, I will suggest only that Rawls does attempt to bring Kant's view closer to his own in his subsequent treatment of Kant by emphasizing Kant's own replacement of the metaphysical argument of *Groundwork* III with the "fact of reason" argument of the *Critique of Practical Reason*, which Rawls interprets along lines at least somewhat more favorable to his own, supposedly historically situated conception of the democratic self. So let us turn now to Rawls's interpretation of Kant himself rather than his Kantian interpretation of his own theory of justice, and see whether this stratagem will work.

16.2. Rawls's Interpretation of Kant

Rawls featured Kant in his course on the history of moral philosophy throughout his years at Harvard. Barbara Herman's edition of Rawls's *Lectures on the History of Moral Philosophy* was based on the final iteration of these lectures, and the ten lectures on Kant comprise a monograph of 180 pages within this book, which also includes five lectures on Hume and two each on Leibniz and Hegel. (Several lectures on the moral philosophy of Joseph Butler were later included in Samuel Freeman's edition of Rawls's *Lectures on the History of Political Philosophy*, which is striking for its omission of any lectures on Kant's own political philosophy; see Rawls 2007.)

Much of what Rawls had to say about Kant had already been made public, more compactly, in the Stanford lecture "Themes in Kant's Moral Philosophy" published in 1989. In these materials Rawls presents a constructivist interpretation of Kant's *moral* philosophy, rather than a constructivist *political* philosophy beginning from a Kantian, moral conception of the self, and this approach can be considered to have launched the constructivist approach to moral philosophy in general of Onora O'Neill, Christine Korsgaard, and others that will be discussed in the next chapter. But even when he is expounding Kantian constructivism as a general moral rather than merely political philosophy, Rawls stresses that the "relatively complex conception of the person [that] plays a central role in specifying the content of [Kant's] moral view" is not itself constructed out of anything more elementary (Rawls 1989, p. 513). What is constructed by Kant, according to Rawls, is "the *content* of the doctrine," that is, "the totality of particular categorical imperatives (general precepts) . . . that pass the test of the" categorical imperative, or "CI-procedure" as Rawls calls it (pp. 513–14). The conception of the self that is the basis of Kant's constructivist moral theory is not itself constructed in any way, nor is the categorical imperative or CI-procedure; that "is simply *laid out*"—the basis of the construction is "the conception of free and equal persons as reasonable and rational, a conception that is *mirrored* in the [CI-]procedure" (p. 514).[17] The construction lies solely in the derivation of particular moral precepts—in Kant's own language, the juridical and ethical duties enumerated in the *Metaphysics of Morals*—through the application of the categorical imperative to certain actual and empirically known features of the human condition: "The CI-procedure adapts the categorical imperative to our circumstances by taking into account the normal conditions of human life and our situation as finite beings with needs in the order of nature" (p. 498). As previously noted, in the "Kantian interpretation" section of *A Theory of Justice* Rawls had treated the recognition that the categorical imperative needs to be applied to our actual circumstances in the order of nature as distinguishing his own approach in political philosophy from Kant's approach in moral philosophy generally, but such an application is exactly what

---

[17] Reath 2022 makes a useful distinction between construction of the "content" of a moral philosophy and a constructivist approach to its "authority," pp. 52, 58–64. Reath argues that Rawls is a constructivist about the content of morality, i.e., the derivation of more particular duties from the categorical imperative, but a "constituvist" about its authority, i.e., that he derives the latter from an analysis of the conditions of the possibility of agency itself. I do not think the Rawlsian assertions just quoted fit very well with the second part of Reath's interpretation.

Kant provides in the *Metaphysics of Morals*, and had always intended as the key move in the transition to such a metaphysics from its "groundwork" or foundation, and Rawls now seems to recognize that. He makes much more use of the *Metaphysics of Morals* than he did earlier, either in *A Theory of Justice* or "Kantian Constructivism," although still not the Doctrine of Right, only the Doctrine of Virtue (e.g., pp. 505, 507, 515).[18] By locating Kant's constructivism in his derivation of specific duties or moral precepts from the conception of the self and its mirroring CI-procedure to actual facts about the conditions of human life, Rawls makes it clear that he does not see Kantian constructivism as going "all the way down" to some non-moral conception of rationality or personality. As we will see in the following chapter, that does not remain true in other versions of Kantian constructivism in moral theory.

We can focus on the following topics in Rawls's interpretation of Kant: (1) his interpretation of the categorical imperative, or the "CI-procedure"; (2) his interpretation of the moral conception of the self that is the starting-point for the construction in terms of Kant's concept of humanity; (3) his account of "The Sequence of Six Conceptions of the Good" culminating in Kant's conception of the highest good, but specifically the highest good that could be attained by unaided human effort; (4) his account of freedom as freedom in *reasoning*, not libertarian freedom of the *will*; and (5) his interpretation of the "fact of reason" as a coherentist model of justification or "authentication" for the moral law. In his treatment of topics (3), (4), and (5), we will see that Rawls takes pains not merely to avoid appeals to metaphysics and theology, but to argue that Kant himself really avoided them; this would suggest that in Rawls's view Kant's moral philosophy is not a controversial or controvertible comprehensive moral view, for such is defined precisely by including or relying upon metaphysical and/or theological premises. Thus Kant's moral philosophy as Rawls interprets it could be considered as a generally acceptable basis for a theory of justice, not merely the product of an overlapping consensus within an already democratic culture. Rawls does not explicitly say this, or explicitly endorse Kant's moral philosophy as his own, but the much greater attention that he pays to Kant's moral philosophy than to any other suggests that he was himself deeply attracted to it.

16.2.1. The CI-Procedure

Rawls's interpretation of the first formulation of the categorical imperative, its requirement that we act only on maxims that we could also will to be universally

---

[18] Lloyd 2014 lauds Rawls's sympathetic approach to the "greats" of the history of political philosophy but does not note than he did not include Kant's own political philosophy in that category.

accepted, is straightforward and similar to others. Indeed, apart from terminology, it is the same as that offered by Onora O'Neill in her 1975 book *Acting on Principle*, published a dozen years before Rawls went public with his interpretation at Stanford. (O'Neill 2013 is a reprint of the original book with a new introduction.) Since O'Neill's book originated as a 1968 Ph.D. dissertation written under Rawls's supervision, in the absence of a direct statement by either it is hard to know whether O'Neill learned this approach from Rawls or Rawls from O'Neill. It might be best to refer to it as the Rawls-O'Neill model of the categorical imperative, or more precisely of its first formulation: the model draws on the first version of the first formulation of the categorical imperative, ordinarily referred to as the Formula of Universal Law, but also on its second version, usually referred to as the Formula of the Law of Nature—"*Act as if the maxim of your action were to become by your will a* **universal law of nature**" (*G*, 4: 421)—which is in turn associated with what Kant calls in the *Critique of Practical Reason* the "Typic of Pure Practical Judgment"—"ask yourself whether, if the action you propose were to take place by a law of the nature of which you yourself were a part, you could indeed regard it as possible through your will" (*CPracR*, 5: 69). Thus Rawls writes that the CI-procedure

> helps to determine the content of the moral law as it applies to us as reasonable and rational persons endowed with conscience and moral sensibility, and affected by, but not determined by, our natural desires and inclinations.... The CI-procedure adapts the categorical imperative to our circumstances by taking into account the normal conditions of human life and our situation as finite beings with needs in the order of nature.   (Rawls 1989, p. 498)

In introducing this CI-procedure, Rawls takes it for granted that it should be based upon the first formulation of the categorical imperative in the *Groundwork*, and does not comment upon this assumption. In the lectures, he cites Kant's own argument "that it is better when making a moral judgment to proceed always in accordance with the strict method and [to] take as our basis the universal formula of the categorical imperative" (*G* 4: 436–7, cited by Rawls at *LHMP*, p. 182). This remark draws no distinction between the formula of Universal Law on the one hand and the Formula of the Law of Nature and the Typic of Pure Practical Judgment on the other, thus it seems.best to understand the Rawls-O'Neill model as a model of the first formulation of the categorical imperative loosely understood.

Be that as it may, the Rawls-O'Neill model of the CI-procedure, in Rawls's version, consists of the following four steps:

(i) The agent proposes a maxim of action to herself, in the form "I am to do X in circumstances C in order to bring about Y," where X is an action, C the circumstances of the proposed action, and Y the state of affairs that is the end or goal of the proposed action.

(ii) The agent then generalizes or universalizes the maxim, thus considers the general "precept" "Everyone is to do X in circumstances C in order to bring about Y."

(iii) "At the third step we are to transform [the universalized maxim formulated] at [ii] into a law of nature, [namely]: Everyone always does X in circumstances C in order to bring about Y (as if by a law of nature."

(iv) At the fourth step, according to Rawls the "most complicated," "We are to adjoin the law of nature at step [iii] to the existing laws of nature (as these are understood by us) and then calculate as best we can what the order of nature would be once the effects of the newly adjoined law of nature have had a chance to work themselves out" (Rawls 1989, pp. 499–500, cf. *LHMP*, pp. 168–9),

and then, of course, although Rawls does not include this as part of the fourth step, consider whether once the effects of the generalization of the maxim "have worked themselves out" in what Rawls calls the "perturbed social world" of step (iv) we could possibly act in the way proposed at (i) or, even if we can, whether we can still rationally will to act in that way. That is, the CI-procedure tests whether one's maxim at step (i) can be acted upon, possibly or rationally, in the world described at step (iv); that is the test whether one's maxim is consistent with its own universalization. O'Neill calls the realization at step (iii) of the "precept" introduced at Rawls's step (ii) the "universalised typified counterpart" of the universalized maxim, and then applies Kant's tests, whether there is a contradiction in conception or in willing, directly to the universalized typified counterpart of one's maxim,[19] but either way the test required by the categorical imperative is ultimately whether one could will to act upon one's originally proposed maxim if everyone else were also to do so. A proposed maxim might fail the test because the proposed action would not even be possible in such a world, as making a false promise is impossible in a world in which all promises have become impossible (the contradiction in conception test), or it might fail because even though the proposed action—or inaction, such as a refusal ever to render assistance—is logically possible in a world in which that is everyone's policy, still no one could rationally will such a maxim or policy (the contradiction in willing test).[20]

---

[19] O'Neill 2013, pp. 140–2.

[20] Reath 2022 argues that Rawls's "CI-procedure" is not intended "to generate a complete normative conception, nor does he introduce it for that purpose," but rather that "he lays out the 'CI-procedure' in order to exhibit and make sense of other distinctive features of Kant's moral conception—such as the priority of right, the reality of pure practical reason, the idea of morality as based on autonomy of the will, the central role of a rich conception of persons as reasonable and ... rational" (p. 54). Surely Rawls thought of the CI-procedure as grounded in and in that sense expressing those "distinctive features," but he certainly presents the procedure as one that tests particular maxims and the results of the

Rawls's four-step layout of the CI-procedure makes it clear that the reasoning about whether one can act or will to act in the way proposed at step (i) in the "perturbed social world" imagined at step (iv) is causal or consequentialist in at least one sense: the question is whether acting on one's maxim would be consistent with the consequences of the actual universalization of that maxim. As we saw, this has been brought as an objection against Kant's supposedly non-consequentialist moral theory since the time of Schopenhauer if not before. But Rawls's model of the CI-procedure makes it perfectly clear that the test is not whether acting on one's maxim would be consistent with the actual consequences of one's own action on that maxim, but with the universalization of one's maxim that one's conception of oneself and others—that is to say, morality—requires one to imagine. In terms of Rawls's model, what requires the transition from step (i) to step (ii) is not any calculation of the likely consequences of step (i) in the real world, but morality's demand that one treat everyone as equals, thus as entitled to act on the same maxim(s) one proposes to act upon oneself. The CI-procedure tests the morality of proposed maxims by their consistency in the "perturbed social world" that morality itself requires us to imagine, not by their prudence in the actual world. Rawls puts this point by writing that "The principle represented by the CI-procedure applies to us no matter what the consequences may be for our rational interests as we now understand them," that is, prudence; "It is at this point that the force of the priority of pure practical reason," that is, morality, "over empirical practical reason comes into play" (Rawls 1989, p. 500). O'Neill makes the same point by saying that one considers the consequences of the universalized typified counterpart of one's proposed maxim in one's "capacity as universal legislator" (O'Neill 2013, p. 155).

As I said, the Rawls-O'Neill model of the application of the first formulation of the categorical imperative is straightforward and should not be controversial. Where Rawls does depart from or at least amplify Kant is in his account of rational willing, that is, his interpretation of the premise for the application of the contradiction-in-willing test to the conjunction of one's proposed maxim and the perturbed social world. Kant did not really provide a formal account of rational willing, but tacitly assumed some general conception of prudence in addition to the explicitly moral requirement of universalizability: a person who is self-sufficient now and willing to forego assistance from others as the price of not rendering any to them (in a perturbed social world, that is) ought to consider that he might not always be so self-sufficient, and therefore ought to realize that he cannot rationally will such a world whatever he could will right now. Rawls says that Kant's test might be fleshed out with "an appropriate conception of what we

iterated application of which could therefore yield a set of morally permissible and mandatory maxims that would in the ideal comprise a "complete normative conception," i.e., a system of moral duties for human beings.

may call 'true human needs'," a phrase Kant uses several times in the *Metaphysics of Morals* (e.g., *MM*, DV, Introduction, section VIII.2.a, 6: 393). In answering the question "Can I will the perturbed social world" associated with the universalized or precept version of my maxim, for example, "the precept of indifference rather than the perturbed social world associated with a precept of mutual aid ... ? ... I am to take account only of my true human needs (which by assumption, as part of the CI-procedure, I take myself to have and to be the same for everyone)" (Rawls 1989, pp. 501–2). In the *Lectures on the History of Moral Philosophy*, Rawls offers a negative rather than positive characterization: the agent is to employ the CI-procedure subject to "two limits on information," namely "we are to ignore the more particular features of persons, including ourselves, as well as the specific content of their and our final ends and desires," and "we are to reason as if we do not know what place we may have in" the "adjusted social world," as he here calls what he previously called the perturbed social world (*LHMP*, pp. 175–6). Rawls's first account of rationality proceeds as if we can directly enumerate a list of basic true human needs, the second account as if we might arrive at that list by eliminating merely idiosyncratic needs. It might be difficult to determine what is idiosyncratic without already knowing what is common, so it is not clear whether the second approach has any advantage over the first. And without a clear method for determining true human needs, it is not clear whether Rawls's interpretation of rational willing has much advantage over Kant's more general appeal to prudence rather than his passing suggestion that we could agree upon a list of "true human needs." (Kant describes prudence as offering mere "counsels" rather than genuine imperatives at *G*, 4: 418.) What is clear is that Rawls wanted to use the notion of true human needs in his interpretation of the categorical imperative to connect Kant's basic method in moral philosophy to his own use of the idea of primary social goods in the reasoning to the principles of justice in the original position in his own political philosophy.

16.2.2. Rawls and the Categorical Imperative

That being said, let us now turn to Rawls's treatment of Kant's further formulations of the categorical imperative. In the *Lectures*, he hews to Kant's statement in the *Groundwork*, that the further formulations of the categorical imperative beyond the first, that is, the Formula of Universal Law as "typified" through the Formula of the Law of Nature, thus the second formulation, the Formula of Humanity (rational being in its human form), and the third, itself again offered in two versions, the Formulas of Autonomy and of the Realm of Ends, serve primarily to "bring the moral law nearer to intuition" (*LHMP*, p. 211, referring to *G*, 4: 436). They do this ultimately by "elucidat[ing] the ideal of a realm of ends" (*LHMP*, p. 212), that is, by means of the final formulation of the categorical imperative, although preceded by a shift of perspective accomplished by the second formulation, the Formula of Humanity, through which we consider "ourselves and other persons as affected by our proposed action" rather than looking "at a moral situation from the agent's point of view" (*LHMP*, p. 183). Here Rawls's treatment of the relations between the first and second formulations of the categorical imperative is again similar to that previously published by O'Neill.[21] In the *Lectures*, Rawls develops an extended interpretation of Kant's idea of humanity as comprised by the powers of "moral personality, which makes it possible for us to have a good will and a good moral character," as well as "those capacities and skills to be developed by culture: by the arts and sciences and so forth," which make it possible for us to intelligently set ends for ourselves and effectively pursue them; both of these powers need to be nurtured and cultivated by human beings, in early education and throughout our lives. This interpretation of Kant's conception of our duty to perfect our own natural and moral capacities (*MM*, DV, Introduction, section VIII.1, 6: 391–3, and §§13–15, 19–22) is obviously connected to Rawls's own conception of the two moral powers of human beings, or we now see more clearly than ever before how deeply his own conception of the two moral powers is rooted in Kant's conception of humanity, thus how the conception of the person from which Kantian constructivism begins really is Kant's own conception: "Kant means by humanity those of our powers and capacities that characterize us as reasonable and rational persons who belong to the natural world" (*LHMP*, p. 188).[22] What Rawls does not do in the *Lectures*, however, is pick up on Kant's suggestion in the *Groundwork*, prior to his suggestion that the second (and third) formulation(s) (merely) bring the rational idea of morality closer to intuition, that the status of humanity as an end in itself, never to be treated merely as a means, is the *ground* of a possible categorical imperative (*G*, 4: 428), thus that the function of the first formulation of the categorical imperative, therefore of the CI-procedure, is to determine what sorts of maxims we need in order to realize the conception of our humanity in our treatment of ourselves and others. In other words, he does not take the opportunity offered by that remark by Kant to stress how closely his own model of constructivism beginning from a moral conception of the person mirrors Kant's own procedure.[23] He does make this clearer in the 1989 version of his Kant interpretation, although sill without citing Kant's remark at *Groundwork* 4: 428:

---

[21] O'Neill 1989a, pp. 128–9.   [22] Rawls, *LHMP*, p. 188.

[23] Irwin 2009, e.g., p. 944, suggests that Rawls would have done better to ground his conception of the original position and therefore his derivation of the principles of justice on the Kantian conception of humanity as an end in itself rather than just on a pre-theoretical conception of fairness. Irwin does not discuss the lectures on Kant, so he does not mention that Rawls came closer to doing this in the lectures, but still stopped short of acknowledging Kant's remark at *G*, 4: 428 that the status of humanity as an end in itself is the ground of a possible categorical imperative.

[I]t is clear from the Introduction to the *Metaphysics of Morals* that "humanity" means the powers that characterize us as reasonable and rational beings who belong to the natural order. Our humanity is our pure practical reason together with our moral sensibility (our capacity for moral feeling). These two powers together constitute moral personality, and include the power to set ends (*MM* 6: 392); they make a good will and moral character possible. We have a duty to cultivate our natural capacities in order to make ourselves worthy of our humanity (*MM* 6: 387). Thus, the duty to treat humanity, whether in our own person or in the person of others, always as an end, and never simply as a means, is the duty to respect the moral powers both in ourselves and in other persons, and to cultivate our natural capacities so that we can be worthy of those [moral] powers. Modulo shifts of points of view... what particular duties are covered by this duty are ascertained by the first formulation of the categorical imperative.

(Rawls 1989, p. 505)

The last clause of this statement clearly suggests that the function of the first formulation of the categorical imperative is to determine what rules must be followed in order to treat ourselves and others as ends and not merely as means, thus to apply the concept of humanity to ourselves; in that sense, the concept of humanity is the starting-point of the construction of moral principles through the CI-procedure, while this conception of ourselves is not itself constructed through any procedure but is the foundation of Kant's own and Kantian constructivism. Rawls's last statement suggests this without emphasizing it as much as one might have expected.

There are points that could be debated in Rawls's treatment of Kant's concept of humanity. Recent debate has taken three different approaches. One approach has been to argue that it is only an agent's *realization* of the capacity to be moral, that is, the agent's actually being moral, that entitles the agent to moral treatment by others;[24] a second approach has been that what demands respect is humanity as the *capacity* to be moral;[25] a third approach is that humanity is simply the capacity to set ends (as Kant suggests at the passage in *Metaphysics of Morals,* 6: 392 to which Rawls refers), so that is what demands respect—but that it is a requirement of reason not to act inconsistently with the presence of this capacity in *everyone.*[26] As Allen Wood has long argued,[27] the first approach is excluded by Kant's insistence that even those who are themselves immoral must still be treated as ends and not merely as means, even if they are being punished for criminal conduct, and Rawls endorses this point (Rawls 2000, p. 195). What Rawls does, in terms of the subsequent debate, is to combine the second and third approaches:

---

[24] See Dean 2006.
[25] E.g., Timmermann 2006, pp. 79–80, 84–5, and Allison 2011, pp. 215–18.
[26] See Guyer 2016c and 2019.   [27] See Wood 1999, pp. 132–9; Wood 2008, pp. 94, 219.

on his account, all humans deserve moral regard in virtue of their possession of both their capacity to set their own ends and their capacity to be moral—in other words, in virtue of their nature as both rational and reasonable. My own view is that there is something potentially circular or uninformative in the view that humans deserve to be treated morally because of *their* capacity to be moral, and that it may come closer to Kant's own view to locate the origin of moral obligation in the *agent's* humanity or moral personality, that is any agent's obligation, because of her own reason, to treat like cases alike, given her undeniable recognition that others have their own will or the power to set their own ends just as much as she does. But I will not argue this point any further here.[28]

16.2.3. Six Conceptions of the Good

Instead, I will now turn to one of the most innovative features of Rawls's Kant interpretation, his attribution to Kant of a "Sequence of Six Conceptions of the Good" (Rawls 1989, pp. 506–10; Rawls 2000, pp. 219–26). Rawls always stressed the priority of the right over the good, the thesis that Kant formulated in the second *Critique* as the "paradox of method...that the concept of good and evil must not be determined before the moral law (for which, as it would seem, this concept would have to be made the basis) but only (as was done here) after it and by means of it" (*CPracR*, 5: 62–3). As just noted, in spite of his own characterization of Kantian constructivism as beginning with a moral concept of the person, Rawls did not take up Kant's suggestion that the status of humanity as an end in itself is the "ground" of a possible categorical imperative and in that sense a good that precedes the moral law, or of the right in the broad sense in which Rawls is using the latter term.[29] Rawls thus adhered to Kant's position in chapter 2 of the Analytic of Pure Practical Reason in the second *Critique* that "the concept of an object of pure practical reason" follows the recognition of the moral law and does not precede it. The novelty of his interpretation, however, lies in his presentation of a sequence of no fewer than six conceptions of the good.

These are (i) the conception of the good "given by unrestricted empirical practical reason," or the "conception of happiness as organized by the (as opposed to a particular) hypothetical imperative." (Rawls 1989, p. 506; Rawls 2000, p. 220). This refers to an individual's conception of her own happiness, as consisting in the satisfaction of her empirically given desires, although involving the merely prudential use of reason for the organization of those desires into a conjointly satisfiable set and for the determination of effective means to their realization— thus the reference to the hypothetical imperative in the singular, that is, to the

---

[28]   Again, see Guyer 2019.

[29]   In distinction from Kant's own reservation of *Recht* for legally coercible duties, that is.

general principle that to will an end is to will some sufficient means to it[30] (which also entails that a rational agent does not will an end for which she has no possible means). As a conception of the good given by the merely empirical or prudential use of reason, this is not a moral conception, or a concept of an object of pure practical reason. This is also true of (ii) the second conception of the good, "the fulfillment of true human needs" as opposed to a "conception of happiness depend [ing entirely] on the contingencies of our life," that is, whatever desires anyone happens to have (Rawls 1989, p. 507; Rawls 2000, pp. 221–2). But this is not yet a moral conception of the good if one applies it only to oneself. This conception of the good is a necessary but not yet a sufficient condition for acting in accordance with the moral law. (iii) The third conception of the good, "as the fulfillment in everyday life of what Kant calls 'permissible ends'," is the first moral conception of the good: permissible ends are those ends suggested by anyone's conception of happiness, or even just of true human needs, the pursuit of which in particular circumstances "respect[s] the limits of the moral law," or passes the test of the categorical imperative (Rawls 1989, p. 507; Rawls 2000, p. 222). Obviously, morality allows one to pursue only permissible ends of one's own and requires one to promote only permissible ends of others in fulfillment of the duty to promote their happiness (see *MM*, DV, Introduction, section V.B, 6: 388). But even the concept of permissible ends cannot be a complete concept of the good for morality, because there will be circumstances in which the pursuit of one otherwise permissible end of one's own might have to be deferred in the name of some more immediate or more stringent duty, and obviously no one can promote all of the permissible ends of others.

To get closer to a complete conception of the object of morality, Rawls moves on to three further conceptions of the good. The first (iv) seems a bit out of place in the sequence, for it is not clearly an *object* of the good will, but the good will itself, "the familiar conception of the good will...Kant's conception of moral worth" (Rawls 1989, p. 508; Rawls 2000, p. 223). The concept of the good will can be thought of as posterior to rather than prior to the moral law, in the sense that a good will is a will that is determined to act in accordance with the moral law no matter what. Thus the good will is defined by the moral law, or the moral law is the *ratio essendi* of the good will, although in Kant's derivation of the first formulation of the categorical imperative in section I of the *Groundwork* the good will is the *ratio cognoscendi* of the moral law, that is, the means to its discovery. But the good will does not seem like an *object* of practical reason in the ordinary sense, that is, a state of affairs to be brought about by actions done in accordance with principles of practical reason, whether empirical (as in the case of mere happiness) or pure. Perhaps one can think of the good will as a state not of the world but of the will, to

---

[30] Kant, *G*, 4: 417. Here however Kant does not refer to "the hypothetical imperative" in the singular, but to the single *principle* of hypothetical imperatives in the plural.

be brought about by one's determination to act in accordance with the moral law. But the real objects of morality in an obvious sense are Rawls's fifth and sixth conceptions of the good.

(v) The fifth conception of the good is the empire of ends, which Rawls describes as "simply the social world that would come about if everyone were to follow the totality of precepts that arise from the correct application of the CI-procedure." Rawls emphasizes the legislative aspect of the empire of ends, its "moral constitution and regulation . . . specified by the totality of precepts that meet the test of the CI-procedure" (Rawls 1989, p. 508; Rawls 2000, pp. 224–5). These precepts or regulations are what must be followed in order to ensure that each person is treated as an end in herself, not merely a means, which is the first part of the "systematic connection" that Kant's ideal of the empire of ends includes. In "Themes," although not in the *Lectures*, Rawls adds, highlighting the constructed character of the ideal of an empire of ends, that "We then specify in the light of this conception what ends are permissible and what social arrangements are right and just" (Rawls 1989, p. 509), thus what duties of right we have in the empire of ends and what sorts of ends we may adopt in pursuing our own happiness and what ends we might accept or endorse in promoting the happiness of others. He does not emphasize as much as one might think that Kant's own formula, "a whole both of rational beings as ends in themselves and of the ends of his own that each may set himself," does, that the ideal of the empire of ends does not just *regulate* what permissible ends we may adopt or promote but *includes* the promotion of permissible ends, suggested by desires but subject, of course, to regulation by moral law: the unconditional value of persons as ends in themselves in the first clause of the definition both requires and constrains the promotion of particular ends as referred to in the second clause of Kant's definition. That treating persons, both oneself as others, as ends in themselves *includes* promoting particular permissible ends should be clearly presented as part of the conception of the empire of ends.

In particular, doing so would make the transition from Rawls's fifth conception of the good to the sixth more transparent. (vi) The sixth conception is "Kant's conception of the complete good." "This is the good that is attained when the realm of ends exists and each member of it not only has a completely good will but is also fully happy so far as the normal conditions of human life allow." "Often Kant refers to this complete good as the highest good," but Rawls proposes also calling it the "realized realm of ends." Rawls stresses that the realm of ends is "a natural good," or that "this complete good can be approximated in the natural world, at least under reasonably favorable conditions," although as he also stresses the two components of the highest good are "different in their nature" and "incommensurable," that is, the end of happiness cannot be allowed to compromise the demand for morality—"they can be combined into one unified and complete good only by the relation of the strict priority of one [morality] over the other [happiness]" (Rawls 1989, p. 509; Rawls 2000, pp. 225–6). Rawls has to make this last point only because he does not discuss the ambivalence that is present in Kant's several discussions of the highest good in each of the three critiques and in the two works of 1793, the essay on "Theory and Practice" and *Religion within the Boundaries of Mere Reason.* In some places, such as the Canon of Pure Practical Reason in the first *Critique*, Kant suggests that individuals must be able to hope for *their own* highest or complete good in a "world that is future for us" (A811/B839), where God will reward the virtuous with the happiness they deserved but did not receive in the natural world, surrounded as they were by so many vicious people. In other places, however, such as "Theory and Practice," he describes the highest good as "universal happiness combined with and in conformity with the purest morality throughout the world" (*TP*, 8: 279), i.e., *everyone's* happiness combined with and as a product of *everyone's* virtue or morality. It is only if the highest good is understood in the first of these senses that a conflict and a need for the priority of the right over happiness even arises: there can be a conflict, of course, between what morality commands and what might best serve *one's own* happiness. But taken in the second form, morality itself commands the happiness of all, in the sense of what would result from the promotion of everyone's conjointly permissible ends. There can be no conflict in this case between morality and "universal happiness," and this would be clear if both aspects of Kant's own description of the concept of the realm of ends were given full due.

In spite of his claim that the potential conflict between happiness and morality or virtue as two components of the highest good, a danger present only on an individual rather than collective conception of the highest good, can be avoided only by the priority of right over happiness, Rawls otherwise imputes the collective conception of the highest good to Kant. He also assumes that this is a "secular" conception (Rawls 2000, p. 318),[31] a state of affairs to be realized "in the order of nature, when all act, as they can and ought to act, from the totality of precepts that meet the conditions of the CI-procedure" (Rawls 2000, p. 312). Like both Allen Wood and Derek Parfit, Rawls argues that it is not any part of Kant's conception that in the name of the highest good we humans should strive to make happiness proportional to virtue if that means attempting to make the vicious *unhappy*, for example by means of punishment: "I do not believe…that the content of the moral law (as specified by the CI-procedure) enjoins that in a realm of ends people are to act so as to make happiness strictly proportional to virtue," although he acknowledges that Kant does seem to take a proportionality requirement, with

---

[31] This expression was introduced in Reath 1988, which equated a "this-worldly" conception of the highest good with a "secular" one and an "other-worldly" conception with a religious one. The equation of "this-worldly" with "secular" is misleading because Kant supposes that, even if we are to believe that the greatest possible happiness for human beings is to be achieved in the natural history of the species and not in any form of non-natural afterlife, we must still believe that the laws of nature have been written by God with an eye to the demands of morality.

negative as well as positive application, for granted in the *Critique of Practical Reason* (Rawls 2000, p. 313). Without making it explicit, Rawls thereby undercuts any need for a postulate of the existence of God at least as a supreme *judge* who metes out rewards and punishments for virtue. He also eliminates any requirement that in the name of the highest good we must *perfect* our virtue, for which we would need infinite time, or immortality: "the particular highest good of our world is still to be determined," he says, "unless we believe with Origen that God will somehow, in ways unknown to us but compatible with our freedom, see to it that in due time everyone achieves a completely good will" (Rawls 2000, p. 314). Rather, "the highest good of a world depends on what free persons do and on the degree of moral worth they actually achieve," that is, the highest good is something that only can and therefore only should (because ought implies can) be achieved in the natural world and in the natural life spans of human beings, or in the collective life span of the human species. Rawls says that he is simply leaving aside the postulate of immortality (p. 318), which Kant had argued, along with Leibniz, Johann Joachim Spalding, and Moses Mendelssohn, is necessary for the perfection of our virtue,[32] but he is actually removing the premise for that argument. And while Rawls is right to argue that there is no basis in Kant's conception of pure practical reason for his claim that an "impartial reason" requires proportionality between any individual's degree of virtue and degree of happiness (Rawls 2000, p. 315, citing *CPracR*, 5: 110), he does not mention that for Kant even the "secular" conception of the highest good, as the realization of our moral ideal of an empire of ends in the order of nature, requires the postulation of the existence of God as the "author of nature," "the supreme cause of nature having a causality in keeping with the moral disposition" that guarantees that action in accordance with the moral law will have its intended effect (*CPracR*, 5: 125).[33] Rawls wants to leave even the practical rather than theoretical metaphysics of Kant's postulates of pure reason behind as quickly as possible.

16.2.4. Freedom

This is true even in the case of what Kant also sometimes treats as not only the object of a postulate of pure practical reason but as the most important of them, namely freedom. Rawls takes a decidedly anti-metaphysical approach to Kant's treatment of free will. In Rawls's view, "our special status in the world does not mean that we also inhabit a different realm, conceived as ontologically separate

---

[32] On the connection between Kant's postulate of immortality and the views of Spalding and Mendelssohn, see Guyer 2020a, chapter 4.

[33] By this point in his argument for the postulates of pure practical reason, Kant seems to have left behind the worry in the opening of the *Groundwork* that "the niggardly provision of a stepmotherly nature" might reduce the goodness of the good will to mere good intention (*G*, 4: 394).

from the order of nature" (Rawls 2000, p. 307), a realm where our noumenal wills can choose to determine themselves by the moral law no matter what our history in the phenomenal world of nature and its causal laws might seem to entail. Indeed, he goes so far as to argue that a metaphysical interpretation of Kant's argument for the possibility of noumenal freedom is not even "allowed by his text": giving a "metaphysical interpretation" to "intelligible character as permanent and timeless ... is not required by the text and goes against the conclusions of the Dialectic of the first *Critique*, as well as Kant's constantly repeating that what he says about freedom is to be understood from a practical point of view.... Thus, to interpret as a metaphysical doctrine Kant's speaking of reason as not subject to the form of time, yet affecting the course of events," does not merely lead "to hopeless difficulties for Kant's view," but "is not allowed by his text" (Rawls 2000, p. 301). This claim is implausible: while it is certainly true that Kant's idea of the freedom of the noumenal will leads to great or even hopeless difficulties, it is difficult to square Rawls's claim that the *possibility* of noumenal freedom—as opposed to *theoretical knowledge of the actuality* of noumenal freedom—is inconsistent with the "conclusions of the Dialectic of the first *Critique*." On the contrary, Kant takes great pains and many pages to argue there that the third Antinomy, between the spontaneity of the will one the one hand and the thoroughgoing determinism of nature on the other, can be resolved *only* by the distinction between noumena and phenomena, that is, between things in themselves that are not spatio-temporal and appearances that are, and that are therefore causally determined (*CPuR*, A444–51/B472–9, A532–58/B560-86).

In fact, Rawls does not concern himself with Kant's own question, how can we always freely *will* to be moral, and to *act* as pure practical reason tells us that we should, in spite of what the causal laws of the natural world might seem to entail. Instead he argues only that moral *reasoning* is itself free. As he puts it in "Themes,"

> For Kant there is no essential difference between the freedom of the will and freedom of thought. If our mathematical and theoretical reasoning is free, as shown in free judgments, then so is our pure practical reasoning as shown in free deliberative judgments. Here in both cases free judgments are to be distinguished from verbal utterances that simply give voice to, that are the (causal) upshot of, our psychological states and of our wants and attitudes.   (Rawls 1989, p. 523)

Or as he says in his lectures, "For Kant there is no separate problem of the freedom of the will, as if something called 'the will' posed a special problem. For him, there is only the problem of the freedom of reason, both theoretical and practical" (Rawls 2000, p. 281)—which is not, however, a problem at all. Just as we are free when doing geometry, for example, to carry out our proofs in strict accordance with the axioms, postulates, and theorems as stated or already proven, regardless of our feelings, moods, incorrect suggestions of our classmates, or the noise of a passing train or ambulance outside the classroom, so we are free to lay out the CI-procedure on the basis of our conception of ourselves as persons and then to apply the procedure in light of the empirical conditions of human existence, in spite of our mere feelings and inclinations, those of others, and other "alien causes." And the latter freedom follows from the former, Rawls supposes, because of the "unity of reason," or both are comprised in this unity. Rawls maintains that "absolute spontaneity" is nothing other than rationality itself (Rawls 2000, pp. 280–1). He finds no special problem about how we can freely choose to act *in accordance with* our reasoning; he supposes that the freedom of the latter is all the freedom we need. Kant certainly thought no such thing, and even the vast majority of philosophers who would prefer some sort of conditional and scalar conception of freedom of action in contrast to Kant's unconditional and absolute conception of freedom would still recognize a distinction between being able to reason about what is right and being able to do what is right.

Rawls maintains his unusual position even though he recognizes the distinction between *Wille* and *Willkühr* in *Religion within the Boundaries of Mere Reason* (Rawls 2000, pp. 294–8). On Kant's account, as we saw in Part I, *Willkühr* is the faculty of choice or "elective will," the power to choose maxims, fundamental or derivative, for action, thus how to act, while *Wille*, "will" without modifier, is identical to practical reason.[34] And indeed, far from insisting on the freedom of reasoning, Kant adds in the Introduction to the *Metaphysics of Morals*, that "the will"—*Wille*—"which is directed to nothing beyond the law itself, cannot be called either free or unfree, since it is not directed to actions but immediately to giving laws for the maxims of action (and is, therefore, practical reason itself)…. Only choice"—*Willkühr*—"can therefore be called *free*" (*MM*, Introduction, 6: 226). This suggests that for Kant it makes no sense to call reason itself either free or unfree, but even if does make sense to talk of the freedom of reasoning or reason, as Rawls does, it is not what Kant is insisting upon: he insists that we are always free to *act in accordance with reason*, even if we do not always do so, and thinks that this claim can be defended only through an argument that begins in the first *Critique* with the theoretical possibility of a free noumenal will and concludes in the *Groundwork* and *Critique of Practical Reason* with a proof of its actuality, whether by direct insight (*G*, 4: 451–2) or as the condition of the possibility of our awareness of our obligation under the moral law (*CPracR*, 5: 30–1).

To be sure, with this criticism of Rawls's *interpretation* of Kant's conception of free will I do not myself mean to *defend* Kant's argument for noumenal freedom.

---

[34] *G*, 4: 412 is often read to state that will and practical reason are identical; but Kant makes it clear there that this is true only for perfectly rational beings, not for us, in whose case practical reason and will can come apart. This is the assumption of Kant's later, more systematic distinction between *Willkühr* as the power of choice and *Wille* as practical reason. *MM*, Introduction, 6: 213 is better evidence for the identification of *Wille* with practical reason as such, but there Kant can make that identification even for the human case because he has clearly separated *Willkühr* from *Wille*.

I do mean to suggest, however, that in failing to see that Kant's theory of free will is supposed to be a theory of freedom in our *responsiveness* to reasons or reasoning, not or not just a theory of the freedom of reasoning itself, Rawls missed an opportunity to consider whether *some* form of freedom in responsiveness to reasons, which many would consider to be a necessary condition of our practices of praise and blame, reward and punishment, can be provided within his own, thoroughly naturalistic framework. I have argued elsewhere that, especially in his lectures on ethics, Kant did suggest empirical criteria for the "imputability" of or responsibility for actions, a theory that predates and is independent of his transcendental idealist theory of free will.[35] To be sure, Kant recognizes in his lectures that the fulfillment of the empirical criteria for responsibility can come in different degrees, and therefore that freedom of the will actually consists in "degrees of imputability" rather than "absolute spontaneity." This is a far cry from his later theory of free will. Still, it would have been interesting to have had Rawls's reflections on Kant's actual empirical theory of freedom rather than his misinterpretation of Kant's transcendental theory of freedom.

16.2.5. The Authentication of the Moral Law and the Objectivity of Moral Laws

Finally, I comment briefly on several aspects of Rawls's interpretation of Kantian meta-ethics, or his epistemology of morality. There are two issues here: how he supposes Kant to defend the categorical imperative or the moral law itself, and how he understands the objectivity of particular moral precepts or imperatives.

Like many although not all interpreters of Kant, Rawls supposes there to be a significant change in strategy from Kant's "synthetic" proof of the validity of the moral law in section III of the *Groundwork* to the "fact of reason" argument of the *Critique of Practical Reason*. Rawls does not see this, however, as a transition from speculative metaphysics to a purely practical point of view, for he does not see the crucial argument of *Groundwork* III as resting on the assertion that although we know external objects only as phenomena we know ourselves as we really are, which is as self-active beings who are both spontaneous and rational (*G*, 4: 451–2); as some others have, he finds the crucial previous argument in the claim that "every being that cannot act otherwise than *under the* idea *of freedom* is just because of that really free in a practical respect" (4: 448).[36] The argument at *Groundwork* 4: 451–2 does indeed raise insuperable methodological problems for Kant, but he also seems to think in the *Groundwork* that it is absolutely necessary to prove our freedom and subjection to the moral law, because he raises the threat

---

[35] See Guyer 2008b.   [36] E.g., Mieth and Rosenthal 2006.

of a circle or *petitio principii*[37] *after* he has stated the claim that to act under the idea of freedom is really to be free (4: 450) and states that this danger has been averted only *after* he has provided the metaphysical argument (4: 453). The methodological problem with the metaphysical argument is presumably why Kant shifted ground in the *Critique of Practical Reason* to a different argument, which starts from the "fact of reason" that we are immediately conscious of the moral law but can deduce our freedom to act in accordance with it no matter what from that immediate consciousness (*CPracR*, 5: 30–1 and 47). Rawls interprets the fact of reason as "the fact that in our common moral consciousness we recognize and acknowledge the moral law as supremely authoritative and directive for us," and argues that "authenticating" this fact consists simply in showing that moral reasoning is just part of or a form of reasoning in general. "In the most general sense, the authentication of a form of reason consists in explaining its place and role within what I shall call the constitution of reason as a whole." Nothing further is either needed or possible; "For Kant there can be no question of justifying reason as such; for reason must answer all questions about itself from its own resources" (Rawls 1989, p. 517, citing *CPuR*, A476–84/B504–12). It is indeed plausible to suppose that there can be no rational justification of the most fundamental principle or principles of reason, on the pain of circularity or infinite regress. But then Rawls also supposes that there can be no further issue about validating our freedom of the will, for as we have just seen he reduces freedom of the will to the freedom of reason, or of reasoning. I have already argued that this is not all that Kant had in mind. We might say that Rawls's interpretation of Kant's idea of the fact of reason is correct as far as it goes, but that it does not go as far as Kant intended, namely to use the indubitable fact of our pure consciousness of the moral law to infer the fact of our freedom to act in accordance with that law, which is an ontological fact about us that is distinct from the moral law. In Kant's own view, our recognition of that freedom may be given along with our consciousness of the moral law, and the latter may be the *ratio cognoscendi* of the former, but the fact of our freedom is metaphysically distinct from our consciousness of the moral law, as it must be in order for freedom to be the ground or *ratio essendi* of the moral law or our obligation under it. To be sure, if Kant's transcendental idealist defense of absolute freedom of the will is rejected, then the extent of human freedom in general, or of the freedom of any particular human being, or of any particular human being at any particular time, becomes an empirical question. But then the latter question does not go away just because *reasoning* may be considered free, as Rawls supposes.

Finally, Rawls links Kant's account of the validation of particular precepts or duties to the account of objectivity that he gave in his earlier statement of Kantian

---

[37] See Schönecker 1999, pp. 329–58; Quarfood 2006; and Berger 2015.

constructivism. As in his account of Kantian constructivism he had rejected any conception of objectivity in morality as the correspondence of our intuitions to independently existing moral facts and argued that the objectivity of moral principles just consists in their being the outcome of a suitable process of construction, as the principles of justice were in his own theory of justice, so too he argues that "in Kant's doctrine. . a correct moral judgment is one that conforms to all the relevant criteria of reasonableness and rationality the total force of which is expressed by the way they are combined into the CI-procedure" (Rawls 2000, p. 244). By the combination of both reasonableness and rationality in the CI-procedure, Rawls means the way that according to Kant maxims as well as claims—such as claims to property in land or contracts—that are suggested by self-interest are tested and limited by the categorical imperative. Once he has moved on from the groundwork for the metaphysics of morals and the critique of pure practical reason to the actual metaphysics of morals as presented in the Doctrines of Right and Virtue, Kant does not indulge in much further method-ological or epistemological discussion. He does not say much more about the status of particular precepts or duties beyond the Introduction to the *Metaphysics of Morals*, where he says that they result from the application of the pure principle of morality valid for all rational beings to the basic, empirically known circum-stances of human beings. But Rawls's interpretation of Kant's procedure as a theory of the objectivity of particular claims about our duties seems entirely correct.[38]

We have now seen how Rawls's own theory of justice was developed as a form of Kantian constructivism, while his interpretation of Kant tried to make him conform as closely as possible to Rawls's version of that constructivism. Although the structure of Rawls's theory of justice was clearly inspired by his understanding of Kant, his actual interpretation of Kant was clearly influenced at some points by his own philosophical assumptions. But neither Rawls's theory of justice nor his Kantian constructivism in moral theory generally attempted to be constructivist "all the way down," and in this his approach was true to Kant. We will now see that subsequent "constructivists," most of whom were students of Rawls at some point in his career, have often gone further—with what success we will now consider.

---

[38] Although, again, this is to reject the weaker interpretation of Rawls's CI-procedure offered by Reath 2022; see n. 20 above.

17

Kantian Constructivism II

From Nagel to Herman

17.1. Constructions from the Concept of a Person

Inspired by Rawls, a number of prominent moral philosophers have attempted to construct morality on the basis of some version of a concept of the person, but, unlike Rawls, hey have tried to start from a concept of the person that is not already explicitly moral. Thus they have not construed constructivism as the construction of more particular moral or political precepts from a more general but already moral starting-point, but have instead tried to get moral conclusions from a non-moral premise. They have thus tried to evade the received wisdom that you cannot get an "ought" from an "is," encapsulated in Moore's "naturalistic fallacy"; rather, like both Hume and Kant, they have attempted to derive "oughts" from the *right* "is."[1] The philosophers to be discussed here include Thomas Nagel, who starts with a metaphysical fact about persons, Christine Korgaard, who starts from a conception of agency, and Adrian Piper, who starts from something more like the logical structure of self-consciousness. The latter two are explicit about their inspiration by Kant. Nagel takes from Kant the idea that morality applies to people on no prior condition about what they want or feel, or requires no prior "motivational factor, but rather creates its own motivation" (*PA*, pp. 12–13)—this is the position that Nagel dubbed "internalism"; it is similar to internalism as understood by Bernard Williams in requiring a reason to be accompanied with its own, internal motivation, but adds that a moral reason creates its own motivation—although while for Kant the determination of the will by the moral law creates the feeling of respect (*G*, 401n.; *CPracR*, 5: 71–6), Nagel does not conceive of motivation as a feeling separate from a reason, but the reason itself. This might suggest that, like Rawls, Nagel held that morality can only begin from some moral premise or conception. But the "second way in which [his] position

---

[1] Thus Sharon Street and Carla Bagnoli have referred to "Humean" as well as "Kantian constructivism": the obvious difference would be to what extent the foundational concept of the person or agent is supposed to be empirical or a priori in origin. See Street 2006, 2008, and 2010, and Bagnoli 2022, pp. 31–40. The literature on constructivism is extensive, with much of it focusing on the limited version by Rawls and the "all the way down" version by Christine Korsgaard. For essays by many of the leading writers on this topic, see Lenman and Shemmer 2012; Bagnoli 2013; and Timmons and Baiasu 2013. See also Shafer 2015. Bagnoli 2022 contains an extensive bibliography.

Kant's Impact on Moral Philosophy. Paul Guyer, Oxford University Press. © Paul Guyer 2024.
DOI: 10.1093/oso/9780199592456.003.0018

resembles Kant's," he says, "is that it assigns a central role in the operation of ethical motives to a certain feature of the agent's metaphysical conception of himself. On Kant's view the conception is that of freedom, whereas on my view it is the conception of oneself as merely a person among others equally real" (*PA*, p. 14). Nagel's focus here is on what we originally identified as the problem of the possibility and nature of the deduction of the categorical imperative. We will also see in this chapter that the issues of the "empty formalism" of the categorical imperative and of the possibility of being free yet immoral are also issues that have driven the recent reconstructions of Kant's moral philosophy. The problem of the highest good has been less prominent, although we will see that in more general terms the issue of the place of happiness in a Kantian morality has figured in the work of Adrian Piper. There has also been recent work on the problem that Schiller raised, that of the place of feeling in Kantian ethics. A number of recent philosophers, including Nancy Sherman, Marcia Baron, Lara Denis, and myself, have addressed that issue,[2] but it has not been foregrounded by the "constructivists" whom I will discuss here, and I will not discuss it—although in this case too Piper's work does touch on this issue.

I will conclude this chapter with a brief discussion of the work of Barbara Herman. She has been connected with several of the self-identified constructivists—for instance, she co-edited the 1997 *Festschrift* for Rawls with Christine Korsgaard and Andrews Reath[3]—but she has never identified herself as a constructivist. In the end, however, her position does come close to that of Rawls's original partial constructivism, so some account of both her affinities and her differences with the self-avowed constructivists, especially Korsgaard, will be a useful way to sum up the chapter.

17.1.1. Thomas Nagel

Nagel (b. 1937), completed his doctoral dissertation under the supervision of Rawls at the end of Rawls's first year as a professor at Harvard. He published the book based on his dissertation, *The Possibility of Altruism*, in 1970, a year before *A Theory of Justice*, thereby becoming the first of Rawls's many students to publish his own important and influential book. He taught at Princeton, where he was one of the founders of *Philosophy and Public Affairs*, and then, in both philosophy and law, at New York University. He made many contributions to general as well as moral and political philosophy.[4] But his first book was his most

---

[2] See Baron 1995, chapters 5–6; Sherman 1997, chapter 4; Denis 2000; Guyer 2010b and 2023.
[3] Reath et al. 1997.
[4] His best-known book after *The Possibility of Altruism* was *The View from Nowhere*, Nagel 1986.

overtly Kantian, so it will be my focus here. As we will see, however, its Kantianism does not go very far.

The book could have been titled "The Possibility of Prudence as well as Altruism," for the argument has two parts. First Nagel argues that prudence—caring about one's own future well-being, or taking potential future needs and desires as reasons for action now just as much as one's current needs and desires are—needs an explanation, but that the explanation is simple: it is a fact that one's future self is the same person as one's present self, and so in considering one's own interests one has just as much reason to care for oneself in the future as one does in the present. Nagel calls this fact a metaphysical fact: he says that his "method is that of metaphysical ethics: moral and other practical requirements are grounded in a metaphysics of action, and finally in a metaphysics of the person" (*PA*, p. 18).[5] At the same time, Nagel does not want to make too strong a claim about metaphysical fact, for example that it could only be known by some kind of a priori rational intuition. "I have no confidence that is a necessary truth that we are constituted as we are, in the fundamental respects which give rise to our susceptibility to moral considerations. But if we were not so constituted, we should be unrecognizably different, and that may be enough for the purpose of the argument" (*PA*, p. 19). We might take this as a signal of methodological modesty; unlike Kant, Nagel is not trying to establish a moral law valid for all possible rational beings. It will suffice to establish the content and possibility of morality for human beings as we know them. In this regard, Nagel is certainly in the same camp as Rawls, who, however he might have described his method at various stages in his career—as a method of reflective equilibrium, Kantian constructivism, overlapping consensus, etc.—likewise never claimed it to be based on rational insight into the nature of all possible rational beings.

Nagel does not say that prudence is part of morality, or, in Kantian terms, that one has a duty to oneself to be prudent—for Kant that would be part but only be part of duty to oneself. Rather, the explanation of prudence is to be a model for the possibility of altruism, with one important shift. The possibility of prudence "depends on an acknowledgment that certain things are not outside" one's current self "to begin with, and that events in [one's] future hold an interest for [one] now because they belong to a single person of whom [one's] present segment is merely one stage" (*PA*, p. 43). Nagel calls this statement "metaphorical" and says that it will be elaborated further, but it really does not need much argument; in his view,

---

[5] This metaphysical assumption is the target of Derek Parfit's subsequent argument in his first book, Parfit 1984, where he argues that concern for one's future self is not easily explained by a metaphysical fact of continuing self-identity but needs an explanation through a content-based psychological relation ("R") to possible future states that are thought of as the continuation, or nearest continuation, of one's present self, which is itself thought of in psychological rather than metaphysical terms. Parfit's psychological rather than metaphysical account of personal identity is actually a revision of Locke's "foresensic" rather than substantival criterion for personal identity (*EHCU*, book II, chapter XXVII), with Locke's strict requirement of memory replaced with the purposely less determinate relation "R."

anyone who does not assume this is basically suffering from dissociation, and is more in need of psychological therapy than philosophical argument. The crucial point that he wants to make, and to carry over to the case of altruism, is that no special motivation, no distinct desire, is necessary to motivate one to care about some interest of a future stage of oneself, just because any normal person already cares about him- or herself as a diachronically extended whole. A "prudential desire is *unnecessary* as a bridge to one's own future, because the connection is already guaranteed by formal conditions on practical reason" (*PA*, p. 43), or, one would have thought Nagel would say, by the metaphysical condition of practical reason, namely that the reasoning is undertaken by a temporally extended self. The situation is not that one now knows that one will have certain needs or desires in the future and one now has a desire that one's future desires can be satisfied, so one now has a reason to take some care about them; one simply sees needs and desires of future stages of oneself as reasons at any time for taking care that they can be satisfied because they are reasons for one and the same self that one now is. Or perhaps one might say that one directly sees both present and future interests of oneself as reasons for action, because they are all interests of the same self; of course interests of *past* stages of oneself are not reasons for action for the simple reason that one cannot change the past, so no present or future actions of one's own can have any effect on the satisfaction of one's past interests. But one's selfhood does extend into the past as well. It had better, because the present, where we think of ourselves as making decisions, is always vanishing into the past.

Nagel places no particular constraints on what can count as a reason for a temporally extended self; his argument is only that reasons are tenseless, so that something that is a reason for one's future self is also a reason for one's present self: "we have a reason to promote any event, actual or possible, if it is tenselessly true that at the time of that event, a reason-predicate applies to it" (*PA*, p. 48). The formal or metaphysical structure of prudential reason does not by itself place any particular substantive constraints on what can count as a reason for oneself at any and all times, although of course it places formal constraints such as that one should not gratify some minor whim now at the cost of destroying the possibility of satisfying pressing needs in the future, etc. (Nagel does not discuss whether discounting the possibility of satisfying future needs because of uncertainty whether one will still be alive at any particular later time might also be part of rationality.) Thus, Nagel's formal or metaphysical account leaves it open that reasons might be furnished by desires for sensory gratification, for intellectual interests, for the well-being of others to whom one has particular connections, such as parents or children, and so on. The formal consideration about the identity of oneself over the whole time of one's life is not inconsistent with a hedonistic view of actual reasons, for example. Thus the metaphysical fact of the extended existence of the self provides a formal constraint on what reasons for action one can have at any time, but hardly provides a complete theory of even just prudential reasons.

The same caveat will apply to Nagel's treatment of altruism. As in the case of prudence, Nagel says, "the problem" of altruism "can be treated without attempting to provide too fine an analysis of benefit and harm, happiness, unhappiness, pleasure, pain, or whatever the principal determinants" of action, "positive and negative, are to be. The question is not why these particular factors motivate, but how, given that they motivate in one way, they can also motivate in another—over time," in the case of prudence, "or across the gap between persons," in the case of altruism (PA, p. 79). The shift that is necessary to go from prudence to altruism is a shift in the relevant metaphysical fact. In the case of prudence, the relevant fact is that in a metaphysical sense one is the same person throughout one's life. The relevant fact in the case of altruism is that different people are the same *sorts* of beings, agents, and we all know that perfectly well, just as well as we know that we are each the same person throughout our life, so that what is a genuine reason in one person is just as much a genuine reason in any other—that is, what is a reason *for* anyone when it occurs *in* anyone is a reason *in* anyone *for everyone*, although of course not everyone will be in the same position to do anything about it in someone else.

> Recognition of the other person's reality, and the possibility of putting yourself in his place, is essential. You see the present situation as a specimen of a more general scheme, in which the characters can be exchanged. The crucial factor injected into this scheme is an attitude which you have towards your own case, or rather an aspect of the view which you take of your own needs, actions, and desires. You attribute to them, in fact, a certain objective interest, and the recognition of others as persons like yourself permits extension of this objective interest to the needs and desires of persons in general, or to those of any particular individual whose situation is being considered.   (PA, p. 83)

The recognition of others as persons like yourself does not in fact just *permit* extension of interest in the satisfaction of your own desires to interest in the satisfaction of theirs, but in some formal, metaphysically grounded sense *requires* it. Insofar as you think that some desire in yourself is an *objective* reason for you to perform some self-regarding action to satisfy it, you think it is an objective reason for *anyone* to perform some action to satisfy it, and likewise think that its occurrence *in* anyone else is a reason *for* anyone, including yourself, to do something to satisfy it. Like cases should be treated alike, after all. That's why Nagel can say that "The rational altruism which I shall defend can be intuitively represented by the following argument, 'How would you like it if someone did that to you?'," because *you* have just as much reason to act with regard to what others would like to happen to them as you take them to have to act with regard to what you would like to happen to you. This is what follows from recognition of the fact, which no one in their right mind can deny, that others are persons just like them.

(That is what sociopaths do deny about others, by their actions if not their words; of course they are not in their right mind.) Although again Nagel does not make this explicit, the duty of altruism is in Kantian terms an imperfect duty of wide obligation: not only must one balance what one can do for others with what one might need to do for oneself, but also of course no one person can help everyone else with an objectively valid need for help, so who one helps will have to be determined by proximity, one's own capabilities and resources, and even one's own preferences among the permissible needs of others.

Although he does not make any reference to this fact, I believe that Nagel's argument for altruism is similar to what is in my view Kant's deepest argument for the moral law, his argument that it is just a fact that all human beings have their own wills, and that to act toward any human being (in fact, oneself included) as if it did not have its own will—to use it merely as a means and not treat it as an end in itself, that is, as a being that gets to set its own ends—is tantamount to denying this fact, that is, to deny a fact that one cannot but assert, and thus a self-contradiction, violation of the most fundamental law of reason. Kant's argument turns on the nature of *reason*, if you like, whereas Nagel's turns on the nature of *reasons*, but they are in the same ballpark. Nagel's theory provides only the formal foundation for an ethics of altruism, that is, it leaves open what the objective reasons for action actually are, thus what one must actually do for others, while Kant adds to his most formal level of moral argument the further argument that if one would oneself want help from others, which in real human life is sometimes unavoidable, but must also generalize, then one must also be prepared to help others, with whatever their permissible desires might actually be, and to the extent called for and possible within one's actual circumstances. Nevertheless, Nagel's argument does capture an important aspect of Kant's thought.

17.1.2. Christine Korsgaard

Korsgaard (b. 1952) completed her Ph.D. at Harvard, under the supervision of Rawls, almost two decades after Nagel. Her approach is like Nagel's insofar as much of her concern is with what it takes for someone to be an agent over time. A key difference is that her argument from the condition of one's own agency to concern for that of others does not depend on a simple metaphysical fact, but rather on what we might call a social theory of intersubjectivity, inspired by Ludwig Wittgenstein's "private language" argument. On this point she goes beyond anything directly argued by Kant. Korsgaard's position developed in three stages, although the first of these is her interpretation of Kant rather than a position asserted in her own voice. This is her interpretation of Kant's Formula of Humanity, from 1986, in which she offers an argument from the value that any subject contingently places on any end of action to the value that one necessarily places on oneself. In *The Sources of Normativity*, Korsgaard's Tanner Lectures published in 1996, the same year that she republished "Kant's Formula of Humanity" in her collection *Creating the Kingdom of Ends*, she transforms the argument that she imputed to Kant to her own argument from the value that anyone places on their particular "practical identity" such as parent, teacher, etc., to the value that one must place on oneself as an agent at all, and then appeals to Wittgenstein's private language argument to establish that reasoning, including practical reasoning, is necessarily social, from which she infers that everyone must set the same value on everyone's underlying agency that they set on their own. Finally, in *Self-Constitution*, published in 2009, Korsgaard argues against "particularistic willing," coming at agency from another side in order to argument that an agent must employ universally valid rather than particularistic reasons in order to function as an agent rather than as a heap of impulses at all, and then relying on the Wittgensteinian argument from a decade earlier to argue that such reasons must be not just intrasubjectively but also intersubjectively valid. Korsgaard's argument that a person can be a genuine agent rather than just a heap of impulses only by acting in accordance with universalistic reasons would seem to leave her open to the objection made by Ulrich two centuries earlier and Sidgwick a century earlier that if any agent's true will is necessarily rational there can be no explanation of immoral behavior at all. Korsgaard bites this bullet, arguing that apparently immoral action must indeed be the result of "defective" reasoning about what reasons are in fact universal rather than of genuinely malicious or even merely morally indifferent intent.[6]

Creating the Kingdom of Ends comprises thirteen papers originally published between 1983 and 1993. The first seven are directly on Kant, the eighth on Aristotle and Kant, and the remainder on general issues in moral philosophy. The papers on Kant include one on section I of the *Groundwork*, one on the Formula of Universal Law, one on the Formula of Humanity, and then papers on the right to lie, on freedom, and on the kingdom of ends (thus, although not so titled, on Kant's third formulation of the categorical imperative). Our focus here will be on the paper "Kant's Formula of Humanity," originally published in *Kant-Studien* in 1986. This paper presents the most distinctive aspect of Korsgaard's

---

[6] Korsgaard's work has drawn much attention, both from her large number of students and from philosophers and critics outside of her circle. To date more attention has been focused on several of her 1986 papers reprinted in *CKE* and her argument in *SN* than on *SC*. Wood 1999, pp. 124–32, offers an interpretation of Kant's purported derivation of the unconditional value of humanity from the conditional value of particular objects of the will that is similar to Korsgaard's 1986 argument. Korsgaard's argument is criticized as an interpretation of Kant by Guyer 1998b and Schneewind 1998b (Korsgaard 1998 is her response); FitzPatrick 2005; Timmermann 2006; Stern 2013; Wuerth 2014, chapters 8 and 9; and others. The commentaries by G. A. Cohen and Raymond Guess in Korsgaard 1996b address her argument there from anyone's particular "practical identity" to their valuation of humanity itself. FitzPatrick 2013 and Guyer 2013 are criticisms of Korsgaard's approach in *SC*. Schapiro et al. 2022, is a collection of papers on Korsgaard by former students and colleagues, although they are not focused on the meta-ethical issue of constructivism.

early Kant interpretation and prepares the way for her own arguments in *The Sources of Normativity* and *Self-Constitution*. The argument is that "when we act we take ourselves to be acting reasonably...we suppose that our end is, in this sense objectively good"; but that since we do not suppose normal ends of action, whether becoming a doctor or getting an ice cream cone, even if we consider them to be "objectively" good, to be *unconditionally* good, good no matter what, thus a sufficient reason for action no matter what, yet "Reason seeks the 'unconditioned,'" we must suppose that there is something unconditionally good that lends its value to that which is objectively but merely conditionally good. "In any case where anything is conditioned in any way, reason seeks out its conditions, not resting until the 'unconditioned condition' is discovered (if possible)" (*KFH*, pp. 116–17). Korsgaard's interpretation of Kant's argument is then that when "you make a choice...you believe that what you have opted for is a good thing," but that the objective value of a choice that is only conditionally good has to be explained by something unconditionally good, and the only candidate for "what makes the object of your rational choice is that it *is* the object of a rational choice," that "rational choice itself *makes* its object good," which is possible only because rational choice itself is supposed to be objectively but *unconditionally* good (*KFH*, pp. 121–2). Further, she supposes Kant to argue that:

> If you view yourself as having a value-conferring status in virtue of your power of rational choice, you must view anyone who has the power of rational choice as having, in virtue of that power, a value-conferring status. This will mean that what you make good by means of your rational choice must be harmonious with what another can make good by means of her rational choice—for the good is a consistent, harmonious object shared by all rational beings. (*KFH*, p. 123)

In other words, your particular end, whatever it might be, is not good because *your* value-conferring status is uniquely unconditionally valuable; it is good because value-conferring status in general is uniquely valuable, so *everyone's* value-conferring status is equally unconditionally valuable. That, in Korsgaard's view of Kant, is what makes everyone an end in him- or herself, and everyone's ends into ends for each of us.

There are numerous issues with this interpretation of Kant. One is how closely it fits with Kant's own words in the passage in which he introduces the Formula of Humanity. There he says that "rational beings" (such as ourselves) "are called *persons* because their nature already marks them out as an end in itself, that is, as something that may not be used merely as a means, and hence so far limits all choice" (*G*, 4: 428); and this appeal to what "nature marks out" looks like a brute appeal to fact rather than the conclusion of any sort of inference. However, at the end of the relevant paragraph Kant does say that without "beings the existence of which is in itself an end...nothing of *absolute worth* would be found anywhere;

but if all worth were conditional and therefore contingent, then no supreme practical principle for reason could be found anywhere." This sounds like the argument that Korsgaard imputes to Kant. But now a more than local textual issue arises, namely a fundamental methodological issue for Kant. In the *Critique of Pure Reason*, he does it make it clear that while it is the nature of reason always to *seek* something unconditioned to provide a sufficient reason for anything and everything that is conditioned, but he also insists that reason itself does not *give* the unconditioned; and, at least in the theoretical context, the unconditioned *never can be given*, because in that context only intuition gives objects (or more precisely, intuition is a necessary condition for an object being given), and intuition is *never* unconditioned—beyond any space there is always more space, before any cause there is always another cause, and so on (see especially *CPuR*, A307–8/B364–5). To suppose that, just because reason always seeks the unconditioned it also gives the unconditioned, is precisely the error that underlies all dogmatic metaphysics. At the very least, the argument that Korsgaard imputes to Kant would have to be accompanied by an explanation of why this warning, which is conclusive in the case of theoretical reason, does not hold in the case of practical reason. In fact, in the *Critique of Practical Reason* Kant does appeal to reason's search for the unconditioned to explain why the highest good is the necessary *object* of morality, but he makes this argument only *after* the fundamental principle of morality has been established (at least to Kant's own satisfaction).

It might seem as if Korsgaard had acknowledged that the unconditioned for morality, that is, the unconditioned value of value-conferring rational choice, is not immediately given when she said that reason does not rest "until the 'unconditioned condition' is discovered (if possible)"; that might have been taken to acknowledge that to seek the unconditioned is not the same as to give or be given the unconditioned. She acknowledges that the arguments of the first two sections of the *Groundwork* are supposed to be "analytic" or "regressive," but she interprets that to mean that "If there is a categorical imperative, then there is fully rational action" (*KFH*, p. 117), and then seems to assume that since the categorical imperative *is* real and indubitable, there really must be rational action, so the "if possible" condition must be discharged. The challenge is only to explain how, not to prove that. This is a contestable interpretation of Kant's method in the *Groundwork*; indeed, he himself says that the existence of everyone as a rational ground for everyone is put forward only as a "postulate" for which grounds will be found only in the *third* section of the *Groundwork* (*G*, 4: 429n.). In Kant's own view, it seems, there is not supposed to be a conclusive argument for the Formula of Humanity, or for the possibility of the categorical imperative in general, in the first two sections of the *Groundwork*; only in its section III is the question "How is a Categorical Imperative Possible?" supposed to be answered (*G*, 4: 453). And then of course there is the question whether the postulate that rational being or humanity is an end in itself is finally proven by the mere presupposition that "every being that cannot act otherwise than *under the idea of freedom* is just because of that really free in a practical sense" (G, 4: 448), or whether a threatening circularity is broken only by metaphysical insight that we really are or have self-active reason (G, 4: 451–2). Korsgaard thinks that the mere distinction between the theoretical and practical points of view with which Kant introduces the latter passage is enough to justify the presupposition that we (all) really are rational and therefore ends in ourselves, but it is certainly possible to read Kant himself as saying that the distinction between the theoretical and practical points of view itself has to be justified by the immediately following metaphysics of self-active reason, which he explicitly says breaks the threatening circularity in the proof that morality is not a phantom of the brain (G, 4: 453)—by no means an uncontroversial claim.

Textual issues aside, there is also an obvious philosophical issue with the argument that Korsgaard imputes to Kant. This is the Humean point—clearly stated in the *Enquiry concerning the Principles of Morals*, to which Kant had access through its early translation into German—that chains of instrumental reasoning do indeed terminate, but terminate in passions for which no further reason can be given. They do not terminate in a sufficient, let alone unconditioned reason; they just terminate:

> It appears evident, that the ultimate ends of human actions can never, in any case, be accounted for by *reason*, but recommend themselves entirely to the sentiments and affections of mankind, without any dependence on the intellectual faculties. Ask a man, *why he uses exercise*; he will answer, *because he desires to keep his health.* If you then enquire, *why he desires health*, he will readily reply, *because sickness is painful.* If you push your enquiries further, and desire a reason, *why he hates pain*, it is impossible he can ever give any. This is an ultimate end, and is never referred to any other object.[7]

Hume supposes that explanations of the values of particular ends do come to an end, but the end is not rational nature at all—he gives no hint that one has to value oneself as a rational being in order to dislike pain, after all, although disliking pain gives one plenty of reason for other actions, such as exercising. A fortiori, there is no suggestion in Hume that explanations of choices must come to the *same* end in everyone; some people, after all, even seem to enjoy pain.

This Humean objection casts doubt on an assumption that Korsgaard makes right from the start of her argument, namely that the conditional values that are conferred by our unconditionally valuable value-conferring selves are themselves *objective*. In what sense is the value of something I happen to care about very

---

[7] Hume, *EPM*, appendix 1, p. 88.

much, and let's suppose at no great detriment to any one else's values and ends, for example, my passion for Kant interpretation, objective? What does that even mean? That everyone else should like it? That everyone else should recognize its value to me? If the objectivity of the value of my value-conferring self is to be deduced from the objective value of my particular ends or objects, then if the value of the latter is not obviously objective, neither is the value of the former. Yet if the objectivity of the value of my particular ends were to be derived from the objective value of my value-conferring self, then the value of the latter must simply be assumed, and there is no need for an argument *to* the unconditional value of the value-conferring self. But then it also seems as if Korsgaard must end up with some sort of intuitionistic realism, that is, the unconditional value of the self would be something objective, simply to be recognized, rather than reached by any sort of argument, or construction. Even if Korsgaard's description of Kant's regress from conditioned to unconditioned value is allowed, either the objectivity of the conditioned value has to be assumed to be transmitted to the unconditioned source of value, which seems un-Kantian, or the objectivity of the unconditioned value has to be simply assumed, which seems at odds with the project of constructivism all the way down. But if the value of the value-conferring self is not objective, then the inference from the value of my value-conferring self to me to that of everyone's value-conferring self to everyone seems in trouble.

Korsgaard's inference from the value of one's own capacity for rational choice to oneself to the value of everyone's capacity for rational choice to everyone thus seems too quick. That becomes a central issue in her own position in *The Sources of Normativity*, to which we turn next. The central argument of this work transforms Kant's supposed inference from the objective but conditioned value of particular ends to the objective and unconditioned value of value-conferring selves into an inference from particular "practical identities" to the value of humanity as the general human identity. A practical identity is a role that serves as a framework for more particular values and choices: for example, one's identity as "a mother or a citizen or a Quaker" gives one reasons for particular actions, such as nurturing one's child or voting or going to a weekly meeting, that other persons with other practical identities do not have: a father has reasons for some different actions regarding his children than a mother has, a childless aunt or uncle has reasons for different actions regarding nephews or nieces than their parents have, a citizen of one country who is a permanent resident of another has reasons for different voting behavior than the citizens of the country where she is a permanent resident, and so on. "Circumstances may cause you to call the practical importance of an identity into question: falling in love with a Montague may make you think being a Capulet does not matter at all," Korsgaard notes (*SN*, p. 120). But, she argues, "What is not contingent is that you must be governed by *some* conception of your practical identity" at some time, otherwise "you will lose your grip on yourself as having any reason to do one thing rather than another," that is, without some practical identity or identities nothing will be able to count as a *reason* for you, as opposed to a momentary whim (*SN*, pp. 120–1). (Here is the germ of Korsgaard's argument against the self as a heap of impulses in *Self-Constitution*.) And further, she supposes, reasons go down further than the particular reasons you can have within the framework of some practical identity, for you must have some reason for adopting some particular practical identity or identities in the first place, or, when it comes to that, changing them as your circumstances change—as you transition gender-identity, or decide to go through the arduous process of changing your citizenship, or decide to become a lawyer after you have already earned a Ph.D. in philosophy and taught for half-a-dozen years. Korsgaard then assumes that reasons for your choice of a practical identity, so to speak reasons for the framework for your reasons, can only come from your underlying identity as a human being: a

> reason for conforming to your particular practical identities is not a reason that *springs from* one of those particular practical identities. It is a reason that springs from your humanity itself, from your identity simply as a *human being*, a reflective animal who needs reasons to act and live. And so it is a reason you have only if you treat your humanity as a practical, normative, form of identity, that is, if you value yourself as a human being.   (*SN*, p. 121)

Precisely because there is nothing unique about your underlying identity as a human being, but that is the same in everyone, it seems that what you value in yourself, as the source of the value of your more particular practical identity or identities, is what everyone must value in themselves, and what everyone should value in everyone precisely because its value is more fundamental than that of the particular practical identities that distinguish people from one another. But this inference is problematic: it is by no means clear that to now value being a lawyer over being a philosopher, there has to be some distinct value that you place on being a human who can be either. Now liking the idea of being a lawyer rather than a philosopher may be reason enough. (If you are a Kantian, of course, you will have to test this new preference for moral permissibility, given all the relevant circumstances. But it is not obvious that the ground of the test of permissibility is the same as any underlying reason for the preference.)

In developing her argument in *The Sources of Normativity*, however, Korsgaard does not simply argue from the purported value of practical identities, or from a supposition of their objectivity, to the objectivity of the "practical, normative, form of identity" of being human as such. Rather, she appeals to Wittgenstein's "private language" argument, still much in the air at Harvard when she was a student, that is, his argument against the possibility of private languages, to defend the idea that (at least some) reasons are inherently intersubjective. Just as the meanings of words must be inherently shareable rather than private, because otherwise there is no criterion or constraint on the correct use of terms, even if one just wants to talk to oneself, so too reasons must be inherently shareable, public rather than private. "The solution to these problems must be to show that reasons are not private, but public in their very essence" (*SN*, pp. 134–5). She does not want to go the route of "substantive moral realism," to be sure, that is, to suppose that reasons are external to individual human beings, waiting to be discovered like planets in some remote galaxy; reasons depend on humans, on what we value, but, she claims, "what both enables us and forces us to share our reasons is, in a deep sense, our *social nature*" (*SN*, p. 135). Reasons can be "incidentally private," presumably in the sense that, although a reason might be valid for multiple persons in the same circumstances there might only be one or a few persons who happen to find themselves in those circumstances, but "To act on a reason is already, essentially, to act on a consideration whose normative force may be shared with others" (p. 136). Presumably the idea is that, just as in order for a term to have a genuine, determinate meaning, I must be able to explain that to others as well as myself, or formulate a rule for its use that others could employ as well as myself, so for something to count as a reason for me I must be able to explain it to others, or formulate a rule for my actions (not just speech-acts) that others could also use.

Korsgaard does not, in my view, go very far to defend the comparison between the publicity of meaning and the publicity of reasons, nor does she go very far to show how her assertions of the inherent publicity of reasons cohere with the possible idiosyncrasy of particular practical identities.[8] Suppose that my chosen identity as a professor of the history of philosophy gives me reasons to make some more particular choices, such as subscribing to certain journals, in what sense are those reasons "public" other than that someone or anyone else can recognize the validity of some hypothetical imperative such as "if you want to be a professor of the history of philosophy, be sure to subscribe to the *Journal of the History of Philosophy*"? Does anyone else have to agree that I have a good reason for wanting to be such a professor? Let alone that my generic identity as a reflective human being gives me a reason for wanting to do that, as opposed to becoming a professor of the history of architecture, or a doctor, lawyer, or chef, while at the same time *your* generic identity as a human being gives *you* a reason for wanting to assume one of these other "practical identities"? That does not seem very plausible. This version of Korsgaard's argument too seems open to the essentially Humean objection that practical reasoning must come to an end *someplace*, but not necessarily in any publicly shareable reason. While my choice to be a philosophy professor gives me all sorts of particular reasons for action, must I have a *reason* for that choice, as opposed to a mere *preference*? As a reflective person, I may well need to convince myself and perhaps I succeed in convincing myself

---

[8] See also Herman 2001, p. 166.

that being a philosophy professor has social value, maybe not as much as being the inventor of a new vaccine but more than being something else, say an opioid manufacturer. But it remains unclear in what sense my human identity gives me a reason for my chosen identity as a philosopher, let alone a reason for anyone else to approve of my choice. Nor is it clear how the reverse direction might work, how my chosen identity really gives me a reason to value my identity as a human being, let alone anyone or everyone else's. Korsgaard's argument seems implausible as well as remote from Kant. In fact, Kant makes it clear that, although we each have an imperfect duty of self-perfection, of finding some way to develop and employ our potential natural talents, he also makes it clear that we all have latitude in selecting in what way to perfect our talents, and that any particular preference must again of course pass the permissibility test of morality but is not in any way derivable from morality (*MM*, DV, §19).

In *Self-Constitution*, Korsgaard reprises her previous argument "that in order to be a person—that is, to have reasons—you must constitute yourself as a particular person, [but] that, in order to do that, you must commit yourself to your value as a person-in-general, that is, as a rational agent." She then says that in the later book she "will argue for the same conclusion, but with a more direct focus on agency—on what is necessary to constitute yourself as the author of your actions" (*SC*, p. 25). This focus is on what it takes to constitute ourselves as "unified agents" rather than mere heaps of impulses, and her argument is that it takes acting on reasons that are universal rather than "particularistic." "If our reasons did not have to be universal," she says, "then they could be completely particular—it would be possible to have a reason that applies only to the case before you, and has no implications for any other case" (pp. 72–3). But a reason like that, she argues, is no reason at all, it is no different than a momentary whim, for it gives you no reason to carry through on what seems like a good idea from one moment to the next, and could leave you an unconnected heap of impulses, at the mercy of such impulses rather than a genuine agent at all. Such a reason would not carry with it an interest in or ground for personal identity, whether as conceived by Locke, Nagel, or Parfit. This might be conceded, but it leaves open the possibility that what might count as a reason *for me* for a sufficiently long time to "constitute" *me* a unified agent is no reason at all for you: a unifying reason might be, so to speak, intra- but not interpersonally universal. In her example of a "young Russian nobleman" who needs more than momentary whim to count as a unified agent, Korsgaard states:

> The argument from [actually, against] particularlistic willing shows why the young Russian nobleman must will his maxim as a universal law, for if he does not, he will be a mere heap of unrelated impulses. The argument ... shows that he must will it as a public law, with normative force for his later self. For if he does not, he will be just a mere heap of private reasons, and that is no better, and really no different, from having a particularistic will.   (*SC*, p. 204)

But this passage clearly leaps from a reason having normative force *for one's later self* to its being *public,* or having normative force *for everyone. Self-Constitution* does not develop a new argument for that transition, so must rely on the argument for the public nature of reasons offered in *The Sources of Normativity,* as well as relying on the previous work for an argument from the purportedly public nature of reasons to the generic identity of being human as a value *of everyone for everyone* (SC, p. 192). There is no new argument for this transition either.

What *Self-Constitution* does offer is an explicit embrace of a conclusion that was only implicit in Korsgaard's earlier work, namely that if one can be a "unified agent" only by acting on reasons, indeed reasons that ultimately carry down to the recognition of the generic value of human being as such, then the only explanation of action in conflict with such reasons, thus of immoral action, is "defective action," action done in accordance with a merely apparent reason or law that does not actually constitute the agent a unified agent rather than a mere heap. And Korsgaard attributes this view to Kant too, who, according to her, "thinks that an action based on the principle of self-love is *defective* as an action, rather than merely bad by some external standard" (SC, p. 162). On Kant's account, to act immorally is to act in accordance with an axiom that subordinates morality to self-love, so on Korsgaard's interpretation of Kant the person who acts out of self-love *thinks* she is acting in accordance with a genuine principle that gives genuine reasons, but in fact since self-love might suggest anything at any time, she is not acting on a principle at all, thus is a mere heap of impulses rather than a unified agent. As such, apparently, she has no evil intent; she has the perfectly good intent of acting on principle, but is just confused about what counts as a principle.

It is difficult to see how this fits with Kant's view in part 1 of the *Religion* that the principle of self-love *can* be a fundamental maxim, or more precisely that subordinating morality to self-love can be a fundamental maxim, although the wrong one. More generally, it is hard to see how *denying* agency to the person acting out of self-love is compatible with any conception of personal responsibility, or in Kant's terms "imputability" for her actions. Korsgaard's constructivism appears to come at the cost of Kant's own solution to the problem of imputable immorality originally raised by Ulrich in 1788.

I will leave discussion and criticism of Korsgaard's version of constructivism here, and turn to a different account of how to derive morality from a conception of the person, that of Adrian Piper.

17.1.3. Adrian Piper

Adrian Piper (b. 1948) also completed her Ph.D. at Harvard under Rawls, indeed at the same time as Korsgaard. She had already established herself as a path-breaking visual and conceptual artist in New York before starting graduate school in philosophy, and after completing her Ph.D. for many years pursued a dual career as both a professional philosopher and an artist. She is certainly the only philosopher ever to receive a full-floor career retrospective at the Museum of Modern Art (the show also traveled to Los Angeles and Munich),[9] Piper's international renown as an artist has for many overshadowed her accomplishments in philosophy, although philosophers can be pleased that the citation for her 2023 Harvard University Medal in the Arts cites her philosophical as well as artistic accomplishments. Her decision to publish the two volumes of her *magnum opus Rationality and the Structure of the Self* (second edition, 2013) online rather than to abridge it for print publication may have led to the work receiving less attention than it deserves. Nevertheless, *Rationality and the Structure of the Self* is an important work in meta-ethics and moral psychology, inspired by Kant but dealing decisively with the history of a considerable portion of twentieth-century moral theory along the way. The work consists of two volumes, the first a critique of a "Humean" approach to its subjects and the second the defense of a "Kantian" approach. These terms are placed within scare-quotes to indicate that, even though Piper's work is thoroughly informed by detailed knowledge of both Hume and Kant, the book is far from being an historical work. The "Humean" model criticized in volume 1 of *Rationality and the Structure of the Self* is the "Belief-Desire Model" that all practical reasoning begins with preferences not set by reason itself, combined with the "Utility-Maximizing Model" that reason functions purely instrumentally in determining how best to realize the goals set by such non-rational preferences, while the "Kantian" view is that reason itself sets the overriding ends of practical reasoning. Piper defends a "Kantian" view. While I have just suggested that Korsgaard's reconstruction of Kant leaves itself open to Humean objection, Piper may be thought of as trying to block any objection to her version of Kantian constructivism from that quarter. Beyond that, her major contribution might be seen as a reasonable response to the problem of the possibility of imputable immorality formulated by Ulrich.[10]

Piper surveys numerous versions of "Humeanism," including not only the paradigmatic version of Richard Brandt; no doubt controversially, she also considers the view of Rawls a form of Humean instrumentalism. The gist of her criticism is that any purely preference-based conception of practical rationality, such as Harry Frankfurt's model of second-order endorsement[11] but in her view even one such as Rawls's model of "reflective endorsement," must leave the coherence of any temporally extended manifold of an individual's choices at the mercy of some preference that can itself always be changed, and thus allows for no realization of a stable, unified self acting over time. As she summarizes her criticism before the decisive chapter of volume 2, there is "nothing inherent in

---

[9] The catalogue is Piper 2018.   [10] This section draws on Guyer 2018b.
[11] See Frankfurt 1988.

the unreconstructed utility maximization model of rationality that requires a rational agent to be psychologically consistent, and no resources within the conventional constraints of this model for inferring from mere *psychological* inconsistency any violation" of any norm, whether interpersonal, as we would assume moral norms to be, or even intrapersonal, as we might assume prudential norms or counsels to be. One might think that "utility theory" is merely a "truism about always doing what we most want to do," but Piper's criticism is that without the framework for structured selfhood that only a "Kantian" model of the self offers, there is not even a "we" or an "I" that can have a coherent conception of what it most wants to do (*RSS*, vol. 2, p. 163). The "Humean" self is indeed just a bundle, not only of impressions and ideas but also of wants with no consistency constraints. This may not seem fair to the historical Hume, or at least the mature Hume of the *Enquiry Concerning the Principles of Morals*, for whom "tranquillity" was a chief moral good, in the form of a quality immediately agreeable to oneself, the achievement of which would presumably require the satisfaction of strong psychological consistency constraints.[12] But it seems a fair criticism of much more recent Humeanism.

If it is Hume's bundle theory of the self that underlies the problems of the Humean model of practical rationality (even though this was ignored by Hume himself in his own practical ethics),[13] it is Kant's conception of the unity of apperception that drives Piper's model of Kantian rationality. This is important, because unlike other versions of contemporary "Kantian constructivism" to which Piper's approach might be compared, her argument does not depend upon any special conception of *practical* reason, but on a conception of *reason* or *rationality* as such, comprising most explicitly a conception of consistency that is derived from logic but applied to choice. In particular, this is a strategic divergence from Korsgaard's versions of constructivism, either her earlier version in *The Sources of Normativity*, where commitment to the moral law is argued to be the necessary condition of having a *practical* identity, or her later version in *Self-Constitution*, where the argument turns on a conception of what it is to be a unified self acting on a reason. Piper's view is rather that commitment to morality is implicated as the condition for including intentions and choices in a self that is unified by the conditions of rationality as such. In other words, namely Kant's words, the guiding-thread of Piper's approach is "that the critique of a pure practical reason, if it is to be carried through completely, be able at the same time to present the unity of practical with speculative reason in a common principle, since there can, in the end, be only one and the same reason, which must be distinguished merely in its application" (*G*, 4: 391). To be clear, Piper herself does not use the term

---

[12] Hume, *EPM*, section 7, p. 63.
[13] For the distinction between meta-ethics and normative ethics as that between moral theory and practical ethics, a philosopher's catalogue of particular duties and/or virtues, see Heydt 2018.

"constructivism" as a designation for her position. Rather, she designates her position as a species of "Rationalism." This would be because she does not consider the fundamental principles of rationality as such as something "constructed,"[14] but as the necessary conditions of coherent thought in general. Just what the relation of those conditions to flesh-and-blood human beings is will be the central issue in what follows.

Although Kant does insist on the unity of reason, thus that what many more recent writers (although influenced by Aristotle) call practical reason is just the application of reason as such to action than cognition, for Kant there is a special issue about the possibility of reason in its practical application, namely whether the application of the one and only reason that there is to the realm of practice, that is, to our choices, can be *efficacious*, or whether we can act in accordance with the deliverances of reason even when our empirical circumstances seem to suggest that we will not or even cannot so act. This is the challenge of showing that "pure reason of itself alone suffices to determine the will" rather than that "it can be a determining ground of the will only as empirically conditioned," the challenge that leads Kant so say that "It is therefore incumbent upon the *Critique of Practical Reason* as such to prevent empirically conditioned reason from presuming that it, alone and exclusively, furnishes the determining ground of the will" (*CPracR*, 5: 15–16). Like other recent writers, Piper does not want to follow Kant in his transcendental idealist solution to the problem of free will, that is, his supposition that the efficacy or practicality of pure reason can be secured only by establishing the theoretical *possibility* of a free will at the noumenal level by means of the distinction between appearances and things-in-themselves and then the *actuality* of the freedom to be rational by inference from our undeniable obligation to act in accordance with the moral law. Instead, one of the most valuable parts of her work, and in my own view a necessary feature of any contemporary version of Kantian moral philosophy, is her *empirical* account of how reason can in fact establish a firm foothold among our desires, one that is firm enough so that even when we are tempted to violate its norms we still seek to preserve at the very least the appearance (in an ordinary sense) of rationality, which Piper labels "pseudorationality." Piper does not help herself to Kant's own assurance that pure reason can always be practical no matter what, but she does show in detail how we can learn to guide our choices by reason and how we attempt to preserve the appearance of reason even when we do not really want to be rational.

Piper's recognition and diagnosis of pseudorationality is important because it shows, in spite of some language that might suggest otherwise, that she does not succumb to the fantasy of assuming that it is a *conceptual* or *metaphysical* necessity that we must choose rationally if we are to choose at all, as Korsgaard

---

[14] In this regard Piper's position remains closer to Rawls's conception of Kantian constructivism than that of the other philosophers who have chosen to call themselves constructivists.

does. Thus Piper avoids Korsgaard's conclusion that moral failure can be explained only as defective reasoning about what morality requires rather than as a direct choice not to be moral. Rather, she recognizes that human beings often have a genuine choice whether *to be rational*, and they do not always choose to be rational, although they are disposed to preserve the *appearance* of rationality not only to others but to themselves as well. A chief virtue of Piper's work is her illuminating account of rationality and irrationality in practice, which in my view is more psychological than metaphysical. A separate question, though, is whether she has a more compelling account than Korsgaard does of why a rational *self* must pay moral regard to *other* selves. We will return to this crucial issue. But first, let us consider Piper's model of the rational self.

Piper's formal account of the rational structure of the self is presented in chapters 2 through 4 of volume 2 of *Rationality and the Structure of the Self*, while chapters 5 through 8 develop her moral psychology, chapters 5 and 6 offering her positive account of how reason influences action and 7 and 8 her analysis of pseudorationality. Chapter 9 lies at the intersection of meta-ethics and moral psychology, with an account of how imperatives arise from the application of norms to our psychology, and the remaining chapters 10 and 11 deal with the moral issue of inclusiveness and its opposite, xenophobia. Here of course the issue of the moral self's relation to other selves comes to the fore.

Chapter 2 is aimed at showing that, "without satisfying at least two familiar and very weak consistency requirements of theoretical reason that are deeply embedded in the structure of a unified self, we could not be motivationally effective agents at all" (*RSS*, vol. 2, p. 52). Both here and in chapter 3, which concerns the concept of a "genuine preference," Piper argues at length that the standard propositional calculus applies to "subsentential" elements as well, laying the groundwork for the claim that the most fundamental logical or formal requirements of rationality, such as the necessity of avoiding self-contradiction, also apply to the domain of choice, modeled as a choice between representations of possible actions rather than as propositions about possible alternatives or alternative maxims. The point of Piper's painstaking logical work in this chapter is to demonstrate that there can be such a thing as contradictory intentions, not just contradictory propositions, and that such intentions need to be avoided in order to have a unified self.

In particular, Piper argues that unified selfhood requires the "two familiar and very weak consistency requirements" that she calls "horizontal" and "vertical consistency." Horizontal consistency requires "that I must conceive all the things and properties that are simultaneously rationally intelligible to me as logically consistent with one another" (*RSS*, vol. 2, p. 85). This means that not only must the various beliefs that I hold simultaneously be consistent rather than contradictory with one another, but also that the various intentions I might be regarded as having at the same time must also be consistent with one another. Vertical consistency requires "that if I recognize some thing or property as a certain kind of thing, I must also be able to conceive it as of the same higher-order kind as is the kind of thing I originally recognized it to be. So, for example, if I recognize something as a three-dimensional thing, I must also be able to conceive it as a thing of a certain length; if I recognize going to the store as a tedious errand, I must also be able to recognize it as nothing extraordinary" (*RSS*, vol. 2, pp. 85–6). In other words, I must be able to move up from more concrete and determinate conceptions of things to less concrete and determinate ones, and, one would think, back down again as well, thus preserving coherence in my conceptions of things— and intentions—by not, for example, conceiving of one and the same thing as both three-dimensional and yet as lacking one of the standard three dimensions, namely length. Piper's second illustration of vertical consistency is clear-cut: the idea seems to be that if I hold the maxim of not avoiding tedious errands when necessary and also conceive of going to the store as a tedious errand, then I would still accept rather than reject the intention of going to the store when necessary; this would seem to hold whether it being necessary for me to go to the store is a frequent or extraordinary occurrence in my life. But my more important concern with this phase of her argument is that while horizontal and vertical consistency certainly seem like necessary conditions of unified thought of any kind, thus of unified selfhood, they do not seem nearly sufficient, for unified selfhood seems to be something that exists over time, even if with development and revision, and the kind of consistency that the unified self needs is surely as much diachronic as synchronic.

Any complaint here may be more about emphasis than substance, for Piper certainly does recognize the need for diachronic consistency in the unified self. At the beginning of the discussion of horizontal and vertical consistency, she alludes to the fact that an "agent's perspective changes over time, and with changes in her state, character, surroundings, and history," evolving "both progressively and regressively as the agent evolves over time," although she there focuses only on the conditions necessary to make "the sum total of things and properties" represented by the agent "simultaneously rationally intelligible to [the] agent at a particular moment" (*RSS*, vol. 2, p. 84). But as the chapter continues, Piper adds to the conditions of rational selfhood what she calls the requirement of self-consciousness or the "self-consciousness property," or the concept of "*my experience*" (*RSS*, vol. 2, p. 97), and this requirement, inspired by Kant's conception of the unity of apperception rather than by a special account of agency, seems to imply a conception of oneself as a temporally extended subject of particular representations, intentions, and ultimately choices and actions, with a requirement of diachronic consistency among those states and not just synchronic horizontal and vertical consistency. Piper does not say this explicitly, but when she refers to "concepts of properties that attach to [an agent] as a *subject* of experience, i.e. to the way she experiences... events, objects, and states of affairs, for example, being surprised by something, or open-minded to something, or desiring something," and then further argues that "In order for an agent to regard his experience of different things as objects of his experiences ... he must be capable of viewing such experiences as not only *affecting* him, but also as being partly *determined* by him" (*RSS*, vol. 2, p. 98), she is surely describing the temporally extended experience of a temporally extended self. Being surprised by something, for example, is a temporally extended experience, even if not a very extended one, involving a change of mental state, over several moments at least, from complacent ignorance to startled recognition, and being open-minded is being disposed to allow one's beliefs, desires, and intentions to change in response to new information rather than to hold them fixed in spite of new information, perhaps over a longer period of time than that needed to be surprised. Only a temporally extended self can be open-minded, or for that matter close-minded.

That it is actually the requirement of diachronic consistency (but also willingness to change in response to new information) that transforms the merely necessary conditions of synchronic horizontal and vertical consistency into something more like the sufficient conditions for unified selfhood becomes clear in Piper's chapter 4, on "The Concept of a Genuine Preference." This chapter includes the statements that "Practical reasoning just is an application of theoretically rational rules of causal inference to the special-case event of intentionally conceptualized behavior of a goal-oriented kind," thus that "if decision theory is a formalization of practical reasoning, then it is a special case of the classical logic that formulates theoretical reason" (*RSS*, vol. 2, p. 112). Both the reference to causal inference and that to goal-oriented behavior take us into the realm of the diachronic and not merely synchronic consistency, since a goal is typically something that one aims to realize at some time later than the moment when it is first formulated and causal inference concerns how one thinks one can get from now to then. The temporally extended character of the unified selfhood that Piper is discussing becomes even more explicit when she writes that:

a conscious and intentional chooser [has] to satisfy two necessary conditions:

(a) she must be able to form and apply consistently through time the concept of a thing's ranking superiority—and therefore some other thing's ranking inferiority—over a series of pairwise comparisons; and

(b) she must remember the relation of the two alternatives she is presently ranking to the third she is not.   (*RSS*, vol. 2, p. 116)

(a) explicitly says that a unified agent has to apply its ranking of things (possible objects of action or actions) consistently "through time," and (b) adds that such an agent has to remember its previous pairwise rankings in order to consistently order multiple rankings—and remembering obviously is possible only for a being with a temporally extended experience. The concept of a genuine preference is then of a preference that can survive standard logical requirements such as transitivity in all pairwise rankings involving it as well as horizontal and vertical consistency in its conceptualization. An agent can have multiple genuine preferences as long as they are each fully transitive with regard to relative rankings of relevant preferences and are consistent with each other. They have to fit together coherently in an agent's "perspective" or "experience," thus "genuine preferences as defined in [Piper's] variable term calculus are integrated into an agent's perspective as some among many other experiences that also include thoughts, beliefs, perceptions, and emotions... this requirement, together with that of horizontal and vertical consistency, secures the rational intelligibility and logical consistency of a chooser's preference and the self-determining agency of that chooser" (*RSS*, vol. 2, p. 259). The point of all this, worked out with formal detail, is that "This approach subordinates the utility maximization model of rationality to the more general and universal requirements of classical logical consistency, and so divests it"—the utility-maximization model, that is—"of its pretensions to universality of application" (*RSS*, vol. 2, p. 263). The rational agent is governed by an ideal of logical consistency, not utility maximization; utilitarianism is not a sufficient characterization of rationality.

It might seem as if Piper's account of the structure of the rational self just places certain formal constraints on a person's preferences, even if not merely that of utility maximization. But her thesis is rather that "acting on her original resolve maintains the horizontal and vertical consistency of" an agent's "experience over time and at each moment is itself a reason. That is, preserving a unified and internally coherent self is a *good* that *justifies*" the agent's "resolve even though that unified self fails to maximize utility on" the particular occasion of some choice-point in this history of her resolute action (*RSS*, vol. 2, p. 176, emphases added). She then glosses this claim by stating that it

> is not about a contingent psychological preference for consistency, but rather about the metaphysical consistency that genuine preference—indeed, any kind of preference—presupposes: I may or may not have a particular liking for consistency; but unless I am a unified and internally consistent self in the first place, the issue of my psychological likes and dislikes cannot arise.... although preserving an internally coherent self in this sense is a good, it is not an end, goal or intentional object that an agent can adopt or at which he can aim. Therefore while it can be a justifying reason for action, it cannot be the object of a preference.   (*RSS*, vol. 2, p. 177)

Therefore it presumably cannot be surrendered in the case in which maintaining does not after all promise maximal utility.

Piper's position may sound like that of Korsgaard in *Self-Constitution*, which is, namely, that a unified agent, in Piper's terms, or an agent that is not a mere heap, in Korsgaard's, cannot but act rationally, although it might fail to correctly infer what is rational in some particular case. One important difference between the two positions is that, while Korsgaard just relies on the invocation of the "private language" argument in *The Sources of Normativity* for her insistence that intrapersonal reasons are interpersonally universal, Piper provides a detailed model of synchronic and diachronic logical consistency to determine what can count as a reason in the intrapersonal case, without immediately inferring that intrapersonal reasons are also interpersonal. Again, we will return to her introduction of the intersubjective validity of reasons later in her argument. But before we get to that, another important difference is that Piper does not in fact succumb to the idea that an agent is an agent at all only if she is a unified agent, and thus run the risk of not being able to explain immoral action except as defective reasoning once the necessary link between agency and morality has been drawn. In spite of her reference to "metaphysical consistency" in the last quotation, Piper is clear that the rationality of the self is an *ideal* to which human beings can and do aspire, but *not* some sort of metaphysical necessity. To the contrary; one of the most interesting part of Piper's work is her moral *psychology*, in which she argues that human beings acknowledge the ideal of rationality, often fall short of it, but show some level of allegiance to the ideal in the way that they fall short. Piper's rich description of the forms of human *pseudorationality* make it clear that she ultimately thinks that flesh-and-blood human beings have a psychological disposition to preserve the unity of their selfhood in many cases but at least the appearance of unified selfhood in yet others, and this recognition is not compatible with a metaphysical necessity that actual human beings preserve actual consistency. If there were such a necessity, people would never have to strive so hard to preserve the mere appearance of it.

Piper is committed to a normative position that unified selfhood is a good that human beings ought to strive to realize, along with the claim in moral psychology that they often do but even when they do not they at least strive to preserve the appearance of it to others and even to themselves. She asks, for example, what sort of reason a would-be dieter has for sticking to his resolve to diet. The would-be dieter is called Myron. Even if he is inclined at time t_3 to stuff himself instead of practicing the restraint on which he had resolved at t_1,

> Myron at t_3 still has a reason to abide by Myron-at-t_1's resolve to diet. The reason is that his resolve at t_1 makes coherent and intelligible his sticking to his diet at t_3, whereas it makes abandoning his diet at t_3 incoherent and disorienting: Sitting stuffed, queasy and stupefied at his dinner table after having gorged himself on food he had for good reason resolved to forego, Myron is naturally confounded by the empty plates and distended expanse of stomach before him. He asks

himself, Did he really eat all that? And Why? To where did the sober and disciplined person he was at t_1 disappear? Myron chooses to avoid this condition of disconnected bewilderment by sticking to his diet at t_3, quite aside from the threat of precommitment or cost in resources of abandoning it. Once again, acting on a genuine preference is itself a good that, by ensuring the internal unity and coherence of his self at each moment and through time, justifies Myron's resolve.   (*RSS*, vol. 2, p. 177)

Myron seems to have a *genuine choice* whether or not to stick to his diet at dinner-time, thus there is no *metaphysical* necessity that he maintain his resolve. Rather, his reason for striving to maintain a unified self, should he choose to act upon it, is that an irresolute, "disconnected" self is bewildering and all things considered *unpleasant*, in spite of the momentary pleasure promised by the prospect of abandoning his diet and stuffing himself. And if it is in this way that preserving a unified self is a good, then it can also be the object of a preference, although since a unified self is a structure or relation among preferences (and beliefs, emotions, etc.) that can only be manifest over time, it is in some sense not of the same order as the particular object of a particular preference ("A triple-scoop sundae now!"), and choosing to act to realize or preserve it is not incompatible with having a first-order preference that is incompatible with that aim ("I wish I could have that sundae now, but I will not!").

Piper's conception of a unified self could also be read as a response to Derek Parfit's "relation R": selfhood is psychological, not metaphysical, but also has to be established, and is not simply given; we need to *make* our later psychological state a "continuant" of our present one. Thus, chapters 5 and 6 of Piper's volume 2 can be understood only on the assumption that she does posit a psychological disposition but not a metaphysical necessity to *maintain* unified selfhood, with the logical rules defining such unity serving as norms to be realized or, as she shows in chapters 7 and 8, at least honored in the breach. Chapter 5 begins with another suggestion of the metaphysical necessity of unified selfhood, and argues that it is because such selfhood is a precondition of any particular rational choice that it cannot itself be seen as the object of any particular choice, thus in that sense as a good (*RSS*, vol. 2, p. 192, see also 194, 198). But that Piper's claim is really psychological is revealed in the statement that "if the promise of rational intelligibility is the carrot that disposes an agent to seek only those ends that satisfy the ... consistency criteria, the threat of psychosis is the stick that discourages her deviation from them" (*RSS*, vol. 2, p. 191): such a disposition is a psychological characteristic of a flesh-and-blood agent, the threat of psychosis is something disturbing and unpleasant to a normal human being, so conversely the prospect of avoiding such psychosis will be appealing, whether you call it a particular good or not. Further, Piper describes "the highest-order disposition to literal self-preservation as a kind of sentinel that repels all ... threats to the theoretically rational unity of the self, filtering out inconsistent or conceptually anomalous beliefs, desires, and impulses, and admitting in only those that qualify as genuine preferences" (*RSS*, vol. 2, p. 201); this describes a causally efficacious psychological disposition. And then she describes the commitment to coherence, including the coherence of genuine preferences, as something to which the agent must become "habituated" through a "long-term" "project of moral self-improvement" (*RSS*, vol. 2, p. 209), success at which depends upon a variety of circumstances, including a "community of spontaneous agents" with adequate "material resources" (*RSS*, vol. 2, p. 233), something which neither has been nor is guaranteed for all human beings, and which can hardly be considered a metaphysical necessity of human existence. It is rather a causal condition for flourishing human existence. Piper also observes that, once the psychological disposition toward unified rather than psychotic selfhood "does take hold, it will bear a relation to individual act-tokens most of the time, even if the requirements of duty are violated occasionally, and even if one then need not be preoccupied with these requirements most of the time" (*RSS*, vol. 2, p. 209); this is an eminently reasonable thing to say, but it could not be said if unified selfhood were a metaphysically necessary condition of genuine action. It is the kind of thing that you can say about a psychological disposition that is usually but not always efficacious. A "motivationally effective intellect," as Piper calls it (*RSS*, vol. 2, p. 213), is not a metaphysical necessity but a desirable psychological possibility for human beings in fortunate circumstances. Piper also calls it an *ideal* of rational motivation (*RSS*, vol. 2, p. 228)—something at which we can and should aim, but not something that is automatically given. Further, Piper makes no suggestion that failures to live up to this ideal are due only to faulty reasoning; they could be due to anything, including free choice if there is such a thing. She also characterizes this ideal as one of interiority as opposed to mere spontaneity: "The second ideal is grounded in the value of interiority; of a vivid and extended life of the mind that includes imagination, intellection, and reflection; these are the foundations of transpersonal rationality" (*RSS*, vol. 2, p. 233). This is an ideal that will appeal to most people once they understand and experience it, and that will motivate them; but there is no metaphysical necessity that human beings all recognize this value. Rationality can "flower" and undergo "development" and "growth": these are things that can happen to psychological dispositions, not to metaphysical necessities.

Having left the talk of the metaphysical necessity rather than psychological value of unified selfhood behind, Piper offers a moving account of its components (chapter 6) and of the ways in which we try to preserve at least the appearance of it, as much for our own benefit as for anyone else's, even when we are undermining it (chapters 7 and 8). The former comes in her account of "moral interiority," the latter in her account of "pseudorationality." Interiority depends upon "modal imagination," the ability to imagine oneself in different circumstances than actually obtain, which in turn leads to the ability to imagine the interior state of others (one thinks here of Adam Smith, though he is not one of the Smiths in Piper's otherwise comprehensive bibliography). Surprisingly, it is in Piper's account of interiority that her pivot to the intersubjective character of moral reasoning occurs, for she describes this ability as the foundation of impartiality and compassion, which consists in empathy, sympathy, and recognition of the need for symmetry in response to the suffering of others (*RSS*, vol. 2, p. 241), and is the opposite of self-absorption (*RSS*, vol. 2, p. 248). Piper explains how both ordinary and aesthetic experience can foster compassion and ameliorate the tendency to self-absorption (*RSS*, vol. 2, p. 254–5). Her argument that genuine impartiality requires avoiding *both* self-absorption but also "vicarious possession" by another—identifying so completely with another's needs that one loses sight of one's own—is particularly illuminating (*RSS*, vol. 2, p. 266). In a passage that might sound like updated Bishop Butler, she concludes that "strict impartiality requires the ability to balance the demands and interests of the self with those of others in accordance with a normative principle biased toward neither" (*RSS*, vol. 2, p. 287).[15] This could also remind one of Kant's eventual conclusion, after the many twists and turns of his critique but then recognition of the moral significance of happiness, that "since all *others* with the exception of myself would not be *all*...the law making benevolence a duty will include myself, as object of benevolence" (*MM*, DV, §27, 6: 451). Among constructivists, Piper uniquely reconstructs this important aspect of Kant's mature ethics.

Piper's analysis of pseudorationality then describes how we try to preserve the appearance of unified selfhood and its particular features even when we are not really aiming at it. Kant is actually the inspiration for Piper's account of pseudorationality although Kant uses no such term. One way one could put Kant's point, although not quite the way Piper does, is that while Kant characterizes rationality in practice, as in his comment about benevolence, as the recognition that one counts no less but also no more than all others, pseudorationality consists in insisting that the requirements of rationality apply to all others but not to oneself, at least when one thinks one can get away with that; one does not deny the demands of morality, but makes an exception for oneself (*G*, 4: 424). Piper instead invokes Kant's definition of evil from *Religion within the Boundaries of Mere Reason*, where, as she reports, Kant defines evil as the "subordinat[ion of] the requirements of principle to the demands of desire," where we then, Piper adds, "rationalize this by minimizing the authority of principle and magnifying the value of desire" (*RSS*, vol. 2, p. 294). The point is that we still try to preserve the structure of rationality over all, but hope to get away with adjustments that will allow what is just the current structure of our desire, so to speak, to mimic the

---

[15] See Butler 2017, Preface and Sermon 1, esp. pp. 13–14 and 18–19.

structure of rationality. Pseudorationality is then non-exhaustively analyzed into denial, dissociation, and rationalization. "In *denial* we suppress awareness of an anomalous particular, property, or state of affairs, by failing to recognize it as instantiating concepts supplied by our unified conceptual scheme," thereby releasing it from the requirements of horizontal and vertical consistency. "In *dissociation*, by contrast, the anomaly is not banished from awareness entirely, but rather identified solely in terms of the negation of some subset of the concepts that constitute the agent's perception," thereby preserving the appearance of horizontal consistency, or, as Piper says, satisfying this requirement "degeneratively." And *"rationalization* consists in biased predication: in applying a higher-order concept too broadly or too narrowly to something, ignoring or minimizing properties of the thing that do not instantiate this concept, and magnifying properties of it that do," this time in order to preserve the appearance of, or degeneratively satisfy, the requirement of vertical consistency (*RSS*, vol. 2, p. 292). Piper provides rich illustration of these forms of psuedorationality; for our purposes the general point is just that insofar as agents doing wrong strive to preserve at least the appearance of rationality, they must recognize the ideal of rationality and its appeal, but not as forcefully as they feel the pull of some desire. All of this makes sense only if we recognize rationality as a *norm* and an *ideal* with some, indeed considerable *motivational* and thus *psychological* pull on even wrong-doing human beings, but not as a *metaphysical necessity* or condition of the possibility of action as such. Unified selfhood might be constitutive for the *concept* of a genuinely rational agent, but for flesh-and-blood human beings it can only be a psychologically powerful ideal that is often strong enough to overcome particular desires but that is sometimes honored only in the breach. Although Piper's talk of "degenerate" forms of rationality may sound similar to Korsgaard's talk of "defective" reasoning, her analysis of pseudorationality makes it clear that the idea of unified selfhood or agency is an ideal to which as a matter of psychological fact we aspire, even when we know we are falling short of it, not a metaphysical necessity.

This conclusion does not fit all of Piper's statements, but it seems to me the only way to make sense of her descriptions of the motivational efficacy of the ideal of rationality on the one hand and the pseudorationality of wrong-doing on the other. Let us now consider further the crucial issue of her transition from the ideal of unified selfhood and interiority to the requirement of moral impartiality, which we have seen to be a challenge in the case of Korsgaard. One may well see how the norm of unified *selfhood* calls for consistent choices over time, or what we might think of as trans-momentary, *intrapersonal* impartiality, but how does this norm also entail *interpersonal* or what Piper calls "transpersonal" impartiality? Piper rejects Kant's own position that the application of a universalizability requirement to a proposed maxim will suffice to determine what is morally requisite, prohibited, or permissible on the basis of the classical objection that one can avoid practical self-contradiction by carefully tailoring one's maxim for any proposed action so that its generalization would not undermine that proposed action (*RSS*, vol. 2, pp. 180–3). I have argued that Kant has resources to reply to this objection, but will not rehearse my arguments on this score here.[16] The present question is, how does Piper herself propose to make the transition from unified selfhood to full-blown morality? In what we have seen so far, Piper has shown how the logical requirements on genuine preference and on unified selfhood more generally provide the foundation for "the relationships of trust and responsibility that a stable interpersonal morality must presuppose" (*RSS*, vol. 2, p. 188)—no one could trust another person who does not maintain a unified self, because what that person says, promises, or does at one moment would imply nothing about what he would say, promise, or do at the next. But does acceptance of the requirements of unified selfhood itself entail commitment to the interpersonal principles of morality as normally understood? Is unified selfhood a sufficient as well as a necessary condition for commitment to morality?

The answer to this question again appears to lie not in logic or metaphysics but in moral psychology, confirming the psychological rather than metaphysical interpretation of Piper's conception of unified selfhood that I have suggested. The key move comes in her account of "interiority," although not so much in chapter 6, explicitly devoted to this topic, which presupposes that the move has already been made, but in the final section of chapter 5, on "Transpersonal Rationality and the Ideal of Interiority" (*RSS*, vol. 2, pp. 233–9), which completes the account of "How Reason Causes Action." The idea, although once again I have to add some words to what Piper explicitly says, is that although it might seem logically possible to gain control over one's impulses by horizontal consistency, vertical consistency, and trans-temporal consistency within one's own personal set of concepts, in fact, that is to say, in psychological reality, one does this by using interpersonally shared concepts with their relations of horizontal, vertical, and trans-temporal consistency. The key idea seems to be that self-conscious agents, who develop the capacity to reflect upon themselves and in so doing to imagine alternatives to their present feelings and desires that would better realize the norms of consistency, thereby also learn to imagine the mental and emotional conditions of others and to respond to them in a non-impulsive way. "Thus interiorized agents of necessity develop the ethical capacities for impersonality, disinterest, selflessness, and impartiality that are engendered by the pleasures of abstract speculation and inquiry, in direct proportion to the vividness, clarity and power of the interior universes they are forced by circumstances to create." "Interiorized agents" do not automatically act upon such considerations, and indeed their ability to imagine the interior state of others also makes them able

---

[16] See Guyer 2007c, pp. 124–6. There are of course many approaches to this issue; see the discussion of Marcus Singer in chapter 15.3 above.

to carry out "calculated revenge, betrayal, deception, and self-aggrandizement," or to do so better than merely impulsive, unreflective agents could do; but memory—presumably memory of indignities and injuries they themselves have suffered—and imagination—imagination of how others feel in such cases—provide "the intrapersonal foundation for the negative moral emotions of guilt, shame, and resentment" and "the interpersonal foundation for the positive moral emotions of empathy, sympathy, pity and compassion" (*RSS*, vol. 2, p. 237). The idea seems to be that the conditions for unified selfhood provide the conditions for the development of moral emotions, and these lead to moral principles, although they do not guarantee that even interiorized agents will always act in accordance with these principles. The "interiorized agent makes a comparative judgment about the superiority of her capacity for interiority itself. She is causally influenced"—although presumably not necessarily determined—"by the impartial directives it engenders because these define and make intelligible to her the kind of self she is. Interiority, then, is a necessary condition of transpersonal rationality; and this, in turn, is a necessary condition for the development of a recognizable morality" (*RSS*, vol. 2, p. 238). But the latter necessity, at least, seems psychological rather than metaphysical. Reflectiveness or self-consciousness naturally tends toward sympathy and impartiality, although it is not in the end a logically or metaphysically sufficient condition for that, nor even when it does generate moral principles does it in any sense guarantee morally correct action. Piper's account is thus, again, superficially similar to but substantively different from Korsgaard's: while Korsgaard tries to derive the intersubjective validity of reasons from what is essentially a theory of meaning, Piper demonstrates the actual role of sympathy and other acknowledgements of others in the psychological development of a unified self. This seems to me the direction that a reconstruction of Kant for contemporary philosophy has to go, although it may threaten Kant's own distinction between what is purely rational and what is "anthropological" in a doctrine of human duties (see again *MM*, Introduction, 6: 217).

Piper's use of the word "sympathy" makes one think of Adam Smith again. But it is not the only thing here that makes one think of Smith. In *The Theory of Moral Sentiments*, Smith transformed the view of the relation between reason and emotion proposed by his teacher Hutcheson and his friend Hume into the view that general principles sum up the particular responses of individuals with well-developed impartial spectators within their breasts.[17] This is not a criticism of Piper, but as a confirmation of the psychological rather than metaphysical interpretation of her argument to which I find myself drawn.

In fact, Kant himself was tempted at least sometimes in his career by an ultimately psychological as well as a more purely rationalist foundation for his

[17] See Smith 1976, part III, section 4, chapter 7, esp. pp. 159–61.

approach to morality.[18] In his lectures on ethics in the form in which they were given from the mid-1770s until the publication of his critical works in practical philosophy, he presented "self-consistency" in the use of our "powers," "choice," or freedom itself as the "essential end" of mankind and as the basis of our duties, in the first instance to ourselves but also to others.[19] About the basis of this claim itself he is less than clear, saying only that freedom "is the highest degree of life." This sounds more like an empirical or psychological claim—it is in the self-consistent exercise of freedom that we *feel* most fully alive—but Kant's comment is hardly decisive. In Kant's earliest recorded thoughts about moral philosophy however, namely some of the notes he wrote in his own copy of his 1764 book *Observations on the Feeling of the Beautiful and Sublime,* he seems to have tried out both a psychological and a rationalist argument for the foundational status of the self-consistent use of freedom. He suggests a psychological argument in remarks like these: "There may quite well be stimulations that the human being prefers to freedom for a moment, but he certainly must feel sorry right after that,"[20] and "if I was free before nothing can present a more dreadful prospect of sorrow and despair to me than that in the future my state shall not reside in my own will, but in the will of another."[21] These sorts of remarks suggest that anyone who has ever experienced freedom will *like* it, and will therefore be disposed to preserve it from being undermined from intrapersonal inconsistency in its use as well as from abridgement by others. This psychological strand in Kant's thought is different from the logical line of thought that he suggests when he says that "In subjection there is not only something externally dangerous but also a certain ugliness and a contradiction that at the same time indicates its unlawfulness.... But that the human being himself should, as it were, need no soul and have no will of his own, and that another soul should move my limbs is absurd and perverse."[22] "Absurd" sounds like a logical rather than psychological term, and "contradiction" surely is; thus Kant seems to be saying that there is a logical absurdity, a violation of the principle of (non-)contradiction, that is, the principle that a contradiction is always false, in treating a being with a will of its own—another being, but for that matter oneself as well—as if it did not have one.[23] Kant's thought seems to be that to *act* toward a being with a will of its own as if it did not have one is also to *assert* both that it has a will and that it does not, thus to assert a self-contradiction, the most fundamental violation of reason that is possible. I referred to this logical strand in Kant's thought in arguing that there is something genuinely Kantian in

---

[18] See esp. my 2011 American Philosophical Association Eastern Division Presidential Address, Guyer 2012b.

[19] Kant, *Moral Philosophy Collins,* 27: 343–6.

[20] Kant 2011, p. 130 (Kant's notes in his copy of the *Observations on the Feeling of the Beautiful and Sublime,* 20:94). Or "There may well be attractions that a person prefers to freedom for a moment, but this must make him sorry in the end," from Kant 2005, p. 13.

[21] Kant 2011, p. 128 (20:92); Kant 2005, p. 12.   [22] Kant 2011, p. 129 (20:93); Kant 2005, p. 12.

[23] Again, see Guyer 2019.

Thomas Nagel's explanation of the possibility of altruism. Here I am suggesting that Piper's psychological account of impartiality also captures a genuine aspect of Kant's thought that has not been emphasized by others in the Rawlsian tradition—although Rawls's own emphasis on the possibility of stability in society in part III of *A Theory of Justice*, which I have not discussed, might also be considered essentially psychological in its approach. My argument that there is much in Piper's work that should be regarded as moral psychology rather than logic and metaphysics should hardly be taken as a criticism of her work. It might instead be seen as a necessary step for the appropriation of Kant's moral philosophy in a post-analytic era, in which a rigid distinction between conceptual analysis and empirical science cannot be maintained. Piper understandably wants logic and psychology to stay together, but without denying the desirability of that I will say that her work on moral psychology in *Rationality and the Structure of the Self* is an important work in the contemporary reception of Kantian moral philosophy.

17.2. Construction from Rationality Itself

In contrast to the philosophers we have just considered, Onora O'Neill (b. 1941) is a constructivist who has attempted to derive morality from the character of rationality as such rather than from a conception of the person, agent, or rational self. Like Korsgaard, O'Neill has sometimes presented her version of Kant's derivation of the fundamental principle of morality as beginning from a concept of agency or rational agency, but her predominant approach to the derivation and justification has been based on a "vindication of reason" as such, so her work merits a discussion separate from the previous section.[24] O'Neill herself has embraced the label of constructivism for her approach to Kant's moral philosophy, stating that

> The Kantian grounding of reason, as of morality, cannot be foundationalist. Anything that could count as foundations would have to be transcendent, and so alien. Kant's strategy is rather to give a constructivist account of the authority of reason, whose supreme principle is no more than the maxim of refraining from acting or thinking on principles that cannot be adopted by all potential agents, regardless of their variable characteristics.   (O'Neill 1989b, p. 64)

---

[24] In addition to O'Neill 2013 (originally 1975) and O'Neill 1989a, O'Neill's chief works related to Kant include the essay collections O'Neill 2000, O'Neill 2015a, and O'Neill 2018. Archard et al. 2013, and Sensen 2013b, are two collections devoted to O'Neill's work.

O'Neill's central argument is that nothing more than a conception of rationality as being prepared to accept only such reasons for belief or action as are acceptable to others is necessary to derive the fundamental principle of morality, the categorical imperative (she does not distinguish the two), and indeed the fundamental principles of theoretical reasoning as well. She thus proposes to ground her version of Kantian constructivism on a more minimalist conception of rationality than Rawls, who always assumed that to play its constructivist role rationality needed to be characterized by the two aspects he called the reasonable and the rational, associated with the two moral powers to have a sense of justice and a conception of the good. O'Neill is explicit that her version of Kantian constructivism is more radical than that of Rawls: while not only in *A Theory of Justice* but also in "*Political Liberalism* Rawls concluded that constructivist methods can be used to identify principles of justice, but not other principles of morality," on her own account "Kant's conception of ethical justification is more radically constructivist than the one that Rawls proposes." It does not propose to reach only others who are "already-like minded," as Rawls's method in *Political Liberalism* does, but presupposes "only a plurality of uncoordinated agents," and is the "project of working, indeed building, from wherever a plurality of diverse agents with unspecified beliefs and situations begins, without presupposing the legitimacy of existing powers and institutions, beliefs or norms, and thereby addressing the task of seeking—constructing—principles that can count as reasons for all of them." "Kant was committed to establishing a conception of reasonableness or practical reason...that would hold for any plurality of interacting beings" (O'Neill 1999, pp. 71, 76, 82, 83, 85). One question for O'Neill's reconstruction of Kant's moral philosophy will certainly be whether it can succeed with as minimal a conception of rationality as she proposes.

That O'Neill's approach to Kant would be so much more radical than Rawls's was not evident in her first work, *Acting on Principle: An Essay on Kantian Ethics*, published in 1975 (under O'Neill's then married name Onora Nell) but based on a dissertation she had completed at Harvard and under Rawls's supervision in 1968. O'Neill took her first degree at Somerville College, Oxford, where she studied with Elizabeth Anscombe and Philippa Foot, before doing her graduate work; after Harvard, she taught at Barnard College of Columbia University, then at the University of Essex from 1977 to 1992, when she moved to Cambridge. There she was both Professor of Philosophy and Principal of Newnham College, the women's college founded by Henry and Eleanor Sidgwick. In recognition of her application of Kantian principles to issues of public concern such as global justice and medical ethics, and her central participation in many public commissions and foundations in Britain, in 1999 she was created a life peer as Baroness O'Neill of Bengarve, a designation reflecting her Irish ancestry, and later designated as a Member of the Order of the Companions of Honour. In her application of Kantian principles to public issues in such works as *Faces of Hunger* (O'Neill

1986) and several books on medical ethics (O'Neill 2002a, 2002b) and in the recognition for such work she is distinguished from any philosopher discussed in this entire volume. In 2013, O'Neill published a second edition of *Acting on Principle*, with an unchanged text but with a reflective and informative introduction. In this work, O'Neill presented a model for the application of the categorical imperative that, as previously noted, was similar to the one that Rawls presented in his lectures on Kant, not published until many years later; in the absence of any information on whether the teacher influenced the student, the student the teacher, or both developed the approach together, this should simply be referred to as the Rawls-O'Neill model of the categorical imperative. In O'Neill's version, an agent is to apply the categorical imperative by testing whether action on her proposed maxim would be possible or consistent with the "universalised typified counterpart" of the maxim, that is, with the supposition that everyone would act on the maxim (O'Neill 2013, p. 241). The Formula of the Law of Nature brings out the role of the "universalized typified counterpart" in the application of the categorical imperative (the term "typified" coming from *CPracR*, 5: 67–71, and meaning realized in a law-governed domain of actual, or in this case, possible objects). O'Neill's interpretation that an agent has to ask whether acting on her proposed maxim would be consistent with the universalized typified counterpart of the maxim is equivalent to Rawls's interpretation that it has to be possible for an agent to act on her proposed maxim in the "perturbed" or "adjusted social world" that would result from the universalization of the maxim. O'Neill then interprets Kant's argument that the universalization of a maxim might yield a "contradiction in conception" or a "contradiction in willing" as that the universalization of some maxims would simply render acting on those maxims impossible by undermining or removing the condition of possibility of such action, as universalizing a maxim of lying would undermine all trust and make achieving anything by a lying promise impossible, while in other cases the universalization of the proposed maxim would be inconsistent with "certain possible purposes—though never the purposes which are simply the desires of agents" (O'Neill 2013, p. 145), but rather more general purposes that any human being would have (see also O'Neill 1985, especially pp. 96–101). This would seem to presuppose some conception of the general purposes of human beings and thereby perhaps a more substantive conception of rationality than the one that O'Neill later employs. Indeed, in her 1985 paper "Consistency in Action," O'Neill argues that such consistency requires a group of "Principles of Rational Intending," namely that "it is a requirement of rationality not merely to intend all *indispensable* or *necessary* means to that which is fundamentally intended but also to intend some *sufficient* means" to that, that it is a requirement of rationality "to seek to make such means available when they are not," that it is a requirement of rationality "to intend all necessary and some sufficient *components* of whatever is fundamentally intended," that it is a further "requirement of rationality that the various specific intentions we actually adopt in

acting on a given maxim in a certain context be mutually consistent," and finally—
though "There may well be yet further principles that coherent sets of intentions
must observe"—"it is a requirement of rationality that the foreseeable results of
the specific intentions adopted in acting on a given underlying intention be
consistent with the underlying intention" (O'Neill 1985, pp. 91–2). This analysis
of the structural principles of practical rationality seems necessary to make the
derivation of concrete duties from the categorical imperative possible, although it
goes well beyond anything that Kant or for that matter Rawls makes explicit. Still,
it raises the question how well it fits with the minimalist conception of reason that
O'Neill later advocates, as well as leaving open the question whether the derivation
of duties by the "contradiction in willing" test is possible without some account of
basic human needs and primary goods such as Rawls requires in his version of
Kantian constructivism.

But O'Neill's distinctive concern in *Acting on Principle* is to show that the
categorical imperative is "action-guiding," that is, that when it is applied in the
actual circumstances of human life it yields a normative account of the duties of
real human beings. This is in response to the age-old criticism that the categorical
imperative is an "empty formalism," but as O'Neill makes clear in her introduction to the second edition of the book, her argument that Kant's principle is
action-guiding also developed in an atmosphere in which numerous commentators had raised a problem of "relevant descriptions" of maxims for Kant, and in
which her Oxford tutor had raised a problem of relevant descriptions for utilitarianism as well as Kantianism—the problem of how we can know what maxim an
agent is actually acting upon, which can make all the difference to the universalizability of her proposed maxim. As Marcus Singer had shown, even the universalization of a highly specific maxim such as that of the would-be bank robber
Ignaz MacGillicuddy, that all red-haired people with that name should rob banks
on the north-east corners of intersections at 5 PM on Tuesday afternoons, would
not undermine the feasibility of the bank robberies that he intends to commit.
O'Neill's argument is that the problem of the possibility of multiple descriptions of
any intended action and therefore of multiple possible maxims for it might be a
problem for moral *assessment*, that is, third-person assessment of the actions of
another person, and maybe even for first-person assessment of one's own past
actions, when one's actual maxim might not be clear even to oneself (what Kant
considers to be the retrospective application of conscience, although O'Neill never
discussed Kant's account of conscience),[25] it is not a problem in the context of
evaluating one's own proposed maxims—guiding one's own actions. On her
account, the function of the categorical imperative is not to guide us in passing
judgment on the acts of others or even on our past acts, but to guide us in our own

---

[25] Kant's distinction between retrospective and prospective conscience is prominent at *Moral
Philosophy Collins*, 27: 351–7, and *Metaphysics of Morals Vigilantius*, §78, 27: 614–17.

actions, in the evaluation of our own proposed maxims. In Kant's own terms, conscience, which is "an instinct to direct oneself according to moral laws," is "an instinct to direct and not to judge"; it is "idle if it produces no endeavour to carry out what is required to satisfy the moral law"; and should have "*principia* of action" (*Moral Philosophy Collins*, 27: 351, 353, 354). In O'Neill's interpretation of the use of the categorical imperative to guide her own actions, an *agent* asks whether the maxim she is proposing to act upon can pass the test of consistency with its universalized typified counterpart, and the maxim is not some philosopher's cooked-up, highly and artificially particularized proposal like "rob banks only if you are red-haired and it is Tuesday afternoon at 5 PM," but something more general, like "rob banks when you need money and that seems a way to get it" or even better "ignore the law when you need money and that will allow you to get it." It is true that any action can be described in multiple ways and attributed to multiple intentions and motivations, and that an outside observer trying to assess the action of another might be genuinely uncertain as to what is the relevant description of the action and the relevant maxim, or one might even be uncertain of this in one's own case. But no rational agent would seriously consider adopting a maxim like the red-haired Tuesday maxim, but only one like the latter, more general maxims, which would link her desired goal with any necessary and sufficient means available. This is what O'Neill means when she says that "Kant's solution to the problem of relevant descriptions is to claim that any voluntary act has a maxim to which the Categorical Imperative should be applied. This solution is adequate only if there is indeed a one-many correlation between maxims and acts and if we have reason for thinking that a maxim is the appropriate principle for moral assessment" (O'Neill 2013, p. 108). By "moral assessment" she means here an agent's assessment of her own proposed maxim, and her point is that the real maxim of any agent's proposed action is a more general expression of an agent's goal and of the range of actions by which it might be achieved, rather than some artificially specialized description of a possible action. The relevant descriptions of agents' proposed actions and maxims, suitable for the agents' own assessment by the categorical imperative, are "large intended sequences of actions such as 'committing murder' or 'betraying the cause'" (p. 109), not artificially tailored maxims like "Murder only red-haired people at 5 PM on Tuesday afternoons" or "betray only red-haired comrades to red-haired enemies, and only on Tuesdays."

It might seems as if agents can easily deceive themselves about their real maxims, as well as about their fundamental maxims or underlying motivations—respect for the moral law, or self-love in all its many forms—and to some extent that is of course true (*G*, 4: 407). But as O'Neill points out, Kant himself argues, not in the *Groundwork* but in the Doctrine of Virtue of the actual *Metaphysics of Morals*, that part of the duty of self-perfection, the general form of imperfect duty regarding oneself, is the duty to perfect one's moral capacities, and that includes the duty to perfect self-knowledge, including knowledge of one's own intentions, motivations, and maxims. O'Neill quotes Kant's remark that "Moral self-knowledge, which requires one to penetrate into the unfathomable depths and abyss of one's heart, is the beginning of all human wisdom," and a fundamental duty (O'Neill 2013, p. 248, citing *MM*, DV §14, 6: 441).[26] That is, one does not merely have a duty to act on universalizable maxims, but Kant's complete account of the ethical duties that may be derived from the fundamental principle of morality, including the duty of self-perfection as well as the duty to promote the happiness of others, requires agents to do their best to determine what their maxims really are, and not to fob off artificially restricted maxims *on themselves* any more than they should deceive others about their real maxims. Or as Kant puts it in the Vigilantius lectures on the metaphysics of morals (1793–4), "Consciousness must be accompanied with an attitude of sincerity... There are tendencies, indeed, in the souls of many, to make no rigorous judgments of themselves—an urge to dispense with conscience." But as agents we are under a moral obligation to resist this urge, not to be "averse to any close investigation of [our] actions" and the "subjective grounds on which to find a thing right or wrong" (27: 616–17). We all have a duty to determine what our proposed maxims really are—that is a crucial part of applying the test of the categorical imperative to them. Of course, as Kant also recognizes, a person, "in the utmost exertion of his dutifulness, can only get get so far as to be conscientious" (27: 617), and we have no guarantee that we will always discover what our real intended maxim is. But we have a duty to strive to do so, and we can be pretty sure that our real intended maxims are not the artificially restricted ones beloved by philosophers to show that obviously immoral maxims can nevertheless pass the universalization test because they can be generalized without undermining the possibility of our acting upon them.

It seems to me that O'Neill diminishes the importance of her approach to the problem of relevant descriptions in some writings subsequent to *Acting on Principle* in which she suggests that the primary function of agents' maxims is to be the subject of a test for their *moral worth*: because "(it applies to maxims and not to intentions of all sorts) the Categorical Imperative can most plausibly be construed as a test of moral worth rather than of outward rightness" (O'Neill 1985, p. 98). Maxims cannot be tested for moral worth at all unless in addition to specifying agents' goals and the actions intended to be means to them they also include their *underlying* motivation, either respect for the moral law or self-love, which was *not* a feature of maxims on the interpretation of their form that O'Neill gave in *Acting on Principle*, where they had the form "When in circumstances— I will do action ___ in order to achieve goal ***." The assessment of moral worth

---

[26] Not 6: 440 as O'Neill says.

seems to be more a matter for third-person appraisal of agents and their actions than a matter for first-person assessment of proposed maxims, although perhaps agents might be represented as asking themselves "What must I do in order to be morally worthy?" and responding that "I must submit my proposed maxims to the categorical imperative," that is, ask whether the universalized typified counterpart of my maxim would be consistent with my willing to act upon it. But the agent's underlying motivation, even if it is to always act from respect for the moral law, still does not seem to be part of her maxim even on that model. Perhaps this is not an important objection to O'Neill, for even in this paper she does stress the basic point that the primary role of the categorical imperative is for agents to test their own proposed maxims:

> The reason why a universality test in a nonheteronomous ethical theory is primarily one for the use of agents rather than moral spectators is that it is only an agent who can adopt, modify or discard maxims. Although a test of the outward moral status of acts might be of most use and importance to third parties (legislators, judges, educators—those of us who pass judgments on others), because it may be possible (or indeed necessary) to prevent or deter or praise or punish in order to elicit or foster outward action of a certain sort, it is difficult if not impossible for outward regulation or pressure to change an agent's maxim. Surface conformity can be exacted; intentional conformity is more elusive. Precisely because we are considering what a universality test for autonomous beings must be like, we must recognize that the test is one that we can propose to but not impose upon moral agents.   (O'Neill 1985, pp. 88–9)

This passage re-emphasizes the importance of the categorical imperative as a test for one's own proposed maxims rather than as a criterion for the moral appraisal of others or even one's own past self that was central to O'Neill's argument in *Acting on Principle*.

O'Neill's reference to autonomous beings in this passage brings us to another point that she has frequently made since *Acting on Principle*, namely that Kant's conception of autonomy is not the same as that which has more recently been prominent. Already in "Reason and Autonomy in *Grundlegung* III," she distinguished between a contemporary conception of autonomy as independence from external determination of one's actions, in Kantian terms a merely negative conception of freedom, and the properly Kantian notion, a positive conception of autonomy as freedom, as the determination of one's actions by the moral law, which is to say by rationality itself: "Autonomy in many modern accounts is construed empirically as action on reflectively endorsed desires, or as avoiding specific sorts of social and personal dependence," which should be contrasted with "the stricter and stranger Kantian conception of autonomy"; on this stricter and stranger conception, "Maxims of autonomous action . . . must hold equally for all rational agents, whatever their peculiar contingent and variable characteristics, and so must be universalizable" (O'Neill 1989b, pp. 53–4). In "Action, Anthropology and Autonomy," also from 1989, she renews this contrast between autonomy as "a matter of being (relatively) independent of something on which action is often dependent," "a matter of achieving a particular self-sufficiency and independence"—something that children, or colonies, might gradually acquire— and autonomy as "a property of any reasoning being," the "capacity to act on principles even when inclination is absent," again "positive freedom" rather than "negative freedom"; here she adds that "Kantian autonomy is not existentialist radical freedom," a conception that she illustrates with a passage from Iris Murdoch, who however mistakenly thinks that the freedom of the person who is "free, independent, lonely, powerful, rational, responsible" but to no one but himself *is* the freedom or autonomy of "Kantian man," when it obviously is not (O'Neill 1989d, pp. 75–6).[27] A paper originally published fifteen years after these contrasts a contemporary conception of autonomy as "a matter of mere, sheer choice,... not based on *any* law or principle," as well as a more moderate conception of "rational autonomy" which recognizes that individual choice must be accompanied with instrumental rationality," to the genuinely Kantian conception of autonomy as "a matter not merely of choosing principles of action that have the form of law, but of choosing principles of action that both have the *form of law* and *could be principles for all*" (O'Neill 2004a, pp. 126, 131). In this article, O'Neill argues that what recent writers consider to be autonomy is actually what Kant considers to be *heteronomy*, that is, the determination of choice of maxims and actions by factors "alien" or external to reason and the rational will, with only the latter counting as autonomy. O'Neill also notes that Kant uses the contrast between heteronomy and autonomy to contrast principles and moral theories as well as willing: a heteronomous candidate for a moral principle or a moral theory is one that takes anything other than reason and the form of law as its basis, while an autonomous principle or moral theory is one that appeals only to reason and the form of law itself. Of course the contrast between heteronomous and autonomous principles and that between heteronomous and autonomous willing are closely connected: heteronomous willing is just the determination of choice by a heteronomous principle or moral theory, and autonomous willing is just the determination of choice by an autonomous principle or moral theory. So no great harm is done by using the contrast between heteronomy and autonomy loosely enough to cover both principles and acts of willing.

O'Neill's contrast between contemporary conceptions of autonomy and the genuinely Kantian conception of autonomy is important, but is also potentially misleading. This is because it is a crucial feature of the genuinely Kantian moral

---

[27] O'Neill cites Murdoch 1970, p. 80.

law that it allows and indeed requires space for each individual agent to determine her own ends although within a framework of equal regard for the same freedom in others. This is evident in the formulation of the categorical imperative as the principle to treat humanity in every person as an end in itself, where humanity is in turn defined as the ability of each to set her own ends (*G*, 4: 429; *MM*, DV, Introduction, sections V and VIII, 6: 387, 392). It is clear without any appeal to the definition of humanity in the formula of the empire of ends, which enjoins us to seek to establish "a whole of all ends in systematic connection (a whole both of rational beings as ends in themselves and of the ends of his own that each may set himself)" (*G*, 4: 433): what it is to treat each as an end in himself is precisely to allow each to set his own ends, to the extent that this is compatible with *all* being free to set their own ends. This recognition requires reading the paragraph in which Kant introduces the "very fruitful concept" of an empire of ends with some care, for Kant first says that we shall be able to conceive of the empire of ends, as the necessary goal of morality, as such a "whole of all ends in systematic connection" only "if we abstract from the personal differences of rational beings as well as from all the content of their private ends." But since Kant immediately goes on to say that the systematic connection of a whole of all ends *includes* the ends that each may set for himself, this preceding clause can mean only that each person must abstract from the content of her personal ends in order to formulate and adopt the principle that a whole of all ends, including the personal ends of each insofar as they are compatible with the personal ends of all, is the end for all. In this way, at least an aspect of the modern conception of autonomy, that each should be free to set and pursue her own ends, is *included* in the Kantian conception of autonomy as the determination of the will by the moral law— what the moral law requires, in requiring that each be treated as an end in itself and all be treated as ends in systematic connection, is precisely that each be free to set her own ends compatibly with all being free to do so. Kantian autonomy allows for and requires individuality within the framework of universalizability.

The same point is clear in both parts of the *Metaphysics of Morals*.[28] According to the Doctrine of Right, "Right is ... the sum of the conditions under which the choice of one can be united with the choice of another in accordance with a universal law of freedom," and the "Universal Principle of Right," on which all the coercibly enforceable duties of right are founded, is that "Any action is *right* if it can coexist with everyone's freedom in accordance with a universal law, or if on its maxim the freedom of choice of each can coexist with everyone's freedom in accordance with a universal law" (*MM*, DR, Introduction, sections B and C, 6: 230). Like the ground for the adoption of the realm of ends as the goal of morality

---

[28] I simply assume here that Kant's "Universal Principle of Right" and the system of duties of right founded upon it are founded upon the fundamental principle of morality just as much as his system of ethical duties including the duties of virtue are; I have made this argument in numerous places.

in general, this conception of right abstracts from the content of any individual's ends, but the equal freedom of choice it prescribes and protects is nothing other than the freedom of each to set and pursue her own ends insofar as that can coexist with everyone's freedom in accordance with a universal law, that is, insofar but only insofar as the freedom of each to set and pursue her own ends is compatible with the freedom of all to do so. The non-coercibly enforceable duties of virtue, by contrast, do concern ends, but two generic ends that are also imperfect duties, of "wide obligation," namely one's own perfection and the happiness of others. The former includes one's "natural perfection," that is, "the *cultivation* of any *capacities* whatever for furthering ends set by reason," and the "*cultivation of morality* in us" (*MM*, DV, section VIII, 6: 391–2) where of course the successful cultivation of morality will place constraint on the ends that we may pursue with our successfully cultivated natural capacities—precisely the constraint that the ends that we each pursue be compatible with the pursuit of their ends by others. That our imperfect duties to others is to promote their ends insofar as those are "permissible," as consistent with the ends of all, is even more obvious. Kant says that "When it comes to my promoting happiness as an end that is also a duty, this must therefore be the happiness of *other* human beings, *whose* (permitted) *end I thus* make *my own end as well*. It is for them to decide what they count as belonging to their happiness..." (*MM*, DV, section V.B, 6: 388). He argues that one's own happiness is not an end that is also a duty because everyone *naturally* desires their own happiness, and duty is only what one does not naturally desire; this is debatable, because people's mere inclination to short-term gratification often interferes with their rational pursuit of their long-term happiness, and the duty to treat the humanity *in oneself* as well as in others always as an end and never merely a means would seem to require that one has a duty to make one's own long-term happiness an end just as much as one has the duty to make the long-term happiness of others one's own end on the ground of the humanity *in them*. But that aside, the important point here is that happiness consists in the satisfaction that is attendant upon, or consists in, the realization of one's ends, and long-term happiness, "satisfaction with one's state, so long as one is assured of its lasting," is satisfaction in the realization of one's ends over one's lifetime. The duty to promote the happiness of others is thus the duty to promote or assist in the realization of their ends, that is, what they "decide [to] count as belonging to their happiness," as long as their decisions about what counts as belonging to their happiness—their selection of ends—is are permissible, that is, compatible with the permissible decisions of everyone else. If one's own happiness can also be part of the happiness of all that is to be promoted—for as Kant later allows, "all *others* with the exception of myself would not be *all*" (*MM*, DV, §27, 6: 351)—then the end that is also the duty to promote the happiness of all is simply the duty to promote the realization of the ends of each insofar as that is compatible with promoting the ends of all. The duty of virtue as well as the duty of justice is the duty to adopt a framework of universal freedom within which individual ends can be pursued and even must be promoted.

Finally, let us return to O'Neill's "vindication of reason," touched upon at the beginning of this section. In "Vindicating Reason," first published in 1992, and subsequent articles, O'Neill argues that the vindication of reason—and therefore justification of the categorical imperative, the question of which she had set aside in *Acting on Principle* in favor of the question of its action-guiding application (O'Neill 2013, p. 43)—obviously cannot appeal to anything given outside of itself, but neither can it appeal to any determinate principles of reason that are given without explanation by some kind of rational intuition. The rational basis of both thought and action must be recognized as "lawful yet assume no lawgiver" (O'Neill 1992, p. 32). Drawing on Kant's 1786 essay "What is Orientation in Thinking?," O'Neill says that "To reason just is to think in a lawlike (principled) way, without deference to any alien 'law'." She also refers to the three "maxims of the *sensus communis*" that Kant presents in the *Critique of the Power of Judgment* (§40, 5: 293) as well as in the *Jäsche Logic* as "maxims for a plurality-without-preestablished harmony," namely the maxims "to think for [oneself], to think from the standpoint of everyone else, and to think consistently" (O'Neill 1992, p. 33), as not only sufficient to define rationality but as sufficient for the self-justification or vindication of reason. But foremost in her account of reason and its non-alienating, non-heteronomous self-justification is the second of these, the requirement to think from the standpoint of everyone else: in O'Neill's view, all that rationality requires, and what suffices for its own justification, is a generalized version of the categorical imperative, namely "the principle of guiding thinking and doing in ways that others too can follow given that no coordination with others is given from 'outside' by any 'alien' authority" (O'Neill 1992, p. 34). As she puts it, "Kant does not begin from any supposed axioms of reason, of logic or of method" (p. 34), but only from the requirement of reasoning in ways acceptable to all. As she puts it in an essay from a dozen years later, speaking for Kant as well as for herself,

> Those who propose *reasons to accept certain beliefs* to "the world at large" must ensure that all others can in principle *follow* the moves that they make in presenting their thoughts: they must aim for intelligibility, without overtly or covertly assuming prior agreement. Those who propose *reasons for acting* to "the world at large" must aim not only for intelligibility: they must propose principles of action that others not merely can follow in thought, but could adopt as principles of action.   (O'Neill 2004b, p. 47)

All that rationality requires for inquiry and action—and since inquiry is a kind of action, what is required for rational action is what is required for rationality in general—is that one seek the possible assent or agreement of others; and apparently that is something that we all do—naturally?—and require no justification for doing.

This minimalist conception of reason and its self-justification is appealing, but its image of reason pulling itself up by nothing but its own bootstraps, like Baron von Münchhausen, may be too good to be true. For surely it rests on two assumptions or principles: first, that other people, assuming such to exist, *can think like oneself and indeed that one must in some way take heed of that fact*, and second, the law of non-contradiction, so that one cannot both acknowledge that fact and deny it, as well as not acknowledging yet denying any more particular proposition or maxim that one thinks will be accepted by others. That there is no coherent thought without the law of non-contradiction, for if one can both assert and deny the same thing then one cannot meaningfully assert or think anything at all, is the first thing one learns in any logic course (although that is of course like learning that one is speaking prose, for one has been assuming that all along). There is no rationality without the law of non-contradiction, wherever one thinks that principle comes from.

But contradictions require some sort of subject-matter to obtain or to be avoided, and the argument for the necessity of acknowledging that one's thoughts and maxims must be followable by others may be somewhat more complicated. Any version of such an argument would presumably begin by assuming that others do or may exist. That does not seem to be something we know a priori, but neither is it anything anyone can plausibly deny, so let's not worry about that assumption. From there, the argument is presumably not supposed to be a Hobbesian argument, that ignoring the possible assent of others will have negative consequences of one kind or another for oneself, that is, be imprudent—that would seem to be a consequentialist, heteronomous form of argument that is not to be imputed to Kant. O'Neill's law of reason to seek agreement cannot just be Hobbes's rule for avoiding conflict and saving some of one's freedom by each conceding some portion of their freedom to a leviathan. But two other strategies suggest themselves. On one, all persons could be supposed to have some kind of status or intrinsic value that makes it mandatory that one require their possible assent to one's thoughts or actions—and then of course the principle of non-contradiction would apply to one's recognition of that value, as well as to one's derivation of any particular consequences from it in the actual circumstances of one's life and/or that of others. Alternatively, one could suppose that it is just a fact that one can hardly deny that others are capable of assenting to reasons for belief or maxims for action, and then consider treating them in a way that ignores that capability as if it were a denial of that acknowledged fact, and thus as if one has committed a self-contradiction. One way or the other, one would be led to the view that one must pay due regard to the assent of others to one's beliefs and maxims, and thus to the principle that one should adopt only beliefs or maxims that others could also adopt. Of course, not everyone will agree to the beliefs or maxims that you will adopt yourself, but if yours are ones that everyone could adopt and theirs are not, then it is they who are being irrational, not you.

As I suggested at the outset of this work and recalled in the preceding discussion of the work of Adrian Piper, I take these to be the two strategies that Kant himself tried out at the most fundamental level of his moral thought. When he said in the *Groundwork* that their nature marks out rational beings as beings that must be treated as ends and never merely as means (*G*, 4: 428), he is treating such beings as having a certain value that must not be denied; when he said in his lectures on ethics that "freedom is the inner value of the world" (*Moral Philosophy Collins*, 27: 244), then, since freedom is a value that inheres in persons, not something floating about anywhere else, he is saying that persons capable of freely setting their own ends have a certain value that must not be denied; of course, it is only when the principle of non-contradiction is also brought on board that it follows that what must be asserted of persons also cannot be denied of them. When Kant wrote very early in his career, in his notes in his own copy of the *Observations on the Feeling of the Beautiful and Sublime*, that "The sole naturally necessary good of a human being in relation to the wills of others is equality (freedom)" (Kant 2011, p. 102; Kant 2005, p. 21), he may also be voicing the premise of this argument. But in the same notes, he may be suggesting the alternative argument that humans have their own wills, that we know that, and that it is a self-contradiction to entail in a way equivalent to denying it. Thus when he says that in "subjection," in treating a human being, who does have a will of his own, as if he had "no will of its own," there is "a contradiction" and something "absurd," for him a term of logical criticism, he is suggesting that the fact that every human has her own will is a fact that we cannot deny, so that treating anyone as if she did not have her own will—as a mere means to whatever one might will oneself rather than as an end in her own right—is tantamount to a self-contradiction.

In the end, it seems to me that Kant never conclusively committed himself to one of these styles of argument rather than to other, and I will not venture to see whether one is more persuasive than the other, thus I will not judge that he should have. I do conclude, however, that O'Neill's vindication of reason falls short of acknowledging both the substantive and the logical premises from which Kant's moral philosophy actually begins. If that is so, then we might conclude that the project of constructivism "all the way down" has foundered, and that something like Rawls's original view that the moral conception of persons as free and equal is not itself constructed but is the starting-point for any further construction of moral and political principles is both the better interpretation of Kant and the more plausible foundation for moral philosophy. As a number of authors have argued, this also means that the contrast between "moral realism" and "constructivism" that has framed so much contemporary meta-ethics is poorly framed, or at least not suitable for understanding Kant. The starting-point of Kant's project in moral philosophy, and therefore in political philosophy, is either a real fact or a real value: the fact that everyone has their own will, or the unconditional value of humanity. This is not "constructed." From that starting point, combined with the most basic principle of reason, the law of non-contradiction, or the requirement of universalizability, together with certain empirical but inescapable facts about the human condition, more specific duties, in Kant's terminology the perfect and imperfect duties of right and virtue, can be derived. Kant's position is thus a combination of realism and constructivism.[29]

17.3. Barbara Herman

A brief look at the work of Barbara Herman can supplement these conclusions. Herman (b. 1945) was an undergraduate at Cornell, then started a Ph.D. program in history at Harvard before switching to philosophy. Perhaps her background in history explains her greater attention to the application of Kant's abstract conception of duty in the context of everyday life, what she calls "middle theory" (e.g., Herman 1993, p. 233), than we often find among Kantian moral philosophers. Herman is often identified as a student of John Rawls, but while she was certainly a student at Harvard at the time when Rawls published *A Theory of Justice*, her primary dissertation advisor was actually Stanley Cavell, with Rawls as the second reader. (I enjoyed the same arrangement.) Unlike the closest students of Rawls, Herman has never, so far as I am aware, identified herself as a constructivist, let alone a "restricted" constructivist or one "all the way down." This is in part because she does not think of the foundational value of humanity as an end in itself as "self-conferred," as Korsgaard has, and in part because she does not think that the "CI-procedure" provides anything like an algorithmic or mechanical method for the derivation of duties as Rawls and O'Neill might be taken to suggest. Thus, in her most recent work she writes that "When it comes to the account of our duties, what they are and how they guide action, there remains," among other (unnamed) interpreters of Kant,

an ill-fated emphases on generating duties and obligations by way of the *Groundwork*'s "categorical imperative procedure," I believe and will argue that there is no such procedure. For the derivation of duties, we have to look elsewhere. When we do, we find an account of duties that presents their function not so much as rules for action or volition, but as nodes or transit points on a deliberative map to a coordinated system of ends and actions and institutions

---

[29] For good treatments of this point, see Stern 2013, p. 38; Sensen 2013; Cadilha and Lisboa 2022, pp. 10–11; Garcia 2022, p. 25; and Reath 2022, pp. 65–7.

whose shared aim is our realizing the value of free and equal persons in a morally supportive social world.   (Herman 2021, p. 73)

Herman's use of the phrase "free and equal persons" cannot but remind us of Rawls's "Kantian interpretation" in the central §40 of *A Theory of Justice*. The equal value of free persons thus seems to be the starting-point for Herman's account of duties and obligations, something that, as in Rawls, is given rather than constructed. Herman's terms for how we get from that starting point to particular obligations, not by a "categorical imperative procedure" but through "nodes and transit points on a deliberative map," is at least as metaphorical as anyone's use of "construction," but what she means is that the idea of the equal value of free persons, or as she often puts it of "rational agency," is an *ideal* and *goal* that we must keep in mind as we work our way through thinking about how best to structure the institutions of human social life—the basic structure of society, in Rawls's terms—and the characteristic demands of daily human life—although not so much the artificially constructed "trolley-car problems" of Philippa Foot, Derek Parfit, and so many others.

As I have suggested, Herman devotes much more of her work to the question of how we apply this abstract ideal in everyday life than to the question of the source of this ideal itself. This is true of her first collection of essays, *The Practice of Moral Judgment* (Herman 1993), her second collection, *Moral Literacy* (Herman 2007), her most recent collection (Herman 2022), and her most extended systematic work, *The Moral Habitat* (Herman 2021). But in the concluding essay of *The Practice of Moral Judgment* and in several essays in *Moral Literacy*, Herman does provide an interpretation of what she takes to be Kant's foundational move, in the latter case explicitly distinguishing her approach from that of Korsgaard. She takes her key from Kant's conception of autonomy in the *Groundwork*: a good will must be a free will, the only way for a will to be free is for it to follow a law entirely of its own, not imposed on it from without, whether by mere inclination of the agent's own or by mere inclinations of anyone else—and then this law is defined not so much by the universality of its form but substantively, as nothing other than the law to preserve and promote freedom, or rational agency, itself. Herman's overarching concern is then to characterize the kinds of obligations and social practices that preserve and promote rational agency rather than destroying, undermining, or compromising it.

Herman remains closest to the traditional focus on the categorical imperative in "Leaving Deontology Behind," the concluding essay in *The Practice of Moral Judgment*, although even there she rejects the assumption that Kant intended it as a decision-procedure for candidate maxims of action. Here she proposes to "see what follows from taking the *Groundwork* opening at face value," that is, its claim that the only thing that is unconditionally good is a good will. The conclusions that she draws from this are that "The domain of 'the good' is rational activity and agency: that is, willing [itself]. Objects and events are not possible bearers of value. They can be thought of as good only insofar as they are possible ends of rational willing." It is the willing itself that must be good, thus "The activity of rational willing brings value into a world that, absent rational beings, could have none" (Herman 1993, pp. 213–14). Her inference is that the willing and action of rational beings, or their actions as willed, thus rational agency, *is* the value in the world. She continues that "the right question to ask is whether a standard of practical rationality provides a real answer to the problem of deontology: can formal rational constraints be or constitute a conception of *value*?" (p. 215). Her answer is yes: the conception of rational agency works the way a conception of value should, for it specifies an end that is to be preserved and promoted in our choice of particular maxims and actions. It does everything that you could want a conception of value to do. Another way to put the issue, she says, is to ask whether a principle, or the principles of "practical rationality" can be a "final end." The answer to this question is that "if we accept that the defining feature of ends is that they are sources of reasons that shape action, then principles can be ends" (p. 216). In particular, Herman argues in this essay, the successive formulations of the categorical imperative in the *Groundwork* (a sequence of formulations that Kant repeats nowhere else) "interpret the arguments of the CI procedure in terms that reveal the aspects of rational agency that generate contradictions under universalization": the formulas of "Universal Law takes the viewpoint of the agent acting; Humanity, the perspective of the person acted upon; Autonomy and the Kingdom of Ends, the place of the agent a community of like persons" (p. 227). But specifically, what these formulae do is reveal the conditions under which free, rational agency must be preserved and promoted: in the contexts of the agent's own willing, in the context of the effect of the agent's willing upon particular others, and in the context of the potential effect of the agent's willing upon the entire human community, or the entire community of rational beings, if that is something different. She adds that, since "the capacity to act for reasons all the way down is defining of rational agency" (p. 228), we must act only in ways that preserve and promote the capacity to act for reasons, but we must also not "violate the separateness condition of rational wills" (p. 230). so we must act only in ways to preserve and promote rational agency in ourselves *and in others*, not subordinating the will of others or their capacity to act for their own reasons to ours. Thus Herman concludes that "The upshot of the sequence of interpretations" of the categorical imperative "is a robust conception of embodied, social—that is to say, human—rational agency. Actions whose maxims have the form of universal law"—but here one has to add, on her own account, that comply with the other formulae of the categorical imperative as well—"express respect for rational agency by taking the fact that all rational agents are ultimate sources of reasons to be a regulative norm for all action" (p. 237).

"Leaving Deontology Behind" thus states the basis for all of Herman's work on "middle theory" that precedes and follows that essay: the latter work is directed in more detail than can be recounted here to exactly how we best preserve and promote rational agency in ourselves and others. In this relatively early essay Herman makes more of a concession to the idea of a "CI-procedure" and to universalizability as a test of the permissibility of maxims than she does in later work. In several of the essays collected in *Moral Literacy* Herman suggests an approach to Kant that hews even more closely to the argument by elimination that Kant proffers in the second part of the first section of the *Groundwork* and the first part of the second section and in the first chapter of the Analytic of the *Critique of Practical Reason* than did her statements in the earlier essay. By Kant's argument from elimination I mean his argument that "material" bases, inclinations or the objects of inclination, can never offer more than contingent, particular maxims of action, so that any maxims that are to be necessary and universal, such as moral maxims must be, can only come from the formal nature of willing itself. "The standard of value or conception of the good in terms of which we conceive our actions cannot be alien to the will" (Herman 2007, p. 170, from the essay "Bootstrapping," first published in 2002, which is a critique of Korsgaard as well as of Harry Frankfurt's view of "second-order" endorsement of "first-order" desires, which on Herman's view offers no escape from the contingency of desire). The argument of this paper is that for Kant the distinctively human will is not simply a power to act in accordance with the representation of any law, as Kant's first definition at *Groundwork,* 4: 412 might suggest, but it is the power to act in accordance with the representation of "the law that is constitutive of the will's own causal power," which is in turn "the principle of best reasons," or the principle of acting only on what seem good reasons, reasons compatible with the preservation and promotion of rational agency itself (p. 171). Herman objects to Korsgaard's earliest statement of her "self-constitution" view that to act in accordance with reasons is *ipso facto* to act in accordance with intersubjectively valid reasons that it leaves a gap that can only be closed with "an additional and . . . essential portion of metaphysics," namely Kant's "account of why the only possible law of an autonomous will is the moral law" (p. 167), which she believes is revealed by Kant's argument by elimination. A crucial point here is that for Herman the value of acting in ways that preserve and promote rational agency itself is not self-conferred as a condition of valuing anything else, as in the Korsgaard of 1986 or 1996, but is simply revealed by the process of elimination. Thus her position comes closer to Rawls's position in his Kant lectures (which she edited shortly before publishing "Bootstrapping") and to the kind of hybrid position that has a realist foundation underlying a constructivist approach to particular maxims or obligations, although, as noted previously, Herman avoids labeling her approach with any of these common meta-ethical terms.

Herman's interpretation of Kant's position thus comes close to my own, which I express by saying that our moral task is to preserve and promote maximal yet equal freedom in all—that is what she is capturing in her expression "rational agency," "agency" connoting the freedom to set our own ends and "rational" that each of us must do so in ways compatible with the equal freedom of all. However, she is content with Kant's argument for elimination for this conclusion; thus she does not acknowledge the first *Critique*'s insistence that arguments in transcendental philosophy should be ostensive and not merely apagogic. Correspondingly, she does not refer to Kant's assertion in the *Collins* lectures that freedom is the "inner value of the world" and that therefore the object of morality is the greatest possible (intra- and interpersonally) consistent use of freedom (27: 244). Nor does she refer to Kant's early suggestion that (in her terms) the separateness of wills is just a fact that we must avoid denying because of reason's most general law, the law of non-contradiction, not because of any special conception of *practical* rationality. However, her claim that the moral law is the *causal* law of the moral will, adopted from the opening of the third section of the *Groundwork* (4: 446), does suggest that she recognizes the need for a factual rather than itself constructed starting-point for Kant's moral theory—a fact of reason, after all.

However, Herman's construal of the moral law as the causal law of the moral will does raise the classical objection to Kant's equation of the free will with the moral law, already raised in the discussion of Korsgaard, the question whether "There is still room to talk about faulty action as free action." Her answer seems analogous to Korsgaard's: "Faulty action is derived from misrepresented value, from an agent's defective volitional judgment about what is best.... Faulty action is thus imputable to the autonomous will, since the principle of the maxim is a representation—albeit a *mis*representation—of the will's own law" (Herman 2007, p. 172). Herman doubles down on this approach in "The Will and Its Objects," one of the chapters of *Moral Literacy* first published only in that book. Here she formulates the classical "worry that if human choice is only free when maxims of action are subjected to the condition of 'qualifying as universal law,' contramoral choice is unfree" (Herman 2007, p. 242). But her solution remains that willing must be willed in accordance with the will's own law, namely the moral law, thus that the only explanation of contramoral willing is that we "*mis*represent" the moral law, "as we may when nonrational influences affect or interfere with our representation of the will's own law (as they can our representation of any law)" (p. 246). Here Herman seems to allow "nonrational" or "alien" influences on our will after all, presumably that what in Kant's view count as mere inclinations can simply interfere with our clear view of the moral law and its authority. What she does not allow any room for is the *Religion*'s insistence that mere inclinations are *never* themselves the source of evil, which is rather always our free choice to subordinate the moral law, which on Kant's view we all always know perfectly well, to self-interest or self-love. There does not seem to be room for intentional evil or contramorality on Herman's account anymore than on Korsgaard's.[30]

More generally, thinking of individual free acts and their relations to other free acts rather than just thinking of freedom in general reveals possible sites for free but evil actions. It might seem that an action is either free or not, but that is too simple. For one, at least apparently, freely choose an act that destroys or compromises the possibility of other free acts, whether by oneself or by others. An act of suicide might be free, but destroy all further possibility of free acts by the suicide, and possibly compromise the freedom of others as well, for example by voiding a life-insurance policy that might have paid for the continued education of a dependent. An act of homicide or maiming might be freely undertaken by the perpetrator, but will destroy or compromise the freedom of the victim. Understanding the possibility of evil requires logical space for free actions that destroy freedom without themselves being self-contradictory, as well as for the free choice to commit such actions and not their commission from mere misrepresentation of the moral law. On Kant's own account, no one merely misrepresents the moral law, although people try to carve out exceptions from it for themselves all the time.

As already mentioned, much of Herman's effort is focused on what she calls "middle theory," the derivation of the particular duties and obligations of human beings, although not by any strict deduction by means of a CI-procedure. Her discussions of the imperfect duties of self-perfection and the promotion of the happiness of others in *Moral Literacy* and *The Moral Habit* are especially rich and rewarding. However, there is one point in the treatment of "Obligatory Ends" when she makes a closer connection between the two imperfect duties than Kant does. In both the Introduction to the Doctrine of Virtue (section VIII.2, 6: 393) and its section §27 (6: 450–1), Kant derives the duty to promote the happiness of others from the morally necessary universalization of one's own merely natural desire that others help one realize one's own happiness when one's own means turn out to be insufficient (which they surely will at some point or other, whatever the momentarily strong and rich person might think). This is as pure an application of the Formula of Universal Law as we find outside of the illustration of the first formulation of the categorical imperative in the *Groundwork*. Herman proposes a different argument for this duty, however, one that treats promoting the happiness of others as a means to one's own self-perfection: "Our own rational abilities are in many ways dependent on those of others...We are, from the

---

[30] Herman does acknowledge Kant's conception of radical evil in a later paper on Kant's *Religion*, "Religion and the Highest Good," first published in 2018, but she there says that "'Radical evil' is... identified as the permanent subjective instability of moral character that mars even the best of us" (Herman 2022, p. 197), but without quite saying that Kant insists that radical evil is the product of an entirely free choice (*Willkühr*), or explaining how this conception of radical evil fits with her previous interpretation of contramoral action as due to mere misrepresentation.

beginning of our lives, involved with others as a way of becoming who we are. And if we do not get this connection right, our rational agency is impaired." Indeed, Herman does not stop there, but also argues, in a manner reminiscent of earlier (anti-Hobbesian) moralists such as Richard Cumberland and Francis Hutcheson, that the well-being of others is not only instrumental to the preservation and promotion of our own rational agency, "but also that their well-being is a source of pleasure to us, something that makes our lives go well" (Herman 2007, pp. 267–8). The worry here is not that Herman's argument brings in empirical considerations here—Kant makes it clear in the Introduction to the *Metaphysics of Morals* that the derivation of our particularly human obligations does require the application of the pure principle of morality to the empirical circumstances of human existence, which surely do include our developmental dependence on each other, for one thing (6: 217). But Kant does not explicitly make the first argument for the duty to promote the happiness of others that Herman attributes to him, although perhaps he should have. More disconcertingly, perhaps, her second argument for this duty makes it subservient to our own *happiness*, which seems distinctly un-Kantian.

In spite of the several problems I have mentioned, Herman's position is like my own in splitting the difference between unrestricted constructivism and an equally unrestricted moral realism: she certainly recognizes that the particular duties and obligations of human beings are to be derived, in "middle theory," by the application of the moral law to the realities of the human condition, and are not otherwise written on some mysterious tablets handed to us by some moral reality. The fundamental value of rational agency, however, like the fundamental value of freedom on my interpretation of at least one of Kant's arguments, is not constructed or self-conferred, but is simply there. That is an element of moral realism.

This brings us back to my suggestion that Herman's position ends up closer to Rawls's original, restricted constructivism than the unrestricted constructivism of other Rawlsians such as Korsgaard and O'Neill. In the middle section of *The Moral Habitat*, which is titled "Making the Turn to Kant" and is Herman's richest discussion of Kant's imperfect duties, the previously most neglected part of his system of duties, Herman premises that "arguments *to* duties should have...value claims as premises" (Herman 2021, p. 77). This can be taken as a statement of Herman's endorsement of a basic realism about value underlying the construction of our duties and obligations. She continues:

Kant himself sees the "What's it for?" question as appropriate and inevitable. There is ample evidence of an answer in the Kantian corpus that the point of our duties and permissions is to create a habitat for free, equal, and self-directing human persons to develop and expression their rational natures. As a habitat, it is an environment suited to such persons, together, over time. As a created habitat, it has laws, but they are moral laws, not laws of nature.... The duties associated with positive law along with the duties governing interpersonal relations and duties to the self are the vehicles for habitat construction.   (Herman 2021, p. 78)

So Herman does use the term "construction" although not "constructivism": it is the moral habitat that must be constructed, but not the value of free, equal, and self-directing persons themselves. Herman's claim that it is the moral habitat that must be constructed also suggests that moral construction must be a real-world process—sustained, collective action—of transforming the natural world into a moral world, not a merely philosophical project of deriving the concepts of our duties from some more fundamental concept.

Herman goes beyond Rawls, and I think beyond Kant himself, in arguing further that the development of a just society, or in Rawls's terms of a just basic structure of society, is not merely part of morality but the necessary condition for the realization of individual morality; here again, she seems to neglect Kant's *Religion*, with its argument that the "change of heart" from evil to good is in principle possible for anyone at anytime, although it may be supported by the development of what Kant calls the "ethico-civil community"—which he decidedly distinguishes from the "juridico-civil community" (*RBMR*, 6: 94). Whether Herman's stronger position or Kant's own weaker one is more plausible is perhaps a question that can only be decided empirically, not a priori. Nevertheless, Herman's return in her latest work to a formulation so redolent of Rawls's original "Kantian interpretation" completes an encirclement of the intervening attempts at a more radical form of constructivism all the way down, and suggests that their more moderate interpretation of Kant, which I share, might be the more plausible one.

Conclusion

After such a long journey, what have we learned?

I said at the outset that I would distinguish between those interpretations and ensuing criticisms of Kant that have seen the requirement of the universalizability of our maxims as the foundation of his conception of morality and those that have found his fundamental moral insight in the ideal of maximal yet equal freedom for all rational beings. We have now seen how while philosophers such as Pistorius, Hegel, Mill, and other more recent writers have criticized Kant for the apparent difficulties in actually deriving duties from the requirement of universal law, philosophers such as T. H. Green, Josiah Royce, H. J. Paton, and John Rawls have developed in their own, insightful ways the ideal that each human being should develop and realize their own conception of a good life, but in a way that does not privilege their goals over those of others or free them from a broad obligation to assist others in setting and realizing their own ends in life. Indeed, even John Stuart Mill developed his version of this idea in *On Liberty*, although he did not seem to have realized that he was following the path that had been blazed by Kant. To use Kant's favored term, the true followers of Kant are those who have realized that what we now think of individual autonomy can only and must be realized within the framework of Kant's conception of morality, the adoption by each of the law that grants equal value to the freedom of all.

Kant himself tried out several different strategies for grounding this moral ideal without settling on just one, and subsequent philosophers have likewise tried to ground it in different ways. Perhaps the secret of the best foundation for morality has yet to be discovered, or perhaps it is the simplest thing in the world: since everyone values their own freedom, even above any of their particular ends, and even if they do not put it to themselves this way, and, as Richard Hooker pointed out at the very beginning of modernity, the essence of rationality is just that like cases should be treated alike, insofar as they are rational everyone should recognize that others value their own freedom just as much as they themselves do, and moreover that others may sometimes need and want their assistance in realizing their own goals just as much as they themselves want such assistance from others.

Next, Kant was convinced that we are always free to do the right thing no matter what our prior history seems to predict, and resorted to his controversial doctrine of transcendental idealism to secure the possibility of such a radical conception of freedom. From Ulrich to Sidgwick to Moore to Rawls, few have been willing to accept Kant's conviction of such unrestricted freedom. Here a

Kant's Impact on Moral Philosophy. Paul Guyer, Oxford University Press. © Paul Guyer 2024.
DOI: 10.1093/oso/9780199592456.003.0019

conception of human freedom as something that must be realized in the natural world, where it is always ever realized only in some degree or other, varying in degree between different individuals and even within particular lives, seems the only plausible conception—but precisely for this reason the fullest realization of maximal yet equal freedom does turn out to be a goal that we can and must work towards, not something that is somehow, somewhere already given. Only when we realize that freedom is not already guaranteed in some noumenal world can it be seen as the end that is also a duty that it properly is.

Finally, Kant was lampooned from the earliest days for an inhuman conception of moral motivation, one that excluded all natural feelings of affection and respect from any role in morally worthy action. As we saw in our contrast between the limited strategic goal of Kant's examples in the first section of his *Groundwork for the Metaphysics of Morals* and the refined psychology of such late works as *Religion within the Boundaries of Mere Reason* and the *Metaphysics of Morals*, this is a canard that should long ago have been laid to rest, and the subtlest Kantians since have recognized this point.

We have repeatedly touched on these and other issues in this review of Kant's impact on the subsequent history of moral philosophy. There is no doubt much more to be said about everything and everyone that I have discussed. Still, three lessons is always a good number to learn, so I shall be pleased if my readers do take away these three points from this work.

Bibliography

I. Primary Sources

Achenwall, Gottfried, 2019. *Natural Law*, edited by Pauline Kleingeld, translated by Corinna Vermuelen, with an introduction by Paul Guyer. London: Bloomsbury.

Anonymous, 1785a. Review of Kant, *Grundlegung zur Metaphysik der Sitten. Allgemeine Literatur-Zeitung* 80 (7 April): 21–3. Reprinted in Landau, 1991, pp. 135–9.

Anonymous, 1785b. Review of Kant, *Grundlage zur Metaphysik der Sitten. Gothaische gelehrte Zeitungen* (17 and 20 August): 66. Stück, pp. 533–6; 67. Stück, pp. 537–44; 67. Stück, Beilage, pp. 545–60. In Landau, 1991, pp. 183–97.

Anonymous, 1786a. Review of Kant, *Grundlegung zur Metaphysik der Sitten. Tübingsche gelehrte Anzeigen* 14 (16 February): 105–12. In Landau, 1991, pp. 277–83.

Anonymous, 1786b. Review of Kant, *Grundlegung zur Metaphysik der Sitten. Kritische Beyträge zur neuesten Geschichte der Gelehrsamkeit.* Erstes Stück: 202–13. In Landau, 1991, pp. 318–23.

Anscombe, G. E. M., 1957. *Intention.* London: Routledge & Kegan Paul.

Anscombe, G. E. M., 1958. "Modern Moral Philosophy." *Philosophy* 33/124: 1–19.

Austin, J. L., 1955. *How to Do Things with Words.* Oxford: Clarendon Press.

Baier, Kurt, 1959. *The Moral Point of View.* Ithaca, NY: Cornell University Press.

Baier, Kurt, 1995. *Rationality and the Moral Order: The Social Roots of Rationality and Morality.* LaSalle, IL: Open Court.

Baumgarten, Gottlieb Baumgarten, 2013. *Metaphysics* (1739), translated by Coutney D. Fugate and John Hymers. London: Bloomsbury.

Baumgarten, Alexander Gottlieb, 2019. *Anfangsgründer der praktischen Metaphysik* (Latin-German edition), translated by Alexander Aichele. Hamburg: Verlag Felix Meiner.

Baumgarten, Alexander Gottlieb, 2020. *Elements of First Practical Philosophy: A Critical Translation with Kant's Reflections on Moral Philosophy*, translated by Courtney D. Fugate and John Hymers. London: Bloomsbury.

Bosanquet, Bernard, 1894. *The Philosophical Theory of the State.* London: Macmillan (4th edition, 1923).

Bosanquet, Bernard, 1912. *The Principle of Individuality and Value.* London: Macmillan.

Bosanquet, Bernard, 1913. *The Value and Destiny of the Individual.* London: Macmillan.

Bradley, Francis Herbert, 1876. *Ethical Studies.* Oxford: Clarendon Press (2nd edition, 1927).

Butler, Joseph, 2017. *Fifteen Sermons and Other Writings on Ethics* (1726), edited by David McNaughton. Oxford: Oxford University Press.

Caird, Edward, 1866. *Ethical Philosophy.* Glasgow: James Maclehose.

Caird, Edward, 1877. *A Critical Account of the Philosophy of Kant.* Glasgow: James Maclehose.

Caird, Edward, 1883. *Hegel.* Edinburgh: William Blackwood.

Caird, Edward, 1889. *The Critical Philosophy of Immanuel Kant.* 2 vols. Glasgow: James Maclehose; New York: Macmillan.

Caird, Edward, 1893. *The Evolution of Religion.* Glasgow: James Maclehose.

Caird, Edward, 1904. *The Evolution of Theology in the Greek Philosophers*. Glasgow: James Maclehose.

Caird, Edward, 2008. *Lectures on Moral* Philosophy. In C. Tyler, ed., *Unpublished Manuscripts in British Idealism*. Exeter: Imprint Academic, vol. 2, pp. 40–152.

Cicero, Marcus Tullius, 1783. *Abhandlung über die menschlichen Pflichten*, translated by Christian Garve. Breslau: Whilhelm Gottlieb Korn (new edition, 1787).

Clarke, Samuel, 1998. *A Demonstration of the Being and Attributes of God and Other Writings*, edited by Ezio Vailati. Cambridge: Cambridge University Press.

Cudworth, Ralph, 1996. *A Treatise concerning Eternal and Immutable Morality*, edited by Sarah Hutton. Cambridge: Cambridge University Press.

Cumberland, Richard, 2005. *A Treatise of the Laws of Nature* (1672), translated by John Maxwell (1737), edited by Jon Parkin. Indianapolis: Liberty Fund.

Eberhard, Johann August, 1781. *Sittenlehre der Vernunft*. Berlin: Friedrich Nicolai (2nd edition, 1786). Reprinted, Hildesheim: Georg Olms, 2011.

Fichte, Johann Gottlieb, 1956. *The Vocation of Man*, edited by Roderick M. Chisholm. Indianapolis: Bobbs-Merrill.

Fichte, Johann Gottlieb. 1982, *The Science of Knowledge*, edited and translated by Peter Heath and John Lachs. Cambridge: Cambridge University Press.

Fichte, Johann Gottlieb, 1992. *Foundations of Transcendental Philosophy: (Wissenschaftslehre) Nova Methodo (1796/99)*, edited and translated by Daniel Breazeale. Ithaca, NY, and London: Cornell University Press.

Fichte, Johann Gottlieb, 2000. *Foundations of Natural Right*, edited and translated by Michael J. Bauer and Frederick Neuhouser. Cambridge: Cambridge University Press.

Fichte, Johann Gottlieb, 2005. *The System of Ethics According the Principles of the Wissenschaftslehre*, edited and translated by Daniel Breazeale and Günter Zöller. Cambridge: Cambridge University Press.

Fichte, Johann Gottlieb, 2010. *Attempt at a Critique of All Revelation*, edited by Allen Wood, translated by Garrett Green. Cambridge: Cambridge University Press.

Foot, Philippa, 1972. "Morality as a System of Categorical Imperatives." *Philosophical Review* 81: 305–16.

Forster, E. M., 1910. *Howards End*. New York and London: G. P. Putnam & Sons, 1910.

Frankfurt, Harry G., 1988. *The Importance of What we Care about: Philosophical Essays*. Cambridge: Cambridge University Press.

Garve, Christian, 1783. *Philosophische Anmerkungen und Abhandlungen zu Ciceros Büchern von den Pflichten*, 3 vols. Breslau: Wilhelm Gottlieb Korn (new edition, 1787).

Garve, Christian, 1792. *Versuche über verschiedene Gegenstände aus der Moral, der Literatur, und dem gesellschaftlichen Leben*, part 1. Breslau: Wilhelm Gottlieb Korn.

Gesang, Bernward, ed., 2007. *Kants vergessener Rezensent: Die Kritik der theoretischen und praktischen Philosophie Kants in fünf frühen Rezensionen von Hermann Andreas Pistorius*. Kant-Forschungen Band 18. Hamburg: Felix Meiner Verlag.

Green, Thomas Hill, 1885–6. *Works of Thomas Hill Green*, edited by R. L. Nettleship, 3 vols. London: Longman, Green, & Co.

Green, Thomas Hill, 2003. *Prolegomena to Ethics*, edited by David Brink. Oxford: Clarendon Press.

Grice, H. P., 1989. *Studies in the Ways of Words*. Cambridge, MA: Harvard University Press, 1989.

Hare, R. M., 1952. *The Language of Morals*. Oxford: Clarendon Press.

Hare, R. M., 1963. *Freedom and Reason*. Oxford: Clarendon Press.

Hegel, Georg Wilhelm Friedrich, 1802–3. "Über die wissenschaftliche Behandlung des Naturrechts, seine Stelle in der praktischen Philosophie und sein Verhältnis zu den positiven Rechtswissenschaften." *Kritisches Journal der Philosophie* 2/2 (November–December 1802), and 2/3 (May–June 1803). Translated as Hegel 1975.

Hegel, Georg Wilhelm Friedrich, 1821. *Naturrecht und Staatswissenschaft im Grundrisse/ Grundlinien der Philosophie des Rechts*. Berlin. Translated as Hegel 1991.

Hegel, Georg Wilhelm Friedrich, 1942. *The Philosophy of Right*, translated by T. M Knox. Oxford: Clarendon Press.

Hegel, Georg Wilhelm Friederich, 1970. *Enzyklopädie der philosophischen Wissenschaften im Grundrisse* (1830), edited by Friedhelm Nicolin and Otto Pöggeler. Hamburg: Felix Meiner Verlag.

Hegel, Georg Wilhelm Friedrich, 1975. *Natural Law: The Scientific Ways of Treating Natural Law, its Place in Moral Philosophy, and its Relation to the Positive Sciences of Law*, translated by T. M. Knox, introduction by H. B. Acton. Philadelphia: University of Pennsylvania Press.

Hegel, Georg Wilhelm Friedrich, 1977. *Faith and Knowledge*, translated by Walter Cerf and H. S. Harris. Albany, NY: State University Press of New York.

Hegel, Georg Wilhelm Friedrich, 1991. *Elements of the Philosophy of Right*, edited by Allen W. Wood, translated by H. B. Nisbet. Cambridge: Cambridge University Press.

Hegel, Georg Wilhelm Friedrich, 2007. *Lectures on the Philosophy of Spirit of 1827–8*, translated by Robert R. Williams. Oxford: Oxford University Press.

Hegel, Georg Wilhelm Friedrich, 2018. *The Phenomenology of Spirit*, translated by Michael Inwood. Oxford: Oxford University Press.

Herbart, Johann Friedrich, 1808. *Allgemeine Practische Philosophie*. Göttingen: Justus Friedrich Danckwerts.

Herman, Barbara, 1993. *The Practice of Moral Judgment*. Cambridge, MA: Harvard University Press.

Herman, Barbara, 2007. *Moral Literacy*. Cambridge, MA: Harvard University Press.

Herman, Barbara, 2021. *The Moral Habitat*. Oxford: Oxford University Press.

Herman, Barbara, 2022. *Kantian Commitments: Essays in Moral Theory and Practice*. Oxford: Oxford University Press.

Home, Heinrich, 1790–1. *Grundsäzte der Kritik*, letzte verbesserte Auflage, translated by Johann Nicolaus Meinhard. Leipzig: Dyck; Vienna: Schrämbl. (See also Kames, Henry Home, Lord.)

Hooker, Richard, 2013. *Of the Laws of Ecclesiastical Polity* (1593), edited by Arthur Stephen McGrade, 3 vols. Oxford: Oxford University Press.

Hume, David, 1998. *An Enquiry concerning the Principles of Morals* (1751), edited by Tom L. Beauchamp. Oxford: Clarendon Press.

Hume, David, 2007. *A Treatise of Human Nature*, edited by David Fate Norton and Mary J. Norton, 2 vols. Oxford: Clarendon Press.

Hutcheson, Francis, 2002. *Essay on the Nature and Conduct of the Passions, with Illustrations on the Moral Sense* (1728), edited by Aaron Garrett. Indianapolis: Liberty Fund.

Hutcheson, Francis, 2008. *Inquiry into the Original of our Ideas of Beauty and Virtue* (1725, 4th edition 1738), edited by Wolfgang Leidhold (2nd edition). Indianapolis: Liberty Fund.

Imhof, Silvan, and Jörg Noller, eds, 2021. *Kants freiheitsbegriff (1786–1800): Dokumentation einer Debatte*, Kant-Forschungen Band 26. Hamburg: Felix Meiner Verlag.

Jacobi, Friedrich Heinrich, 1994. *The Main Philosophical Writings and the Novel* Allwill, translated by George di Giovanni. Toronto and Montreal: McGill-Queens University Press.

Jones, Henry, 1909. *Idealism as a Practical Creed*. Glasgow: James Maclehose.

Jones, Henry, 1910. *Working Faith of the Social Reformer*. London: Macmillan.

Kames, Henry Home, Lord, 2005. *Elements of Criticism*, 6th edition, edited by Peter Jones, 2 vols. Indianapolis: Liberty Fund.

Kant, Immanuel, 1792. "Über das radikale Böse in der menschlichen Natur." *Berlinische Monatschrift* (April): 329–84. (*RBMR*, Part One)

Kant, Immanuel, 1838. *Religion within the Boundary of Pure Reason*, translated by J. William Semple. Edinburgh: Thomas Clark.

Kant, Immanuel, 1900–. *Kants gesammelte Schriften*, edited by the Royal Prussian, later German and Berlin-Brandenburg Academy of Sciences. 29 vols. Berlin: Georg Reimer, later Walter de Gruyter & Co.

Kant, Immanuel, 1960. *Religion within the Limits of Reason Alone*, translated by T. M. Greene and Hoyt H. Hudson. New edition with introduction by John R. Silber: New York: Harper & Row.

Kant, Immanuel, 1992a. *Theoretical Philosophy 1755–1770*, translated and edited by David Walford, with the collaboration of Ralf Meerbote. Cambridge: Cambridge University Press.

Kant, Immanuel, 1992b. *Lectures on Logic*, translated and edited by J. Michael Young. Cambridge: Cambridge University Press.

Kant, Immanuel, 1993. *Opus postumum*, edited by Eckart Förster, translated by Eckart Förster and Michael Rosen. Cambridge: Cambridge University Press.

Kant, Immanuel, 1996a. *Practical Philosophy*, edited and translated by Mary J. Gregor. Cambridge: Cambridge University Press.

Kant, Immanuel, 1996b. *Religion and Rational Theology*, edited and translated by Allen W. Wood and George di Giovanni. Cambridge: Cambridge University Press.

Kant, Immanuel, 1997. *Lectures on Ethics*, edited by J. B. Schneewind, translated by Peter Heath. Cambridge: Cambridge University Press.

Kant, Immanuel, 1998. *Critique of Pure Reason*, edited and translated by Paul Guyer and Allen W. Wood. Cambridge: Cambridge University Press.

Kant, Immanuel, 2000. *Critique of the Power of Judgment*, edited by Paul Guyer, translated by Paul Guyer and Eric Matthews. Cambridge: Cambridge University Press.

Kant, Immanuel, 2004. *Vorlesung zur Moralphilosophie*, edited by Werner Stark and Manfred Kuehn. Berlin and New York: Walter de Gruyter & Co.

Kant, Immanuel, 2005. *Notes and Fragments*, edited by Paul Guyer, translated by Curtis Bowman, Paul Guyer, and Frederick Rauscher. Cambridge: Cambridge University Press.

Kant, Immanuel, 2007. *Anthropology, History, and Education*, edited by Günter Zöller and Robert B. Louden, translated by Mary Gregor, Paul Guyer, Robert B. Louden, Holly Wilson, Allen W. Wood, Günter Zöller, and Arnulf Zweig. Cambridge: Cambridge University Press.

Kant, Immanuel, 2011. *Observations on the Feeling of the Beautiful and Sublime and Other Writings*, edited by Patrick Frierson and Paul Guyer. Cambridge: Cambridge University Press.

Kant, Immanuel, 2012. *Lectures on Anthropology*, edited by Allen W. Wood and Robert B. Louden. Cambridge: Cambridge University Press.

Korsgaard, Christine M., 1985. "Kant's Formula of Universal Law." *Pacific Philosophical Quarterly* 66: 24–47. Reprinted in Korsgaard 1996a, pp. 77–105.

Korsgaard, Christine M., 1986. "Kant's Formula of Humanity." *Kant-Studien* 77: 183–202. Reprinted in Korsgaard 1996a, pp. 106–32.

Korsgaard, Christine M., 1996a. *Creating the Kingdom of Ends*. Cambridge: Cambridge University Press.

Korsgaard, Christine M., 1996b. *The Sources of Normativity*, edited by Onora O'Neill. Cambridge: Cambridge University Press.

Korsgaard, Christine M., 1998. "Motivation, Metaphysics, and the Value of the Self: A Reply to Ginsborg, Guyer, and Schneewind." *Ethics* 109: 49–66.

Korsgaard, Christine M., 2009. *Self-Constitution: Agency, Identity, and Integrity*. Oxford: Oxford University Press.

Landau, Albert, ed., 1991. *Rezensionen zur kritischen Philosophie 1781–87*. Bebra: Albert Landau Verlag.

Leibniz, Gottfried Wilhelm, 1969. *Philosophical Papers and Letters* (2nd edition), edited by Leroy E. Loemker. Dordrecht: D. Reidel.

Lessing, Gotthold Ephraim, 1984. *Laocoön: An Essay on the Limits of Painting and Poetry*, translated by Edward Allen McCormick, with an introduction by Michael Fried. Baltimore, MD: Johns Hopkins University Press.

Locke, John, 1967. *Two Treatises of Government*, edited by Peter Laslett. Cambridge: Cambridge University Press.

Locke, John, 1975. *An Essay concerning Human Understanding*, edited by P. H. Nidditch. Oxford: Clarendon Press.

McDowell, John, 1978. "Are Moral Requirements Hypothetical Imperatives?" *Proceedings of the Aristotelian Society*, supplementary vol. 52: 13–29.

McTaggart, John McTaggart Ellis, 1908. "The Unreality of Time," *Mind* NS 17: 457–74.

Maimon, Salomon, 2010. *Essay on Transcendental Philosophy*, translated by N. Midley, H. Somers-Hall, A. Welchman, and M. Reglitz. London: Continuum.

Mendelssohn, Moses, 1983. *Jerusalem, or on Religion Power and Judaism*, translated by Allan Arkush. Hanover: Brandeis University Press.

Mill, John Stuart, 1956–91. *Collected Works of John Stuart Mill*, edited by John M. Robson. 33 vols. Toronto and London: University of Toronto Press and Routledge & Kegan Paul.

Mill, John Stuart, 1969. *Essays on Ethics, Religion and Society*. Mill 1956–91, vol. 10.

Moore, George Edward, 1898. "Freedom." *Mind*, NS 7/26: 179–204.

Moore, George Edward, 1912. *Ethics*. London: Williams & Norgate. Later reprints, Oxford: Oxford University Press.

Moore, George Edward, 1993. *Principia Ethica*. Revised edition with preface to the 2nd edition and other papers, edited by Thomas Baldwin. Cambridge: Cambridge University Press.

Muirhead, J. H., 1932. *Rule and End in Morals*. Oxford: Oxford University Press.

Murdoch, Iris, 1970. *The Sovereignty of the Good*. London: Routledge & Kegan Paul.

Nagel, Thomas, 1970. *The Possibility of Altruism*. Oxford: Clarendon Press.

Nagel, Thomas, 1986. *The View from Nowhere*. New York: Oxford University Press.

Nehamas, Alexander, 1983. "How One Becomes What One Is." *Philosophical Review* 92: 385–417.

Nehamas, Alexander, 2000. *The Art of Living: Socratic Reflections from Plato to Foucault*. Berkeley and Los Angeles: University of California Press.

Nietzsche, Friedrich, 1986. *Human, All Too Human*, translated by R. J. Hollingdale. Cambridge: Cambridge University Press.

Nietzsche, Friedrich, 2001. *The Gay Science*, edited by Bernard Williams, translated by Josefine Nauckhoff. Cambridge: Cambridge University Press.

Nietzsche, Friedrich, 2002. *Beyond Good and Evil*, edited by Rolf-Peter Horstmann and Judith Norman. Cambridge: Cambridge University Press.

Nietzsche, Friedrich, 2007. *On the Genealogy of Morality*, edited by Keith Ansell-Pearson, translated by Carol Diethe (revised edition). Cambridge: Cambridge University Press.

Noller, Jörg, and John Walsh, eds, 2022. *Kant's Early Critics on Freedom of the Will.* Cambridge: Cambridge University Press.

O'Neill, Onora, 1985. "Consistency in Action." In Nelson Potter and Mark Timmons, eds, *Universality and Morality: Essays on Ethical Universalizability*. Dordrecht: D. Reidel, pp. 159–86. Reprinted in O'Neill 1989a, pp. 81–104.

O'Neill, Onora, 1986. *Faces of Hunger: An Essay on Poverty, Justice and Development.* London: Allen & Unwin.

O'Neill, Onora, 1989a. *Constructions of Reason: Explorations of Kant's Practical Philosophy.* Cambridge: Cambridge University Press.

O'Neill, Onora, 1989b. "Reason and Autonomy in *Grundlegung* III." In Otfried Höffe, ed., *Grundlegung zur Metaphysik der Sitten: Ein kooperative Kommentar.* Frankfurt am Main: Vittorio Klostermann. Reprinted in O'Neill 1989b, pp. 51–65.

O'Neill, Onora, 1989c. "Universal Laws and Ends-in-Themselves." *Monist* (1989). Reprinted in O'Neill 1989b, pp. 126–44.

O'Neill, Onora, 1989d. "Action, Anthropology, and Autonomy." In O'Neill 1989a, pp. 66–77.

O'Neill, Onora, 1992. "Vindicating Reason." In Paul Guyer, ed., *The Cambridge Companion to Kant.* Cambridge: Cambridge University Press, pp. 280–308. Reprinted in O'Neill 2015a, pp. 13–27.

O'Neill, Onora, 1999. "Constructivism in Rawls and Kant." Earlier version in Julian Nida-Rumelin, ed., *Rationality, Realism, Revision: Proceedings of the 3rd International Conference of the Society for Analytical Philosophy.* Berlin: Walter de Gruyter, 1999); final version in O'Neill 2015a, pp. 69–85.

O'Neill, Onora, 2000. *Bounds of Justice.* Cambridge: Cambridge University Press.

O'Neill, Onora, 2001. "Sidgwick on Practical Reason." In Harrison 2001, pp. 83–9.

O'Neill, Onora, 2002a. *Autonomy and Trust in Bioethics: The Gifford Lectures, 2001.* Cambridge: Cambridge University Press.

O'Neill, Onora, 2002b. *A Question of Trust: The BBC Reith Lectures 2002.* Cambridge: Cambridge University Press.

O'Neill, Onora, 2003. "Constructivism in Rawls and Kant." In Freeman 2003, pp. 347–67.

O'Neill, Onora, 2004a. "Self-Legislation, Autonomy, and the Form of Law." In Herta Nagl-Docerkal and Rudolf Langthaler, eds, *Recht—Geschichte—Religion: Die Bedeutung Kants in der Gegenwart, Deutsche Zeitschrift für Philosophie*, Sonderband 9. Berlin: Akademie Verlag, pp. 11–26. Reprinted in O'Neill 2015a, pp. 121–36.

O'Neill, Onora, 2004b. O'Neill, "Kant: Rationality as Practical Reason." In Alfred J. Mele and Piers Rawling, eds, *The Oxford Handbook of Rationality.* Oxford: Oxford University Press, pp. 93–109. Reprinted in O'Neill 2015a, pp. 38–55.

O'Neill, Onora, 2013. *Acting on Principle: An Essay on Kantian Ethics.* New York: Columbia University Press, 1975; 2nd edition, Cambridge: Cambridge University Press, 2013.

O'Neill, Onora, 2015a. *Constructing Authorities: Reason, Politics, and Interpretation in Kant's Philosophy.* Cambridge: Cambridge University Press.

O'Neill, Onora, 2015b. "Changing Constructions." In Brooks and Nussbaum 2015, pp. 57–72.

O'Neill, Onora, 2018. *From Principles to Practice: Normativity and Judgment in Ethics and Politics.* Cambridge: Cambridge University Press.

Parfit, Derek, 1984. *Reasons and Persons*. Oxford: Clarendon Press.

Parfit, Derek, 2011–17. *On What Matters*, edited by Samuel Scheffler, 3 vols. Oxford: Oxford University Press.

Paton, Herbert James, 1927. *The Good Will: A Study in the Coherence Theory of Goodness*. London: George Allen & Unwin.

Paton, Herbert James, 1936. *Kant's Metaphysic of Experience*, 2 vols. London: George Allen and Unwin.

Paton, Herbert James, 1947. *The Categorical Imperative: A Study in Kant's Moral Philosophy*. London: Hutchinson.

Piper, Adrian, 2013. *Rationality and the Structure of the Self* (2nd edition). Available at the website of the Adrian Piper Research Archive, Berlin, <http://www.adrianpiper.com/rss/index.shtml>.

Piper, Adrian, 2018. *A Synthesis of Intuitions: 1965–2016*, edited by Emily Hall. New York: Museum of Modern Art.

Pistorius, Herman Andreas, 1786. Review of Kant, *Groundlegung zur Metaphysik der Sitten*. *Allgemeine deutsche Bibliothek* 66/2 (May): 447–63. Reprinted in Landau 1991, pp. 354–67, and Gesang 2007, pp. 26–38, cited here from the latter.

Pistorius, Hermann Andreas, 1794. Review of Kant, *Critique of Practical Reason*. *Allgemeine deutsche Bibliothek* 117/1: 78–105. Reprinted in Gesang 2007, pp. 78–98.

Popper, Karl R., 1961. *The Logic of Scientific Discovery*. London: Routledge & Kegan Paul.

Popper, Karl R., 1963. *Conjectures and Refutations: The Growth of Scientific Knowledge*. London: Routledge & Kegan Paul.

Prichard, H. A., 1909. *Kant's Theory of Knowledge*. Oxford: Clarendon Press.

Prichard, H. A., 1912. "Does Moral Philosophy Rest on a Mistake?" *Mind*, NS 21: 21–37. Reprinted in Prichard, *Moral Obligation: Essays and Lectures*, edited by W. D. Ross. Oxford: Clarendon Press, 1949; cited here from the most recent edition, Prichard 2002, pp. 7–20.

Prichard, H. A., 1929. "Duty and Interest." In Prichard 2002, pp. 21–49.

Prichard, H. A., 2002. *Moral Writings*, edited by Jim McAdam. Oxford Clarendon Press.

Prichard, H. A., undated. "Kant's *Fundamental Principles of the Metaphysics of Morals*." In Prichard 2002, pp. 50–76.

Pufendorf, Samuel, 2003. *The Whole Duty of Man, According to the Law of Nature*, translated by Andrew Tooke (1691), with two Discourses and a Commentary by Jean Barbeyrac (1718), translated by David Saunders, edited by Ian Hunter and David Saunders. Indianapolis: Liberty Fund.

Pufendorf, Samuel, 2009. *Two Books of the Elements of Universal Jurisprudence*, translated by William Abbott Oldfather (1931), edited by Thomas Behme. Indianapolis: Liberty Fund.

Rawls, John, 1971. *A Theory of Justice*. Cambridge, MA: Harvard University Press. Cited here from revised edition, 1999.

Rawls, John, 1975. "A Kantian Conception of Equality." *Cambridge Review* 96: 94–9. Reprinted in and cited here from Rawls 1999, pp. 254–66.

Rawls, John, 1980. "Kantian Constructivism in Moral Theory." *Journal of Philosophy* 77: 515–72. Reprinted in and cited here from Rawls 1999, pp. 303–58.

Rawls, John, 1985. "Justice as Fairness: Political Not Metaphysical." *Philosophy and Public Affairs* 14: 223–52. Reprinted in Rawls 1999, pp. 388–414.

Rawls, John, 1989. "Themes in Kant's Moral Philosophy." In *Kant's Transcendental Deductions: The Three "Critiques" and the "Opus Postumum"*, edited by Eckart Förster.

Stanford, CA: Stanford University Press, pp. 81–113. Reprinted in and cited here from Rawls 1999, pp. 497–528.

Rawls, John, 1993. *Political Liberalism*. New York: Columbia University Press. Expanded edition, 2005.

Rawls, John, 1999. *Collected Papers*, edited by Samuel Freeman. Cambridge, MA: Harvard University Press.

Rawls, John, 2000. *Lectures on the History of Moral Philosophy*, edited by Barbara Herman. Cambridge, MA: Harvard University Press.

Rawls, John, 2007. *Lectures on the History of Political Philosophy*, edited by Samuel Freeman. Cambridge, MA: Harvard University Press.

Reidy, David A., 2014. "From Philosophical Theology to Democratic Theory: Early Postcards from an Intellectual Journey." In Mandle and Reidy 2014, pp. 9–30.

Reinhold, Carl Leonhard, 1792. *Briefe über die Kantische Philosophie*, vol. 2. Leipzig: Göschen.

Reinhold, Carl Leonhard, 1794. [Review of Kant's *Religion within the Boundaries of Mere Reason*.] *Allgemeine Literatur-Zeitung* 86–90 (13–15 March), cols 681–8, 689–96, 697–704, 705–12, 713–15, at col. 683.

Reinhold, Carl Leonhard, 1797. "Einige Bemerkungen über die in der Einleitung zu den metaphysischen Anfangsgründen der Rechstlehre von I. Kant aufgestellten Begriffe von der Freyheit des Willens." In Reinhold, *Auswahl vermischter Schriften*, vol. 2. Jena: Mauke, pp. 364–400. Translated in Noller and Walsh 2022, pp. 238–49.

Reinhold, Karl Leonhard, 1983–. *Korrespondenzausgabe*, founded by Reinhard Lauth *et al.*, edited by Faustino Fabianelli, Kurt Hiller, and Ives Radrizzani. Stuttgart-Bad Canstatt: Frommann-Holzboog.

Reinhold, Karl Leonhard, 2005. *Letters on the Kantian Philosophy*, edited by Karl Ameriks, translated by James Hebbeler. Cambridge: Cambridge University Press.

Reinhold, Karl Leonhard, 2007–. *Gesammelte Schriften: Kommentierte Ausgabe*, edited by Martin Bondeli. Basel: Schwabe.

Reinhold, Karl Leonhard, 2010. *Versuch einer neuen Theorie des menschlichen Vorstellungsvermögen*, edited by Ernst-Otto Onasch, 2 vols. Hamburg: Felix Meiner Verlag.

Reinhold, Karl Leonhard, 2011. *Essay on a New Theory of the Human Capacity for Representation*, translated by Tim Mehigan and Barry Empson. Berlin and Boston: Walter de Gruyter & Co.

Ross, W. D., 1930. *The Right and the Good*. Oxford: Clarendon Press.

Ross, W. D., 1939. *The Foundations of Ethics*. Oxford: Clarendon Press.

Ross, W.D. (Sir David), 1954. *Kant's Ethical Theory: A Commentary on the* Grundlegung zur Metaphysik der Sitten. Oxford: Clarendon Press.

Royce, Josiah, 1886. *California: A Study of American Character: From the Conquest in 1846 to the Second Vigilance Committee in San Francisco*. Boston: Houghton Mifflin.

Royce, Josiah, 1892. *The Spirit of Modern Philosophy*. Boston: Houghton Mifflin.

Royce, Josiah, 1899, 1901. *The World and the Individual*, 1st and 2nd series. New York: Macmillan.

Royce, Josiah, 1919. *Lectures on Modern Idealism*, edited by Jacob Loewenberg. New Haven: Yale University Press.

Royce, Josiah, 1995. *The Philosophy of Loyalty*. Introduction by John J. McDermott. Nashville, TN: Vanderbilt University Press.

Royce, Josiah, 2001. *The Problem of Christianity* (New edition). Washington, DC: Catholic University of America Press.

Schelling, Friedrich Wilhelm Joseph, 1856–61. *Sämmtliche Werke*, edited by Karl F. A. Schelling, part 1, vols 1–10, part 2, vols 1–4. Stuttgart: Cotta.

Schelling, Friedrich Wilhelm Joseph, 1978. *The System of Transcendental Idealism*, translated by Peter L. Heath, with an introduction by Michael Vater. Charlottesville, VA: University of Virgina Press.

Schelling, Friedrich Wilhelm Joseph, 1985. *Ausgewählte Schriften*, 6 vols. Frankfurt am Main: Suhrkamp Verlag.

Schelling, Friedrich Wilhelm Joseph, 2006. *Philosophical Investigations into the Essence of Human Freedom*. translated by Jeff Love and Johannes Schmidt. Albany, NY: SUNY Press.

Schiller, Friedrich, 1966. *Schillers Werke*, edited by Herbert Kraft, 4 vols. Frankfurt am Main: Insel Verlag.

Schiller, Friedrich, 2005. *Schiller's "On Grace and Dignity" in its Cultural Context: Essays and a New Translation*, edited by Jane V. Curran and Christopher Fricker. Rochester, NY: Camden House. (This edition includes the German text of the essay.)

Schmid, Carl Christian Erhard, 1788. *Kritik der reinen Vernunft im Grundrisse für Vorlesungen* (2nd edition). Jena: Cröker. (First edition, 1786).

Schmid, Carl Christian Erhard, 1790. *Versuch einer Moralphilosophie*. Jena: Cröker.

Schmid, Carl Christian Erhard, 1795. *Grundriß des Naturrechts: Für Vorlesungen*. Jena and Leipzig: Gabler.

Schmid, Carl Christian Erhard, 1798. *Wörterbuch zur leichteren Gebrauch der Kantischen Schriften* (4th edition). Jena: Cröker. Facsimile edition with an introduction by Norbert Hinske. Darmstadt: Wissenschaftliche Buchgesellschaft, 1976.

Schopenhauer, Arthur, 2009. *The Two Fundamental Problems of Ethics*, translated and edited by Christopher Janaway. Cambridge: Cambridge University Press.

Schopenhauer, Arthur, 2010–18. *The World as Will and Representation*, translated and edited by Judith Norman, Alistair Welchman, and Christopher Janaway, with introductions by Christopher Janaway, 2 vols. Cambridge: Cambridge University Press.

Schopenhauer, Arthur, 2012. *On the Fourfold Root of the Principle of Sufficient Reason and Other Writings*, translated and edited by David E. Cartwright, Edward E. Erdmann, and Christopher Janaway. Cambridge: Cambridge University Press.

Shaftesbury, Anthony Ashley Cooper, Third Earl of, 1999. *Characteristicks of Men, Manners, Opinions, Times*, Edited by Philip Ayres, 2 vols. Oxford: Clarendon Press.

Sidgwick, Henry, 1874. *The Methods of Ethics* (1st edition). London: Macmillan.

Sidgwick, Henry, 1896. *Outlines of the History of Ethics* (4rth edition). London: Macmillan.

Sidgwick, Henry, 1902. *Lectures on The Ethics of T.H. Green, Herbert Spencer, and J. Martineau*, edited by E. E. Constance Jones. London: Macmillan.

Sidgwick, Henry, 1905. *Lectures on the Philosophy of Kant and Other Philosophical Lectures and Essays*, edited by James Ward. London: Macmillan.

Sidgwick, Henry, 1907. *The Methods of Ethics* (7th edition). London: Macmillan.

Singer, Marcus George, 1961. *Generalization in Ethics: An Essay in the Logic of Ethics, with the Rudiments of a System of Moral Philosophy*. New York: Alfred A. Knopf; with a new preface, New York: Atheneum, 1971.

Smart, J. J. J. C., and Bernard Williams, 1973. *Utilitarianism: For and Against*. Cambridge: Cambridge University Press.

Smith, Adam, 1976. *The Theory of Moral Sentiments*, edited by D. D. Raphael and A. L. Macfie. Oxford: Clarendon Press.

Tittel, Gottlob August, 1786. *Über Herrn Kants Moralreform*. Frankfurt and Leipzig: Gebrüder Pfähler.

Ulrich, Johann August Heinrich, 1788. *Eleurotheriologie, oder über Freyheit und Notwendigkeit.* Jena: Cröker.

von Humboldt, Wilhelm, 1969. *The Limits of State Action,* edited by J. B. Burrow. Cambridge: Cambridge University Press.

Walschots, Michael, ed., 2023. *Kant's* Critique of Practical Reason: *Background Source Materials.* Cambridge: Cambridge University Press.

Williams, Bernard, 1972. *Morality: An Introduction to Ethics.* Harmondsworth: Penguin. Reprinted Cambridge: Cambridge University Press, 1976.

Williams, Bernard, 1974-5. "The Truth in Relativism." *Proceedings of the Aristotelian Society* 75: 215-28. Reprinted in Williams 1982, pp. 132-43.

Williams, Bernard, 1976a. "Moral Luck." *Proceedings of the Aristotelian Society,* supplementary vol. 50: 115-35. Reprinted in Williams 1982, pp. 20-39.

Williams, Bernard, 1976b. "Persons, Character and Morality." In Amélie O. Rorty, ed., *The Identities of Persons.* Berkeley and Los Angeles: University of California Press. Reprinted in *Moral Luck,* pp. 1-19.

Williams, Bernard, 1980. "Internal and External Reasons." In *Rational Action,* edited by Ross Harrison. Cambridge: Cambridge University Press. Reprinted in *Moral Luck,* pp. 102-13.

Williams, Bernard, 1982. *Moral Luck: Philosophical Papers 1973-1980* (Cambridge: Cambridge University Press.

Williams, Bernard, 1985. *Ethics and the Limits of Philosophy.* Cambridge, MA: Harvard University Press.

Williams, Bernard, 2006. "An Essay on Collingwood." In Williams, *The Sense of the Past: Essays in the History of Philosophy,* edited by Myles Burnyeat. Princeton: Princeton University Press, pp. 341-58.

Winckelmann, Johann Joachim, 2006. *History of the Art of Antiquity,* edited by Alex Potts, translated by Harry Francis Mallgrave. Los Angeles: Getty Research Institute.

Wolff, Christian, 1733. *Vernünfftige Gedancken von der Menschen Thun und Lassen, zur Beförderung ihrer Glückseligkeit* (4th edition). Frankfurt and Leipzig: Renger; facsimile edition with introduction by Hans Werner Arndt, Hildesheim: Georg Olms, 1996.

Wolff, Christian, 1985. *Oratio de Sinarum philosophia practica/Rede über die praktische Philosophie der Chinesen* [1721, 1st authorized edition 1726], edited and translated by Michael Albrecht. Hamburg: Felix Meiner Verlag.

II. Secondary Sources

Al-Azm, Sadik, 1972. *The Origins of Kant's Arguments in the Antinomies* (Oxford: Clarendon Press, 1972).

Albrecht, Michael, 1994. "Kants Maximenethik und ihre Begründung." *Kant-Studien* 85: 129-46; translated as "Kant's Justification of the Role of Maxims in Ethics," in Ameriks and Höffe 2009, pp. 134-55.

Allard, James W., 2005. *The Logical Foundations of Bradley's Metaphysics: Judgement, Inference, and Truth.* Cambridge: Cambridge University Press.

Allison, Henry E., 1983. *Kant's Transcendental Idealism: An Interpretation and Defense.* New Haven: Yale University Press. 2nd edition, 2004.

Allison, Henry E., 1990. *Kant's Theory of Freedom.* Cambridge: Cambridge University Press.

Allison, Henry E., 2004. *Kant's Transcendental Idealism: An Interpretation and Defense* (2nd edition). New Haven and London: Yale University Press.

Allison, Henry E., 2011. *Kant's* Groundwork for the Metaphysics of Morals: *A Commentary*. Oxford: Oxford University Press, 2011.

Allison, Henry E., 2020. *Kant's Conception of Freedom: A Developmental and Critical Analysis*. Cambridge: Cambridge University Press.

Aly, Götz, 2014. *Why the Germans? Why the Jews? Envy, Race Hatred, and the Prehistory of the Holocaust*. New York: Metropolitan Books.

Ameriks, Karl, 1981. "Kant's Deduction of Freedom and Morality." *Journal of the History of Philosophy* 19: 53–79.

Ameriks, Karl, 2000. *Kant's Theory of Mind: An Analysis of the Paralogisms of Pure Reason* (1982) New edition. Oxford: Clarendon Press.

Ameriks, Karl, 2012. "Ambiguities in the Will: Reinhold and Kant, *Briefe II*." In Stolz, Heinz, and Bondeli 2012, pp. 71–90.

Ameriks, Karl, and Otfried Höffe, eds, 2009. *Kant's Moral and Legal Philosophy*, translated by Nicholas Walker. Cambridge: Cambridge University Press.

Anderson, R. Lanier, 1998. "Truth and Objectivity in Perspectivism." *Synthese* 115: 1–32.

Anderson, R. Lanier, 2005. "Nietzsche on Truth, Illusion, and Redemption." *European Journal of Philosophy* 13: 185–225.

Anderson, R. Lanier, 2011. "On the Nobility of Nietzsche's Priests." In May 2011, pp. 24–55.

Anderson, R. Lanier, 2018. "The Psychology of Perspectivism: A Question for Nietzsche Studies Now." *Journal of Nietzsche Studies* 49: 221–8.

Anderson-Gold, Sharon, and Pablo Muchnik, eds, 2010. *Kant's Anatomy of Evil*. Cambridge: Cambridge University Press.

Anscombe, G. E. M., 1958. "Modern Moral Philosophy," *Philosophy* 33: 1–19. Reprinted in Anscombe, *Collected Philosophical Papers*, 3 vols. Minneapolis: University of Minnesota Press, 1981, vol. 3, pp. 26–42.

Ansell Pearson, Keith, ed., 2006. *A Companion to Nietzsche*. Malden, MA: Blackwell.

Archard, David, Monique Deveaux, Neil Manson, and Daniel Weinstock, eds, 2013. *Reading O'Neill*. London: Routledge.

Atwell, John E., 1995. *Schopenhauer on the Character of the World: The Metaphysics of the Will*. Berkeley and Los Angeles: University of California Press.

Audi, Robert, 1996. "Intuitionism, Pluralism, and the Foundations of Ethics." In Walter Sinnott-Armstrong and Mark Timmons, eds, *Moral Knowledge: New Readings in Moral Epistemology*. Oxford: Oxford University Press, pp. 101–36.

Aune, Bruce, 1979. *Kant's Theory of Morals*. Princeton: Princeton University Press.

Bagnoli, Carla, ed., 2013. *Constructivism in Ethics*. Cambridge: Cambridge University Press.

Bagnoli, Carla, 2022. *Ethical Constructivism*. Cambridge: Cambridge University Press.

Baiasu, Sorin, 2020. "Free Will and Determinism: A Solution to the Kantian Paradox." In Manja Kisner and Jörg Noller, eds, *The Concept of Will in Classical German Philosophy: Between Ethics, Politics, and Metaphysics*. Berlin and Boston: Walter de Gruyter & Co., pp. 7–28.

Bailey, Tom, 2013. "Nietzsche the Kantian?" In John Richardson and Ken Gemes, eds, *The Oxford Handbook of Nietzsche*. Oxford: Oxford University Press, pp. 134–59.

Baldwin, Thomas, 1990. *G. E. Moore*. London: Routledge.

Barkan, Leonard, 1999. *Unearthing the Past: Archaeology and Aesthetics in the Making of Renaissance Culture*. New Haven and London: Yale University Press.

Baron, Marcia, 1995. *Kantian Ethics Almost without Apology*. Ithaca, NY, and London: Cornell University Press.

Baron, Marcia W., Philip Pettit, and Michael Slote, 1997. *Three Methods of Ethics: A Debate* Oxford: Blackwell.

Baum, Manfred, 2012. "Kants Replik auf Reinhold." In Stolz, Heinz, and Bondeli 2012, pp. 153–63.

Baxley, Anne Margaret, 2008. "Pleasure, Freedom, and Grace: Schiller's 'Completion' of Kant's Ethics." *Inquiry* 51: 1–15

Beck, Lewis White, 1960. *A Commentary to Kant's* Critique of Practical Reason. Chicago: University of Chicago Press.

Beck, Lewis White, 1962. "Les deux concepts kantiens du vouloir dans leur context politique." *Annales d philosophie politique* 4: 119–37. Translated as "Kant's Two Concepts of the Will in Their Political Context" in Beck, *Studies in the Philosophy of Kant*. Indianapolis: Bobbs-Merrill, 1965, pp. 215–29.

Beck, Lewis White, 1969. *Early German Philosophy: Kant and his Predecessors*. Cambridge, MA: Harvard University Press.

Beck, Lewis White, 1975. *The Actor and the Spectator*. New Haven: Yale University Press.

Beiser, Frederick C., 1987. *The Fate of Reason: German Philosophy from Kant to Fichte*. Cambridge, MA: Harvard University Press.

Beiser, Frederick C., 1992. "Kant's Intellectual Development: 1746–1781." In Guyer 1992b, pp. 26–51.

Beiser, Frederick C., 2002. *German Idealism: The Struggle Against Subjectivism, 1781–1801*. Cambridge, MA: Harvard University Press.

Beiser, Frederick C., 2005a. *Hegel*. London: Routledge.

Beiser, Frederick C., 2005b. *Schiller as Philosopher: A Re-examination*. Oxford: Clarendon Press.

Beiser, Frederick C., 2022. *Johann Friedrich Herbart: Grandfather of Analytic Philosophy*. Oxford: Oxford University Press.

Bennett, Jonathan F., 1966. *Kant's Analytic*. Cambridge: Cambridge University Press.

Bennett, Jonathan F., 1974. *Kant's Dialectic*. Cambridge: Cambridge University Press.

Berger, Larissa, 2015. "Der 'Zirkel' im dritten Abschnitt der *Grundlegung*: Eine neue Interpretation und ein Literaturbericht." In Dieter Schönecker, ed., *Kants Begründung von Freiheit und Moral in* Grundlegung III. Paderborn: Mentis Verlag, pp. 9–82.

Bird, Graham, 1962. *Kant's Theory of Knowledge*. London: Routledge & Kegan Paul.

Bird, Graham, 2006. *The Revolutionary Kant: A Commentary on the* Critique of Pure Reason. Chicago and LaSalle, IL: Open Court.

Bondeli, Martin, 2012. "Zu Reinholds Auffassung von Willensfreiheit in den *Briefen II*." In Stolz, Heinz, and Bondeli 2012, pp. 125–52.

Brooks, Thom, and Martha C. Nussbaum, eds, 2015. *Rawls's* Political Liberalism. New York: Columbia University Press.

Boucher, David, 2009. "Henry Jones: Idealism as a Practical Creed." In William Sweet, ed., *The Moral, Social, and Political Philosophy of the British Idealists*. Exeter: Imprint Academic, pp. 137–51.

Bowie, Andrew, 1993. *Schelling and Modern European Philosophy*. London: Routledge.

Boyle, Nicholas, 2000. *Goethe: The Poet and the Age*, vol. 2. *Revolution and Renunciation*. Oxford: Clarendon Press.

Brandt, Reinhard, 1999. *Kommentar zu Kants Anthropologie*. Kant-Forschungen 10. Hamburg: Felix Meiner Verlag.

Breazeale, Daniel, 2006. "The 'Mixed Method' of Fichte's *Grundlage des Naturrechts* and the Limits of Transcendental *Reellephilosophie*." In *Rights, Bodies and Recognition: New Essays on Fichte's* Foundations of Natural Right, edited by Tom Rockmore and Daniel Breazeale. Aldershot: Ashgate, pp. 117–37.

Breazeale, Daniel, 2007. "Die Synthetische(n) Methode(n) des Philosophierens: Kantische Fragen, Fichtesche Antwortungen." In *Kant und der Frühidealismus*, edited by Jürgen Stolzenberg. Hamburg: Felix Meiner Verlag, pp. 81–102.

Brink, David, 2003. *Perfectionism and the Common Good: Themes in the Philosophy of T. H. Green*. Oxford: Clarendon Press.

Broad, Charlie Dunbar, 1930. *Five Types of Ethical Theory*. London: Routledge & Kegan Paul.

Cadilha, Susana, and Francisco Lisboa, 2022. "Vulnerabilities in Kantian Constructivism: Why they Matter for Objective Normativity." *Kant Yearbook* 14: 1–21.

Callcutt, Daniel, ed., 2008. *Reading Bernard Williams*. London: Routledge.

Cartwright, David E., 1999. "Schopenhauer's Narrower Sense of Morality." In Janaway, editor, 1999, pp. 252–92.

Cartwright, David E., 2010. *Schopenhauer: A Biography*. Cambridge: Cambridge University Press.

Chappell, Richard Yetter, 2021. *Parfit's Ethics*. Cambridge: Cambridge University Press.

Chappell, Sophie-Grace, and Nicholas Smyth, 2023. "Bernard Williams." *Stanford Encyclopedia of Philosophy*, edited by Edward Zalta and Uri Nodelman. Summer, 2023. <https://plato.stanford.edu/entries/williams-bernard/> (Accessed April 7, 2023)

Chignell, Andrew, 2007. "Belief in Kant." *Philosophical Review* 116: 23–60.

Chignell, Andrew, 2013. "Rational Hope, Moral Order, and the Revolution of the Will." In *The Divine Order, the Human Order, and the Order of Nature: Historical Perspectives*, edited by Eric Watkins. Oxford: Oxford University Press, pp. 197–218.

Chignell, Andrew, 2021a. "Belief or faith." In Wuerth 2021, pp. 61–3.

Chignell, Andrew, 2021b. "Hope." In Wuerth 2021, pp. 220–2.

Cholbi, Michael, 2016. *Understanding Kant's Ethics*. Cambridge: Cambridge University Press.

Clark, Maudemarie, 1990. *Nietzsche on Truth and Illusion*. Cambridge: Cambridge University Press.

Clarke, James A., 2016. "Fichte's Independence Thesis." In Gottlieb 2016, pp. 52–71.

Cooper, John M., 2012. *Pursuits of Wisdom: Six Ways of Life in Ancient Philosophy from Socrates to Plotinus*. Princeton: Princeton University Press.

Crisp, Roger, 2015. *The Cosmos of Duty: Henry Sidgwick's* Methods of Ethics. Oxford: Oxford University Press.

Crisp, Roger, 2020. "On *Seeing* What is Right: Sidgwick, Kant, and Philosophical Intuitionism," In Paytas and Henning 2020, pp. 107–17.

Cummiskey, David, 1996. *Kantian Consequentlism*. New York: Oxford University Press.

Dalferth, Ingolf, 2014. "Radical Evil and Human Freedom." In Michalson 2014, pp. 58–78.

Dancy, Jonathan, 1993. *Moral Reasons*. Oxford: Blackwell.

Dancy, Jonathan, 2004. *Ethics without Principles*. Oxford: Oxford University Press.

Dancy, Jonathan, ed., 1997. *Reading Parfit*. Oxford: Blackwell.

Danto, Arthur, 1965. *Nietzsche as Philosopher*. New York: Macmillan.

Dean, Richard, 2006. *The Value of Morality in Kant's Moral Theory*. Oxford: Clarendon Press.

De Lazari-Radek, Katarzyna, 2017. "Sidgwick." In Golob and Timmermann 2017, pp. 509–20.

De Lazari-Radek, Katarzyna, and Peter Singer, 2014. *The Point of View of the Universe: Sidgwick and Contemporary Ethics*. Oxford: Oxford University Press.

Denis, Lara, 2000. "Kant's Cold Sage and the Sublimity of Apathy." *Kantian Review* 4: 48–73.

Denis, Lara, ed., 2010. *Kant's* Metaphysics of Morals: *A Critical Guide*. Cambridge: Cambridge University Press.

DiCenso, James J., 2011. *Kant, Religion, and Politics*. Cambridge: Cambridge University Press.

DiCenso, James J., 2012. *Kant's* Religion within the Boundaries of Mere Reason: *A Commentary*. Cambridge: Cambridge University Press.

di Giovanni, George, 2005. *Freedom and Religion in Kant and his Immediate Successors*. Cambridge: Cambridge University Press.

di Giovanni, George, ed., 2010. *Karl Leonhard Reinhold and the Enlightenment*. Dordrecht: Springer.

Dimova-Cookson, Maria, 2001. *T. H. Green's Moral and Political Philosophy*. London: Palgrave.

Dimova-Cookson, Maria, and W. J. Mander, eds, 2006. *T. H. Green: Ethics, Metaphysics, and Political Philosophy*. Oxford: Clarendon Press.

Edmonds, David, 2023. *Parfit: A Philosopher and his Mission to Save Morality*. Princeton: Princeton University Press.

Ehrenspeck, Yvonne, 1998. *Versprechungen des Ästhetischen: Die Entstehung eines modernen Bildungsprojekt*. Opladen: Leske + Budrich.

Evans, Richard J., 2015. "Was the 'Final Solution' Unique?" In Evans, *The Third Reich in History and Memory*. New York: Oxford University Press, pp. 365–89.

Falduto, Antonino, 2014. *The Faculties of the Human Mind and the Case of Moral Feeling in Kant's Philosophy*. Kant-Studien Ergänzungshefte 177. Berlin and Boston: Walter de Gruyter & Co.

Falkenburg, Brigitte, 2020. *Kant's Cosmology: From the Pre-Critical System to the Antinomy of Pure Reason*. Cham: Springer.

Firestone, Chris L., and Nathan Jacobs. 2008. *In Defense of Kant's Religion*. Bloomington and Indianapolis: Indiana University Press.

Firestone, Chris L., and Stephen R. Palmquist, eds, 2006. *Kant and the New Philosophy of Religion*. Bloomington and Indianapolis: Indiana University Press.

FitzPatrick, William J., 2005. "The Practical Turn in Ethical Theory: Korsgaard's Constructivism, Realism, and the Nature of Normativity." *Ethics* 115: 651–91.

FitzPatrick, William J., 2013. "How Not to Be an Ethical Constructivist: A Critique of Korsgaard's Neo-Kantian Constitutivism." In Bagnoli 2013, pp. 41–62.

Forrester, Katrina, 2019. *In the Shadow of Justice: Postwar Liberalism and the Remaking of Political Philosophy*. Cambridge, MA: Harvard University Press.

Foust, Matthew A., 2012. *Loyalty to Loyalty*. New York: Fordham University Press.

Freeman, Samuel, 2007. *Rawls*. London: Routledge.

Freeman, Samuel, ed., 2003. *The Cambridge Companion to Rawls*. Cambridge: Cambridge University Press.

Freyenhagen, Fabian, 2012. "The Empty Formalism Objection Revisited: §135R and Recent Kantian Responses." In Thom Brooks, ed., *Hegel's Philosophy of Right*. Chichester: Wiley-Blackwell, pp. 43–72.

Fugate, Courtney D., 2012. "On a Supposed Solution to the Reinhold/Sidgwick Problem in Kant's *Metaphysics of Morals*." *European Journal of Philosophy* 23: 349–73.

Fulda, Hans-Friedrich, 2003. *Georg Wilhelm Friedrich Hegel*. Munich: C. H. Beck.

Gališanka, Andrius, 2019. *John Rawls: The Path to a Theory of Justice*. Cambridge, MA: Harvard University Press.

Gardiner, Patrick, 1963. *Schopenhauer*. Baltimore, MD: Penguin.

Garcia, Ernesto V., 2022. "Three Rival Versions of Kantian Constructivism." *Kant Yearbook* 14: 23–43.

García Mills, Nicolás, 2017. "Realizing the Good: Hegel's Critique of Kantian Morality." *European Journal of Philosophy* 26: 195–212.

Gaut, Berys, 2002. "Justifying Moral Pluralism." In Stratton-Lake 2002, pp. 137–60.

Geiger, Ido, 2007. *The Founding Act of Modern Ethical Life: Hegel's Critique of Kant's Moral and Political Philosophy*. Stanford, CA: Stanford University Press.

Gemes, Ken, 2009. "Nietzsche on Free Will, Autonomy, and the Sovereign Individual." In Gemes and May 2009, pp. 33–49.

Gemes, Ken, 2013. "Life's Perspectives." In Gemes and Richardson 2013, pp. 553–76.

Gemes, Ken, and John Richardson, 2013. *The Oxford Handbook of Nietzsche*. Oxford: Oxford University Press.

Gemes, Ken, and Simon May, eds, 2009. *Nietzsche on Freedom and Autonomy*. Oxford: Oxford University Press.

Gewirth, Alan, 1977. *Reason and Morality*. Chicago: University of Chicago Press.

Golob, Sacha, and Jens Timmermann, eds, 2017. *The Cambridge History of Moral Philosophy*. Cambridge: Cambridge University Press.

Gottlieb, Gabriel, ed., 2016. *Fichte's* Foundations of Natural Right: *A Critical Guide*. Cambridge: Cambridge University Press.

Gregor, Mary J., 1963. *Laws of Freedom: A Study of Kant's Method of Applying the Categorical Imperative in the* Metaphysik der Sitten. Oxford: Basil Blackwell.

Grenberg, Jeanine, 2013. *Kant's Defense of Common Moral Experience: A Phenomenological Account*. Cambridge: Cambridge University Press.

Guyer, Paul, 1983. "Kant's Intentions in the Refutation of Idealism." *Philosophical Review* 92: 329–83.

Guyer, Paul, 1987. *Kant and the Claims of Knowledge*. Cambridge: Cambridge University Press.

Guyer, Paul, 1990. "Feeling and Freedom: Kant on Aesthetics and Morality." *Journal of Aesthetics and Art Criticism* 48: 137–46. Reprinted in Guyer 1993a, chapter 1.

Guyer, Paul, 1992a. Review of Henry E. Allison, *Kant's Theory of Freedom*. *Journal of Philosophy* 89: 99–110.

Guyer, Paul, ed., 1992b. *The Cambridge Companion to Kant*. Cambridge: Cambridge University Press.

Guyer, Paul, 1993a. *Kant and the Experience of Freedom*. Cambridge: Cambridge University Press.

Guyer, Paul, 1993b. "Kant's Morality of Law and Morality of Freedom." In Russell B. Dancy, ed., *Kant and Critique: New Essays in Honor of W. B. Werkmeister*. Dordrecht: Kluwer, pp. 43–89. Reprinted in Guyer 2000, pp. 129–71.

Guyer, Paul, 1995. "The Possibility of the Categorical Imperative." *Philosophical Review* 104: 353–85. Reprinted in Guyer 2000, pp. 172–206.

Guyer, Paul, 1997. "Kantian Foundations for Liberalism." *Jahrbuch für Recht und Ethik* 5: 121–40. Reprinted in Guyer 2000, pp. 235–61.

Guyer, Paul, 1998a. "Life, Liberty, and Property: Rawls and the Reconstruction of Kant's Political Philosophy." In Dieter Hüning and Burkhard Tuschling, eds, *Recht, Staat und Völkerrecht bei Immanuel Kant*. Schriften zur Rechtstheorie 186. Berlin: Duncker & Humblot, 1998, pp. 273–91. Reprinted in Guyer 2000, pp. 262–86.

Guyer, Paul, 1998b. "The Value of Reason and the Value of Freedom." *Ethics* 109: 22–35.

Guyer, Paul, 1999. "Schopenhauer, Kant, and the Methods of Philosophy." In Janaway 1999, pp. 93–137.

Guyer, Paul, 2000. *Kant on Freedom, Law, and Happiness.* Cambridge: Cambridge University Press.

Guyer, Paul, 2001. "From Nature to Morality: Kant's New Argument in the 'Critique of Teleological Judgment'." In Hans Friedrich Fulda and Jürgen Stolzenberg, eds, *Architektonik und System in der Philosophie Kants.* Hamburg: Felix Meiner Verlag, pp. 375–404. Reprinted in Guyer 2005a, pp. 314–42.

Guyer, Paul, 2002. "Kant's Deductions of the Principles of Right." In Timmons 2002, pp. 24–64. Reprinted in Guyer 2005a, pp. 198–242.

Guyer, Paul, 2005a. *Kant's System of Nature and Freedom: Selected Essays.* Oxford: Clarendon Press.

Guyer, Paul, 2005b. "Kant's System of Duties." In Guyer 2005a, pp. 243–74.

Guyer, Paul, 2007a. "Naturalistic and Transcendental Moments in Kant's Moral Philosophy." *Inquiry* 50: 444–64.

Guyer, Paul, 2007b. "The Ideal of Beauty and the Necessity of Grace: Kant and Schiller on Aesthetics and Ethics." In Walter Hinderer, ed. *Friedrich Schiller and the Path to Modernity.* Würzburg: Königshausen & Neuman, pp. 187–204.

Guyer, Paul, 2007c. *Kant's* Groundwork for the Metaphysics of Morals: *A Reader's Guide.* London: Continuum.

Guyer, Paul, 2008a. *Knowledge, Reason, and Taste: Kant's Response to Hume.* Princeton: Princeton University Press.

Guyer, Paul, 2008b. "Proving Ourselves Free." In Valerio Rhoden et al., editors, *Recht und Frieden in der Philosophie Kants: Akten des X. Internationalen Kant Kongresses.* Berlin: Walter de Gruyter, 2008, vol. 1, pp. 115–37. Reprinted in Guyer 2016a, pp. 146–62.

Guyer, Paul, 2009a. "Ist und Soll: Von Hume bis Kant, und nun." In Heiner F. Klemme, ed., *Kant und die Zukunft der Aufklärung.* Berlin and New York: Walter de Gruyter & Co., pp. 210–32; translation as "Is and Ought: From Hume to Kant, and Now," in Guyer 2016, pp. 21–35.

Guyer, Paul, 2009b. "The Crooked Timber of Mankind." In Amélie Oksenberg Rorty and James Schmidt, eds, *Kant's* Idea for a Universal History with a Cosmopolitan Aim: *A Critical Guide.* Cambridge: Cambridge University Press, pp. 129–49.

Guyer, Paul, 2010a. "The Obligation to be Virtuous: Kant's Conception of the *Tugendverpflichtung,*" *Social Philosophy and Policy* 27: 206–32. Reprinted in Guyer 2016a, pp. 216–34.

Guyer, Paul, 2010b. "Moral Feelings in the *Metaphysics of Morals.*" In Lara Denis, ed., *Kant's* Metaphysics of Morals: *A Critical Guide.* Cambridge: Cambridge University Press, pp. 130–51. Reprinted in Guyer 2016a, pp. 235–59.

Guyer, Paul, 2011a. "Kantian Perfectionism." In Lawrence Jost and Julian Wuerth, eds, *Perfecting Virtue: New Essays on Kantian Ethics and Virtue Ethics.* Cambridge: Cambridge University Press, pp. 194–214. Reprinted in Guyer 2016a, pp. 70–86.

Guyer, Paul, 2011b. "Examples of Moral Possibility." In Klas Roth and Chris W. Surprenant, eds, *Kant and Education: Interpretations and Commentary.* London: Routledge, pp. 124–38. Reprinted in Guyer 2016a, pp. 260–72.

Guyer, Paul, 2012a. "Schopenhauer, Kant and Compassion." *Kantian Review* 17: 403–29.

Guyer, Paul, 2012b. "A Passion for Reason: Hume, Kant, and the Motivation for Morality." *Proceedings and Addresses of the American Philosophical Association* 86: 4–21. Reprinted in Guyer 2016a, pp. 201–15.

Guyer, Paul, 2013. "Constructivism and Self-Constitution." In Timmons and Baiasu 2013, pp. 176–200.

Guyer, Paul, 2014a. *Kant* (2nd edition). London: Routledge.

Guyer, Paul, 2014b. "Rawls and the History of Moral Philosophy: The Cases of Smith and Kant." In Mandle and Reidy 2014, pp. 546–66.

Guyer, Paul, 2014c. *A History of Modern Aesthetics*, 3 vols. Cambridge: Cambridge University Press.

Guyer, Paul, 2014d. "The Inescapability of Contingency: The Form and Content of Freedom in Kant and Hegel." In Mario Eggers, ed., *Philosophie nach Kant*. Berlin and New York: Walter de Gruyter & Co., pp. 539–62.

Guyer, Paul, 2015a. "Fichte's Transcendental Ethics." In Sebastian Gardner and Matthew Grist, eds, *The Transcendental Turn*. (Oxford: Oxford University Press, pp. 135–58.

Guyer, Paul, 2015b. "The Scottish Reception of Kant." In Gordon Graham, ed., *Scottish Philosophy in the Nineteenth and Twentieth Centuries*. Oxford: Oxford University Press, pp. 118–53.

Guyer, Paul, 2016a. *Virtues of Freedom: Selected Essays on Kant*. Oxford: Oxford University Press.

Guyer, Paul, 2016b. "Kant, Mendelssohn, and Immortality." In Thomas Höwing, ed., *The Highest Good in Kant's Philosophy*. Berlin and Boston: Walter de Gruyter, pp. 157–79.

Guyer, Paul, 2016c. "Setting and Pursuing Ends: Internal and External Freedom." In Guyer 2016a, pp. 87–104.

Guyer, Paul, 2016d. "The Twofold Morality of Kantian *Recht*." *Kant-Studien* 107: 34–63.

Guyer, Paul, 2017. "Absolute Idealism and the Rejection of Kantian Dualism." In Karl Ameriks, ed., *The Cambridge Companion to German Idealism* (2nd edition). Cambridge: Cambridge University Press, pp. 43–64.

Guyer, Paul, 2018a. "Principles of Justice, Primary Goods, and Categories of Right: Rawls and Kant." *Kantian Review* 23: 581–613.

Guyer, Paul, 2018b. "Moral Metaphysics or Moral Psychology? Adrian Piper's *Rationality and the Structure of the Self.*" *Critique.* <https://wp.me/ptwJK-1tp>; also at <http://www.adrianpiper.com/rss/symposium.shtml>.

Guyer, Paul, 2018c. "The Struggle for Freedom: Freedom of Will in Reinhold and Kant." In Eric Watkins, ed., *Kant on Persons, and Agency*. Cambridge: Cambridge University Press, pp. 120–37.

Guyer, Paul, 2018d. "Moral Metaphysics or Moral Psychology? Adrian Piper's *Rationality and the Structure of the Self.*" *Critique* (October). <https://wp.me/ptwJK-1tp>; also at <http://www.adrianpiper.com/rss/symposium.shtml>.

Guyer, Paul, 2019. *Kant on the Rationality of Morality*. Cambridge: Cambridge University Press.

Guyer, Paul, 2020a. *Reason and Experience in Mendelssohn and Kant*. Oxford: Oxford University Press.

Guyer, Paul, 2020b. "Freedom and Happiness: Sidgwick's Critique of Kant." In Tyler Paytas and Tim Henning, eds, *Kantian and Sidgwickian Ethics: The Cosmos of Duty Above and the Moral Law Within*. London: Routledge, pp. 141–62.

Guyer, Paul, 2022. "The Empire of Ends." *Proceedings and Addresses of the American Philosophical Association* 96: 204–37.

Guyer, Paul, 2023. "Schiller and Kant on Grace and Beauty." In Antonino Falduto and Tim Mehigan, eds, *The Palgrave Handbook of the Philosophy of Friedrich Schiller*. Cham: Palgrave Macmillan, pp. 459–76.

Guyer, Paul, forthcoming (a). "Metaphysics as a Rigorous Science." *Revista di Filosofia*.

Guyer, Paul, forthcoming (b). "Living in Accordance with Nature: Kant and Stoicism." In Melissa Merritt, editor, *Kant and Stoicism*. Cambridge: Cambridge University Press.

Guyer, Paul, and Rolf-Peter Horstmann, 2023. *Idealism in Modern Philosophy*. Oxford: Oxford University Press.

Hall, David D., 2019. *The Puritans: A Transatlantic History*. Princeton: Princeton University Press, 2019.

Hamlyn, D. W., 1980. *Schopenhauer*. London: Routledge & Kegan Paul.

Hannan, Barbara, 2009. *The Riddle of the World: A Reconsideration of Schopenhauer's Philosophy*. Oxford: Oxford University Press.

Harrison, Ross, ed., 2001. *Henry Sidgwick*. Proceedings of the British Academy 109. Oxford: Oxford University Press.

Henrich, Dieter, 1957-8. "Hutcheson und Kant." *Kant-Studien* 49: 49-69. Translated in Ameriks and Höffe 2009, pp. 29-57.

Henrich, Dieter, 1958-59. "Hegels Theorie über den Zufall." *Kant-Studien* 50: 131-48. Reprinted in Henrich, *Hegel im Kontext*. Frankfurt am Main: Suhrkamp Verlag, 1971, pp. 157-86.

Henrich, Dieter, 1960. "The Concept of Moral Insight and Kant's Doctrine of the Fact of Reason." In Dieter Henrich, W. Schulz, and Karl Heinz Volkmann-Schluck, eds, *Die Gegenwart der Griechen im neueren Denken: Festschrift für Hans-Gerg Gadamer zum 60. Geburtstag*, edited by. Tübingen: J. C. B. Mohr, pp. 77-15 (in German). Translated by Manfred Kuehn in Henrich 1994, pp. 55-88.

Henrich, Dieter, 1963. "Über Kants früheste Ethik." *Kant-Studien* 54: 404-31.

Henrich, Dieter, 1966. "Fichtes ursprüngliche Einsicht." In Dieter Henrich and Hans Wagner, eds, *Subjektivität und Metaphysik: Festschrift für Wolfgang Cramer*. Frankfurt am Main: Vittorio Klostermann, pp. 188-232.

Henrich, Dieter, 1967. *Fichtes ursprüngliche Einsicht*. Frankfurt am Main: Vittorio Klostermann.

Henrich, Dieter, 1975. "Die Deduktion des Sittengesetzes: Über die Gründe der Dunkelheit des leztzten Abschnittes von Kants *Grundlegung der Metaphysik der Sitten*." In Alexander Schwann, ed., *Denken im Schatten des Nihilismus*. Darmstadt: Wissenschaftliche Buchgesellschaft, pp. 55-112. Abridged English translation in Paul Guyer, ed., *Kant's* Groundwork of the Metaphysics of Morals: *Critical Essays*. Lanham, MD: Rowman & Littlefield, 1998, pp. 303-41.

Henrich, Dieter, 1982. "Fichte's Original Insight." Translated by David R. Lachterman. In Darrel Christensen et al., eds, *Contemporary German Philosophy*, vol. 1. University Park, PA: Pennsylvania State University Press, pp. 15-53.

Henrich, Dieter, 1994. *The Unity of Reason: Essays on Kant's Philosophy*, edited by Richard Velkley. Cambridge, MA: Harvard University Press.

Henrich, Dieter, 2003. *Between Kant and Hegel: Lectures on German Idealism*, translated by David S. Pacini. Cambridge, MA: Harvard University Press.

Henrich, Dieter, 2004. *Grundlegung aus dem Ich: Untersuchungen zur Vorgeschichte des Idealismus, Tübingen-Jena 1790-1794*, 2 vols. Frankfurt am Main: Suhrkamp Verlag.

Henson, Richard, 1979. "What Kant might have Said: Moral Worth and the Overdetermination of Dutiful Action." *Philosophical Review* 88: 39-54.

Herman Barbara, 1981. "The Value of Acting from the Motive of Duty." *Philosophical Review* 90: 359-82.

Herman, Barbara, 2001. "Bootstrapping." In Herman 2007, pp. 154-75.

Herman, Barbara, 2011. "A Mismatch of Methods." In Parfit 2011, vol. 2, pp. 83-115.

Heuer, Ulrike, and Gerald Lang, eds, 2012. *Luck, Value, and Commitment: Themes from the Ethics of Bernard Williams.* Oxford: Oxford University Press.

Heydt, Colin, 2018. *Moral Philosophy in Eighteenth-Century Britain: God, Self, and Other.* Oxford: Oxford University Press.

Hill, R. Kevin, 2003. *Nietzsche's Critiques: The Kantian Foundations of his Thought.* Oxford: Clarendon Press.

Hill, Thomas E., Jr., 1972. "The Kingdom of Ends." In Lewis White Beck, ed., *Proceedings of the Third International Kant Congress.* Dordrecht: D. Reidel. Reprinted in Hill 1992, pp. 58–66.

Hill, Thomas E. Jr., 1985. "Kant's Argument for the Rationality of Moral Conduct." *Pacific Philosophical Quarterly* 66: 3–23. Reprinted in Hill 1992, pp. 97–122.

Hill, Thomas E., Jr, 1992. *Dignity and Practical Reason in Kant's Moral Theory.* Ithaca, NY, and London: Cornell University Press.

Hill, Thomas E., Jr., 2000. "Kant on Punishment: A Coherent Mix of Deterrence and Retribution?" In Hill, *Respect, Pluralism, and Justice: Kantian Perspectives.* Oxford: Oxford University Press, pp. 173–99.

Hill, Thomas E., Jr., and Arnulf Zweig, trs, 2002. [Kant,] *Groundwork for the Metaphysics of Morals.* Oxford: Oxford University Press.

Höffe, Otfried, ed., 1989. *Grundlegung zur Metaphysik der Sitten: Ein kooperativer Kommentar.* Frankfurt am Main: Vittorio Klostermann.

Höffe, Otfried, 1994. *Kant,* translated by Marshall Farrier. Albany, NY: SUNY Press.

Höffe, Otfried, ed., 2011. *Immanuel Kant: Schriften zur Geschichtsphilosophie.* Berlin: Akademie Verlag.

Höffe, Otfried, and Annemarie Pieper, eds, 1995. *F. W. J. Schelling: Über as Wesen der menschlichen Freiheit.* Berlin: Akademie Verlag.

Hohfeld, Wesley Newcomb, 1919. *Fundamental Legal Conceptions as Applied in Judicial Reasoning.* New Haven: Yale University Press.

Honneth, Axel, 1995. *The Struggle for Recognition: The Moral Grammar of Social Conflict.* Cambridge: Polity Press.

Horn, Christoph, and Dieter Schönecker, eds, 2006. *Groundwork for the Metaphysics of Morals.* Berlin and New York: Walter de Gruyter & Co.

Horstmann, Rolf-Peter and Dina Emundts, 2002. *G. W. F. Hegel: Eine Einführung.* Stuttgart: Reclam.

Huddleston, Andrew, 2019. *Nietzsche on the Decadence and Flourishing of Culture.* Oxford: Oxford University Press.

Hunter, Ian, 2001. *Rival Enlightenments: Civil and Metaphysical Philosophy in Early Modern Germany.* Cambridge: Cambridge University Press.

Hurka, Thomas, 2014. *British Ethical Theorists from Sidgwick to Ewing.* Oxford: Oxford University Press.

Hurka, Thomas, 2021. "Moore's Moral Philosophy." *Stanford Encyclopedia of Philosophy* <https://plato.stanford.edu/entries//moore-moral/> (Accessed April 3, 2023).

Hutchinson, Brian, 2001. *G. E. Moore's Ethical Theory: Resistance and Reconciliation.* Cambridge: Cambridge University Press.

Hylton, Peter, 1990. *Russell, Idealism and the Emergence of Analytic Philosophy.* Oxford: Oxford University Press.

Inwood, M. J., 1983. *Hegel.* London: Routledge.

Insole, Christopher J., 2013. *Kant and the Creation of Freedom: A Theological Problem.* Oxford: Oxford University Press.

Irwin, Terence, 1984. "Morality and Personality: Kant and Green." In Allen W. Wood, ed., *Self and Nature in Kant's Philosophy*. Ithaca, NY: Cornell University Press, pp. 31–56.

Irwin, Terence, 2008. *The Development of Ethics: A Historical and Critical Study*, vol. 2. *From Suarez to Rousseau*. Oxford: Oxford University Press.

Irwin, Terence, 2009. *The Development of Ethics: A Historical and Critical Study*, vol. 3. *From Kant to Rawls*. Oxford: Oxford University Press.

Jaeschke, Walter, and Andreas Arndt, 2012. *Die Klassische Deutsche Philosophie nach Kant: Systeme der reinen Vernunft und ihre Kritik, 1785–1845*. Munich: C. H. Beck.

Janaway, Christopher, 1989. *Self and World in Schopenhauer's Philosophy*. Oxford: Clarendon Press.

Janaway, Christopher, ed., 1998. *Willing and Nothingness: Schopenhauer as Nietzsche's Educator*. Oxford: Clarendon Press.

Janaway, Christopher, ed., 1999. *The Cambridge Companion to Schopenauer*. Cambridge: Cambridge University Press.

Janaway, Christopher, 2007. *Beyond Selflessness: Reading Nietzsche's* Genealogy. Oxford: Oxford University Press.

Jenkins, Mark, 2006. *Bernard Williams*. London: Acumen.

Jodl, Friedrich, 1929. *Geschichte der Ethik als philosophischer Wissenschaft* (4th edition). Reprint, Essen: Phaidon.

Johnson, Robert N., 2011. *Self-Improvement: An Essay in Kantian Ethics*. Oxford: Oxford University Press.

Jones, Henry, and J. H. Muirhead, 1921. *The Life and Philosophy of Edward Caird*. Glasgow: Maclehose, Jackson.

Kagan, Shelly, 1989. *The Limits of Morality*. Oxford: Clarendon Press.

Kahn, Samuel, 2021. *Kant's Theory of Conscience*. Cambridge: Cambridge University Press.

Kaufmann, Walter, 1968. *Nietzsche: Philosopher, Psychologist, Antichrist* (3rd edition). Princeton: Princeton University Press.

Keene, Carol A., 2009. "The Interplay of Bradley's Social and Moral Philosophy." In Sweet 2009, pp. 87–100.

Kemp Smith, Norman, 1923. *A Commentary to Kant's "Critique of Pure Reason."* (2nd edition). London: Macmillan.

Kim, Halla, 2015. *Kant and the Foundations of Morality*. Lanham, MD: Lexington Books.

Kirchin, Simon, ed., 2017. *Reading Parfit: On What Matters*. London: Routledge.

Kitcher, Philip, 2022. *The Main Enterprise of the World: Rethinking Education*. New York: Oxford University Press.

Kitcher, Philip, 2023. *On John Stuart Mill*. New York: Columbia University Press.

Kleingeld, Pauline, 1995. *Fortschritt und Vernunft: Zur Geschichtsphilosophie Kants*. Würzburg: Königshausen & Neumann.

Kleingeld, Pauline, 2012. *Kant and Cosmopolitanism: The Philosophical Ideal of World Citizenship*. Cambridge: Cambridge University Press.

Klemke, E. D., ed., 1969. *Studies in the Philosophy of G. E. Moore*. Chicago: Quadrangle Books.

Klemme, Heiner F., 2017. *Kants "Grundlegung zur Metaphysik der Sitten": Ein systematischer Kommentar*. Stuttgart: Reclam.

Klemme, Heiner F., 2023. *Die Selbsterhaltung der Vernunft: Kant und die Modernität seines Denkens*. Frankfurt am Main: Vittorio Klostermann.

Knowles, Dudley, 2002. *Hegel and the* Philosophy of Right. London: Routledge.

Korsgaard, Christine M., 1983. "Two Distinctions in Goodness." *Philosophical Review* 92: 169–95. Reprinted in Korsgaard 1996, pp. 249–74.

Kosch, Michelle, 2008. *Freedom and Reason in Kant, Schelling, and Kierkegaard.* Oxford: Oxford University Press.

Kosch, Michelle, 2014. "Idealism and Freedom in Schelling's *Freiheitsschrift.*" In Lara Ostaric, ed., *Interpreting Schelling: Critical Essays.* Cambridge: Cambridge University Press, pp. 145–59.

Kosch, Michelle, 2015. "Agency and Self-Sufficiency in Fichte's Ethics," *Philosophy and Phenomenological Research* 91: 348–80.

Kosch, Michelle, 2018. *Fichte's Ethics.* Oxford: Oxford University Press.

Krasnoff, Larry, 2014. "Kantian Constructivism." In Mandle and Reidy 2014, pp. 73–87.

Kuehn, Manfred, 2001. *Immanuel Kant: A Biography.* Cambridge: Cambridge University Press.

Kuehn, Manfred, 2012. *Johann Gottlieb Fichte: Ein deutscher Philosoph.* Munich: C. H. Beck.

Kuklick, Bruce, 1972. *Josiah Royce: An Intellectual Biography.* Indianapolis: Bobbs-Merrill.

Kuklick, Bruce, 1977. *The Rise of American Philosophy.* New Haven: Yale University Press.

Laden, Anthony Simon, 2014. "Constructivism as Rhetoric." In Mandle and Reidy 2014, pp. 59–72.

Lamont, W. D., 1934. *Introduction to Green's Moral Philosophy.* London: George Allen & Unwin.

Lange, Friedrich Albert, 1925. *The History of Materialism and Criticism of its Present Importance,* translated by Ernest Chester Thomas, introduction by Bertrand Russell. London: Routledge & Kegan Paul.

Langton, Rae, 2007. "Objective and Unconditioned Value." *Philosophical Review* 116: 157–86.

La Vopa, Anthony J., 2001. *Fichte: The Self and the Calling of Philosophy, 1762–1799.* Cambridge: Cambridge University Press.

Laywine, Alison, 1995. *Kant's Early Metaphysics and the Origins of the Critical Philosophy.* Atascadero, CA: Ridgeview Publishing.

Lazzari, Alessandro, 2004. *"Das Eine, Was der Menschheit Noth ist": Einheit und Freiheit in der Philosophie Karl Leonhard Reinholds (1789–1792).* Stuttgart-Bad Canstatt: Frommann-Holzboog.

Leiter, Brian, 2002. *Nietzsche on Morality.* London: Routledge.

Leiter, Brian, 2009. "Nietzsche's Theory of the Will." In Gemes and May 2009, pp. 107–26.

Leiter, Brian, 2011. "Who is the 'Sovereign Individual? Nietzsche on Freedom." In May 2011, pp. 101–19.

Leiter, Brian, and Neil Sinhababu, eds, 2007. *Nietzsche and Morality.* Oxford: Clarendon Press.

Lenman, James, and Yonatan Schemmer, eds, 2012. *Constructivism in Practical Philosophy.* Oxford: Oxford University Press.

Levy, Paul, 1979. *Moore: G. E. Moore and the Cambridge Apostles.* New York: Holt, Rinehart, & Winston.

Lipscomb, Benjamin J. B. 2022. *The Women are up to Something: How Elizabeth Anscombe, Philippa Foot, Mary Midgley, and Iris Murdoch Revolutionized Ethics.* New York: Oxford University Press.

Lloyd, S. A., 2014. "Learning from the History of Political Philosophy." In Mandle and Reidy 2014, pp. 526–45.

Louden, Robert B., 2000. *Kant's Impure Ethics.* New York: Oxford University Press.

Louden, Robert B., 2011. *Kant's Human Being: Essays on his Theory of Human Nature.* New York: Oxford University Press.

Ludwig, Bernd, 2020. *Aufklärung über die Sittlichkeit: Zu Kants Grundlegung einer Metapysik der Sitten*. Frankfurt am Main: Vittorio Klostermann.

McCarty, Richard, 2009. *Kant's Theory of Action*. Oxford: Oxford University Press.

McCumber, John, 2014. *Understanding Hegel's Mature Critique of Kant*. Stanford, CA: Stanford University Press.

Mac Cumhaill, Clare, and Rachel Wiseman, 2022. *Metaphysical Beasts: How Four Women Brought Philosophy Back to Life*. New York: Doubleday.

MacEwen, Philip, 2009. "The Moral and Social Philosophy of Edward Caird." In Sweet 2009, pp. 51–64.

McLaughlin, Peter, 1990. *Kant's Critique of Teleology in Biological Explanation: Antinomy and Teleology*. Lewiston, NY: Edwin Mellen Press.

McMahan, Jeff, ed., forthcoming. *Derek Parfit: His Life and Work*. Oxford: Oxford University Press.

Maffettone, Sebastiano, 2011. *Rawls: An Introduction*. Cambridge: Polity Press.

Magee, Bryan, 1983. *The Philosophy of Schopenhauer*. Oxford: Clarendon Press.

Magnus, Bernd, and Kathleen M. Higgins, eds, 1996. *The Cambridge Companion to Nietzsche*. Cambridge: Cambridge University Press.

Mander, W. J., 1994. *An Introduction to Bradley's Metaphysics*. Oxford: Clarendon Press.

Mander, W. J., 2011. *British Idealism: A History*. Oxford: Oxford University Press.

Mander, W. J., ed., 2014. *The Oxford Handbook of British Philosophy in the Nineteenth Century*. Oxford: Oxford University Press.

Mander, W. J., 2016. *Idealist Ethics*. Oxford: Oxford University Press.

Mander, W. J., 2020. *The Unknowable: A Study in Nineteenth-Century British Metaphysics*. Oxford: Oxford University Press.

Mandle, Jon, and David A. Reidy, eds, 2014. *A Companion to Rawls*. Chichester: Wiley-Blackwell.

Mariña, Jacqueline, 2021. "It's All about Power: The Deep Structure of Kant's Categorical Imperative and its Three Formulations." In Ansgar Lyssy and Christopher Yeomans, eds, *Kant on Humanity, Morality, and Legality: Practical Dimensions of Normativity*. Cham: Palgrave Macmillan, pp. 67–90.

Marquard, Odo, 1995. "Grund und Existenz in Gott." In Höffe and Pieper 1995, pp. 55–60.

Martin, Wayne, 2019. "Fichte on Freedom." In Steven Hoeltzel, ed., *The Palgrave Fichte Handbook*. Cham: Palgrave Macmillan, pp. 285–306.

Marx, Karianne J., 2011. *The Usefulness of the Kantian Philosophy: How Karl Leonhard Reinhold's Commitment to Enlightenment Influences his Reception of Kant*. Berlin and Boston: Walter de Gruyter & Co.

May, Simon, ed., 2011. *Nietzsche's On the Genealogy of Morality: A Critical Guide*. Cambridge: Cambridge University Press.

Michalson, Gordon E., ed., 2014. *Kant's Religion within the Boundaries of Mere Reason: A Critical Guide*. Cambridge: Cambridge University Press.

Mieth, Corinna, and Jacob Rosenthal, 2006. "'Freedom must be Presupposed as a Property of the Will of All Rational Beings'." In Horn and Schönecker 2006, pp. 247–84.

Miller, Eddis N., 2015. *Kant's Religion within the Boundaries of Mere Reason: A Reader's Guide*. London: Bloomsbury.

Moran, Kate A., 2022. *Kant's Ethics*. Cambridge: Cambridge University Press.

Morgan, Seiriol, 2005. "The Missing Formal Proof of Humanity's Radical Evil in Kant's Religion." *Philosophical Review* 114: 63–114.

Moyar, Dean, 2011. *Hegel's Conscience*. New York: Oxford University Press.

Moyar, Dean, 2021. *Hegel's Value: Justice as the Living Good*. New York: Oxford University Press.

Muchnik, Pablo, 2009. *Kant's Theory of Evil: An Essay on the Dangers of Self-Love and the Aprioricity of History*. Lanham, MD: Lexington Books.

Mure, G. R. G., 1940. *An Introduction to Hegel*. Oxford: Clarendon Press.

Nakano-Okuno, Mariko, 2020. "Kant and Sidgwick on Freedom of Will, Morality, and Responsibility." In Paytas and Henning 2020, pp. 162–83.

Nehamas, Alexander, 1985. *Nietzsche: Life as Literature*. Cambridge, MA: Harvard University Press.

Nehamas, Alexander, 1986. "Will to Knowledge, Will to Ignorance, and Will to Power in *Beyond Good and Evil*." In Yirmiahu Yovel, ed., *Nietzsche as Affirmative Thinker: Papers Presented at the Fifth Jerusalem Philosophical Encounter, April 1983*. The Hague: Martinus Nijhoff, pp. 90–108.

Nehamas, Alexander, 2017. "Nietzsche on Truth and the Value of Falsehood." *Journal of Nietzsche Studies* 48: 319–46.

Neill, Alex, and Christopher Janaway, eds, 2009. *Better Consciousness: Schopenhauer's Philosophy of Value*. Chichester: Wiley-Blackwell.

Nell, Onora, 1975. *See* O'Neill 2013.

Neuhouser, Frederick, 1990. *Fichte's Theory of Subjectivity*. Cambridge: Cambridge University Press.

Neuhouser, Frederick, 2016. "Fichte's Separation of Right from Morality." In Gottlieb 2016, pp. 32–51.

Nicholson, Peter, 2006. "Green's 'Eternal Consciousness'." In Dimova-Cookson and Mander 2006, pp. 139–59.

Noller, Jörg, 2016. *Die Bestimmung des Willens: Zum Problem individuellet Freiheit im Ausgang von Kant* (2nd edition). Freiburg and Munich: Verlag Karl Alber.

Norman, Judith, and Alistair Welchmann, eds, 2023. *Schopenhauer's* The World as Will and Representation: *A Critical Guide*. Cambridge: Cambridge University Press.

Nuccetelli, Susana, and Gary Seay, eds, 2007. *Themes from G. E. Moore: New Essays in Epistemology and Ethics*. Oxford: Oxford University Press.

O'Hagan, Timothy, 1987. "On Hegel's Critique of Kant's Moral and Political Philosophy." In Stephen Priest, ed., *Hegel's Critique of Kant*. Oxford: Oxford University Press, pp. 135–60.

Oppenheim, Frank M., 2005. *Reverence for the Relations of Life: Re-Imagining Pragmatism via Royce's Interactions with Peirce, James, and Dewey*. Notre Dame, IN: University of Notre Dame Press.

Palmquist, Stephen R., 2016. *Comprehensive Commentary on Kant's* Religion within the Bounds of Mere Reason. Chichester: Wiley-Blackwell.

Parker, Kelly A., 2008. "Josiah Royce: Idealism, Transcendentalism, Pragmatism." In Cheryl Misak, ed., *The Oxford Handbook of American Philosophy*. Oxford: Oxford University Press, pp. 110–24.

Pasternack, Lawrence R., 2014. *Routledge Philosophy Guidebook to Kant on* Religion within the Boundaries of Mere Reason. London: Routledge.

Paton, Herbert James, 1936. *Kant's Metaphysic of Experience*, 2 vols. London: George Allen and Unwin.

Paton, Herbert James, 1947. *The Categorical Imperative: A Study in Kant's Moral Philosophy*. London: Hutchinson University Library.

Paytas, Tyler, 2020. "Beneficent Governor of the Cosmos: Kant and Sidgwick on the Moral Necessity of God." In Paytas and Henning 2020, pp. 210–44.

Paytas, Tyler and Tim Henning, eds, 2020. *Kantian and Sidgwickian Ethics: The Cosmos of Duty Above and the Moral Law Within*. London: Routledge.

Phillips, David, 2011. *Sidgwickian Ethics*. New York: Oxford University Press.

Phillips, David, 2019. *Rossian Ethics: W. D. Ross and Contemporary Moral Theory*. Oxford: Oxford University Press.

Phillips, David, 2022. *Sidgwick's* The Methods of Ethics: *A Guide*. New York: Oxford University Press.

Pieper, Annemarie, 1995. "Zum Problem der Herkunft des Bösen I: Die Wurzel des Bösen im Selbst," in Höffe and Pieper 1995, pp. 91–110.

Pinkard, Terry, 2000. *Hegel: A Biography*. Cambridge: Cambridge University Press.

Pinkard, Terry, 2002. *German Philosophy 1760–1860: The Legacy of Idealism*. Cambridge: Cambridge University Press.

Pippin, Robert B., 2008. *Hegel's Practical Philosophy: Rational Agency as Ethical Life*. Cambridge: Cambridge University Press.

Pippin, Robert B., 2009. "How to Overcome Oneself: Nietzsche on Freedom." In Gemes and May 2009, pp. 69–88.

Poellner, Peter, 2011. "*Ressentiment* and Morality." In May 2011, pp. 120–41.

Potts, Alex, 1994. *Flesh and the Ideal: Winckelmann and the Origins of Art*. New Haven and London: Yale University Press.

Proops, Ian, 2021. *The Fiery Test of Critique: A Reading of Kant's Dialectic*. Oxford: Oxford University Press.

Putnam, Hilary, 1979. *Meaning and the Moral Sciences*. London: Routledge & Kegan Paul.

Quarfood, Marcel, 2006. "The Circle and the Two Standpoints." In Horn and Schönecker 2006, pp. 285–300.

Rawling, Piers, 2023. *Deontology*. Cambridge: Cambridge University Press.

Reath, Andrews, 1988. "Two Conceptions of the Highest Good in Kant." *Journal of the History of Philosophy* 26: 593–619.

Reath, Andrews, 1997. "Legislating for a Realm of Ends: The Social Dimension of Autonomy." In Andrews Reath, Barbara Herman, and Christine M. Korsgaard, eds, *Reclaiming the History of Ethics: Essays for John Rawls*. Cambridge: Cambridge University Press, pp. 214–39. Reprinted in Reath, *Agency and Autonomy in Kant's Moral Theory*. Oxford: Oxford University Press, 2006, pp. 173–95.

Reath, Andrews, 2022. "Kantian Constructivism and Kantian Constitutivism: Some Reflections." *Kant Yearbook* 14: 45–67.

Reath, Andrews, Barbara Herman, and Christine M. Korsgaard, eds, 1997. *Reclaiming the History of Ethics: Essays for John Rawls*. Cambridge: Cambridge University Press.

Regan, Tom, 1986. *Bloomsbury's Prophet: G. E. Moore and the Development of his Moral Philosophy*. Philadelphia: Temple University Press.

Reginster, Bernard, 2007. "The Will to Power and the Ethics of Creativity." In Leiter and Sinhababu 2007, pp. 32–56.

Reginster, Bernard, 2021. *The Will to Nothingness: An Essay on Nietzsche's* On the Genealogy of Morality. Oxford: Oxford University Press.

Reginster, Bernard, 2023. "Resignation." In Norman and Welchman 2023, pp. 26–48.

Reich, Klaus, 1935. *Kant und die Ethik der Griechen*. Tübingen: Mohr (Siebeck). Reprinted in Reich, *Gesammelte Schriften*, edited by Manfred Baum, Udo Ramell, Klaus Reisinger, and Gertrud Scholz. Hamburg: Felix Meiner Verlag, 2001, pp. 113–46. In English as "Kant and Greek Ethics," translated by W. H. Walsh, *Mind*, NS 48 (1939): 338–54, 446–63.

Richardson, Henry S., 2006. "Deontological Ethics." In *Encyclopedia of Philosophy* (2nd edition), edited by Donald M. Borchert, 10 vols. Farmington Hills: Thomson Gale, vol. 2, pp. 713–15.

Richardson, John, 1996. *Nietzsche's System*. New York: Oxford University Press.

Richardson John, 2009. "Nietzsche's Freedoms." In Ken Gemes and Simon May, eds, *Nietzsche on Freedom and Morality*. Oxford: Oxford University Press, pp. 127–50.

Richardson, John and Ken Gemes, eds, 2013. *The Oxford Handbook of Nietzsche*. Oxford: Oxford University Press.

Richter, Duncan, 2000. *Ethics After Anscombe: Post "Modern Moral Philosophy."* Dordrecht: Kluwer.

Richter, Duncan, 2011. *Anscombe's Moral Philosophy*. Lanham, MD: Lexington Books.

Ripstein, Arthur, 2009. *Force and Freedom: Kant's Legal and Political Philosophy*. Cambridge, MA: Harvard University Press.

Risse, Mathias, 2007. "Nietzschean 'Animal Psychology' versus Kantian Ethics." In Leiter and Sinhababu 2007, pp. 32–56.

Robertson, Simon, 2017. "Anti-Theory: Anscombe, Foot and Williams." In Golob and Timmermann 2017, pp. 678–91.

Rosen, Michael, 2022. *In the Shadow of God: Kant, Hegel, and the Passage from Heaven to History*. Cambridge, MA: Harvard University Press.

Sala, Giovanni B., 2004. *Kants "Kritik der praktischen Vernunft": Ein Kommentar*. Darmstadt: Wissenschaftliche Buchgesellschaft.

Sarkar, Husain, 2018. *Kant and Parfit: The Groundwork of Morals*. London: Routledge.

Scanlon, T. M., 1998. *What we Owe to Each Other*. Cambridge, MA: Harvard University Press.

Scanlon, T. M., 2003. "Rawls on Justification." In Freeman 2003, pp. 139–67.

Scanlon, T. M., 2011. "How I am Not a Kantian," in Parfit 2011, vol. 2, pp. 116–39.

Schacht, Richard, 1983. *Nietzsche*. London: Routledge & Kegan Paul.

Schafer, Karl, 2015. "Realism and Constructivism in Kantian Metaethics," 1 and 2. *Philosophy Compass* 10: 690–701, 702–13.

Schapiro, Tamar, Kyla Ebels-Duggan, and Sharon Street, eds, 2022. *Normativity and Agency: Themes from the Philosophy of Christine M. Korsgaard*. Oxford: Oxford University Press.

Schilpp, Paul Arthur, ed., 1942. *The Philosophy of G. E. Moore*. The Library of Living Philosophers. Evanston, IL: Northwestern University Press.

Schilpp, Paul Arthur, 1960. *Kant's Pre-Critical Ethics* (2nd edition). Evanston, IL: Northwestern University Press. (1st edition, 1938).

Schmucker, Josef, 1961. *Die Ursprünge der Ethik Kants*. Meisenheim am Glan: Verlag Anton Hain.

Schneewind, Jerome B, 1977. *Sidgwick's Ethics and Victorian Moral Philosophy*. Oxford: Clarendon Press.

Schneewind, Jerome B, ed., 1996. *Reason, Ethics, and Society: Themes from Kurt Baier, with His Responses*. Chicago: Open Court.

Schneewind, Jerome B., 1998a. *The Invention of Autonomy*. Cambridge: Cambridge University Press.

Schneewind, Jerome B., 1998b. "Korsgaard and the Unconditional in Morality." *Ethics* 109: 36–8.

Schönecker, Dieter, 1999. *Kant: Grundlegung III: Die Deduktion des kategorischen Imperativs*. Freiburg and Munich: Karl Alber Verlag.

Schönecker, Dieter, 2005. *Kants Begriff transzendentaler und praktischer Freiheit: Eine entwicklungsgeschichtliche Studie.* Berlin and New York: Walter de Gruyter & Co.

Schönecker, Dieter, ed., 2015. *Kants Begründung von Freiheit und Moral in Grundlegung III: Neue Interpretationen.* Münster: Mentis Verlag.

Schönecker, Dieter, and Allen W. Wood, 2015. *Immanuel Kant's* Groundwork for the Metaphysics of Morals: *A Commentary,* translated by Nicholas Walker. Cambridge, MA: Harvard University Press.

Schönfeld, Martin, 2000. *The Philosophy of the Young Kant: The Precritical Project.* New York: Oxford University Press.

Schultz, Bart, 2004. *Henry Sidgwick: Eye of the Universe.* Cambridge: Cambridge University Press.

Schultz, Bart, 2014. "Henry Sidgwick." In Mander 2014, pp. 461–82.

Schultz, Bart, 2017. *The Happiness Philosophers: The Lives and Works of the Great Utilitarians.* Princeton: Princeton University Press.

Seanor, Douglas, and Nick Fotion, eds, 1988. *Hare and Critics: Essays on Moral Thinking.* Oxford: Clarendon Press.

Sedgwick, Sally, 2008. *Kant's* Groundwork for the Metaphysics of Morals: *An Introduction.* Cambridge: Cambridge University Press.

Sedgwick, Sally, 2012. *Hegel's Critique of Kant: From Dichotomy to Identity.* Oxford: Oxford University Press.

Segula, Marco, 2023. "The Sciences in *The World as Will and Representation.*" In Norman and Welchman 2023, pp. 224–44.

Sensen, Oliver, 2011. *Kant on Human Dignity.* Berlin and New York: Walter de Gruyter & Co.

Sensen, Oliver, 2013a. "Kant's Constructivism." In Bagnoli 2013, pp. 63–81.

Sensen, Oliver, ed., 2013b. *Kant on Moral Autonomy.* Cambridge: Cambridge University Press.

Shapshay, Sandra, 2019. *Reconstructing Schopenhauer's Ethics: Hope, Compassion, and Animal Welfare.* Oxford: Oxford University Press.

Shaw, William H., 1995. *Moore on Right and Wrong: The Normative Ethics of G. E. Moore.* Dordrecht: Kluwer.

Shaw, William H., 2020. *Moore's Ethics.* Cambridge: Cambridge University Press.

Sherman, Nancy, 1997. *Making a Necessity of Virtue: Aristotle and Kant on Virtue.* Cambridge: Cambridge University Press.

Siep, Ludwig, 1979. *Anerkennung als Prinzip der praktischen Philosophie.* Freiburg: Alber.

Silber, John R., 1960. "The Ethical Significance of Kant's Religion." In Kant, *Religion within the Limits of Reason Alone,* translated by Theodore M. Greene and Hoyt H. Hudson (2nd edition). New York: Harper & Row, pp. lxxix–cxxxiv.

Silber, John R., 1963. "The Importance of the Highest Good in Kant's Ethics." *Ethics* 73: 179–97.

Silber, John R., 2012. *Kant's Ethics: The Good, Freedom, and the Will.* Berlin and Boston: Walter de Gruyter & Co.

Simonhy, Avital, 2009. "A Liberal Commitment to the Common Good: T. H. Green's Social and Political Morality." In Sweet 2009, pp. 31–50.

Sinclair, Neil, ed., 2019. *The Naturalistic Fallacy.* Cambridge: Cambridge University Press.

Singer, Marcus G., 1961. *Generalization in Ethics: An Essay in the Logic of Ethics.* New York: Alfred A. Knopf.

Singer, Peter, ed., 2017. *Does Anything Really Matter? Essays on Objectivity.* Oxford: Oxford University Press.

Skorupski, John, 2021. *Being and Freedom: On Late Modern Ethics in Europe*. Oxford: Oxford University Press.

Solomon, Robert, 1996. "Nietzsche *ad hominem*: Perspectivism, Personality, and *Ressentiment* Revisited." In Magnus and Higgins 1996, pp. 180–222.

Stang, Nicholas F, 2021. *"On the Form and Principles of the Sensible and Intelligible World."* In Wuerth 2021, pp. 573–6.

Stäudlin, Carl Friedrich, 1822. *Geschichte der Moralphilosophie*. Hannover: Helwing.

Stern, Robert, 2013. "Moral Skepticism, Constructivism, and the Value of Humanity." In Bagnoli 2013, pp. 22–40.

Stern, Robert, 2017. "British Idealism." In Sacha Golob and Jens Timmermann, eds, *The Cambridge History of Moral Philosophy*. Cambridge: Cambridge University Press, pp. 535–48.

Stolz, Violetta, Marion Heinz, and Martin Bondeli, eds, 2012. *Wille, Willkür, Freiheit: Reinholds Freiheitkonzeption im Kontext der Philosophie des 18. Jahrhunderts*. Berlin and Boston: Walter de Gruyter & Co.

Stratton-Lake, Philip, ed., 2002. *Ethical Intuitionism: Re-evaluations*. Oxford: Oxford University Press.

Strawson, Peter F., 1966. *The Bounds of Sense: An Essay on Kant's* Critique of Pure Reason. London: Methuen.

Street, Sharon, 2006. "A Darwinian Dilemma for Realist Theories of Value." *Philosopical Studies* 109: 109–66.

Street, Sharon, 2008. "Constructivism about Reasons." *Oxford Studies in Metaethics* 3: 207–45.

Street, Sharon, 2010. "What is Constructivism in Ethics and Metaethics?" *Philosophy Compass* 5: 363–431.

Sullivan, Roger, 1989. *Immanuel Kant's Moral Theory*. Cambridge: Cambridge University Press.

Sussman, David, 2005. "Perversity of the Heart," *Philosophical Review* 114: 153–77.

Sweet, William, ed., 2009. *The Moral, Social, and Political Philosophy of the British Idealists*. Exeter: Academic Imprint.

Sylvester, Robert Peter, 1990. *The Moral Philosophy of G. E. Moore*. Philadelphia: Temple University Press.

Taylor, Charles, 1975. *Hegel*. Cambridge: Cambridge University Press.

Taylor, Robert S., 2011. *Reconstructing Rawls: The Kantian Foundations of Justice as Fairness*. University Park, PA: Pennsylvania State University Press.

Thomas, Alan, ed., 2007. *Bernard Williams: Contemporary Philosophers in Focus*. Cambridge: Cambridge University Press.

Thomas, Geoffrey, 1987. *The Moral Philosophy of T. H. Green*. Oxford: Clarendon Press.

Timmermann, Jens, 2003. *Sittengesetz und Freiheit: Untersuchungen zu Immanuel Kants Theorie des freien Willens*. Berlin and New York: Walter de Gruyter & Co.

Timmermann, Jens, 2006. "Values without Regress: Kant's 'Formula of Humanity' Revisited." *European Journal of Philosophy* 14: 69–93.

Timmermann, Jens, 2007. *Kant's* Groundwork of the Metaphysics of Morals: *A Commentary*. Cambridge: Cambridge University Press.

Timmermann, Jens, 2015. "What's Wrong with 'Deontology'?" *Proceedings of the Aristotelian Society* 115: 75–92.

Timmermann, Jens, 2022. *Kant's Will at the Crossroads: An Essay on the Failings of Practical Rationality*. Oxford: Oxford University Press.

Timmons, Mark, ed., 2002. *Kant's* Metaphysics of Morals: *Interpretative Essays.* Oxford: Oxford University Press, 2002.

Timmons, Mark, and Sorin Baiasu, eds, 2013. *Kant on Practical Justification: Interpretive Essays.* New York: Oxford University Press.

Tonelli, Giorgio, 1994. *Kant's* Critique of Pure Reason *within the Tradition of Modern Logic,* edited by David H. Chandler. Hildesheim: Georg Olms.

Trampota, Andreas, Oliver Sensen, and Jens Timmermann, eds, 2013. *Kant's* Tugendlehre: *A Comprehensive Commentary.* Berlin and Boston: Walter de Gruyter & Co.

Tuck, Richard, 2016. *The Sleeping Sovereign: The Invention of Modern Democracy.* Cambridge: Cambridge University Press.

Uleman, Jennifer, 2010. *An Introduction to Kant's Moral Philosophy.* Cambridge: Cambridge University Press.

Valenza, Pierluigi, ed., 2006. *K.L Reinhold: Am Vorhof des Idealismus.* Pisa and Rome: Instituti Editoriali Poligrafica Internaztionali.

Van Tongeren, Paul J. M., 2006. "Nietzsche and Ethics." In Ansell Pearson 2006, pp. 389–403.

van Zantwijk, Tamilo, 2010. "Carl Christian Erhard Schmid." In Heiner F. Klemme and Manfred Kuehn, eds, *The Dictionary of Eighteenth-century German Philosophers*, 3 vols. London: Continuum, vol. 3, pp. 1034–7.

Varden, Helga, 2020. *Sex, Love, and Gender: A Kantian Theory.* Oxford: Oxford University Press.

Vincent, Andrew, 2014. "The Ethics of British Idealism: Bradley, Green, and Bosanquet." In W.J. Mander, ed., *The Oxford Handbook of British Philosophy in the Nineteenth Century.* Oxford: Oxford University Press, pp. 423–39.

Vincent, Andrew, and Raymond Plant, 1984. *Philosophy, Politics, and Citizenship: The Social Thought of the British Idealists.* Oxford: Blackwell.

Walker, Ralph C. S., 2022. *Objective Imperatives: An Exploration of Kant's Moral Philosophy.* Oxford: Oxford University Press.

Wallace, R. Jay, 2007. "*Ressentiment,* Value, and Self-Vindication: Making Sense of Nietzsche's Slave Revolt." In Leiter and Sinhababu 2007, pp. 110–37.

Walschots, Michael H., 2021. "Kant and Consequentialism in Context: The Second Critique's Response to Pistorius." *Archiv für Geschichte der Philosophie* 103: 313–40.

Walschots, Michael H., 2022. "Kant and the Duty to Act from Duty." *History of Philosophy Quarterly* 39: 59–75.

Walschots, Michael H., forthcoming. "Kant and the Duty to Act from Duty." *History of Philosophy Quarterly.*

Walsh, John, 2020. "The Fact of Freedom: Reinhold's Theory of Free Will Reconsidered," in Majna Kisner and Jörg Noller, eds, *The Concept of Will in Classical German Philosophy.* Berlin and Boston: Walter de Gruyter & Co., pp. 89–104.

Walsh, W. H., 1969. *Hegelian Ethics.* London: Macmillan.

Walsh, W. H., 1972. "Herbert James Paton: 1887–1969," *Proceedings of the British Academy 1970* 56 (published in 1972): 293–308.

Ward, Keith, 1972. *The Development of Kant's View of Ethics.* Oxford: Basil Blackwell.

Ware, Owen, 2020. *Fichte's Moral Philosophy.* Oxford: Oxford University Press.

Weldon, T. D., 1958. *Kant's* Critique of Pure Reason (2nd edition). Oxford: Clarendon Press.

Westphal, Kenneth, 1991. "Hegel's Critique of Kant's Moral World View." *Philosophical Topics* 19: 133–76.

Wicks, Robert, 2023. "Schopenhauer, Universal Guilt, and Asceticism." In Norman and Welchman 2023, 2023, pp. 179–99.

Wilford, Paul T., and Samuel A. Stoner, eds, 2021. *Kant and the Possibility of Progress: From Modern Hopes to Postmodern Anxieties*. Philadelphia: University of Pennsylvania Press.

Williams, T. C., 1968. *The Concept of the Categorical Imperative: A Study of the Place of the Categorical Imperative in Kant's Ethical Theory*. Oxford: Clarendon Press.

Wolff, Robert Paul, 1973. *The Autonomy of Reason: A Commentary on Kant's* Groundwork of the Metaphysics of Morals. New York: Harper & Row.

Wood, Allen W., 1970. *Kant's Moral Religion*. Ithaca, NY, and London: Cornell University Press.

Wood, Allen W., 1984. "Kant's Compatibilism." In Wood, ed., *Self and Nature in Kant's Philosophy*. Ithaca, NY, and London: Cornell University Press, pp. 73–101.

Wood, Allen W., 1990. *Hegel's Ethical Thought*. Cambridge: Cambridge University Press.

Wood, Allen W., 1997. "Hegel's Critique of Morality." In Ludwig Siep, ed., *G. W. F. Hegel: Grundlinien der Philosophie des Rechts*. Berlin: Akademie Verlag, pp. 147–66.

Wood, Allen W., 1999. *Kant's Ethical Thought*. Cambridge: Cambridge University Press.

Wood, Allen W., 2001. "The Moral Law as a System of Formulas." In Hans-Friedrich Fulda and Jürgen Stolzenberg, eds, *Architechtonik und System in der Philosophie Kants*. Hamburg: Felix Meiner Verlag, pp. 287–306.

Wood, Allen W., 2006. "The Supreme Principle of Morality." In Paul Guyer, ed., *The Cambridge Companion to Kant and Modern Philosophy*. Cambridge: Cambridge University Press, pp. 342–80.

Wood, Allen W., 2008. *Kantian Ethics*. Cambridge: Cambridge University Press.

Wood, Allen W., 2010. "The Moral Theory of German Idealism." In Dean Moyar, ed., *The Routledge Companion to Nineteenth Century Philosophy*. London: Routledge, 2010, pp. 104–30.

Wood, Allen W., 2011. "Humanity as an End in Itself." In Parfit 2011, vol. 2, pp. 58–82.

Wood, Allen W., 2014. "The Evil in Human Nature." In Michalson 2014, pp. 31–57.

Wood, Allen W., 2016. *Fichte's Ethical Thought*. Oxford: Oxford University Press.

Wood, Allen W., 2017. *Kant's Formulations of the Categorical Imperative*. Cambridge: Cambridge University Press.

Wood, Allen W., 2020. *Kant and Religion*. Cambridge: Cambridge University Press.

Wuerth, Julian, 2014. *Kant on Mind, Action, and Ethics*. Oxford: Oxford University Press.

Wuerth, Julian, ed., 2021. *The Cambridge Kant Companion*. Cambridge: Cambridge University Press.

Wulf, Andrea, 2022. *Magnificent Rebels: The First Romantics and the Invention of the Self*. New York: Alfred A. Knopf.

Yeomans, Christopher, 2012. *Freedom and Reflection: Hegel and the Logic of Agency*. New York: Oxford University Press.

Yovel, Yirmiahu, 1980. *Kant and the Philosophy of History*. Princeton: Princeton University Press.

Young, Julian, 1987. *Willing and Unwilling: A Study in the Philosophy of Schopenhauer*. Dordrecht: Martinus Nijhoff.

Young, Julian, 2005. *Schopenhauer*. London: Routledge.

Young, Julian, 2010. *Friedrich Nietzsche: A Philosophical Biography*. Cambridge: Cambridge University Press.

Zöller, Günter, 1998. *Fichte's Transcendental Philosophy: The Original Duplicity of Intelligence and Will*. Cambridge: Cambridge University Press.

Index

For the benefit of digital users, indexed terms that span two pages (e.g., 52–53) may, on occasion, appear on only one of those pages.